Charit

Administration
Handbook

Charity Administration Handbook

Fourth Edition

Don Bawtree MA FCA BDO Stoy Hayward

Kate Kirkland BA (Hons) FRSA

Tottel Publishing Ltd, Maxwelton House, 41–43 Boltro Road, Haywards Heath, West Sussex, RH16 1BJ

© Tottel Publishing Ltd 2008

A CIP Catalogue record for this book is available from the British Library.

ISBN 978 1 84592 239 9

Typeset by Kerrypress Ltd, Luton, Beds
Printed and bound in Great Britain by Antony Rowe, Chippenham, Wilts

About this book

Background

At the time of writing this fourth edition, the Charities Act is in the early stages of implementation. The regime in Scotland under OSCR and the Scottish 2005 Act is still evolving and the position in Northern Ireland is at an even earlier stage. At the same time the *Companies Act 2006* is being introduced, with inevitable knock on effects to the charity sector. These changes are all in the financial/regulatory regime – there are of course a myriad other changes continuing across the sector in all the walks of life! There is a great deal of change, and much of it adds to the charity administrators worry list!

Many charity administrators bring business skills into their first voluntary sector job. They understand accounts, VAT and human resource management. But what happens if they fail to appreciate that charities operate in a different regulatory framework to businesses, or that that framework has itself changed radically in the last few years?

This book provides a first point of reference for the charity administrator, especially in relation to finance and charity administration matters. It covers a wide range of topics from accounts to regulations for commercial participators, from PAYE administration to the implications of the Disability Discrimination Act. This fourth edition includes new chapters on the new heads of charity, public benefit, and substantial donor legislation.

To some questions it will give the complete answer, to others it will act as a signpost pointing you in the right direction where you can obtain the information that you need.

Inevitably there will be some who think some sections are too brief, and others who feel that some sections are too long or irrelevant. We hope that where a section is not directly relevant to your situation you may still find the information useful in broadening your understanding of issues faced by others in the sector. Either way any comments or suggestions for improving on the coverage or content will be taken in the spirit in which they are intended!

When Kate and Don started the first edition of this book, they worked together at BDO Stoy Hayward. Don still heads up the charity work at BDO while Kate is now Head of Secretariat at the Royal Air Force Benevolent Fund, but continues to do some governance consultancy work. The firm aims to take a holistic approach to our clients, to understand their activities as widely as possible, and help them achieve their mission. This requires the BDO team to have a good understanding of many issues, and so we are grateful to many members of the BDO charity unit for their help and advice in putting this book together. Once again we are grateful for the following staff across the organisation who have helped update this latest edition: James Aston, Keith Breckell, Stuart Bruce, Clare Colborne, Shane Crooks, Simon Davis, Ian MacFarlane, Francine Hill, Sue Ladell, Peter Lewis, Anne Logan, David Neal, Stuart Pepper, Graham Poulteney, Philip Rego, Jaimin Shah, James Sumpter, Ernie Turner and Bruce Williams. Finally thanks to Caroline Catford for co-ordinating the updating of this latest version.

February 2008

Contents

Contents

Contents

Contents

Contents

Contents

Contents

Contents

Table of Statutes

Table of Statutes

Table of Statutes

Table of Statutory Instruments

Table of Statutory Instruments

Table of Cases

Table of Cases

Useful Addresses

Action with Communities in Rural England (ACRE)
Somerford Court
Somerford Road
Cirencester
Gloucestershire
GL7 1TW
Tel: (01285) 653477
Fax: (01285) 654537
www.acre.org.uk

Advisory, Conciliation and Arbitration Service (ACAS)
Head Office
Brandon House
180 Borough High Street
London
SE1 1LW
Tel: (020) 7210 3613
Fax: (020) 7210 3645
www.acas.org.uk

Almshouse Association (The)
Billingbear Lodge
Maidenhead Road
Wokingham
Berkshire
RG40 5RU
Tel: (01344) 452922
Fax: (01344) 862062
www.almshouses.org

Arts Council of England
2 Pear Tree Court
London
EC1R ODS
Tel: 0845 300 6200
Fax: (020) 7608 4100
www.artscouncil.org.uk

Arts Council of Northern Ireland
77 Malone Road
Belfast
BT9 6AQ
Tel: (028) 90 385 200
Fax: (028) 90 661 715
www.artscouncil-ni.org

Arts Council of Wales
9 Museum Place
Cardiff
CF10 3NX
Tel: (029) 20 376 500
Fax: (029) 20 221 447
www.artswales.org

Association of Charitable Foundations (ACF)
Central House
14 Upper Woburn Place
London
WC1H OAE
Tel: (020) 7255 4499
Fax: (020) 7255 4496
www.acf.org.uk

Association of Charity Officers (ACO)
Five Ways
57/59 Hatfield Road
Potters Bar
Herts
EN6 1HS
Tel: (01707) 651777
Fax: (01707) 660477

Association of Chief Executives of Voluntary Organisations (ACEVO)
1 New Oxford Street
London
WC1A 1NU
Tel: (0845) 345 8481
Fax: (0845) 345 8482
www.acevo.org.uk

Big Lottery Fund
1 Plough Place
London
EC4A 1DE
Tel: (020) 7211 1800
Fax: (020) 7211 1750
www.biglotteryfund.org.uk

Useful Addresses

British Quality Foundations (The)
32–34 Great Peter Street
London
SW1P 2QX
Tel: (020) 7654 5000
Fax: (020) 7654 5001
www.quality-foundation.co.uk

British Standards (BSI)
389 Chiswick High Road
London
W4 4AL
Tel: (020) 8996 9001
Fax: (020) 8996 7001
www.bsi-global.com

Business in the Community
137 Shepherdess Walk
London
N1 7RQ
Tel: (020) 7566 8650
Fax: (020) 7253 1877
www.bitc.org.uk

Charities Advisory Trust
Radius Works
Back Lane
Hampstead
London
NW3 1HL
Tel: (020) 7794 9835
Fax: (020) 7431 3739
www.charitiesadvisorytrust.org.uk

Charities Aid Foundation (CAF)
25 Kings Hill Avenue
Kings Hill
West Malling
Kent
ME19 4TA
Tel: (01732) 520 000
Fax: (01732) 520 001
www.cafonline.org

Charities Evaluation Services
4 Coldbath Square
London
EC1R 5HL
Tel: (020) 7713 5722
Fax: (020) 7713 5692
www.ces-vol.org.uk/

Charities Tax Group (CTG)
Church House
Great Smith Street
London
SW1P 3AZ
Tel: (020) 7222 1265
Fax: (020) 7222 1250
www.ctrg.org.uk

Charity Commission Direct
PO Box 1227
Liverpool
L69 3UG
Tel: 0845 300 0218
Fax: 0151 7031 555
Offices in London, Liverpool,
Newport and Taunton
www.charity-commission.gov.uk

Charity Finance Directors' Group
3rd Floor
Downstream Building
1 London Bridge
London
SE1 9BG
Tel: 0845 345 3192
Fax: 0845 345 3193
www.cfdg.org.uk

Communities Scotland
Thistle House
91 Haymarket Terrace
Edinburgh
Midlothian
EH12 5HE
Tel: (0131) 313 0044
Fax: (0131) 313 2680
www.lc.communitiesscotland.gov.uk

Community Foundation Network
Arena House
66–68 Pentonville Road
London
N1 9HS
Tel: (020) 7713 9326
Fax: (020) 7713 9327
www.communityfoundations.org.uk/

Community Matters
12–20 Baron Street
London
N1 9LL
Tel: (020) 7837 7887
Fax: (020) 7278 9253
www.communitymatters.org.uk

Community Network
Ground Floor
12–20 Baron Street
London
N1 9LL
Tel: (020) 7923 5250
Fax: (020) 7713 8163
www.community-network.org

Companies House (Registrar of Companies)
Crown Way
Maindy
Cardiff
CF4 3UZ
Tel: 0870 33 33 636
Fax: (01222) 380 900
www.companieshouse.gov.uk

Co-operative & Community Finance
Brunswick Court
Brunswick Square
Bristol
BS2 8PE
Tel: 01179 166 750
Fax: 01179 166 751
www.icof.co.uk

Directory of Social Change
24 Stephenson Way
London
NW1 2DP
Tel: (020) 7391 4800
Fax: (020) 7391 4808
General Contact No: 08450 77 77 07
www.dsc.org.uk

Disability Rights Commission
See **Equality and Human Rights Commission**

Equality and Human Rights Commission
3 More London
Riverside Tooley Street
London
SE1 2RG
Tel: (020) 3117 0235
Fax: 01925 884 275
www.equalityhumanrights.com

Ethical Investment Research Service (EIRIS)
80–84 Bondway
London
SW8 1SF
Tel: (020) 7840 5700
Fax: (020) 7591 6001
www.eiris.org.uk

Heritage Lottery Fund
7 Holbein Place
London
SW1W 8NR
Tel: (020) 7591 6000
Fax: (020) 7591 6001

HMRC Charities
St Johns House
Merton Road
Bootle
Merseyside
L69 9BB
Tel: 08453 02 02 03
www.hmrc.gov.uk/charities

Housing Corporation (The)
Maple House
149 Tottenham Court Road
London
W1T 7BN
Tel: 0845 230 7000
Fax: (020) 7393 2111
www.housingcorp.gov.uk

Independent Complaints Reviewer to the Charity Commission Report
See **Charity Commission Direct**

Industrial Common Ownership Movement (ICOM)
See **Co-operative & Community Finance**

Inland Revenue Charities
See **HMRC Charites**

**Institute of Chartered Account-
ants in England & Wales**
Chartered Accountants' Hall
PO Box 433
London
EC2 2BJ
Tel: (020) 7920 8100
Fax: (020) 7920 0547
www.icaew.co.uk

**Institute of Chartered Account-
ants of Scotland**
21 Haymarket Yards
Edinburgh
EH12 5BH
Tel: (0131) 347 0100
Fax: (0131) 347 0105
www.icas.org.uk

Institute of Fundraising
Park Place
12 Lawn Lane
London
SW8 1UD
Tel: (020) 7840 1000
Fax: (020) 7840 1001
www.institute-of-fundraising.org.uk

**InterChange Legal Advisory
Service**
InterChange Studios
Hampstead Town Hall Centre
213 Haverstock Hill
London
NW3 4QP
Tel: (020) 7692 5860
Fax: (020) 7813 7493
www.interchange.org.uk/legal

Investors in People UK
7–10 Chandos Street
London
W1G 9DQ
Tel: (020) 7467 1900
Fax: (020) 7636 2386
General Contact No: (020) 7467 1946
www.investorsinpeople.co.uk

Law Society of Scotland
26 Drumsheugh Gardens
Edinburgh
EH3 7YR
Tel: (0131) 226 7411
Fax: (0131) 225 2934
www.lawscot.org.uk

**Legislation Monitoring Service for
Charities, Voluntary Organisations
and their Advisers**
12 Little College Street
London
SW1P 3SH
Tel: (020) 7222 1265
Fax: (020) 7222 1250
www.lmsconline.org

**National Association for Voluntary
and Community Action (NAVCA)**
The Tower
2 Furnival Square
Sheffield
S1 4QL
Tel: (0114) 278 6636
Fax: (0114) 278 7004
www.navca.org.uk

**National Association of Volunteer
Bureaux**
New Oxford House
16 Waterloo Street
Birmingham
B2 5UG
Tel: (0121) 633 4555
Fax: (0121) 633 4043
www.navb.org.uk

National Centre for Volunteering
See **Volunteering England**

**National Council for Voluntary
Organisations (NCVO)**
Regent's Wharf
8 All Saints Street
London
N1 9RL
Tel: (020) 7713 6161
Fax: (020) 7713 6300
www.ncvo-vol.org.uk

National Housing Federation (NHF)
Lion Court
25 Proctor Street
London
WC1V 6NY
Tel: (020) 7067 1010
Fax: (020) 7067 1011
www.housing.org.uk

National Lottery Charities Board (NLCB)
See **Big Lottery Fund**

New Opportunities Fund
See **Big Lottery Fund**

Northern Ireland Council for Voluntary Action (NICVA)
61 Duncairn Gardens
Belfast
BT15 2GB
Tel: (028) 9087 7777
Fax: (028) 9087 7799
www.nicva.org

Office of the Scottish Charity Regulator (OSCR)
2nd Floor
Quadrant House
9 Riverside Drive
Dundee
DD1 4NY
Tel: 01382 220446
www.oscr.org.uk

Official Custodian for Charities
See **Charity Commission Direct**

Refugee Council
240–250 Ferndale Road
Brixton
London
SW9 8BB
Tel: (020) 7346 6700
Fax: (020) 7346 6701
General Contact No: (020) 7346 6700
www.refugeecouncil.org.uk

Scottish Arts Council
12 Manor Place
Edinburgh
EH3 7DD
Tel: (0131) 226 6051
Fax: (0131) 225 9833
www.scottisharts.org.uk

Scottish Charities Office
See **Office of the Scottish Charity Regulator (OSCR)**

Scottish Council for Voluntary Organisations (SCVO)
Mansfield
Traquair Centre
15 Mansfield Place
Edinburgh
EH3 6BB
Tel: (0131) 556 3882
Fax: (0131) 556 0279
General Contact No: 0800 169 0022
www.scvo.org.uk

Sport England
3rd Floor
Victoria House
Bloomsbury Square
London
WC1B 4SE
Tel: (020) 7273 1551
Fax: (020) 7383 5740
www.sportengland.org

Sportscotland
Caledonia House
South Gyle
Edinburgh
EH12 9DQ
Tel: (0131) 317 7200
Fax: (0131) 317 7202
www.sportscotland.org.uk/

Sports Council of Wales
Sophia Gardens
Cardiff
CF11 9SW
Tel: 0845 045 0904
Fax: 0845 846 0014
www.sports-council-wales.co.uk

Useful Addresses

Sports Northern Ireland
House of Sport
Upper Malone Road
Belfast
BT9 5LA
Tel: (028) 90 381 222
Fax: (028) 90 682 757
www.sportni.net

Tai Cymru/Housing for Wales
25–30 Lambourne Crescent
Llanishen
Cardiff
CF4 5ZJ
Tel: 01222 741 500
Fax: 01222 741 501
www.housinginwales.co.uk
(general website on Welsh housing)

United Kingdom Accreditation Service (UKAS)
21–47 High Street
Feltham
Middlesex
TW13 4UN
Tel: (020) 8917 8400
Fax: (020) 8917 8500
www.ukas.com

Volunteering England
Regent's Wharf
8 All Saints Street
London
N1 9RL
Tel: 0845 305 6979
Fax: (020) 7520 8910
www.volunteering.org.uk

Wales Council for Voluntary Action (WCVA)
Baltic House
Mount Stuart Square
Cardiff Bay
Cardiff
CF10 5FH
Tel: (029) 2043 1700
Fax: (029) 2043 1701
www.wcva.org.uk

Other Useful Websites

Local Government Information Unit
www.lgiu.gov.uk

HM Treasury
www.hm-treasury.gov.uk

UK Fundraising Information for Charities
www.fundraising.co.uk

Criminal Records Bureau (CRB)
Information Line: 0870 9090811
www.crb.gov.uk

To contact the authors:

Don Bawtree
Partner, Charity Unit
BDO Stoy Hayward
Emerald House
Epsom
Surrey
KT17 1HS
Tel: (01372) 734 306
e-mail: don.bawtree@bdo.co.uk

Kate Kirkland
16 Westpoint
49 Putney Hill
London
SW15 6RU
Tel: (020) 8788 0559
e-mail: kate_kirkland@btinternet.com
M: 07900 246012

1   Accounting Reference Dates and Periods

1.1   Accounts for all charities, except those too small to be registered, have to be prepared in line with a timetable determined by law. The relevant legislation varies, however, according to the charity's legal structure, whether or not it is registered, the registering or regulating body and its location.

1.2   The *Charities Act 1992* introduced the concept of a financial year for unincorporated registered charities (the parts relating to accounts are now consolidated into the *Charities Act 1993*). Prior to the passing of the Act those charities were required to prepare accounts for consecutive periods not exceeding fifteen months. The *Charities Act 2006* has made no changes to the *Charities Act 1993* provisions. The draft *Charities (Accounts and Reports) Regulations 2008* do not propose changes to the Accounting Reference Date provisions.

1.3   A charity's financial year-end is known as its Accounting Reference Date (ARD), and the financial period running up to that date is known as the Accounting Reference Period (ARP).

UNINCORPORATED REGISTERED CHARITIES

1.4   The *Charities (Accounts and Reports) Regulations 2005* set out how a charity's first financial year should be determined.

- The first financial 'year' of an unincorporated charity (such as a trust or association) runs from the date of the charity's formation to a date, chosen by the trustees as the ARD, or a date within seven days either side of the ARD. The ARD is determined by the trustees and must be at least six, but no more than eighteen, months after the date the charity was established. There is no requirement to file a separate form recording this date with the Charity Commission (for English and Welsh charities) or HMRC or OSCR (for Scottish charities).

CHARITABLE COMPANIES REGISTERED WITH THE CHARITY COMMISSION

1.5   Companies automatically have their first year-end, i.e. their ARD, as the last day of the month which is twelve months from their incorporation date. This may be altered by the directors (i.e. the charity trustees) selecting another date, and filing the relevant form (form 225) with Companies House. See 1.16 below.

1.6   The permitted duration of accounting periods, and rules governing their changes, are the same as for unincorporated charities, although the legislation is set out in the *Companies Act 1985, ss 224* and *225*. One important difference, however, is that the *Companies Act 1985* permits the lengthening or shortening of the accounting period during the original period. The *Charities Act 1993* is silent on this matter.

OTHER TYPES OF CHARITY

1.7   Excepted charities should comply with the Regulations for registered charities unless other legislation applies.

1.8 Accounting Reference Dates and Periods

1.8 Unless other legislation or other legal obligation exists, exempt charities are required to make up consecutive statements of account relating to a period of not more than fifteen months. [*Charities Act 1993 s 46*].

1.9 All industrial and provident societies must choose a year-end between 31 August and 31 January, unless the Regulator has granted permission for the use of another date. [*Industrial and Provident Societies Act 1965, s 39*].

1.10 The Scottish Parliament has approved new Accounting Regulations and the *Charities Accounts (Scotland) Regulations 2006* apply to financial years starting on or after 1 April 2006.

1.11 The ARD of a charity required to register with OSCR is shown in the Scottish register. Existing charities entered on the Register on 1 April 2006; charitable companies incorporated before 1 April 2006 and charities established in countries other than Scotland before 1 April 2006, but registered afterwards, will all retain their existing ARD. Charities entered on the Register after 1 April 2006, that are not charitable companies or charities established in counties other than Scotland can decide their accounting reference date. The date must not be less than six months or more than 18 months after the date the charity was entered in the Register.

1.12 Charitable companies incorporated after 1 April 2006 or charities established after 1 April 2006 in counties other than Scotland and entered in the register can choose an ARD not less than six months or more than 18 months after the date the charity was incorporated or established.

AMENDING THE ACCOUNTING REFERENCE DATE

1.13 Accounts can always be made up to a date within seven days either side of the ARD in order to facilitate the production of accounts based on a 52-week year, rather than on a calendar year. References to 'financial year' and 'twelve months' in the *Charities (Accounts and Reports) Regulations 2005* allow for this minor variation, as do the *Companies Act 1985* and the Scottish Regulations.

1.14 After the ARD has been set for the first financial year, the trustees of unincorporated charities can choose to amend it to a date between six and eighteen months of the previous ARD if there are exceptional reasons to do so. The regulations only permit such a change of year-end if the previous two accounting periods were for twelve months, otherwise prior permission of the Commission must be obtained. The reasons for a change in the ARD will need to be disclosed in the accounts of any charity required to prepare accruals accounts.

1.15 *Section 225* of the *Companies Act 1985* contains similar provisions for amending the ARD. However, although the maximum length of an extended accounting period is the same, i.e. eighteen months, the *Companies Act 1985* does not specify a minimum length of time for shortened accounting periods. Also, the minimum length of time which must pass before a company's ARD can subsequently be altered is five years, in contrast to the two permitted for unincorporated charities, although exceptions are permitted to bring subsidiary company year-ends into line with those of their parent undertaking. In this instance the ARD may be shortened without limitation.

1.16 The change of ARD can be made by filing Form 225 with Companies House. The new ARD must be registered before the filing deadline of the current ARD ie usually 10 months after the current ARD.

1.17   The *Charities Accounts (Scotland) Regulations 2006* provide different provisions for Scottish Charities and those charities incorporated or established outside of Scotland but required to register with OSCR. Scottish registered charity trustees may specify a new ARD for either the current financial year or the immediately preceding financial year as long as the financial year is no longer than 18 months and the charity does not have a financial year that exceeds 12 months in any five-year period. A notice of the change must be given to OSCR within three months of the date of the decision to change the ARD. Where a charity is removed from the Register, its ARP will begin on the day after its previous full financial year end and end on the date of its removal from the register.

2   Accounts: General Requirements

2.1   All charities are required to maintain accounting records and to prepare annual accounts. The detailed requirements are complex due to the interaction of different regulatory regimes around the UK, different legal structures, and different activities. For most large charities, the charities SORP will be the appropriate framework for statutory accounting and reporting, and reference should be made to the Charities Accounts Regulations.

2.2   There are no standards applying to the production of internal, or management accounts. However most charities would expect to be able to produce monthly accounts in a format which is consistent or reconcilable with their statutory report. In addition, management accounts will typically include:

- Variance analysis against budget and prior periods

- Forecasts

- Commentary

- Analysis by cost centre or operational unit

- Management style cash flows.

These are not usually included in annual reports (though some constitutions require additional information).

Management accounts will often exclude:

- Cash flow as required by FRS 1

- Statutory disclosures

- Defined benefit pension scheme adjustments

- Revaluations

- Branch results

- Subsidiary or overseas activities

- Fund analysis.

2.3   Trustees should review their management accounting information and consider which information is appropriate for them to receive regularly and which information can be left to the year end. The more that is left to the year end, the more difficult it is to predict the overall shape and impression of the statutory report, and equally importantly, the trustees will not be able to discharge their responsibilities for the overall management of the charity's affairs.

SORP

2.4   The Statement of Recommended Practice on Accounting by Charities (SORP) applies to all charities in the United Kingdom producing accruals accounts, regardless of whether they are incorporated or unincorporated, unless another SORP, such as the one for housing associations, applies. Although there is no statutory requirement for charities to comply with the SORP, the Charity Commission expects charities to model their accounts on

4

it and would require a charity to justify the reasons for any non-compliance. The Accounting Regulations, draw heavily upon the SORP and make direct reference to the SORP.

Scotland

2.5   The SORP applies to Scottish charities. Most Scottish charities have to follow the *Charities and Trustee Investment (Scotland) Act 2005 (CTISA 2005)* and the *Charities Accounts (Scotland) Regulations 2006.*

ALLOWANCE FOR SIZE

2.6   An accounting regime suitable for large charities would be inappropriate for many others — more than 60% of charities have an annual income of less than £10,000. Therefore the detailed requirements of the accounting regime are graduated according to the size of the charity, as shown in Table 1. Charitable companies must produce annual reports and accounts and send them to the Charity Commission, together with an annual return, and must follow the requirements set out in the *Companies Act 1985* for the form of the report and accounts. The type of scrutiny required will depend on the company's size.

Table 1   Charities Act 1993 (as amended) requirements for unincorporated charities

Size	Type of Accounts	Annual Report	Scrutiny	Annual Report and Accounts Filing	Charity Commission Annual Return
Up to £10k annual income or expenditure	Receipts and Payments or Accruals accounts	Simplified	None routinely required	Charity Commission may request	Simple
More than £10k income or expenditure but not more than £100k income	Receipts and Payments (plus Statement of Assets and Liabilities) or Accruals accounts	Simplified	Independent examination or audit	Must be sent to the Charity Commission	Full
More than £100k income but not more than £500k income	Accruals accounts	Simplified	Independent examination or audit (if income is over £250,000 the examiner must be from a specified body)	Must be sent to the Charity Commission	Full
More than £500k income or expenditure £2.8m	Accruals accounts	Full	Audit	Must be sent to the Charity Commission	Full

2.7   Trustees of registered charities in England and Wales with income or expenditure in excess of £10,000 must file the charity's statutory annual accounts and annual report with the Charity Commission within ten months of the charity's financial year-end. [*Charities Act 1993, s 45*]. If the charity's income and expenditure is below £10,000 the annual report and accounts need only to be filed on request. [*Charities Act 1993, s 45(3A)*].

Limited companies: whether guarantee or with share capital, have slightly different requirements. They can never produce receipts and payments accounts, need also to include a directors' report, and audits of charitable companies are conducted under the Companies Act unless they are not small companies (if income over £5.6m and assets over £2.8m)

STANDARD OF RECORD-KEEPING

2.8   The standards to which the books of account should be maintained is defined by law, although the sort of accounting records (i.e. cash books or computerised records) is not legally defined. *Charities Act 1993, s 41* requires trustees of unincorporated charities to keep accounting records which:

- can disclose at any time, with reasonable accuracy, the charity's financial position;

- will enable the trustees to prepare accounts which comply with the annual charity accounting requirements;

- are sufficient to show and explain all the charity's financial transactions; and

- record the charity's assets and liabilities.

2.9   The accounting records should contain entries from day to day showing income and expenditure and recording the acquisition of assets and liabilities. This does not mean that the accounting records have to be written up on a daily basis, a sensible target for smaller charities is at least to produce a trial balance once a month. It will not always be practicable to include accounting data from diverse operations, such as local volunteer groups, on such a regular basis.

RETENTION OF RECORDS

2.10   *Section 41* of the *Charities Act 1993* requires unincorporated charities to keep accounting records for at least six years from the end of the financial year in which they are made (i.e. for seven years). This requirement differs from requirements of *s 222* of the *Companies Act 1985* which stipulate that records of private companies must be retained for three years (charitable companies are private, rather than public, companies). However, as HMRC can make adjustments to PAYE deductions going back six years and VAT inquiries may also go back six years, all charities would be well advised to keep financial records for at least seven years.

2.11   Financial records include:

- books of account;

- minutes of meetings authorising expenditure;

- other authorisations of expenditure;

- documentation relating to the verification of the receipt of income;

- documentation relating to the verification of expenditure;

- bank statements; and

- records of assets and liabilities.

2.12   Claims under the *Consumer Protection Act 1987* can go back ten years, so it is advisable to keep records of the purchase or sale of major goods for at least that length of time.

ACCRUALS OR RECEIPTS AND PAYMENTS ACCOUNTS

2.13   Depending on their size, or the requirements of their governing document or funders, some smaller charities are required to prepare accounts on an accruals basis. Those that are not required to do so may choose between preparing them on an accruals basis or a receipts and payments basis.

2.14   Accrual accounts give a true and fair view of an organisation's financial affairs as they show all transactions affecting the accounting period, whether or not they are represented as a cash transaction, i.e. monthly accounts would show, for example, an amount equivalent to one-twelfth of an annual payment for rent. Charities preparing accounts on an accruals basis should follow the format recommended by the Statement of Recommended Practice on Accounting for Charities (SORP) unless another SORP applies.

2.15   Receipts and payment accounts are a factual record summarising all the cash transactions made during the relevant period and listing the charity's remaining cash and non-cash assets and its liabilities. Accounting standards do not generally apply to such accounts, because they do not purport to give a true and fair view of either the financial activities for the year or the state of affairs at the year-end. The Charity Commission has issued a guide, 'Receipts and Payments Accounts pack', for charities preparing annual accounts on the receipts and payment basis.

2.16   The formats for the accounts of some charities are not governed, however, by the Charities SORP, but by recommendations or regulations that are more specific to a particular type of organisation, as shown in Table 3.

Table 2   Accounts requirements for particular types of charity

Type of charity	Requirement
Housing associations/Registered Social Landlords (RSLs)	Accruals accounts prepared in accordance with the Accounting Requirements for Registered Social Landlords General Determination 2006 and the SORP for RSLs
Universities	Accruals accounts prepared under the Further and Higher Education SORP
Non-departmental public bodies	Accruals accounts prepared in accordance with HM Treasury guidance, supplemented by Charities SORP

2.17 Accounts: General Requirements

2.17   In addition, excepted charities, especially denominational churches, have modified accounting requirements under their own rules. These broadly follow the requirements of the Charities SORP but reference should be made to each particular set of rules.

AUDIT REQUIREMENT

2.18   Many charities will be required to have their annual accounts audited or otherwise subjected to some form of external scrutiny. For unincorporated charities this scrutiny will be in the form of an independent examination or an audit, whereas charitable and other limited companies will be required to have an audit or an examination if they are small charitable companies i.e. if their annual income is less than £500K and they have less than £2.8m of assets. Industrial and provident societies have similar audit requirements to limited companies under the *Industrial and Provident Societies Act 1968, s 3*.

2.19   The Charity Commission has powers under *ss 43(4)–(6)* of the *Charities Act 1993* to make an order requiring the audit of accounts, e.g. if audited accounts have not been produced within ten months of the end of the relevant financial year or if the Commissioners consider it desirable to have a full audit of accounts that have been independently examined. In certain circumstances the trustees can be jointly and severally liable for the cost of such an audit.

PUBLIC RIGHT TO SEE ACCOUNTS

2.20   The *Charities Act 1993* requires the trustees of all charities in England and Wales to send a copy of the charity's most recent accounts to any member of the public who requests a copy in writing, within two months of the request. [*Charities Act 1993, s 47(2)*]. Failure to do so may result, on conviction, in a fine. The trustees may charge a reasonable fee in respect of the cost of complying with such a request. [*Charities Act 1993, s 47(2)(b)*].

FURTHER INFORMATION

2.21   Charity Commission publications

Accounting and Reporting by Charities: Statement of Recommended Practice (SORP 2005)

CC16:   'Receipts and Payments Accounts Pack'

CC17:   'Accruals Accounts Pack'

CC63a: 'Independent Examination of Charity Accounts: Directions and Guidance Notes'.

3   Accounts: Summary Financial Statements

SUMMARY FINANCIAL INFORMATION AND STATEMENTS

3.1   Many charities publish financial information in a format different from their statutory financial statements. This is usually in an Annual Report or Annual Review, but may also occur in other instances such as fund-raising literature. It should be noted that the full auditor's report must not be reproduced in conjunction with any accounts other than the complete financial statements reported on by the auditors.

3.2   The Charities SORP 2005 refers to some charities publishing summary financial information or summaries in a format different to the statutory accounts. The SORP encompasses a wide range of summary information, but states that there are two basic types of summaries: (1) summarised financial statements, and (2) summary financial information.

3.3   The SORP acknowledges that the publications within which summary financial information and statements are included will vary considerably and accordingly it is not practicable to give detailed recommendations on the content of summary financial information. However, it does provide some general principles to be followed that are included below.

TERMINOLOGY

3.4   Statutory accounts are well defined by the SORP, legislation and accounting standards. Management accounts are not governed by any regulatory framework, as they are produced for internal use by management and trustees. Summary accounts are rarely produced for public consumption, except by charities and public companies.

3.5   The accounting requirements of the *Charities Act 1993* and subsequent amending acts do not include reference to summarised financial statements and information. Therefore trustees of unincorporated charities may produce summarised financial statements on an extra-statutory basis, whilst in the case of charitable companies the specific provisions of the *Companies Act 1985* concerning non-statutory financial statements apply.

3.6   The *Companies Act 1985* distinguishes between summary accounts and non-statutory accounts. The legislation relating to summary accounts is contained in *SI 1995/2092*, a section that relates only to public companies and thus does not apply to charitable companies. However, the *Part VII Chapter 1 Section 240(3)–(5)* relating to non-statutory accounts applies to all companies including charitable companies. This distinction between summary accounts and non-statutory accounts is helpful terminology consistent to that relating to summarised financial statements used by the SORP. Charities sometimes include their full (or almost full) annual accounts in a document, before they have been audited and approved by the trustees. The SORP states that summary financial information should contain information on the Statement of Financial Activities and/or the balance sheet, should be consistent with the full accounts and should not be misleading either by omission or amalgamation.

3.7   Accounts: Summary Financial Statements

UNINCORPORATED CHARITIES

3.7   Whenever the full audited accounts are provided, the auditor's report and the annual report should also be attached.

3.8   Whenever accounts contain less information than the full audited statutory accounts the trustees must decide whether they form summarised financial statements or summary financial information. Summarised financial statements are usually closer to the full accounts than summary financial information. Table 3 sets out some of the characteristics of summarised financial statements and summary financial information, based on the SORP and the *Companies Act*. In some cases it will be a matter of judgement as to which term is correct.

Table 3   Contrasting Characteristics of Summarised Financial Statements and Summarised Financial Information

Characteristics of summarised financial statements	Characteristics of summary financial information
Includes a summary of the SOFA and/or Balance Sheet.	Draws information from only parts of the accounts.
The summary is derived from the statutory accounts.	May be based on interim accounts or other financial information as well as statutory accounts.
A financial statement that purports to be a SOFA or balance sheet or summary thereof.	Makes no reference to either the SOFA or balance sheet.
Represents the entire finances of a charity, or a charity group.	Represents analysis eg. of a particular activity or region.

3.9   If trustees are still not sure whether the information represents summarised financial statements or summary financial information, then a good test is to ask whether or not the information is intended as a substitute for the full accounts (i.e. do you expect members to vote on the annual accounts relying more on the summary information than the full accounts, as often happens?).

3.10   Once the status of the information has been determined the trustees must append the appropriate signed statement to the accounts, encompassing the SORP's requirements. Summarised financial statements should be accompanied by a statement, similar to the following, with the words in italics being amended as necessary:

'These summary financial statements are not the statutory accounts, but a summary relating to both the Statement of Financial Activities and the balance sheet. The full financial statements, from which the summary is derived *have/have not* been audited. The audit report was *unqualified/qualified/contained an emphasis of matter—further details are provided in the summary statements. This summary is for the branch only, and has been extracted from the full accounts of "name of main charity"*. The full accounts, annual report and auditor's report may be obtained from (insert address). The annual report and accounts, which were approved on (insert date), *have/have not* been filed with the Charity Commission.

Signed on behalf of the Trustees ...'

3.11   References to 'audit' should be amended to 'examination' or 'independent examination' as necessary. Only registered charities need to refer to the filing requirement.

3.12   Summarised financial information, in whatever form, must be accompanied by a statement on behalf of the Trustees such as:

> 'This summarised information is provided in order to (state purpose of the information, e.g. assist readers' understanding of the costs incurred in running the project). This information *is/is not* derived from the charity's full annual accounts, *which have/have not been audited/independently examined*. The most recent full accounts, annual report and auditor's report may be obtained from (insert address).
>
> Signed on behalf of the trustees . . .'

Auditor's/Examiner's statement

3.13   There is no statutory requirement for auditors of an unincorporated charity to report on summarised financial statements. However, if the full accounts have been audited or externally scrutinised then the SORP recommends that the auditor or examiner should attach a statement to the summarised financial statements (but not summarised financial information) giving an opinion as to whether or not the summary financial statements are consistent with the full annual accounts.

3.14   The auditor's statement for unincorporated charities is prescribed in the Audit Practice Board's Practice Note 11 (Revised). It sets out the addressee, the respective responsibilities of the trustees and auditors, the basis of the opinion and the opinion itself which should state whether or not the summary accounts are consistent with the full financial statements. If they are inconsistent, then such inconsistencies must be set out and explained.

3.15   No such specimen wording has been issued in respect of independent examiners. However, the SORP requires that their report should follow the same principles as the auditor's statement, including an opinion as to the consistency of the figures.

3.16   Unless agreed as a special assignment, auditors would not report on summary financial information as any further allusion to the audit report may attract deeper credibility to the information than is, in fact, justified. There is no requirement for auditors to review such information and they will only do so if their name is to be associated with it in any way.

CHARITABLE COMPANIES

3.17   Charitable companies should follow the above principles but, in addition, the *Companies Act 1985* requires them to state whether or not the relevant statutory accounts have been filed with the Registrar of Companies.

3.18   The *Companies Act 1985* specifically prohibits publication of an audit report with non-statutory accounts.

3.19   Accounts: Summary Financial Statements

INDUSTRIAL AND PROVIDENT SOCIETIES

3.19   There is no specific reference in the legislation applicable to summary information produced by Industrial and Provident Societies, and so the SORP guidance applying to unincorporated charities should be followed.

SCOTTISH CHARITIES

3.20   Scottish charities should follow all of the above except for the references to the Charity Commission.

3.21   OSCR and the Scottish Charity Accounting Regulations make no mention of summary financial statements or information.

INCONSISTENCIES

3.22   If the auditors consider that there are inconsistencies, then they will refer to this matter in their report to the trustees. If the auditors are not satisfied with the nature of the trustees' statement they will not permit any report they have produced for the trustees to be published.

3.23   The summarised accounts should be consistent with the full accounts. This means that information has been accurately extracted from the full accounts and has been summarised in a way that is not unduly selective or incompatible with the statutory headings. Other information which may be necessary to ensure consistency (for instance a post-balance sheet event or information relating to an exceptional item) or which is fundamental to understanding the figures should also be included.

COMMUNICATING FINANCIAL INFORMATION WITH GRAPHICS

3.24   When producing summary accounts many charities make the information more accessible by presenting it in diagrammatic form. The key advantages of using graphics to portray financial information are as follows:

- assessment of the financial position is easier;

- relationships between sets of data are portrayed more effectively;

- essential elements are communicated faster;

- the presentation has visual appeal.

3.25   However, certain factors can make diagrammatic presentations worse than useless: mismatched scales, poor selection of data, and lack of accompanying narrative can all create a misleading impression.

3.26   Graphs, bar charts, and scatter or radar diagrams, can be used to depict relationships and trends. Pie charts are best for illustrating the breakdown of a constituent whole but less suitable for illustrating absolute growth or decline. They cannot reflect the components of, for instance, a balance sheet which includes negative items. In this instance either a vertical or horizontal bar chart would be more effective. Bar charts can also be used to reflect key ratios, such as the proportion of expenditure going on direct charitable support in comparison with total expenditure.

4   Advertising

4.1   Charities and their trading subsidiaries advertise in a variety of circum-
        stances, for example to:

- promote their services;

- fund-raise;

- campaign;

- recruit staff, volunteers or trustees; and

- communicate other needs, e.g. to let or sell premises.

They use a wide range of media including:

- newspapers and magazines;

- posters and flyers;

- radio, television and cinema;

- direct mail;

- products, such as carrier bags, tee shirts, etc;

- text messaging; and

- the internet, email, bulletin boards, etc.

4.2   Charities should ensure that all their advertising complies with relevant
        legislation and codes of practice. In some instances legal advice will be
        necessary, as the legislation relating to advertising is substantial and complex.
        Failures in compliance can result in bad publicity, with resulting loss of public
        support, and in some instances charities may be fined, or subject to a court
        injunction. Other sanctions include withdrawal of trading privileges, referral
        to the Office of Fair Trading and disqualification from industry awards.

CODES OF PRACTICE

4.3   The advertising industry is subject to self-regulation. The Advertising
        Standards Authority (ASA) is the independent body, set up by the industry,
        that regulates the content of advertisements, sales promotions and direct
        marketing in the UK. The ASA ensures that standards are kept high by
        applying the advertising standards codes. The ASA can stop misleading,
        harmful or offensive advertising. It can also ensure that sales promotions are
        run fairly and resolve problems with mail order purchases. It can help reduce
        unwanted business mail sent either through the post, by email, or by text
        message. The ASA monitors advertisements to spot problems and can inves-
        tigate complaints from any member of the public about advertisements, sales
        promotions and direct marketing. It needs to receive only one complaint
        before it can launch an investigation. Adjudications are published on the
        ASA's website, *www.asa.org.uk*, every Wednesday.

4.4   The advertising standards codes are separated into codes for TV, radio, and all
        other media. The codes can downloaded in full from the ASA's website.
        There are also rules for Teletext advertisements, Interactive advertisements

and the scheduling of television advertisements. The main principles on which all the codes are based are that advertisements should not mislead, cause harm, or offend.

4.5   The advertising industry takes responsibility for writing the advertising standard codes and enforcing the ASA rulings through the Committee of Advertising Practice (CAP). CAP's Broadcast Committee is contracted by the broadcast regulator, Ofcom, to write and enforce codes of practice that govern TV and radio advertising on channels and stations licensed by Ofcom and on interactive television services, TV shopping channels and Teletext services. CAP's Non-Broadcast Committee writes and enforces the British Code of Advertising, Sales Promotion and Direct Marketing, which regulates the content of advertisements in print, on posters, in new media and the cinema and covers all sales promotions, the use of personal data for direct marketing and the delivery of mail order goods or refunds. This Code does not, however, regulate claims organisations make on their websites, or flyposting, premium rate services and phone lines, most advertisements that originate outside the UK, private classified advertisements, private correspondence, such as that between companies and their customers, telephone selling, editorial content of books, newspapers and journals, regular competitions such as crosswords, packaging, tickets, timetables and price lists.

Non-broadcast advertising

4.6   The British Code of Advertising, Sales Promotion and Direct Marketing can be downloaded free from *www.cap.org.uk* or *www.asa.org.uk*. It states that advertisements should be legal, decent, honest and truthful, and be prepared with a sense of responsibility to consumers and society. Marketing communications should respect the principles of fair competition generally accepted in business and should not bring advertising into disrepute. Marketing communications should comply with the law and not incite anyone to break it. No advertisement should mislead by inaccuracy, ambiguity, exaggeration, omission or otherwise and marketers should not exploit the credulity, lack of knowledge or inexperience of consumers. Before distributing or submitting a marketing communication for publication the organisation must hold documentary evidence to prove that all claims, whether direct or implied, are capable of objective substantiation. Advertisements should contain nothing that is likely to cause serious or widespread offence, particularly on the grounds of race, religion, sex, sexual orientation or disability. Advertisements may be distasteful without necessarily conflicting with this requirement. Advertisements should not cause fear or distress without good reason. Shocking images should not be used merely to attract attention. Marketers may give a view about any matter, provided it is clear that they are expressing their opinion rather than stating a fact. Any stated prices should include VAT and marketers must make it clear if stocks are limited. Comparative claims are permitted, but they should neither mislead nor be likely to mislead, and advertisements should not discredit or denigrate products or services of competitors.

4.7   The Code contains specific rules about certain types of promotion, including prize promotions and charity-linked promotions. All promotions run by third parties (e.g. commercial companies) claiming that participation will benefit registered charities or causes must:

- name each charity or cause that will benefit, and be able to show the ASA or CAP the formal agreement with those benefiting from the promotion;

- if the beneficiary is not a registered charity, define its nature and objectives;

- specify exactly what will be gained by the named charity or cause and state the basis on which the contribution will be calculated;

- state if the promoter has imposed a limit on its contributions;

- not limit consumers' contributions. If an amount is stated for each purchase, there should be no cut-off point for contributions. If a target total is stated, extra money collected should be given to the named charity or cause on the same basis as contributions below that level;

- be able to show that targets set are realistic;

- not exaggerate the benefit to the charity or cause derived from individual purchases of the promoted product;

- if asked, make available to consumers a current or final total of contributions made;

- take particular care when appealing to children.

4.8   The Code contains detailed rules for advertising, promotions or direct marketing aimed at or featuring children, motoring, environmental claims, health and beauty products and therapies, including medicines, vitamins, minerals and other food supplements, cosmetics, hair and scalp products and services, weight control, employment and business opportunities, financial products, betting and gaming, tobacco, and alcoholic drinks. Rules about advertising gambling come into force in September 2007.

4.9   The Committee of Advertising Practice offers a Copy Advice Service which is a free, fast and confidential way to check non-broadcast advertising, aimed at selling goods or services or fund-raising, before it is published (see *www.cap.org.uk*).

Broadcast advertising

4.10   Two sets of rules apply to broadcast advertisements – a set for TV and a set for radio. Copies of both the Radio Advertising Standards Code and the TV Advertising Standards code can be downloaded from the BCAP section of the CAP website (*www.cap.org.uk*) or the ASA website (*www.asa.org.uk*). Both codes are framed to ensure that radio and TV advertisements are 'legal, decent, honest and truthful' and do not mislead or cause harm or serious or widespread offence.

4.11   Key points in both codes include the following:

- Advertising must be clearly distinguishable from programming;

- Advertisements must comply with the requirements of the *Control of Misleading Advertisements Regulations 1998* (as amended);

- All factual claims need substantiation and advertisers must provide supporting written evidence if claims are likely to be challenged;

4.12 Advertising

- Environmental claims must be supported by sound factual evidence and should follow DEFRA's Green Claims Code (see *www.defra.gov.uk/environment*);

- Any comparisons should be fair and should not denigrate the products or services of another producer either directly or by implication;

- Advertisements that include reference to premium rate telephone services must comply with the PhonepayPlus (formerly ICSTIS – the Independent Committee for the Supervision of Standards of Telephone Information Services) code of practice which can be downloaded from *www.phonepayplus.org.uk*. In particular pricing information must be given as 'calls cost xp per minute at all times' or as the total maximum cost of the complete message or service to the consumer;

- Advertisements must not include sounds likely to create a safety hazard.

4.12 Charity advertisers must be required to give licensees the following assurances:

- that they do not involve themselves in transactions in which members of their governing body or staff have a financial interest;

- that the response to their proposed advertising, whether in cash or kind or services, will be applied solely to the purposes specified or implied in the advertising;

- that they will not publish or otherwise disclose the names of contributors without their prior permission and that they otherwise comply with the requirements of current Data Protection Legislation.

Licensees may need to seek assurances on other matters where appropriate and should reserve the right to reconsider the acceptability of advertising where it doubts the validity of any information provided.

4.13 There are special rules in the Radio Advertising Standards Code for specific categories of advertising and all radio advertisements relating to the following must be sent to the Radio Advertising Clearance Centre for vetting prior to broadcast:

- Advertising aimed specifically at children (those aged below 16 years);

- Child voiceovers;

- Testimonials;

- Environmental claims;

- Consumer credit, investment and complex financial advertising;

- Political, industrial and public controversy matters (including COI/Government and Council campaigns), Political Advertisers, Humanitarian Advertisers, Trade Unions and similar bodies;

- Alcoholic drink;

- Medical products (including medicines), treatments, services and establishments, Health products and services (including pharmaceutical products and services offering advice on personal medical problems, e.g. private clinics offering cosmetic surgery, therapists);

- Health and/or beauty treatments and claims;
- Food and nutrition claims;
- Dietary supplements; slimming products, treatments and establishments;
- Contraception, condoms and family planning products and services; pregnancy-testing products and services;
- Sanitary protection products;
- Anti-AIDS, anti-drugs and solvent abuse messages;
- Sex shops, stripograms, etc;
- Consumer advice services;
- Competitions, lotteries, betting and gaming;
- Dating, introduction or marriage agencies or services;
- 18-certificate films and videos;
- UK-wide media;
- Websites featuring products and services which fall under 'special categories' within this Code;
- Religious advertising;
- Divination and the supernatural;
- Charities.

4.14   Charities may advertise on the radio or TV for funds or the donation of products or services for charitable purposes providing they comply with all relevant rules on charity advertising, such as the rules on political, industrial and public controversy, environmental claims, and religion, faith and related systems of belief. In addition, charity advertising on TV must reflect a broad sense of ethical responsibility.

4.15   Radio and TV advertisements soliciting donations or promoting the needs and objects of UK bodies whose activities are financed wholly or mainly from donations may only be accepted from registered charities or those able to produce satisfactory evidence that their charitable status has been officially recognised. Non-UK based charities may also be accepted for advertising if satisfactory bona fides can be established.

4.16   Broadcast appeals must:

- avoid presenting an exaggerated impression of the scale or nature of the social problem to which the work of the charity is addressed;
- respect the dignity of those on whose behalf an appeal is made;
- not misrepresent or mislead in any way the charity, its field of activity, or the use to which donations will be put;
- not contain comparisons with other charities;
- not address any fund-raising messages specifically to children;

4.17 Advertising

- handle with care and discretion matters likely to arouse strong emotions in the audience;

- not suggest anyone will lack proper feeling or fail in any responsibility if they do not support the charity.

4.17   If a commercial advertiser promotes a charity in a radio or TV advertisement the following conditions apply in addition to the requirements of *Part II* of the *Charities Act 1992* as amended by the *Charities Act 2006*:

- The advertiser must provide the TV station with evidence of the charity's consent to the proposed advertising.

- If advertisements include an offer to donate part of the proceeds of sales to charity each advertisement must specify which individual charity or group of charities will benefit and clarify how the donations will be calculated; the advertisement must specify what proportion of the consideration paid for the goods or services will be received by the charity for each sale made (e.g. '£1 per sale' or '10% of the purchase price') and must not simply refer to 'x% of the profits' or 'all profits to Charity X'; such offers must not depend on sales reaching a given level, or be subject to any similar condition. Offers of this kind in connection with advertisements for medical products are unacceptable.

4.18   The TV Advertising Standards Code is very similar to that for radio advertising, though there are some differences, for example the TV Code includes a ban on subliminal advertising, i.e. the showing of images for a very brief duration that could influence viewers without them being fully aware of what has been done. TV advertisements must not:

- use expressions reserved for important news and public service announcements (e.g. 'news flash');

- use a situation, performance or style reminiscent of a programme in a way that might confuse viewers as to whether they are watching a programme or an advertisement;

- refer to themselves in a way that might lead viewers to believe they are watching a programme (e.g. by adopting the title 'Programme');

- include extracts from broadcasts of parliamentary proceedings;

- feature, visually or orally, anyone who regularly presents news or current affairs on television.

4.19   TV advertising for religious charities may include appeals for funds if the charities reliably demonstrate:

- that any proceeds will be devoted solely to the benefit of identified categories of disadvantaged third parties;

- that the conveying of that benefit will not be associated with any other objective (e.g. proselytising).

4.20   When drawing up radio advertisements charities can consult the Radio Advertising Clearance Centre, which vets all national radio commercials and certain local and regional commercials before broadcasting. Similarly, almost all TV advertisements are vetted before broadcast by the Broadcast Advertising Clearance Centre, which can offer guidance.

Text Services

4.21   The Advertising Standards Code for Text Services can be downloaded from the ASA's website (*www.asa.org.uk*). It sets out the rules for advertising standards and the separation of advertisements from editorial material.

Premium Rate Services

4.22   PhonepayPlus is the regulatory body for Premium Rate Services. Its Code of Practice can be downloaded from the website *www.phonepayplus.org.uk*. Premium Rate Services typically offer information and entertainment services via fixed or mobile phones, fax, PCs or interactive digital TVs. They are not used by many charities, but some commercial organisations claim that part of the cost of calls to their numbers will be donated to charity.

4.23   The PhonepayPlus Code states that promotional material for fund-raising and charitable promotions must make clear:

- either the total sum per call or the amount per minute that will be paid to the beneficiary;

- the identity of the beneficiary;

- any restrictions or conditions attached to the contribution to the beneficiary.

Programme sponsorship

4.24   When the Independent Television Commission (ITC) was replaced by Ofcom at the end of 2003, Ofcom took over responsibility for the ITC Code of Programme Sponsorship, which covers programmes that are paid, or part paid, for by an advertiser with a view to promoting their name, trade mark, activities, products or other commercial interest. The Code of programme sponsorship can be downloaded from *www.ofcom.org.uk*.

4.25   There are two key principles that underpin the regulation of programme sponsorship:

- To ensure that programmes are not distorted for commercial purposes. A sponsor must not influence the content or scheduling of a programme in such a way as to affect the editorial independence and responsibility of the broadcaster.

- To maintain a distinction between advertising and sponsor credits. This is to ensure that credits are not used to extend the time allowed for advertising.

4.26   Charities considering programme sponsorship should be aware that the code prohibits sponsored programmes from promoting the sponsor itself or its activities, even if it addresses issues within the sponsor's field of activity.

Consumer legislation

4.27   Many laws have been passed to protect consumers from misleading advertisements. The *Trade Descriptions Act 1968* makes it an offence to apply a false trade description to goods, to supply or offer to supply goods to which a false trade description is applied, or to knowingly or recklessly make false statements about services, facilities or accommodation. Charities with shops should ensure that staff or volunteers do not apply false trade descriptions to goods, either verbally or in writing. Charities organising overseas challenge events will also need to take particular care.

4.28 The *Consumer Protection Act 1987* prohibits the sale of unsafe goods and makes it an offence to give misleading indications as to the price at which any goods, services, accommodation or facilities are available. Charities engaged in primary purpose trading as well as trading subsidiaries must comply with this Act. Guidance is available in the Department for Business, Enterprise & Regulatory Reform's Code of Practice for Traders on Price Indication.

4.29 The *Control of Misleading Advertisements (Amendment) Regulations 2000* allow the Director General of Fair Trading to consider complaints about misleading advertisements and where necessary bring an injunction to stop the advertisements.

REQUIREMENT TO STATE REGISTERED STATUS

4.30 A registered charity, if its gross income in its last financial year exceeded £10,000, is required under the *Charities Act 1993 s 5* as amended to state in English (or Welsh in the case of a Welsh charity) the fact that it is a registered charity in all advertisements, notices, and other documents issued by or on behalf of the charity and soliciting money or other property for the benefit of the charity. This applies whether the solicitation is express or implied, and whether the money or other property is to be given for any consideration or not. The charity's registered number does not need to be stated, though it is common practice to do so. Any trustee or staff member who authorises an advertisement that fails to state that the charity is a registered charity is guilty of an offence and liable on summary conviction to a fine. In practice it is prudent for any registered charity, notwithstanding its current level of income, to comply with this requirement. Excepted charities that are not voluntarily registered must not state that they are a registered charity. Exempt charities may state that they are a charity exempt from registration and give their HMRC number.

VAT ON ADVERTISING

4.31 Charities can both provide and purchase advertising services. The VAT treatment to be applied to advertisements is likely to be different in each circumstance. The reliefs available for a charity's advertisements are not available to its trading subsidiary.

4.32 The selling of advertising space by a charity is always regarded as a business activity. Normally any advertising would be treated as a standard-rated taxable supply by the charity. However, as a concession for charities selling advertising space in brochures where at least half of the total number of advertisements in each publication are clearly from private individuals, then all the advertisement income generated can be treated as donations. This means the income in such circumstances can be treated as outside the scope of VAT. HMRC, in their guidance, quote the example of a private advertisement being 'Good wishes from John and Susan Smith', which is contrasted with a business advert including as the wording 'John and Susan Smith, Grocers, 49 High Street'. Should the number of private advertisements in a brochure amount to less than half the total, then all the income is regarded as consideration for a supply. The standard rate of VAT will apply except where the supply is made:

- to another charity and is eligible for zero rating (see **4.24**);

- in connection with an exempt fund-raising activity and eligible for exemption, unless overridden by zero rating in the point above;

- to a person who does not 'belong' in the EU; or

- to a person who 'belongs' in a different EU Member State in connection with the business activity of that person.

Advertising purchased by a charity

4.33   All types of advertising purchased by a charity in a third party medium qualify for zero rating, including advertisements on television, cinema, billboards, buses, in newspapers, programmes, annuals, leaflets and other publications, and on internet sites.

4.34   Marketing and advertising of items to targeted individuals or groups are excluded from zero-rate relief. Customs state that this exclusion includes telesales and direct mail by post, fax or e-mail. However, certain items addressed to targeted individuals or groups will be zero-rated because of the relief granted to pre-printed fund-raising appeals and by the general relief available on certain items of printed matter.

4.35   Relief is also extended, by concession, to goods used by charities in connection with collecting monetary donations. There are three specific goods that qualify:

- certain printed stationery;

- collection boxes; and

- lapel stickers and similar tokens.

4.36   Pre-printed appeal letters, return envelopes and collecting envelopes continue to qualify for zero rating. The concession also applies to all kinds of collecting boxes and receptacles used for collecting money. The relief for lapel stickers and similar tokens extends to small items designed to be worn on clothing, such as paper stickers, ribbons, metal pins and badges, that are given freely in acknowledgment of a donation. It does not extend to clothing (of any material), mugs or similar commemorative items, Christmas cards or calendars.

4.37   Where an advertisement is carried by television, radio or cinema, the zero rate applies only to the cost of the broadcasting or screening of the advertisement, not to the cost of making it. This is in contrast to advertisements in printed media where design and preparation costs for artwork, typesetting, etc. that are closely linked to the production of a qualifying printed media advertisement are zero-rated.

4.38   To obtain zero rating, the charity will need to give the supplier a declaration in the approved format. If this has been overlooked, it is generally possible to correct the position subsequently, subject to any applicable capping provisions.

4.39   Advertising

TAX ON INCOME FROM ADVERTISING

4.39   Since the sale of goods or services constitutes a trade, it follows that the provision of advertising by a charity will also constitute a trade, and one which is almost certainly taxable unless part of a wider activity, such as publishing. The sale of advertising in a charity's publication about its own activities, or in a journal on a subject which a charitable institution or association promotes, will be part of that trade. If the production of the publication is in accordance with or ancillary to the primary purpose of the charity, the advertising revenue forms part of the income of that trade and is usually exempt from tax.

4.40   HMRC draws a clear distinction between advertising and sponsorship. Where references to a sponsor amount to no more than an acknowledgement of the sponsor's contribution, then that sponsorship will not be regarded as trading income. However, HMRC will regard a reference to a sponsor that incorporates either the sponsor's logo, the sponsor's corporate colours, or a mention of the sponsor's products or services, as supplying advertising. Such an advertisement will normally be regarded as taxable unless it relates to a primary purpose of the charity, for example, advertising an exhibition or show to be held by an agricultural society.

FURTHER INFORMATION

4.41   The Committee of Advertising Practice
Mid City Place
71 High Holborn
London
WC1V 6QT
Tel: 020 7492 2222
E-mail: enquiries@cap.org.uk
www.asa.org.uk
www.cap.org.uk

Broadcast Advertising Clearance Centre (for clearance on TV commercials)
4 Roger Street
2nd Floor
London
WC1N 2JX
Tel: 020 7339 4700
www.bacc.org.uk

Radio Advertising Clearance Centre (for clearance on radio commercials)
77 Shaftesbury Avenue
London
W1D 5DU
Tel: 020 7306 2620
E-mail: adclear@racc.co.uk
www.racc.org.uk

PhonepayPlus
Clove Building
4 Maguire Street
London

SE1 2NQ
Tel: 020 7940 7474
www.phonepayplus.org.uk

The Office of Fair Trading
Fleetbank House
2–6 Salisbury Square
London
EC4Y 8JX
www.oft.gov.uk

Trading Standards Central
www.tradingstandards.gov.uk

5 Alcohol

5.1   Charities may want to sell or provide alcohol to people attending fund-raising events or as a way of improving the recreational or educational facilities they offer. The sale of alcohol is a complex subject and professional advice is likely to be required to ensure that the law is not broken and that all the tax and VAT implications have been taken into account. This applies whether the sale is made by:

- the charity;
- other charitable organisations using the charity's premises;
- non-charitable bodies hiring the premises.

5.2   Charities considering providing alcohol must ensure that they comply with:

- their governing document;
- the terms of their lease or freehold title;
- charity law;
- tax and VAT legislation;
- the licensing laws.

GOVERNING DOCUMENT

5.3   Some charities have a governing document that forbids or restricts the sale or consumption of alcohol. If there is such a restriction, the charity has either to abide by it or to apply to the Charity Commission for a Scheme to amend or remove the restriction. (Scottish charities will have to apply to the Office of the Scottish Charity Regulator (OSCR)). The Commission will only make such a Scheme if the charity can demonstrate that the removal of the restriction will enable it to pursue its charitable objects more effectively.

LEASE OR TITLE DEED

5.4   A lease or freehold title deed may contain a covenant forbidding the sale of alcohol, usually to prevent disturbance to neighbouring properties or for moral or religious reasons. The Charity Commission has no power to amend these types of restrictions. If the charity wishes to amend them, it would need to come to an arrangement with the person or people who have the benefit of the covenant. In most instances this will be the landlord or other landowners. If it proves extremely difficult to trace the covenant beneficiary, the charity could apply to the Land Tribunal to have the covenant released, though this is usually a lengthy process. Professional advice will be necessary.

CHARITABLE ACTIVITY OR TRADING?

5.5   Providing a pub or social club type service is not a charitable purpose, even in most cases under the *Recreational Charities Act 1958*, so organisations whose main or sole purpose is to provide such services cannot be registered as charities. However, charities may engage in a trade that is 'ancillary' to their main purpose or covered by certain concessions. 'Ancillary' activities are those that are not part of the charity's main purpose, but which are under-taken as an integral part of providing or meeting the charity's primary purpose. For example, if a charitable theatre provides a bar or restaurant for its patrons, the sale of alcohol would be an ancillary trade. Charities are also permitted to sell alcohol at small, one-off fund-raising events.

5.6   Alcohol can only be supplied on charity premises if, in addition to its provision being ancillary to the charity's purpose:

- it is not prohibited by the charity's governing document or any covenants relating to the charity's property;

- the accommodation of the bar does not hinder the use of the premises for the charity's charitable purposes;

- the bar is only open at times when the charity's premises are being used for charitable purposes;

- the use of the bar is limited to those participating in, watching or using the charity's services.

5.7   Providing that the running of the bar meets the conditions outlined above, the Charity Commission does not place any restrictions on the turnover or size of the bar, or the opening times, though these will have to comply with the Licensing Laws.

TAX

5.8   If a charity is supplying alcohol as a trade, any profits will be liable to tax unless the activity is ancillary or covered by the Inland Revenue's extra-statutory concession or the turnover is within the limits for the exemption for small trades, i.e.:

- the annual turnover will be no greater than £5,000;

- if the turnover is greater than £5,000, it will be no greater than 25% of the charity's total gross income, subject to an overall limit of £50,000.

5.9   If profits are liable for tax, the trustees should remember their duty to minimise the charity's tax liabilities. They should operate the bar through a subsidiary trading company that donates its profits to the charity by Gift Aid. If they fail to do this the trustees may be personally liable to repay to the charity any tax incurred unnecessarily. Further information can be obtained from HMRC's website at *www.hmrc.gov.uk/charities/trading*.

5.10   Charities selling alcohol should display a notice setting out the conditions for use of the bar. The Charity Commission and HMRC stress that if they find a blind eye being turned to non-patrons using the bar, the charity will risk having their entire bar profits assessed for tax.

5.11   The retail sale of alcohol is liable to VAT at the standard rate, regardless of whether the supply is by a charity, a company controlled by a charity, or an independent club, if the supplying organisation is VAT registered. For a charity that is not VAT registered sales of alcohol should be included as taxable turnover for VAT registration purposes. Further information is available from HMRC's website at *www.hmrc.gov.uk/charities/trading*, but professional advice may be required.

5.12 Alcohol

SOCIAL CLUBS

5.12 Trading activities unconnected with a charity's main purpose, for example, undertaken purely to raise funds, are not regarded as being ancillary to a primary purpose and therefore should not be carried out by a charity. If the trustees want to raise money from the sale of alcohol, or from permitting others to hire the charity's premises for events at which alcohol will be supplied, then they will usually have to set up a trading subsidiary and trade through this or trade though an agreement with an existing trading subsidiary. If the trustees want to provide a social club, they should form an independent club. Charity law would not permit trustees to run a bar as a separate section of the charity, nor would it agree that the degree of separation was sufficient if a sub-committee of the charity oversaw the bar. The separation of the bar from the charity must be absolutely clear. If trustees decide to set up an independent club then it will be the responsibility of those managing the club to ensure that it is properly constituted and licensed. The use of part of a charity's premises as a separate club, under a lease or licence, will mean that rate relief will be restricted to the part of the premises used for charitable purposes.

5.13 A bar or social club could be located on a charity's premises, but the charity would need to have a formal agreement, such as an occupational licence or lease, in place between itself and the bar. If the charity owns the premises the trustees would need to check that their governing document included a power allowing the charity to let or sub-let the charity's property. The trustees will also need to check if their title deeds or land certificates allow them to let or sub-let to a non-charitable company. If the charity leases the premises in which it proposes to provide alcohol, the trustees will have to check that the terms of the lease give them power to sub-let to a non-charitable organisation. If it does not, they will have to enter into negotiations with their landlord to amend the terms of the lease.

5.14 The terms on which the charity permits another organisation to run a bar on its premises must not involve any subsidy from the charity to the separate body, even if that body is wholly owned by the charity. The bar must pay for its share of the cost of floor space, heating, lighting, maintenance, business rates, etc. The part of the premises no longer used for charitable purposes will not be entitled to any relief from business rates.

OTHER CONSIDERATIONS

5.15 If a charity is considering selling alcohol on its premises, or allowing another organisation to sell alcohol from the charity's premises, in addition to the points already covered above it must also take into account the following:

- How will the sale or storage of alcohol affect the charity's insurance?

- Will the sale of alcohol require an application to the local authority for planning permission for change of use?

- Will the toilet facilities be adequate? Will any necessary structural alterations to the bar area or toilet facilities require building regulations or Fire Authority approval?

- What arrangements will have to be made to ensure that children under the age of 14 are not allowed access to the bar area or that no one under the age of 18 can purchase or consume alcohol on the premises?

- Will food be provided on five or more occasions in any five-week period? If so, will the premises also have to be registered with the local authority under the *Food Premises (Registration) Regulations 1991*?

- Will the sale of alcohol put rate relief at risk, as rating relief requires the premises to be used wholly or mainly for charitable purposes?

- Do the charity's users, supporters, funders or donors have any religious or moral beliefs that would make the supply of alcohol ill advised?

LICENSING

5.16   The *Licensing Act 2003* came into force on 24 November 2005 and made substantial changes to previous licensing legislation. The Act established a single integrated scheme for licensing premises used to sell or supply alcohol, to provide regulated entertainment, or to provide late night refreshment in England and Wales. Licensable activities may only be carried on under, and in accordance with, a premises licence, a club premises certificate, or a temporary event notice.

Premises licences

5.17   Charities, or their trading subsidiaries, who sell or supply alcohol on their premises on a regular basis or who engage in regulated entertainment activities must apply to the relevant licensing authority for a premises licence. The main licensing authorities in England and Wales are:

- District Councils in England;

- A County Council in England where there is no District Council;

- A County Council or County Borough Council in Wales;

- A Borough Council in London.

5.18   Premises licences will not be time limited (unless requested), nor subject to renewal every three years (as was previously the case for liquor licences). Application forms can usually be downloaded from the local authority's website. The application form has to be accompanied by an operating schedule, setting out details including the licensable activities to be carried out and the proposed hours that the relevant licensable activities are to take place, a plan of the premises in a prescribed format, a form containing the consent of the proposed designated premises supervisor, and the prescribed fee. Copies of the application must be sent to the responsible authorities (public bodies such as the Chief Officer of Police, the Fire Authority, the Health & Safety Authority, the Local Planning Authority, the Environmental Health Authority and the body responsible for the Protection of Children) on the same day as the application is given to the relevant licensing authority.

5.19   Notice of an application for a premises licence, or for the variation of an existing licence, must be advertised at the premises concerned for 28 consecutive days, starting the day after the application is given to the relevant licensing authority. In addition to this, notice of an application must be published in a local newspaper (or if there is none, in a local newsletter, circular or similar document) circulating in the vicinity of the premises, at least once during the ten working days after the application is given to the relevant licensing authority.

5.20   The notice must state:

- the name of the applicant;

- the postal address of the premises, or if none, a description to allow it to be identified;

- a statement of the licensable activities that the applicant proposes to carry on;

- the postal and website address (if any) where the relevant licensing authority's register is kept and can be inspected;

- the date by which an interested party or responsible authority may make representations;

- that representations may be made in writing;

- that it is an offence knowingly or recklessly to make a false statement in connection with an application, and the maximum fine for which a person is liable on summary conviction for the offence.

5.21   In the case of an application to vary a premises licence, the notice must also briefly describe the proposed variation.

5.22   Where no relevant representations are made by responsible authorities or interested parties the licensing authority must grant the licence application subject only to the mandatory conditions and such other conditions as are consistent with the operating schedule. If relevant representations are received, the licensing authority must hold a hearing and consider the representations (unless all parties agree that this is unnecessary). This may result in the rejection of the application, the refusal to specify a premises supervisor (if the licensable activities relate to the supply of alcohol), the exclusion of a licensable activity, or the attachment of conditions to the licence in all cases if this is necessary for the promotion of one or more of the licensing objectives.

5.23   Any premises where alcohol is supplied under a premises licence must have a 'Designated Premises Supervisor' (DPS), who will be named in the operating schedule. The DPS will not necessarily be the licence holder for the premises but they will be the premises' point of contact at all times for licensing authorities, or the police or fire services if problems occur at the premises. The DPS must, however, be a personal licence holder (see below). The DPS does not have to be on the premises at all times when alcohol is being sold, but it is expected that they will spend a significant amount of time on the premises and should be contactable should problems arise.

Personal licences

5.24   The *Licensing Act 2003* establishes a regime for the granting of personal licences to individuals to supply, or to authorise the supply of alcohol. The personal licence is separate from the licence that authorises the premises to be used for the supply of alcohol. The licensing of individuals separately from the licensing of premises permits the movement of personal licence holders from one premise to another, allowing greater flexibility.

5.25   The personal licence relates only to the supply of alcohol under a premises licence. An individual will not require a personal licence for the other licensable activities, the provision of regulated entertainment or late night refreshment, or for the supply of alcohol under a club premises certificate or temporary event notice (although personal licence holders will be able to give 50 temporary event notices each year instead of the limit of five for non-personal licence holders).

5.26   A personal licence does not authorise its holder to supply alcohol anywhere, but only from establishments with a premises licence authorising the supply of alcohol in accordance with the premises licence. An individual may hold only one personal licence at any one time.

5.27   All premises licences authorising the supply of alcohol must have an identi-fied personal licence holder known as the 'Designated Premises Supervisor' (DPS). This ensures there is always one specified individual who can be readily identified at a premises where a premises licence is in force. This person will usually be responsible for the day-to-day running of the premises. More than one individual at the licensed premises may hold a personal licence, although it is not necessary for all staff to be licensed. All supplies of alcohol under a premises licence must be made by, or under the authority of, a personal licence holder. However, this does not mean that only personal licence holders can make such sales or must be personally present at every transaction.

5.28   Applicants for personal licences will need to obtain an accredited qualification first. The aim of the qualification is to ensure that licence holders are aware of licensing law and the wider social responsibilities attached to the sale of alcohol. Details of accredited personal licence qualification providers are available from the Department for Culture Media and Sport. All applications will be subject to criminal records checks and licences will not be granted to people with convictions involving serious crime, serious dishonesty, control-led drugs and offences created by the *Licensing Act 2003*.

5.29   A personal licence is issued for ten years in the first instance and can be renewed on application for a further ten years if the licence holder has not been convicted of any relevant or foreign offence.

Club Premises Certificates

5.30   The *Licensing Act 2003* recognises that volunteer and social clubs give rise to different issues for licensing law than commercially run premises selling direct to the public. These clubs (such as the Royal British Legion, working men's or cricket or rugby clubs) are generally organisations where members join together for a particular social, sporting or political purpose and then combine to purchase alcohol in bulk for its members. Most such clubs will not be charities.

5.31   Volunteer and social clubs carry on activities from premises to which public access is restricted and alcohol is supplied other than for profit. Therefore the *Licensing Act 2003* preserves aspects of earlier alcohol licensing law which applied to 'registered members clubs' and affords clubs special treatment outside the normal premises licence arrangements.

5.32   'Qualifying clubs' are those that meet specified criteria set out in the *Licensing Act 2003*, i.e:

- club rules must not allow individuals to be admitted as candidates for membership with access to membership privileges until at least two days have elapsed between nomination and admission to membership;

- club rules must not allow admission as a member and access to membership privileges to be granted to individuals where there is no prior nomination and application until at least two days have elapsed;

- the club is established and conducted in good faith as a club;

- the club has at least 25 members;

- alcohol is not supplied to members on the premises otherwise than by or on behalf of the club.

5.33   Qualifying clubs can apply to the relevant licensing authority for a club premises certificate that gives them authority to supply alcohol and conduct other 'qualifying club activities' from their premises. The grant of a club premises certificate means that a club is entitled to certain benefits, which include the authority to supply alcohol to its members and sell it to guests without the need for any member or employee to hold a personal licence, and the absence of a requirement to specify a Designated Premises Supervisor (DPS). There are also more limited rights of entry for the police and other authorised persons, as the premises are considered private and not generally open to the public.

5.34   The arrangements for applying for club premises certificates are extremely similar to those in respect of premises licences. For example, similar provisions apply regarding the requirement for advertisement of applications and the making of representations to the licensing authority as apply in the case of applications for premises licences.

Temporary Event Notices

5.35   The *Licensing Act 2003* introduced a light touch system of permitted temporary activities to replace the old occasional licences and occasional permissions previously granted in connection with short-term alcohol and public entertainment licensing. The system involves an event organiser (the 'premises user') giving a temporary event notice (TEN) to the licensing authority and copying this to the police.

5.36   TENs can be used to authorise relatively small-scale ad hoc charity events, such as fundraising events at which alcohol will be supplied or regulated entertainment provided, held in or on any premises that do not have a premises licence, and that involve no more than 499 people at any one time. The premises user must, no later than ten working days before the day on which the event is to start, give duplicate copies of the notice to the relevant licensing authority, together with the fee of £21. A copy of the notice must also be given to the relevant chief officer of police no later than ten working days before the day on which the event is to start. Anyone aged 18 or over can give a maximum of five TENs per calendar year. Personal licence holders can give a maximum of 50 TENs per calendar year. TENs are subject to other maximum limits, as set out below.

5.37   Each event covered by a TEN can last up to 96 hours and no more than 12 TENs can be given in respect of any particular premises in any calendar year, subject to a maximum aggregate duration of the periods covered by TENs at any individual premises of 15 days in any year. There must be a minimum of 24 hours between events notified by a premises user or associates of that premises user in respect of the same premises.

5.38   If the criteria set out above are met, only the police may intervene to prevent an event covered by a TEN notice taking place or agree a modification of the arrangements for such an event and then only on crime prevention grounds.

Scottish charities

5.39   Scottish charities have to comply with the tax and VAT legislation outlined above and with any covenants or other conditions set out in their governing document or other documentation relating to lease or ownership of property. Otherwise they should follow Scottish legislation and regulations concerning liquor sales and licensing.

FURTHER INFORMATION

5.40   Further details and guidance about providing alcohol on charity premises are contained in the Charity Commission's booklet CC27 'Providing Alcohol on Charity Premises' and further information about the *Licensing Act 2003* can be found on the website for the Department of Culture, Media and Sport (*www.culture.gov.uk*).

6   Almshouses

6.1   The first recorded almshouse was founded by King Athelstan in York in the 10th century AD. The oldest almshouse charity still in existence is the Hospital of St Oswald in Worcester, which was founded circa 990. Today 1,800 separate almshouse charities provide some 36,000 needy people, mostly elderly, with a high standard of affordable housing. Many older almshouses are of historic interest or architectural merit.

6.2   Almshouses provide three main types of housing:

- Flats, cottages or bungalows specially designed for the elderly, usually with no communal facilities or warden, but often linked by an alarm system to a control centre.

- 'Sheltered Housing' usually with some communal rooms where residents can mix socially, guest rooms and facilities such as laundry or hairdressing. There is almost always a resident warden to provide security and discreet help enabling residents to maintain as much independence as possible.

- 'Very Sheltered Housing' or 'Extra Care Schemes' for frailer or more dependent people, allowing them independence and privacy yet at the same time providing the extra help they need.

6.3   Each almshouse charity is independent and run by trustees in accordance with its governing instrument. This specifies the area of benefit and the qualification of beneficiaries. Most almshouse charities are for older people but some provide homes for people with mental illness or learning difficulties, and there are some with no age restriction.

THE ALMSHOUSE ASSOCIATION

6.4   Many almshouse charities are members of the Almshouse Association whose aims and objects are to:

- advise members on any matters concerning almshouses and the welfare of the elderly;

- promote improvements in almshouses;

- promote study and research into all matters affecting almshouses;

- make grants or loans to members;

- keep under review existing and proposed legislation affecting almshouses and take action when necessary;

- encourage the provision of almshouses.

6.5   Membership provides a number of benefits including:

- grants and interest-free loans available towards the cost of repairs and improvements to almshouse property;

- a panel of architects with specialised knowledge of almshouses and of the procedures for obtaining housing subsidies;

- financial guidance, including the preparation of feasibility projections and draft budget of income and expenditure;

- the opportunity to insure through the Association's comprehensive insurance policy, which has been specially tailored to the needs of almshouses.

PRIMARY PURPOSE TRADING

6.6   The provision of housing or sheltered housing by a charity whose objects include the relief of poverty, or something similar such as the provision of housing for the needy, in return for payment, constitutes primary purpose trading. Therefore almshouse charities can charge residents for the services they provide and do not need to structure payments through a subsidiary trading company.

67   Almshouse residents are not tenants. They do not have a legal interest in the accommodation in which they live, but occupy it as beneficiaries of the charity. The trustees of each almshouse charity formally appoint residents, in accordance with the trusts of the charity. Residents do not pay rent. They occupy the premises under licence and make a Weekly Maintenance Contribution (WMC) as well as paying for any additional support and services, such as heating, lighting or meals, provided by the charity.

6.8   The WMC is set by the trustees and should not cause hardship to individual residents. It should not normally exceed the Rent Officer's informal assessment of equivalent fair rent (where applicable) and should never be greater than the maximum Housing Benefit payable for each unit. Trustees should ensure that residents are receiving their due entitlement to benefits from statutory sources, such as pension credit and housing benefit. Almshouse charities, like other charities for the relief of the poor, must take care not to use the charity's funds in a way that replaces assistance that people could obtain from the State, as this would be relieving the State, rather than a poor person. Therefore when assessing whether or not the WMC will cause hardship, the charity should count as part of a person's income any State benefit that the person is entitled to receive, even if the person concerned has not claimed the benefit, or refuses to claim the benefit. However, it is legitimate for trustees to use the charity's funds to relieve temporary need resulting from a delay in the payment of State benefits.

6.9   The trustees have responsibility for ensuring that income from the WMC, together with any other income (e.g. investment income), produces sufficient, but no more than sufficient, income to cover the cost of maintaining the almshouses and any essential services provided in them including insurance, repairs, internal and external redecoration, and any other estimated future expenditure (e.g. for updating or refurbishment) highlighted in quinquennial inspection reports.

6.10   The Charity Commission encourages the trustees of almshouse charities to accumulate income and build up reserves in order to establish and maintain:

- an Extraordinary Repair Fund (ERF) for major 'one-off' repairs and improvements (such as re-roofing or providing a new central heating system), or for rebuilding; and

6.11 Almshouses

- a Cyclical Maintenance Fund (CMF) for ordinary items of maintenance and repair which recur at infrequent but regular intervals, such as external and internal decoration.

6.11 If the trustees formally set up an ERF or CMF, they are, in effect, creating a special trust; money held within these special trusts can only be applied for the stated purposes. Where, however, the trustees earmark money as a discretionary fund, the money may at any time be used for the general purposes of the charity.

COUNCIL TAX

6.12 Council Tax is usually paid by individual residents and trustees should ensure that residents claim any Council Tax Benefit to which they are entitled.

STANDARDS

6.13 Almshouses can provide shelter and services to meet people's needs, but they should not provide a standard of housing or services that more than meets people's needs. Trustees and staff should, however, remember that being 'poor' or 'needy' is not the same as being 'destitute'. 'Poor' refers to not having the things in life that most people take for granted and what constitutes this will change with time. For example, indoor sanitation was far from universally available 100 years ago and a television set, regarded today almost as a necessity, was regarded as a luxury only 50 years ago. Someone who normally has an adequate standard of living could also qualify as a beneficiary if they are suffering temporary hardship, perhaps as a result of sickness, an accident or redundancy.

6.14 Trustees have a duty under the *Defective Premises Act 1972* to keep gas, electrical, water and heating installations in proper working order and to replace or repair them when necessary as a result of fair wear and tear.

6.15 Almshouse charities may find it difficult to attract beneficiaries if the buildings have not been kept in a good state of repair, or if they offer only basic accommodation lacking in comforts and facilities nowadays usually taken for granted. Trustees considering embarking on a major programme of repair or modernisation should contact the Almshouse Association, as it has great experience in these matters and can be of particular assistance to trustees through its panel of architects and building surveyors. Members of this panel will undertake a simple feasibility study without charge but subject to agreed fees when the work proceeds.

6.16 For major projects, the Almshouse Association recommends that a development agent (project manager) should be appointed to handle the formalities other than the architect's responsibilities (which are restricted to design, planning approvals and contract control). A local or national housing association can be appointed as the development agent. This is likely to be particularly helpful to trustees who have little or no experience of this type of project and feel daunted by the practicalities involved. It is a requirement of the Housing Corporation if they have funded all or part of the project. It is essential, however, that trustees retain overall control and a proper system of reporting and consultation covering the whole project from initial feasibility study to completion of the works must be put into place.

6.17   If a charity does not have funds for the necessary repair or modernisation of its property, public funding in the form of a grant or loan may be available from either central or local government funds, though this is likely to entail registration with the Housing Corporation as a housing association. Such registration subjects the charity to the supervision of the Corporation and brings with it certain obligations. The availability of finance is another area in which the Almshouse Association has considerable experience.

6.18   There may be a few cases where buildings are so run down, or would be so expensive to modernise, that despite the best efforts of the trustees, it proves impossible to fill vacancies or to raise sufficient money to make the buildings habitable by today's standards. In these circumstances the trustees will have to consider the following options:

- the sale of part of the property and the use of the proceeds to develop the remaining buildings;

- the sale of the existing site and the use of the proceeds to build or convert other property in the vicinity to produce a smaller number of almshouses;

- the appointment of an experienced RSL as a trustee;

- the sale of the premises and the transfer of the proceeds of sale to another permanently endowed almshouse charity in the vicinity which caters for a similar beneficiary class.

6.19   Trustees considering these options should ask the Charity Commission if a Scheme or Order will be necessary.

LEGISLATION

6.20   Almshouse charities in England and Wales are governed by trust law and the *Charities Acts 1992* and *1993* as amended by *the Charities Act 2006*. They must be registered with the Charity Commission. Almshouse charities in Scotland are subject to Scottish charity law and must be registered with the Office of the Scottish Charity Regulator.

6.21   Almshouse charities can apply for registration as Registered Social Landlords (RSLs):

- English charities should apply to the Housing Corporation;

- Welsh charities should apply to the National Assembly for Wales;

- Scottish charities should apply to Communities Scotland.

6.22   RSLs have to comply with their Regulators' regulations which include special accounting provisions. The Housing Corporation requires RSLs to establish internal financial controls including internal audit and require larger almshouse charities to have an Internal Audit Sub-Committee.

6.23   The Housing Corporation, in accordance with the *Housing Act 1996*, has published criteria for the deregistration of RSLs. These permit RSLs providing 50 dwellings or less to be considered for deregistration.

6.24 Almshouses

Change of purpose

6.24   Unless the governing document contains a power of amendment, the trustees cannot alter it. However, they have a duty under *s 13(5)* of the *Charities Act 1993* (as amended by the *Charities Act 2006*) to apply to the Charity Commission for directions if the purpose of the charity can no longer be carried out.

Housing Act 1996

6.25   Except in the case of a company incorporated under the *Companies Act 1985*, the *Housing Act 1996* requires that the consent of the Charity Commission is obtained to any variation of the objects of a RSL which is also a registered charity, even if it has power in its governing instrument to make the amendment. However, before giving their consent the Commission must consult the Housing Corporation. The Commission must also consult the Housing Corporation about changes to the objects of RSLs which are registered charities, where the Commission proposes to make a Scheme to change the objects.

Mortgaging land

6.26   Trustees may wish to mortgage the charity's land in order to raise money to build new almshouses or carry out major repairs. Future income will be used to repay the sum borrowed and the interest charged. If the charity is a RSL the consent of the Housing Corporation is required. If the charity is not a RSL the new procedure under *s 27* of the *Charities Act 2006* applies, and the trustees – before committing the charity to the transaction – must obtain advice from a person they reasonably believe to have sufficient ability and experience in financial matters to advise them, and who has no personal interest in the making of the loan, confirming that:

● the loan is necessary to finance the proposed expenditure;

● the terms are reasonable;

● the charity can afford the repayment terms.

Sale or lease of land

6.27   Trustees may wish to dispose of land belonging to a charity which is held either as investment property, or as functional property for a number of reasons:

● The land may have become surplus to requirements.

● It may be in the interests of the beneficiaries to relocate the almshouse to another site.

● The sale may increase investment income.

6.28   Again there are a number of situations which require different treatment:

(*a*)   The charity is a registered social landlord, or the land has been grant-aided by the Housing Corporation. In this instance the consent of the Housing Corporation is required.

(b)   The charity is not in category (a) and either there is no power in its governing document to dispose of land or the trustees are unable to follow the procedure set out in (c) below, the consent of the Charity Commission under *s 36(1)* of the *Charities Act 1993* may be required. If so the formalities prescribed under *s 37* must be observed.

(c)   The charity is not in category (a) and the trustees have an express or implied power to dispose of land, and the land is not held on trust for use for charitable purposes. Before committing themselves to the transaction, the trustees are obliged by *s 36(2)* of the *Charities Act 1993* to:

●   obtain a written report from a qualified surveyor covering all matters set out in the *Charities (Qualified Surveyors' Reports) Regulations 1992*;

●   advertise the land for sale as advised by the surveyor (unless the surveyor advises positively against this; and

●   reach a decision that the terms of the proposed transaction are the best reasonably obtainable for the charity.

The formalities prescribed under *s 37* must then be observed.

(d)   The charity is not in category (a) and the land is held on trust for use for charitable purposes, but there is a power to sell or lease it, the procedure set out in (b) above must be followed, but in addition trustees must normally publish notices inviting members of the public to make representations to them about the proposed sale or lease, and must take account of any representations received before deciding whether or not to proceed. Again, the documentation must comply with the prescribed formalities.

6.29   The *Trusts of Land and Appointment of Trustees Act 1996* gives trustees a general statutory power to sell, or to grant a lease over, land owned by a charity. However, this power can only be exercised in furtherance of the objects of the charity. It may be necessary for the Charity Commission to make a Scheme to authorise the disposal of any land which is held on trusts which provide for the land to be used as an almshouse.

Connected persons

6.30   Any disposal of land by a charity, which is not in category (a), to a connected person or to a trustee or nominee of a connected person, will require the consent of the Charity Commission under *s 36(1)* of the *Charities Act 1993*. 'Connected person' is defined in *Sch 5* to that Act and includes:

●   a charity trustee or trustee for the charity;

●   a person who is a donor of any land to the charity;

●   a child (including stepchild or illegitimate child), parent, grandchild, grandparent, brother or sister of any trustee or donor of land;

●   an officer, agent or employee of the charity;

●   the spouse (or a person living with another as that person's husband or wife) of any of the above people;

- an institution which is controlled by any of the above people; or

- a body corporate in which any of the above people have a substantial interest.

Investments

6.31   Unless the governing document contains specific investment powers, the trustees will have to invest in accordance with the *Trustee Act 2000* (see CHAPTER 75).

ACCOUNTS

6.32   Generally speaking, charitable almshouses have to comply with the accounting regulations for charities. If they are registered with the Housing Corporation, they are required to comply with *The Accounting Requirements for Registered Social Landlords General Determination 1997* and *The Accounting Requirements for Registered Social Landlords (Amending) Determination 1998.* The *Housing Act 1996* requires them to submit accounts, audited by a qualified auditor in the specified form, to the Housing Corporation within six months of the end of the accounting period. They should also comply with the Statement of Recommended Practice (SORP), 'Accounting by Registered Social Landlords'.

6.33   Statements of accounts of all 'local charities for the relief of poverty' (which includes most almshouse charities) should be sent to the appropriate local authority in whose area the charity operates. Until statements of accounts are sent to the appropriate local authority, trustees must make the statements of account available for public inspection and provide copies of the statements to the public at a reasonable cost.

RESIDENTS

Filling vacancies

6.34   Almshouse charities should deliver their services regardless of gender, marital status, race, religion, or sexual orientation, unless the governing document provides otherwise. It is good practice for almshouse charities to have an equal opportunities policy along the lines of 'the charity is committed to the principles of equal opportunities and observes the letter and spirit of anti-discrimination legislation as far as the governing document allows'.

6.35   Under *s 43* of the *Sex Discrimination Act 1975* charities can limit their services to people of a particular gender if this is necessary in order to comply with their governing instrument. Almshouse charities that are established to provide housing for just one gender must not extend the beneficiary class to include both genders, if the only reason for so doing is to attempt to comply with the Act.

6.36   *Section 34* of the *Race Relations Act 1976* excepts from its general provisions discrimination by a charity where discrimination is necessary in order to comply with any provision in a charitable instrument for conferring benefits on persons of a class defined otherwise than by reference to colour. Therefore, if the governing document restricts beneficiaries to one particular racial group (this must be defined not by colour but by reference to race, nationality or ethnic or national origins) then the trustees would be exempt from prosecution under the *Race Relations Act 1976* if they advertised for residents from that racial group.

6.37   Similarly *s 58* of the *Equality Act 2006* permits charities to restrict benefits to people of a particular religion in order to comply with their governing instrument.

6.38   Provided there is no reason to believe that an applicant would disrupt the good conduct of an almshouse and the peace and quiet of the other residents, almshouse accommodation should always be allotted to those in greatest need who meet the criteria specified in the governing document. The Charity Commission normally permits vacancies to be filled from a waiting list for up to 12 months, after which vacancies must be advertised.

6.39   Some local authorities have the right to nominate people to fill vacancies in almshouses, particularly ones that have been built or improved with the aid of a grant from a local authority or the Housing Corporation. In such instances, those nominated must fulfil the criteria contained in the governing document, i.e. the same criteria as any other applicant. Trustees have the right to turn down any person they believe would be unsuitable, explaining their reasons to the nominating body.

6.40   Applicants should be visited by a trustee or member of staff to find out if they are sufficiently independent to care for themselves in an almshouse and to explain to the applicant what moving to the almshouse would entail, including details of the WMC, the role of the Warden (if applicable), the circumstances in which they would be asked to leave, the policy on pets, upkeep of gardens, laundry, etc.

6.41   New residents should be made welcome and given a letter of appointment setting out the terms of the appointment, level of WMC and arrangements for notifying changes. It is good practice to provide them with a resident's handbook, including details of how they can obtain domiciliary support, how residents are consulted about any major changes, the Residents' Committees (if applicable), the complaints procedure, arrangements for visitors, etc.

Alteration in the circumstances of residents

6.42   Given that beneficiaries may occupy their residence for many years, it is likely that changes in their circumstances will occur during their occupancy. Examples of such changes include:

- changes in marital status, either by bereavement, or by a new marriage;

- other changes in status, i.e. new partner, death of partner; death of sibling, child living with parents leaves;

- in charities with a religious qualification, change of denomination, e.g. from Church of England to Roman Catholicism, or change of church attended;

- change in financial status, e.g. receipt of a legacy.

6.43   Normally, trustees should ask a resident to leave almshouse accommodation if their change of circumstance would have disqualified him or her as an applicant if it had happened before their appointment. However, it would not be a breach of trust for them not to do so in every case. The treatment of a resident is a matter for the discretion of the trustees, and before making such a decision, they should consider relevant factors such as:

- the wishes of the resident;

- the age of the resident (and the possible unsettling effect of asking him or her to leave);

- the health and physical capacity of the resident;

- the alternatives open to the resident;

- the relative merits of any other applicants for appointment; and

- any other pertinent factors (such as possible adverse publicity).

Complaints procedure

6.44   The Almshouse Association recommends as good practice that all almshouse charities have a complaints procedure available for residents. Their suggested model complaints procedure is reproduced as Annex H of 'Standards of almshouse management: a guide to good practice'. Under *s 51(2)(d)* of the *Housing Act 1996*, all almshouse charities which are Registered Social Landlords with the Housing Corporation, or almshouse charities formerly registered with the Housing Corporation and in receipt of a housing grant, have a regulatory obligation to maintain a complaints procedure.

MAINTAINING EFFECTIVENESS

6.45   If the trustees believe that there are insufficient needy people in their area of benefit and they have taken steps to search out potential beneficiaries without success, then they should consider approaching the Charity Commission for a Scheme to do one or more of the following:

- extend the area of benefit;

- amend the purposes of the charity, so the almshouses can be sold and the resources used in some other way to support poor people;

- give the charity's assets to another charity providing shelter for a disadvantaged group of people.

6.46   The Charity Commission has power under *s 21* of the *Charities Act 1993* to transfer to the Official Custodian for Charities land or other assets belonging to a charity that they consider to be at risk.

FURTHER INFORMATION

6.47   Further information and advice can be obtained from the Almshouse Association, the Housing Corporation, Communities Scotland and Cynulliad Cenedlaethol Cymru/National Assembly for Wales.

The Almshouse Association
Billingbear Lodge
Carters Hill
Wokingham
Berkshire
RG40 5RU

Tel: 01344 452 922
Fax: 01344 862 062
Email: naa@almshouses.org
www.almshouses.org

The Housing Corporation
Maple House
147 Tottenham Court Road
London
W1T 7BN
Tel: 0845 230 7000
Email: enquiries@housingcorp.gov.uk
www.housingcorp.gov.uk

Communities Scotland
Thistle House
91 Haymarket Terrace
Edinburgh
EH12 5HE
Tel: 0131 313 0044
Fax: 0131 313 2680
Email: enquiries @communitiesscotland.gov.uk
www.communitiesscotland.gov.uk

Cynulliad Cenedlaethol Cymru/National Assembly for Wales
Cathays Park
Cardiff
CF10 3NQ
Tel: 0845 010 5500
www.assemblywales.org

7   Annual Returns

CHARITY COMMISSION

7.1   In order to keep the Charity Commission's register of charities up to date and allow the Commission to discharge its monitoring responsibilities, all registered charities whose gross annual income or total expenditure is in excess of £10,000 are required by *s 48* of the *Charities Act 1993* to prepare an Annual Return, giving details of administration, financial management and governance, and send it to the Charity Commission within ten months of the end of the financial year to which the return relates. This Annual Return is in addition to the trustees' annual report and accounts required by *s 45*.

7.2   The Annual Return for 2007 is made up of three parts and a Reporting a Serious Incident (RSI) statement:

- Part A, the Annual Update, asks for basic information to keep the Charity Commission's register of charities up to date and includes a new section about the charity;

- Part B asks for financial information, which the Commission will use to identify trends in the resources available to charities and in expenditure by charities;

- Part C, the Summary Information Return (SIR), asks for key qualitative and quantitative information.

7.3   Trustees have a legal obligation to report serious incidents to the Charity Commission. The nature of reportable incidents and information about how to report them is explained fully in the guidance notes. In signing the declaration at the end of the Return, the trustee signatory will be certifying that any such incident occurring in the year in question has been reported to the Charity Commission.

7.4   How many parts of the Annual Return a charity will be required to complete will depend on their income in the financial period ending in 2007, as shown in Table 4 below. Although charities with gross annual income of £10,000 or less are not legally obliged to complete an Annual Return form, they must complete Part A, so the Charity Commission can keep the register up to date.

Table 4 Annual Return – Summary of Requirements

	Annual return			
Income in the financial period ending in 2007	*Annual Update (Part A)*	*Reporting serious incidents declaration*	*Financial Information (Part B)*	*Summary Information Return (Part C)*
£10K or below	√			
>£10k – £25k	√			

>£25k – £500k	√	√		
>£500k – £1m	√	√	√	
>£1m	√	√	√	√

7.5   The Return should be signed by a trustee. Any amendments to the charity's governing document, objects, area of benefit, or a change of bank account that have not already been reported to the Charity Commission and that are not noted in the Annual Update form or Parts B or C of the Annual Return should be set out in a covering letter and sent to the Commission with the completed Annual Return.

7.6   Persistent failure to submit an Annual Return without a reasonable excuse is an offence punishable by a fine. *Section 48(3)* of the *Charities Act 1993*, however, gives the Commissioners power to waive the requirement to produce an Annual Return for a particular charity or class of charities.

7.7   Trustees and staff can get help and advice on completing the Annual Return from the Charity Commission's website (*www.charity-commission.gov.uk*) or by calling Charity Commission Direct on 0845 300 0218 between 0800 – 2000hrs on Mondays – Fridays and between 0900 – 1300hrs on Saturdays.

7.8   Most of the information entered on the Annual Update will be open to public inspection. Charities that wish to exclude their address, or the names of their trustees, can apply for a dispensation from this if they can make a good case, such as being at risk of serious violence or intimidation.

COMPANIES HOUSE

7.9   Charitable companies are also required by *s 363* of the *Companies Act 1985* to submit an Annual Return each year (form 363A which is blank or form 363S which is already filled in) in order to keep the register of companies up to date. The form must be signed by a director (a trustee) or the company secretary and returned within 28 days of the return date together with a filing fee. Failure to file the return within the prescribed time period results in a fine.

7.10   The annual return contains the following information:

- the name of the company;

- its registered number;

- the type of company it is, for example, private or public;

- the registered office address of the company;

- the address where certain company registers are kept if not at the registered office;

- the principal business activities of the company;

- the name and address of the company secretary;

- the name, usual residential address, date of birth, nationality and business occupation of all the company's directors;

7.11 Annual Returns

- the date to which the annual return is made up (the made-up date).

7.11 If the company has share capital, the annual return must also contain:

- the nominal value of total issued share capital;

- the names and addresses of shareholders and the number and type of shares they hold or transfer from other shareholders.

7.12 Directors of charitable companies can protect their addresses from public scrutiny as a result of changes to the *Companies Act*. An applicant must pay a statutory fee of £100 and submit form 723B to the Administrator at Companies House giving details of the perceived risk and supporting evidence plus a service address. Companies House will seek independent evidence from the police and other appropriate authorities in determining whether a confidentiality order should be granted. If granted, a confidentiality order lasts for five years and can be renewed if the risk remains.

7.13 Guidance booklets and statutory forms are available, free of charge from Companies House (see *www.companieshouse.gov.uk*) or by telephoning Companies House on 0870 3333636.

SCOTLAND

7.14 Since April 2006, all charities registered with the Office of the Scottish Charity Regulator (OSCR) are required to submit their accounts to OSCR with their Annual Return form and (where issued) the supplementary Monitoring Return form. Submission will take place according to the charity's financial year end. OSCR sends out Annual Return Forms soon after a charity's Accounting Period End Date.

7.15 Charities must submit accounts for the Accounting Period End Date and send them to OSCR at the same time as the completed Annual Return form. OSCR does not require accounts prior to that date unless they have been previously requested.

7.16 Help in completing the Annual Return form is available from:

- OSCR's website (*www.oscr.org.uk*)

- A telephone helpline (01382 220446) between 0830 – 1600 hrs Monday – Friday

- By e-mailing info@oscr.org.uk

8   Amateur Sport Charities

8.1   The *Charities Act 2006* defines the advancement of amateur sport as a charitable purpose. Amateur sport is defined as 'sports or games which promote health by involving physical or mental skill or exertion and which are undertaken on an amateur basis'. Sport will therefore no longer have to be allied to another charitable purpose, such as the advancement of education or the promotion of recreation. The Act will expand the range of sports clubs that can register as charities. However, charities that advance amateur sport will have to satisfy the public benefit test.

8.2   Examples of the sorts of charities and purposes that will fall under this head include:

- Community amateur sports clubs, such as local football clubs, tennis clubs, hockey clubs;

- Multisports centres;

- Clubs and organisations concerned with the promotion of a particular sport or game, such as governing bodies established to promote and set standards in a particular sport, chess clubs, bridge clubs.

8.3   To be registered as charitable, the Charity Commission publication RR11 'Charitable Status and Sport' states that sports clubs need to promote a sport that promotes physical or mental health and that is not so dangerous that the risks mean that it does not benefit the public. They must have open membership, membership that is affordable to the majority of the community and facilities that are available to all members regardless of skill. Any coaching provided must be available to all. Charitable clubs must not have social members and any non-playing members must be volunteers or helpers.

8.4   Charitable sports clubs can run competitive teams, leagues and ladders and can allocate facilities to allow competitive teams to train and play. However, they must bear in mind that the club must be promoting community participation and therefore give equal treatment to less skilful or less competitive players.

8.5   The *Charities Act 2006* does not define the term 'amateur'. This may cause problems, particularly if the courts define amateur as it is defined in *Sch 18* of the *Finance Act 2002* in relation to community amateur sports clubs, which prohibits all payments to players. At the moment some clubs make small payments to players, which would not be sufficient for a player to live off, to encourage them to continue to play for that particular club and to cover some of their expenses.

8.6   There may be circumstances where it could be argued that the promotion of amateur sport could lead to charitable disbenefits. For example the RSPCA is opposed to angling and some medical charities are opposed to boxing.

8.7   If a charitable sports club has a bar the Charity Commission advise that it should be run through a separate company.

FURTHER INFORMATION

8.7   Charity Commission RR11 'Charitable Status and Sport'

9 Animal Welfare Charities

9.1 Before 2007 the advancement of animal welfare was not, of itself, a charitable activity. Animal charities whose main purpose was to benefit humanity could be registered under the fourth head, i.e. other purposes beneficial to the community. Preventing humans being cruel to animals or enabling them to care for animals was seen as upholding human dignity and a manifestation of the finer side of human nature. This reasoning reflects the principle that the moral improvement of the public is a charitable purpose. However, *s 2* of the *Charities Act 2006* lists the advancement of animal welfare as a charitable purpose.

9.2 The advancement of animal welfare includes any purpose directed towards the prevention or suppression of cruelty to animals or the prevention or relief of suffering by animals. Examples of the sorts of charities and charitable purposes falling within this description include:

- Charities promoting kindness to animals and to prevent or suppress cruelty to animals;

- Animal sanctuaries;

- The provision of veterinary care and treatment;

- Charities concerned with the care and re-homing of animals that are abandoned, mistreated or lost;

- Feral animal control, e.g. neutering.

9.3 Animal welfare charities have always had to demonstrate that they provide public benefit as they fell under the traditional fourth head.

9.4 Organisations directly or indirectly concerned with animal welfare may have more than one charitable purpose. Charities promoting vegetarianism may be concerned with both the rights of animals and the advancement of the health of humans. Charities providing low-cost or free veterinary services may also be relieving poverty. Zoos may be advancing education.

9.5 The *Animal Welfare Act 2006* does not impose a duty of care towards animals, because animals could not sue to enforce the duty, though that is undoubtedly its effect. Animal welfare charities will be acting within the law if they publicise the new law, which sets out five basic needs for animals:

- A suitable environment;

- A suitable diet;

- The ability to exhibit normal behaviour;

- Housing apart from other animals where appropriate;

- To be protected from pain, suffering, injury and disease.

10   Armed Forces and Emergency Services Charities

10.1   Promoting the efficiency of the armed forces is a long standing charitable purpose. The *Preamble* to the *1601 Statute of Elizabeth* referred to 'maintenance of sick and maimed soldiers and mariners' and 'setting out soldiers' (levying a tax to equip soldiers). The promotion of the efficiency of the armed forces of the Crown or of the efficiency of the police, fire and rescue services or ambulance services was included in the *Charities Act 2006* as a separate purpose because of the importance of these services to the nation.

10.2   It is charitable to promote the efficiency of the armed forces of the Crown as a means of defending the country. That includes ensuring that the armed forces are properly trained and equipped during times of conflict. It also includes providing facilities and benefits for the armed forces. Similarly it is also charitable to promote the efficiency of the police, fire, rescue or ambulance services as they exist for the prevention and detection of crime, the preservation of public order and to protect the public.

10.3   The Charity Commission give the following as examples of the sorts of charities and charitable purposes falling within this description:

- Increasing technical knowledge of members of the services through the provision of educational resources, competitions and prizes;

- Increasing physical fitness of members of the services through the provision of sporting facilities, equipment and sporting competitions;

- Providing opportunities for service personnel to gain additional experience relevant to their jobs (e.g. aeroplane clubs for RAF personnel);

- Supporting messes (NCOs and Officers) and institutes (other ranks), including the provision of chattels (items of plate, etc);

- Providing and maintaining band instruments and equipment;

- Promoting and strengthening bonds between allied units;

- Providing memorials to commemorate the fallen or victories;

- Maintaining chapels (e.g. regimental chapels in cathedrals) or churches;

- Researching the military history of a regiment or other unit, and publishing books about it;

- Maintaining a museum or other collection for the preservation of artefacts connected with a military unit or service and supporting military and service museums generally;

- Encouraging esprit de corps (loyalty of a member to the unit to which he or she belongs and recognition of the honour of the unit);

- Providing associations which support a unit and enable serving and former members to mix together;

- Providing facilities for military training (e.g. drill halls);

- Encouraging recruitment to the services (e.g. through exhibitions, air displays etc);

10.4 Armed Forces and Emergency Services Charities

- Benevolent funds for serving members, ex-serving members, widows/widowers of serving or ex-serving members, the dependants of serving or ex-serving members who are in need;

- Provision of an emergency air or sea rescue service and equipment.

10.4　Under the *Charities Act 2006* the promotion of the efficiency of the armed forces or emergency services will no longer be presumed to be of public benefit. In meeting the public benefit test the issue of whether private benefit is more than incidental is likely to arise. Where a private benefit is conferred it is not necessary for the benefit to be merely incidental to the charitable purpose in order to qualify as charitable, if the conferral of that benefit itself constitutes the furtherance of an organisation's charitable purpose. For example, it is not a problem that individual servicemen benefit from being recruited to the armed forces.

10.5　There will be an overlap between this purpose and other charitable purposes. For example, a number of military charities relieve poverty and a number relieve unemployment. Similarly the emergency services save lives and the ambulance service promotes the advancement of health. It is unclear at present whether military charities established purely for the support of ex-service personnel could be registered under this head. It could be argued that knowing you will be looked after in retirement aids recruitment and hence promotes efficiency. On the other hand the activities of ex-service charities may fall under other heads, such as the prevention and relief of poverty, or the relief of those in need by reason of youth, age, ill-health, disability, financial hardship or other disadvantage.

11   Arts, Culture, Heritage and Science Charities

11.1   Until the enactment of the *Charities Act 2006* most charitable organisations working in the fields of the arts, culture, heritage or science qualified as charities under the traditional second head, the advancement of education, or under the fourth head, other purposes beneficial to the community. Now the advancement of the arts, culture, heritage or science is recognised as a charitable purpose in its own right.

11.2   What the term 'culture' means in a legal sense is difficult to say. The Charity Commission's commentary on the descriptions of charitable purposes in the *Charities Act 2006* says 'Culture' is a broad term often used in the context of advancing art or heritage.'

11.3   The advancement of art covers a wide range of charitable activity including the promotion of various forms of art nationally and locally and at a professional and amateur level, the provision of arts facilities and encouraging high standards of art. 'Art' includes abstract, conceptual and performance art and representational and figurative art. The Charity Commission has stated that charities concerned with the advancement of art, whether visual arts or the performing arts such as music, dance and theatre, will need to satisfy a criterion of merit, details of which can be found in their publication RR10 'Museums and Art Galleries'.

11.4   'Heritage' is usually defined as part of a country's local or national history and traditions which are passed down through successive generations. Advancing heritage includes charities for the preservation of historic land and buildings. It also includes activities concerned with preserving or maintaining a particular tradition where the benefit to the public in preserving it can be shown. Further guidance can be found in the Charity Commission's publication RR9 'Preservation and conservation'.

11.5   The advancement of science includes scientific research and charities connected with various learned societies and institutions.

11.6   The sorts of charities that fall under the head of the advancement of the arts, culture, heritage or science include:

- Art galleries, arts festivals and arts councils;

- Charities that promote, or encourage high standards of, the arts of drama, ballet, music, singing, literature, sculpture, painting, cinema, mime, etc, e.g. theatres, cinemas and concert halls; choirs; orchestras; music, operatic and dramatic societies;

- The promotion of crafts and craftsmanship;

- Local or national history or archaeology societies;

- Local arts societies;

- Charities that preserve ancient sites or buildings;

- Charities that preserve a specified monument, building or complex of historic/architectural importance, or the preservation of historic buildings in general, such as building preservation trusts;

11.7 Arts, Culture, Heritage and Science Charities

- The preservation of historical traditions, such as carnivals, country/folk dancing societies, Scottish country dancing and highland dancing societies, eisteddfords, folk clubs, etc;

- Scientific research projects;

- Charities connected with various learned societies and institutions, e.g. the Royal Society, the Royal College of Surgeons; the Royal College of Nursing; the Royal Geographical Society.

11.7   Traditionally most arts, culture, heritage and science institutions have been tested for their public benefit nature under the head of the advancement of education. They were judged to provide public benefit if they were of educational value to the community. In 1916 the courts held that preservation of land of beauty for the benefit of the nation was charitable and in 1943 the Royal Choral Society's objects were held to be charitable on the grounds that they promoted aesthetic education. However, in 1955 the English Folk Dance and Song Society was not granted charitable status as it was held that the main emphasis was on the pleasure derived by the performers, i.e. the private benefit outweighed the public benefit. Most arts, culture, heritage and science charities should not have difficulty in demonstrating that they provide public benefit, providing any private benefit is purely incidental.

FURTHER INFORMATION

11.8   Charity Commission RR9 'Preservation and conservation'

Charity Commission RR10 'Museums and Art Galleries'

Museums Association
24 Calvin Street
London
E1 6NW
Tel: 0207 426 6950

12   Associations

12.1   An association is formed when two or more people come together to do something lawful for the purpose of benefiting themselves or others, but which is not intended to make a profit for themselves or others. To be an association the parties should also have an intention to create a legal relationship between themselves, though this does not need to be explicitly stated. This is what differentiates an association from a group of friends, even though the founding members of an association may be a group of friends.

UNINCORPORATED ASSOCIATIONS

12.2   An unincorporated charitable association is an association whose objects are charitable in law and which is not registered as a company or an industrial and provident society, and is not incorporated under statute or royal charter. An unincorporated charity does not need to be called an association to have that legal structure; it may well be known as a society, club, campaign or even a trust. The unincorporated association is the most common constitutional form adopted by charities in Scotland.

Governing document

12.3   The governing document of an unincorporated charitable association is its constitution or rules. It sets out the purpose, or objects, of the association, who can become a member, and the procedural rules for holding meetings, deciding policy and action, electing the governing body, etc. The procedure for amending the governing document will depend on whether it contains a power of amendment. Even if there is a power of amendment, changes to the objects clause or the Trustees' powers will usually require authorisation by the Charity Commission.

12.4   English and Welsh charities can obtain a model governing documents from the Charity Commission or the Charity Law Association. Scottish charities can obtain a model governing document from the Scottish Council for Voluntary Organisations. The model documents can be adapted to suit a particular charity's needs.

Advantages

12.5   The unincorporated association structure is particularly suitable for membership organisations where it is important that the people ultimately in control of the organisation are democratically elected from amongst the membership by the membership. It has the advantage of being simple and flexible and unincorporated associations can be set up or wound up easily and cheaply.

Disadvantages

12.6   The main disadvantage of using the unincorporated organisation structure is that the charity itself has no legal identity, so the members of the governing body can be held personally liable for the charity's debts and for other claims. The charity cannot enter into contracts or agreements in its own name. Land, property and other assets have to be held by the trustees individually, or by holding trustees, or a custodian trustee. All contracts have to be entered into by individuals, such as the trustees, a sub-group of the trustees, or holding or custodian trustees. The signatories and/or the governing body could be held personally liable for a breach of contract. Similarly if someone wants to take legal action against the charity, the lawsuit would be against the individuals who comprise the governing body or individuals who authorised the action in question. If a charity wanted to take legal action against another party, it would have to do so in the name of an individual or individuals.

EUROPEAN ASSOCIATIONS

12.7   No other European country has a body equivalent to the Charity Commission. For regulatory purposes, charities are grouped with mutual societies in many other European countries. The different approaches to charity law, tax reliefs and other concessions give rise to problems for charities trying to work throughout Europe. Proposals have therefore been put forward to operate a new legal entity, a European association. This would be an incorporated body operating in several European countries and would have a different legal structure to the English association.

13   Auditors

13.1   'Auditor' is often a generic title used to apply to the person carrying out the external scrutiny of the accounts at the year-end. In fact only a minority of charities require an audit in the true sense. This chapter only applies to auditors in the strictest legal sense, although some of the principles may be usefully applied in other cases.

13.2   For most registered charities, the auditor will be appointed by virtue of the *Companies Act 2006* or the *Charities Act 1993*, as amended by the *Charities Act 2006*. Auditors of companies which are below the Companies Act statutory audit threshold will report under the terms of the Charities Act, in common with auditors of non limited company charities. An equivalent regime operates in Scotland.

APPOINTMENT

13.3   The first auditors of a charitable company are appointed by the company directors/trustees, and thereafter by the shareholders/members by ordinary resolution. However, there is no need to reappoint the auditors each year – an auditor will automatically be deemed to be reappointed except in five cases:

- if he was appointed by the directors;

- if the company's articles require actual reappointment;

- if enough members have given notice to the company under *Companies Act 2006, s 488*;

- if there has been a resolution that the auditor should not be reappointed; or

- if the directors decide that they do not need auditors for the following year.

13.4   Unincorporated charities often apply the same regime as companies either from custom, or because of the requirements of the constitution.

13.5   There is no detailed guidance from the Commission on appointing auditors, but OSCR carries the following advice which it applies to both auditors and examiners:

> 'In appointing an independent examiner or auditor charity trustees should take into consideration the degree of complexity of the charity's accounts and structure. The more complex the organisation and accounts the higher the level of qualification or experience required of the independent examiner or auditor'.

13.6   In deciding who to appoint as an independent examiner charity trustees should consider the type of accounts the charity prepares and ensure the independent examiner or auditor:

- is independent of the management and administration of the charity;

- is eligible under the regulations to act as an independent examiner or auditor;

13.7   Auditors

- is eligible under their professional body's rules and regulations to act as an independent examiner or auditor;

- has experience of accounts to the same level and degree of complexity.

13.7   To be independent the independent examiner or auditor should have no connection with the charity trustees that might inhibit their ability to carry out an impartial examination. Whether a connection exists will depend on the circumstances of a particular charity, but the following people will normally be considered to have a connection:

- the charity trustees or anyone else who is closely involved in the administration of the charity;

- a major donor or major beneficiary of the charity;

- a close relative, spouse, partner, business partner or employee of any of the people mentioned above.

13.8   The Charity Commission can order a charity to be audited and, in certain circumstances, can also appoint the auditor. In such a case the costs of the audit are recoverable from the trustees or, if the Commission think this impractical, from the funds of the charity.

REMOVAL AND RESIGNATION

13.9   The members of a company can remove the auditors at any time by ordinary resolution with special notice. However, this is rarely used as it requires a general meeting of the members. Therefore in practice the procedure for removing auditors for charities of all legal structures tends to be the same, namely that the incumbent is asked to resign his office, thereby creating a casual vacancy, which the directors or trustees then fill by their chosen appointment. This appointment is then formally ratified in general meeting, usually the annual general meeting. The governing documents of unincorporated charities usually provide the trustees with the power to fill such casual vacancies.

13.10   Increasingly such changes in appointment only occur after discussions with the incumbent auditor and a tender process including written and verbal presentations. It is therefore rare for the auditor to be unaware of a forthcoming change and to be unprepared for resignation.

13.11   Both the *Companies Act 1985*, the *Charities Act 1993* and Scottish Regulations have procedures to follow on a change of auditors, in addition to the protocols which accountancy firms follow on a change of professional appointment.

13.12   The auditor of an unincorporated charity is required under the *Charities Act Regulations* and the Scottish Regulations to inform the trustees in writing if there are any circumstances connected with his ceasing to hold office which ought to be brought to their attention, or, if there are no such circumstances, to issue a statement to that effect. If there are any relevant circumstances to report, then a copy of this letter should be sent by the auditor to the Charity Commission. In Scotland, if the auditor so requests, a statement has to be included in the trustees' report.

13.13   Similarly, under the *Companies Act 2006, s 519*, an outgoing auditor of a limited company must deposit at the registered office of the company a similar statement of matters which should be brought to the attention of the members or creditors of the company. If there are any such circumstances then the statement must be filed with the Registrar of Companies within 28 days.

QUALIFICATIONS

13.14   An auditor of a registered charity, whether a limited company or unincorporated, must be eligible under the *Companies Act 1985*, which requires the auditor to be a member of a recognised supervisory body, and eligible under those rules. The recognised bodies are:

- The Institute of Chartered Accountants in England and Wales,

- The Institute of Chartered Accountants in Scotland,

- The Institute of Chartered Accountants in Ireland,

- The Association of Authorised Public Accountants, and

- The Association of Chartered Certified Accountants.

13.15   The same rules broadly apply to industrial and provident societies.

POWERS

13.16   The auditors or examiners of an unincorporated charity have rights. They have a right of access to any books, documents and other records (however kept) which relate to the charity concerned and which the auditor or examiner considers necessary to inspect. They are also entitled to require such information and explanations from past or present officers or employees of the charity as they consider necessary.

13.17   The rights of company auditors are slightly different under *Companies Act 2006, s 499*. The right of access in this instance pertains to the company's books, accounts and vouchers, and the auditor has a right to require information from the company's officers, defined as the directors and the company secretary, anyone holding any such information, and anyone to whom those criteria applied at the relevant time.

13.18   The rights of the auditor of an industrial and provident society are very similar to the rights of a company auditor.

13.19   The main difference between the rights of a company auditor and the rights of an auditor of an unincorporated charity is the right of the charity examiner or auditor to require information from not just present officers of the company, as the *Companies Act 1985* prescribes, but also past officers and employees. This is a slightly different power to that which exists under the Companies Act.

DUTIES

13.20   All auditors have a statutory duty to report in the prescribed form on the accounts. The style of this report is highly stylised, and is set out in standards issued by the Auditing Practices Board.

13.21 Auditors

13.21   The *Companies Act 2006*, the *Charities Act 1993* and the Scottish *Charity Accounting Regulations* all require the auditor to consider the following areas in his report, although the legislation differs slightly in the precise wording:

- whether the accounts have been prepared in accordance with the relevant financial reporting framework and show a true and fair view;

- whether the directors report/annual report is consistent with the accounts; (at the time of writing this requirement is being clarified by OSCR)

- whether proper accounting records have been kept and whether the accounts agree with those records; and

- whether all information and explanations to which he is entitled have been given.

13.22   Additionally, company auditors are required to report by exception if proper returns have not been received from branches not visited by them, or if a company has claimed exemption from the requirement to prepare group accounts to which it was not entitled. Company auditors are also required to make good any omission from the accounts of disclosures of emoluments received by directors. [*Companies Act 2006, s 798*].

13.23   One change introduced by the *Companies Act 2006* is that audit reports are signed by an individual, rather than just by a firm. This individual will usually be the engagement partner, referred to in the legislation as the senior statutory auditor.

Audit thresholds

13.24   Audit thresholds are harmonised with the full implementation of the *Charities Act 2006* and the relevant parts of the *Companies Act 2006*. At that point the audit requirement is the same across England, Wales and Scotland (minor differences in respect of groups and the exact scope of the report are unintentional and likely to be resolved by revised legislation). Audit thresholds are subject to consultation, and therefore may change, but at the time of writing the regime from 1 April 2008 will be as follows.

All charities other than exempt charities are required to have an audit if income is over £500,000 or assets are over £2.8 million and income is over £100,000. Where the charity is a company, the audit will be conducted under the *Companies Act 2006* unless the company is exempt from audit as a small or dormant company. A small company has income below £5.6 million and a balance sheet total below £2.8m, and in this case the audit will be conducted under the *Charities Act 1993*. This nuance will be reflected in the audit report itself and the terms of engagement, but in practice has no discernible impact on the audit process itself.

Conduct of the audit

13.25   The audit of a charity is fundamentally no different from any other external audit, although it is governed by Practice Note 11 issued by the APB, which sets out the special features of charities and how the auditor should interpret auditing standards.

The auditor should provide a planning document, which should be seen by those charged with governance, and a report after the audit, often referred to as a management letter. The formal report on the accounts will usually only be signed after the charity has provided the auditor with a letter of representation, covering issues where the auditor is especially relying on the trustees' confirmation of certain matters.

Auditors will always discuss the risk of fraud in the organisation, following international auditing standards, and charity auditors have a duty to report to the regulator where they are aware of matters which they consider to be of material significance to the Regulator. These reports will often be discussed with trustees first, but do not have to be. Reporting issues are broadly those matters which would be subject to a serious incident report to the Charity Commission.

CHARITIES RECEIVING SUBSTANTIAL PUBLIC FUNDS

13.26   Some charities, including charities in the NHS, receive substantial public funds and have their accounts audited by the Comptroller and Auditor General or by auditors from the Audit Commission. The Charity Commission has powers to disapply the audit and independent examination provisions of *Part VI* of the *Charities Act 1993* in instances where a charity's accounts are scrutinised by these bodies.

14   Borrowings

14.1   All types of charity may borrow, provided that their governing document contains a clause permitting them to do so. This clause is usually incorporated into most governing documents at the charity's formation. However, trustees should be aware of any potential limitation in their powers which may exist, for example restricting a charity from borrowing at over a certain rate of interest, or from offering certain types of security. Aternatively trustees may be able to rely on implied powers to borrow based on the *Trusts of Land and Appointment of Trustees Act 1996* and the *Trustee Act 2000*. Charities that trade have an implied power to borrow in support of their trade, and trustees may borrow on an unsecured basis in relation to charity land and buildings. However some lenders will be cautious about lending on the basis of implied powers, and advice may be needed from lawyers or the Charity Commission.

14.2   Charity Commission consent for borrowing will not normally be given where the borrowing is to acquire investments.

14.3   There is no distinction between loans and bank overdrafts, and so the processes described below, especially in relation to charging and security, apply equally to both.

14.4   Whatever the powers of the trustees, they should never act imprudently. This responsibility can impose a greater burden on those with a financial background, who may need to guide their colleagues on the full implications of larger borrowing decisions. Where the sum is substantial a smaller finance group can be established to consider the impact of a loan, to examine budgets and cash flow forecasts, and most importantly to confirm that the charity not only needs the borrowing, but has the ability to service and repay the loan. Professional advice may be needed.

14.5   Charities must keep a record of any loans. Details will be needed to ensure that the routine payments and accounting are accurate both in respect of capital repayment and any interest due. Sometimes confusion arises over whether an amount was intended as a loan or as a gift. Where supposed donors request their money back on the basis that it was intended as a loan it will be particularly useful for an organisation to demonstrate that it has operational procedures in place for recording all loans, whether interest bearing or not.

TYPES OF BORROWING

14.6   The range of loan finance available to a charity is as great as the range available to individuals or commercial organisations. Some commercial lending is designed to be tax efficient in the hands of a commercial company, or is preferred because it enables a business to present its accounts in a certain way. These advantages, which are not attractive to charitable organisations, may make these forms of lending less competitive as a result. Trustees should not assume that the same considerations which inform their judgements in commerce automatically apply in the charity context.

14.7   Loans from banks or other financial institutions will usually require some form of security. If this is to be land, then the *Charities Act 1993, s 38* procedures must be followed. These require the trustees to obtain an Order of the Court or of the Charity Commission, or written professional advice (this can be from an external source or from a suitably qualified trustee or member of staff) about whether or not the loan is necessary, whether the terms of the loan are reasonable, and whether the charity has the ability to repay the loan on those terms. Since the *Charities Act 2006* it has been possible to structure mortgages in such a way that further advances can be added on to an existing mortgage without it having to be treated as an entirely separate transaction.

14.8   Other security, such as a floating charge over book debts, may be granted without the need for statutory procedures, although again the governing document should be consulted. It is possible for individuals to guarantee loans instead of the charity granting security. Banks are accustomed to this approach in the context of small businesses, but any guarantor needs to be aware that the commitment is not merely a cosmetic exercise to enable a charity to obtain a loan. Banks can and do call in guaranteed loans, and do go to the guarantor for any losses realised, even though this process may sometimes extend over several years.

14.9   Charities also have access to sources of lending which are not available to other organisations. These include benefactors and trustees, other charities, and specialist lending institutions. Benefactors and trustees are often pre-pared to make interest-free loans, and these can be easier to appeal for than outright donations. Once the money has been passed over there is always the hope that it will be converted into a donation subsequently. Where individuals make substantial loans interest free it should be clear that the lender has no control over the application of any investment income arising, to avoid personal tax complications for the lender. [*ICTA 1988, s 660*].

14.10   More recently there has been increasing interest in other forms of funding to charities, often described as venture philanthropy. This may represent a mixture of funding grants, loans and other support, and often will involve more intervention and performance measurement from the funder. The funder will often be a charity set up for this purpose

14.11   Often trustees may wish to support their own charity through loans. Where they are interest bearing, the interest received may comprise a benefit to the trustee and would therefore be in breach of trust unless specifically author-ised by the governing document. Where such loans are made interest free, the charity should be conscious of the possibility of a conflict of interest arising between the future needs of the charity and the trustee personally. Obvious problems may arise if a trustee has committed a significant sum to the charity, which then begins to get into financial difficulties. Similarly, over-dependence on one source of finance, be it loan or donation, can impair the trustees' ability to act objectively in the best interests of the charity.

Interest

14.12   If any interest is paid to the lender, and if the interest is calculated by reference to a debt which is intended or capable of being outstanding for more than a year, then the interest should be paid to the lender net of basic rate tax, and the tax deducted accounted for to HMRC.

14.13   The Charity Commission guidance is that interest may also be secured by property without jeopardising the *s 38* procedures. Interest rate swaps may or may not need Commission consent – again it will depend on the powers of the trustees, whether or not the swap is incidental to the main borrowing, and whether or not it is speculative.

Loan to or from trading subsidiaries

14.14   The relationship between the charity and its trading subsidiary is discussed in CHAPTER 120. Usually it is the charity that lends money to its subsidiary, but occasionally a subsidiary is in a position to lend money to the charity and, as the subsidiary is usually under the control of the charity trustees, this is a readily available source of finance for the charity. The directors of the trading subsidiary should be prepared to resist such requests for finance if it is not in the best interests of the company. The directors of the trading subsidiary need to act responsibly towards that entity in isolation, and should not jeopardise its solvency out of a desire to help out the parent body.

Other sources of finance

14.15   On a more commercial basis, there are also organisations which lend on formal terms to charities. Some of these are special interest charities support-ing particular types of charitable endeavour (for instance, the Architectural Heritage Fund), others are charities supporting the sector more widely, such as Charities Aid Foundation's loan services. Beyond the charitable sector organisations like Industrial Common Ownership Finance Ltd and social banks will lend to social enterprises co-operatives, social enterprises, commu-nity businesses, development trusts and businesses developed from the chari-table and voluntary sector. Futurebuilders England is a government-backed fund offering support and investment to third sector organisations to deliver public services. It offers loans, grants and support to build the capacity of third sector organisations who want to deliver better public services.

14.16   Finally, charities should not always assume that loans are to be avoided. Sometimes the trustees should actively consider whether taking out a loan could be the best means of achieving the charity's objects: for instance, where an immediate need requires cash, where fund-raising pledges are still being honoured, or as an alternative to holding surplus cash in reserves. In this situation a charity may accept that it can afford to operate without a large working capital reserve if it has security available, for instance, in the form of property, against which it can borrow in an emergency.

14.17   The ability to obtain loans should therefore be factored into any reserves policies and the assessment of free reserves would normally offset secured borrowings against the relevant asset. Since some of the loan will be payable in the short term, the free reserve calculation should take into account the debt falling due within one year.

15   Branches

15.1   The precise status of any form of branch network can have far-reaching consequences. It is important therefore to ensure that this status is clear to everybody concerned before taking actions which may have repercussions for either the main charity or the other groups.

15.2   Branches are defined in the SORP as 'entities or administrative bodies set up, for example, to conduct a particular aspect of the business of the charity, or to conduct the business of the charity in a particular geographical area'.

DEFINITIONS

15.3   Branches may be called by many names: the following list is not exhaustive, but is set out to help the reader consider to what extent any internal arrangement may in fact fall within the definition. Branches are variously called: branch, group, region, area, Friends, supporters, league, chapter and project. The branch may or may not be formally constituted. It may operate at a considerable distance from the parent organisation, and it may or may not hold itself accountable to the parent charity. None of these factors are of fundamental importance to the status of a branch, although together they may begin to indicate more clearly the legal position.

15.4   The key issue is one of autonomy, or control. Who does, or should, exercise control over the affairs of the branch? This should be answered not on the basis of the current state of the relationship with the branch, but on the underlying facts. Reference should be made to the constitutional position and the administrative arrangements. The SORP lists some characteristics of a non-autonomous branch as follows:

- it uses the name of the reporting (i.e. main) charity within its title;

- it exclusively raises funds for the main charity and/or for its own local activities;

- it uses the main charity's registration number to receive tax relief on its activities;

- it is perceived by the public to be the main charity's local representative, or its representative for a particular purpose;

- it receives support from the main charity through advice, publicity materials, etc.;

- it provides finance for the main charity's primary purpose activities;

- it is staffed by employees of the main charity;

- its funds are the legal property of the main charity, whether or not a local bank account is operated.

15.5   A branch may therefore be simply part of the administrative machinery of the main charity, or a separate legal entity. Constitutional arrangements such as power of appointment, removal and veto must be examined. Where the status is still unclear following the applications of the various tests listed, then legal advice may be needed, or advice should be sought from the Charity Commission. Informal fund-raising groups are not necessarily either branches or even charities in their own right.

FRIENDS

15.6   Several charities have organisations linked to them known as 'Friends' and there are thousands of such charities either registered as 'Friends' or using that word in their working name. Usually Friends are a means of involving a wide circle of people who wish to support the charity without becoming legally responsible for it. Sometimes the reason for setting up a group of Friends is because some supporters are willing to raise funds for the charity but wish to control where the funds are applied by imposing some form of restriction on the transfer of the funds. Whether or not the Friends organisation is a separate registered charity, it may be necessary for the accounts to be consolidated into the main charity's accounts. Determination of the precise status of 'the Friends' will be vital here, and FRS 2 and the SORP between them provide guidance on the definition of control.

CLARIFICATION IMPORTANT

15.7   The reasons for determining the status of branches include identifying all the risks that the main charity bears, which may be increased by a lack of central control. For instance, a contractual liability in a branch may follow through to the main charity, but may be the type of liability that the trustees of the main charity would never have accepted in their own right. Other issues include tax exposure, conformity with the charity's health and safety and HR policies, protection of the brand and coordinating fundraising activities.

15.8   Charities with branches or dispersed operations therefore need to clarify their own legal structures, and then ensure that systems operate which maximise the efficiency of the organisation, minimise the risk, and also preserve the goodwill and co-operation of the local staff and volunteers at branch level. The systems in operation will need to cover a wide range of topics, but especially they will need to cover accounting and tax matters, and the use of delegated authorities.

OPERATIONAL AUTHORITY

15.9   The authorities within which a local branch can operate should be clearly set out in a standard form used by the main charity with all its branch operations. These agreements may take several different forms, and will depend on the exact nature of the relationship. However, they typically fall into certain categories:

- a full branch constitution incorporating the relationship with the main charity;
- a separate agreement covering specific areas; and
- a 'franchise' agreement.

15.10   In all cases, it is important for the main charity to have confidence in certain key areas, namely:

- the delegated authority for the local committee to enter into contractual agreements, and operate local bank accounts;

- the terms of reference of local committees;

- the geographical area, or other important limitation, on the branch's activity;

- the adoption of policies and safeguards instituted by the centre;

- the terms and conditions of local employment arrangements;

- the approach to fundraising, and the use of the national charity's name; and

- the operation of a sound system of internal controls.

15.11   Many of these issues will be addressed when the branch is first formed, but thereafter it is important for the trustees to be able to monitor the activities of the local branch. This will require some form of reporting back to the centre, a need which may be underlined by year-end accounting needs, and tax factors.

15.12   A charity whose branches are not autonomous should include the financial performance of branches within its annual accounts, consolidated on a line by line basis gross, not net. Where branches hold general purpose funds it is common for the annual accounts to highlight these in the reserves analysis, perhaps even as designated funds. The requirement for trustees to include branch activities in the main charity's accounts underlines the need for them to exercise a proper level of management control during the year.

FINANCIAL REPORTING

15.13   Where a branch network is seen as being a part of the main organisation, then it is possible for the combined activities of the branches to create a tax liability. This liability can be caused either by the branches undertaking transactions and activities which were not approved by the centre, or simply by the scale of the activities which, when combined, trigger either a requirement to be registered for VAT, or become sufficiently large for HMRC to regard the scale of activity as taxable. For this reason many organisations run centralised functions for branches providing not only accounting but also other administrative support.

15.14   Where branches do their own accounting it is important for the centre to receive regular financial reports from the branches, in a format that allows the central finance department to collate and review them within a meaningful timeframe. In some cases, depending on the structure adopted, it may be necessary for the local branch to be reporting on two entities, the charitable activity and a trading subsidiary.

15.15   Whatever the regularity of the financial reporting, the annual accounts will certainly need to incorporate the material results of non-autonomous branches. It will therefore be necessary in these circumstances to plan the year-end accounting work, and the audit (or examination), further ahead than would be necessary for a stand-alone entity. The likely programme is as follows.

15.16   Branches

Table 5   Typical audit schedule for charity with branches

Timescale	Work
3–6 months before the year-end	Agree a format for the year-end accounts package with main charity finance department, local branch accountants and auditors
Near the year-end	Issue accounts pack to branches and explain the reason for any changes from previous years. Notify them of any changes in the audit arrangements
1–2 months after the year-end	Collect accounts from branches, review and query as appropriate
Later	Audit of local results if carried out centrally, and feedback to branches on results of consolidation exercise

15.16   Although financial information may be returned from branches throughout the year, often the annual exercise is the most detailed and the most complete. Advantage should be taken of the information presented at this stage to gain a thorough understanding of local operations.

AUDIT

15.17   Whether or not an audit is required at local level will be a matter for individual consideration in each case. However, the following factors will need to be taken into consideration by both the main charity's auditor and the finance department.

- Does the national or local constitution require some form of audit or examination?

- Do any local funding arrangements require audit/examination?

- Can the main auditor express an opinion on the accounts of the whole organisation based on records available at the centre?

- Can the main auditor report on individual branches from the centre, or does a local auditor need to be involved?

- Who should bear the cost of local audit work?

- Can the work of internal audit be relied on in this area?

15.18   The auditors of charitable companies have a duty under the *Companies Act 1985* to state if proper returns adequate for their audit have not been received from branches not visited by them. The *Companies Acts* do not define branches.

VAT

15.19   Where the branch organisation also forms part of the VAT registration, then the branches will need to submit quarterly returns in line with the main charity. As an administrative convenience the centre may structure its affairs so that no money is passed either way at this stage, but all transactions are handled on a 'current account' maintained between the branch and the centre, with any cash balance being settled up later.

TRADING SUBSIDIARIES

15.20   If a trading subsidiary is operated by the main charity, then a branch may also operate as a branch of the subsidiary. This will require a second set of books to be maintained by branches, which may be undesirable. Added complications such as this are particularly unwelcome where the branch is operated by volunteers, whose goodwill (and patience) is important to the success of the local operation.

PRACTICAL APPROACHES

15.21   To reduce the complexity of administering branch structures, the following approaches are often applied.

●   A tiered organisation is set up, with more complex or larger branches being entitled to undertake a wider range of activities than smaller or simpler branches.

●   Branches are allocated to groupings, usually geographic regions, and intervening layers of management and support are used.

●   An internal audit function is developed which also has a support role to the branches.

●   Branches are restricted in the range of activity which they can undertake, with the centre taking the view that, for instance, fund-raising opportunities foregone are less of a cost than the administration of small sums, with the concomitant risk.

●   Detailed system manuals and procedures, possibly involving some sort of centralised banking arrangements, are imposed from the centre.

●   All trading activities are undertaken by the centre, with branches acting like an agent.

BANKING

15.22   Banking arrangements can also be used both to help and control local branches. The exact needs of the charity will determine the bank selected, but where branches are involved, often the need for easy local banking, overnight clearing to a central account, and the operation of a local account as part of the main account will be additional factors to take into account when selecting a bank. Where branches are mainly fund-raising groups, then the nature of the money being banked may also affect the choice of banker. For example, some banks are more geared up than others to receive and handle large volumes of coinage.

OVERSEAS BRANCHES

15.23   Branches do not operate in the UK alone. It has been a common misconception that once a charity has passed money over to its overseas operations its trust obligations have been discharged. The definition of the autonomy of an overseas branch is essentially the same as the definition for a branch in the UK, with some obvious exceptions. Therefore, where an overseas branch is operating as part of the UK charity, then it is fully accountable to the trustees in the UK.

15.24   This aspect of overseas branch operations is emphasised by *ICTA 1988, s 506* which states that an application of funds overseas is not qualifying, or charitable, expenditure unless the charity has taken reasonable steps when making the transfer to ensure that it is applied for charitable purposes.

15.25   In some cases the treatment of overseas activities may be slightly different in practice compared with the comparable treatment of a similar situation in the UK. For instance, equipment sent to a branch in the UK will continue to be recorded as an asset of the charity, but may be written out of the books if despatched to an overseas project as it would not be cost-effective to recover it. Such policies do not alter the trustees' underlying duty to protect the assets, however. For instance, it would probably still be appropriate to obtain adequate insurance cover for the equipment.

OTHER BRANCH RELATIONSHIPS

15.26   Some organisations describe themselves as having branches when the relationship does not fit into the definition for non-autonomous branches described above. For instance, umbrella bodies and connected charities fall outside the 'branch' definition, as do relationships such as that between an Anglican diocese and parochial church councils.

16   Budgets

GENERAL CONSIDERATIONS

16.1   A budget is the financial representation of the organisation's plans for a future period. Many of the aspects of budgeting are the same for a charity as they are for a commercial enterprise, or indeed for an individual. There are, however, certain features of a charity's affairs which make the budget process more fraught than in these other situations. One of these is the frequency with which volunteer treasurers, with little formal training in the subject, are put in the position of having to produce budgets (or accounts) and explain them. Some general principles are therefore set out below, followed by points of more detailed application to charities.

Why budget?

16.2   A budget provides an element of internal control for a charity. It sets out the income the organisation intends to generate and how it intends to apply its resources, and enables the trustees to monitor the financial progress against that plan. Without the budget, the actual results noted during and after the year are of only limited value. Figures can only be compared with those of previous years, which may have been subject to all sorts of distortions.

Budget bases

16.3   Because a budget is looking ahead it has to be based on certain assumptions, both in the detail and in the overall plan of the charity. It is important that these are clearly understood by the users of the budget if it is to be of any use. Normally budgets end up as tough but realistic estimates; tough enough to make the organisation seek to be efficient and dynamic, but realistic enough not to lure the trustees into dangerous over- or under-spending.

16.4   Most organisations will base next year's figures on a mixture of what happened last year and expectations for next year, together with external factors such as changes in tax recoveries, inflation and so on. It follows that those preparing the budget need access to information. Alternative approaches include zero based budgets (similar to priority based budgets) where the budget is drawn up starting from scratch, and every line of income and expenditure is challenged. This can be a very time consuming exercise but it is useful to adopt this approach occasionally as it helps to identify priorities. Outcome focused managers often prefer activity based budgeting which groups costs according to specific outcomes or activities, rather than by departments or units.

16.5   An 'ideal' budget is a budget that sets out the results if everything was perfect. It has the two great disadvantages, first of deluding the reader into thinking that it will happen, and therefore taking decisions accordingly, and second also of only ever reporting negative variances (i.e. bad news) from then on. However, where a budget which includes some sensitivity analysis is presented, an optimistic version as well as a likely version could be used to show the organisation what might be achievable.

16.6 Budgets

16.6   A budget should not just concentrate on income and expenditure, any more than should the management accounts. Unless a balance sheet is also presented, it is difficult to be certain that the overall impact of a course of action has been understood. For instance, an increase in income applied totally to purchasing an asset, such as a property, could lead to financial difficulties, even though total income exceeded total expenditure. For the same reason, a cash flow statement should also be produced, although sometimes this may be derived from the balance sheet and the Statement of Financial Activities (SOFA).

Setting the budget

16.7   The budget should not drive the charity. The charity should have its own strategic or operational plan from which the budget is derived. The effect of preparing the budget may lead to some plans being curtailed, or funds identified that are available to spend. For these reasons, the budget setting process should be an inclusive one, working both top down and bottom up. The overall budget parameters, such as the proportion of income to be allocated to particular services, should be determined by the trustees, the team leaders can then develop their plans and budgets in this context and feed them back up for consolidation and review. The consolidated budget is then reviewed, negotiated and amended until it is accepted by the trustees. In larger organisations this process may take several months. It may be necessary to be preparing next year's budgets before the previous year's accounts are finalised. Ideally, the budget for the next period will be part of a longer cycle, say a three-year plan, which will therefore be continuously updated.

THE VIEW OF THE CHARITY COMMISSION

16.8   The Charity Commission has increasingly laid greater emphasis on the need for budgeting procedures in charities and drawn attention to them in a number of leaflets described below.

Internal Financial Controls

16.9   CC8 'Internal Financial Controls for Charities' states that proper and realistic estimates of expected income and expenditure should be made in order to have full control over the charity's finances. The budgets and accounts should only be approved by the trustees after discussion, and only if the trustees understand the financial information.

Charities and trading

16.10   When establishing a trading subsidiary the Charity Commission advises the trustees to take certain budgetary considerations into account. The subsidiary should be financially viable as soon as possible. Normally it is expected that this will be within the first five years of its operation, although in practice many smaller charities would be expecting viability within 12 months. Other factors include how any inter-entity debts are to be settled, the timing of Gift Aid payments, and the return to be achieved on any initial investment.

Charities' reserves

16.11   Charities should realistically assess their reserves needs as 'an essential part of good financial management practice', advises the Charity Commission in CC19 'Charities' Reserves'. The reserves policy should be informed by income and expenditure forecasts, and an analysis of future needs, opportunities, risks and contingencies.

CHARITY v COMMERCIAL BUDGETING

16.12   The following additional complexities must be taken into account when producing a charity's budget. These are unlikely to be relevant in comparably sized commercial enterprises. Many of these factors are as relevant to the production of management accounts as they are to the production of budgets.

Outcomes

16.13   The budget is not the ultimate determinant of the projected success or otherwise of the organisation, in the same way that the accounts are not primarily concerned with surplus or deficit. The budget should be driven by the plan to achieve the outcomes specified in the plan. The budget should therefore put any surplus or deficit into the context of other factors.

Branches

16.14   Branch results should be planned, either in summary in the centre, or from detailed budgets submitted by them individually. This lengthens the budgeting process.

Investments

16.15   The total return on investments, both capital and income, should be forecast; this can be based on the investment manager's own predictions, and the required returns to which the manager operates.

Gifts in kind/donated facilities

16.16   Often gifts in kind and donated facilities are omitted from the budget. If they are central to the charity then they should be included as part of the fundamental measurement of the operation. Even where they are less important, their inclusion will reduce variances requiring explanations on management accounts, and in some cases will ensure that performance ratios are more accurately anticipated. Where overheads are allocated out to projects and departments, then the exclusion of donated facilities can seriously distort the assessment of the costs of individual units.

Funds

16.17   Funds need separate presentation. Designated funds might be grouped together with general funds, or treated as a memorandum, depending on their significance. Restricted funds should be presented separately from the general fund, although it is likely that the level of detail will be less than on the general fund as income and expenditure will often comprise grants, discrete items, or allocations from general fund items.

17   Capital Gains Tax

DEFINITION

17.1   A capital gain arises when an asset which has increased in value is given away, sold, exchanged or disposed of in any other way, other than in the course of trade. Tax is charged on the increase in value with an allowance made for the length of time the asset has been owned. This allowance takes the form of an indexation allowance based on the Retail Price Index and applies to individuals and trusts up to 5 April 1998 and to companies. From 6 April 1998, individuals and trusts are entitled to taper relief, which reduces the gain by a percentage. This percentage varies according to the length of time the asset has been owned since April 1998 and whether or not it is a business asset. Companies, industrial and provident societies, and unincorporated associations do not pay capital gains tax, instead they pay corporation tax on their profits which will include any capital gains. However, trusts do pay capital gains tax on any non-exempt capital gains.

17.2   The Chancellor announced changes in his 2007 Pre-Budget Report which, if enacted, will abolish both indexation allowance and taper relief and subject any capital gains realised to a flat 18% rate of taxation. At the time of writing these proposals are the subject of much debate between the Government and interested parties. The changes ultimately introduced may not take the exact form envisaged by the Chancellor's Pre-Budget Report.

17.3   Most capital gains made by charities are exempt from tax provided that the gain is used for charitable purposes. This exemption from capital gains tax can be lost, however, where the charity has incurred non-charitable expenditure, i.e. expenditure for non-charitable purposes, such as funding a trading subsidiary. The exemption is not lost, however, if the proceeds of the sale of an asset, excluding the gain, are spent on a non-charitable purpose. [*Taxation of Chargeable Gains Act 1992, s 256*]. When an asset forms part of a charity's permanent endowment, the terms of the endowment may require gains made from the sale of the asset to be reinvested in similar assets. Where this is the case the gain will be exempt from capital gains tax.

GAINS

17.4   A chargeable gain on which capital gains tax is payable can arise on the disposal of an asset by sale or gift. Where the disposal is not at arm's length, e.g. in the case of a gift to a beneficiary of the charity, the market value of the asset is normally substituted for any proceeds. Allowable deductions in arriving at the chargeable gain are the cost of the asset, expenditure on improvement or enhancement of the asset, the incidental costs of acquisition and disposal and any available indexation allowance or taper relief.

LOSSES

17.5   Capital losses occurring in the same or an earlier period may be deducted from chargeable gains in calculating the liability to capital gains tax. Losses are calculated in the same way as gains, except that indexation allowance and taper relief do not apply (see **17.1** above). The legislation makes no reference to capital losses made by charities and it is arguable whether it must be implied from the legislation that because a gain is generally not a chargeable gain, a loss is not allowable. This point is only relevant where a charity has at some time made capital losses and is subject to tax on its chargeable gains because, for example, it has incurred non–charitable expenditure. Where a charity has a loss of tax exemption because of the rules relating to non–charitable expenditure, it can choose by election what income or gains are taxed. A charity may elect to pay tax on its chargeable gains and seek to argue that capital losses are deductible.

LOSS OF CHARITABLE STATUS

17.6   In a body set up as a trust the trustees are liable for the trust's taxes and can be held personally liable if the trust cannot pay its taxes. Where a charitable trust is wound up, or its objects cease to be charitable, there is a deemed disposal of all the trust's assets at their market value and any gain arising will be subject to capital gains tax unless they are passed to another charity to be applied for charitable purposes. Where there is a non–exempt capital gain and the assets held were acquired using the proceeds from the disposal of other assets with an exempt gain accrued at the time, that original gain also becomes taxable. The gain is assessed on individuals who are trustees at the time when the disposals were made. Therefore, if it is likely that a trust will cease to be charitable at some future date, trustees should be aware of these provisions and should seek an indemnity on retirement as gains made when they were trustees could become subject to tax at a much later date.

GIFTS TO CHARITY

17.7   When a donor wishes to give an asset to a charity, or sell it to the charity at less than its market value, its value is assumed to be an amount that does not give rise to a gain or a loss, so the donor does not have to pay capital gains tax. [*Taxation of Chargeable Gains Act 1992, ss 257, 258*]. Similar rules apply to gifts and sales below market value to institutions listed in the *Inheritance Tax Act 1984*, such as universities, museums and art galleries. If the sale of an asset would make a loss the donor may wish to consider selling the asset to a third party, offsetting the loss against any capital gains they have made in order to reduce their overall liability for capital gains tax, and donating the proceeds of the sale to a charity under Gift Aid, thus increasing the value of the gift to the charity. If the donor is a higher rate tax payer then he may claim additional income tax relief on his Gift Aid donation. From April 2000 individuals and companies can also get tax relief for the value of gifts to charity of quoted securities, unit trusts and certain other investments when calculating their income or profits for tax purposes.

17.8   From April 2002 the tax relief referred to above for qualifying investments was extended to include gifts of land or buildings to a charity.

TRADING COMPANIES

17.9   A charity's subsidiary trading company is fully liable for corporation tax on any capital gains it makes from the sale or disposal of assets. The tax liability can be avoided, however, by using Gift Aid to pass the taxable gains to the charity.

17.10   It may be advisable for the charity, rather than the trading subsidiary, to own assets which could give rise to capital gains. Professional advice should be sought.

18 Charitable Purposes

WHAT IS A CHARITY?

18.1 The modern concept of charity has evolved from the preamble to the *Charitable Uses Act 1601* (since repealed), popularly known as the *Statute of Elizabeth I*, which listed the following as being regarded as charitable:

- relief of aged, impotent (weak or powerless) and poor people;

- maintenance of sick and maimed soldiers and mariners;

- maintenance of schools of learning, free schools, and scholars in universities;

- repair of bridges, ports, havens, causeways, churches, sea banks and highways;

- education and preferment (advancement) of orphans;

- relief, stock or maintenance of houses of correction;

- marriages of poor maids;

- supportation, aid and help of young tradesmen, handicraftsmen and persons decayed (fallen into misfortune);

- relief or redemption of prisoners or captives; and

- aid or ease of any poor inhabitants concerning payment of fifteens (a tax on movable property), setting out soldiers (a tax to equip soldiers), and other taxes.

18.2 The Courts have subsequently based their decisions on what is, or is not, regarded as a charitable purpose from these by analogy. This allows purposes that could not have been imagined in 1601, to become charitable today. So, for example, 'the preferment of orphans' is analogous to 'the provision of orphanages' which is analogous to 'caring for disadvantaged children', which is analogous to 'caring for children suffering from sexual abuse'. Therefore an organisation such as the NSPCC can be registered as a charity even though its purposes were not included in the preamble to the *Charitable Uses Act 1601*.

18.3 In 1891 in a landmark case, which subsequently has become known as the *Pemsel* case, the judge, Lord MacNaghten, drew on the *1601 Act* and an 1804 definition of charitable objects to group charitable purposes into four 'heads' or categories (*Income Tax Special Purpose Comrs v Pemsel [1891] AC 531*). These are:

- the relief of poverty;

- the advancement of education;

- the advancement of religion; and

- other purposes beneficial to the community in a way recognised as charitable.

18.4 In July 2001 the then Prime Minister commissioned a review of the law and regulation of charities and other not-for-profit organisations. The review was carried out by the Government's Strategy Unit, and the findings were published in September 2002 in a report entitled 'Private Action, Public Benefit'. The Strategy Unit found that the four categories or heads of charity defined by *Pemsel* did not accurately reflect the range of organisations that are, or should be, charitable today. It recommended that in future all charities should have to demonstrate public benefit, rather than some purposes being presumed to be for the public benefit. It also recommended that there should be a new definition of charity, i.e. a charity should be an organisation that provides public benefit and which has one or more of a number of defined purposes. Following a period of public consultation many of the recommendations were included in a new Act, the *Charities Act 2006*.

18.5   *Section 1* of the *Charities Act 2006* provides a general statutory definition of 'charity' for the first time. For the purposes of the law in England and Wales a charity is an institution which is established for charitable purposes only and is subject to the control of the High Court. A charitable purpose is defined as one of the purposes listed in the Act and for the public benefit.

CHARITABLE PURPOSES

18.6   *Section 2* of the *Charities Act 2006* contains the first statutory definition of 'charitable purposes', i.e. a purpose is charitable if it meets two criteria:

- it must fall under one or more of the thirteen descriptions or 'heads' of charity defined in *s 2(2)* of the Act, and

- it is for the benefit of the public.

18.7   The descriptions or 'heads' of charity defined in *s 2(2)* are:

(1)   the prevention or relief of poverty (see CHAPTER 93);

(2)   the advancement of education (see CHAPTER 41);

(3)   the advancement of religion (CHAPTER 102);

(4)   the advancement of health or the saving of lives (see CHAPTER 59);

(5)   the advancement of citizenship or community development (see CHAPTER 21);

(6)   the advancement of the arts, culture, heritage or science (see CHAPTER 11);

(7)   the advancement of amateur sport (see CHAPTER 8);

(8)   the advancement of human rights, conflict resolution or reconciliation or the promotion of religious or racial harmony or equality and diversity (see CHAPTER 63);

(9)   the advancement of environmental protection or improvement (see CHAPTER 44);

(10)   the relief of those in need by reason of youth, age, ill-health, disability, financial hardship or other disadvantage (see CHAPTER 129);

(11)   the advancement of animal welfare (see CHAPTER 9);

(12)   the promotion of the efficiency of the armed forces of the Crown, or of the efficiency of the police, fire and rescue services or ambulance services (see CHAPTER 10);

(13)   any other purposes not defined above but which were recognised as charitable under charity law in force before the *Charities Act 2006* came into force, or by virtue of *s 1* of the *Recreational Charities Act 1958*, or any purposes that may reasonably be regarded as analogous to, or within the spirit of, purposes already recognised as charitable (see CHAPTER 20).

18.8   In the above descriptions:

- 'religion' includes a religion which involves belief in more than one god and a religion which does not involve belief in a god;

- the advancement of health includes the prevention or relief of sickness, disease or human suffering;

- head 5 includes rural or urban regeneration, and the promotion of civic responsibility, volunteering, the voluntary sector or the effectiveness and efficiency of charities;

- in head 7 'sport' means sports or games that promote health by involving physical or mental skill or exertion;

- head 10 includes relief given by providing accommodation or care;

- in head 12 'fire rescue services' means services provided by fire and rescue authorities under *Part 2* of the *Fire and Rescue Services Act 2004.*

18.9   These 13 new heads of charity will apply from when the relevant sections of the *Charities Act 2006* come into force, which is expected to be in the Spring of 2008. In the meantime the four *Pemsel* heads remain in place.

CATCH-ALL OBJECTS

18.10   When drafting a charity's objects it is possible to make them very wide, e.g. 'to relieve poverty, advance education, and advance religion anywhere in the world and do all such other things that may benefit the community in a way recognised as charitable', and then go on to add more specific clauses indicating the type of work and areas in which the charity will initially operate.

PUBLIC BENEFIT

18.11   Charities established for the relief of poverty, the advancement of education or the advancement of religion have been presumed to benefit the public. *Section 3* of the *Charities Act 2006* removes that presumption and once the provisions in the Act relating to public benefit come into force, which is expected to be in early 2008, all charities will have to be able to demonstrate how their purposes benefit the public.

18.12   The Act does not define 'public benefit' and the concept of public benefit will remain in common law. In guidance issued in 2005 the Charity Commission defined the principles that would show whether an organisation provided benefits to the public as:

- there must be an identifiable benefit, though this can take many different forms;

- the benefit will be assessed in the light of modern conditions;

- the benefit must be to the public at large, or to a sufficient section of the public;
- any private benefit must be incidental;
- those who are less well off must not be entirely excluded from benefit.

18.13   The benefit to the public, whether tangible or intangible, should be capable of being identified. Tangible benefits will usually be obvious and measurable. Intangible benefits may be more difficult to measure, but should be identifiable, for example an increased sense of well-being. It is not sufficient for some benefit to result. Positive benefits must outweigh any harm that results from achieving a particular purpose.

18.14   Benefits can be direct and indirect. Most charitable purposes will provide direct benefits to individuals, for example an improvement in their financial position or their health. Indirect benefits, such as the benefits to care home residents when a charity provides training for care staff in order to improve their performance, can also be taken into account when assessing if an organisation provides sufficient benefit to the public.

18.15   Perceptions of public benefit will change over time due to changing social and economic conditions and changes in society's values. Purposes once regarded as beneficial may no longer be regarded as beneficial today and vice versa. Therefore public benefit must be assessed in the light of current conditions.

18.16   Judging whether a sufficient section of the public receives a benefit is not simply a matter of numbers. If a charity's benefits are open to anyone who falls within the beneficiary group, who chooses to take advantage of them, it will be judged as providing benefit to the public, even if the numbers assisted are relatively small. This would be the case for charities established to assist those with rare diseases.

18.17   Any private benefits arising from a charity's purposes must be incidental. A charity established for the purpose of urban regeneration, for example, will inevitably provide private benefits to individuals or companies in the area being regenerated. However, this is legitimate if it is incidental to the charity's main purposes, providing that the amount of private benefit is reasonable in the circumstances.

18.18   Some charities, such as care homes, schools, private hospitals, theatres and heritage centres, may charge for their services. However, if the fees charged are so high that they effectively exclude the less well off from accessing the service, the organisation will fail the public benefit test unless it can demonstrate that the less well off are not wholly excluded from any direct or indirect benefits. This would be the case if the charity offered tickets to the less well off at concessionary prices, or, in the case of educational charities, offered scholarships or bursaries, or, in the case of private hospitals, allowed its facilities to be used by the NHS.

18.19   *Section 4* of the Act requires the Charity Commission to issue guidance on the operation of the public benefit requirement and to revise its guidance from time to time, for example if there are changes in society which bring about developments in the legal concept of public benefit. Draft guidance is currently the subject of public consultation, and final guidance is expected to be issued in October 2007 and will be available on the Charity Commission's website (*www.charity-commission.gov.uk*).

18.20   Charitable Purposes

18.20   The Charity Commission's guidance on public benefit will not be legally
binding on charity trustees, though trustees will be required to take it into
account when doing anything to which the guidance is relevant.

19   Charitable Status

19.1   Organisations in England and Wales operating on a not-for-profit basis will be charities by definition if their objects or purposes are wholly and exclusively charitable (see CHAPTER 18) and they provide a public benefit.

CHARITABLE STATUS INDEPENDENT OF REGISTRATION

19.2   Most charities with an income of more than £5,000 are required by *s 3A* of the *Charities Act 2006* to register with the Charity Commission (see CHAPTER 101) but it is not this registration that grants them charitable status, it is meeting the criteria for a charity outlined above.

CHARITABLE STATUS NOT DEPENDENT ON LEGAL STRUCTURE

19.3   An organisation's status as a charity is a completely separate matter from the legal structure it chooses to use. Thus a benevolent society that adopts the legal structure of a company or an industrial and provident society will be charitable provided that:

- its objects are wholly and exclusively charitable;
- it provides a public benefit.

ADVANTAGES OF CHARITABLE STATUS

19.4   Having charitable status brings and confers a number of tax and other advantages.

- Being a charity attracts funding and other support from the general public as, on the whole, the British public regard charities as 'a good thing'.
- Some funding bodies can give grants only to registered charities.
- Charities are entitled to 80% business rate relief, with a further 20% at the discretion of the local authority (see CHAPTER 97).
- Charities enjoy a number of tax reliefs (see CHAPTER 118).
- Charities are entitled to call on the Charity Commission for support and guidance and the Commission's role as a regulator enhances public confidence in charities as it detects and deters abuse.

DISADVANTAGES OF CHARITABLE STATUS

19.5   There are, however, some disadvantages attached to being a charity including the following.

- Some needy people have a negative attitude to receiving 'charity' and therefore will not seek help.
- Charities have to comply with charity law and regulation in addition to legislation relating to their legal structure. Charity law restricts their political and campaigning activities and requires them to structure

certain trading activities through subsidiary trading companies which may, in turn, add to their operating costs.

- With some exceptions, members of the governing body cannot be paid. This can result in their not giving sufficient time to their duties.

- In some instances charity trustees can be held personally liable for their actions and this can deter some people from being willing to act as trustees.

- Charity trustees have to act in the best interests of the charity, with prudence and within the law and the charity's governing document. This may produce a conflict with their personal code of ethics, e.g. they may be unable to exclude certain investments from the charity's portfolio that they themselves would not wish to hold.

DECLARATION OF CHARITABLE STATUS

19.6   *Section 5* of *Charities Act 1993* requires all registered charitable trusts and associations with an annual income of more than £10,000 to include a statement of charitable status on the following documents:

- all notices, advertisements and other documents soliciting money or other property for the benefit of the charity,

- cheques, bills of exchange, promissory notes and orders for money or goods, and

- bills, invoices, receipts and letters of credit.

Welsh charities may use 'elusen cafrestredig' on documents wholly in Welsh.

19.7   *Section 68* of the *Charities Act 1993* requires charitable companies whose name does not include the words 'charity' or 'charitable' to include a statement indicating their charitable status on a similar range of documents and also on:

- all business letters;

- all notices and other official publications; and

- all conveyances purporting to be executed by the company.

19.8   While there is no statute or case law yet on whether these requirements apply to e-mails or to information on websites, the general consensus is that they do.

20   Charities for Other Purposes

20.1   The thirteenth head of charity defined in the *Charities Act 2006* is 'other purposes currently recognised as charitable and any new charitable purposes that may be recognised in the future as being similar to another charitable purpose'. It will therefore include charities and purposes previously recognised as charitable under the *Pemsel* fourth head that do not come under any of the other 12 heads defined in the *Charities Act 2006*.

20.2   Charity Commission guidance gives the following examples of charities and charitable purposes that fall under this head:

- The provision of facilities for recreation and other leisure time occupation in the interests of social welfare with the object of improving the conditions of life for the persons for whom they are intended;

- The provision of public works and services and the provision of public amenities (such as the repair of bridges, ports, havens, causeways and highways, the provision of water and lighting, a cemetery or crematorium, as well as the provision of public facilities such as libraries, reading rooms and public conveniences);

- The relief of unemployment;

- The defence of the country (such as trusts for national or local defence);

- The promotion of certain patriotic purposes, such as war memorials;

- The social relief, resettlement and rehabilitation of persons under a disability or deprivation (including disaster funds);

- The promotion of industry and commerce;

- The promotion of agriculture and horticulture;

- Gifts for the benefit of a particular locality (such as trusts for the general benefit of the inhabitants of a particular place); the beautification of a town; civic societies;

- The promotion of mental or moral improvement;

- The promotion of the moral or spiritual welfare or improvement of the community;

- The preservation of public order;

- Promoting the sound administration and development of the law;

- The promotion of ethical standards of conduct and compliance with the law in the public and private sectors;

- The rehabilitation of ex-offenders and the prevention of crime.

20.3   Charities for other purposes must, like all charities, be for purposes that are wholly and exclusively charitable, and must be for public benefit. For example, in order to gain charitable status an organisation established for the relief of unemployment will need to show that:

- it is set up for the primary purpose of relieving unemployment for the public benefit;

20.4   Charities for Other Purposes

- its activities are designed to relieve unemployment generally or to relieve unemployment in a significant section of the community;

- any benefit accruing to private interests must be strictly incidental to the charity's primary purpose.

20.4   Charitable purposes have been extended and developed over the years by decisions of the courts and the Charity Commission on the basis of analogy with purposes originally held to be charitable. This development of the law reflects changes in social conditions. The process will continue into the foreseeable future.

FURTHER INFORMATION

20.5   Charity Commission RR1a 'Recognising New Charitable Purposes'

Charity Commission RR3 'The Relief of Unemployment'

21   Citizenship and Community Development Charities

21.1   The advancement of citizenship or community development is one of the new heads of charity defined in the *Charities Act 2006*. It includes the charitable purpose of urban and rural regeneration, which had previously been recognised by the Charity Commission as a charitable purpose in its own right, and the promotion of civic responsibility, volunteering, the voluntary sector and the efficiency and effectiveness of charities.

21.2   The advancement of citizenship or community development includes a broad range of charitable purposes, focussed on developing the community as a whole rather than on individuals. The sorts of charities that fall under this head include:

- Charities that promote good citizenship and civic responsibility, such as Scout and Guide Groups and good citizenship award schemes;

- Charities that promote urban and rural regeneration, such as community regeneration trusts;

- Charities that promote volunteering, such as Volunteer Centres and Time Banks;

- Charities that promote the voluntary sector, such as NCVO;

- Charities that promote the efficiency and effectiveness of charities and the effective use of charitable resources, such as CAF, Charity Evaluation Service, and CFDG;

- Charities that promote community capacity building, such as community development trusts;

- Charities concerned with social investment, such as the Foundation for Social Entrepreneurs.

21.3   For most organisations wishing to register as charities under this head it should be relatively easy to demonstrate that their purposes are exclusively charitable and that they provide public benefit, as they are established to benefit the community rather than individuals. However, demonstrating that they provide public benefit and that any private benefits are incidental and proportionate may be more difficult for charities promoting urban and rural regeneration, than for those promoting community capacity building, as private individuals and businesses often benefit when an area is regenerated.

PROMOTION OF URBAN AND RURAL REGENERATION

Charitable purpose

21.4   In its publication RR2 'Promotion of Urban and Rural Regeneration', the Charity Commission gives the following example of an objects clause that would be acceptable: 'The promotion for the public benefit of urban or rural regeneration in areas of social and economic deprivation (and in particular [specify area]) by all or any of the following means: [specify activities]'.

21.5   Citizenship and Community Development Charities

Criteria for charitable status

21.5   For a regeneration organisation to be granted charitable status it would need to show that:

- it has effective criteria for determining whether or not an area is in need of regeneration;

- its activities will cover a broad spectrum of regeneration work including at least three of the activities listed in 21.10 below;

- the public benefit arising will outweigh any private benefit which may be conferred on individuals or companies in the area and that the organisation has clear criteria by which this can be determined;

- its objects are exclusively charitable.

Public v private benefit

21.6   Most tangible benefits of regeneration appear to go to individuals, for example in the form of increased property prices, or to companies rather than to the wider public. For an organisation to be charitable its purposes and activities must be for public benefit and any private benefit that does arise should do so only as a side effect of the achievement of the charitable purpose. Therefore a regeneration organisation applying for charitable status will need to demonstrate that its activities will not result in an unacceptable level of private benefit.

21.7   If the main problems in an area are poor housing and high crime, but unemployment is low, charitable status would not be granted to a regeneration organisation that intends to focus on activities to regenerate the area by further reducing the level of unemployment as this would have only a marginal effect on deprivation in the area, i.e. the private benefit accruing to local employers from schemes to reduce unemployment would be likely to be greater than the benefit accruing to the public.

21.8   Criteria that might be used to weigh up the balance between public and private benefit include:

- the increase in the number of homes for sale and house prices;

- the change in the waiting list for social housing;

- the change in the rate of participation of local people in community events;

- the increase in public amenities;

- the change in the health of the local population;

- the reduction in unemployment;

- the reduction in unemployment benefit compared with the amount that the charity would have to pay an employer to take on unemployed people;

- the change in the crime rate.

21.9   In assessing whether an organisation is set up for public or private benefit the Charity Commission will take into account the support and participation of a large part of the community in developing the regeneration plans, the impact of the organisation's activities on the local community and the composition of the trustee body. This should be independent of companies or funding bodies that stand to gain from the regeneration activities. If some of the trustees are likely to gain personally from the regeneration the charity's governing document must contain provision for the declaration of interests. Trustees with an interest should absent themselves from discussions in which they may have a conflict of interest and may not vote on them. The charity's promoters should be able to demonstrate that having an individual with a private interest as a trustee is to the benefit of the charity, notwithstanding the potential conflict.

Regeneration activities

21.10   The types of activities that an urban or rural regeneration charity might carry out include:

- providing, maintaining and improving public amenities;

- providing, maintaining and improving recreational facilities;

- preserving buildings in the area that are of historic or architectural interest;

- conserving, maintaining or improving environmental features such as docks, canals, public footpaths, etc.;

- providing, maintaining and improving roads and accessibility to main transport routes;

- providing public healthcare facilities;

- providing childcare facilities;

- promoting public safety and the prevention of crime.

21.11   They can also carry out activities that would also qualify as charitable under the heads of the relief of poverty, or the advancement of education, or other purposes currently recognised as charitable and any new charitable purposes which are similar to another charitable purpose, such as:

- providing financial assistance to people in need;

- providing housing for those in need;

- improving housing standards generally in an area of deprivation;

- helping unemployed people to find employment;

- providing education, training, work experience and advice to unemployed people with the aim of helping them gain employment;

- providing financial or technical assistance to new businesses;

- providing financial or technical assistance to existing businesses where it would enable them to employ and train unemployed people;

- providing land or buildings to businesses on favourable terms in order to create training and employment opportunities for unemployed people.

21.12 Citizenship and Community Development Charities

Accounting requirements

21.12 These may well be complex depending on the activities carried out and the way in which the charity works, ie as a front-line operation or as a co-ordinating body subcontracting some of the work to other charitable or non-charitable organisations. Specialist advice will be needed.

21.13 If a regeneration charity owns land or property the trustees will have to decide whether it should be accounted for as functional property or investment property, particularly where the property has been used for both purposes. As with charities for the relief of unemployment, if the charity provides land or property to a business start-up on favourable terms the trustees will similarly have to decide whether it should be accounted for as functional property or investment property. Again, as with charities for the relief of unemployment, where payment is made to a commercial company to take on unemployed people the charity will need to agree with the company the economic cost of employing and training such staff. The charity should not pay an amount in excess of the economic cost.

PROMOTION OF COMMUNITY CAPACITY BUILDING

Charitable purpose

21.14 In its publication RR5 'The promotion of community capacity building', the Charity Commission gives the following example of an objects clause that would be acceptable: 'To develop the capacity and skills of the members of the [socially and economically] [socially] disadvantaged community of [specify area] in such a way that they are better able to identify, and help meet, their needs and to participate more fully in society'.

Criteria for charitable status

21.15 For a community capacity building organisation to be granted charitable status it would need to show that:

- It carries out its activities amongst members of a socially and economically disadvantaged community or, in some cases, a community which is simply socially disadvantaged;

- The purpose of those activities is the improvement of the capacity and skills of those who take part in them;

- Those activities are capable of improving the capacity and skills of those who take part in them;

- Any personal benefit derived by individuals or groups from the organisation's activities is incidental to the wider benefit to the public;

- It has objects in a form which describe the purpose and the benefits flowing from it with sufficient clarity and which are exclusively charitable.

Public v private benefit

21.16 To be a charity, an organisation promoting community capacity building must be set up for the benefit of the public. This means that any personal benefits must be ancillary or incidental to the wider benefits to the public flowing from its activities. The Charity Commission state in RR5 'The promotion of community capacity building' that personal benefit to members of a community from the work of a community capacity building organisation will be acceptable, because it is that very benefit to individuals, for example improved skills, confidence and capacity (eg an improved ability to present arguments orally or in writing), that will deliver the necessary benefit to the public.

21.17   The personal advantage that people might derive subsequently from the application of those skills, for example in the job market, would not be objectionable either, as it would be considered incidental to the wider public benefit to the public that comes from having acquired or improved skills – in the same way that the personal benefits which flow to individuals from education are seen as incidental.

21.18   When community capacity building is directed at disadvantaged communities indirect benefit to the public arises from:

- the increase in skills, competencies and self confidence on the part of members of such communities;

- the more effective, efficient and sustainable delivery of services to such communities;

- the promotion of social cohesion.

21.19   In determining the balance between public and personal benefit arising from the proposed activities organisations will need to consider the benefits to any groups with whom they will work. The extent to which groups may become better organised, better informed and more focused may not always be incidental to the wider benefit to the public. The sort of benefits that will need to be considered particularly carefully are those:

- arising from activities which bring significant benefits to individuals (for example, giving detailed advice on how to set up and run a business);

- arising from activities which bring significant benefits to a small group of individuals (such as a savings club);

- arising from activities directed towards members of a non-charitable group which is concerned with the personal interests of its members (such as a residents' association or a shopkeepers' association).

21.20   Certain activities may be recognised as charitable if carried out by a charity established for the relief of poverty, but not if carried out by an organisation established to advance community development.

Community capacity building activities

21.21   The types of activities carried out by charities established for community capacity building will combine encouragement with practical assistance, and help members of the community to help themselves. They may include:

- providing support and assistance to members of the community that enables them to identify and deal with problems that affect them as members of that community

- developing structures which enable them to be better placed to co-operate with each other and deal with organisations in the wider community;

- providing advice and support for evaluation of projects;

- nurturing networking and the sharing of experiences as part of the learning process;

- enabling groups to consolidate and build upon existing skills;

- providing training or instruction of any sort, including formal training (e.g. in the use of a PC or the preparation of accounts);

- providing advice/support as to how to identify needs or priorities of groups, or to plan projects and their implementation (e.g. drawing up business plans, budgets, funding applications);

- equipping with or developing transferable skills such as team-working and problem solving;

- developing peoples' capacity to organise structures and practices within their organisations (e.g. through training in meeting skills, management methods and techniques for projects and people);

- developing peoples' capacity for working within structures outside their group(s) (e.g. by coaching in negotiation, assertiveness and advocacy).

FURTHER INFORMATION

21.22   RR2 'Promotion of urban and rural regeneration'. Charity Commission, March 1999

RS12 'The Regeneration Game: the range, role and profile of regeneration charities'. Charity Commission, October 2006

RR5 'The promotion of community capacity building'. Charity Commission, November 2000.

22 Charity Commission

INTRODUCTION

22.1 The Charity Commission is the independent regulator of charities in England and Wales. It has a staff of almost 500 based in offices in Liverpool, London, Newport and Taunton and its expenditure in 2006 amounted to £31.83m. At the end of March 2007 there were 190,469 charities on its register. The Charity Commission is a non-ministerial government department, accountable to Parliament and the courts for promoting the effective use of charitable resources, giving information and advice to charities, investigating misconduct and abuse, and maintaining a public register of all charities with the exception of those that are exempted or excepted from registration. Its remit extends to England and Wales only, although the Commission has some supervisory powers over Scottish charities that are controlled from England or Wales. Scottish charities are regulated by the Office of the Scottish Charity Regulator (see CHAPTER 108). Charities in Northern Ireland are currently regulated by the Department for Social Development though there are plans to establish a Charity Commission for Northern Ireland (see CHAPTER 87).

22.2 The Charity Commission is not subject to the direction or control of Ministers. *Section 6(1)–(4)* of the *Charities Act 2006* underlines this by stating that 'In the exercise of its functions the Commission shall not be subject to the direction or control of any Minister of the Crown or other government department'. However, Cabinet Office Ministers have some functions in relation to the Charity Commission including:

- Appointing the Charity Commission Board Members, after a fair and open competition;

- Replying to questions in Parliament about the Commission;

- Making orders to give effect to changes in charities' constitutions which are regulated by Acts of Parliament and have been agreed by the Commission;

and the Treasury has administrative control relating to expenditure.

22.3 The *Charities Act 2006* contains a number of measures designed to modernise the Charity Commission's functions and powers as regulator, increase its accountability, and preserve its independence from Ministers. The Commission has become a body corporate, the Charity Commission for England and Wales, and the office of Charity Commissioner for England and Wales has been abolished. The Commission now has a non-executive Board, consisting of nine Members of the Commission, which is responsible for its governance, and a Chief Executive responsible for its management.

22.4 The Commission has been playing the role of both regulator and adviser to charities. However, the *Charities Act 2006* sets out the Commission's objectives, general functions and general duties which make it clear that the Commission's future role will focus more on regulation than support. The Commission is required to state in its Annual Report how it has met or discharged its objectives, functions and duties.

22.5 Charity Commission

CHARITY COMMISSION'S OBJECTIVES, FUNCTIONS AND DUTIES

22.5 The *Charities Act 2006* sets out the Commission's objectives as:

- The public confidence objective, i.e. to increase public trust and confidence in charities;

- The public benefit objective, i.e. to promote awareness and understanding of the operation of the public benefit requirement;

- The compliance objective, i.e. to promote compliance by charity trustees with their legal obligations in exercising control and management of the administration of their charities;

- The charitable resources objective, i.e to promote the effective use of charitable resources;

- The accountability objective, i.e. to enhance the accountability of charities to donors, beneficiaries and the general public.

22.6 The Commission's general functions are set out in the Act as follows:

- Determining whether institutions are, or are not, charities;

- Encouraging and facilitating the better administration of charities;

- Identifying and investigating apparent misconduct or mismanagement in the administration of charities and taking remedial or protective action in connection with misconduct or mismanagement therein;

- Determining whether public collections certificates should be issued, and remain in force, in respect of public charitable collections;

- Obtaining, evaluating and disseminating information in connection with the performance of any of the Commission's functions or meeting any of its objectives (this includes the maintenance of an accurate and up-to-date register of charities);

- Giving information or advice, or making proposals, to any Minister of the Crown on matters relating to any of the Commission's functions or meeting any of its objectives.

22.7 The Commission's general duties relate to the way in which the Commission carries out its functions and manages its affairs. They are defined in the Act as follows:

- 'So far as is reasonably practicable the Commission must, in performing its functions, act in a way which is compatible with its objectives and which it considers most appropriate for the purpose of meeting those objectives;

- So far as is reasonably practicable the Commission must, in performing its functions, act in a way which is compatible with the encouragement of all forms of charitable giving and with voluntary participation in charity work;

- In performing its functions the Commission must have regard to the need to use its resources in the most efficient, effective and economic way;

- In performing its functions the Commission must, so far as relevant, have regard to the principles of best regulatory practice (including the principles under which regulatory activities should be proportionate, accountable, consistent, transparent and targeted only at cases in which action is needed);

- In performing its functions the Commission must, in appropriate cases, have regard to the desirability of facilitating innovation by or on behalf of charities;

- In managing its affairs the Commission must have regard to such generally accepted principles of good corporate governance as it is reasonable to regard as applicable to it.'

NEW POWERS

22.8   The *Charities Act 2006* gives the Commission the power to do anything which is calculated to facilitate, or is conducive or incidental to, the performance of any of its functions or general duties. It also gives the Commission the following new powers to ensure that charities' property, assets and reputation are protected:

- The power to remove a person from membership of a charity when a formal inquiry under *s 8* of the *Charities Act 1993* has been opened. This is in addition to their powers under the *Charities Act 1993* to suspend or remove a person from their position of trustee, officer, employee or agent;

- The power to direct trustees, officers or employees of a charity to take specific actions to protect a charity when a *s 8* inquiry has been opened;

- The power to direct charity trustees to apply charity property for the purposes of the charity (this power can be used without opening a *s 8* inquiry);

- The power to determine who the members of the charity are at any time during a *s 8* inquiry or upon the application of the charity;

- The power, following the opening of a *s 8* inquiry and having obtained a warrant from a Magistrate, to enter premises and seize documents (including electronic mail), prevent interference with or destruction of documents, make copies of them and obtain further information from the charity about the existence and whereabouts of such documents;

- The power to use its discretion regarding whether or not publicity is needed for a Scheme.

THE CHARITY TRIBUNAL

22.9   The *Charities Act 2006* creates a new Charity Tribunal to deal with appeals against decisions of the Commission. Until now many charities have been deterred from challenging a decision of the Commission because to do so would have entailed taking the case to the High Court, which is difficult and expensive. The Tribunal will be able to hear appeals against a wide range of decisions, set out in *Sch 4* of the Act, including decisions to register a charity, to remove a charity from the register, and to institute an inquiry or investigation into a charity. The Act allows a party to proceedings before the Tribunal to appeal to the High Court against a decision of the Tribunals and the Attorney General will be able to intervene in a Tribunal or appeal in respect of which he is not a party.

22.10   Customer service complaints, such as complaints about the time the Commission has taken to deal with a matter, will not come within the jurisdiction of the Tribunal but will continue to be dealt with by the Commission's internal complaints system and the Independent Complaints Reviewer.

22.11   *Section 2B* of the Act provides that a charity complainant will only have to pay costs if the Tribunal considers that the charity has acted vexatiously, frivolously or unreasonably. The Tribunal may instruct the Commission to pay all or part of the claimant's costs if it considers that a decision, direction or order of the Commission which is the subject of the proceedings was unreasonable.

CHARITIES ACT 1993

22.12   Other sections of the *Charities Act 1993* that have been amended by the *Charities Act 2006* include those relating to registration (see CHAPTER 101), the application of property cy-pres (see CHAPTER 107), *s 8* inquiries (see CHAPTER 74), publicity requirements for schemes (see CHAPTER 107), powers to give advice and guidance (see CHAPTER 122), restrictions on mortgaging (see CHAPTER 78), auditing of charities that are not companies (see CHAPTER 47), amending memorandum and articles of association (see CHAPTER 83), remuneration of trustees, waiver of trustee's disqualification and powers to relieve trustees from liability for breach of trust (see CHAPTER 121), trustee indemnity insurance (see CHAPTER 122), and powers to spend capital (see CHAPTER 53).

Sections of the *Charities Act 1993* that remain in place include:

- *Sections 6* and *7* which gives the Commission the power to direct a charity to change its name in certain circumstances;

- *Section 8* which gives the Commission the power to institute an inquiry;

- *Section 9* which gives the Commission the power to request information about a charity;

- *Section 19* which gives the Commission the power to appoint a receiver and manager;

- *Section 21* which gives the courts power to vest in the Official Custodian any land held by or in trust for a charity;

- *Sections 24* and *25* which give the courts or the Commission power to establish common investment funds and common deposit schemes;

- *Section 31* which gives the Commission the power to order taxation of a solicitor's bill.

OFFICIAL CUSTODIAN

22.13   The Official Custodian for Charities is an employee of the Charity Commission who has powers under *s 21* of the *Charities Act 1993* to act in a similar role to that of a custodian trustee for charities in respect of any charity land which is placed (or 'vested') in the Official Custodian by means of an Order or Scheme made by the Charity Commission or, in rare cases, by the High Court. Using the Official Custodian to hold land saves unincorporated charities from going to the trouble and expense of transferring title to land every time a trustee ceases to hold office, or from having to appoint a custodian trustee or holding trustees. Another role of the Official Custodian is to hold title to cash and investments as a protective measure during the carrying out of certain formal enquiries. Currently there is no charge for either service.

22.14   Responsibility for managing charity land held by the Official Custodian remains with the charity trustees and they can do the same sort of things with it that they could if ownership were vested in them. The charity trustees, not the Official Custodian, are deemed to be the landlord for the purpose of the *Landlord and Tenant Act 1927.*

22.15   If the Charity Commission has instituted an inquiry under *s 18(1)* of the *Charities Act 1993* and found misconduct of management, or found that a charity's assets needed protection, they can make an order requiring the charity's property to be transferred to the Official Custodian, though in practice this only happens on rare occasions.

22.16   In the past the Official Custodian of Charities also held investments on behalf of some charities. However, *s 23* of the *Charities Act 1993* required the Official Custodian to divest herself of all property except land, making charity trustees take greater responsibility for the management of charity investments.

FURTHER INFORMATION

22.17   Charities Act 2006: What Trustees Need to Know, The Office of the Third Sector, 2007.

The Charity Commission CC13 'The Official Custodian for Charities' Land Holding Services'

The Independent Complaints Reviewer
New Premier House (Second Floor)
150 Southampton Row
London
WC1B 5AL
Telephone: 020 7278 6251
Fax: 020 7278 9675
E-mail: enquiries@icr.gsi.gov.uk
www.icrev.org.uk/

23   Children and Vulnerable Adults

23.1   Many charities work with children or adults who are vulnerable due to their age, mental ability or health. The trustees of such charities must ensure that policies are in place and implemented to safeguard the children or vulnerable adults that the charity is supporting, either in the UK or overseas, and minimise the risk of any harm being done to them. The policies and working practices should also be designed to protect staff and volunteers working with children or vulnerable adults from false accusations.

23.2   The protection policy must be approved and endorsed by the trustees and should be based on the following principles:

- The welfare of the child or vulnerable adult is paramount;

- All children and vulnerable adults without exception have the right to protection from abuse, regardless of gender, ethnicity, disability, sexuality or beliefs;

- All suspicions and allegations about abuse will be taken seriously by trustees, staff and volunteers, and responded to swiftly and appropriately (this may require a referral to children's services or the Police);

- All the charity's trustees, staff and volunteers have a responsibility to report concerns.

23.3   All those working with children or vulnerable adults should be made aware of:

- good practice;

- the types of practice that can never be sanctioned;

- how to respond to suspicions and allegations;

- how to ensure confidentiality;

- what systems are in place to ensure that all those working with children or vulnerable adults are routinely and regularly monitored.

23.4   Charities working with children must comply with the *Protection of Children Act 1999* and the *Criminal Justice and Courts Services Act 2000*. It is an offence for any organisation to offer paid or unpaid employment involving regular contact with young people under the age of 18 to anyone who has been convicted of certain specified offences, or included on lists of people considered unsuitable for such work held by the Department for Education and Skills (List 99) and the Department of Health (PoCA list). It is also an offence for people convicted of such offences to apply for work with young people. *Schedule 4* of the *Criminal Justice and Courts Services Act 2000* lists the offences that would automatically ban the offender from working with children (these include various kinds of violence and sexual offences). The *Criminal Justice and Courts Services Act 2000* disqualifies certain individuals from holding a range of positions in children's charities, which includes charity trusteeship. The Charity Commission does not have the authority to give a waiver for this type of disqualification.

23.5   The Safeguarding Children and Safer Recruitment in Education guidance, which is underpinned by regulations, came into force in January 2007. This consolidated guidance sets out the responsibilities of all local authorities and

94

the education sector, including educational charities, to safeguard and promote the welfare of children and young people.

23.6   Charities working with vulnerable adults must comply with the *Care Standards Act 2000*. This Act aims to improve the quality of care services and protect vulnerable people who use these services. It created a Protection of Vulnerable Adults (POVA) list, similar to the provisions for children. Individuals will be included on the list if they have abused, neglected or otherwise harmed vulnerable adults whether or not in the course of employment; acting as a workforce ban.

23.7   In 2006 the Department of Health set up the Dignity in Care initiative to ensure all older people are treated with dignity when using health and social care services. It will ensure that only those who are suitable will be able to care for those most in need.

CRIMINAL RECORDS BUREAU (CRB) CHECKS

23.8   The law covering checks carried out by the CRB is very complex. Each charity and its trustees must find out if they are legally entitled and/or legally required to obtain CRB disclosures. If in doubt they should seek advice, e.g. from a solicitor.

23.9   Staff and volunteers working with, or applying to work with, children or vulnerable adults, must be checked with the Criminal Records Bureau (CRB) prior to their taking up paid or unpaid work. The standard disclosure lists all convictions (spent and unspent), cautions, reprimands and warnings held on the Police National Computer, and where appropriate it also includes details from:

- the Protection of Children Act (PoCA) list of people banned from working with children in social or health care,

- information that is held under *s 142* of the *Education Act 2002* (formerly known as List 99) which details people banned from working in schools and further education institutes,

- the Protection of Vulnerable Adults (PoVA) list, and disqualifications from working with children or vulnerable adults.

23.10 Those whose work regularly involves caring for, training, supervising or being in sole charge of a child or vulnerable adult must be subject to an enhanced disclosure, which provides the same information as that included in a standard check plus additional relevant and proportionate information held by the local police forces.

23.11 In 2006 the Charity Commission decided that its charity registration process needed review to ensure that charities were carrying out CRB checks on trustees of charities working with children or vulnerable adults. When organisations working with children or vulnerable adults apply for registration the Commission now requires proof that satisfactory CRB checks have been obtained for all the trustees.

23.12 There are some specific legal requirements which mean that CRB checks must be carried out for some trustee positions. In broad terms where it is a legal requirement for checks to be carried out, it is because there is a higher level of access to or control over the beneficiaries. These are:

- governors of independent schools;

- trustees of charities which are 'child care organisations'; and

- trustees of charities which work with vulnerable adults and who personally provide care to them.

Checks should be carried out regularly for continuing trustees.

23.13 The person who is to be checked must complete and sign an application to the CRB to make the disclosure. This must then be countersigned by a representative of an organisation which is registered with the CRB, known as a 'registered body'. Both the person concerned and the registered body will receive the subsequent disclosure.

23.14 Because registered bodies have to undertake to process a certain number of requests every year and to follow certain procedures set out by the CRB, it is not practical for most charities to be registered bodies themselves. A lot of charities therefore use a third party registered body, known as an 'umbrella body', to undertake the checks for them. In this case the charity can decide whether it wants to receive the CRB disclosure or whether it wants the umbrella body to interpret the information on its behalf.

23.15 Having to CRB check staff is costly for many charities. Fees were increased in 2006 to £31 per person for a standard disclosure and to £36 for an enhanced disclosure. At present there is no charge for disclosures for volunteers.

23.16 The fee for registration as a 'registered body' with the CRB is £300, plus £5 for each additional registered signatory. Registered persons must adhere to the CRB code of practice that requires them to:

- have a written policy on the recruitment of ex-offenders;

- store criminal record disclosures securely and dispose of them once used;

- consider carefully the relevance of any criminal convictions when assessing a person's suitability for employment.

CHANGES TO THE LEGISLATION

23.17 The *Safeguarding Vulnerable Groups Act 2006* introduces a new vetting and barring scheme for those who work with children and vulnerable adults. The Act aims to help avoid harm, or risk of harm, to children and vulnerable adults by preventing those who are deemed unsuitable to work with children and vulnerable adults from gaining access to them through their work. The scheme is due for introduction from Autumn 2008 and will introduce a single list of those barred from working with children and a separate, but aligned, list of those barred from working with vulnerable adults. These will replace List 99, the PoCA list, the PoVA list, and the disqualification orders regime. The Independent Safeguarding Authority, which was previously known as the Independent Barring Board, will be the new non-departmental public body created to take consistent expert decisions as to who should be included in the new lists of people who will be barred from working with children and/or vulnerable adults.

23.18 Under the *Safeguarding Vulnerable Groups Act 2006*:

- there will be tough penalties for those employers who fail in their responsibility to carry out the necessary checks or recruit people for paid or unpaid work who are not members of the scheme – including fines of up to £5,000;

- it will be a criminal offence for a barred individual to even seek a job in regulated activity working in close contact with children or vulnerable adults;

- employers and parents will be able to make an online check that a prospective employee is a member of the scheme and thus not barred;

- vetting decisions will be reviewed when new information becomes available and employers who have registered an interest will be notified when an individual ceases to be a member of the scheme.

REPORTING ABUSE

23.19   The Charity Commission has stated that it will take a zero tolerance approach to the abuse of vulnerable beneficiaries and to the lack of adequate measures to protect vulnerable beneficiaries. Where a child or vulnerable adult has been abused, or where abuse is suspected, the matter should be reported immediately to the Police and to other relevant regulatory bodies, including the Charity Commission. The trustees should also inform the Commission if the charity has been the subject of any criminal investigation or if another regulator or agency has imposed any formal sanction on it. If the trustees fail to report a serious incident to the Commission as soon as they become aware of it, they must do so as part of the Annual Return (see CHAPTER 7).

FURTHER INFORMATION

23.20   *The Protection of Children Act 1999: A practical guide to the Act for all organisations working with children.* Department of Health, 2000. Available at:

www.dh.gov.uk/PublicationsAndStatistics/Publications

Protection of Vulnerable Adults (POVA) scheme in England and Wales for care homes and domiciliary care agencies: a practical guide. Department of Health, 2004. Available at: *www.dh.gov.uk/PublicationsAndStatistics/Publications*

The Department for Education and Skills: *www.everychildmatters.gov.uk/socialcare/safeguarding*

The Department of Health: *www.dh.gov.uk/en/Policyandguidance/Healthandsocialcaretopics/ Socialcare/ Vulnerableadults/index.htm*

Safeguarding Children and Young People: a manual for child protection and safe practice. Churches Child Protection Advisory Service, 2004

Positively safe: a guide to developing safeguarding practices. National Council of Voluntary Child Care Organisations, 2005.

Firstcheck: a step by step guide to help organisations prepare child protection policies and procedures. NSPCC, 2006

NSPCC Child Protection in Sport Unit: *www.thecpsu.org.uk*

Keeping Children Safe: A Toolkit for Child Protection, www.keepingchildrensafe.org.uk, 2006

24   Commercial Participators

24.1   The *Charities Act 1992* was intended to promote public giving to charity by increasing public confidence in them. One of the ways in which it sought to do this was by giving the public clearer information about just how much a charity would receive when a commercial venture claimed to be giving a proportion of their profits, or a certain amount per item sold, to a charity.

24.2   In 1988 the Woodfield Report recommended that whenever goods or services were offered for sale with the indication that some part of the proceeds was to be donated to charity, the public should be given information about which charity, or charities, were to benefit (and, if more than one, in what proportion) and the manner in which the amount the charities would receive would be calculated. Doubts were expressed about the practicality of Woodfield's suggestions, but, notwithstanding these, the *1992 Charities Act* contained sections that dealt with relationships between charities and commercial ventures, known as commercial participators.

Definition

24.3   *Section 58(1)* of the *Charities Act 1992* defines a commercial participator as:

'In relation to any charitable institution ... any person who

- carries on for gain a business other than a fund-raising business, but

- in the course of that business, engages in any promotional venture in the course of which it is represented that charitable contributions are to be given to or applied for the benefit of the institution'.

24.4   A charity's own trading company could be argued to come within that definition, but the *Deregulation and Contracting Out Act 1994, s 25* clarified that a trading company owned by a charitable institution is not a commercial participator.

Examples of commercial participators

24.5   An example of a commercial participation is when a tea company encourages the public to buy its particular brand of tea, by advertising that for every packet sold they will donate 20p to a named charity.

24.6   Similarly some banks and financial institutions enter into joint promotional ventures with charities by issuing credit cards that bear the name and/or logo of a charity, sometimes together with an illustration of the charity's work. The arrangement benefits both parties. In return for the charity mailing its database of donors and supporters, the bank agrees to give the charity a fee for each card issued, and a small percentage of the expenditure on the card.

24.7   Again, when there is a disaster, for example an earthquake or the loss of a lifeboat, some businesses will decide to donate a proportion of their sales or profits to a named charity helping the victims. Even when they have no formal agreement with the charity concerned, if they advertise what they are doing in advance, they become commercial participators and must comply with the Act.

How the public will be reassured

24.8   The legislation regarding commercial participation was designed to open arrangements between commercial participators and charities to public scrutiny in two ways:

●   any commercial participator who claims to be assisting a charity will have to have an agreement with the charity and make its claims only in accordance with that agreement; or

●   any representations made by the commercial participator must be accompanied by a statement which clarifies specified matters relating to those representations, such as the proportion of the proceeds the charity will receive.

The agreement between the charity and the commercial participator

24.9   *Section 59(2)* of the *Charities Act 1992* requires there to be an agreement between any commercial participator who represents that part of the proceeds will be donated to charity, and the charity concerned. The agreement must be in writing and must be signed by or on behalf of the charitable institution and the commercial participator. The agreement must specify:

●   the name and address of each of the parties;

●   the date on which the agreement was signed;

●   the duration of the agreement;

●   any terms relating to the early termination of the agreement;

●   any terms relating to the variation of the agreement during that period.

24.10   In addition *s 60* requires that the agreement must also contain the following:

●   A statement of its principal objectives and the methods to be used in pursuit of those objectives. For each method specified there should be a description of the types of charitable contributions which are to be donated and of the circumstances in which they are to be given.

●   Provision as to the manner in which the parties will determine:

(a)   if there is more than one charitable institution party to the agreement, the proportion in which the institutions which are so party are respectively to benefit under the agreement; and

(b)   the proportion of the consideration given for goods or services sold or supplied by the commercial participator, or of any other proceeds of a promotional venture undertaken by him, which is to be given to or applied for the benefit of the charitable institution; or

   (c) the sums by way of donations the commercial participator will make in connection with the sale or supply of any goods or services sold or supplied by him.

- Provision as to any amount by way of remuneration or expenses which the commercial participator is to be entitled to receive in respect of things done by him in pursuance of the agreement and the manner in which any such amount is to be determined.

24.11 Following the Government's Strategy Unit recommendation that the existing legislation be amended to require that a more specific statement of the return that will be made to the charity, *s 67* of the *Charities Act 2006* amends *s 60* of the *1992 Act* so solicitation statements will now need to include the amount the commercial participator will be paid, if that is known at the time when the statement is made or, if the specific amount is not known, a reasonably accurate estimate of what they will receive, instead of just the method by which the amount will be determined.

24.12 The regulations require that monies should be paid over by the commercial participator to the charitable institution within 28 days of receipt, unless other arrangements are specified in the agreement.

Tripartite agreements

24.13 The regulations are written in a way that presupposes that the agreement is made between a charity and a commercial participator. However, the involvement of a commercial participator often means that some type of trading is taking place. Unless the trading activity is part of the charity's primary purpose, it will be carried out by the charity's trading subsidiary, therefore the commercial participator will need to contract with the charity's trading company, rather than with the charity. The charity could sign an agreement with the commercial participator if it was a principal in the arrangement, and the charity's trading company was merely acting as the charity's agent. However, it is most important that the charity is not a principal, because to be so would mean that the charity was engaging in non-primary purpose trading activity, which would be a breach of charity law. The charity would also be receiving income that would not be covered by one of the exemptions from income tax set out in the *Income and Corporation Taxes Act 1988, s 505*, and as a result would have to pay tax on the income it received from the deal with the commercial participator.

24.14 Ventures involving commercial participators will therefore require an agreement between the commercial participator and the charity's trading company and, in order to comply with the *Charities Act 1992, s 59(2)*, an agreement between the charity and the commercial participator.

24.15 Given that the commercial exploitation of a charity's name, logo and goodwill is not primary purpose trading, many charities will have appointed their trading companies as licensees to exploit these on their behalf, thus avoiding a breach of charity law and any possible tax liability that could arise if a charity raised money in this way. However, the *Charities Act 1992, s 59(2)* makes it absolutely clear that any agreement allowing a commercial participator to exploit the name of a charitable institution has to be between the institution and the commercial participator. It cannot be between a charitable institution's trading company and a commercial participator.

24.16   One solution is to set up tripartite agreements between the charity, its trading company and the commercial participator. This solution is not, however, as straightforward as it first appears. In drawing up such an agreement it is important to show that the charity is not a principal in the arrangement; rather, the charity's sole purpose in entering into the agreement must be to demonstrate that it has no objection to the agreement between its trading company and the commercial participator. The charity must not take any role in the agreement that suggests that the charity itself is trading with the commercial participator, or that suggests that the charity was supplying a service to the trading company, as this could render ineffective the covenanted payment of profits from the trading company to the charity, because it could then be argued that the trading company was making covenanted payment in return for the services supplied.

24.17   Great care must be taken in drafting tripartite agreements and structuring the ways the charity receives money from the commercial participator if any liability for tax is to be minimised. As well as considering how income from the deal may be taxed, the VAT implications of the deal must also be considered. HMRC have confirmed that arrangements between charitable institutions and commercial participators for the licensing of the charity's name will attract VAT.

24.18   In relation to Affinity Card Schemes, where the contractual arrangements allow a clear separation between payments for promotional services, and contributions for which the charity is not obliged to do anything in return, only the initial payment (typically one-fifth) will attract VAT. Also, following a Court of Appeal decision (*Customs & Excise Commissioners v Civil Service Motoring Association [1998] STC 111*), in some cases payments may be treated as exempt from VAT. This is an area which needs to be assessed on a case-by-case basis.

Transitional provisions

24.19   The *Charities Act 1992* and regulations do not contain any transitional provisions for agreements entered into prior to 1 March 1995. So if a charity's trading company is party to an existing agreement with a commercial participator that commenced before 1 March 1995 but which is still extant, then the charity will have to enter into a supplemental agreement with the commercial participator in order to conform with the Act.

Retailer as a commercial participator

24.20   If, for example, a tea company agrees to give a named charity 5p for every packet of tea sold that carries printed details of the promotion, the tea company is clearly a commercial participator. But if the tea is sold in a supermarket, is the supermarket also a commercial participator? By displaying the tea on their shelves the supermarket is clearly promoting it for sale, so it could be argued that it is a commercial participator and should have an agreement with the charity concerned. However, this clearly was not the intention of the 1992 Act.

Christmas cards

24.21   Many charities sell Christmas cards using a commercial participator. In recent years there has been considerable media interest highlighting the extent to which charities actually benefit from these arrangements. The Charity Commission and the Advertising Standards Authority believe it is important that the public does not get the impression that charities benefit more from such arrangements than is actually the case. The Commission suggests that any statement on the packaging of the cards should inform the public what the net donation to the charity will be after all expenses have been paid. Many of the public are not aware that in most instances charities make much more profit per card from cards sold through the charity's own mail order catalogues or in their charity shops than when cards supporting the charity are sold in supermarkets and chain stores.

Television advertisements

24.22   If a commercial participator promotes a charity in a television programme, in addition to the requirements of *Part II* of the *Charities Act 1992* the following conditions apply:

- The advertiser must provide the TV station with evidence of the charity's consent.

- If sale proceeds are to be donated, the basis on which the donation will be calculated must be made clear; conditions such as sales reaching a particular level before donations are made are not acceptable.

- Offers in relation to medical products are not acceptable.

Enforceability

24.23   Breaching the requirements for the *Charities Act 1992, s 59* agreements is a criminal offence giving rise to a maximum fine of £500. The Court may also grant an injunction to a charity if the commercial participator solicits money for the charity without an agreement.

24.24   Penalties for failing to comply with the *Charities Act 1992, s 59* requirements for agreements attach to the commercial participator, not the charity. It will be in a charity's long-term interest to make a potential commercial participator aware of this legislation, though doing so may not be the most positive way to commence negotiations and might even deter some companies from entering into such arrangements.

24.25   If a charity has entered into an agreement that is defective, then an order of the court will be required to enforce it. There may be some circumstances in which a commercial participator wishes to enforce an agreement, for example because the charity is not making an agreed payment for goods the commercial participator has agreed to provide at a heavily discounted price as part of the agreement. However, it is much more likely that a charity would wish to enforce an agreement, for example because the commercial participator is holding on to the proceeds and not passing them onto the charity within the agreed timescale.

24.26   The legislation requires the commercial participator to pay sums due to the charity within 28 days of receipt or such other period as may be agreed. If the commercial participator pays the money to the charity's trading company, which then keeps it until the end of its financial year, when it covenants its profits to the charity, then the commercial participator may be guilty of a criminal offence!

24.27   Agreements are only needed if the commercial participator makes a 'repre-sentation'. However, *s 58(6)(a)* of the *Charities Act 1992* defines a representa-tion very widely:

> ' "represent" and "solicit" mean respectively represent and solicit in any manner whatever, whether expressly or impliedly and whether done:
>
> - by speaking directly to the person or persons to whom the representation or solicitation is addressed (whether when in his or their presence or not); or
>
> - by means of a statement published in any newspaper, film or radio or television programme ...'

24.28   If a spokesperson for a commercial participator is giving a television interview and mentions their company's support for a charity it would obviously not be practical for them to give all the details that must be specified in the statement. Similarly, if a shop assistant wears a charity's T-shirt of their own choosing it would be ridiculous to suggest that the shop should put up a sign saying that X% of the sales of all items in the shop will be donated to T-shirt charity. However, if the shop had a policy requiring all their assistants to wear one particular charity's T-shirts, then this could be interpreted as the shop supporting a particular charity and therefore a representation was being made.

24.29   Failure to make the statement required by the *Charities Act 1992, s 59* is a criminal offence carrying a maximum penalty of £5,000. [*Charities Act 1992, s 60(7)*]. The penalty can be imposed for each offence, i.e. for each item sold without the required statement being made, so selling 100 items at £1 each without the required statement could cost a commercial participator £500,000. The risk involved in the agreement not fully satisfying the regula-tions, and the commercial participator being found guilty of a criminal offence and fined as a result, may be sufficient to deter potential commercial participators from considering such deals. Charities themselves may become less willing to suggest them, fearing the bad publicity that would result from their involvement in a deal that leads to a company being fined as a result of breaching charity law.

Limitations of the controls on commercial participation

24.30   The *Charities Act 1992* contains no controls over commercial participators who seek to raise money for general charitable purposes, such as the homeless rather than for particular charities. The unscrupulous may use this to exploit the public's willingness to give to charity but any scandals will undermine the Act's attempts to increase public confidence in charities.

24.31   Most deals require such complex, and therefore costly, agreements between a charity, its trading company, and a commercial participator that many poten-tial commercial participators may believe the risks associated with entering into such arrangements will surpass the benefits they are likely to gain.

CHARITY COMMISSION GUIDANCE

24.32   In autumn 2002 the Charity Commission published a Regulatory Study 'Charities and Commercial Partners'. When charities are considering enter-ing into agreements with commercial partners the Commission recom-mended that:

24.33   Commercial Participators

- Charities should recognise the value of their name and the potential value to a commercial organisation of being associated with it. Professional advice on valuing the charity's name may be necessary. Any arrangement should be a fair deal for the charity.

- Charities need to establish what they expect to gain from a partnership before entering into an agreement and set up mechanisms to monitor and review the partnership.

- Proposed commercial partnerships should be thoroughly researched and charities should consider taking professional advice on the relevant issues, including the fund-raising potential and the legal and tax implications. The credentials of the company should be checked and references obtained from other charities with whom they have had a similar relationship.

- Charities should not sign an agreement drawn up by the commercial partner without seeking appropriate advice.

- Where relevant, charities must ensure that commercial partnerships comply with *Part II* of the *Charities Act 1992* and the *Charitable Institutions (Fund-raising) Regulations 1994*. If the agreement is to be between a commercial company and a charity's trading subsidiary, the charity should ensure that appropriate licensing arrangements are in place between the charity and its trading subsidiary. (Charities must now also comply with *s 67* of the *Charities Act 2006*.)

- Charities should establish an ethical policy to help them determine whether or not a particular partnership would be appropriate and in the best interests of the charity and to help a potential partner understand the charity's values.

- The ethical policy and any commercial partnerships should be included in the charity's annual report.

- Charities should take steps to ensure that they have identified and managed the risks associated with a commercial partnership.

- The expectations of both the charity and commercial company should be agreed before any commercial agreement is entered into and both parties should be sure that they can manage them effectively and appropriately.

FURTHER INFORMATION

24.33   RS2 'Charities and Commercial Partners' Charity Commission Regulatory Study.

25   Common Investment Funds and Common Deposit Funds

COMMON INVESTMENT FUNDS

25.1   Common investment funds (CIFs), and the closely related common deposit funds (CDFs) are means by which charities can pool the funds they have available for investment and obtain certain advantages that are not available to them through conventional investment products. CIFs and CDFs are charities in their own right and only charities may invest in them.

25.2   CIFs are similar to unit trusts. They allow charities to diversify their investments to reduce risk, they are tax-efficient, administratively simple and cost-effective. CIFs are established by Charity Commission Schemes, using the Commission's powers under *s 24* of the *Charities Act 1993*. Most CIFs are open to all charities, or to a particular class of charities, to invest in. They are run professionally by their operators and are usually commercial investment products.

25.3   Persons and firms that engage in specific types of activity (called 'regulated activity') must be authorised to do so by the FSA. Establishing and/or operating a CIF, if that is done by way of business, may be a regulated activity and therefore the persons or firms may need to be authorised by the FSA. Acting as trustee of an authorised unit trust by way of business is also a regulated activity. In practice, this will often mean that the fund manager and corporate trustee of a CIF will be engaging in regulated activity. A fund manager and/or corporate trustee that is authorised to engage in regulated activity will be monitored and supervised by the FSA.

25.4   CIFs take in and invest the assets of participating charities who are in turn entitled to a share of the capital and income of the fund proportionate to their investment, held in 'units'. CIFs are controlled by the Charity Commission and have a separate set of accounting regulations.

Any charity in England and Wales may participate in a CIF unless its constitution specifically prohibits it, or the terms of the CIF specifically disqualify it. The *Charities Act 2006* also made CIFs available for Scottish and Northern Irish Charities.

25.5   CIFs are administered by professional fund managers and operate like unit trusts. A charity's money is thus being spread over a wider range of investments than would otherwise be possible for a portfolio of this size. This has the advantage of reducing overall risk to each participating charity. The charity gains in other ways too: individual dealing fees are reduced and all income is paid gross, reducing paperwork for the charity administrator and improving cash flow.

25.6   Commonly a CIF has two pools of funds: income units and accumulation units. Income units pay a regular income stream, whereas accumulation units are rolled into the value of the fund and the income is reinvested to increase its value.

25.7   At the end of 2006 there were over 43 CIFs worth together over £13.1 billion. These are primarily UK equity based funds, but there are also a number of bond / gilt funds, property funds and absolute return funds available.

25.8 Common Investment Funds and Common Deposit Funds

Powers and policy

25.8 Each CIF has its own powers and policies which are available from the fund manager on request. Charities considering investing in a CIF should obtain this information first and review it before making a decision to invest. Issues to consider will include the cost structure, the fund manager and the fund's performance.

Charges

25.9 Annual management and administration charges typically range between 0.15% to 1.00%pa of the value of the units, although initial charges or a minimum fee may also apply. Most funds distribute income quarterly.

Performance

25.10 Because CIFs invest in a range of investments, their performance can be expected to be predictable and broadly in line with market conditions. The wm company publishes regular reports of CIF performance.

ETHICAL CIFS

25.11 Charities are allowed to adopt ethical investment policies in particular circumstances (see 75.28). Trustees may therefore only place funds in an ethical CIF if the CIF excludes investments that the charity would be permitted to exclude. A number of CIFs will exclude tobacco companies from their investment portfolios, and many others adopt a socially responsible stance. This means that they try and use the size of their shareholding to influence corporate policy over environmental issues.

INVESTMENT PORTFOLIOS

25.12 Occasionally charities set up a fund that they refer to as a common investment fund. Unless this is established as a CIF by the court or by a Scheme of the Charity Commission, then this term is a misnomer and should be avoided. It is more likely to be simply an investment portfolio which has been combined as the result of common accounting for a number of restricted funds or subsidiary trusts. Occasionally charities operate informal investment schemes together with other charities. This may constitute a breach of trust by the charities, so the scheme should be formalised with the Charity Commission.

25.13 A pooling scheme establishes a particular type of common investment fund whose main characteristic is that the pooling scheme and the participating charities must all have exactly the same trustees. A pooling scheme allows a body of trustees who administer more than one charity to combine funds from any or all of those charities for investment purposes: this contrasts with the CIFs which are the subject of this guidance and which are open to different trustees of different charities.

COMMON DEPOSIT FUNDS

25.14 Common deposit funds (CDFs) are used to pool cash deposits from several charities in suitable income yielding accounts and are themselves charities.

CDFs can only be created by the Court or by a Scheme of the Charity Commission using its powers under *s 25* of the *Charities Act 1993*, and are not available to Scottish charities. Each participating charity is entitled to repayment of the sums it has deposited in the CDF plus interest. CDFs do not have the general power of investment set out in the *Trustee Act 2000*.

Advantages

25.15 The cash deposited in a CDF is pooled and invested in the money market: sterling deposits with banks, building societies and local and central government. Because the money is pooled, larger sums are available for investment and interest rates are generally higher than a single charity could obtain from an individual bank or building society deposit. There are few account charges and interest is paid gross. A CDF may therefore be particularly suitable for charities depositing smaller sums. They also have the advantage of spreading the risk if any one deposit taker should fail.

25.16 CDFs are useful for short-term investment, for example investing income being held pending expenditure for the purposes of the charity. However, they are not considered suitable for longer-term investment as there is no protection against inflation. The benefits of CDFs are as follows:

- charities obtain money market rates of interest;

- the account is in the name of the charity, therefore there is no need to change the names of the account holders if trustees change;

- interest is paid gross;

- participating charities have easy access to funds;

- regular statements are provided.

25.17 As with common investment funds, an investment in a CDF cannot be assigned or sold.

25.18 It is not uncommon for charities to establish informal common deposit funds, whereby they seek to obtain higher interest rate returns by combining cash balances. These may constitute unauthorised common deposit funds, which would again represent a breach of trust by all the trustees. There is also the risk of the charity operating the scheme contravening the banking regulations.

THE TRUSTEE ACT 2000

25.19 The *Trustee Act 2000* allows trustees to invest assets held on trust in the same range of investments as an absolute owner, unless this would override any express powers or restrictions in a trust's governing document. One effect of the Act is that charity trustees to whom the Act applies will be able to make 'shared-control' investments, i.e. investments in which two or more charities are joint owners. Although the Act may reduce the need to make pooling schemes, they are still likely to be attractive to many charities. There will almost certainly be circumstances in which trustees will prefer to pool investments under the authority of a pooling Scheme rather than under the proposed general power.

25.20 Common Investment Funds and Common Deposit Funds

25.20 *Sections 4* and *5* of the *Trustee Act 2000* impose standard investment duties on trustees. Where investments are pooled in a pool charity established by a pooling Scheme, these duties must be exercised by trustees:

- as trustees of each participating charity in respect of each contribution it makes to the pool; and

- as trustees of the pool charity in respect of the investments which the pool charity makes.

25.21 Where the new statutory power of investment is relied upon to make shared control investments, it appears that the standard investment duties must be exercised:

- as trustees of each participating charity in respect of each contribution it makes to the jointly held investment fund; and

- as trustees of the jointly held investment fund in respect of each investment made by the fund; and

- as trustees of each participating charity in respect of each investment made by the fund.

25.22 Pooling schemes include specific machinery for ensuring equitable treatment between the charities contributing funds to the pool. This guidance would not be available to trustees who simply relied on the statutory power of investment. They would need to take particular care that the systems they put in place instead were suitable and adequate.

25.23 The feature that distinguishes a 'pool charity' from other CIFs is that all charities eligible to participate must, at the time when any particular contribution is made to the pool, be administered by exactly the same body of trustees that the pooling scheme appoints as the charity trustee(s) of the pool charity. If a charity that has contributed to the pool subsequently comes to be administered by a separate body of trustees, it does not have to withdraw those funds from the pool but it cannot make any further contributions.

Pool charities and CIFs which are not pool charities

25.24 No distinction is made between pool charities and CIFs in the *Charities Act 1993*, but they are treated differently under the *Charities (Accounts and Reports) Regulations*, the *Financial Services Act 1986 (Restriction and Exemption) Order 1999* and the *Trustee Act 2000*. The general power of investment applies to pool charities but does not apply to CIFs.

FURTHER INFORMATION

25.25 Charity Commission CC14 'Investment of Charitable Funds'

26   Community Amateur Sports Clubs

26.1   There are about 110,000 amateur sports club in the UK, involved in over 100 sports. Until 2002 they could not obtain any tax reliefs similar to those available for charities. However, the *Finance Act 2002* allowed some sports clubs to register as Community Amateur Sports Clubs (CASCs) and obtain tax reliefs that were similar to, but not as extensive as, those available for charities. By 2007 4,380 clubs had registered as CASCs, saving £20.3m in tax.

26.2   In 2002 the Charity Commission recognised that the promotion of community participation in healthy recreation by providing facilities for playing particular sports was a charitable purpose, allowing some amateur sports clubs to apply for charitable status. The *Charities Act 2006* defines the advancement of amateur sport as a charitable purpose and should extend the range of clubs that could register as charities.

26.3   Those running amateur sports clubs should consider whether they are eligible to register with HMRC as a CASC, or to register with the Charity Commission as a charity. If they are not eligible they should consider whether the benefits to be gained from tax relief would outweigh the changes necessary to become eligible, or whether they should remain as they are.

REGISTERED CASCS

26.4   A sports club which is:

- open to the whole community,

- organised on an amateur basis, and

- has as its main purpose the provision of facilities for, and promotion of participation in, one or more eligible sports (HMRC maintain a list of 113 eligible sports).can apply to HMRC to be registered as a CASC.

26.5   A club is open to the whole community if:

- membership is open to all without discrimination;

- the facilities of the club are available to members without discrimination; and

- the fees are set at a level that do not pose a significant obstacle to membership or use of the facilities.

26.6   Discrimination includes indirect discrimination on grounds of:

- ethnicity, nationality, sexual orientation, religion or beliefs; and

- sex, age or disability except as a necessary consequence of the requirements of a particular sport.

This does not however prevent a club from having different classes of membership.

26.7   A club is organised on an amateur basis if:

- players are not paid for playing, though reimbursement of expenses is permitted;

109

26.8   Community Amateur Sports Clubs

- it is non-profit making, i.e. its constitution requires that any surplus income or gains must be reinvested in the club and any surpluses or assets cannot be distributed to members or third parties (though this does not prevent donations by the club to charities or to other clubs that are registered as community amateur sports clubs);

- it provides for members and their guests only the ordinary benefits of an amateur sports club; and

- its constitution states that on the dissolution of the club the net assets must be applied for approved sporting or charitable purposes.

26.8   A club is allowed to:

- enter into agreements with members for the supply to the club of goods or services, such as ground maintenance or coaching, or

- employ and pay remuneration to staff who are also members of the club,

provided the terms are approved by the governing body of the club without the member concerned being present and are agreed with the member on an arm's length basis.

26.9   Where a club satisfies the requirements of registration as a CASC it is eligible for exemption from Corporation Tax on:

- profits from trading where the turnover limit of the trade is less than £30,000 p.a.;

- interest received without limit;

- income from property where the gross income is less than £20,000 p.a.;

- chargeable gains without limit;

where the whole of the income or gains are applied for qualifying purposes. Apportionment rules apply where a club is not registered for the whole period.

26.10   Registered CASCs are eligible for 80% mandatory business rate relief and a further 20% relief at the discretion of the local authority.

26.11   Membership fees are not considered to be donations and are therefore not eligible for Gift Aid. However, other donations made by individuals and companies are eligible for Gift Aid. Gifts by individuals will be free of inheritance tax and gifts of chargeable assets by individuals and companies will be free of capital gains tax. Businesses that give goods or equipment that they make, sell or use will get tax relief for their gifts.

26.12   HMRC may terminate registration where it appears to them that a club is no longer entitled to be registered. A club has the right of appeal to the Commissioners of HMRC against any such decision. There is no provision in the *Finance Act 2002* for a club to de-register. Therefore before applying to be a CASC, club members need to agree that they want to maintain the club for the continuing use of the community. If members want to make money by selling the ground to developers, then CASC status is not appropriate. If a CASC ceases to operate, its assets have to be passed on in accordance with the legislation to another CASC, or to the governing body of an eligible sport or a charity.

CHARITABLE SPORTS CLUBS

26.13   Charities must have exclusively charitable purposes and any sports club wishing to register as a charity would have to stop its non-charitable activities (although they could be carried out by a separate non-charitable club). To qualify for charitable status a sports club must also:

- promote community participation in healthy recreation by providing facilities for playing sport;

- be organised on an amateur basis;

- have membership and facilities that are open to all without discrimination;

- not use a test of skill to determine eligibility for membership;

- have membership fees that are affordable.

26.14   The Charity Commission defines healthy recreation as an activity which, if practised with reasonable frequency, will tend to make the participant healthier. The sports regarded by the Commission as healthy are not the same as those listed for eligibility as a CASC. For example, the Commission do not currently recognise snooker, motor sports, gliding or rifle shooting as healthy sports, though this could be challenged in the courts.

26.15   Charitable sports clubs can run competitive teams, leagues and ladders and can allocate facilities to allow competitive teams to train and play. However, they must bear in mind that the club must be promoting community participation and therefore give equal treatment to less skilful or less competitive players. Coaching, if available, must be given for all levels of skill.

26.16   Charitable sports clubs cannot have a separate group of social members. If there is a bar at the club the Charity Commission recommends that it is run by a separate company.

26.17   The tax benefits available to charitable sports clubs are more extensive than those available to registered CASCs. Charitable sports clubs are exempt from corporation tax:

- on all profits derived from trade in fulfilling their charitable purpose;

- on all profits not derived from the fulfilment of their charitable purpose on the lower of 25% of their turnover or £50,000;

- on all interest received;

- on all capital gains.

26.18   Charitable sports clubs are eligible for 80% mandatory business rate relief and a further 20% relief at the discretion of the local authority.

26.19   The tax benefits for those donating to charitable sports clubs are the same as those for donors to registered CASCs. Membership fees are not eligible for Gift Aid. However other donations made by individuals and companies to charitable sports clubs are eligible for Gift Aid. Gifts by individuals will be free of inheritance tax and gifts of chargeable assets by individuals and companies will be free of capital gains tax. Businesses that give goods or equipment that they make, sell or use will get tax relief for their gifts.

26.20   In addition the following benefits are available:

111

26.21   Community Amateur Sports Clubs

- Special VAT treatment in some circumstances;

- Gifts of quoted shares, certain securities, land and/or buildings can be made by both individuals and companies with the benefit of income and corporation tax relief respectively.

26.21   Charities can also raise funds from the public, and from grant-making trusts and local government more easily than can non-charitable bodies.

26.22   One major potential advantage of charitable status over CASC tax status is in relation to VAT on the construction of buildings. This arises because the construction of a building that a charity intends to use for a relevant charitable purpose does not attract a VAT charge. The advantage arises because most Sports Clubs cannot recover VAT on their expenditure in full. So by avoiding it being charged in the first place substantial amounts of VAT could be saved. In order to qualify the building must be used for a relevant charitable purpose. This is use either for a non-business purpose or use of a building 'as a village hall or similarly in providing social or recreational facilities for a local community'. There is therefore, a strong possibility that if a Club registers as a charity it can take advantage of this relief.

FURTHER INFORMATION

26.23   *www.cascinfo.co.uk*

www.hmrc.gov.uk/casc

www.runningsports.org

27   Compact

27.1   The Compact, established in 1998, is a framework for partnership between government and the voluntary and community sector in England to improve their relationship for mutual advantage. The Compact was the result of consultation across Government and the voluntary and community sectors: although it is not a legally binding agreement, the Compact has been successfully used in public law cases.

27.2   The idea behind the Compact is to improve working relationships between organisations like charities and their public funder, and to try to ensure that both parties have compatible expectations. A significant financial outworking of the Compact is the application of full cost recovery.

27.3   The Compact is supported by five codes of good practice covering: funding and procurement, community groups, BME groups, volunteering and consultation and policy appraisal. These address the mutual rights and responsibilities which local government and related bodies, and the voluntary and community sector should reflect in their relationships with VCOs. These codes can be obtained or downloaded from the Compact Commission's website (*www.thecompact.org.uk*).

27.4   There are also local compacts between the sector, local authorities and other local public bodies.

27.5   The National Assembly for Wales' Voluntary Sector Scheme is the equivalent to the Compact in England. The Scheme sets out the broad principles and shared values which govern the relationship between the National Assembly and the voluntary and community sector in Wales.

27.6   An equivalent compact also operates in Scotland: the Compact between the Scottish Executive and the voluntary sector. The Scottish Compact is an agreement between the Scottish Executive, its agencies, non-departmental public bodies and the voluntary sector on the principles of working in partnership.

KEY PRINCIPLES

Reproduced below is the summary of the Compact's key principles:

- A healthy voluntary and community sector is part of a democratic society;

- Working in partnership with the voluntary and community sector can result in better policy and services and better outcomes for the community;

- Partnership requires strong relationships (e.g. integrity and openness);

- Government can play a role as funder of the voluntary and community sector;

- The independence of the voluntary and community sector should be respected.

27.8 Compact

Government undertakes to

- Promote the Compact across Government;
- Respect the independence of the voluntary and community sector;
- Consult early enough to make a difference;
- Recognise the cost of doing business when funding public service delivery.

The voluntary and community sector undertakes to

- Operate through open and accountable organisations;
- Involve all stakeholders and embrace diversity;
- Contribute constructively to public policy.

Government and the voluntary and community sector together undertake to

- Work together to improve outcomes for the community.

All public authorities should acknowledge and adhere to these principles.

27.7   The Charity Commission recognise the significance of compacts in their publication CC37 'Charities and Public Service Delivery'. For instance they state that:

> 'Under the terms of the Compact and its Funding and Procurement Code (and the Code of Practice for Funding the Voluntary Sector in Wales), full cost recovery should apply in any case where a public authority is purchasing a service from a charity, unless the charity decides to forego full cost recovery.
>
> Where a public authority is not purchasing a service but simply supporting charitable activity then the level of support given is something that can be negotiated between the charity and the authority but is ultimately at the discretion of the authority.

28   Companies

28.1   There are three legal structures commonly adopted by charities: a company limited by guarantee or shares, a trust or an unincorporated association. Most larger charities are set up as companies limited by guarantee. These are always private companies, not public ones.

28.2   The *Charities Act 2006* introduced a new legal structure, the Charitable Incorporated Organisation. This structure is likely to become available for charities to use in the summer of 2008. The CIO is an alternative structure to a limited company, especially designed for charities, and has an equivalent in Scotland in the SCIO. The Charity Commission cite the following advantages of CIOs:

- A single registration – a charity which is also a company (a charitable company) has to register with the Registrar of Companies at Companies House and the Commission. A CIO will only need to register with the Commission (or OSCR in the case of SCIO).

- Less onerous requirements for preparing accounts – small CIOs will be able to prepare receipts and payments accounts, larger charities will prepare accruals accounts.

- One annual return – charitable companies have to prepare an annual return under company law and (normally) a separate return under charity law.

- Reduced filing requirements – CIOs will only have to send accounts, reports and returns to the Charity Commission/OSCR. Charitable companies have to send accounts to both the Charity Commission/OSCR and Companies House.

- Lower costs for charities – Companies House filing fees will be avoided.

- Simpler constitutional form – the model forms of constitution will include fewer fixed governance provisions than is the case with companies.

- More straightforward arrangements for merger and reconstruction – the *Charities Act 2006* contains a number of provisions designed to facilitate merger and reconstruction which are not available to charitable companies.

LIMITED COMPANIES

28.3   Charities use the structure of a limited company for two different purposes: to conduct their own affairs, or as a vehicle for conducting non-charitable activities, such as trading. Where a limited company is used to carry out the charity's objects, the constitution may be either that of a company limited by guarantee or a company limited by shares. Subsidiary trading companies are usually companies limited by shares, with the charity owning all the shares.

28.4   A company limited by guarantee is an incorporated organisation, i.e. it has a legal personality of its own, separate from its members, so it can take action and enter into legal agreements in its own name. Other types of incorporated

28.5 Companies

organisations include industrial and provident societies, companies with a share capital, and bodies set up under Royal Charter or by Act of Parliament.

28.5   A registered charity which is also a guarantee company is subject to the same regime as any other limited company, with one or two minor exceptions. As a result it has to consider not only charity legislation, but also the *Companies Acts*. Unlike charity law, company law broadly applies consistently across the United Kingdom.

Advantages of incorporation

28.6   There are a number of reasons for incorporation as a company. The primary motive for incorporation as a limited company is usually the desire to limit the liability of trustees in the event of a claim against the charity, however arising. The effectiveness of this protection is dependent on the circumstances and directors should not assume blanket immunity. Generally where the directors have acted in good faith, and the claim arises through normal business operations, or a contractual claim, then the protection is effective, but reference should be made to CHAPTER 91.

28.7   Secondly, a body corporate, such as a company, is a legal person in its own right. This means that it can enter into contracts and own assets such as investments or properties. There is no need for such items to be held by individuals acting on behalf of the charity.

28.8   Thirdly, a company has perpetual succession. This means that there is no need to transfer contracts, leases, title deeds, etc. to new signatories whenever the persons who originally signed them cease to be trustees.

28.9   Incorporated organisations also have the advantage of permanence. They continue to exist until they are formally dissolved and cannot merely 'fade away'.

Disadvantages of incorporation

28.10   Incorporation brings with it additional paperwork and costs, such as filing fees and the staff costs of complying with company legislation. Audit fees may also be higher.

28.11   Companies have to make the names of their directors publicly available. In certain circumstances this might prevent people from being willing to act as trustees.

Companies limited by guarantee

28.12   The advantages for a charity in being formed as a guarantee company are that, in certain circumstances, the liability of the members of the company for the debts of the company in the event of the company being unable to meet its own debts is limited to the amount of their guarantee – usually a nominal sum such as £10, and there is no necessity to issue certificates of membership. In contrast the trustees of an unincorporated organisation, such as a trust or an association, are personally (jointly and severally with all trustees) liable for the debts of the organisation if it is unable to pay them.

28.13   A company limited by guarantee is generally recommended as the most suitable structure for a charity that employs staff, owns property or investments, or is involved in contracts or other operations which involve significant risk.

28.14   The governing document of a company limited by guarantee is its memorandum and articles of association, see CHAPTER 83. In all cases a company has two important tiers in its governing structure: the members and the directors.

Members and directors

28.15   The members of a company limited by guarantee are those people who, having agreed to become members, have their names entered on the register of members. Because the company has no shares, no share certificate is issued to the member, although the company may issue a membership certificate. However, in any case, it is prudent for a new member to confirm willingness to be a member, in writing as a formal record. Unlike shareholders, members of a company limited by guarantee have no right to a dividend or to participate in the assets of the company on its winding up. The directors are those people elected by the members to govern the company. Directors are usually, but not necessarily, members.

28.16   Under company legislation a company need only have one member and it can also have only one director. However, in the case of a charitable company the Charity Commission would usually require there to be a minimum of three directors.

28.17   The members of the company are not necessarily the same as the people commonly referred to as the 'members' of a charitable organisation. Often the 'membership' is a much looser grouping of supporters, or interested people, who receive information or take part in activities in return for a subscription, and who may even elect committee members. They are not automatically the same as the members recognised under the *Companies Acts*. It is important to maintain a proper register of the legal membership, as the company needs to obtain the sanction of its members for certain transactions.

Charitable companies limited by shares

28.18   While it is more usual for charities to adopt the format of being limited by guarantee rather than by shares, some charities do choose to have shareholders in much the same way as a commercial limited company, except that no profit can accrue to the shareholders of a charitable company. Although similar to other limited companies, special rules apply to charitable companies, whatever their form or constitution.

Company law requirements

28.19   The formalities of the *Companies Acts* apply to guarantee companies throughout the UK. In particular this means that any changes in directors, the company secretary and the registered office need to be filed with Companies House. In addition an annual return needs to be completed each year and filed, as well as the annual return made to the Charity Commission.

28.20   Guarantee companies have broadly the same accounting and audit rules as other limited companies. However, there are two main differences:

117

- Guarantee companies must file their full memorandum and articles with the Registrar of Companies on incorporation. Companies limited by shares must register a memorandum but may adopt model articles set out in Table A accompanying the *Companies Act* under which the company was incorporated. Insofar as no articles are registered, or those registered do not contradict or exclude Table A, the provisions of that Table will be deemed to apply.

- Charitable guarantee companies are entitled to drop the word 'limited' from their title. Where this is done, then letters and orders must refer to the fact that the charity is a limited company. These disclosure requirements are additional to those required by the *Charities Act 1993*. To obtain the exemption the charity must submit a statutory declaration to the Registrar of Companies.

Procedures

28.21   The Charity Commission has the power to petition the High Court for the winding up of a charitable company if they have opened an inquiry under the *Charities Act 1993, s 8*, and are satisfied that they should exercise their powers for the protection of the charity.

28.22   The *Companies Acts* lay down procedures for the alteration of a company's memorandum and articles of association. Where such changes relate to a company's objects, its memorandum, or to a clause in its articles concerning how property can be applied, then the written consent of the Charity Commission is required in advance, and that consent must be copied to the Registrar of Companies with the company's own filing.

28.23   A charity, whether a company or not, should not act in breach of its own constitution or in breach of trust. Companies have a power to ratify constitutional breaches in certain circumstances. However, this power is specifically limited for charitable companies, so that such an act can only be ratified if the incident in question was a commercial transaction, and the other party did not know that the transaction was beyond the powers of the company. [*Charities Act 1993, s 65*].

28.24   Certain other transactions that are permitted by the *Companies Acts* need the prior written consent of the Charity Commission if they are to be carried out by charitable companies. They all relate to transactions, either directly or indirectly, with directors or connected parties.

Directors

28.25   The trustees of an incorporated charity are the company directors in law. Often charities have senior executives whose job title includes the word director, for instance, 'Director of Resources'. Unless formally appointed to the board, this staff member is not a director in terms of the *Companies Acts*. Two situations need care. First, the trustees need to be aware of their responsibilities both as charity trustees and as company directors, and to understand that they have responsibilities under both charity and company law. Second, the senior executive staff should avoid acting in the capacity of directors, or else they risk becoming shadow directors, i.e. persons in accordance with whose directions or instructions the directors of the company are accustomed to act. Company law treats shadow directors in the same way as other directors.

The secretary

28.26   In addition to members and directors, every company is required to have a secretary. The secretary cannot be the same person as a sole director, but could be another director. The role of the secretary in a private company is typically either a nominal one, mainly confined to signing statutory returns, or is developed to a wider role as 'the chief administrative officer of the company'. In either case, the secretary is an officer of the company and has certain liabilities and responsibilities under the *Companies Acts*. From 6 April 2008, private companies are not required to have a secretary although they may do so if they wish. Any document that needs to be signed by two persons on behalf of a private company may be signed by two directors or a sole director and a person so authorised by the sole director.

Registers

28.27   All companies are obliged to maintain certain registers, either at their principal place of business or at their registered office. These registers include registers of members, directors and secretaries, mortgages and charges, and debenture holders. Often these registers are maintained manually in a combined company register book, but they can be kept and maintained on specialised computer software.

Accounting and audit requirements

28.28   Limited companies are required to have an audit under the *Companies Acts* if their income is over £5.6m or their balance sheet total is over £2.8m. A charitable company's audit report over these thresholds will therefore refer to the *Companies Acts*. Below these thresholds the audit will be conducted under the *Charities Act 2006*, and the independent examination regime applies in the same way to companies as it does to unincorporated charities.

28.29   The audit regime described above represents a significant change from the prevailing regime prior to the implementation of the *Companies Act 2006*, the *Charities Act 2006* and the *Charities and Trustee Investment (Scotland) Act 2005*. The harmonisation of these regimes has been a welcome simplification.

28.30   All charitable and private companies are required to file accounts and a directors' report with the Registrar of Companies within ten months of the year-end. The accounts must comply with the prescribed format and other disclosure requirements of the *Companies Acts*, but in practice this allows charities to adopt the SORP in full, since certain sections of the prescribed formats may be amended by the company. As from 6 April 2008 the period for filing accounts of a private company at Companies House is reduced from ten months to nine months.

Requirement to state name

28.31   Companies must state their full name on all business letters, notices, official publications, cheques, orders for money, invoices, receipts and similar documents. On all business letters and order forms it must also state the company's country of registration, registration number and the address of the registered office.

Members' rights

28.32   Rights of members under the *Companies Acts* , include:

- the right to receive a copy of the statutory accounts;

- the right to call a general meeting;

- the right to remove the directors;

- the right to remove the auditors.

Annual General Meetings

28.33   Private companies are not required to hold an annual general meeting unless they are required to do so by their articles.

The Companies Acts

28.34   Reference to the *Companies Acts* refer to the *Companies Act 1985* and the *Companies Act 2006*. The *Companies Act 2006* received its Royal Assent on 8 November 2006 and is being introduced in stages. Some sections are already in force, others will commence on 6 April 2008 and 1 October 2008 with the remainder being introduced on 1 October 2009. It is important to note that until a particular section of the *Companies Act 2006* becomes law, the relevant section of the 1985 Act still applies.

Forms

28.35   Many of the transactions carried out by a company need to be supported by forms filed with Companies House (either Companies House, Crown Way, Cardiff, CF14 3UZ, or for companies registered in Scotland, Companies House, 37 Castle Terrace, Edinburgh, EH1 2EB). These forms are often subject to minor amendment and it is always worth checking that the charity is using the current version. The list shown in Table 7 is not exhaustive, as many of the forms relate to transactions in which charitable companies are most unlikely to participate. These are not listed here, and neither are those forms specifically needed only on incorporation.

28.36   All forms listed below are posted on Companies House's website. They can be printed off, completed, signed and returned to Companies House. The forms marked * can be filed electronically.

28.37   Limited companies are subject to corporation tax on their income. However, most charitable companies will avoid corporation tax by operating within the exemptions available to them, and trading companies will avoid corporation tax by donating their profits to their parent charity using Gift Aid.

Table 6   Companies House forms commonly used by charities

Form number	Subject matter
30(5)(a) to (c)	Omitting the word 'limited' from company name
88(2)*	Return of allotment of shares
123*	Increase in authorised share capital
225*	Notice of accounting reference date (for a newly incorporated company)
287*	Change in situation of registered office
288a*	Appointment of director or secretary
288b*	Resignation of director or secretary
288c*	Change of particulars for director or secretary
353*	Location of register of members if kept somewhere other than its registered office
363a*	Annual return
391	Notice of resolution removing auditor
652(a)	Application for striking off

DORMANT COMPANIES

28.38   A charitable company is dormant if there have been no significant accounting transactions during a financial year. A dormant company must comply with all parts of the *Companies Acts* regarding the preparation and submission of annual reports and accounts, as well as directors' reports but is exempted from the requirement to have an audit.

29   Contract Income

29.1   Contracts are agreements that are legally enforceable by the courts. Contracts usually take the form of signed documents, but a written contract is not essential for the vast majority of legally enforceable contracts. A legally enforceable contract can exist without it being in writing except in certain situations. Charities enter into a wide range of contracts in the normal course of business – this chapter focuses particularly on contract income.

29.2   The SORP's glossary explains that 'it is not always easy in practice to decide whether a particular arrangement is or is not intended by the parties to be a legally binding contract for the supply of services. If, under the arrangement, the payer, rather than the recipient charity, has taken the lead in identifying the services to be provided, or if the arrangement provides for damages to be paid in the case of a breach of its terms, rather than, say, for total or partial refund of the payment, it is more probable that there is a contract for the supply of services. If there is no such contract, the rights and obligations of the parties will depend primarily on the law of trusts and conditional gifts, rather than on the law of contract.'

29.3   Even with this help, it is often unclear whether or not a particular arrangement is a contract. This is because charities often enter into arrangements with organisations that are either based overseas or not in the commercial sector. As a result arrangements are often either informal, or described as agreements, memoranda of understandings or even as grants. It can be a fine judgement to decide between a performance related, restricted grant and a contract – often the best indicator is whether or not the charity is entitled to make any profit. Even this can be difficult to judge, as many funding terms will allow some sort of 'contribution' to other costs. The SORP reflects this confusion in allowing 'grants' to be presented in different places. However, it is important to distinguish contracts from other forms of income as the definition may alter the tax and VAT treatment, the ability for charities to accumulate profit, and enforceability.

29.4   For a contract to be valid a number of conditions have to be met.

- There must be at least two parties with the capacity to enter into a contract. If charities wish to enter into contracts, the corporate body, in the case of an incorporated charity, or the governing body, in the case of an unincorporated charity, must have the power to enter into contracts, the contracts must be within the charity's objects, and those signing the contract must be authorised to do so.

- An offer must be made and must be accepted clearly and without qualification. Although the acceptance of the offer must be unconditional, the offer can stipulate that the contract comes into being only if certain conditions are met.

- An offer and an acceptance form a contract only if there is sufficient certainty as to what has been agreed.

- There must be consideration, i.e. something of material value must be given in exchange for what is offered, either at the time the contract is entered into or within some agreed time period in the future. For a contract to exist, the amount of the consideration does not have to reflect the value of what is offered, e.g. a peppercorn or £1 could be exchanged for a year's lease on a prime office building.

- The parties to the contract must intend to create a legally binding agreement. The courts almost always find that arrangements of a business nature where one party is paid to provide goods or services for another are intended to be legally binding agreements.

JOINT OR JOINT AND SEVERAL LIABILITY

29.5   If two or more charities agree to provide a service under a contract, for example, to run a day centre for a local authority, their liability could be joint, or joint and several. All parties to the contract should be clear what liability they are taking on and if it is joint and several (i.e. each party is potentially liable to provide the full amount or service even if they have only agreed to provide a small proportion) this should be an explicit part of the agreement. This is because the potential consequences of joint and several liability are likely to be very different from joint liability, where each party to the contract is only liable for the share it has contracted to provide.

Contracting with government

29.6   Many charities generate contract income, and this is a growth area as central and local government look to the voluntary sector to help in service delivery. As a result, for many charities their contracts will relate to public service delivery. In the past it has been understood that charities were not generally able to subsidise statutory provision through voluntary income. This understanding changed when the Charity Commission published their opinion on Wigan Leisure and Culture Trust and Trafford Community Leisure Trust, when they concluded that the law does not prevent charities from using their own funds to provide services on behalf of public authorities, even if a public authority has a legal duty to provide a service.

29.7   Because contracting with government has become so important to the sector, the Charity Commission have published guidance on this aspect of contract activity and set out the following general principles, which may equally apply to other forms of contract income:

- Understand the risks: Any charity that is considering public service delivery should weigh up the risks and the opportunities. It is important to recognise and manage risks, and ensure they are appropriately shared between the charity and the public authority. Trustees must not agree to any contract or funding agreement unless they are satisfied that its terms are in the charity's interests. They should therefore consider the need for professional (legal and accountancy) advice on the terms of such documents;

- Stick to your mission: make sure that the contract is within the charity's powers and resources and will not, even inadvertently, divert the charity from its mission;

- Guard your independence: in the context of public service delivery this refers in part to charities making sure they retain independence to campaign, but also means that charities should not be dominated by one customer who can virtually control the charity;

- Know your worth. This means that a charity should:

    — understand the full cost of the charity's services;

    — recognise the charity's scope to deliver and any limitations,

    — identify any unique or distinctive qualities of the charity's services; and

    — use these and other relevant factors to set a price for those services.

29.8   Full cost recovery should apply in any case where a public authority is purchasing a service from a charity, unless it is in the charity's interests to forego full cost recovery. Charities are allowed to achieve a surplus on funding agreements.

COST RECOVERY

29.9   Over recent years there has been a long running battle for charities to ensure that they cover all their costs when obtaining contracts. This is particularly important because a contractual relationship is all about performance, and so a charity may be obliged to fulfil its contractual obligations whether or not it has the funds. Where funding is received by grant, then the charity's obligation is to apply the funds properly; when the funds are exhausted the obligation usually finishes. Often agreements combine elements of grant and contract language, but this is a key reason for being clear on the distinction. The Charities SORP helps here.

29.10   To ensure that a charity recovers all its costs, it needs to be clear on its own costs and it needs to be robust in negotiations with the customer. ACEVO has published specific guidance on full cost recovery which allocates all costs out to services on a template approach, and in line with public sector finance rules.

29.11   Central and local government compacts are designed to help the relationship between charities and statutory purchasers. The first Local Compact was published in 1999 by Dorset County and 99% of England is now covered by a Local Compact. Crucially, compacts include the express statement recognizing that it is legitimate for voluntary and community organisations to include the relevant element of overhead costs in their estimates for providing a particular service. Therefore charities should expect and negotiate for full cost recovery in any case where a public authority is purchasing a service from them, unless the charity decides it is in its beneficiaries' interests to forego full cost recovery.

29.12   Most government contracts will only be won after some sort of tendering process. The EU Treaty governs all public sector procurement processes in the UK. Contracts will fall into one of three categories: services, supplies, or works contracts, and different rules apply at national, regional and local level. Finally, the tender process will also be governed by the size of the contract. As a result any decision to begin tendering and then running such contracts should only be taken after the trustees are confident that they have the necessary dedicated resource to keep track of developments and requirements both in the tendering process and throughout the life of the contract.

TAX CONSIDERATIONS

29.13   Providing services for public bodies under contract is likely to be primary purpose trading. Income generated will not be subject to tax, providing that any profit is applied for charitable purposes (see CHAPTER 118). Premises used to provide the service will qualify for business rate relief (see CHAPTER 97). Providing a service for a fee is regarded as a business activity so, depending on the nature and scale of activities, the charity may have to register for VAT and add VAT to its fees. Where this is the case the charity may be able to recover the VAT element of its own expenditure in providing the service.

29.14   Where a charitable company carries out substantial business with a public body, or where the public body is represented on the trustee board, the charity could be regarded as a 'regulated' company under local government law. Particular care should be taken where a public authority has a shareholding, or can apply control by restricting the company's activities by placing non-commercial conditions on any funding, or limiting the company to trade solely with the local authority.

CONTRACT RISK

29.15   Trustees should make sure that services to be provided under contract fall within their charitable objects, or else they will be acting in breach of trust and could be personally liable for the performance of the contract and for any damages payable if they do not fulfil the terms of the contract. For example, a charity whose objects are limited to providing musical education for children should not contract with the local authority to provide musical education for all residents of the area.

29.16   Trustees are legally responsible for contracts to which an employee of the charity has committed them. Therefore trustees should ensure that the charity has good internal control procedures that require significant contracts to be brought to their attention and approved by them before they are signed.

29.17   Charities should not enter into contracts unless they are reasonably certain they have enough liquid assets (e.g. cash) to meet their liabilities. The contractual terms should always be studied carefully. Many charities wishing to return leased office equipment, such as photocopiers, have found to their cost that early termination of the lease triggers large penalty payments.

29.18   Unincorporated charities entering into contracts should consider whether or not it would be prudent to become incorporated in order to reduce the trustees' risk of personal liability for contracts.

29.19   Charities carrying out services under contract are likely to need public liability insurance, indemnity insurance and commercial insurances such as fire, theft, vehicle and employer/occupier liability insurance.

CONTRACTUAL RIGHTS FOR THIRD PARTIES

29.20   Charities and their trading subsidiaries enter into a large number of legal contracts many of which involve third parties. The *Contracts (Rights of Third Parties) Act 1999* gives third parties contractual rights in certain circumstances.

29.21 Contract Income

29.21   *Section 1* of the Act gives a third party the right to enforce a contractual term in circumstances where the contract expressly provides for it, or the contractual term purports to confer a benefit on the third party. To qualify for the right to enforce, the third party must be identified in the contract by name, class or description.

29.22   Qualifying third parties have the right to enforce any contractual term that confers a benefit on the third party, including terms that exclude or limit a third party's liability. Any rights that the third party acquire under the Act are in addition to those already available under existing law. The Act only passes the benefits of contracts, not their burdens. So if charity A and charity B agree that charity C will make a payment this cannot be enforced unless charity C expressly joins into the contract.

29.23   The following types of contracts are excluded from the Act:

- employment contracts;

- contracts under bills of exchange, promissory notes or other negotiable instruments;

- contracts for carriage of goods that are subject to the rules of the appropriate international transport convention.

30 Corporate Governance

30.1 There have been a number of major reports on corporate governance published in the last fifteen years including:

- the Cadbury Committee's report on the Financial Aspects of Corporate Governance;

- the Greenbury Report on Directors' Remuneration;

- the Hampel Committee's Report which extended the work of the Cadbury Committee and its 'Combined Code' which was derived from its own final report and those of the Cadbury and Greenbury Committees. The Combined Code requires directors to report on all internal controls, not just internal financial controls;

- the Turnbull Report that produced guidance for directors on risk, internal control and governance;

- the Higgs Report on the role and effectiveness of non-executive directors.

The higher-profile collapses of a number of large US firms such as Enron Corporation and Worldcash led to the US federal government passing the Sarbanes Oxley Act in 2002, in an attempt to restore public confidence in corporate governance.

30.2 Corporate governance is not the same as charity governance, though it is similar in many ways. On the one hand charity trustees are not accountable to the owners of the charity in the way that corporate directors are accountable to shareholders. Charities have no 'owners', as such, and the trustees are required to act in the interests of present and future beneficiaries. However, on the other hand the role directors play in the strategic leadership, direction and monitoring of a commercial company is very similar to the role trustees play in governing a charity. While the reports listed above focus on improving standards of governance of commercial companies, many of their recommendations are just as applicable to the governance of charities. Similarly the Report of the Committee into Standards in Public Life (the Nolan Report) and the National Housing Federation's report 'Competence and Accountability on Housing Association Governance' contain recommendations that are applicable and appropriate to the governance of a wide range of charities.

CADBURY COMMITTEE

30.3 The Cadbury Committee's report covered the control and reporting functions of boards and the role of auditors. The Committee developed a Code of Best Practice to be adopted by listed companies and reported upon in their annual report and accounts. The code is based on principles of openness, integrity and accountability, all of which find a ready echo in the voluntary sector.

30.4 The Cadbury code recommends the following.

- **The Board of Directors** The code requires all directors to meet regularly in order to retain full and proper control over the entity. There should be clear lines of delegated authority and divisions of responsibility.

30.5   Corporate Governance

- **Non-Executive Directors** Non-executive directors should be independent in every way and appointed for a specific period.

- **Executive Directors** Contracts should not exceed three years. There should be a separate remuneration committee made up of non-executive directors to determine executive directors' remuneration.

- **Reporting and Controls** The board should ensure that an objective and professional relationship is maintained with auditors. The board should establish an audit committee comprising at least three non-executive directors with written terms of reference dealing clearly with its authority and duties. The directors should report on their responsibilities for the accounts, the effectiveness of the system of internal control, and whether the business is a going concern, with supporting assumptions or qualifications as necessary.

Audit committees

30.5   Cadbury lists the following advantages of establishing an audit committee. An audit committee can help to:

- improve the quality of financial reporting by reviewing the financial statements on behalf of the board;

- create a climate of discipline and control which will reduce the opportunity for fraud;

- enable the non-executive directors to contribute an independent judgement and play a positive role;

- help the finance director by providing a forum in which he can raise issues of concern and which she can use to get things done which might otherwise be difficult;

- strengthen the position of the external auditor, by providing a channel of communication and forum for issues of concern;

- provide a framework within which the external auditor can assert his independence in the event of a dispute with management;

- strengthen the position of the internal audit function; and

- increase public confidence in the accounts.

Specimen terms of reference are suggested by Cadbury. These cover constitution, membership, attendance at meetings, frequency of meetings (at least twice a year), authority, duties and reporting procedures.

GREENBURY COMMITTEE

30.6   The Greenbury Committee's report focused on directors' remuneration. As directors of charitable companies are, in the main, unpaid this report has limited relevance for the voluntary sector. However, the Charity Commission is showing an increasing willingness to permit charities to remunerate trustees and has agreed that a small number of remunerated chief executives can be trustees of the charity that employs them. The *Charities Act 2006, s 36* provides for the remuneration of trustees for providing services to a charity, such as marketing consultancy or decorating, in certain circumstances, but not for their service as trustees, providing that the trustee board as a whole reasonably believe it to be in the charity's interest to do so. A general principle stated in the Greenbury Report that does have relevance for the voluntary sector was the need for companies to establish a remuneration committee made up of non-executive directors, to set and review the remuneration of directors. Setting and reviewing the remuneration of the Chief Executive Officer is a responsibility that many charities do not currently discharge effectively, and yet it is a subject that chief executives are naturally reluctant to raise. If this responsibility is not carried out by the board acting as a whole, the trustees should establish a remuneration sub-committee to set and review the chief executive's remuneration.

HAMPEL COMMITTEE

30.7   Like the Cadbury Committee's recommendations, the Hampel Committee's recommendations also have relevance for the voluntary sector. Hampel extended Cadbury's work to include the need for directors to be accountable for the internal control and risk management of all aspects of the governance and management of companies, not just financial governance and management. Hampel recommended that the board should maintain a sound internal control system and that the directors, at least annually, should review the system's effectiveness and report to shareholders that they have done so. Where no internal audit function exists the Hampel Committee recommended that the board should consider whether or not such a function was needed.

TURNBULL COMMITTEE

30.8   The Turnbull Committee Report was published in September 1999 and sets out the need for companies to establish good internal control and risk management systems. Principle D.2 of the Turnbull Combined Code states: 'The board should maintain a sound system of internal control to safeguard shareholders' investment and the company's assets'. Provision D.2.1 of the code states that: 'The board should, at least annually, conduct a review of the effectiveness of the group's system of internal control and should report to shareholders that they have done so. The review should cover all controls including financial, operational and compliance controls and risk management'. Provision D.2.2: 'Companies that do not have an internal audit system should from time to time review the need for one'.

30.9   The Combined Code does not suggest increased regulation for regulation's sake. Rather it recognises the need to ensure that there is a risk-based approach to developing sound business practices in order to protect the shareholders' interests. It states that all companies need clear systems of internal controls that are part of the normal management and governance processes of the organisation, embedded within the organisation's operations, and not seen treated as a separate exercise undertaken to meet regulatory requirements. The guidance also recommends that companies should be able to respond promptly to risks arising from both within and outside the company.

30.10   Although the Turnbull Report recommendations apply at the moment only to listed companies, they are likely in time to have a significant effect on charities. More and more charities will establish an internal audit function, carried out by the charity's own staff, or by an external firm of auditors, or by consortia arrangements in which a number of charities combine resources to provide a shared internal audit function.

30.11   Categories of significant risk to be assessed include organisational, operational, financial and compliance risks. For a charity these might include risks arising from bad publicity or restructuring the management structure, inappropriate treatment of beneficiaries or the introduction of new services, misallocation of restricted funding or a declining trend in income from a particular source, and failure to comply with the charity's ethical investment policy or to account correctly for VAT.

30.12   The Board should take responsibility for deciding the acceptable level of risk, the threat of risks crystallising, the charity's ability to contain the impact of risks crystallising and the cost to benefit ratio of operating internal controls. It will need to consider how to evaluate and manage key risks, how to effectively control areas of known weakness, how to monitor the implementation of measures to eliminate or control risk, and whether more assessment and monitoring are needed.

30.13   Periodically the Board will need to consider any changes to significant, known risk factors, the organisation's ability to respond quickly and effectively to changes in its operating environment, the quality of its control monitoring, any incidents of major control failures and the effectiveness of its year-ending reporting process.

HIGGS REPORT

30.14   The Higgs Report reviewed the role and effectiveness of non-executive directors and made recommendations to advance and reflect best practice in corporate governance through revisions to the Combined Code. Recommendations that are relevant to charities include:

- The number of meetings of the board and its main committees should be stated in the annual report, together with the attendance of individual directors.

- The board should be of an appropriate size. Not so large as to be unwieldy, but of a sufficient size that the balance of skills and experience is appropriate for the requirements of the business.

- The division of responsibilities between the chairman and the chief executive should be set out in writing and agreed by the board.

- The non-executive directors should meet at least once a year without the chairman or executive directors present and the annual report should include a statement on whether such meetings have occurred.

- Prior to appointment, potential new non-executive directors should carry out due diligence on the board and on the company to satisfy themselves that they have the knowledge, skills, experience and time to make a positive contribution to the board.

- There should be a nomination committee of the board to conduct the process for board appointments and make recommendations to the board.

- The nomination committee should evaluate the balance of skills, knowledge and experience on the board and prepare a description of the role and capabilities required for a particular appointment.

- On appointment non-executive directors should receive a letter setting out what is expected of them.

- The nomination committee should provide support to the board on succession planning.

- A comprehensive induction programme should be provided to non-executive directors.

- The chairman should address the developmental needs of the board as a whole with a view to enhancing its effectiveness.

- The performance of the board, its committees and its individual members should be evaluated at least once a year. The annual report should state whether such performance reviews are taking place and how they are conducted.

- The chairman should assess what information is required by the board. Non-executive directors should satisfy themselves that they have appropriate information of sufficient quality to make sound judgements.

- A non-executive director should normally be expected to serve two three-year terms, though a longer term will exceptionally be appropriate.

- On appointment, non-executive directors should undertake that they will have sufficient time to meet what is expected of them, taking into account their other commitments. If a non-executive director is offered appointments elsewhere, the chairman should be informed before any new appointment is accepted.

- The nomination committee should annually review the time required of non-executive directors. The performance evaluation should assess whether non-executive directors are devoting enough time to fulfilling their duties.

- A full-time executive director should not take on more than one non-executive directorship, nor become chairman, of a major company. No individual should chair more than one major company.

- Where a non-executive director has concerns about the way in which a company is being run or about a course of action proposed by the board, these should be raised with the chairman and their fellow directors. Non-executive directors should ensure their concerns are recorded in the minutes of the board meetings if they cannot be resolved.

- On resignation, a non-executive director should inform the chairman in writing, for circulation to the board, of the reasons for resignation.

- The remuneration committee should comprise at least three members, all of whom should be independent non-executive directors. It should have published terms of reference.

- No one non-executive director should sit on all three principal board committees (audit, nomination and remuneration) simultaneously.

- Companies should provide appropriate directors' and officers' insurance and supply details of their insurance cover to potential non-executive directors before they are appointed.

- All non-executive directors, and in particular chairmen of the principal board committees, should attend the annual general meeting to discuss issues raised in relation to their role.

- Boards should recognise that non-executive directors may find it instructive to attend meetings with major investors from time to time and should be able to do so if they choose.

NOLAN COMMITTEE

30.15   The Nolan Committee Report looked at good governance for public spending bodies and set out seven principles to govern the conduct for those in public life. The principles have relevance for the governance of most charities, and particularly those that are non-departmental public bodies and those that derive the majority of their income from public funds. The seven principles are:

- Selflessness

- Integrity

- Objectivity

- Accountability

- Openness

- Honesty

- Leadership.

30.16   NCVO has produced a Model Code of Conduct for Voluntary Sector Boards (see Chapter 54) based on the seven Nolan principles. It suggests that the model code be used as a guide to good practice, rather than as a definitive code. In summary the code sets out that trustees should behave with:

- Selflessness: acting in the best interests of the charity as a whole, and not seeking to gain financial or other material benefits for themselves, their families, their friends or the organisation they work for or represent.

- Integrity: not placing themselves under financial or other obligations to individuals or organisations that might seek to influence them; not only avoiding impropriety but avoiding situations that might lead to suggestions of impropriety; and not accepting gifts and hospitality that could be seen as influencing their judgement.

- Objectivity: making sure that all their actions and decisions are made solely on merit.

- Accountability: acting in ways that preserve public confidence in the charity and being prepared to give account to all the charity's stakeholders for all their actions and decisions.

- Openness: handling all confidential material with due care, but otherwise being as open as possible about the trustees' actions and decisions, and the reasons for them.

- Honesty: declaring any conflicts of interest and resolving them in the interests of the charity.

- Leadership: setting a good example of corporate leadership and developing a good, constructive working relationship with the staff.

NATIONAL HOUSING FEDERATION

30.17   The National Housing Federation (formerly known as the National Federation of Housing Associations) held an Inquiry into Housing Association Governance in 1995. Its report, 'Competence and Accountability' (the Hancock Report), contained a draft Code of Governance, designed to improve the competence and accountability of housing associations (now known as registered social landlords), but much of which is relevant to many other types of voluntary organisation.

30.18   Amongst the Code's recommendations are the following:

- the Board should be given a clear statement of their role, with the emphasis of this role being on directing rather than managing;

- the Board should be given a clear statement of the role of Board members, the Chair, the Treasurer and any other honorary officers and the Chief Executive;

- the maximum size of the Board should be 15;

- there should be formal, published and open selection procedures for Board members and comprehensive induction arrangements; and

- there should be regular assessment of Board members' performance.

COMPANIES ACT 2006

30.19   *Section 170* to *177 of* the *Companies Act 2006* sets out the general duties of company directors (see CHAPTER 35).

31   Corporation Tax

31.1   Charities that are companies, industrial and provident societies, or unincorporated associations are within the scope of corporation tax. Corporation tax is payable on taxable profits in an accounting period, which is normally their financial year. Profits include both income and capital gains though in the case of most charities these will be exempt from tax.

SELF-ASSESSMENT

31.2   Where a charity or its subsidiary trading company has taxable income or gains, it is required to notify HMRC within 12 months from the end of its accounting period, unless it has made a corporation tax return in respect of that period. Where HMRC know that an entity may be liable to corporation tax it will issue it with a notice to file a corporation tax return. The return must be submitted within 12 months of the period-end. Under the self-assessment provisions, an entity is also required to make payment of corporation tax according to its calculation of tax payable. No assessments are made but HMRC have until 12 months after the tax return filing date to raise any queries by starting an enquiry. Companies and charities that come within the scope of corporation tax are liable to penalties for failing to notify HMRC that they are liable to corporation tax, or for failing to submit a corporation tax return on time, and interest is charged on any corporation tax paid late.

EXEMPTION

31.3   The rules of corporation tax are the same for charities as they are for commercial companies except that charities are exempt from corporation tax on certain classes of income and gains.

Section 505 exemptions

31.4   The main exemptions from corporation tax on income are to be found in *s 505* of *Income and Corporation Taxes Act 1988*. This section provides exemption from tax on:

- profits or gains arising in respect of rent or other receipts from land, wherever situated, provided that the land is vested in the company for charitable purposes and the income is only applied to charitable purposes;

- interest, annuities, annual payments, dividends, etc. arising in the UK or overseas where the income in question forms part of the income of a charity or is, according to rules and regulations established by Act of Parliament, Charter, Decree, Deed of Trust or Will, applicable to charitable purposes only, so far as any of this income is applied to charitable purposes only;

- certain public revenue dividends to the extent that they are applicable and applied only for the repair of any cathedral, college, church, chapel or building used only for divine worship;

- the profits of a trade carried on by a charity if the profits are applied solely for the purposes of the charity and either the trade is exercised in

134

the course of the actual carrying out of a primary purpose of the charity or the work in connection with the trade is mainly carried on by beneficiaries of the charity; and

- profits accruing to a charity from a lottery if the lottery is an exempt lottery within the meaning of the *Gambling Act 2005* by virtue of *Part 1* or *4* of *Sch 11* to that Act and the lottery is promoted in accordance with a lottery operating licence within the meaning of *Part 5* of that Act or the lottery is promoted and conducted in accordance with *Articles 133* or *135* of the *Betting, Gaming, Lotteries and Amusements* (*Northern Ireland*) *Order 1985* and the profits are applied solely to the charity's purposes.

EXEMPTION FOR SMALL TRADING AND OTHER INCOME

31.5   From April 2000 there is a tax exemption for the profits of small scale trading activities that are not otherwise exempt from tax. This applies to trading profits and other casual profits, such as sponsorship and some royalties, provided that the total turnover from all taxable activities is within certain limits. It also applies if, at the beginning of the period, there was a reasonable expectation that turnover would be within those limits, even if they are later exceeded. HMRC may ask for evidence to support any argument that the turnover was greater than originally expected. The annual turnover limit is £5,000 or, if greater, 25% of the charity's total income from all sources but is subject to an overall limit of £50,000.

Other exemptions

31.6   There are a number of provisions for charging tax on certain types of income or gains where a specific exemption is made for charities.

- Charities are exempt from the special charges relating to Certificates of Deposit if the profits or gains are applied to charitable purposes only.

- Charities are exempt from the offshore funds legislation if the gains are applicable and applied for charitable purposes.

- Charities are exempt from the accrued interest scheme which applies on a transfer of certain interest bearing securities where the interest is applied for charitable purposes only.

- The charge to tax where a pension fund surplus is repaid to an employer does not apply where the employer is a charity.

- Charities do not have to pay corporation tax on capital gains if they are applied for charitable purposes.

- Charities are exempt from tax on non-trading gains on intangible fixed assets such as intellectual property.

Conditions

31.7   Most of the above exemptions require that the income or gains are applied only for charitable purposes. There are therefore three requirements: first that the money is applied, second that it is for charitable purposes and third that it is not also for any other purpose. Strictly, because corporation tax is an annual tax, the income or gains should be applied in the same year in which they arise. In practice, HMRC do not appear to insist on this, subject to the rules for charitable expenditure. If a charity applies its income in any matter permitted by its governing document then it should be arguable that the income is applied for charitable purposes only. Application includes spending the money on legitimate administration expenses of the charity, investing in funds held for charitable purposes or applying it according to an order or advice given by the Charity Commission. Where, however, income is left uninvested or applied for non-charitable purposes, the charity is probably acting in breach of its governing document and the income or gains may become taxable.

TRADING

31.8   Where a charity is carrying on trading activities there are additional conditions which must be satisfied for the trading profits to be exempt from tax. Normally, a trade involves the sale of goods or services as part of a commercial enterprise but for tax purposes, a single or occasional venture may also be treated as a trade where a number of criteria are met (known as the *Badges of Trade*) including the intention to make a profit. The fact that the profits are a form of fund-raising for the charity is irrelevant in deciding whether or not a trading activity exists. Unless within the small trading exemption, the two additional conditions which must be satisfied if trading profits are to be exempt from tax are that the trade must be exercised in the course of the actual carrying out of a primary purpose of the charity or the work in connection with the trade must be mainly carried out by beneficiaries of the charity and any profits must be applied solely for the purposes of the charity.

Primary purpose trading

31.9   Examples of primary purpose trades are:

- the provision of educational services by a charitable school;

- the holding of an exhibition by a charitable art gallery or museum;

- the sale of tickets for a theatrical production staged by a charitable theatre company;

- the provision of health care services or residential accommodation by a care charity;

- the sale of certain educational goods by a charitable art gallery or museum.

Ancillary trading

31.10   Additionally, the exemption from tax on trading profits extends to activities which are ancillary to the carrying out of a primary purpose. Examples of ancillary trading are:

- the renting of accommodation to students by a university or college;

- sales of goods or services for the benefits of students, or the provision of a crèche for the children of students, by a school or college;

- the sale of food and drink to patrons of a charitable art gallery, museum or theatre;

- the sale of confectionery, toiletries and flowers to patients and their visitors by a League of Friends hospital shop.

31.11   Prior to 22 March 2006, the above activities could not be extended without putting the tax exemption under *s 505* at risk. For example, if a museum sold a range of goods some of which were not educational, or a college rented accommodation to tourists during the holiday periods, or a theatre restaurant or bar was open to members of the general public the whole of the exemption for all primary purpose trading activities was lost, unless the amounts involved were small in themselves and the turnover of that part of the trade was less than 10% of the total turnover.

Split trades

31.12   A change was introduced in the *Finance Act 2006* allowing trades to be split into primary purpose and non-primary purpose elements, and each constituent trade taxed separately with the former being tax exempt and the latter taxable. Likewise, where the work in connection with a trade is carried out partly, but not mainly, by beneficiaries of a charity that part is treated as a primary purpose trade and any profits are tax exempt; the remainder of the trade is taxed separately and any profits are likely to be taxable unless the small trading exemption applies. When calculating profits there should be a reasonable apportionment of income and expenses between the primary purpose and the non-primary purpose elements of the trade. This change applies for charitable companies' chargeable periods beginning on or after 22 March 2006 (budget day).

Concession for fund-raising

31.13   By concession, HMRC do not seek to tax the profits of some small-scale events arranged to raise funds for charity, but the organisation must comply fully with the terms of the concession. This concession applies to 'bazaars, jumble sales, gymkhanas, carnivals, fireworks displays and similar activities arranged by voluntary organisations or charities for the purposes of raising funds for charity'. The following conditions must, however, also be satisfied:

- the activities are supported substantially because the public are aware that any profits will be devoted to charity;

- no more than 15 events of the same kind at the same location may be held in any year, unless the weekly gross takings do not exceed £1,000;

- the profits are transferred to charities or are otherwise applied for charitable purposes.

31.14   The list of events quoted is not exhaustive and the concession will often apply to other similar events such as fêtes, concerts, dinners, dances and sports matches.

Donated goods

31.15   A number of charities raise funds by selling donated goods either as a regular activity in charity shops or as an occasional activity at e.g. a jumble sale or fête.

Provided that the goods are not subjected to significant refurbishment, or used or processed to make other goods, e.g. cloth being made up into garments, such sales are not a trading activity. The sales are simply the realisation of the value of the donated goods. This is so even where the donated goods are sorted, cleaned and minor repairs are made.

Sponsorship

31.16   Business sponsorship is also a common method used by charities to raise funds but it can easily amount to a trading activity, either as a separate trade or as part of another trade. If the sponsorship payments are not made in return for goods or services provided by the charity, they will normally be classed as charitable donations and, therefore, not taxable. However, where the charity agrees to provide some goods or services, including publicity, advertising or entertaining, in return for the sponsorship payments, the arrangement may be treated as trading.

31.17   Unless it amounts to advertising, merely acknowledging a sponsor's contribution will not normally make sponsorship a trading activity. HMRC regard a reference to a sponsor as an advertisement if it incorporates either the sponsor's logo, the sponsor's corporate colours or mention of the sponsor's products or services. Similarly, HMRC will normally treat sponsorship payments as trading income if the sponsor is allowed use of the charity's mailing list or logo; or if the charity endorses the sponsor's products or services; or the charity grants the sponsor exclusive rights to sell its goods or services on the charity's premises. Nevertheless, if the sponsorship income forms part of another trade, rather than a trade in itself, and that trade is a primary purpose trade then the profits will be exempt from tax. An example of this would be where a business sponsors a charitable theatre's stage production.

Affinity credit cards

31.18   The fees received by a charity from the issue or use of credit cards bearing the name of the charity is trading income, which is not from a primary purpose or ancillary trade and is therefore taxable. It may be possible to arrange for series of payments to be made for the use of the charity's logo by separate agreement, in which the charity is not obliged to do anything in return. The payments should be exempt from tax as annual payments. A separate agreement would be needed for the use of the charity's mailing list and promotional activities as fees received for these services would be taxable. If the arrangement is structured through a charity's trading subsidiary, care is needed over the agreement between the charity and its subsidiary for the use of the charity's name.

Royalties

31.19   The taxation treatment of royalties depends on their nature and what the charity does or has done in return. In most cases they will be taxable, either as trading income or under *Schedule D, Case VI, s 18* of the *Income and Corporation Taxes Act 1988*, for which there is no specific exemption outside the exemption for small trading and other income. In some cases where the charity has done nothing to earn the royalty, the royalty fees could be treated as an annual payment, which would be exempt from corporation tax.

Calculation of profit

31.20   Having established that a charity is carrying on a trade which is not for a primary purpose or within the concessions, the actual profit of the trade must be calculated in order to arrive at any tax liability. In arriving at these profits, the charity will be able to deduct not only the direct expenditure of the trade but also a proportion of other indirect overheads which may be partly attributable, such as the running costs of the premises, salaries and administration costs. It may also be possible to organise events that amount to trading activities so as to minimise the profit. This can be achieved by the charity setting a minimum charge and inviting an additional voluntary donation. However, promotional material and tickets must clearly state that:

- only the minimum charge need be paid;

- further contributions are entirely discretionary;

- no additional benefit is secured by making an additional payment.

Costs can be deducted from this in order to arrive at the taxable profit. If this is done then only the minimum charge qualifies as taxable income.

31.21   Costs can be deducted from this in order to arrive at the taxable profit. If this is done then only the minimum charge qualifies as taxable income.

31.22   If a charity makes a loss from a trading activity, the loss will be regarded as charitable expenditure if the activities are within the charity's objects. If they are not, the loss may be regarded as non-charitable expenditure, which can result in a proportion of the charity's income losing exemption from corporation tax (see below).

Loss of exemptions

Accounting periods beginning after 22 March 2006

31.23   Where a charity's income and gains are not applied solely to charitable purposes, its exemption from tax may be restricted. Calculation of the restriction in tax relief for accounting periods beginning before 22 March 2006 is discussed in the next section. Legislation introduced in the *Finance Act 2006* applies for accounting periods beginning on or after 22 March 2006.

31.24   Restriction of tax relief may apply where:

- an item of expenditure is incurred wholly for non-charitable purposes;

- an item of expenditure is incurred partly for charitable purposes and partly for non-charitable purposes; or

- a charity is treated as incurring non-charitable expenditure.

Charitable and non-charitable expenditure

31.25   Charitable expenditure is that which the charity has incurred for charitable purposes only. It will include such items as charitable grants and expenditure incurred on the administration of the charity. It is important to note that charitable expenditure does not include investments that the charity has made or loans which are accepted as charitable. This is because the making of an investment is not generally regarded as expenditure. However, if the charity makes a non-charitable (non-qualifying) loan or investment this is treated for tax purposes as non–charitable expenditure.

31.26   Non-charitable expenditure is not defined other than by the fact that 'charitable expenditure' is defined as expenditure 'exclusively for charitable purposes'. The following expenditure is considered non-charitable:

- expenditure which is not incurred for charitable purposes only;

- any payments to an overseas body where the charity has not taken reasonable steps to ensure the payment will be applied for charitable purposes;

- any investments and/or loans made by the charity which are not qualifying investments and loans;

- losses arising from non-primary purpose trading or deemed non-primary purpose trading;

- amounts treated as non-charitable expenditure as a result of certain transactions with substantial donors. For detailed guidance on transactions with substantial donors see CHAPTER 40 Donations and Fundraising.

Relievable income and gains

31.27   A charity's relievable income and gains is its income and gains that qualify for relief or exemption from tax. It includes the following:

- Gift Aid donations;

- income from land such as rental income;

- interest received;

- profits from a charity's primary purpose trading activity;

- certain annual payments (e.g. certain royalties);

- and capital gains.

31.28   Receivable income does not include income which does not qualify for tax exemption, for example, the profits of non-charitable (non-primary purpose) trading or amounts taxable under tax anti-avoidance provisions.

31.29   Additionally, legacies and other donations that are outside the scope of tax altogether, for example, donations made outside the Gift Aid regime, are not relievable income.

Restriction to a charity's tax relief

31.30   If a charity incurs non-charitable expenditure or is treated as incurring such expenditure (for example, under the rules for transactions with substantial donors), it loses tax exemption on an equivalent amount of relievable income and gains. Furthermore, unlike the previous rules (see below), there is now no *de minimis* limit before the restrictions on relief take effect.

EXAMPLE

31.31   A charity has gross Gift Aid income of £67,000 and gross rental income of £33,000 in a chargeable period. It is entitled to tax exemption on these sources of relievable income, totalling £100,000. However, the charity spends £80,000 in charitable grants and administration and makes a non-charitable loan of £20,000 to its trading subsidiary. The tax consequence of making the non-charitable loan is that tax relief is disallowed in respect of £20,000 relievable income which otherwise would have been exempt from tax.

31.32   The charity may by notice to HMRC specify the order in which the different sources of relievable income and gains are restricted. Where HMRC require the charity to give such a notice, and the charity fails to do so within 30 days, HMRC will determine the order. If a charity has incurred non-charitable expenditure it should complete a Self Assessment / Corporation Tax Return for the chargeable period concerned and account for any resulting tax liability. If the return provides details of the order in which tax exemption for relievable income and gains is to be restricted then HMRC will accept this as sufficient notice.

Carrying back of excess non-charitable expenditure

31.33   The amount of non-charitable expenditure incurred by a charity in a chargeable period may be greater than the relievable income and gains in that period. Where this is the case any excess non-charitable expenditure is set against the remainder of the total income and gains of the charity for the period. 'Total income and gains' is the sum of the charity's relievable income and gains plus all other sources of income or gains, whether chargeable to tax or not (e.g. non-taxable grants, donations outside of gifts aid, legacies, etc.)

31.34   If any excess of non-charitable expenditure remains then that excess is carried back to the previous chargeable period, where it is treated as non-charitable expenditure of that period. Any further excess is carried back and dealt with similarly in earlier periods ending up to six years before the end of the current period.

31.35   There is no provision for non-charitable expenditure to be carried forward. The six-year carry-back period may include periods beginning before 22 March 2006. In that case, the restriction cannot exceed the amount that would have been restricted under the old rules (see below).

Examples of non-charitable expenditure

31.36   In their guidance, HMRC cite the following as examples of potentially non-charitable expenditure.

Payments outside the terms of the charity's governing document

31.37   Charitable expenditure not specifically authorised by the terms of a charity's governing document will not necessarily be treated as non-charitable expenditure. In considering the tax treatment of such expenditure HMRC may seek the views of the relevant charity regulator.

31.38   If a charity's governing document specifically prohibits or restricts certain expenditure, it will be treated as non-charitable expenditure.

Accumulation

31.39   The bulk of charitable exemptions from tax stipulate that income from the exempt source must be 'applied to charitable purposes only' in order for the exemption to apply.

31.40   Charities on occasion accumulate income or build up reserves. It is questionable whether this is an application of funds to charitable purposes only.

31.41   HMRC have stated that they will challenge accumulations of income where income is not invested but kept in cash or in a current account; or if it becomes apparent that investment decisions are not made exclusively for the benefit of the charity.

Payments overseas

31.42   Where a payment is made or committed to an overseas body, the onus is on the charity that makes that payment to show that it has taken reasonable steps to ensure that the payment will be applied for charitable purposes. If it has not done so, the payment is deemed to be non-charitable expenditure.

There was a similar requirement under the old rules. There was a complex set of rules which restricted the amount of a charity's income which was exempt from tax. This restriction depended upon the amount of a charity's qualifying expenditure and relevant income and gains. Qualifying expenditure (now termed 'charitable expenditure' under the new rules above) was expenditure incurred for charitable purposes only. Relevant income and gains were any income or gains which were taxable or which would have been taxable without the main exemptions provided by the *Income and Corporation Taxes Act 1988*. In this context, expenditure included any money spent by the charity in the year for whatever purpose and, as stated above, could include certain trading losses. Tax exemptions were lost when a charity's income and gains were £10,000 or more, its relevant income and gains exceeded its qualifying expenditure and the charity had incurred non-qualifying expenditure. Examples of non-qualifying expenditure would be losses from a trade which was not a primary purpose trade, or a loan which broadly was not made for charitable purposes by way of investment or for the benefit of the charity.

Net relevant income

31.43   The first stage in assessing whether or not the charity's income was exempt from tax was to ascertain whether the relevant income of the year exceeded the qualifying expenditure of that year. If it did not, the rules did not apply.

Non-qualifying expenditure

31.44   The next stage was to ascertain whether or not there was non-qualifying expenditure for that year. Where there was both non-qualifying expenditure and a shortfall of qualifying expenditure over relevant income and gains, then there was a loss of tax exemption. The non-qualifying expenditure gave rise to a loss of exemption but it was restricted in that year to the shortfall of qualifying expenditure. For example:

Relevant income	£100,000
Qualifying expenditure	£75,000
Non-qualifying expenditure	£120,000
Loss of exemption	£100,000 – £75,000 = £25,000

31.45   If, as in the above example, the non-qualifying expenditure for the year exceeded the shortfall of qualifying expenditure, the charity was retrospectively deemed to have incurred non-qualifying expenditure in the previous year, the amount being equal to the surplus non-qualifying expenditure. In the above example this would be £95,000, i.e. £120,000 – £25,000. The calculations must then be repeated for the previous year to see if, retrospectively, tax exemption was also lost in that year. As long as there was a surplus of non-qualifying expenditure, the charity had to carry it back for up to six years. Surpluses of non-qualifying expenditure did not, however, have to be carried forward.

31.46   There was one limitation on the carry-back principle. Expenditure was not carried back if the charity could show that it represented expenditure of non-taxable sums, i.e. sums which were not taxable in any event, with or without exemption, such as donations outside of Gift Aid and legacies. In these circumstances, the amount of non-qualifying expenditure which would otherwise be carried back was compared with the non-taxable sums received, so that only the excess, if any, was carried back. If in the above example, the charity had received donations in the year of £80,000, the amount carried back to the earlier year would only have been the additional £15,000.

31.47   The limit of £10,000 on a charity's income and gains after which tax exemptions were lost was set in 1986 when this legislation was introduced. It had not been increased since that date and therefore, in real terms, its value deteriorated over time.

31.48   From April 2002 to March 2006 there was a starting rate of corporation tax on the first £10,000 of profits of NIL. This allowed charities flexibility in retaining funds in trading subsidiaries rather than having to pay up all profits in order to avoid paying corporation tax and then providing loans or share capital to expand their activities.

32   Custodian Trustee

32.1   A custodian trustee is a corporate body, commonly a bank, insurance company or local authority, which looks after the documents or other evidence of the title to an unincorporated organisation's property or investments on behalf of the trustees as a whole. Custodian trustees are empowered to act in accordance with rules set out in the *Public Trustee Act 1906, s 14*. The Charity Commission will permit a charity to have all its investments and land held by just one custodian trustee.

METHOD OF APPOINTMENT

32.2   A custodian trustee can be appointed under *s 4(1)* of the *Public Trustee Act 1906* in any of the following ways:

- by the governing document of the charity when it is first established;

- by the person or persons with power to appoint trustees;

- by an Order or Scheme of the Court.

The Charity Commission can also appoint a custodian trustee by an Order or Scheme under *s 16* of the *Charities Act 1993*.

RESPONSIBILITIES

32.3   A custodian trustee is not a charity trustee and the responsibilities of custodian trustees are very different from those of charity trustees. The activities of custodian trustees are limited to holding legal title to investments or land, receiving income from these assets and remitting income to the charity. They play no further part in the management of the charity or its assets. They cannot act on behalf of the managing trustees, even if there are none.

32.4   Custodian trustees must act on the instructions of the charity trustees unless doing so would be unlawful or a breach of trust. If a custodian trustee acts unlawfully or commits a breach of trust while acting on the instructions of the charity trustees, legal liability rests with the charity trustees. However, if a custodian trustee commits a breach of trust by acting outside the terms of its agreement with the charity whose assets they hold, the custodian trustee will be legally liable.

ADVANTAGES OF HAVING A CUSTODIAN TRUSTEE

32.5   Unincorporated charities often choose to use a custodian trustee, or a group of holding trustees (see CHAPTER 61) to hold title to their land or investments. This is because unincorporated charities cannot hold their investments or land in the name of the charity, as an unincorporated body has no legal personality of its own. If the trustees hold legal title, expense is incurred every time there is a change in the governing body and legal title has to be transferred to the new body of trustees.

FEES

32.6   Custodian trustees usually charge a fee for their services. Under general law all charity trustees have the power to appoint a custodian trustee, but they may not remunerate a custodian trustee unless the charity's governing document contains a clear power permitting such a payment or if, more rarely, the Charity Commission has made an Order or Scheme allowing the trustees to remunerate a custodian trustee.

32.7   Some corporate bodies, including charities, local authorities and trust corporations set up to serve religious denominations, such as the Church of England's Diocesan Boards of Finance, are willing to act as custodian trustees without remuneration.

TERMINATION

32.8   If a charity wishes to dispense with the services of its custodian trustee, the trusteeship must be terminated by an Order of the Court or the Charity Commission acting under the *Public Trustee Act 1906, s 4(1)(a)*.

FURTHER INFORMATION

32.9   Charity Commission operational guidance OG 39 *www.charity-commission.gov.uk*

33   Data Protection

33.1   The *Data Protection Act 1998* came into force on 1 March 2000 and substantially altered previous data protection laws. It applies to any organisation that collects or uses information about recognisable living individuals which is kept on a computer, or other electronic retrieval system, or recorded as part of a relevant filing system i.e. a system containing a set of data structured by name of individual or other criteria which make information relating to a specific individual readily accessible. Paper records held by organisations on 23 October 1998 did not have to comply with most of the Act until October 2007, but all information added to the files after 23 October 1998 has to comply as soon as it is added.

33.2   The *Data Protection Act 1998* applies to processing personal data by which individuals can be identified. This includes expressions of opinion that identify the individual as well as visual data such as photographs and videos. Processing has a very wide meaning in the Act. It includes looking at personal data on a screen, and storing, sorting and analysing it.

33.3   The Act gives rights to individuals (data subjects) and imposes duties on the collecting organisation (the data controller) and its employees who hold and process personal data. Charities should consider giving one member of staff overall responsibility for ensuring that all the charity's data processing complies with the legislation and ensure that all staff, particularly those in fund-raising, supporter management and operational departments, are aware of the legislation and know who to contact for detailed advice.

DATA SUBJECTS

33.4   A data subject is any living individual whose personal data is obtained, held, used and otherwise processed by an organisation within the meaning of the data protection legislation. Examples of the types of individuals charities hold data on are current and former employees, job applicants, current and former beneficiaries and potential beneficiaries, donors, etc. A data subject need not be a United Kingdom national or resident.

CONSENT

33.5   The *Data Protection Act 1998* refers to two types of consent: 'consent' and 'explicit consent'. Consent is not defined in the Act, but in the EC Directive that led to the Act consent is defined as '... any freely given specific and informed indication of his wishes by which the data subject signifies his agreement to personal data relating to him being processed'. The fact that the data subject must 'signify' his agreement indicates that there must be active communication between the data subject and the data controller. Data controllers cannot infer consent from non-response to a communication, though a data subject may 'signify' agreement other than in writing. Consent obtained under duress or on the basis of misleading information will not be a valid basis for processing. Consent must be appropriate to the circumstances. Where 'explicit consent' is required for the processing of sensitive data the data subject must give absolutely clear consent, i.e. the consent must cover the specific detail of the processing, the particular type of data to be processed (or even the specific information), the purposes of the processing and any special aspects of the processing that may affect the individual, such as disclosures that may be made of the data. There are circumstances, however, in which the processing of personal data does not require consent, including circumstances where the processing of data is necessary to perform a contract or for the administration of justice.

DATA CONTROLLERS

33.6   A data controller is an individual or organisation that determines the purposes for which, and the manner in which, personal data are, or are to be, processed. A data controller must be a legal person, i.e. an individual, or a corporate body, or an unincorporated body of people.

Data processors

33.7   A data processor, in relation to personal data, is a person, other than an employee of the data controller, who processes personal data on behalf of the data controller, for example a mailing house.

Recipient

33.8   A recipient, in relation to personal data, is any person to whom the data is disclosed, including any person to whom it is disclosed in the course of processing the data for the data controller.

PERSONAL DATA

33.9   Personal data is any data that relates to a living individual and from which a living individual could be identified. It can be as little as name, address, telephone number and e-mail address, or it may include, for example, information about a person's state of health, educational qualifications or financial circumstances. Images captured by CCTV cameras that could be matched to a photograph, a physical description or a physical person would be personal data, as would email addresses that clearly identify an individual, e.g. don.bawtree@bdo.co.uk. Information about an individual working for another charity in the same field would be personal data, whereas information about the charity they worked for is not personal data.

SENSITIVE PERSONAL DATA

33.10   Because of their sensitive nature some types of personal data have been defined as 'sensitive personal data' by the Act and are subject to a stricter data protection regime. Sensitive personal data relate to:

- Racial or ethnic origin;
- Political opinions;
- Religious beliefs or other beliefs of a similar nature;
- Membership of a trade union;
- Physical or mental health or condition;
- Sexual life;
- Commission or alleged commission of any offence;

- Proceedings and sentences for any offence – committed or alleged.

33.11   Sensitive personal data cannot be processed unless one of a number of conditions are satisfied. The two most significant of these conditions are: (i) that the data subject must give explicit consent to the processing of the data; and (ii) processing must be necessary for the purpose of exercising or performing any right or obligation which is conferred or imposed by law on the data controller in connection with employment.

PROCESSING

33.12   Processing includes virtually anything that can be done with data, including typing data into a computer, storing it on a hard drive, copying it onto a disk, or reading it from a computer screen. Processing also includes collecting, recording, holding, retrieval, consultation, use, disclosure, combining, blocking and destruction of data.

33.13   All organisations, including charities, must comply with data protection rules when:

- asking for personal information on questionnaires or application forms;
- active or passive collection or dissemination of personal data on the internet or the organisation's intranet or extranet;
- sending personal data within or outside the organisation by e-mail or telephone;
- direct marketing;
- compiling and using mailing lists;
- compiling personal data for inclusion in directories or publications;
- using existing personal data for new purposes;
- using third parties to carry out any processing;
- dealing with employment issues;
- monitoring employees' use of the telephone, computer, internet and email.

NOTIFICATION

33.14   The registration procedure in the *1984 Act* has been replaced by a simplified notification system. A charity that is a data controller has a duty to notify the Information Commissioner about its processing operations with personal data. It must provide the Commissioner with information about:

- the name and address of the data controller, or his nominated representative;
- the personal data processed by the charity;
- the categories of individuals whose data are processed;
- the purposes for which data are processed;
- any recipients to whom the data are disclosed;

- the countries or territories outside the European Economic Area to which data are transferred. (The export of personal data to non-EEA countries is now illegal unless the data controller can show that the country of the transferee is 'safe' for data protection purposes or one of the exemptions in the Act applies.);

- the data security measures employed to protect the personal data.

33.15   Notification has to be renewed every year. The fee for renewal is currently £35. The register of data controllers can be found at *www.ico.gov.uk/ tools_and_resources.aspx*.

DATA PROTECTION PRINCIPLES

33.16   The *Data Protection Act 1998* sets out eight data protection principles that must be observed by all employees of charities that are data controllers. They are:

(i) Personal data shall be processed fairly and lawfully and, in particular, shall not be processed unless certain conditions are met, i.e. the data subject must have given consent, or explicit consent in the case of sensitive personal data, and the processing must be necessary;

(ii) Personal data shall be obtained only for one or more specified and lawful purposes and shall not be further processed in any manner incompatible with such purpose(s);

(iii) Personal data shall be adequate, relevant and not excessive in relation to the purpose(s) for which they are processed;

(iv) Personal data shall be accurate and, where necessary, kept up to date;

(v) Personal data processed for any purpose (s) shall not be kept longer than is necessary for that purpose(s);

(vi) Personal data shall be processed in accordance with the rights of data subjects under the *Data Protection Act 1998*;

(vii) Appropriate technical and organisational measures shall be taken against unauthorised or unlawful processing of personal data and against accidental loss or destruction of, or damage to, personal data;

(viii) Personal data shall not be transferred to a country or territory outside the European Economic Area, unless that country or territory ensures an adequate level of protection of the rights and freedoms of data subjects in relation to the processing of personal data.

33.17   Breaches of the principles may result in a complaint by the individual concerned, a claim for compensation by the individual concerned, or possible enforcement action by the Information Commissioner.

DATA SUBJECTS' RIGHTS

33.18   Any data subject may demand to see and/or have a copy of all personal data held and processed about him. The data subject has the right to be given a description of the personal data, the purposes for which they are being processed, and those to whom they are or may be disclosed. A subject access request must be made in writing, including by electronic means, and the data controller has the right to charge an appropriate fee (currently the maximum is £10 in most cases). A data controller must respond to a subject access request promptly, and in any case within 40 days of the receipt of the request, or the receipt of the information needed to satisfy himself as to the identity of the person making the request, or the receipt of the fee.

33.19   Data subjects have a right to object to the processing of their personal data where such processing may cause substantial and unwarranted damage or distress. This right applies in relation to perfectly lawful processing that is unwanted by the data subject for a specified and justifiable reason because it is causing or likely to cause them to suffer loss or harm, or upset or anguish of a real nature, over and above annoyance level.

33.20   Data subjects may apply to the Court for an order requiring a data controller to correct, block, erase or destroy any personal data relating to them that is incorrect or misleading or that contains information and/or opinions that are based on inaccurate data.

33.21   Every individual has the right to request by written notice that organisations, including charities, stop, or do not begin, processing their personal data for the purpose of direct marketing. When a data controller receives such a notice he must comply as soon as he can, and usually within 28 days. The data subject may apply to the Court for an order if the data controller fails to comply with the notice.

33.22   Individuals have rights in relation to decisions that significantly affect them that are made using solely automated means, i.e. with no human involvement. Where decisions are automated the data subject should be informed. Within 21 days of the data subject being informed of the decision, they have the right to ask for the decision to be reconsidered and for information about the basis on which the decision was made. The data collector should respond within 21 days. For example, an individual has the right to object to recruitment decisions being based purely on the basis of psychometric testing and can insist on a human evaluation being made.

33.23   Finally any data subject can claim compensation through the Courts for any damage, or damage and distress, suffered as a result of a breach of the Act by a data controller unless the data controller is able to prove that he took such care as was reasonable in all the circumstances to comply with the Act.

EXEMPTIONS TO DATA SUBJECTS' RIGHTS

33.24   The rights of data subjects can be restricted on the following grounds:

- National security;
- Crime and taxation;
- Health, education and social work;
- Regulatory activities;
- Journalism, literature and art;
- Research, history and statistics;
- Legal privilege;
- Confidential references given by the Data Controller.

OBTAINING DATA SUBJECTS' CONSENT

33.25   When collecting personal data charities must provide data subjects with the following:

- The name of the organisation or individual that will be processing the data, for example the charity, its trading company, or both;

- The primary purpose of the processing, e.g. to record a donation, send a publication, provide services;

- Details of any other purposes that the data will be used for, e.g. sending information about the charity or mail order catalogues;

- Details of any third parties to whom the data may be disclosed;

- Details of how the data subject can opt out of having their data used for anything other than the primary purpose.

DIRECT MARKETING ACTIVITIES

33.26   The *Data Protection Act 1998* covers all direct marketing activities across all media channels. The *Privacy and Electronic Communications Regulations 2003* contain extra requirements which must be complied with if an organisation is carrying out direct marketing via electronic communications.

33.27   When charities collect personal information from individuals they cannot use it for direct marketing purposes unless they make it clear at the time the data is collected that it may be used for direct marketing activities. It is good practice to give individuals the opportunity to opt out of receiving further marketing materials each time they are contacted by the charity or contact the charity. Promotional literature should include an opt in or an opt out statement along the lines of 'Please tick the box if you are happy to receive further information about the charity and its activities' or 'Please tick the box if you do not want to receive further information'. Charities must not send further information to individuals who have indicated that they do not wish to receive it.

33.28   Some individuals may have opted out from some or all types of direct mail through the Mail Preference Service. Charities should not send mailshots to people on the Mail Preference Service list unless they have received some other indication that the person would be willing to accept direct mail from the charity.

33.29   Charities must not make unsolicited telephone calls to individuals who have informed them that they do not wish to receive such calls, or to individuals on the Telephone Preference Service list, unless the individual has told the charity they do not object. Charities must not make automated calls (pre-recorded phone messages) without getting the individual's consent first. Similarly charities must not send unsolicited marketing by electronic mail (email, text, voice, picture and video messages) without getting the individual's permission first.

33.30   Charities must not send unsolicited marketing materials by fax to any number on the Fax Preference Service list, unless the individual has told the charity they do not object, or to individuals who have told the charity they object to such communications.

INFORMATION COMMISSIONER

33.31   The Information Commissioner is responsible for enforcing both the *Data Protection Act 1998* and the *Telecommunications (Data Protection and Privacy) Regulations 1999*. The Commissioner has a number of duties including:

- to promote the following of good practice by data controllers;

- to disseminate information about the Act and how it works;

- to encourage the development of Codes of Practice, setting out guidance as to good practice;

- to maintain a register of data controllers;

- to prosecute persons in respect of offences committed under the Act.

33.32   In pursuing his duties the Information Commissioner can:

- hear complaints from individuals;

- enter a data controller's premises and carry out an inspection, if it is suspected that any of the Data Protection Principles are being contravened or if there is another suspected offence under the Act;

- serve an information notice on a data controller requesting information about a suspected breach of Data Protection Principles;

- serve an enforcement notice upon a data controller who the Commissioner is satisfied has contravened, or is contravening, any of the Data Protection Principles, requiring the data controller to take, or refrain from taking, specified steps or to refrain from processing any personal data altogether, or from processing for a specified purpose or in a specified manner.

OFFENCES UNDER THE ACT

33.33   Offences under the Act include:

- non-compliance with the Data Protection Principles;

- processing personal data without notifying the Information Commissioner;

- failure to notify the Information Commissioner of changes to the notification register entry;

- failure to comply with subject access requests, or information notices, or enforcement notices;

- unlawful obtaining of personal data;

- unlawful selling of personal data.

33.34   Proceedings for a criminal offence under the Act will be commenced in England and Wales by the Information Commission or the Director of Public Prosecutions, in Scotland by the Procurator Fiscal, and in Northern Ireland by the Information Commissioner or the Director of Public Prosecutions for Northern Ireland. A person found guilty of an offence under the Act can be sentenced on summary conviction to a fine not exceeding the statutory maximum (currently £5,000), or on conviction on indictment to an unlimited fine.

33.35   If a corporate body commits a criminal offence under the Act, any company director, trustee, manager, secretary or similar officer is personally guilty of the offence, in addition to the corporate body, if the offence was committed with his/her consent or connivance, or the offence is attributable to any neglect on his/her part.

FURTHER INFORMATION

33.36   Information Commissioner
Wycliffe House
Water Lane
Wilmslow
Cheshire
SK9 5AF
Information line: 01625 545745
Website: *www.dataprotection.gov.uk*
E-mail: data@dataprotection.gov.uk

Direct Marketing Association
Tel: 020 7321 2525
Website: *www.dma.org.uk*

Mail Preference Service (020 7766 4410)

Telephone Preference Service (0845 070 0707)

Fax Preference Service (0845 070 0702)

34   Devolution and Regionalisation

34.1   The devolution of political power to Scotland, Wales and Northern Ireland and to the English regions has had an impact on many charities, particularly charities based in England but working UK-wide. Devolution has an impact on how charities need to position themselves in order to gain credibility with funding bodies, how they deliver services, how they exercise their political leverage and how they hold themselves accountable.

34.2   Charities need to question the impact of devolution on their overall strategy, decision-making, structure, governance, service delivery, campaigning, and fund-raising, financial and human resource strategies. They also need to consider if they need to build new relationships with potential and existing funders and new alliances with other voluntary organisations. In some instances devolution has led to charities restructuring, transforming their national branches into autonomous organisations or adopting a federal structure, in order to take advantage of the opportunities presented by devolution.

SCOTTISH PARLIAMENT

34.3   The *Scotland Act 1998* laid out the legislative details of the Scottish Parliament which took up its full powers in July 1999. It is written in terms of reserved powers, prescribing everything over which the Westminster Parliament retains control. The UK Parliament retains powers over:

- UK foreign policy, including European Union policy;
- UK defence and national security;
- UK fiscal, economic and monetary system;
- Common markets for UK goods and services;
- The constitution;
- Social security;
- Employment legislation;
- Transport safety and regulation;
- Company law;
- Certain other matters presently subject to UK or GB regulation, including the National Lottery and equality rights legislation.

34.4   All remaining areas are automatically devolved to the Scottish Parliament including:

- Agriculture, forestry and fishing;
- Education and training;
- Environment;
- Gaelic;
- Health;
- Housing;

- Law and home affairs;
- Local government;
- Natural and built heritage;
- Planning;
- Police and fire services;
- Prisons;
- Social work;
- Sports and the arts;
- Statistics and public records;
- Tourism and economic development;
- Transport.

34.5   The Scottish Parliament can introduce new legislation and amend or repeal existing legislation on devolved matters. Committees and individual Members of the Scottish Parliament can introduce legislation and the Parliament can consider legislation promoted by an external body, such as a Scottish charity. Charities operating in Scotland can therefore influence policy and provide information and expertise on a wide range of issues being debated by the Parliament. Committees of the Scottish Parliament seek evidence on a regular basis from voluntary organisations on a broad range of policy issues.

Relationship to Westminster

34.6   The UK Parliament remains sovereign but Westminster MPs can no longer debate or question Ministers on devolved matters. A Secretary of State for Scotland remains in the UK Cabinet and represents the interests of Scotland in the UK Parliament. MPs from Scotland continue to sit at Westminster.

34.7   Most of the funding for Scotland's public expenditure programme continues to be met through the 'Block' and formula process under which the UK government previously transferred money to the Scottish Office.

WALES

34.8   The *Government of Wales Act 1998* laid out the legislative details of the National Assembly for Wales which also took up its full powers in July 1999. The *Government of Wales Act 2006* has introduced the ability of the National Assembly for Wales to make its own legislation on devolved matters including:

- Agriculture, fisheries, forestry and rural development;
- Ancient monuments and historic buildings;
- Culture;
- Economic development;
- Education and training;
- Environment;

34.9   Devolution and Regionalisation

- Fire and rescue services and promotion of fire safety;
- Food;
- Health and health services;
- Highways and transport;
- Housing;
- Local government;
- Public administration;
- Social welfare;
- Sport and recreation;
- Tourism;
- Town and county planning;
- Water and flood defence;
- Welsh language.

34.9   The role of the Welsh Assembly Government is to:

- Make decisions;
- Develop and implement policy;
- Exercise functions;
- Make subordinate legislation (e.g. regulations and statutory guidance);
- Propose Assembly Measures (Welsh laws).

Relationship to Westminster

34.10   Westminster retains responsibility for criminal justice, immigration, taxation, defence, and foreign affairs.

NORTHERN IRELAND ASSEMBLY

34.11   The Northern Ireland Assembly took up its powers in December 1999, following the Belfast (Good Friday) Agreement. After long periods of suspension and the restoration of Direct Rule, the Assembly was restored on 8 May 2007. It has full legislative and executive authority to make laws and take decisions on all the functions of the Northern Ireland Departments.

34.12   The Secretary of State for Northern Ireland remains responsible for matters not devolved to the Assembly including law and order, political affairs, policing and criminal justice. It also has responsibility for matters relating to the licensing and legislation concerning firearms and explosives, including fireworks.

REGIONALISATION

34.13   There are nine English regions:

- East of England;

156

- East Midlands;

- London;

- North East;

- North West;

- South East;

- South West;

- West Midlands;

- Yorkshire and the Humber.

With the exception of London, all have broadly similar infrastructures.

34.14   Government Offices for the Regions (GORs) were established in 1994, bringing together the existing regional government offices dealing with transport, the environment, education and trade and industry. Their remit is to promote competitiveness, prosperity and quality of life in their region through business enterprise, sustainability and regeneration. They also have a role in identifying issues specific to their region and ensuring that these are fed into the national policy-making process.

34.15   The GORs act as the government sponsoring unit for the Regional Development Agencies (RDAs) which were established in 1999 under the *Regional Development Agencies Act 1998* in each of the English regions except London. GORs provide advice to RDAs about government policies and programmes and guidance relating to the operation of the RDAs.

34.16   Each RDA is managed by a RDA Board, the majority of whose members come from business. Their purpose is to promote the economic, social and physical regeneration of their region. All are required to produce a Regional Economic Strategy that should include input from the voluntary sector and identify key partners, including voluntary organisations, to help implement the strategy.

London

34.17   London differs from the other regions in that it is the only one to have democratic representation. The first elections for the London Mayor and Greater London Assembly, which together form the Greater London Authority (GLA), were held in May 2000. The RDA for London is known as the London Development Agency (LDA). It has broadly similar responsibilities and functions as the other RDAs, though slightly wider as responsibilities for transport and policing are also devolved to the GLA, unlike other RDAs. The LDA came into being in July 2000 and is accountable to the GLA.

The Compact

34.18   The relationship between central government and the voluntary sector is set out in the Compact ('Compact on Relations between Government and the Voluntary and Community Sector in England', The Home Office, 2000). The principles set out in the Compact relate to GORs as well as RDAs. The Compact outlines a new approach to partnership between the government and the voluntary sector in England based on shared values. It was drawn up following extensive consultation with the voluntary and community sector and government departments. The underlying philosophy is that voluntary and community activity is fundamental to the development of a democratic, socially inclusive society. It sets out a list of shared principles and undertakings by the government on issues such as independence of the sector, funding, policy development, and better government and by the voluntary sector on funding and accountability, policy development and consultation, and good practice. For more information about the Compack, see CHAPTER 27.

FURTHER INFORMATION

34.19   Public Information Service
The Scottish Parliament
Edinburgh
EH99 1SP
Tel: 0131 348 5000
Fax: 0131 48 5601
Email: sp.info@scottish.parliament.uk
Website: *www.scottish.parliament.uk*

National Assembly for Wales
Tel: 0845 010 5500
Website: *www.assemblywales.org*

Northern Ireland Assembly
Website: *www.niassembly.gov.uk*

Government Offices for the English Regions
Website: *www.gos.gov.uk*

35   Directors

DIRECTOR

35.1   The word 'director' is used in the voluntary sector in a number of different contexts. The trustees of a charitable company may be referred to as the (company) directors, as may the directors of industrial and provident societies. The most senior member of staff may also be referred to as 'the Director', or others as 'the Director of Operations', 'the Director of Finance', 'the Director of Fund-raising'. Some of these 'directorships' are of no statutory significance, though in some circumstances staff could be judged to be acting in a statutory capacity as shadow directors.

SHADOW DIRECTOR

35.2   A shadow director is defined by *s 251* of the *Companies Act 2006* as being someone 'in accordance with whose directions or instructions the directors of the company are accustomed to act'. Merely providing trustees with information, as a chief executive might do, or advising them, as an accountant or solicitor might do, does not amount to acting as a shadow director. A chief executive who dominated the board of trustees and controlled almost all of the charity's activities could, on the other hand, be regarded as a shadow director.

35.3   Although the *Companies Act 2006* recognises the existence of shadow directors, in practice it is rare for an individual to be held to be a shadow director. Where someone does act as a shadow director then they become liable to incur penalties personally if the company is in default of its obligations under the *Companies Acts* or the *Insolvency Act 1986*.

35.4   In the remainder of this chapter the term 'director' is used to refer to a charitable company's directors (i.e. the trustees/governors/management committee members).

APPOINTMENT

35.5   The first directors are appointed in the company formation process and subsequent directors are appointed in accordance with the company's articles. In practice, when a new commercial company is set up, it is often acquired from formation agents who set up off-the-shelf companies with their own staff as the first directors. These directors then appoint the purchaser's nominees as directors and resign themselves.

35.6   On appointment new directors record their consent to act by signing Companies House form 288a which is then dated and countersigned by the company secretary or another trustee. The Secretary sends the form to Companies House (this process can also be done online), and the directors' details are entered in the register of directors in the charity's statutory books. Members of the public can gain access to the names of directors of a charitable company by contacting Companies House.

35.7   Limited companies, other than public limited companies, sometimes have only one director, but then that person cannot also be the company secretary.

35.8 Directors

A body corporate, e.g. another limited company, can be a company director, in which case an individual will be appointed by the body corporate to act on its behalf. Frequently, the articles of the company will stipulate that there must be a minimum number of directors greater than one. When the *Companies Act 2006* is fully in force a least one director of a private company must be a natural person (as opposed to a company). The office of company secretary will no longer be required, though the company secretariat functions will still need to be carried out.

QUALIFICATIONS

35.8   Any person who has reached the age of 16 and who is not disqualified by law, or prohibited by the charity's articles of association, may become a director of a charitable company.

Disqualification under the Charities Act 1993

35.9   *Section 72* of *Charities Act 1993* disqualifies people from becoming directors (trustees) of a charitable company if they:

- have unspent convictions for offences involving deception or dishonesty;

- are undischarged bankrupts;

- have been at any time removed from trusteeship of a charity by the Charity Commission or the Court in England, Wales or Scotland, because of misconduct;

- are disqualified from being company directors under the *Company Directors Disqualification Act 1986*;

- have failed to make payments under county court administration orders; or

- have made compositions (i.e. come to an arrangement) with their creditors and have not been discharged.

35.10   As soon as someone comes within *s 72*, e.g. the day they are convicted of an offence involving dishonesty, they are automatically disqualified from acting as a trustee. It is a criminal offence to act as a charity trustee while disqualified.

Waiver from disqualification

35.11   Under *s 72(4)* of *Charities Act 1993* the Charity Commission can grant a waiver from disqualification, either generally or in relation to a charity or a specific class of charities. For example, waivers may be given to ex-offenders so that they can serve on the boards of charities working with offenders. Anyone convicted of a relevant offence or who becomes bankrupt and who wishes to remain eligible to be a charity trustee may apply to the Commission for a waiver. Under *s 35* of the *Charities Act 2006*, when it comes into force, the Charity Commission must grant an application for a waiver from disqualification from a person who has been disqualified for more than five years, unless it is satisfied that there are special circumstances for not granting a waiver. However, this does not apply to people who have been disqualified from acting as company directors, or who are undischarged bankrupts, or who have failed to pay under a county court administration order.

Disqualification under the Company Directors Disqualification Act 1986

35.12   Under the *Company Directors Disqualification Act 1986* the Court may disqualify people:

- who have been convicted of criminal offences relating to the promotion, formation, management or liquidation of a company;

- who have been persistently in default of company legislation for filing accounts and other documents;

- who have been found guilty of fraudulent trading or fraud; or

- whose conduct as a director has made them unfit to be involved in the management of a company.

DUTIES

35.13   The duties of company directors are not as onerous as the duties of charity trustees. However, the members of the governing body of a charitable company are both company directors and charity trustees. The *Companies Act 2006* (*ss 171 to 177*) sets out the general duties of company directors as follows:

- Duty to act within powers

    — A director must act in accordance with the company's memorandum and articles of association and must only exercise powers for the purposes for which they are conferred.

- Duty to promote the success of the company

    — A director of a company must act in the way that he considers, in good faith, would be most likely to promote the success of the company and must take into account the likely long-term consequences of any decision, the interests of the company's employees, the need to foster business relationships with suppliers, customers and others, the impact of the company's operations on the community and the environment, the desirability of the company maintaining a reputation for high standards of business conduct, and the need to act fairly as between members of the company.

- Duty to exercise independent judgement

    — This duty is not infringed by a director acting in accordance with an agreement duly entered into by the company that restricts the future exercise of discretion by its directors, or in a way authorised by the company's governing document.

- Duty to exercise reasonable care, skill and diligence

    — A director must exercise the care, skill and diligence that would be exercised by a reasonably diligent person with general knowledge, skill and experience that would be reasonably expected of a person carrying out the functions of a company director, and that would be exercised by someone with the director's general knowledge, skill and experience.

- Duty to avoid conflicts of interest

  — A director must avoid a situation in which he has, or can have, a direct or indirect interest that conflicts, or possibly may conflict, with the interests of the company.

- Duty not to accept benefits from third parties

  — A director may not accept a benefit from a third party for being a director or doing anything as a director. A third party is a person other than the company, an associated body corporate or a person acting on behalf of the company or an associated body corporate.

- Duty to declare interest in proposed transaction or arrangement

  — If a director of a company is directly or indirectly interested in a proposed transaction or arrangement with the company, he must declare the nature and extent of that interest to the other directors.

35.14   Breach of these duties exposes the director to action by the company or its members.

DIRECTORS' MEETINGS

35.15   In order to manage the affairs of the company, the directors need to meet as a group. The frequency of these meetings, what they consider, and how they are transacted will depend on the nature of the company's activities and the internal rules set out within the articles of association or in standing orders. In CC3: '*The Essential Trustee: what you need to know*' the Charity Commission reminds trustees that trusteeship requires 'time, understanding and effort'. Trustees must be 'prepared to take an active part in the running of the charity'. They should 'meet regularly if they are to administer their charity properly. How often that needs to be will depend on the size and nature of the charity'.

35.16   Company directors need to hold an annual general meeting in order to transact the formal business of the year in relation to the annual accounts and appointment and remuneration of auditors. When the *Companies Act 2006* comes fully into force there will no longer be a requirement for a private company to hold an annual general meeting, unless the articles of association explicitly require one to be held. The notice period for calling all general meetings will be reduced to 14 days, even if a special resolution is being proposed. Directors should take their responsibilities seriously. It will be appropriate for them to receive regular progress reports, management accounts and be informed of major developments, and they should consider any recommendations arising from the audit and the auditor's management letter.

Trading subsidiaries

35.17 Where a charity operates a trading subsidiary the directors of the trading subsidiary should meet independently of the charity trustees, and transact business in their capacity as that company's directors.

PERSONAL LIABILITIES

35.18 Although an advantage of incorporation is the limitation of liability, directors of companies can still incur personal liabilities, some of which cannot be covered by insurance. The two most clear-cut situations are where a person acts as a director when disqualified, when a director may be held liable for all of the company's debts incurred whilst he was a director (*Company Directors Disqualification Act 1986, s 15*) or when a company, or industrial and provident society, is insolvent. The risks and effect of insolvency are covered in CHAPTER 69. Directors should be alert not only to actual insolvency, but also to situations where they ought to have known that insolvency was inevitable. Companies cannot indemnify their directors against fines imposed in criminal proceedings, or against penalties imposed by regulatory bodies, or the cost of defending criminal proceedings in which a director is convicted, or the cost of civil proceedings brought by the company against a director in which judgement is given against him [*Companies Act 2006, s 234*].

OFFICE HOLDERS

35.19 A company director is an office holder, i.e. the role of the director is defined not by an employment contract, but by virtue of the office itself. Sometimes this distinction is not just academic, for example, if someone is both an office holder and an employee they could be removed from office as a director under the provisions of the *Companies Act 1985*, but may still have a claim against the company under their rights as an employee.

PAYMENT OF DIRECTORS

35.20 Directors of a charitable company cannot be paid, or otherwise benefit from their office, unless the governing document expressly permits this or unless payment has been authorised by the Charity Commission or the courts.

35.21 A director of a subsidiary trading company who is a trustee of the holding charity cannot be paid for acting as a director of the subsidiary company, unless the governing document of the charity specifically provides for this. However, staff of the charity can be paid for acting as directors of the charity's wholly owned trading subsidiary.

35.22 The Charity Commission has stated that wherever trustees act as directors of a trading subsidiary, two points need to be borne in mind:

● the potential for conflict of interest; and

● that the appointment of trustees as directors cannot be used as a method of paying trustees 'by the back door'.

DISCLOSURE

35.23 There is no requirement to list all the names of a charity's directors on its stationery. However, if one director is named, other than within the text or as

35.24   Directors

a signatory, then all directors must be named. Sometimes a charitable company lists the names of its patrons. 'Patron' is not a legally recognised title, but if any patron is also a director then if this person's name is listed it will be necessary to list all the directors' names as well.

35.24   There is a general trend for companies not to disclose directors' names because of the need to reprint stationery every time there is a change of directors. It may be helpful for parties with whom an organisation is dealing to understand the status of the people who make up the charity's board, so this trend is not necessarily a welcome one.

35.25   The names of directors must be set out in the annual report. The SORP requires charities to list the names of all the trustees on the date the report was approved (or at least 50 if there are more than 50 trustees), and also to list the names of all trustees who served during the year. The *Companies Act 2006, s 416* requires companies to list all the names of directors who served during the financial year (even if there are more than 50), but there is no requirement to list the names of directors at the date of signing. As the SORP annual report requirement applies to incorporated charities only subsidiary trading companies can omit to list the names of directors at the date of signing.

35.26   When the *Companies Act 2006* is fully in force directors will no longer be required to enter their private residential address on the register of directors held at Companies House. They will be able to give the address of the company's registered office as their address.

REMOVAL FROM OFFICE

35.27   Directors may cease to hold their office in a number of ways, the most common being resignation or retirement at the end of an agreed term of office. Notice of a director ceasing to hold office should be filed at Companies House. The notice does not need to be signed by the director resigning, but needs to be signed by another director or by the company secretary.

35.28   Occasionally a director may cease to hold office for more dramatic reasons, for example, as a result of being removed by the Charity Commission, or through failure to comply with the terms of appointment. Often the governing document will set out certain qualifications upon which a director holds office. The most common are some sort of role definition (a member of the local authority) or attendance at a predetermined number of meetings. This latter route has even been used by private companies as an attempt to force out directors, by calling meetings at short notice in extremely difficult to reach locations. Where a director is also a member of the company, ceasing to hold office as a director has no effect on that person's entitlement or rights as a member.

35.29   Directors of charitable companies may be removed by resolution of the members in a general meeting, as long as 14 days' notice of the resolution is provided [*Companies Act 2006, s 168*]. The director has a right to defend himself or herself in writing or at the meeting. [*Companies Act 2006, s 169*].

36   Disability Discrimination

36.1   The *Disability Discrimination Act 2005* makes substantial amendments to the *Disability Discrimination Act 1995* which introduced measures aimed at ending the discrimination faced by many of the 10 million disabled people in Great Britain and gave disabled people new rights in the areas of:

- employment;
- access to goods, facilities and services;
- the management, buying, or renting of land or property;
- educational services.

36.2   The *Disability Discrimination Act 2005* builds on amendments made to the *Disability Discrimination Act 1995* by other legislation passed since the 1995 Act came into force. The *Disability Discrimination Act 2005* requires public bodies to promote equality of opportunity for disabled people. It also introduces new provisions for disabled persons' parking badges and improvements to let dwelling houses, prohibits discrimination against disabled people by general qualifications bodies, and allows the government to set minimum standards so that disabled people can use public transport easily. Most of the *Disability Discrimination Act 2005* applies to Great Britain, but it does not apply to Northern Ireland, as disability discrimination and transport are transferred matters under the *Northern Ireland Act 1998*. The Act applies to all employers (small employers are not exempt) and everyone who provides a service to the public, except the Armed Forces.

36.3   *Section 1* of the *Disability Discrimination Act 1995* defines a person as having a disability for the purposes of the Act where he has a physical or mental impairment which has a substantial and long-term adverse affect on his ability to carry out normal day-to-day activities.

Physical and mental impairments

36.4   Examples of physical impairment include blindness, deafness, heart disease, arthritis, diabetes, progressive neurological conditions, mobility problems, chronic fatigue syndrome. and 'hidden' disabilities such as dyslexia and epilepsy, depending upon the severity of the impairment. Some severe disfigurements are classed as a disability. *Section 18* of the *Disability Discrimination Act 2005* deems people diagnosed with HIV, cancer or MS to be disabled before they experience a substantial adverse affect on their ability to carry out normal day to day activities. The Secretary of State can make regulations excluding certain cancers which do not require substantial treatment from this provision.

36.5   Mental impairments include mental illnesses and conditions usually referred to as 'learning disabilities'. *Section 18* of the *Disability Discrimination Act 2005* removes the requirement in the *Disability Discrimination Act 1995* that a mental illness must be 'clinically well-recognised' before it can amount to a mental impairment. A person with a mental illness will still, however, need to demonstrate that they have an impairment that has a substantial and long-term adverse affect on their ability to carry out normal day-to-day activities.

36.6   The regulations exclude some conditions, for example addiction to alcohol, drugs, nicotine, or any other substance not medically prescribed (but damage to health caused by the addiction may be covered), seasonal conditions such as hay fever if it doesn't aggravate the effects of an existing condition, certain personality disorders, such as exhibitionism and voyeurism, the physical or sexual abuse of others, a tendency to steal or to set fires, and tattoos and body piercing.

Long term

36.7   'Long term' means:

- that the disability has lasted for at least 12 months; or

- that the disability is expected to last for at least 12 months; or

- that in the case of a person expected to live for less than 12 months, the disability is likely to last for the rest of their life.

Normal day-to-day activities

36.8   'Normal day-to-day activities' means the activities that most people carry out on a regular basis. An impairment will be treated as affecting a person's ability to carry out normal day-to-day activities if it affects at least one of the following:

- mobility;

- manual dexterity, e.g. ability to use hands for writing or cooking;

- physical co-ordination;

- continence;

- the ability to lift, carry or move ordinary objects;

- speech, hearing or eyesight;

- memory, or the ability to concentrate, learn or understand;

- understanding the risk of physical danger.

It is not the individual's activities at work that are relevant, but their activities in everyday life.

Substantial

36.9   In deciding whether or not an impairment has a substantial affect on normal day- to-day activities, the Act says that any treatment or correction should not be taken into account, including medical treatment or the use of a prosthesis or other aid (for example, a hearing aid). The only things which are taken into account are glasses or contact lenses. For example, if, as a result of a hearing impairment, a person experiences difficulty hearing someone talking at a sound level which is normal for everyday conversations in a moderately noisy place, it would be reasonable to regard this as having a substantial adverse effect. Being unable to hold a conversation in a very noisy place such as a factory floor would not. If an impairment affects a person's mobility, being unable to travel a short journey as a passenger in a vehicle would reasonably be regarded as having a substantial adverse effect. So would only being able to walk slowly or with unsteady or jerky movements. But experiencing some minor discomfort as a result of walking without help for about 1.5 kilometres or a mile would not. Although a minor impairment may not, on its own, count as 'substantial', if a person has a number of minor impairments they may be held to have a substantial effect.

36.10   The 1995 Act contains some special provisions, for example:

- If an impairment has substantially affected a person's ability to carry out normal day-to-day activities, but does not any more, it will still be counted as having that effect if it is likely to do so again;

- If someone has a progressive condition, and it will substantially affect their ability to carry out normal day-to-day activities in the future, they will be regarded as having an impairment which has a substantial adverse affect from the moment the condition has some effect on their ability to carry out normal day-to-day activities;

- If someone is registered as blind or partially sighted or certified as blind or partially sighted by a consultant ophthalmologist, they will automatically be considered to be disabled;

- People who have had a disability in the past but who are no longer disabled are covered by certain parts of the Act.

Employment

36.11   The *Disability Discrimination Act 1995* abolished the registration scheme that was created under the *Disabled Persons (Employment) Act 1944*, but anyone who was registered as a disabled person under that Act continues to qualify as a disabled person, irrespective of whether or not they meet the definition of disabled in *s 1* of the 1995 Act, as amended by the 2005 Act.

36.12   Since October 2004 it has been against the law for an employer of any size to discriminate against a disabled person because of their disability:

- in the recruitment process;

- in their terms and conditions of employment;

- in chances for promotion, transfer, training or other benefits;

- by dismissing them unfairly

unless the discrimination can be justified.

36.13   In relation to employment, discrimination is justifiable if the reason for it is both material and substantial. For example, a charity leasing offices on the third floor of an old building without a lift would not be expected to install a lift in order to employ someone who used a wheelchair (although the charity would be expected to have looked into the feasibility and cost of making alterations even if it later decided that they were unreasonable), but it would be expected to provide a braille keyboard if a potential employee needed one. In a case that has come before a tribunal (*Tarling v Wisdom Toothbrushes Ltd*) the tribunal held that an employee had been dismissed because of a disability and that it was not reasonable for the employer to ignore advice to buy a special chair costing about £1,000 (but which would have cost the employer £200 to buy given the assistance available) that would have enabled the employee to perform her duties satisfactorily.

36.14 Disability Discrimination

36.14   The *Disability Discrimination Acts* outlaw the following kinds of discrimination for all employers:

- direct discrimination;
- failure to comply with the duty to make reasonable adjustments;
- treating a disabled person less favourably;
- subjecting a disabled person to harassment;
- victimisation of a disabled person.

36.15   The *Disability Discrimination Act* 1995 says that an employer's treatment of a disabled person amounts to direct discrimination if:

- the treatment is on the grounds of his/her disability; and
- the treatment is less favourable than the way in which a person not having that particular disability is (or would be) treated.

36.16   Employers have a duty to make reasonable adjustments for disabled job applicants or staff when a policy or practice, or a physical feature of their premises, places the disabled person at a substantial disadvantage compared with someone who is not disabled. Examples of reasonable adjustments are:

- making adjustments to premises e.g. widening a doorway, providing a ramp, moving furniture to allow wheelchair access, relocating light switches, door handles or shelves;
- altering the person's working hours or allowing flexible working;
- allowing absences during working hours for medical treatment;
- giving additional training;
- acquiring special equipment or modifying existing equipment;
- changing instructions or reference manuals;
- providing additional supervision and/or support;
- allocating some duties to another person.

36.17   The law lists the following factors that may have a bearing on whether or not it will be reasonable for an employer to have to make a particular adjustment:

- how effective the adjustment is in preventing the disadvantage;
- how practical it is;
- the financial and other costs and the extent of any disruption;
- the extent of the employer's financial or other resources;
- the availability to the employer of financial or other help to make the adjustment;
- the size and type of business.

36.18   The law says that an employer's treatment of a disabled person amounts to less favourable treatment if the treatment is for a reason related to their disability and the treatment is less favourable than the way others would be treated. For example, if an employer provides staff with training on a new process in the charity, but does not offer that training to a disabled staff member, they will be treating the disabled employee less favourably.

36.19   A disabled person is subjected to harassment when, for a reason which relates to the person's disability, another person engages in unwanted conduct which may violate the disabled person's dignity or creates an intimidating, hostile, degrading, humiliating or offensive environment for that disabled person.

36.20   It is unlawful for an employer to victimise someone because they have started or taken part in legal proceedings under the *Disability Discrimination Act* or have alleged in good faith that someone else could be in breach of the Act.

36.21   The *Disability Discrimination Act 2005* makes it unlawful for employers, and third parties such as newspapers, to publish, or cause to be published, discriminatory advertisements inviting applications for a job, training or other relevant benefit.

ACCESS TO WORK

36.22   Access to Work is a government scheme operated by local job centres. It provides practical advice and support to disabled people and their employers to help overcome work related obstacles. It can pay a grant towards certain extra employment costs resulting from disability, such as:

- fares to work if transport is difficult;

- a communicator at a job interview for someone with a hearing impairment;

- a support worker, such as a reader if someone has a visual impairment;

- specialist equipment, such as voice activated software;

- adaptations to premises, such as installing an accessible toilet.

36.23   It is important to remember that rights disabled people have through the *Disability Discrimination Acts* are in addition to any other statutory or contractual employment rights that they may have.

Goods and services

36.24   Under the *Disability Discrimination Acts*, it is unlawful for providers of goods and services, whether charged for or free, to treat disabled people less favourably than other people for a reason related to their disability. Since 2004 service providers have had to make 'reasonable adjustments' to the way they deliver their services so that disabled people can use them.

36.25   Examples of reasonable adjustments include:

- installing an induction loop for people who are hearing impaired;

- giving the option to book tickets by email as well as by phone;

- providing disability awareness training for staff who have contact with the public;

- providing larger, well-defined signage for people with impaired vision;

- installing a ramp at the entrance to a building.

36.26 Disability Discrimination

36.26 What is considered a 'reasonable adjustment' for a large organisation like a supermarket may be different to a reasonable adjustment for a small charity shop. What is practical in the service provider's individual situation and what resources the charity may have will be taken into account. Charities will not be required to make changes which are impractical or beyond their means. Failure or refusal to provide a service to a disabled person that is offered to other people is discrimination unless it can be justified.

36.27 In relation to the provision of goods and services discrimination is justifiable if providing an inferior service to the disabled person is necessary in order for the service provider to be able to provide the service to the disabled person, or other members of the public. Similarly the service provider can justify not providing a service to a disabled person if they would otherwise be unable to provide the service at all. A service provider is justified in refusing to enter into a contract with a disabled person if that person is unable to understand the nature of the agreement or to give informed consent. The Act does not require service providers to do anything that would endanger the health and safety of any person, including the disabled person in question, or anything that would fundamentally alter the nature of the service, professional or business.

Land or property

36.28 A disabled person's right to be protected against discrimination in relation to managing, buying, or renting land or property is in addition to their other rights, for example, as a tenant. It is unlawful for landlords and other persons connected with the selling, letting and managing of premises to treat disabled people less favourably for a reason related to their disability, unless they can show that the treatment is justified. Discrimination includes:

- refusing to sell or let a property or offering a property for sale or rent on worse terms to a disabled person;

- treating a disabled person less favourably on a housing waiting list or register;

- unreasonably preventing a tenant from using benefits/facilities or not allowing them to use these facilities in the same way as a landlord would allow other tenants to do;

- evicting a disabled tenant for a reason connected with their disability or harassing them for that reason.

36.29 The *Disability Discrimination Act 2005* makes it unlawful for landlords and managers letting property to discriminate against a disabled tenant or prospective tenant by failing, without justification, to comply with a duty to provide a reasonable adjustment for the disabled person. The new provisions would require a landlord or manager to take reasonable steps to change a policy, practice or procedure that makes it impossible, or unreasonably difficult, for a disabled person to take a letting of the premises, or, where there is a letting already in existence, that make it impossible or difficult for a disabled tenant, or other disabled person lawfully occupying the premises, to enjoy the premises or use a benefit or facility conferred with the lease. For example, a landlord or manager may be obliged, where it was reasonable to do so:

- to allow a tenant who has mobility difficulties to leave his rubbish in another place if he cannot access the designated place;

- to allow an occupier who uses a wheelchair to use an existing accessible entrance at the back of a block of flats even though other tenants cannot use it.

36.30   The provisions would also require a landlord or manager to take reasonable steps to provide an auxiliary aid, such as a clip on receiver that vibrates when the door bell rings for a hearing impaired tenant, or service where that would either:

- enable or facilitate a disabled person's enjoyment of the premises or use of any benefit or facility, such as a communal laundry room, conferred with the letting; or

- (as the case may be) enable or make it easier for a disabled person to take on the tenancy.

36.31   The landlord or manager is not required by the Acts to alter the physical features of the premises, such as widening doorways. However, they may be required to waive terms in a lease that prohibit a tenant from making alterations to the premises without the landlord's consent. The tenant would have to pay for the alterations, agree to reasonable conditions such as reinstatement, and show that the alterations they wished to carry out were necessary because of their disability.

36.32   Landlords who are renting out accommodation in their own homes are not covered by the requirements of the *Disability Discrimination Acts.*

Educational services

36.33   From September 2002 the *Disability Discrimination Act 1995* was extended to education following amendments introduced by the *Special Educational Needs and Disability Act 2001*. The changes make it unlawful for any school or provider of further education, higher education, adult and community education, in England, Wales and Scotland, to discriminate against disabled pupils (both current pupils and prospective pupils). The *Disability Discrimination Act 2005* took things further, giving most public authorities a positive duty to promote disability equality.

Schools

36.34   The *Disability Discrimination Act 2005* applies to all schools in England, Wales and Scotland, including independent schools and pupil referral units. The requirements of the Act are in addition to the duties schools have under the Special Educational Needs Framework and new planning duties that require local education authorities to develop plans to make schools accessible to disabled pupils.

36.35   A school might discriminate against a disabled pupil in two ways:

- **Less favourable treatment**. If a school treats a disabled pupil, or prospective pupil less favourably than another because of their disability, this will be unlawful discrimination unless the school can justify it. For example, a school might tell a parent who wants their daughter with

171

epilepsy to go to a primary school that the school cannot take her unless she stops having fits. This is likely to count as less favourable treatment for a reason related to the child's disability. If the school cannot justify it, it will amount to discrimination;

- **Failing to make a reasonable adjustment**. This can count as discrimination if it places disabled pupils and prospective pupils at a substantial disadvantage compared to non-disabled pupils. For example, a deaf pupil who lip-reads is at a disadvantage if teachers continue to speak while facing away to write on a whiteboard.

36.36   It is unlawful for schools to discriminate in the following ways, unless they can justify the less favourable treatment:

- **Admissions**. Schools must not discriminate against a disabled person in the way they decide who can get into the school, including any rules they use when a school is over-subscribed, in their terms for offering a place at the school, or by refusing an application from a disabled person for admission to the school;

- **Education and associated services**. This includes discrimination against disabled pupils in all aspects of school life such as education, school trips and other extra-curricular activities;

- **Exclusions**. It is unlawful to discriminate against a disabled pupil by excluding them because of their disability. This applies to both permanent and fixed-term exclusions.

36.37   In some cases, a school can treat a disabled pupil 'less favourably' if it can justify this. Its justification must be substantial and relevant to the particular circumstances. A school can justify less favourable treatment if it is because of a permitted form of selection. For example, a child with learning difficulties applies to a school that selects its intake on the basis of academic ability and fails the school's entrance exam. Even though the reason for her performance in the exam was a reason related to her disability, because the school has used objective rules, the less favourable treatment (that she is not offered a place at the school) is likely to be justified.

36.38   If a school does not make reasonable adjustments to avoid putting disabled pupils at a substantial disadvantage, it can justify this if it has a substantial reason which is relevant to the particular circumstances. The Act does not say what 'reasonable' means. It will depend on the circumstances of the particular case and will be decided by the tribunal or appeals panel. However, in deciding what is 'reasonable', a school can take account of:

- its need to maintain academic and other standards;

- its financial position and any grants that may be available;

- the practicalities of making the particular adjustment;

- the health and safety of the disabled pupil and others;

- the interests of other pupils.

36.39   Similarly the Act does not define what a 'substantial disadvantage' is. It will depend on the circumstances of the particular case, and a tribunal or appeals panel would decide what it means. However, in deciding what a substantial disadvantage is, a school can take account of:

- the time and effort it would take the disabled child if the school does not take certain steps to help the child, and how much of a disadvantage this would be to the child;

- the amount of inconvenience, indignity or discomfort a disabled child might suffer;

- the disabled child's possible loss of opportunity or lack of progress compared to other non-disabled children.

36.40   Schools do not need to provide aids or adaptations for disabled children under the Act. They may, however, be under a duty to provide such aids to children under the Special Educational Needs Framework. This might include services such as information available in braille or on audio tape, or personal assistance.

36.41   All local education authorities in England, Wales and Scotland must have accessibility plans to make their schools more accessible to disabled pupils. Maintained schools, independent schools, and non-maintained special schools must produce their own accessibility plans. The plans must be in writing and publicly available. The Department of Education and Science has produced guidance for schools in England and Wales on their planning duties under the Act. This is called 'Accessible schools: planning to increase access to school for disabled pupils', number LEA/0168/2002 available from DfES Publications on 0845 6022260 (available in Braille, large print and audio tape), or from the DfES website at *www.dfes.gov.uk/sen*.

Further and higher education

36.42   All of the information provided under the heading 'Schools' also applies to further and higher education establishments in England, Wales and Scotland. The Commission for Equality and Human Rights has detailed guidance on how further and higher educational establishments should put these changes into effect.

General qualifications bodies

36.43   The *Disability Discrimination Act 2005* prohibits general qualifications bodies from discriminating against disabled people on the grounds of their disability when awarding professional or trade qualifications. General qualifications bodies are required to make reasonable adjustments, such as ensuring that examinations halls are accessible for wheelchair users and that there are disabled toilet facilities.

Public transport

36.44   The *Disability Discrimination Act 1995* gave the government powers to make regulations about the design of and access to newly built public transport vehicles, taxis and services. Public transport termini are covered by this Act so, for example, a deaf person could complain about the lack of minicom or other accessible information at a train station. The *Disability Discrimination Act 2005* introduced provisions requiring rail vehicle accessibility compliance certificates for prescribed rail vehicles.

36.45   Disability Discrimination

Websites

36.45   As a matter of good practice, charities should ensure that their websites can be accessed by people with disabilities. Guidance for those responsible for commissioning or maintaining public-facing websites and web-based services can be found in 'A guide to good practice in commissioning accessible websites' (published in March 2006) which was developed by the British Standards Institution (BSI) and sponsored by the Disability Rights Commission.

COMMISSION FOR EQUALITY AND HUMAN RIGHTS

36.46   In October 2007 the Commission for Equality and Human Rights (CEHR), which was established by the *Equality Act 2006*, took over the responsibilities of the Disability Rights Commission (DRC), the Commission for Racial Equality, and the Equal Opportunities Commission. The CEHR took on all of the powers of the Commissions, which were dissolved under the *Equality Act 2006*, as well as new powers to enforce legislation more effectively and promote equality for all. The CEHR will champion the diverse communities that make up modern Britain in their struggle against discrimination. Its role is to reduce inequality, eliminate all forms of illegal discrimination, strengthen good relations between people and protect human rights. It will promote awareness and understanding of human rights and encourage good practice by public authorities in meeting their *Human Rights Act 1998* obligations. The Commission will cover England, Scotland and Wales. In Scotland and Wales there will be statutory committees responsible for the work of the CEHR.

36.47   In order to carry out its duties, the Commission has a number of specific functions:

● Assisting disabled people to secure their rights, and arranging for legal advice and help where appropriate;

● Providing information and advice to disabled people and to employers and service providers about their rights and duties under the Disability Discrimination Acts;

● Preparing and reviewing statutory codes of practice, which provide practical guidance to employers and service providers on meeting their obligations under the Disability Discrimination Acts and on good practice;

● Providing an independent conciliation service in the event of disputes between disabled people and service providers over access to goods and services, and monitoring the performance of the conciliation service;

● Undertaking formal investigations into how disabled people are treated in a particular organisation or sector, and into unlawful acts by particular organisations;

● Carrying out research to inform discussion and policy-making and to ascertain how well the law affecting the rights of disabled people is working.

36.48   The Commission is as much concerned with educating public opinion and promoting good practice as it is with enforcement. Wherever possible, the Commission aims to work in partnership with employers and service providers, adopting a non-confrontational approach. As well as its advisory and educative role, the Commission has enforcement powers to enable it to fulfil its task of securing civil rights for disabled people. These powers include:

Power to conduct formal investigations

- The Commission may decide to conduct a formal investigation for any purpose connected with the performance of its duties;

- The Commission has power to require any person to give written or oral information for the purposes of a formal investigation.

Power to serve non-discrimination notices

- If through a formal investigation the Commission is satisfied that a person has committed or is committing an unlawful act, it may serve him or her with a non-discrimination notice;

- A non-discrimination notice gives details of the unlawful act and requires him or her not to commit any further unlawful acts of the same kind;

- The notice may also require the person to produce an action plan to ensure compliance with the law. If the Commission considers that an action plan is inadequate it may apply to a county court (or in Scotland to the sheriff) for an order.

Power to enter into an agreement

- As an alternative to taking enforcement action against a person whom it believes has committed an unlawful act, the Commission may enter into a written agreement with them;

- Under such an agreement, the person concerned agrees not to commit any further unlawful acts of the same kind (and to take any other action as may be specified in the agreement), while the Commission agrees not to take any relevant enforcement action;

- If, however, the other party to an agreement fails to comply with their undertakings, the Commission may apply to a county court (or in Scotland to the sheriff) for an order.

Power to act over persistent discrimination

- If a person has been served with a non-discrimination notice or has been found to have committed an act of unlawful discrimination, and is, in the view of the Commission, likely to commit further such acts, it can apply to the county court for an injunction (or in Scotland to the sheriff for an interdict).

Power to provide assistance

- The Commission may grant assistance to an individual who is bringing proceedings in connection with unlawful discrimination. This is a matter for the discretion of the Commission, which will take into account whether the case raises a matter of principle, and whether it is unreasonable to expect the applicant to deal with the case unaided;

- If given, assistance may take the form of legal advice and/or representation, efforts to settle the dispute, or any other assistance which the Commission thinks appropriate.

175

36.49   Disability Discrimination

Power to issue Codes of Practice

- The Commission may prepare and issue Codes of Practice, giving practical guidance to employers, service providers and others concerned with promoting equal opportunities for disabled people and encouraging good practice. Such Codes of Practice must be approved by the Secretary of State and laid before Parliament;

- Failure to observe any provision of a Code of Practice does not make a person liable to proceedings, but a court or tribunal must take into account any provision of a Code that it considers relevant to any proceedings.

Power for conciliation of disputes

- Although no member or employee of the Commission may provide conciliation services in relation to disputes arising under *Part III* of the *Disability Discrimination Act 1995* concerning access to goods and services, the Commission may make arrangements for the provision of conciliation services by another person or persons.

MAKING A COMPLAINT

36.49   A person with a disability who believes that they have been discriminated against can seek advice from the CEHR. If they wish to pursue a claim that they have been unlawfully treated by an employer or potential employer they must bring their complaint to an Employment Tribunal. The complaint must usually be made within three months of the alleged discrimination. A person who believes that a service provider has discriminated against him or her may bring civil proceedings in the County Court (Sheriff's Court in Scotland). Court action must be brought within six months of the alleged discrimination. Industrial tribunals and courts can award compensation for financial loss and for injury to feelings.

GOOD PRACTICE

36.50   Charity trustees and senior managers should ensure that their charity has a policy to ensure inclusion of disabled people and the policy should be communicated to all staff. Staff dealing with employment matters, or the provision of goods, services or facilities or educational services, or the management, buying or renting of land or property, may need to be given additional training so that they are fully aware of the charity's policy, its legal obligations and the duty to make reasonable adjustments.

36.51   The implementation and effectiveness of the charity's policy should be regularly monitored and reviewed. Any acts of discrimination committed by staff or volunteers should be addressed through the charity's disciplinary rules and procedures.

36.52   From time to time charities should consult people with disabilities to ensure that they are meeting their needs. They should establish a feedback and complaints procedure that is easy for people with disabilities to use.

36.53   In some instances long-term sickness could be classified as a disability so it is important that charities have good sickness and absence management policies, and take legal advice if considering dismissing someone on grounds connected to sickness or disability.

36.54   Charities should take steps to ensure that they are complying with the *Disability Discrimination Acts* and are not at risk of claims for discrimination. Successful claims can damage a charity's reputation and even if legal actions are successfully defended, they are costly in staff time and money.

POSITIVE DISCRIMINATION

36.55   Positive discrimination, which generally means employing someone because they come from a deprived group rather than because they are the best candidate, is generally unlawful. However, charities set up to help people with certain kinds of disabilities are permitted to discriminate in their favour and similarly charities providing supported employment may treat one group of severely disabled people more favourably than other people.

36.56   Charities can also take positive action, that is measures designed to counteract the effects of past discrimination and to help abolish stereotyping, to encourage disabled people to take advantage of opportunities for work and training, when under-representation of disabled people has been identified in the previous year. Positive action may include measures such as the introduction of non-discriminatory selection procedures and training programmes. For example, if disabled people are under-represented in its workforce, a charity could include a statement in job advertisements to the effect that 'applications from disabled people are particularly welcomed as disabled people are currently under-represented in our workforce'. Similarly, disabled employees should be encouraged to apply for promotion or transfer opportunities.

36.57   Although it is legal to take positive action to encourage disabled people to apply for jobs or promotion, selection must be based solely on merit. Appointing a less competent candidate because they had a disability would be unlawful.

FURTHER INFORMATION

36.58   Commission for Equality and Human Rights
Kingsgate House
66–74 Victoria Street
London
SW1E 6SW
Tel: 020 7215 8415
Email: news@cehr.org.uk

Equality Online
www.equality-online.org.uk

Directgov
www.direct.gov.uk/en/DisabledPeople

RNIB
105 Judd Street
London
WC1H 9NE
Tel: 020 7388 1266
Email: DDAEnquiries@rnib.org.uk
www.rnib.org.uk

RNID
19–23 Featherstone Street
London
EC1Y 8SL
Tel: 0808 808 0123
Textphone: 0808 808 9000
Email: informationline@rnid.org.uk
www.rnid.org.uk

37   Disaster Appeals

37.1   When a disaster happens there is usually an immediate public response, often before any formal appeal has been launched. This was certainly the case in 1997 following the death of Diana, Princess of Wales. In some instances, such as the Ethiopian Famine, the money raised was not sufficient to meet the needs of all the potential beneficiaries, despite the public's generosity. However, in others too much money is raised and those affected may end up being accused of profiteering from their tragedy. This can happen when the horror of a disaster attracts widespread media coverage and a generous public response, but the need for financial assistance is not great, as only a small number of breadwinners have been lost or those killed were children.

37.2   The Attorney-General has drawn up guidelines, which are issued in the Charity Commission's series of leaflets (CC40 'Disaster Appeals: Attorney-General's Guidelines'), to remove doubts about the precise status of such appeals, to reassure the public that their money will go to the purpose they intended and to ensure that appeals are set up in the most appropriate manner, taking advantage of any tax concessions that might be applicable. These guidelines are merely advisory in Scotland.

37.3   Whenever there is a disaster the Charity Commission will respond with urgency to requests for advice and if a charitable appeal is to be launched they will speed up the normal registration procedures. For example, the World Trade Centre Disaster Fund was set up within three days of 9/11. The Red Cross also operates a disaster appeal scheme with a 24-hour helpline (0800 777100) to assist with the setting up of disaster appeals.

CHARITABLE OR NON-CHARITABLE APPEAL

37.4   One of the first decisions that has to be made is whether the appeal should be charitable or not. The Charity Commission advises that particular care is taken over an appeal to help the victims of a disaster (or their families) where the beneficiaries may be a relatively small number of people. Disaster appeals are not always charitable. A charity cannot be created if it is intended that specific people will have the right to assistance whether or not they are in actual need, or that the benefits are only for particular private individuals. Where a charitable disaster appeal fund is set up, people will only be allowed to benefit on the basis of their proven need.

37.5   The main advantage of a disaster appeal being charitable is that donations can attract tax relief, especially through the Gift Aid scheme. This acts as an incentive to donors and makes the value of donations to the appeal greater. The main disadvantages are that:

- individual beneficiaries cannot be named;

- the amount that can be given to any one affected individual is limited to that appropriate to their needs, with the surplus going to other appropriate charitable purposes; and

- charitable trusts in England and Wales are subject to the regulatory requirements of the Charity Commission.

37.6   Setting up a non-charitable trust has the following advantages:

- the money raised can be for a named individual or individuals;

- no limit is imposed on the amount that can be given to any one affected individual, unless one has been imposed by the terms of the appeal;

- the Charity Commission cannot regulate the trust. Only the Court acting on behalf of the beneficiaries will have control over the trust.

However, a non-charitable trust has the disadvantage of not attracting any tax reliefs or concessions.

WORDING

37.7   If the appeal is to be charitable it must be worded in a way that does not jeopardise an application for charitable status. Even if the appeal is to be non-charitable, care must be taken with the terms so that the public is clear about who will benefit, whether or not their benefit is at the discretion of the trustees, and whether or not all the money raised will go to the beneficiaries and, if not, what will happen to any surplus.

37.8   Where an appeal is for a specific purpose and more money is raised than is needed for that purpose the surplus will belong to the donors. The organisers would then be left with the expensive and arguably pointless exercise of trying to return it to them. For this reason organisers are advised to state what will happen to the surplus if the appeal is over-subscribed or at least state that any surplus will be applied for charitable purposes at the trustees' discretion.

37.9   If a gift is sent before the publication of an appeal the trust will have to write to the donor asking for their permission to add the gift to the appeal fund. Where too many gifts are received to make this practicable, the published appeal should state that all donations already received will be added to the appeal fund unless the donors notify the organisers within, say, ten days, or by a specific date, that this is not their wish.

37.10   The Charity Commission leaflet CC40 'Disaster Appeals: Attorney-General's Guidelines' contains suggested wording for charitable and non-charitable appeals.

APPEALS FOR INDIVIDUALS

37.11   Publicity surrounding an individual, such as the disappearance of Madeleine McCann, can result in the public responding with gifts of money. If launching an appeal for an individual it is important to state clearly whether or not the appeal is for a charitable fund. Again the appeal should make clear to the public whether their gift will go to benefit the individual, or for a charitable purpose including helping the individual insofar as that is charitable.

37.12   It is hard to gauge in advance what the response to an appeal will be. In case more is raised than is appropriate for the needs of the individual, all appeals should make clear what will happen to any surplus. If an appeal is non-charitable it is still possible to specify that any surplus will be given to a charity.

TAX

37.13   HMRC's leaflet 'Appeal Fund Guidance' sets out the tax implications for funds set up in response to an appeal and gives information about tax and

VAT issues for funds set up as trusts. It also explains the tax treatment of people who benefit from a trust. It can be downloaded from *www.hmrc.gov.uk/afg/index.htm.*

38 Dissolution

38.1 There are a number of reasons for a charity ceasing to exist including:

- the achievement of its charitable objects;
- insolvency;
- an inability to raise supporters;
- an inability to raise funds;
- the objects are out of date; and
- the service provided is no longer required.

DISPOSAL OF REMAINING ASSETS

38.2 Most charities have a clause in their governing document enabling them to be wound up and stating what should be done with any remaining assets once all the charity's financial obligations have been met. Commonly such clauses state that the surplus should be given to a charity with similar charitable objects, but sometimes a specific charity is named or the trustees are given complete discretion to exercise in this event. At the time of writing there is confusion over the implications of general dissolution clauses for cross-border charities, and legal advice is needed for individual circumstances.

PROCESS OF CLOSING DOWN

38.3 The process of dissolution, the ending or closing down of an organisation, will depend on whether it is solvent or insolvent and its legal status, i.e. whether it is incorporated or unincorporated.

Insolvent charities

38.4 Incorporated organisations that are insolvent will go into insolvent liquidation. This is a process governed by the *Insolvency Act 1986* in which any remaining assets are disposed of and outstanding liabilities are met insofar as they can be. If an unincorporated organisation becomes insolvent it does not have to go through the formal process of liquidation, as the trustees will be personally liable to meet any financial obligations still outstanding when all the charity's assets have been realised and used to pay outstanding debts. The trustees of unincorporated charities should take all possible steps to reduce their liabilities, such as giving precautionary notice of redundancy to staff, once they suspect that the charity may become insolvent.

Solvent charities

38.5 If a solvent incorporated organisation wishes to wind up it may go through a formal liquidation which is also governed by the *Insolvency Act 1986*. However, a solvent charity is more likely simply to distribute its assets and then apply to be removed from the register of charities. If it is a limited company then it should first go through the striking off procedures at Companies House. Avoiding a formal liquidation is more straightforward and will save on professional fees, but should only be undertaken where the trustees are clear on their financial position and can identify all the interested parties. Companies House provides the following guidance in respect of private companies, which also includes charitable companies.

A private company that is not trading may apply to the Companies Registrar to be struck off the register. It can do this if the company is no longer needed.

The procedure is not an alternative to formal insolvency proceedings where these are appropriate, as creditors are likely to prevent the striking off. Even if the company is struck off and dissolved, creditors and others could apply for it to be restored to the register.

38.6   A private company can apply to be struck off if, *in the previous three months*, it has not:

- traded or otherwise carried on business;

- changed its name;

- for value, disposed of property or rights that, immediately before it ceased to be in business or trade, it held for disposal or gain in the normal course of its business or trade (for example, a company in business to sell apples could not continue selling apples during that three-month period but it could sell the truck it once used to deliver the apples or the warehouse where they were stored);

- engaged in any other activity except one necessary or expedient for making a striking-off application, settling the company's affairs or meeting a statutory requirement (for example, a company may seek professional advice on the application, pay the costs of copying the Form 652a, etc). However, a company can apply for striking off if it has settled trading or business debts in the previous three months.

38.7   A company cannot apply to be struck off if it is the subject, or proposed subject, of:

- any insolvency proceedings (such as liquidation, including where a petition has been presented but has not yet been dealt with); or

- a *s 425* scheme (that is a compromise or arrangement between a company and its creditors or members.

38.8   A solvent Industrial and Provident Society may be wound up by an instrument of dissolution signed by at least three-quarters of its members. An application to terminate a society's registration by instrument of dissolution may be made if:

- the society is solvent and has assets available for distribution;

- three-quarters of the members of the society sign the instrument of dissolution;

- the intended distribution of the remaining assets is in line with the registered rules; and

- the society is up to date in submitting its annual returns. Any outstanding returns must be submitted before an instrument of dissolution can be registered.

38.9   Dissolution

38.9   Solvent unincorporated organisations wind up in accordance with procedures set out in their governing document. If they have permanent endowment unincorporated charities cannot generally be wound up. In this case, trustees should approach the Charity Commission for advice. The Charity Commission may be able to use their powers to amend the terms of the endowment.

38.10   If the governing document of an unincorporated charitable association or a charitable trust does not contain a winding up clause the charity can use all its assets for charitable purposes or give them to another charity or charities to use for purposes within the donor charity's objects. Whatever the governing document says, assets in restricted funds can only be used to discharge liabilities relating to those funds; they cannot be used to pay off general creditors.

Small charities

38.11   The Charity Commission operates a separate regime for small non limited company charities. In this case, 'small' is income under £20,000. This regime essentially represents a more flexible approach to ensuring rigid compliance with the legal requirements where the amounts involved are trivial. This approach is less easy to adopt where there is either permanent endowment or land involved. This approach is a policy, rather than something based strictly in law: trustees should therefore follow the appropriate legal procedures, but the Commission may be less stringent in their response.

38.12   *Section 74* of the *Charities Act 1993* (as amended) enables the trustees of small registered charities to transfer their assets to one or more charities with similar objects by passing a resolution by a two-thirds majority provided that:

- the charity's income from all sources was less than £10,000 in the last financial year;

- the charity does not hold land on trusts which stipulate that the land can be used only for the purposes of the charity;

- the trustees of the recipient charity or charities have indicated that they are willing to accept the assets; and

- the charity is not a body corporate.

Where the charity holds a permanent endowment the resolution must apply also to that property.

Removal from register

38.13   Charitable companies and industrial and provident societies come into existence when they are entered on the register of companies or friendly societies and similarly cease to exist when they are removed from the relevant register. If unincorporated charitable trusts and associations use the powers in their governing documents to dissolve themselves they must inform the Charity Commission if they are registered in England and Wales. [*Charities Act 1993, s 3(7)(b)*]. The Commission will want copies of the final accounts and a certified copy of the resolution to dissolve. The final accounts will need to show closing NIL balances.

38.14   'Time charities' are charities established usually for particular purposes for a limited period of time. They will be subject to specific procedures and trustees should consult with the Charity Commission at the expiry of the time period.

38.15   If a charity's assets include payments under deeds of covenant or GAYE these will need to be formally assigned to another charity and the donors and HMRC notified.

38.16   It should be noted that removal from the register of charities, whether in Scotland or in Engalnd and Wales, does not represent the end of the organisation's life. Removal from the charity register simply confirms the entity is no longer charitable: it is the formal dissolution process that brings an end to the legal entity or trust.

Scotland

38.17   The *Charities and Trustee Investment (Scotland) Act 2005* introduced a requirement for charities to seek consent from OSCR in relation to certain actions a charity may wish to take and also to notify OSCR when certain changes have taken place. These include dissolution and winding up.

39   Dividends

39.1   Charities may receive dividends from the investment of their funds or from a subsidiary, which may have been set up to carry out a trading activity. Dividends from UK companies are received with a tax credit attached. This tax credit can be set against the liability of the recipient to UK tax on the dividend. The gross amount on which tax, if any, is to be paid is the aggregate of the dividend and the tax credit.

39.2   Charities are exempt from UK income tax or corporation tax where the dividend income in question forms part of the income of the charity or if an Act of Parliament, Charter Decree, Deed of Trust or Will is applicable for charitable purposes. The amount is only exempt, however, in so far as it is applied for charitable purposes only. Dividends received by charities from foreign companies are also exempt from income tax and corporation tax, provided that the same conditions apply. In the case of foreign dividends there will usually be an amount of foreign tax paid according to the tax legislation of the country concerned and the provisions of a Double Tax Treaty with the UK. Charities cannot reclaim any foreign tax properly suffered in these circumstances.

39.3   Charities cannot reclaim the UK tax credit on dividends received following changes which took effect from 6 April 1999. Recognising the special position of charities there was a compensation scheme to cushion the impact of the changes. This compensation took the form of a payment to a charity of a percentage of the dividends it received on a sliding scale over five years from 6 April 1999, as shown in Table 8.

39.4   Charities had two years from the end of the tax year in which the dividend was paid to reclaim any compensation due. Therefore the last date upon which a reclaim could have been made was 5/04/2006.

39.5   Charities treated as companies for tax purposes were treated slightly differently. Their time limit was two years from the end of the accounting period in which dividends were paid. For example, if a charitable company received a dividend on 2 April 2004, and their next financial year ended on 30 March 2005, they would have had until 30 March 2007 to claim the compensation.

Table 7   Compensatory payments

Year	%
1999/2000	21
2000/2001	17
2001/2002	13
2002/2003	8
2003/2004	4

40   Donations and Fundraising

INTRODUCTION

40.1   Fundraising is not a charitable activity as defined by law, but is a crucial activity for many organisations in order that they can ensure that they can meet their charitable aims. As the reliance on the voluntary sector to provide services that were traditionally carried out by the state becomes more pronounced, fundraising becomes increasingly important. Fundraised income is important to allow organisations to maintain sustainable levels of funding, particularly those organisations depending principally on project and statutory funding.

40.2   The Charity Commission provides guidance on aspects of fundraising. The Commission's publications CC20 'Charities and FundRaising' and CC20a 'Charities and Fundraising – A Summary' are particularly relevant and can be downloaded from the publications section of the website, *www.charity-commission.gov.uk*.

40.3   Charities depend on a variety of sources for the funding to do their work. The main ones are:

- endowments;

- legacies;

- public donations;

- public appeals;

- grants from trusts, local authorities or The National Lottery;

- contracts with statutory and other bodies;

- fees for services;

- special events, e.g. coffee mornings, jumble sales, concerts, gala balls;

- raffles and lotteries;

- direct mail;

- sponsorship; and

- primary purpose and ancillary trading.

40.4   In addition to these, charities may also obtain funding by recovering income tax paid on donations, from the profits of their trading subsidiaries, and from investment income.

40.5   While the public may regard all the above means of income generation as forms of fundraising, the law draws a distinction between fundraising and trading. Sometimes the distinction is hard to make, but it is important that the charity administrator does so, or seeks advice, because of the charity law and tax implications.

40.6   Donations may have conditions attached to their use (requiring them to be classified as restricted income), but not conditions that create a contractual obligation between the donor and the recipient. The distinction is important when considering their tax treatment, their presentation in the accounts, and in identifying whether or not there is any liability for repayment on non-performance. Donations therefore exclude amounts received under 'service agreements' where those agreements amount to contracts, but include restricted fund income. 'Sponsorship' may be a donation or it may be a contractual trading agreement. The determining factor will be reciprocity, that is, what the sponsor will receive in return for their sponsorship payment.

CASH DONATIONS

40.7   Cash donations are probably the most potentially volatile element of a charity's income stream, especially where the method of collection relies on major events such as flag days which can be affected by factors beyond anyone's control. This volatility should be factored into the planning process and the control system by rigorous interrogation of the premises for predicting this level of income, a budget where the basis for the predicted income figure is clearly understood, and explanations of the final receipts analysed against other known data and comparatives.

40.8   All income received should be subject to a system of internal financial control. Donations are particularly vulnerable to the risk of theft or diversion since they are one-sided transactions: the donation comes in, and nothing comparable to a purchase order or invoice comes into or out of the charity to identify the event. As trustees are responsible for establishing controls, they should therefore pay close attention to donated income. Whilst cash donations are easily fitted into the internal financial control systems, charities should also consider the implications of other types of donations.

DONATED ASSETS

40.9   Traditionally donations are assumed to equate to cash, but in fact charities receive a wide variety of gifted income: assets (gifts in kind), facilities, services, publicity and time. As trustees must always act in the best interests of the charity they should normally accept all donations offered. However, there may be exceptional circumstances when the trustees feel that accepting a donation would be inappropriate, for instance if the source of the donation is an organisation whose aims are directly opposed to the charity's, or where there is a suspicion that the funds are the product of an illegal activity, e.g. money laundering, or where the costs of converting a donated property would exceed the cost of leasing or building a new development.

40.10   Accounting for donated assets will depend on their nature:

- a functional asset, e.g. a minibus to be used by the charity;

- an investment asset, e.g. a valuable picture to be retained for sale in the future;

- goods for resale, e.g. bric-à-brac given to a charity shop;

- goods for distribution, e.g. damaged stock for beneficiaries.

40.11   Assets given for retention by a charity should be shown as income in the period in which they are receivable and taken to the balance sheet. Whatever systems of internal control charities operate should also be applied as far as possible to gifts. In particular, correspondence files should be maintained and any policy on acknowledging gifts adhered to.

40.12 Goods for resale and for distribution are only recognised as income when they are disposed of, either by sale or by distribution. The effect of this, in respect of goods for sale, is that only the sale proceeds are shown in the annual accounts. There will be no stock adjustment. The trustees should not forget that the underlying assets still exist even if a figure representing them does not appear in the accounts. The trustees are still responsible for protecting the assets and insuring them pending disposal.

INTANGIBLES

40.13 The SORP requires intangible assets (e.g. donated facilities, beneficial loans, donated services, some volunteer time) to be valued in the accounts if the charity would have otherwise had to purchase them and the benefit is quantifiable and material. The value to be included should be the cost to the donor. The logic of this disclosure requirement is that the charity reflects the total resource made available to it, and can account for its stewardship of those resources. However, there are problems connected with this accounting and issues for organisations to consider as a result of the new presentation.

40.14 Donated facilities are only recognised when they are used, and so whenever an item of income is recorded, an equal and matching item of expenditure will be required. This therefore has no net effect on any surplus or deficit for the year, and consequently the recording of intangibles tends to be the sort of adjustment which is processed at the year-end, when the audited accounts are being prepared. Sometimes this is the only practicable approach, especially in the case of occasional donations, but where the donated facility is fundamental to the operation of the charity, then the income and expenditure should form part of the budgeting process and the regular management accounting. There are two reasons for this. First, by building the income and expenditure into the budgets, the trustees and staff are fully aware of the total costs of running the operation, and can assess the importance of the intangible income stream. Second, the fewer the changes between the management accounts and the annual accounts, the more confidence the trustees and senior executive staff can have in the financial reporting.

40.15 Trustees should consider the significance of intangible income and ensure that the financial reporting is in line with its significance to the organisation. Often, in larger charities, this income stream is not material and is therefore not reported in the accounts. There is, however, a danger of this policy being self-fulfilling: they are not reported because they are small, and they must be small, because otherwise they would have been reported in the past. Although it is difficult to quantify such intangibles, especially in branch operations, it is not impossible.

ANONYMOUS DONATIONS

40.16 A donor can always request a donation to be anonymous, but generally a charity will want at least one responsible person within the organisation to be able to identify the donor. This is important in order to be able to identify related party transactions, and to ensure that the charity is not a conduit for unlawful activities. Where a donor wants to make a substantial donation completely anonymously, they can do so by using an intermediary charity which can forward the donation in the form of a grant.

40.17   Of course, many charities receive anonymous donations all the time – through things like collecting boxes, collections and raffles. Because of the individual size of these, and the lack of any conditions or tax issues, these do not normally present problems.

40.18   Generally charities cannot recover gift aid on anonymous donations. The exception is where they receive a donation through redirection of a tax recovery when a donor has indicated their desire to benefit the charity on their self-assessment tax form.

COSTS OF RAISING DONATIONS

40.19   There is a cost to attracting donations and this cost will vary depending on the nature of the donation, as well as on the efficiency of the charity and the attractiveness of the ask. For this reason it is difficult to establish useful 'broad brush' benchmarks in fundraising costs. However, both the Institute of Fundraising and the Centre for Interfirm Comparison rank the relative costs of generating voluntary income, from most effective to least effective, under the following headings:

- Legacies;

- Trusts;

- Central fundraising;

- Corporates;

- Committed giving;

- Local fundraising.

REGULATION OF FUNDRAISING

40.20   Every charity fundraising scandal has an impact on the public's willingness to support charities. Regulation is therefore an important way of ensuring that the public is confident that money given to charity will reach its intended destination. When John Major introduced the *Charities Act 1992* he commented that one of the Act's main aims was to open wider the floodgates of giving by ensuring even greater public confidence in charities. *Part II* of the *Charities Act 1992* deals with the control of fundraising, and applies to all registered charities, to exempt and excepted charities and to charitable institutions, i.e. institutions established for charitable, benevolent or philanthropic purposes. An institution established under the laws of another country could qualify as long as its objects were charitable in English law.

40.21   *Sections 58–64* of the Act deal with professional fundraisers in order to protect both charities and the public from unscrupulous fundraisers, and with commercial participators, so that when the public is encouraged to buy a certain product or service on the grounds that the purchase will benefit a charity, they are given access to certain basic information about by how much the charity will actually benefit. *Sections 65–71* deal with public charitable collections.

40.22 The main regulator involved in overseeing charities attracting donations is the Charity Commission in England and Wales, or OSCR in Scotland. Others may get involved depending on the nature of the donation, such as HMRC. In addition other organisations exist to advise and to regulate fundraising in its various aspects. These include:

- The **Institute of Fundraising**, which sets out to be the professional membership body for UK fundraisers, working to promote the highest standards in fundraising practice and management;

- The **Fundraising Standards Board** (FRSB) was launched in 2007, and runs the self-regulation of fundraising scheme in the UK. Charities and organisations that display the scheme's logo are demonstrating that they have signed up to the highest fundraising standards;

- The **Public Fundraising Regulatory Association** (PFRA) regulates the use of face-to-face fundraising by charities and professional fund-raising organisations and works with local authorities to ensure that fundraising sites are used appropriately It enforces a code of practice, which aims to ensure that people's experience of face-to-face fundraising is positive, and uses an accreditation scheme, mystery shopping and feedback from stakeholders and members of the public to monitor members' compliance.

40.23 The *Charities Act 2006* introduced new provisions that require commercial fundraisers collecting on behalf of charities to state how much they will be paid for the appeal and which organisations will benefit. In addition to these provisions, the *Charities Act 2006* also requires that all public collections for charitable purposes in public places obtain a licence from the local authority and the Charity Commission. The new provisions are not due to come into force until 2009.

PROFESSIONAL FUND-RAISERS

40.24 *Section 58* of the *Charities Act 1992* defines professional fundraisers as 'any person who carries on a fundraising business' or 'any other person who for reward solicits money or other property for the benefit of a charitable institution'. At first sight a charity's own subsidiary trading company could be said to come within this definition. However, trading subsidiaries wholly owned by charities are exempted from the regulations.

40.25 The regulations require there to be a written agreement between a professional fundraiser and a charity containing the following:

- the name and address of the parties to the agreement;
- the date on which the agreement was signed by each of those parties;
- the period or duration of the agreement; and
- any terms enabling the agreement to be brought to an end prematurely or altered during the period of the agreement.

40.26 In addition, the agreement must contain the following:

- A statement of the principal objectives for the fundraising and the methods to be used in the pursuit of those objectives;

- If more than one charitable institution is party to the agreement, the proportions in which each charitable institution is respectively to benefit under the agreement;

- Details of the amount and the methods of calculation of expenses and remuneration to be paid to the professional fundraiser under the terms of the agreement.

Exemptions

40.27   As mentioned above, a charity's own trading subsidiary is exempted from the definition of a professional fundraiser and there are also exemptions for:

- charitable institutions;

- companies connected with charitable institutions, e.g. Cards for Christmas, a charitable institution that co-ordinates the sale of Christmas cards for a number of charities;

- low-paid workers, e.g. someone paid a nominal sum of £5 a day, plus expenses, or less than £500 per year, for 'rattling' a collecting tin in the street or organising a fundraising event;

- collectors, e.g. collectors or agents paid by professional fundraisers to solicit funds do not themselves become professional fundraisers;

- celebrities, e.g. well-known people who make an appeal on behalf of a charitable institution on television, radio or in the cinema, even if they receive a fee from the charity or a professional fundraiser.

Using a professional fundraiser

40.28   Employing a professional fundraiser can be the most cost-effective way of raising funds. However, trustees should think carefully before engaging a professional fundraiser, because the public can be hostile to the idea of someone making a profit from fundraising. They need to check whether or not:

- employing a professional fundraiser is essential to achieve their aims;

- all other feasible and less expensive methods of fundraising have been explored; and

- using the charity's own staff or volunteers would be more effective.

40.29   If the services of a professional fundraiser are considered necessary then the charity administrator should:

- look at the guidance available from the Institute of Fundraising;

- prepare a proper form of agreement under the regulations;

- be clear about all the terms in the agreement; and

- look at proper security arrangements to make sure that the risk of wrongdoing such as fraud is minimised.

Breaches of the regulations

40.30   If a professional fundraiser solicits money for the benefit of a charitable institution without a written agreement, the court may, at the request of the charitable institution, grant an injunction. Agreements that do not comply with the *s 59* requirements are enforceable only to the extent as may be provided by a court order.

40.31   Professional fundraisers who breach the *Charities Act 1992, s 60* by failing to indicate one of the following are committing a criminal offence and can be subject to a fine of up to £5,000:

- which charities will benefit;

- how the fundraiser's remuneration will be determined;

- that donors who give more than £50 in response to a telephone appeal must be given notice that they have a right to cancel the donation within seven days of receiving the notification of the right to cancel;

- that donors who give more than £50 in response to a radio or TV appeal by credit or debit card have a right to a refund if they give written notice within seven days of the broadcast.

40.32   When a charity appeals for money the purpose of the appeal should be clearly stated. If the appeal is for general funds then it should be clear to the reader that any specific project described in the appeal literature is only an example of the type of work carried out by the charity. If the appeal is for a specific project then the appeal literature must make clear what will happen to any surplus funds raised or what will happen to money raised if, after a considerable period of time, insufficient funds have been raised to undertake the particular project, for example to repair a church spire. If this is not done then in the event of an insufficient amount of money being raised the trustees must return money given by identifiable donors. Money put into collection boxes or raised at jumble sales or by competitions can be regarded as given by unidentifiable donors. If an appeal raises more money than is required and the appeal did not specify what would happen to any surplus funds then the trustees must write to the Charity Commission for advice on whether a Scheme will be needed to enable the money to be spent on other charitable purposes.

40.33   Funds raised for a special appeal should be accounted for separately as a restricted fund.

Fundraising for other charities

40.34   If a local charity raises funds for another charity by acting as a fundraising agent any literature should make clear which charity the funds raised will benefit. The collecting charity must be certain that the beneficiary organisation is a registered charity before making any claims to that effect. Failure to do so could be an offence under *s 63* of the *Charities Act 1992*.

40.35   The collecting charity will only be able to contribute to the costs of fundraising if the purpose for which funds are being raised comes within the collecting charity's charitable objects. For example, a local breast cancer charity could use some of its funds to raise funds for a national breast cancer charity but could not use its funds to raise funds for a local environmental charity.

40.36 The collecting charity should seek the beneficiary charity's prior consent to the use of its name and should allow the beneficiary charity to approve any fundraising method or literature that will be used. Funds raised will belong to the beneficiary charity, not the collecting charity.

40.37 If a charity agrees to raise funds for capital equipment or buildings the appeal will have fulfilled its charitable objects once the equipment or buildings have been provided. Donors will then have no control of the future use or sale of the equipment or buildings. Therefore to protect the intentions of the donors and their own integrity charities should consider having a legal agreement drawn up that specifies the terms on which the appeal funds will be transferred and places restrictions on the future use of the equipment or buildings for which they have raised funds.

Broadcast appeals

40.38 The BBC's Charity Appeals Advisory Committee and Ofcom have issued codes of conduct and general guidance for charities and broadcasters. Broadcast appeals should not be misleading in any way about a charity's activities or how the money being appealed for will be used. They must deal with the topic sensitively, respecting the dignity of the potential beneficiaries, and not exaggerate the degree of need. Comparisons with other charities should not be made and fundraising messages should not be addressed specifically to children.

CHAIN LETTERS

40.39 These are not prohibited by law, although the Charity Commission has expressed concern about charities using chain letters as a method of fundraising (Report of the Charity Commissioners 1991 and 1993). Once started they are difficult to stop and if they reach their target the charity could then be in the position of misleading the public. The Institute of Fundraising also advises against the use of chain letters. If a chain letter is used to raise money for a charity the letter must state the name of the charity. If the charity is registered and has an income of over £10,000 a year, the fact that the charity is registered must be on every copy of the letter.

COMPETITIONS

40.40 A competition must involve skill that is not at so low a level that almost every entrant could win, i.e. a competition is not the same as a lottery. Competitions are not subject to any specific legislation, but must comply with the British Codes of Advertising and Sales Promotion. Entry fees for competitors may be subject to VAT and the proceeds to corporation tax.

DIRECT MAIL

40.41 If a charity raises funds through direct mail and keeps information about donors it must register under the *Data Protection Act 1998*. All direct mailings should comply with the rules on list and database practice issued by the Advertising Standards Authority and, if appropriate, the rules on distance selling.

TELEPHONE FUNDRAISING

40.42   If a commercial company undertakes telephone fundraising for a charity it will be acting as a professional fundraiser and must therefore have a written agreement with the charity in accordance with *Part II* of the *Charities Act 1992*.

40.43   Telephone fundraising is an increasingly common and successful means of raising money, but can provoke strong negative reactions in some members of the public. The Institute of Fundraising have produced a code of good practice for telephone fundraising, for use by charities and professional telephone fundraising agencies in an attempt to ensure that the method does not fall into disrepute and become illegal. The Code recommends that:

- calls should not be made after 9 pm;

- calls should not be made to people under the age of 16;

- calls should not be made to numbers randomly generated by computers;

- callers should be pleasant and honest and accept termination of the call without argument;

- callers must give their name and the name of the charity on whose behalf they are calling;

- callers must state that the purpose of the call is to raise support; and

- if asked, callers who are deemed to be acting for professional fundraisers should supply the name of the professional fundraising agency and the cost to the charity of each call.

CHALLENGE EVENTS

40.44   Overseas adventure treks and bike rides in which participants have to raise a minimum amount of sponsorship have become a popular way of raising funds in the last few years, particularly as they also generate publicity for the charity and often lead to long-term relationships between the charity and partici-pants. They are also challenging for fundraising departments for a number of reasons, for example:

- they are not package tours but package tour regulations may apply;

- participants are volunteers, but depending on the notional benefit to them and the amount raised by them, they may fall within the definition of professional fundraiser as defined by the *Charities Act*;

- a risk management assessment (including natural phenomena, civil disturbance, safety of participants) must be undertaken. For advice on the risks of travelling to particular locations, charities should consult the Foreign & Commonwealth Office (*www.fco.gov.uk/travel*);

- money raised is a donation, but because participants get something in return there are tax and VAT implications.

Professional advice is likely to be needed by any charity organising such an event for the first time.

40.45   The Department of Business and Regulatory Reform takes the view that if transport and accommodation are provided for participants a challenge event falls within the scope of the *Package Travel, Package Holidays and Package Tours Regulations 1992 (SI 1992/3288)*. These regulations set out requirements that will need to be followed when drawing up contracts between the charity and the participants, when designing brochures and when giving information before travel.

40.46   The Civil Aviation Authority (CAA) may take the view that if flights are provided, the flight arrangements must by protected by an Air Travel Organisers Licence (ATOL bond). The licence holder must lodge bond money with the CAA, so in the event of the airline becoming insolvent, the bond can be used to reimburse anyone unable to travel because of the organiser's failure and to repatriate anyone overseas at the time of the failure.

40.47   Therefore charities or their trading subsidiaries must either have an ATOL bond or must act as the agent for an ATOL bond holder.

40.48   HMRC may regard any fee paid by participants and the sponsorship donations they collect as trading income because the participant gets a benefit from taking part in the event. The scale of most challenge events is such that they do not qualify for the tax concessions that apply to small-scale fundraising events. If an outside organiser runs the challenge event and contracts to give the charity a donation no liability to tax on the amount raised arises. However, in most instances the organiser will want to use the charity's name and logo in promoting the event so HMRC will treat the donation as taxable income. Therefore most charities structure challenge events through their trading subsidiary.

40.49   Charities also have to consider if their challenge events fall within the Tour Operators Margin Scheme (TOMS) for VAT purposes. TOMS applies to those who buy in and sell travel facilities for the direct benefit of the traveller. TOMS means that a charity will have to relate all the direct purchases relating to the event (travel, accommodation, tour guides, etc.) to the sums received in order to calculate the gross profit margin. No VAT can be recovered on the direct purchases. However, events outside the EU are zero-rated so VAT paid on indirect purchases can be recovered.

FACE-TO-FACE DONOR RECRUITMENT

40.50   Face-to-face donor recruitment, in which teams of paid, usually young, fundraisers, clipboard in hand, approach people in the street and talk to them about the charity they are recruiting for, is another fundraising method that has become popular in recent years. Like telephone fundraising, it is unpopular with many people but is very successful at recruiting people under 40 who are not already supporting a charity. The Institute of Fundraising has issued a code of practice on what is referred to as 'personal solicitation for committed gifts'. It has also drawn up a donors' rights charter and an accompanying complaints procedure.

FUNDRAISING EVENTS

40.51   Charities organise a wide variety of fundraising events from gala balls to bingo nights, sponsored walks to bungee jumps, teddy bears picnics to hunger lunches. No matter how worthy the cause these events must comply with relevant legislation. Organisations may need to seek advice on the following.

- Is consent required from the police or local authority?

- If food is to be served, what food hygiene regulations will apply?

- If alcohol is to be served, what are the licensing arrangements?

- Is the charity's insurance adequate to cover any liabilities arising from accidents, cancellations by celebrities, rain, etc.?

- If there is to be a raffle does it need to be registered with the local authority or the Gambling Commission?

- What are the tax and VAT implications?

- Can sponsorship be obtained to cover the costs?

- Have the media been informed?

SUBSTANTIAL DONORS

Introduction

40.52   HMRC have long been concerned at the abuse of charitable status by taxpayers whose level of connection with the charity is such that they are able to control its actions and do so for their own benefit. In seeking to deal with the problem they introduced the substantial donor rules in 2006. They are sweeping, complex and capable of producing arbitrary results. Unfortunately, it is charities, not donors, that are penalised.

Overview

40.53   Transactions between charities and their substantial donors entered into after 22 March 2006 are covered. Substantial donor status however can result from donations made at any time, even before the introduction of the new rules. A substantial donor (which includes anyone connected with him or her) is linked to the charity and any connected charities for the purposes of these rules. Any payment made under any prescribed transaction between the substantial donor/connected persons and the charity/connected charities, is then potentially non-charitable expenditure (see **31.26**) for tax purposes, unless one of the exceptions applies. The exceptions generally exclude arm's length transactions – but not always (see below).

Definition of substantial donor

40.54   In relation to a charity's chargeable period, a substantial donor is a person (individual or company) who makes 'relievable gifts' (see below) which come to:

- at least £25,000 in any 12-month period coinciding to any extent with the charity's chargeable period; or

- an aggregate of at least £100,000 over any six-year period coinciding to any extent with the charity's chargeable period.

40.55 Donations and Fundraising

40.55 What's more, any person who has become a substantial donor under either test remains a substantial donor for a further five chargeable periods from ceasing to meet either test.

Connected persons

40.56 'Person' encompasses a company or trust as well as an individual.

A substantial donor includes connected persons, defined as an individual and his or her spouse or civil partner and the relatives of them both (brother, sister, ancestor or lineal descendant) and their spouses or civil partners. Business associates, companies and trusts can also be included. Gifts made by connected persons all form part of the tally of relievable gifts.

Exclusions to the definition of a substantial donor

40.57 A person is not a substantial donor to a charity if:

- he has not made enough relievable gifts to satisfy the criteria noted above (i.e. at least £25,000 in any 12-month period or an aggregate of at least £100,000 over any six-year);

- the donor is a charity donating to another charity;

- the donor is a housing association or Registered Social Landlord donating to a charity with which it is connected.

40.58 A company which is a wholly-owned subsidiary of one or more charities is excepted from the definition of substantial donor. A standard trading subsidiary arrangement will therefore be excluded but not a joint venture vehicle with non-charities.

40.59 If for any reason a donation does not qualify for tax relief (for example if a donor receives benefits in excess of the statutory 'Gift Aid' benefit limits in consequence of his donation), his donation will not be a 'relievable gift' thus the donor will not be a substantial donor by virtue of that gift alone.

Relievable gifts

40.60 A relievable gift is a donation of cash or property (including non-monetary gifts) to a charity, which qualifies for specified tax reliefs. It includes gifts of:

- Cash, under the individual or company Gift Aid provisions;

- Quoted shares and securities, and real property where the donor has obtained income or corporation tax relief;

- Gifts of assets where the donor has obtained capital gains tax relief;

- Plant or machinery where the donor has received capital allowances;

- Trading stock;

- Amounts donated via payroll giving; and

- Gifts from settlor-interested trusts.

40.61 It does not include gifts where the only tax relief attracted is inheritance tax relief (e.g. a donation made in a will), even where property is re-directed to a charity from an estate by a variation made within two years of a death.

Chargeable periods affected

40.62   The chargeable period for a charitable trust is the tax year ended 5 April. For a charity treated as a company for tax purposes, the chargeable period is its accounting period.

40.63   The effective dates for transactions (not gifts) between the substantial donor and the charity are all dates on or after 22 March 2006. For the purposes of gifts, there is no starting date.

40.64   A transaction can be caught if it is made at any time in the chargeable period, even if it occurs before a donor has made the gifts which qualify him as a substantial donor.

40.65   Once a person is a substantial donor to a charity in respect of a chargeable period he is also treated as a substantial donor in respect of the next five chargeable periods.

40.66   Donors making gifts of £25,000 or more will be substantial donors for at least seven years. A donor making a single £100,000 or more gift acquires substantial donor status for at least 17 years.

Example

●   Mr Jones makes a relievable gift of £100,000 to a charity on 1 January 2010, which falls into the charity's chargeable period ended 31 December 2010.

●   He is a substantial donor in respect of each of the charity's chargeable periods falling wholly or partly within the six year period ended 1 January 2010 and also in respect of the chargeable periods falling wholly or partly within the six year period beginning 1 January 2010.

●   Thus, he is a substantial donor for the charity's chargeable period ended 31 December 2004 through to the chargeable period ended 31 December 2016.

●   He is also a substantial donor in respect of the next five chargeable periods (i.e. to 31 December 2021).

●   In total Mr Jones is a substantial donor of the charity in respect of the 18 year period from 1 January 2004 to 31 December 2021!

●   Therefore, in consequence of his gift, the legislation will apply to any transactions between the charity and Mr Jones between 22 March 2006 and 31 December 2021.

Transactions caught by the legislation

40.68   The transactions covered by these measures are:

●   the sale or letting of property by a charity to a substantial donor or vice versa;

●   the provision of services by a charity to a substantial donor or vice versa;

●   an exchange of property between a charity and a substantial donor;

- the provision of financial assistance (including the provision of a loan, guarantee or indemnity or charitable grants to beneficiaries) by a charity to a substantial donor or vice versa;

- investment by a charity in the business of a substantial donor;

- payment of remuneration (including non-cash benefits) to a substantial donor.

The charge to tax

40.69   Charities can claim exemption from tax on most sources of income, subject to the income being applied solely to charitable purposes. Where a charity incurs non-charitable expenditure, its exemption from tax is restricted. For detailed guidance about non-charitable expenditure see **31.26**.

40.70   Where a charity's transactions with substantial donors are caught by the legislation, the charity is treated as incurring non-charitable expenditure. This applies in the following circumstances:

- Where a charity makes a payment to a substantial donor in the course of or for the purposes of a specified transaction (noted above), the amount of the payment is treated as non-charitable expenditure.

- Where a transaction with a substantial donor takes place on terms that are less beneficial to the charity than the terms which might be expected in an 'arm's length' transaction, the cost to the charity of the difference in terms (as determined by HMRC) is treated as non-charitable expenditure.

Statutory exceptions

40.71   There are statutory exceptions to the treatment of transactions with substantial donors as non-charitable expenditure of the charity.

The following table, produced by HMRC, summarises the exceptions applying to each type of 'caught' transaction:

Transaction	Exception
Sale or letting of property by a charity to a substantial donor	No exception.
Sale or letting of property to a charity by a substantial donor	Transaction excepted if it takes place in the course of a business carried on by the substantial donor, on terms which are no less beneficial to the charity than an arm's length transaction, and is not part of an arrangement to avoid tax.

The provision of services by a charity to a substantial donor	Transaction excepted if the services are provided in the course of the actual carrying out of a primary purpose of the charity, on terms which are no more beneficial to the donor than those on which services are provided to others.
The provision of services to a charity by a substantial donor	Transaction excepted if it takes place in the course of a business carried on by the substantial donor, on terms which are no less beneficial to the charity than an arm's length transaction, and is not part of an arrangement to avoid tax.
An exchange of property between a charity and a substantial donor	No exception (however a disposal at an undervalue to a charity, to which income/corporation tax relief applies or capital gains tax relief applies, shall not be a transaction to which this legislation applies).
The provision of financial assistance by a charity to a substantial donor	No exception.
The provision of financial assistance to a charity by a substantial donor	Transaction excepted if the assistance is on terms which are no less beneficial to the charity than might be expected from an arm's length transaction, and the assistance is not part of an arrangement to avoid any tax.
Investment by a charity in the business of a substantial donor	Transaction excepted if the investment takes the form of a purchase of shares or securities listed on a recognised stock exchange.
Payment of remuneration by a charity to a substantial donor (including the cash equivalent of remuneration paid otherwise than in cash, such as benefits in kind)	Remuneration for services as a trustee will be excepted only where it is approved by the Charity Commission or another regulatory body or by a Court.

Payments by a charity or benefits arising to a substantial donor from a transaction are disregarded if they relate to a donation by the donor and do not exceed the relevant 'Gift Aid' benefit limits (see **117.22**).

Anomalies

40.72   Despite exemption for some transactions at arm's length, there is no exemption whatsoever for the sale, exchange or letting of property by a charity to a substantial donor, even where land is sold for full value satisfying *s 36* of the *Charities Act 1993*.

40.73   In addition, the sale or letting of property to a charity will only be covered by the arm's length exemption if it takes place in the usual course of the donor's business.

40.74   Paradoxically, a sale at an undervalue to a charity is not a transaction caught by the rules.

40.75   Another potential hazard is the provision of financial assistance, including a charitable grant or loan, to a substantial donor, which will be caught even if properly made under the charity's objects and powers. For example, the amount of any grant paid by a charity is treated as non-charitable expenditure if made to a recipient who is (or later becomes) a substantial donor of the charity, or a person connected with a substantial donor.

Conclusion

40.76   All charities should keep records of any of their donors who fall (or may fall) within the 'substantial donor' definition and monitor its transaction with those donors.

40.77   If a charity enters into transactions with a substantial donor, to which none of the statutory exceptions apply, it is expected to complete a self-assessment tax return showing that it has incurred non-charitable expenditure, and to account for the tax due.

40.78   Charities will inevitably be burdened with more extensive record-keeping to avoid triggering a tax liability. Given the extraordinary reach of the rules, the assurance in HMRC guidance that a charity's existing records should be adequate to allow cross-checking against proposed transactions, seems hopelessly wide of the mark.

FURTHER INFORMATION

40.79   Fund-raising is a complex area as charity administrators have to take into account not just charity law, but a wide range of other legislation and there are often complex tax and VAT issues that require professional advice if the charity is to take maximum advantage of the various concessions. Information on the direct tax and VAT implications of fund-raising are given in CHAPTERS 30, 48, 111, 121 and 125. As previously mentioned, further advice can be obtained from the Institute of Fundraising who have drawn up a comprehensive set of Codes of Practice, to highlight what is mandatory in law, what the Institute regards as mandatory requirement and what constitutes advice on best practice. The codes can be downloaded in full from their website (*www.icfm.org.uk*).

41   Educational Charities

DEFINITION OF CHARITABLE PURPOSES

41.1   The advancement of education has long been regarded as a charitable purpose and is listed as such in the *Charities Act 2006*. The advancement of education is wider than the provision of academic education in schools, colleges, universities and other educational institutions and includes less formal education conducted in the community.

41.2   Examples of the sorts of charities and charitable purposes that fall under this heading include:

- Places of education, such as schools, colleges and universities;

- Charities that support schools, colleges and universities, such as Parent Teacher Associations, educational prize funds, the establishment of professorships, scholarships, lectures, etc, student unions, and exam boards;

- Charities that educate the public about a particular subject;

- Pre-school education, such as playgroups;

- Charities that provide apprenticeships, advancement in life and vocational training opportunities, such as providing training for unemployed people;

- Museums;

- Professional bodies;

- Physical and out-of school education for children and young people, such as providing sporting opportunities for children;

- Research projects.

41.3   Over the years the courts have found that a surprisingly wide variety of objects fall under the head of the advancement of education. These have included:

- the provision of holiday camps for Boy Scouts (*Re Alexander (1932) Times, 30 June*);

- to encourage, exercise and maintain standards of crafts both ancient and modern (*IRC v White and A-G (re Clerkenwell Association of Craftsmen) (1980) 55 TC 651*);

- the advancement of the knowledge of dowsing (Charity Commissioners' Annual Report 1966 Appendix A, p 31, The British Society of Dowsers);

- diffusion of knowledge of Egyptology (*Re British School of Egyptian Archaeology, Murray v Public Trustee [1954] 1 WLR 546*).

41.4   It is difficult to be precise as to where the line is drawn between the advancement of education and a non-charitable purpose. Examples of failed educational charitable purposes have included the Margaret Thatcher Foundation (too political), specific training for members of a profession (too much private benefit), and a library of pornography (anti-social). It is clear that the definition of education is wide, and this was emphasised by Lord Hailsham in 1980 when he drew attention to the need for the definition to take account of social developments, which may lead to new areas of education being charitable in line with social values.

PUBLIC BENEFIT

41.5 *Section 3(2)* of the *Charities Act 2006* abolishes the presumption that organisations for the advancement of education provide public benefit. Once the public benefit requirement and provisions come into force, probably in early 2008, all charities for the advancement of education will need to be in a position to demonstrate that they provide public benefit.

ORGANISATIONS INVOLVED IN EDUCATION

41.6 If the range of activities which are classified as charitable is wide, then so are the variety of organisations involved in education, and their charitable status. Excluding the purely state sector, the following are some of the more significant categories or organisations which may be charitable and in some way, advance or provide education:

- universities: mainly exempt charities under the *Charities Act 1993 2 Sch*;

- other higher education institutes (HEIs) and further education colleges which may or may not be charitable;

- state schools: voluntary schools and foundation schools may be charitable in their own right, often depending on the relationship with their Diocese or foundation;

- independent schools: often established as registered charities or linked to a charitable foundation;

- student unions: can be registered charities in their own right, but usually operate within the framework of the university;

- learned societies: registered charities, often established under a Royal Charter;

- pre-school playgroups: may be independent registered charities, or members of the Pre-school Learning Alliance, the umbrella body for England (there are sister organisations in Wales and Scotland);

- voluntary organisations with educational objects which target specific beneficiary groups, e.g. Workers Educational Association, NACRO.

41.7 Educational charities derive income from many sources. Many charge fees for provision of services which may be funded through private or state sources. Higher and Further Education provision is funded at arm's length by Central Government through their respective funding councils or National Assemblies. Many voluntary organisations receive government funding indirectly through subcontracting to provide specific education 'content' to fully accredited HEIs and FE Colleges or Training Providers funded directly through the Learning and Skills Council.

41.8 Charities involved in education may do so by the direct provision of educational services (as do many independent schools) or by the promoting of education either by grants and scholarships, or in a less direct way. Educational charities apply their funds in three main ways:

- providing for the education of individuals;
- giving special benefits for schools and other educational establishments;
- making grants to other educational charities.

41.9   Educational charities should not use their funds to subsidise statutory provision.

ACCOUNTING FOR EDUCATIONAL ACTIVITIES

41.10   There are various accounting requirements which apply to the variety of educational charities already discussed. In general, registered educational charities will comply with the Charities SORP. Other educational charities will have their own accounting requirements stipulated by a government department or will have a separate SORP.

41.11   HEIs and FE Colleges have their own SORP, 'Accounting in Further and Higher Education Institutions'. The appropriate funding bodies also issue further guidance.

41.12   In most respects accounting for schools is similar to accounting for other charities. Schools will often have a number of immaterial restricted funds formed for funding scholarships or prizes, and may also have substantial functional fixed assets in property. Guidance from the Charity Finance Directors' Group in conjunction with NCVO on the presentation of this element of the accounts suggests that it may be useful to categorise these assets in a 'capital (designated) reserve' to distinguish them from reserves that are more accurately described as 'free'.

EDUCATIONAL COSTS

41.13   Many charities not directly involved in education may still incur educational costs. Charities involved in campaigning about health care, for instance, may spend money on educating the public about a particular issue. Sometimes activities may be dual purpose. Advertisements promoting the needs of the homeless, for instance, may be promoting both a campaign for change in government policy with regard to the homeless and the financial needs of a charity for the homeless.

41.14   The presentation of such costs in the statutory accounts needs careful consideration. The suggested headings within which to categorise expenditure on the SOFA include the 'cost of generating funds'. Costs included here should relate only to fund-raising related activities: where the publicity relates to campaigns to change opinions or policies etc., it should be presented as part of charitable expenditure (costs of activities in furtherance of the charity's objects). Sometimes a split of the cost may be appropriate.

EDUCATION AND TAX

41.15   The supply of educational services for a fee will not be taxable if the income falls within the main exemptions for direct tax. Although an independent school's fee income derives from trading, it is primary purpose trading and

41.16 Educational Charities

hence the income from it is not taxable. Schools, colleges and HEIs need to beware of other income generating activities which fall outside their primary purposes, but which seem to fit naturally alongside other operations. Conference facilities, weddings and summer lets, school uniform shops and second-hand bookshops are common examples of fundraising which should, ordinarily, be handled through a separate trading subsidiary. An alternative structure is for all trading, including the provision of education, to be structured through a non–charitable trading company owned and managed by a charitable foundation. With direct reliefs for charities on capital gains tax, stamp duty and other taxes, the alternative structure can give rise to complex tax planning issues.

41.16   Educational services are exempt for VAT purposes if provided by eligible bodies. These are schools, colleges and universities, but will also include registered charities if surpluses arising from educational activities are reapplied to the further provision of education (see 125.8).

41.17   Trading businesses who give used plant or machines, such as second-hand computers, or their own trading stock to schools and colleges do not have to bring market value into account when calculating their profits for tax purposes and therefore do not get taxed on the value of their gift.

42   Employment

Contract of employment

42.1   A contract of employment is a legally binding agreement between employer and employee which is formed when an employee agrees to work for an employer in return for pay and under which the employer and employee have certain mutual obligations. The contract may be made orally, but it should also be put in writing to avoid dispute. Contracts of employment may be of indefinite duration, or for a fixed term.

WRITTEN STATEMENT

42.2   The *Employment Act 2002* requires employers to put some of the main particulars of employment in writing. This written 'statement of employment particulars' is not itself a contract of employment, but it is evidence of the contract of employment. The written statement must be given to all employees who have been or will be employed for at least one month, within two months of the start of their employment and ideally on the first day of their employment. It must include:

- the names of the employer and the employee;

- job title or brief job description;

- the date employment began (and the date the period of continuous employment began);

- remuneration and the intervals at which it is to be paid;

- job location or, if the employee is required or allowed to work in more than one location, an indication of this and of the employer's address;

- hours of work;

- holiday entitlement and pay;

- entitlement to sick leave, including any entitlement to sick pay;

- pension arrangements;

- the amount of notice of termination required of employee and employer;

- where it is not permanent, the period for which the employment is expected to continue or, if it is for a fixed term, the date when it is to end;

- details of the existence of any relevant collective agreements which directly affect the terms and conditions of the employee's employment including, where the employer is not a party, the persons by whom they were made;

- details of the employer's disciplinary and grievance procedures;

- a statement of whether or not a pensions contracting-out certificate is in force.

42.3   If an employee is normally employed in the UK but will be required to work abroad for the same employer for a period of more than one month, the statement must also cover:

42.4   Employment

- the period for which the employment abroad is to last;

- the currency in which the employee is to be paid;

- any additional pay or benefits; and

- the terms relating to the employee's return to the UK.

42.4   Where there are no particulars to be given for one of the required items (for example, where there is no pension entitlement), this must be indicated.

42.5   The note of disciplinary and grievance procedures must:

- include details of any disciplinary rules and any disciplinary or dismissal procedures that apply to the employee;

- specify, by description (for example job title) or by name, the person to whom the employee can apply and the manner in which an application should be made if he or she is dissatisfied with any disciplinary or dismissal decision relating to him or her, or for the purpose of seeking redress of any grievance relating to his or her employment;

- cover any further steps which follow from the making of such an application.

42.6   These requirements do not apply to rules, disciplinary or dismissal decisions, grievances and procedures relating to health or safety at work.

42.7   The written statement can be provided in addition to a letter of engagement or a contract of employment, where these do not include all the information required by law. There is no need to issue a separate written statement if the necessary information has been included in a written contract of employment or letter of engagement. Although the principal statement must take the form of a single document, employers may find it convenient to meet this requirement by attaching photocopies of relevant extracts from staff handbooks or other literature and making it clear in the statement that these contain part of the information required to be given.

42.8   The *Employment Act 2002* gives employees a right to compensation if they are not given a written statement of employment particulars or if their written statement is incomplete. To claim compensation an employee will need to refer the matter to an employment tribunal during their employment or up to three months after the date on which it ends.

42.9   Employees who qualify for a written statement of employment particulars are also entitled to receive written notification whenever a change occurs in one of the particulars that must be included in the statement. This notification need not be a personalised letter but could take the form of, for example, an email sent to all staff or a photocopied notice, provided that a copy is given to each of the affected employees individually. The notification must be given at the earliest opportunity, and in any event within one month of when the change occurs (or, if the change results from the employee being required to work outside the UK for more than one month and if his or her date of departure is earlier than one month after the change occurs, before he or she leaves).

42.10   In most cases the notification must contain explicit particulars of the change. There are, however, a number of exceptions. Particulars of changes in:

- entitlement to sick leave, including any entitlement to sick pay;

- pensions and pension schemes;

- disciplinary rules; and disciplinary or dismissal procedures;

- any further steps which follow from the making of an application under the employer's disciplinary, dismissal or grievance procedures;

may be given by reference to some other document which the employee has a reasonable opportunity of reading in the course of his or her employment (for example on the employer's intranet) or which is made reasonably accessible to him or her in some other way. It is for individual employers to make suitable arrangements to ensure that this requirement is complied with, should they choose to make reference to some other document.

42.11   In addition, particulars of changes in the entitlement of employer and employee to notice of termination of employment may be given by reference to the provisions of the relevant legislation or to those of any relevant collective agreement which the employee has reasonable opportunities of reading in the course of his or her employment, or which is made reasonably accessible to him or her in some other way.

42.12   The itemised pay statement, which most employees are entitled to receive, may be a convenient vehicle for notifying changes in pay, and in other matters, provided that appropriate wording is included which draws attention to the change.

42.13   The fact that employers are required to notify employees of changes to particulars in the written statement does not mean that they are entitled to vary contractually-agreed terms and conditions of employment without their employees' consent. Once terms and conditions of employment have been agreed, any changes should also be negotiated and agreed between employers and employees (or their representatives).

OBLIGATIONS OF EMPLOYMENT

42.14   Where an employer/employee relationship exists both the employer and the employees have duties to each other, some of which are implied by the nature of the contract, some imposed by statute and some that may be written into an agreement. In this respect, charities are no different from any other employer. A charity may, however, have volunteers and a higher than average number of casual workers and persons providing some form of consultancy service. In these cases, an employer/employee relationship does not always exist. It is important, however, for a charity to know whether it is legally an individual's employer or if the individual is self-employed, a contractor, a secondee or a volunteer so that it can ensure that it is fulfilling all its obligations.

42.15   An employer has a duty to provide work when available, to pay the employee and to provide an itemised pay statement, to reimburse certain expenses, to provide a safe working environment as required by the *Health and Safety at Work etc Act 1974*, not to order the employee to do anything dangerous or illegal, and to behave in a reasonable and fair manner. In return, the employee has a duty to behave loyally, reasonably and honestly, to provide services personally, to carry out reasonable instructions and generally co-operate to carry out the work in a competent manner, to adapt to new ways of work, if necessary after training, to pass to the employer copyright for work done in the course of employment, to volunteer relevant information that comes into the employee's possession and to treat confidential information accordingly.

42.16   Additionally, an employee has statutory rights not to be discriminated against on the grounds of racial or ethnic origin, sex, sexual orientation, disability, marital status, religion or belief, or age, unless there is a lawful reason, not to be unfairly dismissed, to receive a minimum period of notice, to belong, or to not belong, to a trade union, to take reasonable time off for public duties (with or without pay), to receive statutory sick pay, and, where appropriate, maternity pay, maternity and paternity leave and parental leave.

42.17   The *Fixed-term Employees* (*Prevention of Less Favourable Treatment*) *Regulations* made under the *Employment Act 2002* require that employees on fixed-term contracts must not be treated any less favourably than comparable permanent employees on the grounds that they are fixed-term employees, unless this is objectively justified. Less favourable treatment in relation to particular contractual terms will be justified where the overall package of terms and conditions is no less favourable than a comparable permanent employee's. The use of successive fixed-term contracts will be limited to a maximum of four years, unless a longer period is objectively justified. Fixed term employees on contracts of two or more years are no longer able to waive their statutory right to receive redundancy payments. If a fixed-term contract ends when a task is completed or when a specified event does or does not happen, it will be classified in law as dismissal. Employees on these contracts will have the right not to be unfairly dismissed, the right to a written statement of reasons for dismissal and the right to statutory redundancy payments. Fixed-term employees will have the right to receive guarantee payments, payments on the grounds of medical suspension and Statutory Sick Pay on the same basis as permanent employees. Detailed guidance is available in the publication 'Fixed-term work: a guide to the Regulations' (PL512) which can be downloaded from the Department for Business, Enterprise & Regulatory Reform's website (*www.berr.gov.uk*). Organisations with staff on fixed-term contracts should ensure that they are fully aware of the implications of these rules, particularly if fixed-term staff are not eligible for the same pension entitlement and other benefits offered to permanent employees.

42.18   There is also a legal requirement for an employer to operate PAYE for the deduction of tax and national insurance contributions from an employee's pay and to provide the employee and HMRC with certain end of year tax information.

VOLUNTEERS

42.19   Volunteers will not normally be regarded as employees for the purposes of employment law provided that they receive no payment other than reimbursement of genuine out-of-pocket expenses. If they receive more than this, however, they may be treated as employees both for the purposes of employment rights and for tax and national insurance purposes. HMRC accept that unpaid volunteers may be reimbursed certain expenses free of tax. These are:

● travel expenses, including travel from home to the usual place of work;

● the cost of specialist clothing;

- the cost of meals taken where the voluntary work occupies more than four hours a day or because it has to be carried out at mealtimes;

- the actual cost of childcare incurred for the person to be available to do the voluntary work.

42.20   Where volunteers use their own cars for travelling, the expenses reimbursed must not be greater than HMRC agreed mileage rates. Any expenses reimbursed in excess of the above are taxable and HMRC may consider that they constitute pay and should be subject to tax under PAYE. Where a charity has a large number of volunteers they may be able to agree with HMRC a flat rate expense allowance, provided that they can show that there is unlikely to be any profit element as far as the volunteer is concerned. However, in a 1997 employment tribunal the payment of a fixed rate of expenses was deemed to be employment. Charities should keep careful records of all expenses reimbursed to volunteers, who should provide evidence of the cost incurred in support of their claim. If the charity does not have such records, HMRC may, in the absence of evidence to the contrary, consider these amounts to be pay.

42.21   Other forms of payment to volunteers, such as honoraria, may result in the 'volunteer' being regarded as an employee for tax and national insurance purposes.

42.22   Paid volunteers may only be reimbursed expenses tax free if the expenditure was necessarily incurred in carrying out the work. This usually limits expenses to the cost of travelling while actually carrying out the work and any expenditure incurred, for example, for materials etc., while doing so. Reimbursement of the cost of travel from home to the normal place of work and meals taken while at work will be taxable. These costs are not related to the job itself but to the circumstances of the employee.

EMPLOYMENT STATUS

42.23   Employment status can be much more difficult to establish in the case of casual, part-time or temporary workers and those on a fixed-term contract. This is an area which is always considered by HMRC when carrying out a PAYE compliance audit and which frequently results in additional sums having to be paid to HMRC, going back for a number of years, for failing to deduct tax under PAYE.

Deciding factors

42.24   A person's employment status depends upon the contract or arrangement with the charity. It does not necessarily depend upon the hours worked, the frequency of the work or whether the person may be self-employed in respect of other work carried out, although these factors must be considered.

42.25   The following are the six main relevant factors, which have been laid down by the courts, to be used in determining whether a person is employed or self-employed but the emphasis to be placed upon any of these factors will depend on the circumstances and it is a question of weighing up all the relevant facts of the case.

- The degree of control exercised by the employer over the employee in terms of responsibility for the work, working hours and how and where the work is carried out. A person in a senior position or carrying out specialist work may be an employee, but will not have a great deal of supervision. He may have authority over other employees, which a self-employed person probably would not. An employee would also be expected to conform with the normal working hours and practices of the employer, whereas a self-employed person carrying out services for an organisation would generally have more freedom provided the necessary tasks were satisfactorily completed.

- A person is more likely to be an employee if the work they are carrying out is being done by other employees, as opposed to being a specialist service which that particular person has been brought in to provide. Casual and temporary employees often fall into this category as they are brought in during busy periods or for seasonal events and work alongside other employees doing the same tasks.

- An employee is not normally expected to have his or her own equipment or to use it in the employment, except in certain trades where it is normal practice for a person to have their own tools. It would be unusual for a self-employed person to require the charity to provide an office, computer and telephone when the work could be carried out just as easily at the person's own office or home. In some cases, however, the work carried out is such that it would not be normal to provide your own equipment whether you were an employee or self-employed. This was the main argument put by HMRC against a video engineer who worked on equipment provided by the TV or film company for whom he was working. The courts held that he was self-employed because he was not in the business of providing his own equipment. The equipment used was not of that nature.

- With a contract of service there is a mutual obligation by the employer to provide work and by the employee to carry it out. A person who is self-employed is under no such obligation to take on work offered until they have contracted to do so and then the contract would normally only be for a specific task or tasks. An employee can normally be asked to carry out a number of tasks during normal working hours and within a general job description.

- Whether the parties treat their relationship as employer/employee, with all the duties this implies, including being personally involved in providing a service to the employer. A self-employed person will not necessarily be expected to undertake the work himself/herself but may subcontract it or use one of his or her own employees. On the other hand, a person may not have any employees or anyone to whom they can subcontract the work and it may require their specialist skills or knowledge but the terms of contract can still be that of a self-employed person.

- Whether the person carrying out the work can really be said to be in business on their own account. This is increasingly becoming the most important test. Persons who are self-employed will normally be responsible for their own work and liable for anything that goes wrong as a result. They will also be expected to correct any errors or make good any deficiencies in their own time and at their own expense. Employers are generally liable for the actions of their employees. A self-employed person is more likely to charge a fee for the services carried out. While this may be charged at an hourly rate, they will not normally be paid for turning up at work. When entering into contracts for the services of a self-employed person, HMRC will look to see how that person is remunerated. A charity will have a stronger argument that the person is self-employed if they pay a fee for a job, however it may be calculated, rather than paying the person an hourly rate for a number of hours worked, since this is generally a sign of casual employment. A person carrying on business on their own account will also normally have other clients and will fit their work in to suit their clients' needs and not work exclusively for one client at a time, as in the case of an employee. It is not, however, sufficient for a person to be taxed as self-employed with regard to other work carried out and charities should not be misled into believing that because a person is treated by HMRC as self-employed in one respect, they will not be treated as an employee in another. For example, doctors with their own practice will normally be self-employed but may well also have contracts with hospitals as employed consultants.

Agreeing status with tax authorities

42.26   Each HMRC tax district has at least one inspector who will deal with enquiries about the status of employees. If they are provided with all the relevant facts they will make a decision as to whether a person is employed or self-employed on behalf of an employer and, based on the facts given, this will be binding on both HMRC and the Contributions Agency for the purposes of national insurance. The Contributions Agency will also deal with these enquiries. Where a charity is in doubt as to status, it should contact its PAYE tax district or the local Contributions Agency office. In making such an enquiry it is important that the charity considers all the relevant factors and bases its argument thereon. It is also much more helpful if there is a written contract or letter of engagement between the parties setting out all the terms of the agreement including those matters referred to above. Alternatively employers can obtain an HMRC 'view' of the employment status of workers by using the Employment Status Indicator (ESI) tool, which is available on HMRC's website. However, this will provide a general guide only which would not be binding on HMRC.

42.27   It is the employer's duty to ensure that PAYE is operated, where necessary, but it is up to individuals to agree their final tax liabilities with HMRC. The PAYE system does not necessarily collect the correct amount of tax due and if individuals feel they have been incorrectly treated as employees they can themselves take the matter up with HMRC and appeal to the Commissioners. It must be said, however, that if an employer operates PAYE HMRC consider that this is evidence that the employer considered a contract of employment existed. On the other hand, the fact that a contract states that it is not to be a contract of employment and that the individual is responsible for their own tax liability cannot alter the real nature of the contract if the terms are such that it is a contract of service rather than a contract for services.

Office holders

42.28   In addition to employees, there are office holders, whose rights and duties are determined by the position they hold, as opposed to a contract of employment. Typically, the office holders for a charity will be the company directors, honorary officers and the company secretary. If these persons are paid for their duties then, for tax purposes, they are treated in the same way as employees.

Agency staff

42.29   Temporary staff employed through an agency are treated as employees of the agency as long as the employer pays the agency for their services. The agency is therefore required to operate PAYE and not the organisation which is using the temporary staff.

EQUAL OPPORTUNITIES IN EMPLOYMENT

42.30   Employers should have written policies to deal with equal opportunities, harassment and bullying and all employees should be informed of the policies. Policies must be enforced and monitored. Employees should not be disadvantaged in the workplace for reasons that have nothing to do with their skills or the performance of their duties. Discrimination has a slightly different meaning in the context of race, sex, sexual orientation, religion or belief and age on the one hand and disability on the other.

42.31   Direct discrimination occurs where a person of one sex/race/sexual orientation/religion/age is treated less favourably than an employer treats or would treat someone of the opposite sex etc. It also covers treatment of a married person or person in a civil partnership which is less favourable than the treatment of a single person. The age discrimination regulations are unique in that the employer can seek to justify a claim of direct age discrimination. In all other areas of discrimination there is no defence to direct discrimination. In order to establish that discrimination has taken place it is not sufficient to show that the treatment is different, it must be shown to be less favourable.

42.32   Indirect discrimination takes place where a person applies a provision, criteria or practice to someone of a particular race, sex, sexual orientation, religion or belief, or age that he would apply equally to someone not of that orientation, religion or belief, etc but which puts them at a disadvantage and cannot be shown as being a proportionate means of achieving a legitimate aim. For example, requiring all employees to be under 5ft 4 is a provision that more women than men can comply with, so it is therefore indirect discrimination. Employers can seek to justify indirect discrimination. This will involve a balancing process, weighing up the discriminatory effect against the legitimate aim of the employer.

42.33   Victimisation is a form of direct discrimination, so employees who raise a grievance, complaint or submit a claim for a prohibited ground are protected against retaliation from their employer. Victimisation occurs when a person is treated less favourably on the ground that he has done (or intends to do or is suspected of having done or intending to do) any of the following:

- brought proceedings under the discrimination Acts;

- given evidence or information in connection with proceedings brought under those Acts;

- otherwise done anything under or by reference to those Acts;

- made an allegation that an act has been committed that would constitute a contravention of those Acts.

42.34   Where allegations are made by the complainant which are false or made under bad faith, then there is no protection against victimisation.

42.35   Harassment in the workplace is often thought to be limited to office banter or misplaced comments but it is more far-reaching than this. Harassment can range from bullying to apparently meaningless comments. It can undermine confidence, lead to stress and affect the performance of all those involved. Harassment is a ground of unlawful discrimination, distinct from direct or indirect. It is defined as engaging in unwanted conduct which has the purpose or effect of violating the complainant's dignity or creating an intimidating, hostile, degrading, humiliating or offensive working environment for the complainant.

42.36   The *Sex Discrimination Act 1975* (as amended), the *Race Relations Act 1976* (updated by the *Race Directive*), the *Disability Discrimination Act 1995*, the *Employment Equality (Religion or Belief) Regulations 2003*, the *Employment Equality (Sexual Orientation) Regulations 2003* and the *Employment Equality (Age) Regulations 2006* prohibit various forms of discrimination in employment and the *Equal Pay Act 1970* ensures that men and women's pay and conditions are the same for like work.

42.37   Under the *Race Relations (Amendment) Act 2000* public authorities and organisations that provide services on their behalf must have due regard to the need to eliminate unlawful discrimination and promote equality of opportunity and good race relations. The *Equality Act 2006* placed a duty on public authorities to promote equality of opportunity between women and men and prohibit sex discrimination and harassment in the exercise of public functions. Many charities are affected by this legislation as they receive funding from public bodies or provide services for local authorities. Therefore these charities must not only avoid discrimination, but must work proactively to overcome it and to promote equality of opportunity. Detailed guidance can be found on the Commission for Equality and Human Rights' website (*www. cehr.org.uk*).

42.38   The *Sex Discrimination (Indirect Discrimination and Burden of Proof) Regulations 2001* require that if the claimant can show a difference in treatment and a difference in sex the onus is on the employer to prove that it is not an act of discrimination.

42.39   Employees with a disability who receive special equipment to carry out their jobs are now fully exempt from paying tax on it, even if it is used outside work.

People with criminal records

42.40   The *Rehabilitation of Offenders Act 1974* gives ex-offenders the right to withhold information about 'spent' convictions and makes it unlawful for an employer to dismiss an employee or refuse to employ someone because they have a spent conviction. There are exceptions in the case of those working with children or vulnerable adults (see CHAPTER 23).

TRANSFER OF UNDERTAKINGS REGULATIONS (TUPE)

42.41   Many charities have recently been taking on work previously done by a local authority or are considering merging with another charity. Where this is the case, or in any other situation where a charity takes on workers previously employed by another employer, they will be affected by the *Transfer of Undertakings (Protection of Employment) Regulations 2006 (TUPE)*. The main implications are that the charity will have to provide their new employees with their existing terms and conditions, with the exception of their occupational pension scheme. The charity is not obliged to give their new employees rights to a comparable occupational pension scheme.

42.42   The Regulations require the outgoing employer to notify the incoming employer, in writing or other readily accessible format, with the following information about employees being transferred:

- The identity of the employees who will transfer;

- The age of the employees;

- Information contained in those employees' statements of employment particulars;

- Information relating to any collective agreement applying to the employees;

- Details of any disciplinary action or grievances raised within the preceding two years;

- Information relating to any court or tribunal claim taken by the employees in the previous two years and details of potential legal action the outgoing employer has reasonable grounds to believe any employee may bring.

42.43   The notification must include information relating to any employee who would have transferred had he or she not been automatically unfairly dismissed prior to the transfer. Notification must be made at least 14 days prior to the transfer or as soon as reasonably practicable in special circumstances.

42.44   *TUPE* also imposes an obligation on a charity to consult with employee representatives about employees likely to be affected by a transfer. This applies not just to employees who are being transferred, but to the charity's existing employees who will be affected by the arrival of new colleagues.

42.45   *TUPE* is a complex and changing area of legislation. Charity administrators who believe they may be affected should seek professional advice.

NATIONAL MINIMUM WAGE

42.46   The National Minimum Wage applies to virtually all workers above compulsory school leaving age, including seasonals, part-timers, casuals, overseas workers even if they are only in the UK for a short time, agency workers and homeworkers who may not otherwise qualify as 'workers' for employment legislation purposes, etc. It does not apply to people running their own business on a self-employed basis, the armed forces, prisoners working under prison rules, or to volunteers who receive only reimbursement of genuine out-of-pocket expenses and no benefits other than the training necessary for them to carry out their volunteer work. It also does not apply to resident members of charitable religious communities (unless they run a school, a further or higher education institute), volunteers who receive a payment towards subsistence and who are working for a charity, voluntary organisation, associated fund-raising body or statutory body and who have been placed with that body by a charity acting in pursuance of its charitable objects (for example volunteers in Emmaus Communities) and volunteers who receive accommodation or meals because it is necessary for them to carry out their work. The National Minimum Wage does apply, however, to volunteers who receive payment above genuine reimbursement of expenses, lump sum expenses, or an honorarium, or training beyond what is needed for them to carry out their volunteer work, or other benefits such as free or discounted admission to fund-raising events, or shop discounts.

42.47   The National Minimum Wage rates are based on the recommendations of the Independent Low Pay Commission and are usually increased each year. Information on current rates is available from the National Minimum Wage Helpline 0845 6000 678. From 1 October 2007 the rates are as follows:

- For workers aged 22 and over £5.52 per hour

- For 18–21 year olds £4.60 per hour

- For 16–17 year olds £3.40 per hour

The rate for the accommodation offset will increase to £30.10 per week (£4.30 per day).

42.48   Some organisations providing care occasionally do so by employing a carer to live with a client. This may entail long periods when the carer must be available for the client but may in fact only work for short periods. The rules relating to whether the national minimum wage should be paid for all hours of availability or on an estimate of the time actually worked are complex and have to be interpreted in terms of four differently defined categories of work, i.e. 'timed work', 'salaried hours work', 'output work' and 'unmeasured work', so professional advice is usually necessary.

42.49   It is a criminal offence to refuse or wilfully neglect to pay the National Minimum Wage. Employers must keep adequate records to show that they are paying their workers the National Minimum Wage.

WORKING TIME REGULATIONS

42.50   The *Working Time Regulations 1998* (amended with effect from 1 August 2003) make it unlawful for employers to require most employees to work for more than 48 hours per week, averaged over a 17-week period unless the employee agrees otherwise in writing, or unless the employee can determine their working hours themselves (e.g. senior managers), or workers choose to work longer hours on a voluntary basis. For employees over the minimum school leaving age but under 18 the limit is eight hours working time a day and 40 hours a week. The Regulations give virtually all workers, including part-timers, freelance workers, agency workers and casuals, the right to:

- 24 days' paid annual holiday (this can include bank holidays) from 1 October 2007, increasing to 28 days from 1 April 2009;

- compensation for untaken leave on termination of employment;

- a 20-minute rest break if the working day is longer than six hours (workers between the school leaving age and 18 are entitled to 30 minutes if the working day is longer than 4.5 hours);

- a rest period of 11 consecutive hours every 24 hours (12 hours' rest between each working day for workers between the school leaving age and 18);

- a weekly rest period of at least 24 hours (two days' weekly rest for workers between the school leaving age and 18);

- a maximum of eight hours work per 24 hours for night workers;

- free health assessments for night workers.

42.51   Workers aged between the school leaving age and 18 must not be required to work between 10pm and 6am or between 11pm and 7am, except in certain circumstances.

SUNDAY WORKING

42.52   The *Employment Rights Act 1996* gives shop workers in England and Wales the right to choose not to work on Sundays and includes measures to protect workers who refuse to work on Sundays. This legislation protects charity employees working in charity shops or, for example, employees working in charitable museums and gelleries.

FAMILY FRIENDLY LEGISLATION

42.53   The *Work and Families Act 2006* introduced new legislation to:

- extend the maximum period that may be prescribed in regulations as the period for which statutory maternity pay, maternity allowance and statutory adoption pay are payable from 26 weeks to 52 weeks;

- introduce a new scheme that will provide certain employees (generally fathers) with a new entitlement to take leave to care for a child and a new entitlement to receive pay while they are on leave, if certain conditions are met;

- widen the scope of the existing law on flexible working to enable more people with caring responsibilities to request to work flexibly;

- provide a new power to increase on one occasion the maximum amount of a week's pay which may be taken into account in the calculation of certain payments (for example, redundancy payments);

- provide a new power to make provision about annual leave.

42.54   The *Work and Families Act 2006* contains a new provision entitling an employer to make reasonable contact with the employee (and vice-versa) while she is on maternity leave, to discuss a range of issues, e.g. to discuss her plans for returning to work, or to keep her informed of important developments at the workplace. The employee should be informed of any relevant promotion opportunities or job vacancies that arise during maternity leave. In addition the Act introduced 'keeping in touch' days whereby an employee on maternity or paternity leave can work for up to 10 days during their statutory maternity pay period without ending the leave or losing entitlement to SMP.

Maternity pay and leave

42.55   The *Maternity and Parental Leave etc.* and the *Paternity and Adoption Leave (Amendment) Regulations 2006* came into force on 1 October 2006 affecting employees whose expected week of childbirth or date for adoption was on or after 1 April 2007.

Maternity leave

42.56   All pregnant employees are entitled to take up to one year's (52 weeks) maternity leave, regardless of length of service with the employer. Maternity leave is a single continuous period and is made up of:

- 26 weeks' **Ordinary Maternity Leave** – during which the contract of employment continues, and during which the employee must continue to receive all her contractual benefits except (unless agreed otherwise) wages or salary; and

- 26 weeks' **Additional Maternity Leave** – during which the contract of employment continues, but only certain terms of that contract apply. Employers and employees may agree between themselves for other terms to continue, although this is not required by law.

42.57   By law an employee must take a minimum of two weeks' (four weeks for those who work in factories) maternity leave immediately following the birth. If an employee has a contractual right to maternity leave in addition to the statutory right set out above, she may take advantage of whichever is the most favourable to her.

42.58   A woman can choose the date when she wishes to start her maternity leave. This can usually be any date from the beginning of the 11th week before the week the baby is due. She must give her employer notification of her pregnancy, the expected week of childbirth and the planned date of the start of maternity leave no later than the end of the 15th week before the expected week of childbirth. Many employees will find it convenient to give notice of the date for the start of statutory maternity pay (SMP) at the same time. The employee can vary the start of her leave provided she gives the employer 28 days' notice. If the woman has her baby or is absent from work due to a pregnancy-related reason after the beginning of the fourth week before the expected week of childbirth, but before the date she has notified, the maternity leave period begins automatically on the day after the first day of her absence.

42.59   Within 28 days of receiving the notice of when an employee wants her maternity leave to start, her employer must confirm to her in writing what her expected date of return is if she takes her full leave (52 weeks). The employer is not entitled to ask the employee if she intends to return to work after maternity leave. The assumption is that the employee will return the day after the leave period ends. If an employee wishes to return to work before the end of her full maternity leave period, she must give her employer eight weeks' notice of her return to work. This notice requirement applies during both ordinary and additional maternity leave. The notice period is the minimum the employer is entitled to expect, but the employer can of course accept less or no notice at their discretion.

42.60   An employee who has notified her employer that she wishes to return to work before the end of her maternity leave is entitled to change her mind. However, in these circumstances she must give her employer notice of this new, later date of return at least eight weeks before the date she had originally notified as her date of return.

42.61   An employee who does not wish to return to work after her maternity leave must give her employer the notice of termination required by her contract of employment. However, it will usually help her employer if she can give as much notice as possible. As long as she specifies the date on which she wishes to terminate the contract (this could be the first day she was due back at work after maternity leave) this will not, of itself, mean that she is no longer entitled to maternity leave or pay for the rest of the maternity leave period.

Maternity pay

42.62   Pregnant employees who meet qualifying conditions based on their length of service and average earnings, and who give the correct notice, are entitled to receive up to 39 weeks' Statutory Maternity Pay (SMP) from their employer. The Government intends to extend the period eventually to one year (see **42.53**). The qualifying conditions are as follows:

●   the woman must have been employed by her employer for a continuous period of at least 26 weeks ending with the week ('the qualifying week') immediately preceding the 14th week before the expected week of her baby's birth;

●   her normal weekly earnings for the period of eight weeks ending with the qualifying week must be equal to or more than the lower earnings limit for National Insurance contributions.

42.63   The rate of SMP is 90% of a woman's average weekly earnings for the first six weeks, followed by the lesser of a flat rate of £112.75 a week from 1 April 2007 or 90% of her average weekly earnings for the remaining 33 weeks. The flat rate is subject to review every April and current rates can be found on the Department for Work and Pensions' website (www.dwp.gov.uk).

42.64   Employers who are liable to pay SMP may reclaim 92% of the amount they pay from HMRC. Small charities may be eligible to claim back 104.5% of the money they pay out in SMP if their total National Insurance liability in the previous tax year was £45,000 or less.

42.65   Women who do not qualify for statutory maternity pay may be entitled to Maternity Allowance. To qualify a woman must have been employed or self-employed in at least 26 of the 66 weeks ending with the week before the expected week of her baby's birth. She must also meet an earnings condition in respect of 13 weeks falling within the 66-week period. Maternity Allowance is paid directly to women by the Department for Work and Pensions and is administered by the Department.

42.66   Employees who take advantage of 'keeping in touch' days and work for up to ten days during their maternity leave should receive contractual pay for the days worked, the detail depending on the agreement reached with the employer over the amount and nature of the work.

Contractual rights during maternity leave

42.67   The contract of employment continues throughout the 26 weeks of Ordinary Maternity Leave, unless either the employer or employee expressly ends it or it expires. During Ordinary Maternity Leave an employee has a statutory right to continue to benefit from the terms and conditions of employment that would have applied to her had she been at work instead of on leave, for example gym membership or private health insurance, except for the terms providing for her wages or salary.

42.68   During her Ordinary Maternity Leave period a woman continues to be employed. This means that this period counts towards her period of continuous employment for the purposes of entitlement to other statutory employment rights (for example, the right to a redundancy payment). It also counts for assessing seniority, pension rights, and other personal length-of-service payments, such as pay increments under her contract of employment.

42.69   When a woman returns to work from Ordinary Maternity Leave she has a right to return to the same job on the same terms and conditions as before her leave began. She is entitled to benefit from any general improvements to the rate of pay, or other terms and conditions, which may have been introduced for her grade or class of work while she was away, as if she had not been away. If a pay rise has been awarded during maternity leave, and, but for her absence she would have received it, her employer should have recalculated her SMP.

42.70   The contract of employment continues throughout Additional Maternity Leave unless either party expressly ends it or it expires. During Additional Maternity leave a woman does not have any statutory entitlement to receive contractual remuneration from her employer. However, if the employee does any of the limited amount of work allowed during maternity leave then it will be a matter for her and her employer to agree the contractual pay she will receive for that work.

42.71   In the absence of any agreement to the contrary, the terms and conditions of the employment contract which apply during Additional Maternity Leave are as set out below:

- The employee is entitled to benefit from her employer's implied obligation to her of trust and confidence;

- She is bound by her implied obligation to her employer of good faith;

- The employee is bound by any terms in her contract relating to:

  — disclosure of confidential information;

  — acceptance of gifts or other benefits;

  — participation in any other business.

- She is entitled to receive whatever period of notice her contract provides for if her employment is terminated (an employee who is pregnant or on maternity leave is protected from dismissal which is wholly or partly related to her pregnancy or maternity leave);

- She must give her employer the notice provided for by her contract of employment if she is terminating her contract;

- She is entitled to any contractual rights to compensation and statutory redundancy pay if she is made redundant;

- Any terms and conditions in the contract of employment relating to disciplinary or grievance procedures will continue to apply.

42.72 During her Additional Maternity Leave period a woman continues to be employed. This means that this period counts towards her period of continuous employment for the purposes of entitlement to other statutory employment rights. However, unlike Ordinary Maternity Leave, the Additional Maternity Leave period is not required to be counted for the purpose of assessing pension rights, and other payments based on an individual employee's length of service, such as pay increases linked to length of service, unless the contract of employment provides for service to accrue during Additional Maternity Leave. In these circumstances the period of employment before the start of Additional Maternity Leave will be 'joined up' with the period of employment on her return to work as if they were continuous.

42.73 During any period of 'paid maternity leave', regardless of whether this is Ordinary or Additional Maternity Leave, the employer's pension contribution should be calculated as if the woman is working normally and receiving the normal remuneration for doing so. 'Paid Maternity Leave' is when the employee is receiving Statutory Maternity Pay or contractual (occupational) maternity pay, or a combination of both. In other words, if an employee takes 26 weeks of Ordinary Maternity Leave followed by 13 weeks of Additional Maternity Leave, returning to work when the period of Statutory Maternity Pay comes to an end, the pension contributions the employer makes should continue throughout the whole period as though the woman was working normally and had taken no maternity leave at all. However, if, rather than returning to work when the period of paid maternity leave came to an end, an employee remains on leave and uses up the rest of her Additional Maternity Leave and is not paid for these final 13 weeks, the employer need not continue the pension contributions during the unpaid leave unless the contract of employment provides otherwise.

42.74 If the rules of the pension scheme require the employee to contribute towards her occupational pension, her contributions should be based on the amount of pay she receives during the maternity leave period i.e. Statutory Maternity Pay, contractual pay, or a combination of both.

42.75 Employees on maternity leave retain their entitlement to statutory annual leave (four weeks' paid leave per year) throughout Ordinary and Additional Maternity Leave. If the employee is also entitled to contractual annual leave (that is, annual leave that is provided by her contract, on top of the four weeks statutory minimum provided by law) she will continue to accrue this additional, contractual entitlement during Ordinary Maternity Leave. She does not, however, have an entitlement to continue accruing contractual annual leave during Additional Maternity Leave unless she has agreed otherwise with her employer.

42.76 It is not possible for an employee to take annual leave at the same time as maternity leave. It will, though, usually be possible for an employee to use any untaken annual leave either before she starts her maternity leave, or once her maternity leave has finished. She could, for example, agree with her employer that she will take two weeks' annual leave immediately before starting maternity leave. This would mean that her last day at work before maternity leave was actually two weeks before her maternity leave began. However, if the baby is born during the annual leave, the maternity leave must start from that point.

42.77 Employers and employees will often find it useful, once the woman has given notice that she is pregnant, to incorporate annual leave arrangements into their planning. This is particularly important if the employee plans to take a whole year's maternity leave, as it is not possible to carry over statutory annual leave from one leave year to the next, or to pay the employee in lieu of any untaken statutory annual leave unless the contract is terminated. It is, of course, up to the employer and the employee to agree between them whether to carry over or provide pay in lieu of any untaken contractual annual leave above the statutory minimum.

42.78 It is unlawful for an employer to select a woman for redundancy or terminate her contract solely or principally because she is pregnant or on maternity leave. An employee made redundant in these circumstances will have a claim for unfair dismissal and may also be able to claim sex discrimination. An employee who has been dismissed in this way should appeal against the dismissal as part of the requirement under the Statutory Dispute Resolution Procedures. Failure by employers or employees to use these statutory procedures could result in an increase or reduction to any compensation awarded. The ACAS Code of Practice on disciplinary and grievance procedures sets out the statutory dispute resolution procedures that should be followed before an employee may, if the dispute is not resolved, complain to an Employment Tribunal.

42.79 Any redundancy must follow the correct procedures. If a redundancy situation arises at any stage during an employee's maternity leave which means it is not practicable for the employer to continue to employ her under her original contract of employment, she is entitled to be offered (before that contract ends) a suitable alternative vacancy, where one is available. This includes a vacancy with an associated employer or with a successor to the original employer. The new contract must take effect immediately on the ending of the original one and must be such that:

- the work to be done by the employee is both suitable and appropriate for her to do in the circumstances; and

- the capacity and place in which she is to be employed and the other terms and conditions of her employment are not substantially less favourable to her than if she had continued to be employed under the original contract.

42.80 If the employer has a suitable alternative vacancy available, but fails to offer it to the employee, the redundancy dismissal will be regarded as an unfair dismissal. If the employer offers the employee a suitable alternative vacancy (she is entitled to a four week trial period in which to decide whether the employment is suitable, and this period may be extended beyond four weeks by written agreement) and she unreasonably refuses it, either before or during the trial period, she may forfeit her right to a redundancy payment.

42.81 If an employee on ordinary or additional maternity leave is made redundant, her maternity leave period comes to an end. She is entitled to receive from her employer a written statement of the reasons for her dismissal, regardless of whether or not she has requested one, and regardless of her length of service. If her employer fails to provide a statement, or provides one that she considers to be inadequate or untrue, she may make a complaint to an employment tribunal, having first followed the Statutory Dispute Resolution Procedures. The employee should also receive her normal notice entitlement, or pay in lieu of notice The employee may also be entitled to a redundancy payment. The employee will still be entitled to Statutory Maternity Pay of up to 39 weeks once she has qualified for it.

Paternity leave

42.82   To qualify for statutory paternity leave an employee must satisfy the following conditions:

- they must have worked continuously for their employer for 26 weeks ending with the 15th week before the baby is due;

- they must have or expect to have responsibility for the child's upbringing, in addition to any responsibility of the mother;

- they must be the biological father of the child, or the mother's husband or partner (partner is defined as a person who lives with the mother and child in an enduring family relationship, but who is not the mother's parent, grandparent, sister, brother, aunt or uncle. Same sex partnerships qualify for paternity leave.)

42.83   Employers can ask their employees to provide a self-certificate as evidence that they meet these eligibility conditions.

42.84   The *Maternity and Parental Leave etc and the Paternity and Adoption Leave (Amendment) Regulations 2006* extend paternity leave to 26 weeks where the mother or adopter has returned to work and has not used up her SMP or SAP.

42.85   In other circumstances eligible employees can choose to take either one week or two consecutive weeks' paternity leave (not odd days). They can choose to start their leave on any day of the week:

- from the date of the child's birth (whether this is earlier or later than expected), or

- from a chosen number of days or weeks after the date of the child's birth (whether this is earlier or later than expected), or

- from a chosen date later than the first day of the week in which the baby is expected to be born.

42.86   Leave must be completed:

- within 56 days of the actual date of birth of the child, or

- if the child is born early, within the period from the actual date of birth up to 56 days after the first day of the expected week of birth.

42.87   Only one period of leave is available to employees irrespective of whether more than one child is born as the result of the same pregnancy.

Paternity pay

42.88   During their paternity leave, most employees are entitled to Statutory Paternity Pay (SPP) from their employers. SPP is paid by employers for either one or two consecutive weeks, as the employee has chosen, at a flat rate of £112.75 a week from 1 April 2007 or 90% of average weekly pay whichever is the lower. The flat rate is subject to review every April and current rates can be found on the Department for Work and Pensions' website (*www.dwp.gov.uk*).

42.89   Employees who have average weekly earnings below the Lower Earnings Limit for National Insurance purposes do not qualify for SPP, but may be able to get Income Support while on paternity leave. Additional financial support may be available through Housing Benefit, Council Tax Benefit, Tax Credits or a Sure Start Maternity Grant. Further information is available from local Jobcentre Plus offices or Social Security offices.

42.90   Any employee wishing to claim SPP must notify their employer of their intention to do so by the end of the 15th week before the baby is due or as soon as practicable after this. They should tell the employer: (i) the week the baby is due; (ii) the amount of paternity leave they intend to take; and (iii) the date when they want their leave to begin. The employer can require this notice to be in writing.

42.91   Employees can change their mind about the date on which they want their leave to start, providing they tell their employer at least 28 days in advance (unless this is not reasonably practicable). Employees must tell their employers the date they expect any payments of SPP to start at least 28 days in advance, unless this is not reasonably practicable.

42.92   Employers can recover the amount of Statutory Paternity Pay (SPP) they pay out in the same way as they can claim back Statutory Maternity Pay.

Contractual rights during paternity leave

42.93   Employees are entitled to the benefit of their normal terms and conditions of employment, except for terms relating to wages or salary (unless their contract of employment provides otherwise), throughout their paternity leave. Where employees have a contractual right to paternity leave as well as the statutory right, they may take advantage of whichever is the more favourable. Any paternity pay to which they have a contractual right reduces the amount of SPP to which they are entitled.

42.94   Employees are entitled to return to the same job following paternity leave. Employees are protected from suffering unfair treatment or dismissal for taking, or seeking to take, paternity leave. Employees who believe they have been treated unfairly can complain to an employment tribunal, providing they have first followed the Statutory Dispute Resolution Procedures.

ADOPTION PAY AND LEAVE

42.95   The *Maternity and Parental Leave etc.* and the *Paternity and Adoption Leave (Amendment) Regulations 2006* came into force on 1 October 2006 affecting adoptions where the expected date of the child's placement, where a child is placed for adoption by an adoption agency within the UK, is on or after 1 April 2007, or, where a child is adopted from overseas, the date the child enters the UK is on or after 1 April 2007.

42.96   If two people are jointly adopting a child they can choose which of them will take adoption leave and pay and which one will take paternity leave and pay. Where an individual is adopting they are entitled to adoption leave and pay and their partner may be eligible for paternity leave and pay.

42.97   Adoption leave and pay entitlements are generally the same as those for maternity pay and leave, though there are some differences where a child is adopted from overseas. Adoption leave is known as Ordinary Adoption Leave (OAL) and Additional Adoption Leave (AAL), and pay as Statutory Adoption Pay (SAP).

42.98   Where a child is placed for adoption by an adoption agency within the UK, the employee must notify their employer of when they want to take their adoption leave no more than seven days after they are notified that they've been matched with a child. The earliest that adoption leave and statutory adoption pay can begin is 14 days before the expected date of placement of the child and the latest it can start is on the date of placement itself. Pay and leave can start on any predetermined date between these two dates.

42.99   When a child is adopted from overseas the adoption leave and pay can start from the date the child enters the country or from a fixed date up to 28 days later. The employee must tell their employer that they will be taking adoption leave within seven days of receiving official notification i.e. (or completing their 26 weeks' service if that is later) and tell them the date they received official notification and the date the child is expected to enter the country. The employee must give their employer 28 days' notice of the actual date they want their adoption leave and SAP to start. To claim SAP they must give their employer the following evidence:

- a copy of the official notification 28 days before the date they wish to claim;

- within 28 days of the child entering Great Britain they must give further evidence of the date of entry, such as a plane ticket or copies of entry clearance documents.

42.100   Adoption pay and leave are not available when the child is already being cared for by the adopter, for example when a stepchild or foster child is being adopted. However, employees adopting a relative from overseas may qualify if they have been assessed and approved as being a suitable adoptive parents.

42.101   Employers can recover the amount of Statutory Adoption Pay (SPP) and Statutory Paternity (Adoption) Pay they pay out in the same way as they can claim back Statutory Maternity Pay.

42.102   Further information on maternity, paternity and adoption leave and pay is available from the Department for Business, Enterprise & Regulatory Reform's website (*www.berr.gov.uk*) and from ACAS (*www.acas.gov.uk*).

Parental leave

42.103   The purpose of parental leave is to care for a child. This means looking after the welfare of a child and can include making arrangements for the good of a child. Caring for a child does not necessarily mean being with the child 24 hours a day. The leave might be taken simply to enable the parents to spend more time with young children, or to accompany a child during a stay in hospital, or to settle a child into new childcare arrangements, or to take a child to stay with grandparents.

42.104   Parents who have one year's service with an employer are entitled to a total of 13 weeks' unpaid parental leave for each child born or adopted. The leave is extended to 18 weeks if the child is entitled to disability living allowance. The leave can start once the child is born or placed for adoption with the employee, or as soon as the employee has completed a year's service, whichever is later. This parental leave is in addition to statutory maternity leave. The leave may be taken at any time up to the child's fifth birthday, or the child's 18th birthday if the child is disabled and entitled to disability living allowance, or within five years of the child's placement for adoption with the family.

42.105   Parental leave must be taken in blocks of no shorter than one week and no more than four weeks may be taken for any one child in any one year. The period can be extended by individual, workforce or collective agreements.

42.106   The employee is normally required to give the employer 21 days' notice of his/her intention to take parental leave. The employer may, on proper notice, delay the leave for up to six months if the business would be disrupted if parental leave were granted. The employer must, however, offer an alternative time when the leave can be taken.

42.107   Further information on parental leave is available at *www.berr.gov.uk* and at *www.acas.gov.uk*.

Leave for dependent emergencies

42.108   All employees have the right to reasonable unpaid time off to deal with unexpected or sudden emergencies relating to dependants, including sons, daughters, spouses, parents or anyone else who lives with the employee as a member of their family, or even a distant relative or neighbour who is solely dependent on the employee. The right is intended to cover unexpected situations, so the worker could take a few days off to arrange care for a dependant who has suddenly become ill, but could not use this right to take a month off to care for the dependant.

Work Flexibility

42.109   The *Employment Act 2002* gave parents of children aged under six, or of disabled children aged under 18, the right to request work flexibility. The *Work and Families Act 2006* extended the right to request flexible working to the carers of adults. To be eligible to make a request under this right:

- a person must be an employee and have worked for their employer continuously for 26 weeks at the date the application is made;

- a person must not have made another application to work flexibly under the right during the past 12 months;

- a parent must:

  — be the parent of a child aged under six, or under eighteen where the child is disabled;

  — have responsibility for the upbringing of the child and be making the application to enable them to care for the child; and

  — be either the mother, father, adopter, guardian, special guardian or foster parent of the child; or married to or the partner of the child's mother, father, adopter, guardian, special guardian or foster parent;

- a carer of an adult who is in need of care must be, or expect to be, caring for a spouse, partner, civil partner or relative; or if not the spouse, partner or a relative, live at the same address as the adult in need of care.

42.110   An employee must set out in writing the proposed new working pattern, the effect this may have on the employer, and how, in their opinion, any such effect might be dealt with. The proposal may relate to hours worked, times at which hours are worked, place of work (including working from home) and any other aspect of his/her terms and conditions as may be specified by regulations. Employers have a statutory duty to consider such requests seriously and may only refuse the application on one of a number of specified grounds set out in legislation including additional costs, detrimental effect on ability to meet customer demand, inability to reorganise work, inability to recruit additional staff, a detrimental impact on quality of performance and insufficiency of work during periods the employee proposes to work or planned structural changes. If an employee is dismissed for requesting flexible working the dismissal will automatically be unfair.

PART-TIMERS' RIGHTS

42.111   Part-time workers have enjoyed the same statutory rights (pro rata) as full-time workers doing comparable jobs for the same employer for some time. The *Part-time Workers* (*Prevention of Less Favourable Treatment*) *Regulations 2000* came into force on 1 July 2000, ensuring that part-time workers must be treated no less favourably in their contractual terms and conditions than comparable full-time workers, unless it is objectively justified. The Regulations encourage employers to adopt a flexible approach to allowing full-time workers to work part-time following a period of absence or a variation of their contract of employment if they wish to do so.

42.112   The Regulations apply to agency workers, homeworkers, casuals and freelance workers as well as employees but not to those who are genuinely self-employed. Part-time workers now have the right to

- the same hourly rate of pay;

- the same rate of overtime pay;

- the same access to company pension schemes;

- the same entitlement to contractual annual leave, and to contractual maternity/paternity/adoption leave and pay, and other benefits;

- the same entitlement to contractual sick pay;

- no less favourable treatment in access to training;

- no less favourable treatment in selection for redundancy.

42.113   The Regulations were amended in 2002 and now:

- allow a part-timer to compare his or her terms and conditions with any comparable full-timer (the comparator), regardless of type of contract (permanent, fixed-term etc.) rather than requiring the comparator to be on the same type of contract;

- allow claims for equal access to occupational pension schemes to be backdated for more than two years.

FIXED-TERM CONTRACTS

42.114   Fixed-term employees include:

- employees hired for a fixed period of time, for example to do seasonal work;

- employees hired for a period which ends when something specific happens, e.g. a grant ends or a person on maternity leave returns;

- employees hired to do a specific task, such as installing new computer systems.

42.115   The *Fixed-term Employees* (*Prevention of Less Favourable Treatment*) *Regulations 2002* and the relevant sections of the *Employment Act 2002* came into effect on 1 October 2002. As a consequence the contractual rights of fixed-term employees must not be less favourable than those of a comparable employee on a permanent contract, unless less favourable treatment is objectively justified. This does not require exact pro rata entitlements; it is sufficient for the fixed-term employee's contractual rights to be, as a whole, at least as favourable as the permanent employee's. Fixed-term employees who believe they have been treated less favourably now have a right to receive a written statement giving the reason for any less favourable treatment.

42.116   Workers on fixed contracts have the same statutory rights to claim unfair dismissal if the contract is not renewed when it ends and there is not a fair reason for the dismissal, such as redundancy. If the employee is redundant they will be entitled to redundancy rights, including redundancy pay after two years' continuous employment.

42.117   Employers must give fixed-term employees the same opportunity to secure permanent employment in their organisation as permanent employees, for example by giving them equal access to details of any available vacancies.

42.118   The regulations limit the use of successive fixed-term contracts. There is no limit on the duration of a first, fixed-term contract. However, if a first, fixed-term contract lasts for four years or more and is renewed the second contract will be regarded as permanent unless the use of a further fixed-term contract is objectively justified. If fixed-term employees have their contracts renewed, or if they are re-engaged on a new fixed-term contract, when they already have a period of four or more years of continuous employment, the renewal or new contract takes effect as a permanent contract, unless the employment on a further fixed-term contract is objectively justified, or the period of four years has been lengthened under a collective or workplace agreement.

42.119   See *www.berr.gov.uk* for more information about fixed-term contracts.

PERMANENT HEALTH INSURANCE

42.120   Voluntary organisations should not set up permanent health insurance schemes that guarantee an employee's salary (or part of it) after they become unfit for work without serious consideration of the long-term implications. Employment tribunals will imply into contracts of employment a term that a sick employee will not be dismissed in a way that deprives him or her of the permanent health insurance cover. This can lead to the voluntary organisation having to employ someone for many years after they cease to work. This will involve continuing substantial national insurance contributions and a possible obligation to provide a period of paid holiday.

TRADES UNION RECOGNITION

42.121   The sections of the *Employment Relations Act 1999* relating to the recognition of trades unions came into force on 6 June 2000. Unions can request recognition if an employer employs at least 21 workers, or an average of 21 workers in the previous 13 weeks. Requests must:

- be in writing;

- identify the union(s) and the bargaining unit;

- state that the request is made under *Sch A1* to the *Trade Union and Labour Relations (Consolidation) Act 1992*;

- be accompanied by a certificate stating that the union is independent.

42.122   The employer has ten working days within which to agree a bargaining unit and that the union is to be recognised, or inform the union that the request has not been accepted, but indicate a willingness to negotiate, in which case an extension of at least 20 working days will be granted.

42.123   If an employer fails to respond, or rejects the application and is unwilling to negotiate, or if no agreement is reached within the extension period, the union may apply to the Central Arbitration Committee (CAC) for a determination as to whether the proposed bargaining unit is appropriate and whether the union has the support of a majority of the workers constituting the bargaining unit.

42.124   If, within ten working days of indicating a willingness to negotiate, the employer proposes that ACAS be requested to assist in the negotiations and the union rejects the proposal, or fails to accept the proposal within ten working days, the union will lose its right to refer the matter to the CAC.

42.125   Once the bargaining unit has been settled, the CAC will issue a declaration that the union is recognised providing that:

- the employer accepts that the union enjoys the support of a majority of the workforce;

- the CAC is satisfied that more than 50% of the bargaining unit are members of the union seeking recognition;

- following a secret ballot, a majority of the bargaining unit who voted and 40% of those eligible to vote within the bargaining unit have supported recognition.

42.126   If the union is unsuccessful the CAC will not entertain another application for three years. Equally derecognition cannot take place until after a period of three years.

42.127   Once a union is recognised the employer and the union must try to reach a procedural agreement for the conduct of collective bargaining, failing which the union may apply to the CAC to have the default procedure implemented. The recognition procedure is legally binding and both the employer and the union can apply to the Court if there is a breach. For breaches of non-binding agreements either party can apply to the CAC.

DISMISSAL

42.128 Employees have the right not to be unfairly dismissed. Dismissal is normally fair only if the employer can show that it is for one of the following reasons:

- a reason related to the employee's conduct;

- a reason related to the employee's capability or qualifications for the job;

- because the employee was redundant;

- because a statutory duty or restriction prohibited the employment being continued, for example if an employee was banned from driving and the employment involved driving;

- some other substantial reason of a kind which justifies the dismissal and that the employer acted reasonably in treating that reason as sufficient for dismissal.

42.129 Dismissals are classed as 'automatically unfair', regardless of the reasonableness of an employer's action, if an employee is exercising their specific rights in relation to:

- pregnancy, including all reasons relating to maternity;

- family reasons, including parental leave, paternity leave (birth and adoption), adoption leave or time off for dependants;

- representation, including acting as an employee representative and trade union membership grounds and union recognition ;

- part-time and fixed-term employees;

- discrimination, including protection against discrimination on the grounds of age, sex, race, disability, sexual orientation and religion or belief;

- pay and working hours, including the Working Time Regulations, annual leave and the National Minimum Wage.

42.130 There is no length of service requirement in relation to making a complaint to an employment tribunal about a dismissal on 'automatically unfair' grounds. In most other circumstances an employee must have at least one year's continuous service before they can make a complaint to an employment tribunal. The length of service requirement is reduced to one month for employees claiming to have been dismissed on medical grounds as a consequence of certain health and safety requirements that should have led to suspension with pay rather than to dismissal.

CONSULTATION ON COLLECTIVE REDUNDANCIES

42.131 The *Collective Redundancies and Transfer of Undertakings* (*Protection of Employment*) (*Amendment*) *Regulations 1999* came into force on 28 July 1999. The Regulations amend the *Trade Union and Labour Relations* (*Consolidation*) *Act 1992* and the *Transfer of Undertakings* (*Protection of Employment*) *Regulations 1981* (*SI 1981/1794*) insofar as they relate to information and consultation. There is a statutory requirement to consult when 20 or more redundancies are proposed at one establishment over a period of 90 days or less. The Regulations require that:

231

- where an employer recognises a union they must negotiate with that union;

- consultation in relation to redundancies must include all employers who might be affected, not just those who may be dismissed;

- employers must comply with requirements in relation to the election of employee representatives, including making suitable arrangements for the election to take place, ensuring that all affected employees may vote and that the voting is conducted in secret.

DISCIPLINARY AND GRIEVANCE PROCEDURES

42.132   The *Employment Act 2002* and the *Employment Act 2002 (Dispute Resolution) Regulations 2004* introduced minimum statutory procedures binding on employers and employees designed to encourage the resolution of disputes in the workplace and stem the rising numbers of Employment tribunal claims. In September 2007 the Government announced a review of the new procedures, as the number of cases being referred to tribunals had not fallen, so the procedures described below may change.

42.133   All employers must issue a written document that sets out their disciplinary rules and the new three-step minimum disciplinary and grievance procedures. This information can either be communicated in the employee's contract, his or her written particulars of employment or the letter sent when offering the employee a job. Alternatively, the employer can set out the details in a statement of change.

Statutory disciplinary and dismissal procedures

42.134   In step one the employer must give the employee a written statement setting out why they have decided to take disciplinary action. In step two the employer must meet the employee, who has the right to be accompanied by a work colleague or trade union representative. The employer should state his case, let the employee respond and then, after the meeting, give the employee the decision. The employer is required to inform the employee that they have a right to appeal against the decision. In step three the employee may appeal against the decision and choose to be accompanied at the appeal meeting, which should ideally be heard by a different or more senior manager. The employer must inform the employee of the decision of the appeal. The employee must appeal to complete the statutory procedure.

42.135   If the statutory procedures are not completed the employee may be able to claim automatic unfair dismissal. However, if the failure to complete the procedure is the employee's fault the employment tribunal will usually reduce his or her compensation.

Statutory grievance procedures

42.136   In step one the employee sets out in writing his or her grievance with the employer. The grievance letter does not need to set out every detail of the complaint as long as the employer can understand the general nature of the complaint being made. It is not necessary for the letter to state explicitly that it is a grievance letter or in pursuance of a grievance procedure. The safest approach for charity administrators is to treat every written complaint as triggering the statutory grievance process.

42.137   In step two the employer arranges a meeting to discuss the employee's grievance. The employee has the right to be accompanied by a work colleague or union representative. At the end of the meeting the employer informs the employee of the decision and the employee's right of appeal. In step three the employee tells the employer if he or she wishes to appeal (and he or she must do so to complete the statutory procedure). If an appeal is requested, a further meeting should be arranged, if possible with a more senior or different manager. Again, the employee has the right to be accompanied. After the appeal meeting, the employee is told of the employer's decision.

42.138   Usually, employment tribunals will reject claims from applicants if employees have not raised the grievance by sending a step one letter. If the employee begins the procedure by sending a step one letter his or her complaint will be accepted by the tribunal, but if the three-step procedure has not been completed and the employee is successful in his or her claim, the compensation will usually be increased or decreased by between 10 and 50 per cent depending on whether it was the employer's or the employee's fault that the procedure was not completed.

REFERENCES

42.139   When recruiting staff it may be desirable to take up references. If references are to be sought this should be stated on the application form. Current employers should not be approached unless the candidate has given express permission. If references are sought, they will be most effective if a job description is included with the request, with structured, relevant questions that will enable the potential employer to gain accurate, further information about the candidate's abilities. Personal information or conjecture about the applicant should not be requested. Completing a reference takes time and proper consideration, so they should only be sought where they are necessary and appropriate. A simple form confirming dates of employment, capacity and particular skills may be all that is needed.

42.140   Job offers are sometimes made 'subject to satisfactory references being received', but this terminology is not advisable. The referee may simply fail to provide any kind of reference or a referee may wrongly indicate the applicant is unsuitable, in which case if the offer is withdrawn on those grounds, the organisation could face legal action by the applicant.

42.141   There is no obligation on an employer to provide a reference. Where references are provided:

- they must be factually accurate, but do not have to be comprehensive;
- they must not be misleading;
- they must be reasonable and fair to both the employee and the person to whom the reference is supplied;
- they must not breach the employer's implied duty of trust and confidence;
- any inaccuracies must not be due to negligence or maliciousness.

233

WHISTLE BLOWING

42.142   The *Public Interest Disclosure Act 1998* promotes accountability in the public, private and voluntary sectors, by offering employees who whistle-blow on their employer's malpractice protection against dismissal and discrimination in certain circumstances. The types of disclosures that qualify are those relating to:

- A breach of a legal obligation;

- A miscarriage of justice;

- A criminal offence;

- A danger to the health and safety of any individual;

- Damage or risk of damage to the environment;

- Concealment of any of the above.

42.143   The Act permits disclosures where an employee has a reasonable belief that one of the events listed above has occurred, is occurring, or is likely to occur. The belief need not be correct – it might be discovered subsequently that the worker was in fact wrong – but the worker must show that he held the belief, and that it was a reasonable belief in the circumstances at the time of disclosure. To be protected disclosures must be:

- made in good faith;

- made in the reasonable belief that the information, and any allegation contained in it, are substantially true; and

- not made for the whistleblower's personal gain.

42.144   Employees do not have to raise a grievance in order to make a protected disclosure. The statutory minimum grievance procedures apply to a protected disclosure only if the employee actually intends that the disclosure constitutes raising the matter with his employer as a grievance.

42.145   Complaints are intended to be made to the employer in the first instance or to a person or body which has been prescribed by the Secretary of State for the purpose of receiving disclosures about the matters concerned, for example the Commissioners for HMRC or the Commission for Social Care Inspection.

42.146   In certain circumstances an employee will be protected even if they make a complaint in the first instance to the media, the police or to their MP. To be protected they would need to show that they had acted in good faith, they believe that the complaint is substantially true and they were not acting out of personal gain. They must also believe that they would suffer a detriment if they complained to their employer in the first instance, or that the evidence would be destroyed if they went to their employer, or that they have previously made substantially the same complaint before and it has not been acted upon.

EMPLOYMENT REGULATIONS FOR CARE HOMES

42.147   The *Care Home Regulations 2001* came into force on 1 April 2002. The definition of 'care home' is wide and may apply to any establishment that provides accommodation with personal care or nursing to the physically or mentally ill, the physically or mentally disabled, or those dependent on drugs or alcohol. The Act requires employers to satisfy themselves that all their employees are physically and mentally fit to complete their duties. Before employing a member of staff the administrator must obtain documentary evidence of all relevant qualifications and two written references. Any gaps in the employment record must be explored. A police check must also be carried out and the Protection of Children and Vulnerable Adults and Nursing and Midwifery Council registers must be checked.

OVERSEAS PERSONNEL

42.148   Organisations deploying staff abroad need to make clear provision in their employment contract for eventualities such as staff having to be repatriated in the event of war, civil conflict, natural disasters, etc. Courts and tribunals have been reluctant to find that employment contracts are 'frustrated' in these circumstances.

SICKNESS ABSENCE

42.149   Failing to manage sickness absence can have a serious impact on the effectiveness and financial resources of a charity. It can be a difficult area to manage because of the sensitive nature of the issues and the need to consider the *Disability Discrimination Acts* (see CHAPTER 36). The Government has produced a 'desk aid' for GPs to help them decide whether or not a patient is fit for work. Charities receiving vague medical certificates from GPs should write to them asking if they have used the guidance in the desk aid when considering whether or not the patient is fit for work.

42.150   When dealing with employees who are on long-term sickness absence charity administrators will need to consider the following:

- in the opinion of the worker's general practitioner/medical consultant, or of the organisation's doctor, when will a return to work be possible?

- would a phased return, such as working part-time or flexible hours, help the employee to get back to work?

- will there be a full recovery or will a return to the same work be inadvisable?

- could the employee return if some assistance were provided?

- Could some reorganisation or redesign of the job speed up a return to work?

- is alternative, lighter or less stressful work available, with retraining if necessary?

- is there a requirement under the *Disability Discrimination Act 1995* to make a reasonable adjustment?

42.151   If, having explored the above options and failed to come up with a solution, a charity wants to dismiss an employee who is on long-term sick leave it must, as a minimum, follow the statutory dismissal and disciplinary procedures. It may be advisable to take legal advice before starting the dismissal process.

42.152 The Employment Appeals Tribunal has decided that employees continue to accrue their entitlement to paid holiday while on long-term sick leave. However, if a worker does not exercise their right to take annual leave within a leave year, then their statutory entitlement to paid holiday will be lost as they are not allowed to carry this over to the next leave year. For example if a person is on sick leave for the whole of a leave year there is no statutory entitlement to annual leave for that year.

Career breaks

42.153 The Employment Appeals Tribunal has decided that in some circumstances there is continuity of employment during long career breaks. For example a woman who took a four-year career break at the end of her maternity leave was found by the Tribunal to have been continuously employed during this period, despite the fact that the particular scheme required the employee to resign from the company at the end of her maternity leave. This finding will have ramifications in relation to rights such as unfair dismissal, redundancy policies and other benefits linked to length of service.

Employee consultation

42.154 The *Information and Consultation of Employees (ICE) Regulations 2004* give employees the right to be:

- informed about the organisation's economic situation;

- informed and consulted about employment prospects; and

- informed and consulted about decisions likely to lead to substantial changes in work organisation or contractual relations, including redundancies and transfers.

42.155 The *ICE Regulations* currently apply to businesses, including charities, with 100 or more employees. From April 2008 they will apply to those with 50 or more employees. The Regulations do not apply to businesses with fewer than 50 employees.

42.156 The Regulations may require charities to establish new arrangements for informing and consulting their employees, though some charities will be able to meet their obligations by means of pre-existing agreements on information and consultation which have workforce support. Detailed guidance is available from ACAS.

43   Entertainment

43.1   Charities get involved in entertaining for a number of reasons, perhaps the most common being fund-raising when events such as balls, concerts and firework displays are organised. However, they may entertain guests on a more private basis, such as to build relationships with potential donors, they may provide public entertainment as part of their primary purposes, and they may run events for social, or semi-social purposes. All these activities are affected differently by tax law, VAT, licensing arrangements and commercial considerations. In addition, many events will be put on with sponsorship from a commercial business which may thereby become a commercial partici-pator under the *Charities Act 1992, s 58*.

PRIMARY PURPOSE ACTIVITIES

43.2   Some organisations undertake to provide entertainment as part of their primary purpose; for example a theatre may run a dramatic production, an orchestra perform a concert, a museum run an exhibition or a special needs group put on a display. Where such events are primary purpose trading there will be no direct tax implication. Furthermore, the exemption from tax for primary purpose trades extends to ancillary activities, so a charity can sell food and drink to visitors attending a play or concert or visiting an art exhibition.

43.3   Where sponsorship is intended to fund a trading activity of the charity, then the sponsorship payments will normally be regarded as part of the income of that trade. Where a charitable theatre receives business sponsorship towards the cost of a production, then that sponsorship income may be regarded as trading income.

FUND-RAISING ACTIVITIES

43.4   Where a charity puts on an entertainment event in order to raise funds then it needs to consider the following. Can the event be undertaken by the charity? Is it taxable? Is it subject to VAT or does it fall within the exemption for fund-raising events? What other licences may be needed? Is it commercially justifiable?

Can the event be undertaken by the charity?

43.5   The constraints on whether the event can be undertaken by the charity or if it needs to be put through a non-charitable trading company, are the governing document of the charity and the tax position. Most governing documents include a power such as 'to raise funds provided that in raising funds the trustees shall not undertake any substantial permanent trading activity and shall comply with any relevant statutory regulations'. Where this, or a similar clause, is present then the charity should be able to set up a fund-raising event. However, the administrator should check with the governing document for any specific exclusions or terms of trust which may impinge on the planned event.

43.6   Entertainment

Is the event taxable?

43.6   The principles of trading and the approach of HMRC are set out in CHAPTER 120. However, it is common for charities to assume that events such as a sponsored premier, or a dinner dance, are simply not a taxable activity. Since many commercial operations provide similar entertainment on a profit-making basis, then this is clearly a misconception and any entertainment run as a fund-raising event should be considered for operation through a trading subsidiary.

43.7   If the event is taxable, then profits will be calculated in the usual way. As with all trading events, overheads can be apportioned, and some goods and services provided at undervalue can be treated as a deduction at full commercial value. This method of calculating the profit should not be relied upon to eliminate all profits on an event where, for instance, celebrities have provided substantial, and therefore expensive, time free of charge. It is intended to apply to small notional costs only. Losses on such events may constitute non-charitable expenditure and thereby trigger a tax charge if offset against relievable income.

43.8   Where an entertainment, or indeed any other fund-raising event, is to be run by a charity, the amount of tax payable may be minimised by making a minimum charge and inviting those attending to make an additional voluntary contribution. HMRC have stated that such donations will not be taxable as long as all the following conditions are satisfied:

- It is clearly stated on all publicity material, including tickets, that anyone paying only the minimum charge will be admitted without further payment.

- The additional payment does not secure any particular benefit (for example, admission to a better seat in the auditorium).

- The extent of further contributions is ultimately left to ticket holders to decide (even if the organiser indicates a desired level of donation).

- For film or theatre performances, concerts, sporting fixtures and similar events the minimum charge is not less than the usual price for the particular seats at a normal commercial event of the same type.

- For dances, dinners and similar functions the sum of the basic minimum charges is not less than the total costs incurred in arranging the event.

Concessions for small-scale fund-raising activities

43.9   Income from entertainment will not be regarded as taxable, even if the entertainment is not primary purpose, if it is covered by the concessions relating to small-scale fund-raising activities. These activities include fêtes, balls, bazaars, gala shows, performances or similar events that do not form part of a series of similar events. A charity can run up to 15 events of any of these types in a year at any one location without having to pay tax on the income generated and they will be exempt for VAT purposes. Furthermore a charity can run any number of small-scale events (e.g. coffee mornings) if the income from such events is under £1,000 a week.

Is it subject to VAT?

43.10   Many events run as entertainment will constitute a business activity and are therefore subject to VAT. The admission to premises for a charge is always regarded as a business supply, and charities should not assume that because the event does no more than cover its cost, or is only a one-off event, they do not have to charge VAT.

43.11   Following the *Finance Act 2000*, events of the type described in 43.9 above are accorded the same treatment for both VAT and direct tax: this removed a long-standing source of irritation for charity administrators who previously had to interpret and apply two sets of rules.

43.12   The location of an event can affect its eligibility for the exemption. The determining factor will again be the likelihood of it distorting competition. An event does not qualify for exemption if the event is likely to place a commercial enterprise at a disadvantage.

43.13   An event does not qualify for VAT exemption where accommodation is provided by the charity organising the event, unless the accommodation does not exceed two nights in total and does not fall within a special scheme known as the Tour Operators' Margin Scheme.

43.14   Where an event is organised on behalf of a charity by a club or a business as agent, then the income passed to the charity is covered by the exemption. As with the direct tax, it is open to an organisation to charge a minimum fee and invite those attending to make an additional donation. These donations will be outside the scope of VAT on the same criteria as those set out above in relation to direct tax.

43.15   In some cases admission charges by an eligible body will also be exempt, if they relate to a museum, gallery, art exhibition, zoo, or a theatrical, musical or choreographic performance of a cultural nature. An eligible body is non-profit making, essentially managed and administered on a voluntary basis, and which applies any profits made by the events to the improvement or continuance of the relevant facilities.

43.16   If a planned event does not fall within the exemption, then the supply of the service is liable to VAT at the standard rate, subject to the charity breaching the VAT registration threshold. It may or may not be an advantage for the event to be exempt. If the event is exempt then there will be no VAT to account for on the income but the VAT incurred on costs will be irrecoverable. On the other hand if the event is taxable then VAT will either have to be deducted from ticket prices, reducing the profit, or ticket prices will have to be increased, which could affect the number sold; but it will be possible to recover VAT charged on costs incurred in running the event. Assuming the event operates at a profit then the exemption should be beneficial, but only a detailed individual analysis of the event will determine the full impact of its VAT status.

What other licences may be needed?

43.17   Charities today are taking on an ever broadening range of fund-raising activities, ranging from trout fishing to ballooning, from barn dances to beach barbecues, from challenge holidays to golf days. This book can only give an indication of the type of events that will require licences or that are subject to other regulations. Detailed advice should be taken before proceeding with any new type of event.

43.18   Stage plays may require licences under the *Theatres Act 1968*, film shows under the *Cinemas Act 1985*, and a licence is normally required for public dancing, music or other public entertainment. Licences may also be required for sporting events where spectators are invited, and for public music entertainments in the open air, even on private land. There are exemptions for lower key events such as garden fêtes and religious services, and fees are not always payable with other applications.

43.19   Where copyright music is to be played, another range of licences and consents will be required, and a broader range of activity than just public performance, for instance a dancing club, would require such a licence. A Performing Right Society licence may cover a variety of situations where music is reproduced, but for live performances permission will need to be sought from the copyright owner. Separate licences are needed in respect of recorded material, and can be obtained from Phonographic Performance Limited or Video Performance Limited. If the event is to be recorded then a licence should be obtained from the Mechanical Copyright Protection Society. More information can be obtained from the Intellectual Property Office – ipo.gov.uk.

43.20   The *Copyright, Designs and Patents Act 1988* means that copyright music is used in public, permission from every writer or composer whose music will be played must be obtained in advance. A Performing Rights Society music licence gives the legal permission to play just about any copyright music in the world repertoire. If copyright music is to be performed a Performing Right Society music licence is required regardless of the ownership of any other type of licence.

43.21   The provision of alcohol is subject to strict regulation (see CHAPTER 5). Similarly, food provided at an event is also subject to regulations issued under the *Food Safety Act 1990*. These apply even to food prepared in private homes for sale at a charity event.

43.22   Where groups of people attend a public event they may represent a public meeting, an assembly, or a procession. These terms have legal connotations which require separate consideration, as each is governed by different legislation, including the *Public Meeting Act 1908*, *Representation of the People Act 1983*, *Public Order Acts*, and even anti-pollution legislation in respect of the use of loudspeakers.

43.23   Finally, charities should ensure that in running any entertainment they comply with local bye-laws. The detailed nature of these requirements suggests that charities should be obtaining professional legal advice before embarking on any event which may require external sanction.

Commercial justification

43.24   It is by no means uncommon for enthusiastic fundraisers, or groups, to create grand entertainments on a lavish scale for fund-raising purposes. The events are always apparently exciting and dynamic, and promise substantial returns to the charity if all goes well. Very often the events are organised at relatively short notice so urgent decisions need to be made if the event is to go ahead, and opportunities not to be missed. In such situations the prudent trustee would do well to remind him or herself of the statutory complications and licensing requirements before allowing the organisation to commit itself to holding an event that has not been thoroughly planned.

43.25   A detailed financial plan should be prepared for any event which is likely to involve the commitment of the charity's resources. The detail should encompass itemised cash flows, on a frequency to match the event: possibly even daily in some cases. The income and expenditure should be properly timed, in order to identify any possibility of the charity being required to provide temporary finance, and the expenditure in particular should be estimated in meticulous detail to ensure that not only have all costs been taken into consideration, but all contingencies have been catered for, such as all insurances including cancellation insurance due to weather or other events, or costs for taxis home late at night.

43.26   The assumptions underlying these forecasts should be rigorously challenged. What is the basis for expecting the suggested numbers? Are any celebrities committed to attending? Are their fees already known? Has the site been 'walked' to assess the equipment needs? These and many other questions need to be asked.

43.27   Before committing to an event, the trustees should be content that the potential reward is sufficient to justify the investment of time and money and the risk to the charity's good name. There is no arithmetic answer to this question, but again there are certain key questions. Has some simple sensitivity analysis been done to indicate the effect of lower than expected numbers on expected income? What is the break-even point? On this basis, is the risk still worthwhile given the impact on the general resources of the charity? If the event fails completely, who can or will underwrite the financial loss, and what will be the effect on future voluntary income and support? Even if the event succeeds, is it of a quality and ethos which supports the overall mission of the charity?

43.28   Even where all these questions are satisfactorily answered, trustees should make a point of keeping in touch with the developments of major events and ensure that information provided to them is factual, and not wishful thinking on behalf of the event organiser. It can be very difficult for such a person to have to admit to impending failure, especially when there is still a hope for success, however slim. The ultimate decision to cancel should be in the hands of the trustees, not the event organiser.

PRIVATE ENTERTAINING

43.29   Trustees and executive staff sometimes incur expenditure in the provision of entertaining. Where the amounts or nature become either material or beyond what is strictly required in the best interests of the charity, then the expense may represent a taxable benefit on the individual, be a breach of trust, or could amount to a personal benefit to a trustee that requires repayment.

43.30   It is unlikely that individual sums involved would be material, but the accumulation of such sums over a period of years can quickly amount to several thousand pounds, and even where this is still not significant to a charity, the profile of the organisation can be damaged by, for instance, imbalanced media coverage. Therefore, charities should establish clear guid-

43.31　Entertainment

ance as to what is an acceptable level of such expenditure, and the circumstances when such expenditure is justified, and then ensure that the guidelines are being followed.

43.31　Such entertaining expenditure is not an allowable deduction in the tax computations of a trading company. It will therefore create a difference between the profits in a trading subsidiary shown in the accounts, and the profits to be taxed, which will be higher. If a Gift Aid payment is based on all the profits chargeable to tax, the effect will be to leave the company with a loss, making it insolvent if the share capital is only of minimal value. This situation is hard to correct without some tax becoming payable, and therefore, wherever possible, such entertainment costs should be limited to a bare minimum, and care taken as to whether they rightly sit in the company or the charity.

43.32　Such entertaining could be construed as non-charitable expenditure in the charity, if it is not incurred solely for charitable purposes. This in turn could lead to a tax charge in the charity.

SEMI-SOCIAL ENTERTAINING

43.33　In some charities the members themselves meet in the furtherance of the charitable objectives, and in the course of these activities begin to operate more on a social level than a charitable one. For instance, local branch volunteers may use the same facilities to hold a training event and to hold a Christmas dinner. Alternatively, an institution or learned society may follow a meeting of its members with a dinner dance.

43.34　Apart from all the other considerations already set out above, this type of activity needs assessing to judge whether or not it ought to be carried out by the charity. The implications may be wide-ranging. Not only is there the potential for charitable property to be misapplied, but events which run at a loss, and claims arising from accidents and other damage, may rest incorrectly with the charity.

43.35　Charities should establish what can and cannot be undertaken using charitable resources. For instance, the Christmas dinner should either be a mechanism for thanking and motivating volunteers, or it should be undertaken entirely separately from the charity's affairs. Where any benefit is provided to volunteers, the tax treatment will need separate consideration.

43.36　Although it is customary for some charity members to meet at dinner dance type events, charities can only justify running dinner dances if they are organised as fund-raising events, which the members attend with a view to raising funds and not with a view to having a subsidised evening out. If there is any doubt, such events are better organised by a separate committee that subsequently transfers any 'profit' to the charity.

43.37　Entertaining staff and even trustees may also create tax liabilities for the individuals. For instance the provision of a sandwich lunch to trustees (directors) of a charitable company is, strictly speaking, an assessable benefit which should be declared on their P11Ds.

44   Environmental Protection Charities

44.1   Charities for the advancement of environmental protection, or improvement fell under the traditional fourth head of other purposes beneficial to the community until they were recognised as a charitable purpose in their own right in the *Charities Act 2006*.

44.2   The advancement of environmental protection or improvement includes preservation and conservation of the natural environment and the promotion of sustainable development. Conservation of the environment includes the conservation of a particular animal, bird, or other species, or wildlife in general; a specific plant species, habitat or area of land, including areas of natural beauty and scientific interest; flora, fauna and the environment generally. Charity Commission guidance states that charities concerned with environmental protection or improvement may need to produce independent expert evidence, that is authoritative and objective, to show that the particular species, land or habitat to be conserved is worthy of conservation. Further guidance on this can be found in their publication RR9 'Preservation and Conservation'.

44.3   Examples of the sorts of charities and charitable purposes falling within this description include:

- Charities concerned with conservation of flora, fauna or the environment generally;

- Charities concerned with conservation of a particular geographical area;

- Charities concerned with conservation of a particular species;

- Zoos;

- The promotion of sustainable development and biodiversity;

- The promotion of recycling and sustainable waste management;

- Research projects into the use of renewable energy sources.

44.4   Charities for the advancement of environmental protection or improvement already have to provide public benefit, so the new legislation will merely consolidate existing practice. To be of public benefit the benefit does not have to be tangible or consciously received by the public. Therefore preservation of a particular plant can be for the public benefit even though the vast majority of the public are unaware that the plant exists.

44.5   There will be some instances where the benefit of protecting a particular animal will be called into question, particularly if it carries disease or damages crops or livestock. Similarly the benefits of clean renewable energy produced by wind farms may have to be weighed against the noise and visual intrusion they create. The Charity Commission will at times have to perform a delicate balancing act when determining the benefit to the public.

44.6   Environmental charities often raise awareness through campaigning activities and therefore have to take account of the Charity Commission's guidance on campaigning and political activities, which is due to be revised in the Autumn of 2007.

44.7 Environmental Protection Charities

FURTHER INFORMATION

44.7   Charity Commission RR9 'Preservation and Conservation'.

45   European Union Legislation and Funding

45.1   The European Union (EU) is a family of 27 democratic European countries, committed to working together for peace and prosperity. It is not a State intended to replace existing States, nor is it just an organisation for international cooperation. The EU is, in fact, unique. Its Member States have set up common institutions to which they delegate some of their sovereignty so that decisions on specific matters of joint interest can be made democratically at European level.

45.2   The UK's membership of the EU impacts on charities in two main ways. EU legislation affects the legal framework in which charities operate and EU funding can be a source of income for some charities, particularly those working to support economic development or those tackling environmental issues.

INFORMATION ON EUROPE

45.3   EUROPA is the portal site of the European Union (*www.europa.eu*). It provides up-to-date coverage of European Union affairs and essential information on European integration. Users can also consult all legislation currently in force or under discussion, access the websites of each of the EU institutions and find out about the policies administered by the European Union under the powers devolved to it by the Maastricht, Amsterdam and Nice Treaties.

LEGAL BACKGROUND

45.4   The European Union adopts legislation in the form of Directives and Regulations. European Directives require Member States to implement their provisions nationally for the benefit of Europe as a whole. Member States have to achieve the results outlined in the directive, but are free to choose how to achieve that result. For example, *Directive 2001/23/EC* required Member States to safeguard employees' rights in the event of a business being transferred to another owner. In the UK employees' rights were protected under the *Transfer of Undertakings (Protection of Employment) Regulations 2006*. One of the main advantages of directives is that high level policy choices can be made at a European level while the details of their implementation are left to national governments.

45.5   Regulations directly implement EU policy in Member States without the need for Member States to enact their own legislation. Regulations become law in all Member States the moment they come into force, without the requirement for any implementing measures to have been taken. The contents of a Regulation can be said to be the law of every Member State overriding conflicting domestic provisions.

45.6   Certain proposals for the future development of European legislation involve charities, in particular the proposals for the harmonisation of VAT throughout Europe, which may result in the loss of zero rating reliefs in the UK. Charities have already suffered from the introduction of VAT, a tax originally introduced in 1973 as both simple to understand and to operate. It is estimated that charities lose £500 million a year through irrecoverable VAT.

45.7 European Union Legislation and Funding

LOBBYING

45.7   Many charities are now seeking to influence the policy formulation and decision-making processes of the European institutions. The European Commission's Transparency Initiative is shaping up to have significant implication for civil society organisations that lobby and campaign at EU level. The Commission has promised to set up a voluntary registration system for lobbyists (or 'interest representatives' to use the language of the European Commission) which will be run by the Commission. There will be incentives to encourage lobbyists to register, such as automatic alerts of consultations on issues of known interest to the lobbyists. There will also be a common code of conduct for all lobbyists developed by the lobbying profession itself, possibly consolidating and improving the existing codes, and a system of monitoring and sanctions to deal with incorrect registrations and breaches of the code of conduct. An excellent briefing that summarises this Initiative and some areas of concern is available from the EU Civil Society Contact Group (*www.act4europe.org*).

45.8   The EU Civil Society Contact Group brings together eight large rights and value based NGO sectors – culture, environment, education, development, human rights, public health, social and women. The members of these sectoral platforms are European NGO networks. They bring together the voices of hundreds of thousands of associations and charities across the Union. The Group aims to represent the views and interests of rights and value based civil societies on major issues that affect them across their sectors of activity. The Group's objective is to encourage and promote a transparent and structured civil dialogue that is accessible, properly facilitated, inclusive, fair, and respectful of the autonomy of NGOs. It promotes lasting access to information, access to justice in matters of concern to civil society, consultation, and integration of all levels of civil society in the European project.

EUROPEAN STRUCTURAL FUNDS 2007–2013

45.9   A new EU budget has been agreed for 2007–13:

- The UK will receive approximately €2.6 billion in Convergence funding for its poorest regions. Cornwall and West Wales and the Valleys will receive full Convergence funding, while the Highlands and Islands will receive phasing-out Convergence funding averaging approximately two-fifths of the intervention rates for the UK's future full Convergence regions.

- The UK will also receive approximately €6.2 billion in Competitiveness funding for its other regions. Of this, South Yorkshire and Merseyside will receive phasing-in Competitiveness funding averaging approximately one-third of the intervention rates for the UK's future full Convergence regions. It will be for the Government, in agreement with the Commission, to decide how the UK's remaining Competitiveness funding should be allocated between its nations and regions.

- Finally, the UK will receive approximately €600 million in Co-operation funding. The Government will also need to agree with the Commission how this should be allocated.

246

45.10   The Structural and Cohesion Funds are the European Union's main instruments for supporting social and economic restructuring across the EU. They account for over one third of the European Union budget and are used to tackle regional disparities and support regional development through actions including developing infrastructure and telecommunications, developing human resources and supporting research and development.

45.11   The Structural and Cohesion Funds are divided into three separate funds:

- European Regional Development Fund (ERDF);
- European Social Fund (ESF);
- Cohesion Fund.

These are used to meet the three objectives of Cohesion and Regional policy, of which the Structural Funds are an instrument: Convergence (ERDF; ESF and Cohesion Fund), Regional Competitiveness and Employment (ERDF; ESF) and European Territorial Co-operation (ERDF).

45.12   Compared to the previous period 2000–2006, the major changes to Cohesion and Regional policy, of which the Funds are an instrument, are:

- More clearly focused on the renewed Growth and Jobs (Lisbon) Agenda, thus stimulating more ownership of the agenda at regional and local level. For instance the level of expenditure to be earmarked for the Lisbon Agenda in the UK is 60 % for Convergence regions and 75 % for regions under the Regional Competitiveness and Employment objective;

- Modernised through a new architecture, including a more strategic approach. The need for each Member State to produce a National Strategic Reference Framework is a good example of this;

- Simpler and more efficient operation, for example, the number of instruments have been reduced from six to three, a new 'proportionality' principle will provide for less bureaucracy, the number of programming steps will be reduced from three to two, national eligibility rules apply instead of Community rules, and Member States and regions are asked to take more responsibility and be more transparent in their management of the Funds.

45.13   The European Commission has given the green light to the new ESF programme for England and Gibraltar for 2007–2013. The programme will invest £4 billion, of which £2 billion will come from the ESF, over seven years in two key priorities:

- extending employment opportunities by tackling barriers to work faced by people who are unemployed or disadvantaged in the labour market;

- developing a skilled and adaptable workforce by training people who lack basic skills and good qualifications.

45.14   Delivery of the funds in England is through Communities and Local Government (CLG), which is the Managing Authority for the European Regional Development Fund (ERDF) (for the 2000–2006 period through the Government Offices in the regions and for the 2007–2013 period through the Regional Development Agencies) and the Department for Work and Pensions (DWP), which is the Managing Authority for the European Social Fund

45.15 European Union Legislation and Funding

(ESF) in England, through Job Centre Plus and the Learning and Skills Council. The Scottish Executive, the Welsh Assembly Government and the Northern Ireland Administration are responsible for regional policy, including delivering the Structural Funds, on their territories.

45.15   Structural Funds have been an important source of income for many charities in recent years, especially for charities established to relieve unemployment or for urban regeneration. Indeed, it is difficult to imagine how the objectives of this funding – to reduce economic, social and regional disparities – could be realised without active involvement of the voluntary sector. Advice on applying for funding can be obtained from NCVO.

FURTHER INFORMATION

45.16   *A Guide to European Union Funding for NGOs.* ECAS, 2006. (Can be ordered from the Directory of Social Change)

www.esf.gov.uk

www.ncvo-vol.org.uk/structuralfunds

46   Ex Gratia Payments

DEFINITION

46.1   An *ex gratia* payment is a payment which the trustees believe they are under a moral obligation to make, but which the trustees are not under any legal obligation to make, and the trustees have no power under the charity's governing document to make the payment, and the trustees cannot justify the payment as being in the interests of the charity. Most *ex gratia* payments made by charities are generally either in the context of an individual leaving the charity's employment, or where a charity receives a legacy due to technical error in drafting a will, though the legacy was clearly intended for another beneficiary. In principle no charitable organisation can ordinarily make such a payment, as they must apply their funds only to charitable purposes. Although the *Charities Act 2006* makes it easier for charities to amend their constitutions, this does not extend to including a power to make *ex gratia* payments.

Principles

46.2   *Ex gratia* payments can be authorised by the court or the Attorney General and the *Charities Act 1993, s 27* gives the Charity Commission the power to authorise an *ex gratia* payment, by issuing an Order. Such a payment may represent an application of the charity's assets, or a waiver of entitlement to receiving something.

46.3   Further guidance is provided in leaflet CC7 '*Ex Gratia* Payments by Charities' which generally expands on *s 27*. In particular, it highlights the distinction between the situation where to refuse payment would be morally wrong, and where to do so would simply create bitter disappointment. The example used is of a legacy where the amount received by the charity was much greater than the testator had intended, to such an extent that an honourable man would conclude that part of the estate received was really intended for someone else. This is a different position to one in which potential beneficiaries are upset because they have not received as much as they had hoped for from the estate, because the testator consciously decided to give elsewhere. Such a distinction is helpful in weighing up whether the charity should approach the Charity Commission for a suitable order.

46.4   The test which will be applied both by the Commission (and the Attorney General) in deciding whether or not to authorise a payment will be whether if the charity were an individual, it would be morally wrong of that individual to refuse to make the payment. Provisions contained in *Sch 1* to the *Housing Act 1996* may (in certain circumstances) preclude the granting of *ex gratia* payments by registered social landlords.

46.5   If an *ex gratia* payment has been made without obtaining the consent of the Charity Commission, then the position should be rectified by informing the Commission and obtaining its advice. This is especially important as such payments fall within the broad responsibilities of the auditor in reporting matters to the Charity Commission under the whistle-blowing requirement.

46.6 Ex Gratia Payments

Such matters are therefore likely to be raised during the audit, and the charity would be acting prudently to regularise matters before they involve further professional time and money.

46.6   There is no concept of materiality in this context. Although minor payments which are effectively *ex gratia* may seem unimportant, neither the legislation nor Charity Commission guidance refer to any *de minimis* levels.

Accounting treatment

46.7   The Charities SORP requires additional disclosure in the accounts of any *ex gratia* payment, whether the value is represented by payment, non-monetary benefit, or waiver of rights to which the charity is entitled, and where the payment is not made as an application of funds or property for charitable purposes but in fulfilment of a compelling moral obligation. The same note should also disclose the nature and date of the authority for such a payment. The authority will be by the court, the Attorney-General or the Charity Commission.

46.8   The SORP clarifies the position regarding redundancy payments. If trustees believe that offering redundancy payments that are in excess of the statutory minimum level helps to motivate and retain staff, and thus benefits the charity, then such redundancy payments will not be regarded as *ex gratia* payments.

INDUSTRIAL AND PROVIDENT SOCIETIES

46.9   The prohibition on making *ex gratia* payments is not dissimilar to that for registered charities – indeed exempt charities also apply to the Charity Commission for authority to make such payments.

NON-CHARITABLE COMPANIES

46.10   These companies can make payments if they are genuine, reasonably incidental to the business, and made for the benefit and prosperity of the organisation (*Parke v Daily News [1962] 2 All ER 929*), but they can also make an *ex gratia* payment to current or past employees if the company has ceased operation or is being transferred to another company. [*Companies Act 1985, s 719*].

SCOTTISH CHARITIES

46.11   Scottish legislation has no comparable power for the authorisation of *ex gratia* payments. If a section of a charity's constitution was written before 15 November 2004 (the day on which the *Charities Bill* was introduced to the Scottish Parliament) and said that a charity could pay trustees in whatever way set out then it can still do so.

TAXATION

46.12   *Ex gratia* payments will not necessarily qualify for tax relief in non-charitable companies. Where the payment is not made wholly and exclusively for the purpose of carrying on a trade, but for something else, it is not allowed. In the unusual instance of substantial payments being made by a charity which are not in fulfilment of its charitable objectives, tax exempt income equivalent to the amount of the payment may lose exemption from tax resulting in a potential tax liability for the charity. In addition to this the tax status of the charity itself may be called into question.

46.13   *Ex gratia* payments may be taxable upon individuals, depending upon their circumstances. It used to be the case that up to £30,000 could be given to an ex-employee *ex gratia* and free of tax. Where such payments are now paid on retirement, the Inland Revenue regard them as relevant benefits under an unapproved retirement benefits scheme (*Income Tax (Earnings and Pensions) Act 2003, s 393*) and therefore taxable in full. Theoretically, such payments can still be made in the case of redundancy or compensation for loss of office, although any payment which flows from the terms of the contract of employment may still be taxable. Payment to an employee in lieu of notice is normally allowable.

HONORARIA

46.14   Honoraria are often *ex gratia*: they are payments made to individuals in return for services rendered to the charity, usually in an administrative capacity, but the amount paid is not intended to reflect the commercial value of the service rendered. Although this can be an effective means of a charity obtaining services at a low cost, honoraria should always be considered carefully before being approved by trustees. Charity legislation in England Wales and Scotland now permits payments to trustees in return for services subject to strict conditions: these are not considered here as 'honoraria'.

46.15   An honorarium is not usually regarded by trustees as a contractual arrangement, giving the individual employment rights or making that person subject to PAYE. This may not be correct. An honorarium is also sometimes wrongly adopted as a means of paying a trustee who perhaps contributes more in time and resources than do other trustees. Somehow naming a payment to a trustee as an honorarium seems to change the trustee's perception. This is an illusion. The rules about payments to trustees apply irrespective of the amount paid or services provided.

46.16   Where a charity has a subsidiary, this should not be used to camouflage such payments. The trustees effectively control the company's assets as well as the charity's and the effect of paying an honorarium through the company is therefore nullified. Where it is appropriate for a company to pay an honorarium in its own right, then it may of course do so.

46.17   Trustees should realistically assess how necessary it is to make such a payment, and ensure that the payment is the best use of its resources. Honoraria should not be used as a means by which a charity can support 'a deserving individual' unless that individual fits in to the general charitable purposes of the charity, in which case support may be better provided through some form of direct charitable expenditure.

OTHER PAYMENTS NEEDING AUTHORITY OR ADVICE

46.18   In addition to *ex gratia* payments there are other types of payment that may require consent or advice from the Charity Commission. For example, there are payments which the trustees have no legal obligation or power to make, but which they believe to be in the best interest of the charity. If the trustees can satisfy the Charity Commission that making such a payment will benefit the charity, the Commissioners can authorise the payment by making an Order under *s 26* of the *Charities Act 1993*. Similarly there may be instances where the trustees are unsure about the correctness of making a payment, perhaps because of a lack of clarity in the wording of their governing document. In these situations the trustees can seek advice from the Charity Commission on an informal basis or in more complex cases under *s 29* of the *Charities Act 1993*. Where trustees have sought the Charity Commission's advice they are protected by law from personal liability for breach of trust.

GIFTS ON RETIREMENT OF A TRUSTEE

46.19   Charities do not need explicit authority to make small gifts to retiring trustees where the value is nominal and the trustees agree that the payment is in the interests of the charity. The rule of thumb definition of what constitutes a small gift is £25.

47   Examination of Accounts

47.1   Under the *Charities Act 1993, s 44 (1)(f)* (as amended) unincorporated charities whose accounting period commences on or after 27 February 2007, whose gross income is £500,000 or less in the relevant financial year and whose gross assets are £2.8m or less at the end of the year may elect to have an independent examination. Where gross assets exceed £2.8m, provided gross income is less than £100,000, then unincorporated charities may still elect to have an independent examination.

47.2   There is, however, no requirement for independent scrutiny where the gross income for the year in question is £10,000 or less.

47.3   Friendly societies and industrial and provident societies are required to appoint auditors under the *Industrial and Provident Societies Act 1968*, unless they are very small.

47.4   A charity may also have an audit requirement as a result of obligations existing outside the statutory framework, such as a requirement within its governing document, another statutory regime, or at the insistence of a donor or financier.

47.5   There are no formal procedures required in opting for an examination, except the normal routines for trustees' decisions. However, the Charity Commission has issued Guidance Notes on the selection of examiners and directions on the carrying out of an independent examination (CC63a 'Independent Examination of Charity Accounts'). These documents support the summary requirements set out in the accounting regulations.

47.6   An independent examination provides some degree of assurance about the annual accounts, but trustees and charity administrators must understand that the examiner is not required to form an opinion as to whether or not the accounts show a true and fair view. The examiner's report will merely indicate whether or not the accounts are in agreement with the underlying accounting records and comply with relevant legislation.

EXAMINER'S REPORT

47.7   Regulations stipulate the nature of the report which the examiner must give, and the powers and rights of the examiner. The report should be addressed, and signed and dated by the examiner, state that it is a report under *s 43*, and specifically cover the matters set out below either by negative assurance, or by a specific statement.

- Negative assurance:

    — whether accounting records have been kept in accordance with the *Charities Act 1993*;

    — whether the accounts accord with those records;

    — whether the accounts comply with the accounting regulations, if full accrual accounts have been prepared.

253

- Specific statement:
    - whether or not any matter has come to the examiner's attention in connection with the examination to which attention should be drawn in order for the reader to reach a proper understanding of the accounts.
- If the circumstance exists, a statement explaining:
    - any material expenditure or actions contrary to the trusts of the charity;
    - that information or explanations have been withheld;
    - any inconsistencies between the accounts, if prepared on an accruals basis, and the annual report.

EXAMINER'S RIGHTS

47.8   The examiner has a statutory right of access to any books, documents and other records, however kept, which relate to the charity concerned. The examiner also has the right to obtain information from past or present trustees, officers and employees. Note that this right extends beyond that conferred on company auditors under the *Companies Act 1985, s 389*, which relates only to current officers of the company.

INDEPENDENCE

47.9   The examiner must be an independent person. The following would normally be considered to be connected and therefore not acceptable as an examiner: a charity trustee or anyone else closely involved with the charity's administration, a major donor to the charity, a major beneficiary of the charity, or a close relative, business partner or employee of any of these.

QUALIFICATIONS

47.10   The *Charities Act 2006* requires that where a charity has gross income over £250,000 the examiner chosen should be a qualified accountant, or a member regulation body including the Associations of Charity Independent Examiners.

47.11   For financial years commencing before 27 February 2007 the Charity Commission recommends that where a charity has gross assets in excess of £1,000,000, or gross income of more than £100,000, then the examiner chosen should be a qualified accountant.

47.12   If the accounts are prepared on an accruals basis, complying in full with the SORP, then the examiner should have a commensurate understanding of the issues involved. Any prospective examiner should be aware of and consider the examination guidelines prior to accepting the appointment.

47.13   If a charity wishes to appoint a firm to undertake an examination, then the appointment should be with an individual in that firm, in which case the name of the firm or company can be added to the report. In all cases a formal letter of engagement between the examiner and the charity should be prepared. This does not need to be reissued each year.

47.14   When choosing an examiner the trustees should have regard to the guidance issued by the Commission. This states that where trustees are unable to obtain the services of a competent examiner on a voluntary basis, then they are not only entitled, but should be prepared, to pay a fee, and regard it as a proper expense of the charity.

EXAMINER'S DUTIES

47.15   Anyone acting as an independent examiner is under a duty of care and must act reasonably and responsibly. If the examiner is a professional accountant a higher duty of care will be expected of him/her.

47.16   The examiner's work should be in accordance with the directions issued by the Charity Commission. In summary the examiner is required to:

- check that the charity is entitled to have an examination, rather than an audit, and that it is entitled to prepare receipts and payments accounts, if applicable;

- obtain an understanding of the charity's structure and financial activities in order to plan the specific procedures;

- record any procedures carried out, and any matters which are important to support eventual conclusions;

- compare the accounts with the accounting records;

- review the accounting records in order to provide a reasonable likelihood of identifying any material failure to maintain them; and

- carry out analytical procedures to identify unusual items or disclosures, and obtain suitable explanations.

47.17   Where the accounts are prepared on an accruals basis the examiner is required to:

- decide whether the accounts comply with the Regulations;

- consider the accounting policies, and material judgments;

- enquire of the trustees about material events after the year-end which may affect the accounts; and

- compare the accounts with the annual report, and consider any inconsistencies.

47.18   In all cases the examiner is required to:

- review and assess all conclusions and evidence, in the light of the required examiner's report set out above;

- inform the Charity Commission in writing if, whilst acting in the capacity as examiner, information or evidence is obtained which gives the examiner reasonable cause to believe that any one or more of the charity trustees has been responsible for deliberate or reckless misconduct in the administration of the charity;

- Where the examiner is exercising their discretion to report matters which may be relevant to the work of the Commission, the examiner

255

47.19   Examination of Accounts

should report the matter in writing to: The Assessments Unit Manager, Charity Commission Direct, PO Box 1227, Liverpool L69 3UG.

47.19   Independent examination is not an audit, and although it may involve test checks of the accounting records it will often not be necessary for source documentation to be inspected by the examiner. If, after carrying out the above procedures, the examiner suspects that the accounts may be materially mis-stated then additional verification work may be undertaken.

48   Excepted Charities

48.1   Traditionally some groups of charities have been excepted from registering with the Charity Commission, including some religious charities, some armed forces charities and some Boy Scout and Girl Guide charities. Excepted charities that registered voluntarily were given a charity number and could ask to be removed from the Charity Commission's register at any time. In 2006 over 100,000 charities in England and Wales were estimated to be excepted from compulsory registration.

48.2   The *Charities Act 2006* requires some of these excepted charities to register with the Charity Commission. Initially only excepted charities with an annual income of £100,000 or over will have to register. Those under the £100,000 threshold will not have to register but they will come under the jurisdiction of the Charity Commission. It is likely that the £100,000 threshold will be lowered over time, but this will not happen before the Act is reviewed in about five years' time.

48.3   The following extract from the Regulatory Impact Assessment sets out the scale of the issue for excepted charities:

Table 8 Number of Excepted Charities affected by the new measures

Type of organisation	Number of charities required to register at £100k threshold
Armed Forces	1,000–2,000
Baptist Union of Great Britain	200–300 (rough estimate by the Commission in July 2003)
British and Foreign Unitarian Association	None
Church in Wales	55
Church of England	1,800–2,000
Fellowship of Independent Evangelical	Less than 75 (estimated)
Grace Baptist Churches	5
Guide Association	No information received
Methodist Church	650
Presbyterian Church of Wales	4 or 5
Religious Society of Friends	Limited number required to register
Roman Catholic	No information received
Scout Association	Unable to estimate (no central figures)
United Reformed Church	Unable to estimate (no central figures)
University of Buckingham	1

48.4   Excepted Charities

i.e. approximately 3,800 to 5,000 excepted charities will be required to register with the Commission.

48.4   The provisions of the 2006 Act make no difference to the position of excepted charitable trusts for the advancement of religion conditional on the upkeep of graves.

48.5   The *School Standards and Framework Act 1998* excepts any foundation established otherwise than under that Act, which has no property other than the premises of any school or schools falling within *subsection (1)(a)* of the Act (and is not an exempt charity), from the requirement to register with the Commission. Charities excepted from the requirement to register under this section will not be affected by the changes to the exceptions regime, as the general income registration threshold for charities would have applied to them in any event.

CHARITIES REGISTERED WITH OTHER BODIES

48.6   Some charities are excepted from registering with the Charity Commission because they are registered with another body. Examples include:

- some Scout and Guide groups;
- some voluntary state schools, provided they hold no property apart from school premises;
- some places of worship; and
- about 25,000 armed forces charities wholly or mainly concerned with the promotion of the efficiency of the armed forces.

SMALL CHARITIES

48.7   Very small charities, i.e. any charity whose income from all sources does not in aggregate amount to more than the registration threshold, are excepted from the requirement to register, as they are felt to be too small to merit the degree of scrutiny that registration brings. [*Charities Act 1993, s 3*]. This threshold was revised and simplified by *s 9* of the 2006 Act. Charities with an annual income below £5,000 will no longer be required to register and existing charities under this threshold will be able to ask to be removed from the register.

PLACES OF WORSHIP

48.8   Places of worship registered under the *Places of Worship Registration Act 1855* are excepted from registering. The exception in respect of registered places of worship should not be misunderstood. All churches are not automatically excepted because of this section: certain properties are registered under the *Places of Worship Registration Act 1855*, but the exception, and rate relief, attaches only to the property (and related buildings) itself, and not to activities undertaken within the property.

48.9   Under the provision of the *Places of Worship Registration Act 1855*, a congregation may apply for a building to be certified as a place of worship by applying to the superintendent registrar in the district where the venue is situated. This excludes churches or chapels of the Church of England, unless it shares a church building with another religious denomination.

REGULATION

48.10 An excepted charity is under a very similar regulatory regime as any registered charity. The general trust and stewardship obligations apply, they can seek advice and support from the Charity Commission and are subject to its powers of investigation. They are bound by the same rules on public collections, and are subject to the same rules for the preparation of accounts. The tax concessions that apply to registered charities also apply to excepted charities. Excepted charities must comply with the *Charities Act 1993* (as amended) requirements on the sale, leasing, mortgage or disposal of land. There are, however, a few key differences. Firstly, by definition, excepted charities will not have a registered charity number (unless they are voluntarily registered). Where it is necessary to produce evidence of charitable status, it is generally acceptable to quote an HMRC reference, making clear that this is a tax reference, and not a registered charity number.

48.11 An excepted charity does not have to file its annual accounts and report with the Charity Commission, unless it is voluntarily registered and has an annual income over £10,000, although the Charity Commission has the power to ask for them. Excepted charities may not have to comply with the Charities Act requirements on the examination and audit of accounts, though most will have their own internal guidance on accounting and audit, which will often be more stringent than the *Charities Act 1993* requirements. For instance, the Church of England rules for Parochial Church Councils (PCCs) do not recognise the light touch regime. They require all PCCs to be examined or audited.

OPERATION OF OTHER CHARITIES

48.12 Excepted charities may also operate other charities. If these are separately constituted or are outside the objects of the excepted charity, then they should not automatically be assumed to fall within the exception. A separate charity operated by an excepted charity may need to be registered in its own right and accounts and audit procedures complied with individually.

SCOTLAND

48.13 Excepted charities do not exist in the same way in Scotland, although a comparable regime relates to designated religious charities.

48.14 *Section 65* of the *Charities and Trustee Investment (Scotland) Act 2005* allows OSCR to designate a charity that meets certain criteria as a designated religious charity. To be designated, the body's main purpose must be the advancement of religion, its main activity must be the regular holding of public worship, it must have been established in Scotland for at least ten years and have a membership of at least 3,000 over the age of 16. In addition, it must have an internal organisation with supervisory and disciplinary functions over all its component parts and have a regime for keeping accounting records which OSCR considers correspond to those for other charities.

48.15   Excepted Charities

48.15   Designated religious charities are exempt from certain provisions of the *Charities and Trustee Investment (Scotland) Act 2005*; they do not need to seek OSCR's consent for certain changes to their constitutions, OSCR may not direct them or their trustees to stop undertaking activities, nor to suspend the charity trustees following its inquiries. The Court of Session may not appoint a judicial factor, appoint a trustee, nor suspend a charity trustee or manager of the religious charity.

49   Exempt Charities

49.1   Exempt charities are bodies that are established for charitable purposes, but which have not been allowed to register with the Charity Commission because it was assumed that they were adequately overseen by other public bodies, such as the Financial Services Authority, the Housing Corporation, the Higher Education Funding Council for England and the Department for Culture, Media and Sport. The *Charities Act 2006* makes sure that these charities are monitored for their compliance with charity law.

49.2   Exempt charities include:

- charitable friendly societies, which must comply with the *Financial Services and Markets Acts 2000* and the *Mutual Societies Order 2001*;

- charitable industrial and provident societies, which are registered in the register of social landlords under *Part 1* of the *Housing Act 1996*;

- higher education corporations, which must comply with the *Education Reform Act 1988*, as amended;

49.3   The 2006 Act puts previously exempt charities into two categories:

- Those already regulated by a body, other than the Charity Commission, which has agreed to take responsibility for ensuring that they comply with charity law. These charities will continue to be exempt and will be regulated by their current regulator, now known as their 'principal regulator'. The Charity Commission will be able to investigate these charities at the request of their principal regulator.

- If no suitable regulator exists then a previously exempt charity will stop being exempt and will have to register with the Charity Commission. Initially only such previously exempt charities with an annual income of over £100,000 will have to register. Those under the £100,000 will not have to register but they will come under the jurisdiction of the Charity Commission. This £100,000 threshold may be reduced in the future but this will not happen until the Act is reviewed in about five years' time.

49.4   Schedule 2 of the *Charities Act 1993* gives a list of exempt charities. *Section 11* of the *Charities Act 2006* amends this list, removing some specified institutions and adding others.

49.5   The Charity Commission has limited powers in connection with the administration of exempt charities as they are subject to the jurisdiction of another supervisory body. The Commission can only exercise its powers under the *Charities Act 1993 s 8* to institute an inquiry into the affairs of an exempt charity if requested to do so by the charity's principal regulator. Exempt charities do not have to comply with the *Charities Act 1993* requirements on the sale, leasing, disposal and mortgaging of land, and do not have to comply with the *Charities Act 1993* requirements relating to the form and content of accounts, audit and annual report. However, they are subject to the more general provisions of the 1993 Act. For instance, they are required to keep proper accounting records, and prepare accounts for periods of up to 15 months. The accounting requirements of their particular principal regulator are likely to be similar to those of the Charity Commission. Under the *Charities Act 1993 s 16* the Charity Commission can make Schemes for the application of property *cy-près* and for the administration of an exempt charity. It can make Orders to vest land in the Official Custodian for Charities (*ss 16* and *21*) and to sanction actions that are in the interests of an exempt charity but not within the trustees' existing powers (*s 26*). The Commission can authorise *ex gratia* payments under *s 27*, accept documents for safekeeping under *s 30*, and waive the disqualification of a trustee under *s 72*. The Commission can also make Schemes under *s 17* to establish common investment funds for exempt charities and under *s 24* to establish common deposit funds.

49.6   *Schedule 5* of the *Charities Act 2006* provides for increased regulation of exempt charities, as parts of the 1993 Act that formerly did not apply to exempt charities now apply. For example, exempt charities are no longer excluded from the Commission's powers to require a charity's name to be changed, or its power to call for documents.

49.7   As with any charity, the trustees (or a trustee) of an exempt charity may write to the Charity Commission for formal advice about a proposed course of action, and in following that advice the trustees will be deemed to have acted in accordance with their trusts. [*Charities Act 1993, s 29*]. This is always subject to the trustees not having reasonable cause to suspect that:

- the advice was given in ignorance of material facts; or

- material facts have changed since the advice was given; or

- a court decision has also been obtained; or

- there are proceedings in hand to obtain a court decision.

49.8   Trustees of exempt charities may be incorporated under the *Charities Act 1993, s 50*, in the same way as those of a registered charity and the Charity Commission can amend, enforce or dissolve their certificates of incorporation (*ss 56, 58* and *61*).

49.9   Exempt charities are subject to the same tax regime as registered charities and the provisions in *Part II* of the *Charities Act 1992* relating to fund-raising also apply to them.

49.10   Exempt charities are not closely controlled by the Charity Commission as this is the role of each principal regulator. The principal regulator has a general duty to do all that it reasonably can to meet the compliance objective in relation to the charity. The compliance objective is defined in the 2006 Act as 'to promote compliance by the charity trustees with their legal obligations in exercising control and management of the administration of the charity'. Trustees of exempt charities need to be aware of their own constitutional requirements, and the principles of charity and trust law generally. In particular, the Charities SORP does not apply only to registered charities, and so an exempt charity should follow it unless another, more specific SORP must be followed. In the context of charitable status, the term 'exempt' has no relevance to the type of supply for VAT purposes.

50   Exemptions from VAT

BACKGROUND

50.1   *European VAT Directive 2006/112* provides the basis for exemptions from VAT in the areas of social welfare and property. These reliefs are enacted in UK law by the *Value Added Tax Act (VATA) 1994, Sch* 9. Charities are most likely to find the following relevant:

- *Group 1:* Land and Buildings

- *Group 6:* Education

- *Group 7:* Health and welfare

- *Group 9:* Trade Unions and Professional Bodies

- *Group 10:* Sporting services provided by Non-profit Making Bodies

- *Group 12:* Fund-raising

- *Group 13:* Cultural services.

50.2   The advantage of an exempt supply is that it is not subject to VAT and charities whose supplies fall within this category may therefore benefit. However, unlike zero-rated supplies, there is normally no relief for input tax on supplies of goods and services used by the charity in making exempt supplies. VAT incurred on the costs of making exempt supplies may only be recovered if it is *de minimis* (see 125.11). A charity making only exempt supplies cannot normally register for VAT.

50.3   The HMRC Notices mentioned in this chapter are available from the National Advice Service or can be accessed or downloaded at www.hmrc.gov.uk. The information contained in these Notices and in this section is for general guidance only, and can never be a substitute for detailed professional guidance.

LAND AND BUILDINGS: GROUP 1

50.4   Charities may buy, sell, lease or rent out properties and may also carry out major refurbishments to such properties. Each of these transactions has VAT implications and, although the legislation in this area is somewhat of a minefield, with careful professional guidance a charity may be able to make significant VAT savings.

50.5   *VATA 1994 Sch 9 Group 1* sets out the general rule that a lease of land, a right over land or licence to occupy land is exempt. The 'election to waive exemption' (also known as the 'option to tax') allows a person (including a charity) to tax some, but not all, supplies of property. It applies on a building by building basis and can be exercised by a person making what would otherwise be an exempt supply in relation to a building or undeveloped land. The election is binding on the owner of the relevant interest in the land/building and does not automatically pass when the interest is disposed of.

Supplies not affected by the option to tax

50.6   Certain supplies remain exempt even though the option to tax has been exercised on the property in question. These are very important for charities and include the following.

- A building or part of a building intended for use as a dwelling or number of dwellings or solely for a relevant residential purpose (see CHAPTER 130). An option to tax can still have effect where:

    — at or before the time of the grant/sale both the parties agree in writing that the vendor will exercise the option to tax; and

    — at the time the supply is made, the purchaser intends to use the property for the purpose of making a zero-rated supply under *VATA 1994 Sch 8 Group 5 Item 1(b)*, i.e. for conversion into one or more dwellings, or for use solely for a relevant residential purpose (e.g. care home, hospice, student residence etc.).

- A building or part of a building intended for use solely for a relevant charitable purpose (see CHAPTER 130), other than as an office.

- A supply of land to a registered housing association which certifies to the supplier that the land is to be used for the construction of dwellings or buildings solely for a relevant residential purpose other than as an office.

50.7   The complex anti-avoidance provisions introduced by the *Finance Act 1997* disapplying the option to tax in specified circumstances are outside the scope of this book, though they are considered in the chapter 'Land and Buildings' in *Tolley's VAT Planning*.

Exercising the option to tax

50.8   The option will have no effect unless written notification of it is given to the National Option To Tax Unit, Glasgow within 30 days of it having been made or such longer period allowed by HMRC. The written notification must state unambiguously which property is involved and the date from which the option has effect. *VATA 1994 Sch 10 Item 2* sets out the general requirements.

50.9   A person wishing to exercise an option to tax land or property from which they have already received exempt income must usually first obtain written permission from HMRC. Also, an option cannot be made retrospectively, although HMRC will usually accept a belated notification of an option, e.g. where VAT has been charged on rents but not notified to them.

Effect of opting to tax

50.10   The option is generally a relieving measure which allows a landlord to recover VAT incurred on, for example, the construction, refurbishment or management of a property. Once a charity has exercised the option for any property it must charge VAT on all future supplies in relation to that property which would otherwise be exempt. For example, it is not possible to exercise the option in order to tax rents, but then to sell on an exempt basis the freehold of a property in future. The option remains effective even if the property is sold and re-acquired.

50.11   Unless the lease specifically provides otherwise, a landlord has a right to add VAT to the rent agreed under the lease following an option to tax – there is nothing in the legislation requiring him to consult his tenant before opting. Tenants that are exempt or partly exempt will suffer irrecoverable input tax if their landlord exercises the option to tax. If partly exempt, the tenant will be unable to recover all their input tax under the partial exemption rules, unless it falls within the *de minimis* limit. Where the exempt input tax of a tenant does not amount to more than £625 per month on average and 50% of total input tax, all such input tax is treated as attributable to taxable supplies and therefore recoverable in full subject to the normal rules.

Revoking the option to tax

50.12   An option to tax can be revoked within three months from the date on which it is made, provided it has not been put into practical effect through the charging of VAT or the recovery of input tax, and provided that the property in question has not been purchased as a VAT free transfer of a going concern. This, therefore, has little practical benefit. Revocation is also allowed 20 or more years after the election has had effect. In all cases, the person exercising the option to tax must obtain the written consent of HMRC to the revocation.

Restrictions on use by a charity

50.13   HMRC take the view that a tenant intending to use a building (or part of one) for a relevant charitable purpose is not required by law to issue a qualifying use certificate to the landlord. This could put the landlord at risk, since he is unable to opt to tax, but there is no onus on the tenant to prove his user status. Landlords who have opted, or who intend to opt, and who receive claims that a building is being used, or is intended for use, for a qualifying purpose, may seek to obtain suitable indemnities from the tenant.

Other supplies of interests in land

50.14   These include the following:

- Payments made to a landlord to surrender a lease or vary the terms of a lease are exempt from VAT, unless the landlord has opted to tax.

- Reverse surrender payments, i.e. where the landlord pays the tenant to surrender his lease, are exempt unless the tenant has exercised the option.

- Inducement payments such as reverse premiums are outside the scope of VAT unless a payment is linked to benefits a tenant will provide outside normal lease terms. Examples of standard rated benefits are tenants carrying out building works to improve the property by undertaking necessary repairs or an upgrade, carrying out fitting-out or refurbishment which is the landlord's responsibility or acting as an anchor tenant.

- Grants of licences to occupy land where the land is unspecified, so that the tenant has unspecified use, are standard rated for VAT.

- Dilapidation payments made to a landlord to cover wear and tear on vacation of a property are outside the scope for VAT.

50.15 Exemptions from VAT

50.15   In general, the area of land and property VAT is highly complex and professional advice should be sought.

EDUCATION: GROUP 6

50.16   The supply of education, research or vocational training by a charity will generally be exempt if it is made for consideration. If the charity is not a school, university or other similarly approved institution, exemption will only apply if it falls within the definition in *VATA 1994 Sch 9 Group 6 note 1(f)*, i.e. 'any other body which is precluded from distributing and does not distribute the profit it makes and which applies those profits to the continuance or improvement of such supplies'. It is therefore important to ensure that, although a charitable organisation may overall be non-profit making, if exemption is desired, then any surplus created by a particular activity should be put back into the same project rather than applied elsewhere. The supply of any goods or services (other than examinations services) which are closely connected to the supply of education, research or vocational training are also exempt provided that they are for the direct use of the pupil, student or trainee. Examples include accommodation, catering, transport and school trips.

50.17   When a charity purchases supplies of education or training, they will be exempt from VAT if supplied by an eligible body such as a university. In the case of research, the supply will be exempt if made by one eligible body to another. However, supplies of research by an eligible body to an ineligible one, e.g. medical research supplied to a commercial enterprise such as a pharmaceutical company, will be taxable at the standard rate.

50.18   Charities should note that, in some cases, it may be beneficial to ensure that VAT is charged on educational services, e.g. where the supply is to a body such as an NHS Trust or a local authority that can generally recover the VAT charged. In that instance, the use of a trading subsidiary structure should be considered.

50.19   HMRC Notice 'Education and Vocational Training' (Notice 701/30) sets out detailed guidance on this area and can be accessed or downloaded at *www.hmrc.gov.uk*. The Notice gives examples of what constitutes 'education', 'research' and 'vocational training'.

HEALTH AND WELFARE: GROUP 7

Welfare

50.20   Welfare services and related goods supplied by charities may qualify for exemption if certain conditions are fulfilled. *VATA 1994 Sch 9 Group 7 items 9 and 10* exempt:

- *Item 9*: the supply, otherwise than for profit, by a charity, state-regulated private welfare institution or agency or public body of welfare services and of goods supplied in connection therewith.

- *Item 10*: the supply, otherwise than for profit, of goods and services incidental to the provision of spiritual welfare by a religious community to a resident member of that community in return for a subscription or other consideration paid as a condition of membership.

266

50.21   Welfare services are defined as financial and other assistance given to people in need, and are directly connected with:

- the provision of care, treatment or instruction designed to promote the physical or mental welfare of elderly, sick, distressed or disabled persons;

- the protection of children and young persons; or

- the provision of spiritual welfare by a religious institution as part of a course of instruction or a retreat, not being a course or a retreat designed primarily to provide recreation or a holiday.

50.22   The three main strands of any welfare services are as follows:

- they will be of help and benefit to the recipient;

- they will be given rather than sold – although HMRC accept that a nominal charge can be made;

- they will be provided to people in need.

50.23   'Care, treatment or instruction' includes the protection, control or guidance of an individual when this is provided to meet physical, personal or domestic needs.

50.24   The exemption does not include the supply of accommodation or catering except where it is ancillary to the provision of care, treatment or instruction.

'Otherwise than for profit'

50.25   This phrase was considered by the Court of Appeal in *Customs & Excise Comrs v Bell Concord Educational Trust Ltd [1989] STC 264*, in the context of education provided by a charity. It was held that the making of a surplus was not an object of the company and that it did not systematically aim to make a profit. The Trust's memorandum and articles provided that no distributions could be made to members and, since the only activity of the charity was the provision of education, it was decided that supplies were made otherwise than for profit. HMRC have interpreted this case as allowing charities to budget for a surplus in setting fees, provided that the surplus is ploughed back directly into the activity in question. Where the charity intends to use the surplus as a subsidy for different activities it is seen as operating for a profit and its activities do not qualify for exemption, even where the subsidised activities are charitable in their own right.

Supplies of welfare services 'at below cost'

50.26   By concession the supply of welfare services and related goods made by charities consistently 'below cost' to people for the relief of distress are non-business supplies and therefore outside the scope of VAT. 'Below cost' means the cost of providing the welfare is subsidised by at least 15% from the charity's own funds. HMRC will need to be satisfied that the subsidised services are available equally to all distressed persons. The service subsidy must be available not only to those people who cannot afford to pay the full rate but also to those who can afford it. Further, it must not be applied conditionally, e.g. only during spells of very cold weather or only to persons living in a certain area or of a certain age. Any services provided for people who are not distressed could attract VAT.

Meals on wheels and catering

50.27   This service is often run by a charity on behalf of a local authority. Any charge made to the recipient for the meals is not consideration paid to the charity but is part of the local authority's non-business income. If the charity makes a charge to the local authority for providing the service, this is a taxable supply of a delivery service and not a welfare supply by the charity. The local authorities can recover the VAT charged.

50.28   Supplies of food and drink by charities from trolleys, canteens or shops are business but exempt when connected with the welfare of those in hospital or prison, or those visiting them (HMRC Notice 701/1/ 'Charities').

The 'protection of children and young persons'

50.29   This exemption is not limited to protection from harm but also includes:

- services designed to improve the well-being of the young; and

- the protection of the young from malign influences.

An example of a welfare service falling within this category is the provision of accommodation in a children's home.

'Spiritual welfare'

50.30   In determining whether a supply qualifies as spiritual welfare HMRC look to the intention behind the supply. Useful indicators include the way in which the supply is advertised and the objects and purpose of the organisation making the supply. A meeting of persons who have suffered a bereavement would qualify where the purpose of the meeting is held out as the provision of spiritual succour. On the other hand, conferences, courses of instruction or retreats cannot be treated as exempt when the spiritual welfare element is an incidental benefit and not the main purpose of the supply. For example, a course in theology is not the provision of spiritual welfare but an educational process. The charity could instead consider whether this supply falls within the education exemption (see **50.16**). As with welfare, the recipient of spiritual welfare must be a person in need of such and not someone who merely wishes to expand their knowledge of spiritual matters.

50.31   Exemption is afforded to the supply of goods only when they are provided by a charity in connection with a welfare service.

HEALTH

50.32   The provision of medical services for a consideration is generally exempt from VAT. From 1 May 2007 the law was amended to clarify that this relates only to the provision of medical care and not to other services provided by medical professionals such as preparing reports for third parties or acting as an expert witness. Most services are exempted under *items 1, 2, 3* and *5* of *Group 7*. This exemption extends to the services of unqualified staff who are supervised by registered staff, e.g. a qualified nurse supervising an unqualified care assistant. Broadly, the services exempted cover most medical and paramedical professionals including doctors, dentists, nurses, ophthalmic opticians, chiropodists and physiotherapists. They do not cover the services of health professionals who are not listed in the register kept by the Health Professional Council, such as acupuncturists.

50.33   The exemption in *Group 4* is a wide exemption to cover the provision of care or medical or surgical treatment in an approved hospital or other institution. This would cover a private hospital, authorised hospices, etc. The exemption does not extend to veterinary hospitals or practices.

TRADE UNIONS AND PROFESSIONAL BODIES: GROUP 9

50.34   *VATA 1994 Sch 9 Group 9* allows for the provision of facilities and advantages to members of clubs, associations and other such organisations, by certain non-profit making bodies, to be treated as VAT exempt. The non-profit making bodies falling into this category would be trade unions, or similar organisations whose main objective is to negotiate the terms and conditions of employment of its members, professional associations whereby membership is restricted to individuals seeking or holding an appropriate qualification, learned or representational associations, and other similar organisations.

50.35   The exemption covers the provision of services and related goods by the qualifying body to its members, provided that they are made available without payment (other than a membership subscription) and provided they relate to the aims of the organisation.

50.36   Exemption does not apply to:

- supplies that do not relate to the body's aims as set out in its rules or constitution;

- the supply of any right of admission to any premises, event, or performance, to which non-members are admitted for a consideration;

- any supplies which are not provided automatically as a result of membership and for which an additional sum is charged; and

- supplies to non-members.

50.37   Where clearly identifiable zero-rated benefits (i.e. a yearbook) are provided in return for membership subscriptions, the subscription may be apportioned between exempt and zero-rated benefits. Such apportionment is allowed by concession only to non-profit making bodies.

SPORTING SERVICES PROVIDED BY NON-PROFIT MAKING BODIES: GROUP 10

50.38   An exemption from VAT for sporting and physical education services supplied by non-profit making bodies to individual sporting participants exempts services closely linked with and essential to sport or physical recreation supplied to individuals taking part in the activity where the supplies are made by:

- a 'non-profit making body' having members, to those of its members who are granted membership for a period of three months or more; and

- a 'non-profit making body' which does not run a membership scheme (e.g. a charity).

50.39   The supply of any services of residential accommodation, catering, bar facilities or transport as well as supplies by local authorities, government departments and non-departmental public bodies such as Sports Councils are specifically excluded.

50.40   A 'non-profit making body' is one whose constitution or articles of association preclude it from distributing surpluses of income over expenditure to its members, shareholders or any other party. However, sporting services will not be excluded from exemption simply because profits on certain activities are used to subsidise other activities (e.g. profits on the bar are used to subsidise subscriptions).

50.41   After several attempts, changes to *Group 10* were introduced with effect from 1 January 2000. The changes are aimed at preventing VAT avoidance by proprietary clubs and to restrict the exemption to genuine non-profit making sports clubs.

50.42   Further details of the exemption and the anti-avoidance measures are contained in HMRC Notice 701/45 'Sport'. These are complex and professional advice should be taken if appropriate.

RELIEF FOR IMPORTATION

50.44   Charities are entitled to special reliefs from VAT on certain imports of goods from a place outside the Member States of the EU. These are not exemptions within *Sch 9* of *VATA 1994*, but are contained in EC law and in UK statutory instruments and statements of practice. They include the following.

- Basic necessities (i.e. food, medicines, clothing, blankets, orthopaedic equipment and crutches, required to meet a person's immediate needs) obtained without charge for distribution free of charge to the needy by a 'relevant organisation'. Excluded are alcoholic beverages, tobacco products, coffee, tea and motor vehicles other than ambulances.

- Goods donated by a person established outside the Member States to a 'relevant organisation' for use to raise funds at occasional charity events for the benefit of the needy also qualify for relief. There must be no commercial intent on the part of the donor. Alcoholic beverages etc. are excluded as above.

- Goods imported by a 'relevant organisation' for distribution or loan, free of charge, to victims of, or for meeting its operating needs in the relief of, a disaster affecting the territory of one or more Member States. This relief applies only if the EC Commission has authorised the importation of the goods.

- Articles donated to or imported by an approved organisation principally engaged in the education of, or the provision of assistance to, blind or handicapped persons for loan, hire or transfer on a non-profit making basis where those goods are specially designed for the education or employment.

50.45   'Relevant organisation' means a State organisation or other approved charitable or philanthropic organisation.

50.46   The above reliefs are conditional on:

- the goods being put to the use or purpose specified; and

- unless specifically allowed, the goods not being lent, hired out or transferred unless to an organisation which would itself be entitled to the
  relief if importing the goods on that date. In the latter case, prior
  notification in writing must be received from HMRC and the goods
  must be used solely in accordance with the relieving provisions.

50.47   Full details of all the goods which qualify for relief are contained in HMRC
         Notice 317 'Imports by Charities'.

FUND-RAISING: GROUP 12

50.48   In the case of charity fund-raising events, it is important that the planning of
         such events extends to ensuring that they fall within the scope of the VAT
         exemption where this is advantageous, as will usually be the case. People
         attending or participating in the event must be aware of its primary fund-
         raising purpose. Social events which incidentally make a profit do not fall
         within the exemption. Nor do events which form part of a social calendar for
         members, for another purpose (such as an AGM) , street collections or flag
         days (which are outside the scope of VAT) , travel packages or the sale of
         goods unless in the context of a qualifying fund-raising event. HMRC have
         advised that this means publicity material, tickets and other items which
         should clearly refer to the fund-raising purpose of the event.

50.49   Prior to 1 April 2000 a fund-raising event was defined as a fête, ball, bazaar,
         gala show, performance or similar event which is separate from, and not
         forming any part of, a series of regularly run or similar events. With effect
         from 1 April 2000, all fund-raising events including participatory, internet
         and 'virtual' events are exempt, subject to the conditions on the number of
         events described in paragraph **50.50** below. Goods and services connected
         with a fund-raising event and within the scope of the exemption include
         admission charges, sponsorship income directly connected to the fund-
         raising event, sales of advertising space in commemorative brochures and
         merchandising income. In relation to merchandising income, if the licence to
         market items connected with the event is granted to third parties, the licence
         fee will be exempt, but the merchandise sold by third parties will be taxable.

50.50   The exemption used to be limited to one-off events. However, with effect
         from 1 April 2000, a charity can now conduct up to 15 fund-raising events of
         any one type in any one location in any one year. In addition an unlimited
         number of small-scale events, such as coffee mornings, where gross takings do
         not exceed £1,000, can now be held and treated as exempt. Events carried out
         more than once or twice a week are more likely to be seen as regular trading
         activities and be excluded from exemption.

50.51   The EC legislation does not specify that fund-raising must be the main
         purpose of the event. Accordingly, in the case of *Newsvendors Benevolent
         Institution, Lon/96/567, July 1996 (14343)* the tribunal found that a charity
         which raised funds through holding a festival dinner and carol concert came
         within the exemption even though the events served other purposes, i.e. the
         dinner dance was originally organised to thank contributors and to enable the
         outgoing festival chairman to hand over to his successor, and the carol concert

was a religious service. However, if the raising of funds is merely an incidental purpose, the event will not qualify for VAT exemption.

50.52   For the purpose of this exemption, 'charity' includes a body corporate which is wholly owned by a charity and whose profits, from whatever source, are payable to a charity by virtue of a deed of covenant or trust or otherwise. The fact that a subsidiary can shed profits using the Gift Aid scheme does not affect the VAT exemption. Where it is advantageous to a charity to maintain taxable trading (e.g. to recover input tax) it should also be possible for a trading subsidiary to achieve this through the charity allowing it to retain some of its profits.

ALTERNATIVE STRUCTURES FOR FUND-RAISING EVENTS

50.53   When a fund-raising event does not qualify for exempt treatment, it is still open to a charity to set a basic minimum charge which will be standard rated, and to invite those attending the event to supplement this with a voluntary donation. The extra contributions will be outside the scope of VAT if all the following conditions are met:

- it is clearly stated on all publicity material, including tickets, that anyone paying only the minimum charge will be admitted without a further payment;

- the extra payment does not give any particular benefit (for example admission to a better position in the stadium or auditorium);

- the extent of further contributions is ultimately left to ticket holders to decide, even if the organiser indicates a desired level of donation;

- for film or theatre performances, concerts, sporting fixtures, etc. the minimum charge is not less than the usual price of the particular seats at a normal commercial event of the same type;

- for dances, dinners and similar functions, the minimum total sum upon which the organisers will be liable to account for VAT will not be less than their total costs incurred in arranging the event.

50.54   If the publicity material for a fund-raising event suggests that those paying a recommended extra amount are more likely to be admitted than those paying merely the basic ticket price, then the extra amount becomes part of the consideration for a supply of services, rather than a pure donation, and as such the full payment is subject to VAT at the standard rate. Further details of the fund-raising exemption can be found in HMRC Notice CWL4 which can be accessed or downloaded at *www.hmrc.gov.uk*.

CULTURAL SERVICES: GROUP 13

50.55   *VATA 1994, Sch 9, Group 13* provides an exemption from VAT since 1 June 1996 (but backdated to 1 January 1990) for admission charges to certain cultural places and events. In particular, it exempts the supply by a public body or an eligible body of a right of admission to:

- a museum, gallery, art exhibition or zoo; or

- a theatrical, musical or choreographic performance of a cultural nature.

A charity may fall within the definition of 'eligible body' where it:

- is precluded from distributing, and does not distribute, any profit it makes;

- applies any profits made from the above-mentioned supplies to the continuance or improvement of the facilities made available by means of the supplies.

50.56   However, the exemption only applies where the body is managed and administered on a voluntary basis by persons who have no direct or indirect financial interest in its activities. HMRC now accept that the financial interest must be actual rather than potential and that no direct or indirect interest exists unless payments are made to a manager/administrator above the market rate, paid as routine overheads or are at all profit-related and there is also a link between the payments and the person's participation in the direction of the charity's activities.

50.57   The decision of the European Court of Justice in the *Zoological Society of London* case, (*[2002] STC 521*), was the first to clarify the law in this area. HMRC now accept that an organisation can be managed and administered on an 'essentially' voluntary basis even when it uses paid employees to carry out most of the day-to-day activities of the organisation. The crucial point is that persons exercising strategic management and control must not be paid. HMRC's policy is that if just one such person manages and administers the charity at the highest level, then exemption cannot be allowed.

FURTHER INFORMATION

50.59   Further detail on the exemption may be found in HMRC Notice and Updates 701/47 'Culture". This can be a complex area and charitable cultural bodies would be prudent to review their VAT status in the light of the guidance therein.

51 Expenses

51.1   Payments by a charity to volunteers, including members of the governing body, or members of staff are generally either remuneration or reimbursement of out-of-pocket expenses. It is important to distinguish between these types of payment and ascertain whether the recipient is a volunteer or staff member for a number of legal reasons and because the tax treatment of the payment may vary as a result.

51.2   'Out-of-pocket' expenses are necessary costs genuinely incurred by staff or volunteers in the nature of the work they do for an organisation. Examples are the cost of any necessary travel, other than the cost of travelling between home and the usual place of work, postage, stationery, telephone calls, cleaning materials for the charity's premises, hotel accommodation if the person is required to be away from home overnight and the cost of providing care for a dependant. It is good practice to issue guidance about the maximum amount that can be claimed for such things as meals, hotels and dependant care.

51.3   Charities should require any person claiming out-of-pocket expenses to produce a receipt for the expenditure unless it is genuinely impossible to do so, e.g. fees for cloakrooms or parking meters. Receipts should be kept by the person responsible for producing the charity's accounts for audit purposes and in case the Charity Commission, OSCR, HMRC or the Benefits Agency asks to see them. Charities should have an appropriate system for authorising claims for expenses.

TAX

51.4   Income tax does not have to be paid on genuine expenses allowed by HMRC, and receipt of such expenses does not affect a person's entitlement to benefits. However, if the charity reimburses expenses to paid staff which HMRC does not allow for employees, such as the cost of travel between home and the usual place of work, these will be subject to tax and national insurance.

51.5   Different tax rules apply to unpaid volunteers. Unpaid volunteers may be reimbursed tax-free for travel expenses between home and the usual place of volunteering, for the actual cost of meals taken because of voluntary work for more than four hours in any one day, or because the voluntary work must be carried out at meal times, and for the cost of dependant care necessary to allow the volunteer to be available for voluntary work.

51.6   Charities have to declare reimbursed expenses on the HMRC form P11D or P9D unless the charity has a dispensation. Dispensations are granted to organisations whose only entries on P11D and/or P9D forms would relate to the reimbursement of expenses genuinely incurred wholly in the course of business or to accommodation paid for directly by the charity to a hotel, guesthouse or other provider on behalf of the employee. If the charity does not have a dispensation the recipients must declare their reimbursed expenses on their income tax self-assessment forms. Therefore good record-keeping is essential.

RIGHT TO BE REIMBURSED

51.7 Employers have a statutory duty under the *Employment Rights Act 1996* to reimburse their employees for expenses incurred in carrying out their employer's requirements. Under the *Trustee Act 1925, s 30(2)* trustees of charitable trusts and associations, including holding and custodian trustees, have a statutory right to be reimbursed for any expense incurred in their service as a trustee. Members of charitable associations who are not trustees do not have a statutory right to have their expenses reimbursed. However, they can be reimbursed if this is not prohibited by the charity's governing document. Trustees of charitable companies do not have a statutory right to have their expenses reimbursed. Their expenses can only be reimbursed if the governing document contains an explicit clause permitting the payment of trustees' expenses or if the members have approved payment. Trustees of charitable industrial and provident societies can have their expenses reimbursed provided that their rules contain a clause explicitly permitting this.

51.8 Expenses reimbursed to trustees must be disclosed in the charity's annual accounts.

EXPENSES OR REMUNERATION?

51.9 Salaries and wages are clearly remuneration. However, some other payments or benefits commonly referred to as 'expenses' may in fact amount to remuneration and therefore be forbidden by law or the charity's governing document. Such payments may also be subject to income tax or could affect the State benefits a person is receiving. Examples of payments to volunteers that are often described as 'expenses' but which are really remuneration include:

- honoraria;
- per diem expenses that are paid regardless of the amount actually spent;
- payments to compensate for loss of earnings;
- payments that the claimant would have incurred anyway, e.g. home telephone line rental; and
- mileage rates above those set by HMRC.

PAYMENTS TO TRUSTEES

51.10 Particular care must be taken with payments to trustees. It is a basic principle of trust law that trustees must not benefit from their trust unless the governing document contains an express power permitting payment, or payment has been authorised by the Charity Commission or the Court. 'Benefit' includes any property, goods, or services which have a monetary value, as well as money. Reimbursing genuine expenses does not produce a benefit for the trustee, it merely prevents them from being worse off as a result of their trusteeship. However, any form of remuneration is a benefit and is therefore a breach of trust unless it falls within the scope of *Charities Act 1993, s 73A*, as amended by the *Charities Act 2006*, or is explicitly authorised by the governing document, the Charity Commission or the Court. If a trustee has received an improper payment or benefit they can be required to repay the amount received to the charity or, if the benefit was in goods or kind, a sum equivalent to the value of the benefit received.

51.11 Expenses

51.11 Some governing documents permit trustees from certain professions, such as solicitors or accountants, to be paid for providing professional services to the charity. In some instances the Charity Commission will authorise payments to trustees for professional services when this is not explicitly allowed in the governing document. *Section 36* of the *Charities Act 2006* permits trustees to be paid for providing specific goods or services to the charity over and above their normal trustee duties in certain circumstances. If a trustee is to benefit in this way the other trustees should consider whether or not it is truly in the best interests of the charity to use that particular trustee or their firm. The discussion should be minuted and the minute should make it clear that the person concerned was not present for that part of the meeting and, if required to do so, had declared their interest.

51.12 The restrictions on paying trustees apply not just to individuals but also to businesses which the trustee owns, or in which the trustee is a partner or has a substantial share holding, or of which the trustee is the managing director. Many governing documents include a clause which prohibits the charity from entering into contracts with a company in which a trustee owns shares amounting to 1% or more of the voting rights.

51.13 Trustees of charitable trusts and associations who are solicitors may ask their partners to undertake paid professional work for the charity, however it must be clear that it is the partner or partners personally that are being hired and not the firm.

51.14 Trustees of charitable companies are under a statutory duty to disclose the nature and extent of any interest in any transaction (*Companies Act 2006, s 182*). This Companies Act requirement is only modified to the extent that the company's articles permit. The governing documents or codes of practice of some unincorporated charities also require trustees to disclose any conflicts of interest. If the governing document of a charitable company permits trustees to be paid, either for their work as directors of a charitable company or for work that they do for the charity, a copy of their service contract or a memorandum setting out the terms of their remuneration must be kept and must be available to company members. Any form of remuneration paid to trustees must be disclosed in the charity's annual accounts.

51.15 Trustees who receive a fee for acting on the board of directors of their charity's wholly owned, non-charitable, trading subsidiary may keep the fee if the governing document of the charity explicitly allows this, or if they have applied to the Charity Commission and been granted authority to keep the fee. Otherwise they must pay the fee to the charity.

PAYMENTS TO MEMBERS

51.16 Members of charities who are not trustees may receive remuneration provided this is not prohibited by the governing document.

52   Friendly Societies

52.1   A very small number of charities are formed as friendly societies. A friendly society is a voluntary mutual organisation whose main purpose is to assist members (usually financially) during sickness, unemployment or retirement, and to provide life assurance. Friendly societies are often confused with industrial and provident societies, which have similar rules. Both are represented in the *Friendly and Industrial and Provident Societies Act 1968*. However, friendly societies have distinct legislation that is generally unfamiliar even to professional advisers because of the relatively small number of charitable friendly societies: in 1996 there were only 72 benevolent friendly societies in existence.

52.2   Under the *Friendly Societies Act 1974* some self-help and benevolent societies, some of which were charitable, could be registered as friendly societies. They were classified as exempt charities and did not have to register with the Charity Commission. After the enactment of the *Charities Act 1993* friendly societies were not allowed to register with the Commission, even if they wanted to, and registration ceased to have effect on those that were already registered. The *Friendly Societies Act 1992* ended the formation of new charitable friendly societies under the *1974 Act*, so since 1993 new charitable organisations have not been able to be structured as friendly societies.

REGULATION

52.3   The *Financial Services and Markets Act 2000* disbanded the Friendly Societies Commission and gave its regulatory powers to the Financial Services Authority. The Authority protects friendly societies and their funds and ensures that they comply with the *Friendly Societies Act 1992* provisions.

TYPES OF FRIENDLY SOCIETY

52.4   Since February 1993, friendly societies can only be incorporated under the *Friendly Societies Act 1992* for purposes defined in *Sch 2*. These purposes are not charitable, comprising mainly long-term insurance business and general insurance business. However, before that date friendly societies could be established for other purposes:

- genuine friendly or mutual assurance societies whose main purposes are assisting members during sickness, unemployment or retirement;

- cattle insurance societies;

- benevolent societies established for benevolent or charitable purposes, and whose benefits are not restricted to members or their relatives;

- working men's clubs;

- specially authorised societies approved by the Treasury which undertake activities such as the promotion of science, literature and fine arts;

- old people's home societies.

52.5   Some benevolent friendly societies, old people's home societies and specially authorised societies are charitable. As exempt charities the parts of the

52.6 Friendly Societies

Charities Act 1993 relating to accounts, audit and property transactions are broadly disapplied. However, the fund-raising provisions under the *Charities Act 1992* apply fully to benevolent societies. Benevolent friendly societies are eligible for all the tax reliefs and other benefits of charitable status if their purpose is wholly charitable and they are for public benefit. Their status is usually a matter for negotiation with HMRC. Specially authorised societies, of which there were 131 in 1996, may exist for charitable or non-charitable purposes.

CONSTITUTION

52.6   A benevolent friendly society has to have certain rules which are prescribed by legislation, setting out its name, registered office, its objects, meeting and voting procedures, how the committee of management (the trustee body) is appointed and removed, investment powers, accounting and audit arrangements, how the books may be inspected, dispute procedures and how the rules may be amended. A general meeting must be held at least every 15 months. The committee must comprise at least two members, and the Act stipulates provisions for the age of members, appointment, co-option and retirement. There must also be a chief executive and a secretary, though the roles can be fulfilled by one person. The chief executive should have the requisite knowledge and experience to discharge his duties, and any changes in this appointment should be notified to the Registrar within 28 days.

52.7   A friendly society may have trustees appointed to hold property and to act in other situations where an unincorporated body cannot reasonably act. This is not the same as taking responsibility for the management and administration of the charity.

52.8   Branches have particular significance in friendly societies, which may be registered as such, or may have instead to register as a separate society.

FINANCES

52.9   Friendly societies have to keep accounting records and maintain an internal control system. The accounting record requirements are very similar to those which apply to charitable limited companies. Auditors must be appointed with similar duties to those set out in the *Companies Act 1985*.

Further Information

52.10   The Financial Services Authority
25 The North Colonnade
Canary Wharf
London
E14 5HS
Website:www.fsa.gov.uk

53   Funds

53.1   The funds of a charity are not simply its cash balances, nor are they necessarily limited to those funds managed by investment or fund managers. The funds are the unexpended balances that represent the wealth of the organisation, including investments and cash, less its liabilities. The funds may be analysed into differing types, as described below, and comprise individual funds or trusts. Certain types of funds retained by a charity or its subsidiary are subject to trust law, which is a complex area often requiring legal advice.

53.2   In day-to-day terms it is important to understand the types of fund operated by a charity in order to understand what resources are available to spend, and for what purpose they may be expended. The definition of the funds therefore has implications for the whole financial management of the charity and will also have bearing on matters such as the internal control procedures and any computerised accounting system selected. Before considering these implications it is important to clarify the types of fund a charity may have.

TYPES OF FUND

Restricted funds

53.3   Restricted funds are funds which are subject to specific trusts, either declared by the donor when making the donation or accepted by the donor in responding to a specific appeal, for example to restore or repair a church spire or to help people in the aftermath of a natural disaster. Restricted funds may be restricted income funds, which are expendable at the discretion of the trustees in line with the nature of the fund, or restricted capital funds, where the fund has to be retained either permanently or for some fixed period of time or until some specific event occurs. In practice the terms 'restricted income fund' and 'restricted capital fund' are little used. Restricted income funds tend to be known simply as 'restricted funds', and restricted capital funds as 'endowment funds'. This convention is followed hereafter in this chapter.

53.4   A restricted fund exists to be applied for a particular purpose, usually defined either by a function or a geographical factor. A gift given to be used in a specified period of time is not a restricted fund on the basis of the time restriction alone. If the charity can legally use the funds immediately on whatever it chooses then the income is simply unrestricted. If the income cannot be used immediately it is deferred as a liability until the relevant future period.

53.5   The SORP clarifies that where funds are provided for fixed assets, the trustees' obligations, and the accounting treatment, will vary. Sometimes the trustees may be required to hold the asset on trust for a specific purpose, on other occasions trustees may have discharged their obligations simply by acquiring the asset. By extension, a gift of a fixed asset is accorded the same treatment as a gift of money to acquire an asset.

53.6   If a restricted fund represents an asset that will be retained for some time by the charity it is logical to reflect the using up of that asset by amortising the restricted fund value over the expected life of the asset, or even the donor's own expectations of how long the asset can reasonably be regarded as restricted.

53.7   Money given to a charity on condition that, for example, the charity raises matching funds or that someone visits a certain country, is not restricted as such conditions do not create a trust obligation.

53.8   Where restricted funds are held, there is an expectation that they will be applied within a reasonable period. If the fund is not applied reasonably quickly, then it should be invested in order to maintain the fund's value pending application and hopefully add to the fund. In some cases, for instance over the life of a major appeal, it may be appropriate for a separate bank account or investment account to be set up to identify the return earned. There is, however, no requirement to operate a separate new bank account for a restricted fund. The notional interest earned can be calculated and credited to the fund.

53.9   If a charity receives a restricted gift for a purpose which it is unable to meet, either for practical reasons or because using assets in this way would constitute a breach of the charity's governing document, then the fund is not restricted. The gift will need to be returned and the donation becomes a liability pending its repayment.

ENDOWMENT FUNDS

53.10   Restricted capital funds, or endowment funds, fall into two further categories, permanent endowment and expendable endowment.

Permanent endowment

53.11   A permanent endowment fund is a capital fund where the trustees have no power to convert the capital into income. The fund has to be maintained at its value indefinitely, although the individual assets making up that fund may in some cases be exchanged. For instance, if a portfolio of shares is left to a charity to generate income for supporting the general purposes of the charity then shares making up the portfolio could, in the absence of any express provision to the contrary, be traded to maximise the investment return. On the other hand, an art collection given to a charity as permanent endowment would have to be preserved largely intact. Items within the collection could be loaned, or even swapped or sold provided the purpose was to enhance the collection. The charity could not sell part of the collection merely to raise income.

Expendable endowment

53.12   An expendable endowment fund is a form of capital fund. The trustees are not obliged to spend the fund until it is converted into income. Usually there is a condition attached to the receipt of the fund stating that the trustees cannot initially convert the capital into income, but may do so at some time in the future, perhaps on the happening of a certain event, or after a fixed period of time.

UNRESTRICTED FUNDS

53.13   If no specific terms of trust govern funds they are unrestricted and can be used for any purpose within the objects of the charity, subject to any power of accumulation within the governing document. If they are left as free funds they are usually referred to as the general fund, or accumulated funds. However, if the trustees decide to set aside amounts for particular purposes these funds are known as designated funds.

Designated funds

53.14   Designated funds should represent the trustees' genuine intentions. Although the trustees remain free to remove the designation, this should only be done if there was a change in a charity's circumstances, e.g. if a planned new building was no longer required. Funds should not be designated merely to reduce the apparent level of a charity's free reserves.

53.15   If a designation is revoked funds shown as designated in one set of accounts, may be released to general funds in the next set. The SORP permits designated funds to be presented as a separate column on the face of the SOFA, although more usually movements on designated funds are shown exclusively in a note to the accounts.

53.16   In assessing the reasonableness of a charity's reserves levels, funders should take note of the level of designated funds. Assuming that they are reasonable both in nature and in quantum, they will reflect prudent management by the charity. For instance, it would be prudent to set aside income to fund future capital expenditure or to meet redundancy liabilities in local authority funded project-based charities. Although designated funds are easy to create and subsequently remove, it would be imprudent for a charity to use designated funds in order to camouflage excess balances. Unconvincing reasons for setting up designated funds, or transfers and releases of such funds year on year for little apparent purpose, serve only to undermine the credibility of the charity's financial reporting.

FINANCIAL MANAGEMENT

Internal controls

53.17   A charity which has a surplus on its restricted funds but a deficit on its unrestricted funds is prima facie insolvent. Since the SORP was introduced and charities are presenting their balance sheets according to type of fund, it has become apparent that quite a number are technically insolvent. As charities can only use funds within the attached terms of trust, it is increasingly important for the internal financial controls to distinguish between types of fund received and to record income properly as soon as possible. This means recording receipts according to the type of appeal, and checking accompanying correspondence to ensure that gifts are not simply assumed to be for general purposes.

53.18   Whenever fund-raising literature is being prepared or despatched, then the finance department should be informed. In this way the nature of incoming funds can be understood and properly accounted for. Early discussion may also make it possible to avoid the accidental creation of restricted funds by making it clear that funds received may be used for wider purposes than is the main subject of the appeal. Such additional wording is also important in case an appeal either raises too much money or fails to reach its target. In both cases some money would otherwise need to be repaid to the donors.

MANAGEMENT ACCOUNTING

53.19   Although not all charities produce management information in SORP format, much of the information presented in a full set of accounts should be capable of extraction directly from the accounting system. This is because the annual accounts are merely a stylised presentation of matters under the control of the charity's trustees throughout the year. Indeed management accounts will be more detailed in places, for instance most charities do not disclose all their fund analysis by every individual fund due to immateriality, whereas these will all need accounting for within the management information system.

53.20   As a result the management accounting system for charities must accommodate not only the traditional nominal ledger expense analysis (natural costs), and probably cost centre and/or project or departmental analysis, but also fund analysis. This extra dimension to the accounting analysis may need to be done on spreadsheets, as the degree of analysis of each figure may be too time consuming to handle when allocating individual items within the main accounts system itself.

53.21   Whatever system is used, the accounting should routinely reflect any allocation of income to the funds and also the deduction of any administration costs relating to the fund. If this element of the accounting is not incorporated into the accounting function then the figures presented in the year-end accounts, especially on the general funds, may be substantially different to expectations.

53.22   Charities differ in their approach to cost allocation by fund. The need for more or less sophisticated methods will depend on both the nature and volume of the individual restricted funds.

53.23   When restricted funds are represented by grants, it may sometimes be possible for a proportion of administration costs to be charged to each fund on an arithmetic basis. These costs could include management and administration, and the costs associated with obtaining the grant. In other cases it may be more appropriate to operate each fund as a separate entity, with the actual costs associated with each fund deducted from that fund.

REVALUATION RESERVES

53.24   Revalution reserves arise when a fixed asset is valued upwards. They represent the difference between the original cost and the current accounts valuation (carrying value). They are of little significance to trustees except as a means of remembering the historical composition of reserves. However, the *Companies Act 1985* requires them to be separately distinguished in the accounts.

ENDOWMENT INCOME AND EXPENDITURE

53.25   In the past trustees have had to credit endowment funds with capital returns, whilst the income return has been available for the general purposes for which the fund was established. The Charity Commission has recognised that changes in taxation and reward schemes have resulted in investment returns arising in a growing variety of ways that are no longer in line with trust law. As a result of these developments the Charity Commission may permit a charity to manage permanent endowment funds on a total return basis. This combines together all forms of return on investments to produce a total return, some of which can be used to meet the needs of present beneficiaries while the remainder is added to capital to help meet the needs of future beneficiaries.

53.26   Expenses incurred in the administration, protection or enhancement of an endowment should normally be charged to it, as should any related depreciation or improvement.

53.27   Registered and excepted charities' accounts will show funds by category as part of their old total reserves. Universities, which are exempt charities, account for restricted income funds differently, as liabilities, since they follow a separate SORP.

54 Governance

54.1 Governing a voluntary organisation is never straightforward. In *Towards Voluntary Sector Codes of Practice* Julian Ashby wrote: 'It (governance) is undertaken by volunteers with limited time but all the responsibilities of company directors. It also has to balance the requirements of different stakeholders and maintain an appropriate relationship with staff. It is a role that is not always well understood or carried out effectively.' Other observers of charity boards might be more inclined to write that it is a role that is frequently misunderstood or carried out ineffectively, or in a manner that causes friction with those employed to help, by people with limited time, and in some instances limited competence, some of whom see their role as being to represent the interests of one particular group of stakeholders.

54.2 Most charities are formed by a small group of individuals who see a need in society and decide to do something about it. In the start-up phase of the organisation, this group will do everything from developing the charity's mission and strategy to stuffing envelopes and washing tea towels. They are unlikely to distinguish between governance and management (see Fig 1).

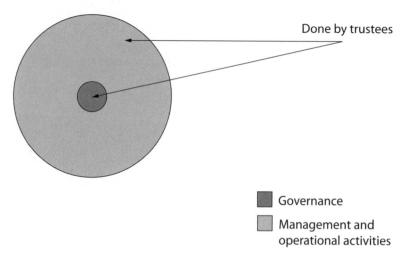

Done by trustees

■ Governance

■ Management and operational activities

Fig 1: Emerging organisation

54.3 If the charity grows, it is likely to attract more volunteers and eventually start to employ paid staff. At this stage the trustees begin to delegate some of the charity's work and there is a separation of the governance and management roles (see Fig 2).

54.4 Finally, in large, professionally staffed organisations, the roles of staff and trustees become largely discrete, with the trustees' role being to govern the charity and the staff's to implement the trustees' policies and strategy and manage the organisation on a day-to-day basis as shown in Fig 3.

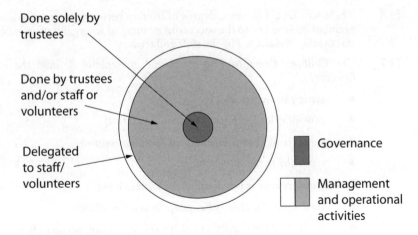

Done solely by
trustees

Done by trustees
and/or staff or
volunteers

Delegated
to staff/
volunteers

Governance

Management
and operational
activities

Fig 2: Small to medium-sized organisation

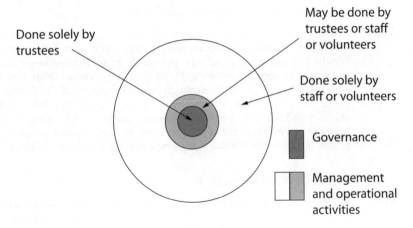

Done solely by
trustees

May be done by
trustees or staff
or volunteers

Done solely by
staff or volunteers

Governance

Management
and operational
activities

Fig 3: Large organisation with professional staff

54.5   However, the picture presented by some commentators of a complete division
between governance and management is oversimplified. They confuse governance with strategic management and limit management to operational
management. 'Governance' is not the same as 'management', but neither is it
totally discrete. Governance is an integral part of the system by which
organisations are managed and controlled. It is too complicated and too
dynamic to be reduced to a simple division of labour with trustees 'governing'
and staff taking responsibility for day-to-day operational management. Trustees should quite rightly focus most of their attention on issues of governance,
such as setting long-term strategy and policy, but from time to time they will
have to carry out management tasks, such as appointing, appraising or
dismissing members of staff. Similarly, operational matters will be the main
focus of the staff's work, but at times they will have a most valuable input into
strategic issues. For example staff input will be essential in the strategic
planning process.

54.6 Governance

54.6   There will always be some degree of overlap between governance and management and the key to the successful running of an organisation is how well this overlap is managed by the staff and trustees.

54.7   The Cadbury Committee on corporate governance defined the roles of directors as:

- setting strategic aims;

- providing leadership to put them into effect;

- supervising the management of the business; and

- reporting to the shareholders.

Charity governance is not dissimilar. Trustees must:

- ensure that the charity has purpose and direction;

- ensure that the charity's work has the desired impact on its beneficiaries;

- provide leadership and direct the staff; and

- be accountable to multiple stakeholders.

54.8   The key difference, however, between charity and corporate governance is that unlike company directors whose objective it is to bring the greatest benefit to shareholders and who personally benefit from their role, charity trustees, with some exceptions, do not benefit personally from their trusteeship and must always act as stewards for the greater good. They must always act in the best interests of the charity's present and future beneficiaries and must set aside their own personal interests and even their personal ethics, for example in avoiding investments in companies producing or selling certain products, unless such restrictions would further the charity's objects.

CODE OF GOVERNANCE

54.9   In 2005 the Charity Commission, the National Council for Voluntary Organisations, the Association of Chief Executives of Voluntary Organisations, Charity Trustee Networks and the Institute of Chartered Secretaries and Administrators developed a code of good governance for voluntary and community organisations. The code was endorsed by The National Hub of Expertise in Governance, which has taken on responsibility for future work on the code. It can be downloaded from *www.governancehub.org.uk*.

54.10   The Code sets out best practice for governing a voluntary or community organisation. It is not mandatory, but organisations that comply with the Code are invited to state that they do so in their Annual Report and other relevant published material. The code aims to help enhance the effectiveness of voluntary and community organisations by:

- clarifying what governance is and how governing bodies can govern effectively;

- giving organisational stakeholders information about the way organisations are governed;

- maintaining and enhancing public confidence in voluntary and community organisations.

54.11   The code sets out seven principles of good governance:

- Board leadership – every organisation should be led and controlled by an effective Board of trustees which collectively ensures delivery of its objects, sets its strategic direction and upholds its values.

- The Board in control – the trustees as a Board should collectively be responsible and accountable for ensuring and monitoring that the organisation is performing well, is solvent, and complies with all its obligations.

- The high performance Board – the Board should have clear responsibilities and functions and should compose and organise itself to discharge them effectively.

- Board review and renewal – the Board should periodically review its own and the organisation's effectiveness and take any necessary steps to ensure that both continue to work well.

- Board delegation – the Board should set out the functions of sub-committees, officers, the chief executive, other staff and agents in clear delegated authorities and should monitor their performance.

- Board trust and integrity – the Board and individual trustees should act according to high ethical standards and ensure that conflicts of interest are properly dealt with.

- The open Board – the Board should be open, responsive and accountable to its users, beneficiaries, members, partners and others with an interest in its work.

Underlying each of these is the principle of equality.

NATIONAL OCCUPATIONAL STANDARDS

54.12   In 2006 the National Council for Voluntary Organisations published National Occupational Standards for trustees and management committee members in the voluntary and community sector, that were developed by a group of representatives from across the sector. National Occupational Standards (NOS) define good practice in the way people carry out tasks, based on the functions of their role. They can be regarded as quality standards for people. They focus on outcomes – what needs to be done, not on how it should be done. NOSs exist for many different occupations including accountancy, personnel management, and business administration. They are often used as a foundation on which National Vocational Qualifications (NVQs) and Scottish Vocational Qualifications (SVQs) are developed. Although there are no plans at present to develop NVQs in governance, the NOS for trustees can be used to plan, structure and review training and learning for trustees.

54.13   Charity administrators can use the NOS for trustees to:

- prepare role descriptions
- plan recruitment of new trustees
- plan induction for new trustees
- design training for trustees

287

- identify board or trustee learning needs
- review trustees' performance
- demonstrate the standards the organisation meets.

54.14   The NOS for trustees and management committee members are comprised of four units. Each unit contains a description of the trustee's role, a unit commentary and an outline of the criteria that a Trustee must meet in performing their role. The four units are:

- Safeguard and promote the values and mission of the organisation
- Determine the strategy and structure of the organisation
- Ensure the organisation operates in an effective, responsible and accountable manner
- Ensure the effective functioning of the Board

54.15   Further information on the NOS for trustees and management committee members can be obtained from the Governance Hub (*www.governance-hub.org.uk*).

55   Governing Document

55.1   The document that sets out the purpose for which a charity is established and how it is to be operated is known as the 'governing document' or the 'governing instrument'. The format of this document will vary according to the legal status of the charity, the most usual being:

- the memorandum and articles of association, if the charity is a company;

- a trust deed, a declaration of trust, or a will, if the charity is a trust;

- a constitution or rules, if the charity is an unincorporated association; or

- rules, if the charity is an industrial and provident society

- a constitution, if the charity is a charitable incorporated organisation.

In addition to the above, some charities will be governed by a Royal Charter or Act of Parliament.

55.2   Trustees and senior staff should know and understand their governing document because it is arguably the charity's most important document, setting out its aims or charitable objects, its rules and the trustees' powers. All trustees should be given a copy of the charity's governing document as soon as they are elected or appointed, as they have a legal obligation to ensure that everything the organisation does complies with it and it provides the framework for everything the charity does. If the governing document is written in language that is difficult to understand, the trustees should also be given a plain English version.

55.3   A charity's governing document sets out the terms of the trust between the charity's donors/funders, the trustees and the beneficiaries. For charitable unincorporated associations, companies and industrial and provident societies the governing document is a type of contract, enforceable in the courts.

55.4   Professional advice is usually needed in drafting a governing document. However, both the Charity Commission and the Charity Law Association have produced model governing documents for English and Welsh charities and the Scottish Council for Voluntary Organisations has produced model documents for Scottish charities. These can be adapted to meet the requirements of particular charities, thus saving the expense of drafting a document from scratch.

55.5   A good governing document will be drafted in such a way that the objects are sufficiently broad to encompass not only what the charity does at present but also what it might expand to do in the future. It should be written in plain English and be reasonably comprehensive, setting out the rules and procedures that are likely to be needed. It is advisable to include a power of amendment.

55.6   While the format of the governing document varies according to an organisation's legal status, most will include details of the charity's:

- name and location;

- objects;

- powers, including any powers to amend the governing document;

- membership;

- governing body, including method of appointment and indemnification;

- meetings, including quorum, procedures, minutes;

- audit requirements;

- use of the seal;

- dissolution.

POWERS

55.7   Charities are strictly speaking only allowed to engage in activities that are directly related to their objects. So a charity established to provide a helpline for people suffering from bereavement can operate a telephone helpline, but may not be able to employ staff, open a bank account, lease premises, etc., as these activities do not directly relieve the suffering of the bereaved, but are merely a means to that end. Charities need powers to undertake these 'means' activities. Some powers will be given by statute or implied, others will be express powers, i.e. set out in the governing document, or included in a general catch-all power in the governing document.

Statutory powers

55.8   Statutory powers are those given under statute, such as the powers charities are given to undertake certain property transactions in the *Charities Act 1993*. Other statutory powers are given to a type of organisation, and therefore apply to all organisations of that type, charitable or otherwise. For example, charitable companies do not need an explicit power of amendment in their governing document because all companies have been granted this power under *s 21* of the *Companies Act 2006*. A charity's governing document can extend a statutory power, for example, to give a charity wider powers of investment than it would otherwise have, or it may restrict a statutory power, for example, narrowing a charitable company's power to amend its governing document.

Implied powers

55.9   Implied powers are those a court would find necessary for an organisation to have in order for it to achieve its charitable objects, such as the power to open a bank account. They can be exercised even when they are not explicit in statute, or in the charity's governing document.

Express powers

55.10   Express powers are those explicitly stated in the charity's governing document because they do not exist under statute and are not so intrinsic to the achievement of the charity's objects that they can be implied. Examples are powers allowing charitable funds to be used to purchase trustee indemnity insurance, and powers to delegate investment fund management.

General powers

55.11   Most governing documents will also include a general, catch-all power, such as the power to take any action that the trustees see fit to achieve the charity's charitable objects. This will enable the organisation to develop its work in the future without having frequently to redraft its governing document or go to the Charity Commission for a Scheme. However, the proposed action must be:

- lawful;

- not one for which an explicit power is needed;

- not explicitly prohibited by the governing document; and

- one which comes within the wording of the general power.

55.12   It is possible for trustees to unintentionally commit a breach of trust by assuming that their catch-all clause allows anything lawful. For example, trustees of a charity with a catch-all clause may think it gives them power to amend any part of their memorandum and articles of association, but *s 64* of the *Charities Act 1993*, as amended by *s 31* of the *Charities Act 2006*, requires them to obtain the Charity Commission's consent to amendments to their objects clause or to provisions directing or restricting the manner in which the charity's property may be used or applied.

Powers relating to money

55.13   Most governing documents will include the power to raise funds and to invite and receive contributions. If this power is not explicit it could be included under a general power or implied. Some governing documents will prohibit the charity from engaging in substantial non-primary purpose trading. Again, most governing documents will include the power to operate a bank account and carry out financial transactions, though this power could be implied if it is not explicit. Raising money through loans or other forms of borrowing requires an explicit power, as does using charitable funds to pay for trustee indemnity insurance. Where there is a statutory obligation to do something, such as to take out employers' liability insurance, the charity does not require a specific power.

Powers relating to property

55.14   If a charity is ever likely to occupy premises, its governing document should contain clauses giving the trustees powers to buy, sell, let, exchange, mortgage, build, etc.

Powers relating to employment

55.15   Companies and industrial and provident societies have an implied power to employ staff. This implied power does not extend to unincorporated charities, though it may be covered by a general power if it is not included as a specific power.

Other powers

55.16   Many charities will have specific powers permitting them to carry out activities that are not directly in furtherance of their objects, but are closely related to them. For example, they may have powers to conduct and publish research, hold conferences or public meetings, advise other charities or public bodies, or undertake joint activities with other organisations whose objects are included in their own.

CONFLICT OF INTEREST

55.17   Some governing documents contain clauses relating to potential conflicts of interest. For example, they may include a clause excluding people from becoming trustees if they have certain types of relationship with a member or members of the charity's staff, or they may explicitly allow users of the charity's services to become trustees subject to certain conditions.

MEMBERSHIP

55.18   If the charity has a membership the governing document will usually describe the various classes of membership, eligibility for membership, rights, responsibilities and benefits of membership, the rights of members to resign and the rights of the charity to terminate an individual's membership.

55.19   If the governing document merely states that these matters can be determined by the members at a general meeting or by the trustees, these decisions become known as the charity's 'rules' or 'standing orders'.

MEETINGS

55.20   Membership charities will have clauses in their governing document relating to the requirements for annual general meetings, including the notice which must be given, the quorum, the business which must be conducted, how voting will take place, the majority required to pass a resolution, etc. The governing document will also contain the procedures for holding general, special or extraordinary meetings.

GOVERNING BODY

55.21   The governing document usually sets out:

- the names of the first members of the governing body;
- the maximum and minimum number of people who can form the governing body;
- criteria of eligibility for membership of the governing body;
- the method of selection, election or appointment;
- the length of term of appointment;
- any limits placed on the number of consecutive terms that can be served;
- procedures for resignation;
- how casual vacancies are filled;

- the powers of the governing body, including powers of delegation;

- the frequency at which the governing body meets;

- the quorum and procedures for meetings.

55.22   It may also specify that honorary officers should be appointed or elected. These will normally be a chairperson, vice-chairperson and honorary treasurer but in some instances there will also be an honorary secretary.

55.23   If the governing document gives the trustees powers to delegate to sub-committees it will often include details of how the sub-committees are to be composed, i.e. exclusively of trustees, or by a mixture of trustee and non-trustee members.

THE SEAL

55.24   The governing documents of many incorporated charities and of some unincorporated charities that have an incorporated trustee board include directions on reporting the use of the seal. The seal is a stamping device used to show that an incorporated body has entered into a legally binding agreement. Industrial and provident societies are required to have a seal. Companies and incorporated trustee bodies are no longer required to have a seal, but may continue to use one if they so wish.

BANK ACCOUNTS

55.25   Some governing documents include clauses setting out:

- that all bank accounts in which the charity's money is lodged must be in the name of the charity;

- which bank the charity is to bank with;

- how many signatories there must be to the charity's account;

- how many signatures are required for each transaction; and

- who the signatories can be, e.g. at least one must be a trustee.

AUDIT AND ACCOUNTS

55.26   The governing document may stipulate:

- the types of financial records that must be kept;

- the types of accounts that must be prepared; and

- the way in which the accounts must be audited.

Frequently the governing document will contain a requirement for a full audit even though this may not be required by statute.

PROPERTY AND INSURANCE

55.27   Provisions relating to the use, upkeep and insurance of property and other assets are frequently contained in a charity's governing document.

INDEMNIFICATION

55.28   The governing document should include a clause to the effect that if trustees act prudently, lawfully and in accordance with their governing document then any liabilities they incur as trustees can be met from the charity's resources. It may also add that trustees will not be held responsible for the wrongful actions of staff or agents provided that they have exercised proper care in their appointment and supervision.

BRANCHES

55.29   Where a charity has a branch structure the governing document often includes the rules governing relationships between the main charity and its branches. The governing document should make it clear whether the branches are autonomous or controlled by, and part of, the main charity.

AMENDING THE GOVERNING DOCUMENT

55.30   Charitable companies frequently do not have an explicit power of amendment in the governing document, because they have this power under company law. An Industrial and Provident Society's rules must include provision for amendment under the *Industrial and Provident Societies Act 1965*. It is an advantage for trusts and unincorporated associations to include a power of amendment in their governing document, as it will save them from having to apply to the Charity Commission for a Scheme should they wish to amend some aspects of their governing document or to the Office of the Scottish Charity Regulator in the case of Scottish charities.

55.31   The *Charities Act 2006* relaxes the restrictions in the *Charities Act 1993* on amending governing documents. When the provisions come into force in late 2007 or early 2008, charitable companies wishing to amend their governing document must follow the requirements of the *2006 Act* and will only need the Charity Commission's consent for amendments to:

- The objects of the charity;

- Any provisions in the governing document that deal with what happens to property on the dissolution of the company;

- Any provisions in the governing document where the amendment would authorise any benefit to the directors or members, or to other people connected to them.

55.32   The 2006 Act makes it easier for unincorporated charities with gross income in their last financial year of no more than £10,000 to update their charitable purposes if these are no longer relevant in modern society. They will no longer have to apply to the Charity Commission for a Scheme. Trustees must be satisfied that the change is in the charity's interests. The updated purposes must consist of or include purposes similar to those being replaced. The trustees must pass a resolution by at least two-thirds of those who vote and send a copy of the resolution to the Commission with the reasons for passing the resolution. The resolution automatically takes effect 60 days after receipt by the Commission, unless the Commission objects to the proposed changes. These provisions are likely to come into effect in 2008.

55.33   The 2006 Act also updates and extends the existing rules to make it easier for unincorporated charities to change their administrative powers and procedures that concern the general running and administration of the charity and the work of the trustees without the Charity Commission's prior approval. The updated power retains an important safeguard for unincorporated associations that have a body of members distinct from the trustees. For these charities the members must hold a meeting to approve the resolution of the trustees. The resolution must be passed by a two–thirds majority on a vote of the members present or by a decision taken without a vote and without any expression of dissent. This provision came into force in February 2007.

DISSOLUTION

55.34   The governing document should specify what happens to any remaining assets if the charity is wound up or dissolved and has met all its financial obligations.

STANDARD GOVERNING DOCUMENTS

55.35   Some large national charities produce a standard governing document that can be used by organisations associated with that charity. These standard governing documents contain both agreed objects and administrative provisions that are specific to a particular type of organisation. The following organisations have a standard governing document which has been approved by the Charity Commission:

- Afro-Caribbean Evangelical Alliance
- Age Concern
- Alpine Garden Society local groups
- Archway Groups
- Arts Council
- Arts Festival Association
- British trust for Conservation Volunteers
- Building preservation Trusts
- CARE (Pregnancy Crisis)
- Charitable Voluntary Music Groups (Making Music)
- Child contact centres
- Childminding Association
- Children's Links
- Choirs
- Churches in fellowship with Assemblies of God
- Citizen's Advice Bureaux
- City Academies
- Civic trust Local Amenity Societies

- Clubs for young people
- Community Associations/centres
- Community Law Centres
- Community transport schemes
- Contact a family
- Council for the protection of rural England
- Councils for voluntary service
- Crossroads Care Attendant Schemes
- DIAL
- Dyslexia Association
- Elim Gospel Foursquare alliance social care companies
- Evangelical Alliance
- Foursquare Gospel Church
- Gateways
- Girl Guides
- Habitat for Humanity
- Halliwick Swimming Therapy Regional associations
- Headway
- Homestart
- Hospital Broadcasting Associations
- Independent Theatre Council
- Inner Wheel Club Benevolent Funds
- International society for Krishna Consciousness
- Jehovah's Witness Congregation
- Kids Club Network
- Ladies' Circles
- Lions Club Charity Trust Fund
- Making Music
- Marriage Resource Groups
- Masonic Lodge Benevolent Funds
- MIND
- Mudiad Ysgolion Meithrin – Cylch Cyfansawdd (combined Parent and toddler groups)
- Mudiad Ysgolion Meithrin – Cylch Meithrin (Playgroup)
- Mudiad Ysgolion Meithrin – Cylch Ti s Fi (Parent and toddler groups)
- National Autistic Society

- National Confederation of Parent teacher Association
- National Operatic and Dramatic Societies
- Neighbourhood Watch Schemes
- NPFA: recreation Ground
- PATA (Playgroup and toddler association)
- PHAB Clubs
- Playgroup Network
- Pre-school extended school partnership
- Pre-school learning alliance
- RELATE
- Riding for the disabled
- Rotary Club trust Funds
- Round table Charitable funds
- Rural community Councils
- Samaritans
- School funds (Secondary Heads Association)
- SCOPE (affiliated groups)
- Scouts
- Sea Rangers
- Spiritual Assembly of Bahai's
- Talking Newspaper Association
- Third Age Trust
- Time banks
- Townswomen's Guilds
- Toy Libraries
- Tree wardens
- Unitarian Meeting Churches
- United Trust services
- Victim support Schemes
- Village Halls (ACRE)
- Vineyard Christian Fellowship
- Wales pre-school playgroup
- Women's Aid Groups
- YMCA
- Young Farmer's Clubs

55.35   Governing Document

- Youth for Christ Centre

56   Grant Making

GIFTS NOT CONTRACTS

56.1   Many charities, such as benevolent funds, make grants to individuals and many make grants to other charities to carry out work that is within their charitable objects. A grant is essentially a gift and as the giving of a grant does not usually create a contract, the recipient's right to a grant cannot be enforced in the courts. The donor charity can, however, attach terms and conditions to a grant, for example stipulating what it must be spent on, though usually this is specified by the potential recipient in their grant application. No matter who sets the terms and conditions, grants can only be used for the purpose for which they were given. If they are spent in any other way the donor charity can require the grant to be repaid, or take action for breach of trust.

56.2   Grants are discretionary payments, so they can be withdrawn or changed by the donor at any time and the recipient has no recourse in law. However, as a matter of good practice a grant-making organisation should not agree to give a grant without being sure that it has the resources to honour its promise and if a recipient fails to satisfy the conditions of a grant those making the grant should attempt to find out why this has happened before they cut off further funding.

TAX TREATMENT

56.3   One-off payments by charities to individuals, for example to purchase essential clothing or a cooker, are treated as donations. The Charitable Disregard Rule, which restricted the amount of regular charitable payments that could be made to an individual to a maximum of £20 a week, was abolished in October 2006. This rule had previously limited the ability of grant-making charities to help some of the most needy people in society, especially those under retirement age who were in receipt of means tested benefits. Pensioners can receive help from charities without it affecting their Pension Credit. Scholarships are not generally taxed as income. [*Income Tax (Trading and Other Income) Act 2005, s 776*]. However, if a company sets up an educational trust to provide scholarships for the children of its employees, the scholarships will be regarded as a benefit for employees and the employees will be taxed on them.

56.4   Grants made by a charity to another organisation are usually outside the scope of tax provided that the grant is to be used for a charitable purpose (however, see 56.5 below).

56.5   Grants made to substantial donors (i.e. those making donations in excess of £25,000 in a 12-month period, or in excess of £100,000 in a six-year period) of a charity may be regarded as non-charitable expenditure and such payments may result in a potential tax liability for the charity. This may be the case even where the grant is within the objects and powers of the charity or made to a stated beneficiary of the charity. Substantial donors may be individuals, companies, partnerships, etc. Please see CHAPTER 118 for details on the substantial donor rules. Charities do not usually make grants to substantial donors, because if the donor can afford to make a substantial donation they are not likely to need the charity's support; however, HMRC gives the following example of how a charity can inadvertently end up making a grant to a substantial donor:

- In February 2008 a charity makes a £5000 grant to a homeless person, Mr Rose.

- Mr Rose later inherits a large sum of money and on 1 December 2009 he makes a single £75,000 Gift Aid donation to the charity which helped him.

- Mr Rose is a substantial donor of the charity in respect of its chargeable period ended 31 December 2008 and each chargeable period to 31 December 2014.

- The amount of the grant is therefore treated as non–charitable expenditure of the chargeable period ended 31 December 2008 and the charity is liable to tax on £5000 of its income for that chargeable period.

- If Mr Rose deferred his donation to 1 January 2010, he would not be regarded as a substantial donor of the charity for its chargeable period ended 31 December 2008 and there would be no tax liability related to the grant.

GRANT-MAKING TRUSTS

56.6   Grant-making trusts are a distinct and important part of the voluntary sector. They disburse funds usually to other charities or to non–charitable, philanthropic organisations to spend on charitable activities. They vary tremendously in size from multi–million pound foundations, such as the Wellcome Trust, to very small trusts set up by individuals. The latter are sometimes referred to as 'private', 'family' or 'personal' trusts, but these terms can be misleading. If a trust is a registered charity it is publicly accountable. The trustees as a body, not the settlor (i.e. the person who provides the capital sum to establish the trust fund), are responsible for making decisions about grants. In practice, however, if the settlor is a trustee their opinion will carry a lot of weight.

56.7   Most grant-making charities require applicants to make a good case for funding. The applicant will be expected to demonstrate that they will use the grant to good effect, producing the desired outcome in a cost-effective manner. They will also need to demonstrate that they have a prudent level of reserves, enough to ensure their future viability but not so much that they are well able themselves to finance the work for which they are seeking funding.

GOOD PRACTICE IN MAKING GRANTS

56.8   Unsuitable applications waste the time and resources of both the party making the application and the grant-making trusts that receive them. This can be minimised if grant-making trusts establish clear guidelines about the type of projects they will and will not fund and make this information readily available, together with details of the typical size of grants made, perhaps maximum and minimum and average size, and their application procedure. This information can be sent directly to organisations that the grant-making trust knows it would be interested in funding and/or supplied to the publishers of directories of grant-making trusts.

56.9   Similarly a grant-making trust should establish clear procedures for processing applications and make the details available to potential applicants. They should:

- give applicants their timetable and procedures for processing grants;

- ask applicants for, and check, their:

   — experience of doing similar work;

   — expected outcomes of the work to be funded;

   — financial competence;

   — current financial position; and

   — names of senior staff/trustees.

56.10   Decision-making procedures should be established taking into account the following points.

- Will any delegated authority be given to staff? If so, what level and what criteria will be used for approving applications?

- What will be the trust's policy for dealing with any conflicts of interest, i.e. funding work of an organisation that employs a trustee of the grant-making trust?

- Notification — how quickly applicants will be told of decisions.

56.11   Giving applicants the reasons why an application has been turned down consumes resources but is helpful to the applicant and can be cost-effective for a grant-making trust in the long run if it serves to educate applicants and deter unsuitable applications in the future.

56.12   When selecting from applications, trustees and staff should judge on substance rather than presentation, except to the extent that the presentation is material. They should also take into consideration whether or not the project needs a variety of funders to ensure its long-term stability and the organisation's demonstrable commitment to equal opportunities in the selection of its staff and beneficiaries.

56.13   Grant-making trusts should confirm grant offers in writing giving details of:

- the amount of the grant;

- the purpose of the grant;

- the duration of the grant;

- any conditions attached;

- the arrangements for payment;

- monitoring and evaluation arrangements; and

- details of circumstances in which the grant might be terminated.

56.14   Grant-makers should check the effectiveness of their funding, if only to guide them in making future funding decisions. Therefore, they should establish monitoring and evaluation procedures. It is best for the grantee and grantor to agree how effectiveness will be measured at the outset. They will need to agree the frequency with which various parameters such as performance measures/outputs/outcomes will be monitored. If a project is jointly funded the funders should consider co-operating with each other on methods of monitoring and/or evaluation.

Dissemination

56.15   It is good practice for funders to encourage organisations that they have funded to disseminate the results of their work, and give details of innovative approaches, etc. to others. If necessary the funder should be prepared to fund the costs of dissemination. Similarly, funders should be prepared to disseminate the results of any evaluations they carry out.

FURTHER INFORMATION

56.16   ACF (Association of Charitable Foundations)
Central House
14 Upper Woburn Place
London WC1H 0AE
Tel: 020 7255 4499
Email: acf@acf.org.uk
Website: *www.afc.org.uk*

The Association of Charity Officers
Five Ways
57/59 Hatfield Road
Potters Bar
Hertfordshire
EN6 1HS
Tel: 01707 651 777
Fax: 01707 660 477
Email: info@aco.uk.net
Website: www.aco.uk.net

57 Groups

57.1 A group structure exists when one legal entity has control over another. The key element in deciding whether or not several entities legally form a group is therefore 'control'. If a group exists, then the responsibilities of the holding entity's trustees may need reassessing, and their relationships redefining, as the holding entity's trustees will be accountable for the activities of the group. It follows from this that the issue is not one of accounting significance only. If the trustees of the holding charity are supposed to be in control of a group of subsidiary operations, then it is legitimate to ensure that the actual degree of control mirrors the accounting treatment, presenting the group's financial activities in one consolidated statement.

57.2 The most common type of group to exist is the charity that operates a trading subsidiary. In this case usually the shares in the subsidiary are owned either by the charity in its own name, or by some individuals on the charity's behalf. The subsidiary exists usually to carry out an aspect of trading which the charity either cannot, or prefers not to, operate itself. The reasons are usually tax driven, either direct tax or VAT, but may also include the need to limit contractual risk, or to conduct an activity not within the objects of the charity.

VAT CONSIDERATIONS

57.3 It should be noted that whilst it is necessary to meet an 'under common control' condition to achieve a 'VAT Group' it is also necessary to obtain HMRCs' approval in advance. A VAT group is VAT registered as a single 'person' with all members using the same VAT registration number. The benefits of a VAT group may be a simplification of VAT reporting obligations or the removal of an obligation to charge VAT on transactions between VAT group members. It is, however, an area in which professional advice is usually appropriate because of the range of complex issues to be considered.

WHAT IS CONTROL?

57.4 In the past commercial organisations have used strict accounting definitions of control to manipulate their accountability. By buying or selling one share, a majority shareholding could become a minority shareholding, thus altering the presentation dramatically. Control is therefore now defined in wider terms. The *Companies Act 1985* defines a group as any corporate body (i.e. not just limited companies), with control over a subsidiary undertaking, which includes unincorporated bodies. The Charities SORP adopts a similar definition, but does not restrict groups to being corporate bodies. For a company the hallmarks of control are if the holding entity:

- holds a majority of the voting rights of another undertaking;

- is a member (i.e. shareholder) of another undertaking and has the right to appoint or remove a majority of its board;

- is a member (i.e. shareholder) of another undertaking and has an agreement with the other members (i.e. shareholders) so that it has control over the voting rights; or

- has the right to exercise a dominant control over another undertaking because of a control contract or provisions contained in the governing document of the subsidiary.

57.5   Control may also exist if the parent entity holds a participating interest (20% or more) and either exercises a dominant influence over the undertaking, or they are managed on a unified basis.

57.6   The SORP applies similar rules to charities that are not company subsidiaries, setting out the following situations:

- parent charity trustees and/or members or employees can appoint or remove most of the subsidiary's trustees;

- the subsidiary's constitution gives the parent's trustees powers to direct the subsidiary trustees;

- the subsidiary's objects are substantially confined to the benefit of the parent.

57.7   Other indicators of control include where the subsidiary's operating and financial policies are in accordance with the main charities or where, whatever the activities of the subsidiary, all the risks and rewards lie with the main charity.

BRANCHES

57.8   Normally the consideration of branches is a different matter to that of groups. A branch is usually either independent, or a part of the main organisation with no separate legal persona. The question of control is still an important one, but in a different context. As far as the accounting treatment is concerned, branches which are not legally autonomous are treated as though they are an integral part of the charity.

THE USES OF TYPES OF GROUPS

57.9   The simplest and most common type of group is described above at **57.2**. However, it is one of a number of options, and charities will adopt differing structures depending upon their needs.

GROUP STRUCTURE

57.10   The simplest way of forming a group is for the shares in the subsidiary company (which should therefore be limited by shares, not by guarantee) to be owned by the holding charity directly or, if the charity is unincorporated, by holding trustees on behalf of the charity. Appropriate documentation should be put in place to ensure that those named on the share certificates hold the shares on trust for the charity and do not legally hold the beneficial ownership of the company themselves.

57.11   In this way the subsidiary is completely controlled by the charity, and a group automatically exists. The shareholders have the right to remove directors, but in practice, once the first directors are appointed, then board membership issues are usually dealt with by the directors themselves.

57.12   The directors of the subsidiary company will have a duty to act in the best interest of that company. Therefore care must be taken to avoid conflicts of interest with the charity. The Charity Commission recommends that this is best achieved by at least one director not being a trustee or employee of the charity, and at least one trustee not being a director.

57.13   In many groups there will be a sharing of office facilities and equipment. This is especially true where a charity fund-raising department operates in the charity's own premises but is attracting income streams such as sponsorships, which may need to be put through the subsidiary trading company.

57.14   In this instance the charity should ensure that there is no hidden subsidy for the subsidiary by way of the free provision of services and facilities. This would represent a non-charitable application of the charity's assets, and would therefore not only be a breach of trust, but could also lead to a tax charge on the charity, reduced rates of VAT recovery, and limit business rate relief.

57.15   Two specific types of intra-group supply may need further consideration. First, if a registered charity is making land available to the subsidiary, then a lease or licence may be required. Because the disposition is to a connected person, an order from the Charity Commission authorising such a transaction will also be required. Second, equipment which is to be used exclusively by the subsidiary should be purchased by the subsidiary. This will affect the ability of the subsidiary to pass all of its profits to the charity under a profit-stripping Gift Aid payment due to the differences between the accounting and tax treatment of fixed asset depreciation. The ramifications of acquiring such equipment should therefore be considered before the purchase is made.

FINANCING THE SUBSIDIARY

57.16   New companies usually need some initial finance to start them off. Unfortunately it is not always easy for the charity to provide this finance, either because applying funds to a small trading operation may constitute non-charitable expenditure for tax purposes, or because the application represents a breach of the trustees' investment powers. Although many charities regard these handicaps as anachronistic, they serve to focus trustees' attention on the commercial and whole business rationale for setting up a subsidiary.

57.17   There are a number of means of providing a subsidiary company with its initial working capital. These are shown in Table 9.

57.18   The recommendation of the Charity Commission is that subsidiaries should be funded normally by long-term secured loans with clear repayment terms and interest which is paid, rather than simply recorded as a book entry. The principles underlying this recommendation apply equally to all charities, not just to those that are registered.

Table 9   Methods of financing a trading subsidiary

Method	Advantages	Disadvantages
Share capital	Makes the subsidiary company more solvent, as share capital is not repayable except in a winding-up situation	Ties up charity money long-term

May not be a qualifying investment
Is unsecured if the company is wound up
Cannot usually be repaid unless the subsidiary company is wound up |
| Interest bearing, secured long-term loan from charity | Is repayable but committed long-term
Lender receives interest | Ties up charity money long-term

May not be a qualifying investment |
| Trading balance from charity | Simple and flexible | May not provide enough resource for the subsidiary company

May be a slippery slope leading to charity money being tied up long-term |
| Commercial loan from a bank, for example | Simplest, and justifies commercial rationale of subsidiary | Probably more expensive than internal sources of capital

Charity cannot guarantee or underwrite finance |
| Retained profits | Simplest, and tax charge can still be avoided if gift aid payment made within nine months of year end after accounts are finalised | May result in tax charge, and reduces cash flow to charity |
| Charity gift or grants | Creates a one-off non-taxable surplus in the subsidiary | Only possible if the subsidiary is in some way fulfilling the charity's objects. Should be discussed with the Charity Commission or OSCR |

ACCOUNTING FOR SUBSIDIARIES

57.19   A parent charity should prepare consolidated accounts including all its subsidiary undertakings except where any of the following apply:

- the gross income of the group is less than the *Charities Act 1993* audit threshold;

- the subsidiary undertakings/results are immaterial to the group;

- the accounts to be aggregated are in liquidation.

57.20   The broad requirements are as follows:

- the SOFA should be consolidated;

- the balance sheet should be presented for the group and the charity;

- a cash flow statement is only required, if relevant, for the group;

- if a separate income and expenditure account is presented, it should be for the group only;

- a note should set out the profit and loss accounts of any subsidiaries; and

- notes to the balance sheet should separate out charity and group items.

57.21   Although much of this is cumbersome and of only limited relevance to most readers, it is not particularly complex. Strictly speaking a separate SOFA is required for the charity as well as the group. However, the Charity Commission will normally accept just the group SOFA if the assets and liabilities of the parent are distinguishable and the results of any subsidiary clearly stated.

57.22   When consolidating accounts, each income and expenditure item is individually consolidated, after adjusting out any inter-entity charges. For instance a management charge from the charity to the subsidiary would not show as income and cost on the consolidated accounts.

57.23   It should be noted that the statutory whistle-blowing requirement for auditors relates not only to charities, but also to any institution or body corporate connected with the charity.

57.24   Because a limited company can have wide commercial objects and can also ratify some *ultra vires* acts in retrospect, the Charity Commission is uneasy about the degree to which activities which could otherwise be undertaken by the charity are being undertaken by a trading company in its stead. There are also other problems. There is always a danger of a charity, having established a group structure, losing sight of the purpose for which it was formed, and the wrong drivers leading to an activity being operated in the wrong entity. For instance the success of the fund-raising department's trading operations may lead to an expansion of its activities to such an extent that rate relief becomes jeopardised. The risk of costs being misallocated and incurring VAT or direct tax penalties has already been referred to. Employment matters can also become blurred, and the true employer not clearly identified. The underlying principle is to regard the subsidiary as a separate commercial operation, with the relationship maintained at arm's length wherever practicable. Issues such as licensing agreements, employment contracts and shared facilities should always be considered not only from the group's perspective, but also from the charity's.

58   Hallmarks of a Well Run Charity

58.1   The principles that the Charity Commission uses to measure registered charities are set out in CC60 'The Hallmarks of a Well Run Charity'. They form a useful guide to trustees in assessing how well they are doing in running their charity. There are six hallmarks, and these are reproduced below from the Commission's Guidance[1].

FOCUS ON IMPACT AND OUTCOMES

58.2   (1) An effective charity considers the impact that it wants to have and actually has on the people who benefit from it, is clear about its objects, vision, mission and values, and how it will achieve them.

In order to demonstrate this, the charity:

- complies with the law by ensuring that its aims and planned activities are within the objects set out in its governing document;

- has a clear idea of its vision, mission, and values (e.g. set out in a written statement that is regularly reviewed) which gives the charity focus, direction and clarity and involves stakeholders both in defining and measuring its efficacy;

- prepares and regularly reviews a written plan outlining the steps it will take to achieve its mission;

- has considered methods of identifying, measuring and learning from the charity's achievements and outcomes, including the positive and negative effects that it has on the people who benefit from the charity, other stakeholders and the community as a whole;

- sets achievable targets and indicators against which success is measured based on the aims of the charity, the needs of the people who benefit from it, the quality of its services and the resources available;

- regularly reviews whether the charity's objects (as set out in its governing document) are up to date and relevant.

FIT FOR PURPOSE

58.3   (2) The structure, policies and procedures of an effective charity enable it to achieve its mission and aims and deliver its services efficiently.

In order to demonstrate this, the charity:

- reviews its organisational and trustee structures and evaluates its achievements and performance against its targets on a regular basis to ensure that it is maximising its potential;

- identifies and regularly assesses the risks that it is exposed to and decides how it will manage them;

---

1 Reproduced with kind permission of the Charity Commission.

- regularly reviews its governing document to ensure that it is up to date and that the trustees have the powers that they need in order to achieve the charity's objects and manage its resources;

- identifies and complies with relevant legislation and takes professional advice where necessary;

- develops and uses written policies and procedures for its employment practices, including the appointment, appraisal, training and development of staff;

- recognises and promotes diversity in beneficiaries, staff and volunteers;

- where it utilises volunteers, cultivates an environment which attracts volunteers to support the aims of the charity and puts in place policies and procedures which recognise their worth and maximise their contribution to the charity;

- has policies and procedures to protect vulnerable groups that it works with including, for example, children and people with a learning disability.

SOUND GOVERNANCE

58.4   (3) An effective charity is run by a clearly identifiable trustee body that has the right balance of skills and experience to run the charity effectively, acts in the best interests of the charity and its beneficiaries, understands its responsibilities and has systems in place to exercise them effectively.

In order to demonstrate this, the charity:

- complies with the law by ensuring that the trustee body is constituted in accordance with the governing document;

- identifies the mix of skills, knowledge and experience necessary for the efficient and effective direction of the charity and ensures that the rotation of trustees provides adequate opportunities for reassessing that mix;

- recruits and selects trustees on the basis of the mix of skills, knowledge, experience and the diversity that they bring to the trustee body, as well as the time they have to do the job well; undertakes all appropriate checks to ensure that a prospective trustee is both eligible and suitable to act in that capacity;

- has a policy for managing conflicts of interest on the trustee body and ensures that trustees understand that they must act solely in the best interests of the charity;

- has an induction programme for trustees which enables them to rapidly become effective and valuable trustees;

- has a trustee body that takes responsibility for evaluating its own performance and for identifying and addressing the individual training needs of trustees;

- has a trustee body that is the right size for the charity – large enough to include the right balance of skills and experience needed to run the charity effectively, but small enough to facilitate discussion and effective decision making;

- has a clear understanding of the respective roles of the trustee body and staff with written role descriptions for trustees and trustee officers (such as the Chair and Treasurer), and has systems in place that the trustee body used to monitor and oversee the way in which their delegated powers are exercised;

- is able to take decisions which further the work of the charity while recognising and managing the risks to the charity's beneficiaries, to itself and to other stakeholders.

MAXIMISES POTENTIAL

58.5   (4) An effective charity manages and uses its resources so as to optimise its potential.

In order to demonstrate this, the charity:

- plans to manage its resources (including finance, skills, knowledge, experience and assets), considers appropriate methods of controlling costs and generating new funding, and monitors actual performance so as to identify any potential problems in good time and take corrective action;

- has robust systems in place for internal financial control and the protection of its funds;

- diversifies its sources of income, for example, to reduce the risk of over dependence on one or two sources;

- has a fund-raising strategy that works within recognised good practice frameworks and considers which methods of fund-raising are appropriate for the charity;

- has robust processes in place for the management and control of all fund-raising activities undertaken by the charity or on its behalf;

- has a strategy in place for both its investments and its reserves which takes into account and plans for the needs of current and future beneficiaries;

- considers and plans for the use of non-cash resources such as volunteers, donated goods, and physical assets for own use or investment;

- considers collaborations and partnerships with other organisations and mergers with other charities to improve efficiency and the better delivery of benefits and services.

ACCOUNTABLE AND TRANSPARENT

58.6   (5) An effective charity is accountable to the public and other stakeholders in a way that is transparent and understandable.

In order to demonstrate this, the charity:

310

- complies with its legal obligation to produce an annual report and accounts which includes an explanation of what the charity has done during the year and, as a matter of good practice, the extent to which it has achieved its charitable aims in a way that internal and external stakeholders can understand;

- complies with relevant legal and good practice obligations for financial reporting, including the Charities SORP and has reporting practices that are honest, open, even-handed (not hiding the bad), clear and comply with the appropriate standards;

- explains its activities and decisions in an open and transparent way while maintaining confidentiality where appropriate, and is able to demonstrate its independence from other bodies. Independence in this context means that the charity must act to carry out its own charitable purposes, and not for the purpose of implementing the policies or directions of a governmental authority, or of any other bodies;

- welcomes both positive and challenging feedback from its stakeholders and has well-publicised, effective and timely procedures for dealing with complaints about the charity and its activities. These explain rights to complain and appeal and give details of the process and likely timescales;

- has a communications strategy that ensures that accurate and timely information is given to stakeholders including the media, donors and beneficiaries.

FLEXIBLE

58.7   (6) An effective charity is flexible enough to influence and adapt to changes in the environment in which it works in order to meet the changing needs of those who use its services.

In order to demonstrate this, the charity:

- has systems in place to gather and analyse information about emerging trends in the environment in which it operates, and their likely impact on the activities of the charity and partner organisations, and uses these to inform its planning processes;

- welcomes feedback from its beneficiaries about the services it provides and the areas where improvements could be made;

- identifies and uses opportunities to influence the environment in which it works to be more conducive to its aims, following the law and good practice when campaigning or lobbying;

- is not complacent but is engaged in a process of continual improvement, using techniques and tools best suited to its size and activities, e.g. recognised quality systems and benchmarking, to improve its own future performance;

- is ready to share good practice with other bodies;

- investigates and makes appropriate use of new technologies to carry out its activities more effectively;

- considers from time to time different methods of carrying out its administrative work, for example buying in external services or collaborative working such as sharing resources such as staff, offices or transport.

58.8   These hallmarks are not all legal requirements, but instead describe an overall principle. As a result some of the detail is more applicable to some charities than others, although the six main principles will apply to all charities.

58.9   The hallmarks are the benchmark used by the Charity Commission in their review visits, and so charities can easily prepare for such visits by comparing their performance with these hallmarks.

58.10   The Commission has recognised that there are a variety of models in the sector for encouraging good practice: here is a comment from a board paper in late 2006:

'The quality assurance process ... used by Age Concern to assess each member against their National Standard ... is the gateway for member charities to use the Age Concern brand and membership. It was agreed that if their Quality Counts standard covered the Hallmarks of an Effective Charity it may be possible to except Age Concern charities that meet their standard from future review visits. It was also possible that the Charity Commission could endorse their standard which they would very much welcome as it would demonstrate to their members that the regulator has confidence in the process.'

59   Health Charities

59.1   The *Charities Act 2006* lists the advancement of health or the saving of lives as a charitable purpose. The advancement of health includes the prevention or relief of sickness, disease or human suffering, as well as the promotion of health. It includes conventional methods as well as complementary, alternative or holistic methods which are concerned with healing mind, body and spirit in the alleviation of symptoms and the curing of illness. Charity Commission guidance states that to be charitable there needs to be sufficient evidence of the efficacy of the method to be used. Assessing the efficacy of different therapies will depend upon what benefits are claimed for it (i.e. whether it is diagnostic, curative, therapeutic and/or palliative) and whether it is offered as a complement to conventional medicine or as an alternative. Each case is considered on its merits but the House of Lords Report (6th Report of the House of Lords Select Committee on Science and Technology, Session 1999 – 2000) on complementary and alternative medicine provides a useful guide.

BENEFICIARIES

59.2   The definition of who qualifies as 'sick' is a wide one, and includes people who are physically or mentally ill, infirm or convalescent, or who have a mental or physical disability, and those suffering from an addiction. The governing document should always be consulted to ensure that potential beneficiaries qualify and that the objects are not too narrowly drawn, for instance some governing documents require people to be both 'sick' and 'poor'. Again before giving assistance trustees need to be sure that:

- the person has a clear need for assistance;
- the benefits or assistance proposed are related to that need;
- the benefits or assistance proposed are not available from other non-charitable sources.

ACTIVITIES

59.3   Charitable purposes falling within this head include:

- The provision of conventional and/or complementary, alternative or holistic medical treatment, care and healing;
- The provision of comforts, items, services and facilities for people who are sick, convalescent, disabled or infirm, e.g. Hospital Radio;
- Medical research;
- The provision of blood transfusion services;
- The promotion of activities that have a proven beneficial effect on health;
- The provision of rescue services, such as lifeboats, mountain rescue, fire, ambulance, air ambulance and first aid services, or which assist the work of the police and rescue services for example by providing emergency radio communication at national and local disasters;

- The provision of life saving or self defence classes;

- The provision of support to hospitals, e.g. Hospital Leagues of Friends;

- The provision of services and facilities for medical staff, such as homes for nurses;

- The maintenance of proper standards of medical practice, e.g. the General Medical Council;

- The provision of assistance to the victims of natural disasters or war or torture or terrorism.

ITEMS AND SERVICES CHARITIES CAN PROVIDE TO SICK PEOPLE

59.4   In its publication CC6 'Charities for the Relief of Sickness', the Charity Commission lists the following items and services as those which it may be appropriate for a charity, established for the relief of sickness, to provide. The list is not intended to be exhaustive. Items that may be given or loaned include:

- bedding

- clothing

- food for special diets

- fuel or the equivalent in savings stamps or pre-charged keys

- heating appliances

- medical or other equipment

- wheelchairs

- televisions or TV licences

- radios

- washing machines

- telephones

- prescription 'season tickets'.

Services that could be provided include:

- bathing

- foot care

- hair washing

- shaving

- aromatherapy, massage and other complementary therapies

- help in the home

- adaptations to the homes of disabled people

- laundering

- meals on wheels

- nursing aid
- physiotherapy in the home
- gardening
- reading
- exchange of library books
- shopping
- sitting-in
- tape-recording books and newspapers
- child-minding
- outings and entertainments
- travelling companions
- counselling.

59.5   Other special arrangements may be made, such as periods of rest or change of environment, treatment at convalescent homes or health clinics, temporary relief for those having the care of a sick person or a person with a disability, help for relatives and friends to visit or care for patients, and transport.

VAT

59.6   Often the provision of services by a charity involved in health care will be under a contract, either with a statutory provider or with an individual. Such a supply is therefore a business supply but it will normally be exempt from VAT if it constitutes a welfare service. Where such welfare services are provided consistently below cost they may be outside the scope of VAT (see CHAPTER 50).

CONTRACTS

59.7   As charities have increasingly been drawn into the contract culture, so there has been a growing need for them to understand the implications of entering into such arrangements. The position is complicated by the lack of distinction between grants, contracts, and such things as 'service level agreements'. In practice every such arrangement will be either a contract or a grant, and its exact nature needs to be identified as it may have consequences for the trustees.

59.8   A contract is a trading obligation which creates rights and expectations between the parties. In a contract, there will be an exchange for value. In this context a charity will provide a service usually on behalf of the health authority or local authority in exchange for an agreed fee. The contractual risk is therefore with the charity to perform its part of the agreement. If it fails, then the other party can take legal action against the charity or, if the charity is unincorporated, against the trustees personally as in this instance it is the trustees who are party to the contract. Although such a contractual arrangement is by definition trading, it is usually primary purpose trading.

59.9   Health Charities

59.9   Where the charity is receiving a grant to help it provide a service, then no such contractual exchange is taking place. However, the charity will still need to account for the use of the grant monies, if only through the statutory accounts. Any unspent grant income should be repaid to the grantor, whereas any profit on a contract, subject to any dispute over performance or costed services, can be kept by the charity and used for any charitable purpose.

RELATIONSHIPS WITH STATUTORY PROVIDERS

59.10   A charity should not use its funds to pay for or provide services that a public body is legally required to provide at public expense. This means that it is permissible for a charity to provide additional services, or to provide a qualitatively better service, as in both of these cases this extra element can be paid for from the charity's own funds.

59.11   A health authority, for instance, may contract with a charity to provide services on its behalf. The contract price should not be subsidised by the charity either financially or by the provision of other services or volunteer time. Where additional features are to be provided these must be in addition to the basic service provided by the authority, albeit through the medium of a contract at a proper price with a charity. This means that in the case of a service which should be provided by the public sector, using public funds, then although there may be a competitive tendering process the charity should only offer to provide the service at the full economic cost.

59.12   It is not always easy to identify what the contracting party is legally obliged to provide out of public funds, and for this reason charities which are new to such arrangements should be extremely careful, obtaining evidence of the public body's responsibilities before entering into the contract. Local authorities often have discretion about the exact nature of the provision to be made, and in this case it will be necessary to consider what the pattern of the service has been in the past, to ensure that the voluntary sector is not simply being seen as a cheap, alternative source of provision.

59.13   It is not uncommon for a representative of the public body to act as a trustee of a charity, either because the charity needs the expertise, or because the public body wishes to have some influence over the relationship. This is an area for potential conflict of interest and should, if possible, be avoided. There is no reason why the representative cannot attend trustee meetings for some or all of the agenda, and simply have observer or adviser status. If the individual is a trustee, it may be necessary for that person not to be involved with any discussion or decision relating to the relationship between the public body and the charity, or for the Charity Commission to be asked to give their specific approval to certain transactions and arrangements.

GIFTS TO HOSPITALS AND DOCTORS' SURGERIES

59.14   Subject to the condition that a charity should not use its funds to pay for statutory services, a charity can make a gift to a hospital provided that the hospital concerned cares for sick people primarily from the charity's area of benefit and that the people will benefit directly from the gift. A charity may also loan equipment to a hospital on terms agreed between them and the hospital which should include details of who is responsible for the cost of maintaining the equipment. Once the equipment is no longer needed it should be returned to the charity.

59.15   Similarly, a charity can also give, loan or provide a grant to purchase equipment for a doctor's surgery, provided that the trustees are satisfied that the equipment is needed, cannot be provided by the doctor out of the practice's funds, and will be used to benefit patients living within the charity's area of benefit.

FURTHER INFORMATION

59.16   CC6 'Charities for the Relief of Sickness'. Charity Commission, March 2000.

60   Her Majesty's Revenue & Customs

CLAIMS ADMINISTRATION

60.1   Her Majesty's Revenue & Customs (HMRC) has a specialist office responsible for the tax affairs of charities, including their subsidiaries. Formerly this was part of the Financial Intermediaries and Claims Office (FICO) but is now known as HM Revenue & Customs Charity Asset & Residence (HMRC Charities). The office will provide help and information to charities and their advisers on taxation matters and these should be addressed to:

HM Revenue & Customs Charity, Asset & Residence
St John's House
Merton Road
Bootle
Merseyside
L69 9BB

60.2   HMRC Charities deals with claims for exemption by charities and their repayment claims. It also examines the accounts of charities and those of their trading subsidiaries whose files have now been, or are being transferred to HMRC Charities from the local districts. In examining claims by charities, HMRC Charities has a continuous programme of on-site inspection visits to check that charities are complying with the requirements of the tax legislation.

INVESTIGATIONS

Special Civil Investigations

60.3   Investigations by HMRC are broadly dealt with at two levels. Special Civil Investigations concentrates on uncovering tax evasion, dealing mainly with the larger more serious cases. Its office is divided into units which deal with serious cases of fraud relating to business accounts, suspected criminal offences in other areas, particularly in connection with fraud relating to the construction industry, Pay As You Earn (PAYE), Gift Aid, special offices handling highly technical areas and covering particular industries and PAYE audit and special trade investigation units. It is outside the scope of this book to deal with the handling of investigations by Special Civil Investigations. At any sign of their involvement, professional advice should be sought immediately, preferably from an accountant or lawyer familiar in dealing with these matters. Investigations by Special Civil Investigations can lead to criminal proceedings as well as very severe financial penalties.

HM Revenue & Customs Charities

60.4   HMRC Charities deals with routine investigations concerning charities, except in relation to PAYE and related matters in connection with employees, which are dealt with by the PAYE district concerned. These offices have a continuous programme of on-site inspection visits, where they will examine the charity's or the company's records to ensure proper compliance with the legislation, regulations and procedures.

Records

60.5   In carrying out a PAYE investigation or compliance audit, HMRC will ask to see all of the charity's or the company's books and records and not merely the payroll calculations. This is because their enquires will include looking at payments to individuals who may be employees but who have not been treated as such and reimbursed expenses and payments relating to employees that may give rise to taxable benefits. It is important that a note is kept of questions asked, replies given and any matters that HMRC consider give rise to additional tax.

Settlements

60.6   Where benefits have been provided to employees that have not been included on forms P11D, HMRC will often seek a global settlement from the organisation rather than make an assessment on each individual employee. Such a settlement may well cover all of the previous six years. In these circumstances the tax will normally be collected on a grossed up basis, i.e. the payment in respect of the employee is treated as a net sum but a penalty will not normally be included. It is often possible to negotiate the amount of such a settlement with HMRC, so it is important to consider what they say at the initial stage and then seek professional advice before agreeing a settlement. An employer is required to make full disclosure to HMRC but is not required to reach agreement on every point at the time the investigation takes place. Any contentious matters can be the subject of further correspondence and/or discussion and negotiation.

Penalties

60.7   A penalty, if charged, will be calculated as a percentage of the tax and NIC underpaid as a result of fraud or neglect. The maximum penalty of 100% of the tax is only ever charged in the most extreme cases and it is normally a lot less. The amount of the reduction depends upon the extent to which all details were disclosed to HMRC, the extent to which the employer co-operated with the inspection and the size and gravity of the offence. HMRC have produced a leaflet on this subject (IR109) which is normally sent to employers before an inspection takes place.

60.8   Interest will also be charged on any tax which the employer has failed to deduct. This will include cases where a person was treated as self-employed but it is later established that the individual concerned should have been treated as an employee. In these circumstances, there is a liability to both tax and National Insurance Contributions (NIC) (employee's and employer's contributions). HMRC do not normally treat payments as being net of deductions. This is not the case, however, where it was clearly the understanding of both parties that PAYE was to have been operated and the employee believed that a net sum was being paid.

Professional advice essential

60.9   The issues involved in these investigations are not always clear and HMRC's view is open to challenge. Professional advice should therefore be taken at an early stage. Because HMRC will normally look back over a number of years, substantial amounts can often be involved.

61   Holding Trustees

61.1   A holding trustee is an individual or a corporate body that is not a trust corporation, that holds investments and/or land on behalf of an unincorporated charity, but who, unlike a custodian trustee, does not have to act in accordance with the rules set out in the *Public Trustee Act 1906*.

61.2   Holding trustees have to act on the instructions of the charity trustees (or 'managing' trustees as charity trustees of charities with holding trustees are sometimes called in order to help distinguish between the roles) unless doing so would be unlawful or a breach of trust. If a holding trustee commits a breach of trust by acting outside the terms of their agreement with the charity, the holding trustee will be legally liable. Unlike custodian trustees, holding trustees are also liable for breaches of trust carried out on the instructions of the charity trustees. Holding trustees should refuse to carry out instructions that would lead to a breach of trust and therefore it is very important for them to have full details of the purposes for which property is held and any conditions attached.

61.3   Unincorporated charities cannot hold assets in the charity's name as they have no legal personality of their own. Therefore they often prefer to use a custodian trustee (see CHAPTER 32) or a small group of holding trustees to hold title to their investments or land, rather than all their trustees, as this avoids the expense of having to transfer legal title to a new body of trustees every time there is a change on the governing body. If a charity has holding trustees the Charity Commission generally requires there to be a minimum of three, but does not stipulate a maximum number.

61.4   Holding trustees hold legal title to investments. They also hold legal title to land if they are individuals, or, if the holding trustee is a corporate body, to land that is not registered with the Land Registry. Holding trustees hold land as joint tenants, so legal advice should be sought before appointing holding trustees to hold land. Holding trustees do not usually have any powers of management.

61.5   Sometimes a charity's governing document will specify who the holding trustees are to be. If not, the charity trustees can appoint suitable individuals or corporate bodies. Unless excluded by the governing document, there is no reason why a charity trustee could not also be a holding trustee of the same charity.

VESTING

61.6   Vesting is the name of the process by which legal ownership of investments or land is passed to holding or custodian trustees. Vesting has to take place whenever a new holding or custodian trustee is appointed.

61.7   Other physical assets, for example, computers or cars, can be held by the trustees of an unincorporated charity without being formally vested in them. The trustees can transfer them simply by handing them over.

62   Honorary Officers

62.1   Most charities find they need to allocate specific responsibilities to certain trustees, usually known as the 'officers' or the 'honorary officers'. Almost all will have a chairperson and a treasurer, as these roles are particularly important. Many will also have a vice–chair and secretary. The honorary officers may have specific roles, functions and responsibilities set out in the charity's governing document, which may also contain procedures for their appointment.

62.2   In addition to their specific functions it is useful to have a small group of trustees who can:

- deal with urgent matters requiring attention between board meetings;

- take the lead in deciding which matters should be brought to the board;

- act as spokespersons for the charity and represent it at public gatherings;

- assist with the recruitment of senior staff;

- act as a link between the trustees and the charity's staff;

- sit on grievance and disciplinary panels.

62.3   The honorary officers should remember that they are 'first amongst equals'. They are agents of the board of trustees and should only act on its behalf where they have delegated authority so to do. The full board should be kept regularly informed of any decisions or activities the honorary officers undertake on its behalf. The honorary officers may play a leading role on the board, but must remember that it is the whole board who are responsible for governing the charity and each member has joint liability for the board's decisions. If the honorary officers take too strong a lead, or form a powerful inner cabal, they risk abusing their power. Other trustees may feel that their contribution is not required, and so the charity loses the skills, experience and commitment these trustees have to offer.

62.4   It is good practice to develop job descriptions and person specifications for the honorary officers and to allow the board of trustees to elect their honorary officers from candidates who meet the criteria. Trusteeship is a group activity and groups usually perform best when their leaders have the support of the majority of team members.

THE CHAIRPERSON

62.5   The role of the chairperson extends well beyond chairing the meetings of the board of trustees. The chairperson has to act as the leader of the board, making sure it fulfils its responsibilities for the governance of the charity and is focused on achieving the charity's mission. Vision and leadership are essential qualities for a good chairperson, together with good people skills and the ability to act with fairness and impartiality. The chairperson must work closely with the chief executive, helping to establish a mutually supportive relationship between the trustees and the staff.

62.6   The chairperson, together with the chief executive and sometimes the other honorary officers, will usually plan and draw up the agendas for board meetings. It is normally the chairperson's responsibility to supervise and appraise the work of the chief executive. The chairperson may also be called upon to act as a spokesperson for the charity and represent it at functions, meetings and in the press and broadcasting media. Other tasks may include authorising action to be taken between meetings of the full board, signing cheques for amounts above those for which authority has been delegated to staff and signing legal documents.

THE VICE-CHAIRPERSON

62.7   The vice-chairperson acts for the chairperson when he or she is not available and undertakes assignments at the request of the chairperson.

THE SECRETARY

62.8   The secretary is responsible for the smooth running of the board of trustees and its committees, including overseeing the preparation and circulation of board papers and agendas, minute taking (this is a particularly important task as these form the legal record of the board's decisions), checking that a quorum is present, booking the meeting room, organising refreshments, etc. The secretary is also responsible for communicating with the members, organising the annual general meeting and any special or extraordinary meetings. Charitable companies may appoint a company secretary, whose duties are to ensure that the charity complies with the requirements of company law as set out in the *Companies Act*, including keeping the Register of Members, Register of Directors and Register of Charges up to date and notifying Companies House of any changes in trustees, preparing and filing the annual return and making sure that the company documents are kept safely. The company secretary does not need to be a director of the company and can therefore be a member of staff. The *Companies Act 2006* removed the requirement for all private companies to have a company secretary.

62.9   Because of the wide-ranging, responsible and continuous nature of the secretary's duties, most organisations large enough to employ staff will assign the secretary's duties to a paid member of staff rather than to a trustee. In many medium to larger-sized organisations most of the secretary's duties will be carried out by the chief executive's assistant. In the largest charities the company secretary's role may be split between a number of people including the Head of Finance and the Head of Human Resources.

62.10   Some charities have both an honorary officer known as the 'secretary' or 'honorary secretary' and a company secretary. If this is the case it is important to distinguish between the role of the honorary secretary and that of the company secretary as each has different legal liabilities. The honorary secretary's role will normally be confined to taking minutes of meetings from which all staff are excluded, acting as an additional member of the small group who may be authorised to take certain actions between meetings, or nominated as the one whom the chairperson is required to consult about certain matters. The honorary secretary would have the same legal liability as any other trustee and would not, for example, be personally liable for failing to submit formal returns, for example to Companies House. The company secretary of a charitable company is an officer of the company by virtue of the *Companies Act 1985* and could be liable to prosecution if he breached the requirements of company law. If found guilty he could be fined or in exceptional circumstances imprisoned.

THE TREASURER

62.11   The role of the treasurer is to take the lead in helping the trustees discharge their financial responsibilities, by making sure that they understand the charity's business plan and budget, the financial implications of their decisions and that they do not expose the charity to undue financial risk. The treasurer should also ensure that the board receives timely, accurate financial reports which present the information trustees require in an 'easy to understand' format, and help the board by interpreting and explaining such matters as charity accounting requirements and the difference between statutory and management accounts. The treasurer will also play a lead role in appointing, monitoring and liaising with the auditors and other professional advisers, such as tax advisers or investment managers, that the board wishes to employ.

62.12   The precise tasks of a treasurer will depend on the size of the charity and the skills of the staff it employs. In any charity duties are likely to include:

- presenting financial reports to the board and the AGM;

- keeping the board aware of its financial responsibilities;

- ensuring that the charity's accounts are prepared in a suitable format;

- ensuring that the accounts and financial systems are examined or audited in accordance with legislation and the charity's governing document;

- liaising with the auditors and any other financial advisers.

62.13   In smaller charities the treasurer may personally maintain the financial records, prepare and monitor budgets and prepare and present financial reports.

62.14   The treasurer need not be a professionally qualified accountant, but should have a sufficient level of commercial and financial acumen to guide the financial affairs of the charity and command the respect of trustees, staff and other key stakeholders, such as major funders. To be effective the treasurer will need to have a thorough understanding of the nature of the charity's work. Detailed knowledge of charity accounting regulations is less necessary than a willingness to acquire it, or knowing when to seek professional advice.

JOB DESCRIPTIONS FOR HONORARY OFFICERS

62.15   The following specimen job descriptions are typical of those in current use.

Job description for a chairperson/vice-chairperson

62.16   The role of the chairperson is to lead the board of trustees, ensuring that it fulfils its responsibilities for the governance of the charity; to work in partnership with the chief executive, helping him or her achieve the aims of the charity; and to optimise the relationship between the board of trustees and the staff/volunteers.

62.17   The responsibilities of the chairperson will include:

- providing leadership for the board of trustees;

- planning an annual cycle of board meetings;

- setting agendas for the board meetings;

- chairing board meetings;

- ensuring that actions agreed at board meetings have been taken;

- liaising with the chief executive to keep an overview of the charity's affairs and to provide any necessary support;

- appraising the performance of the chief executive;

- sitting on appointment and disciplinary panels; and

- representing the charity at functions, meetings and acting as a spokesperson as appropriate.

Person specification for a chairperson/vice-chairperson

62.18   In addition to the qualities needed by all trustees, the chairperson/vice-chairperson should also possess the following:

- leadership skills;

- experience of committee work;

- tact and diplomacy;

- good 'people' skills; and

- impartiality, fairness and the ability to respect confidences.

62.19   In most circumstances the chairperson/vice-chairperson should have knowledge of, or involvement with, the type of work undertaken by the charity, the voluntary sector or other relevant networks.

Job description for a secretary

62.20   The role of the secretary is to support the chairperson by ensuring the smooth functioning of the board. The responsibilities of the secretary will include either doing the following tasks or delegating them to a member of staff and ensuring that they have been carried out:

- preparing agendas with the chairperson and chief executive;

- making the arrangements for meetings (booking the room, arranging for equipment and refreshments, organising facilities for those with special needs, etc.);

- minuting board meetings;

- ensuring that the minutes are signed by the chairperson once they have been approved;

- checking that a quorum is present at board meetings;

- circulating agendas, papers and minutes;

- receiving agenda items from other trustees/staff;

- checking that trustees and staff have carried out action agreed at a previous meeting;

- circulating members with agendas and minutes of the annual general meeting and any special or extraordinary general meetings;

- acting as company secretary (if appointed) where this role is not delegated to a member of staff; and

- sitting on appraisal, recruitment and disciplinary panels as required.

Person specification for a secretary

62.21   In addition to the qualities needed by all trustees, the secretary should also possess the following:

- organisational ability;

- knowledge or experience of business and committee procedures; and

- minute-taking experience, if this is not being delegated to staff.

Job description for a treasurer

62.22   The overall role of a treasurer is to maintain an overview of a charity's affairs, ensuring its financial viability and that proper financial records and procedures are maintained. The responsibilities of the treasurer will include:

- overseeing, approving and presenting budgets, accounts and financial statements;

- being assured that the financial resources of the charity meet its present and future needs;

- the preparation and presentation of financial reports to the board;

- ensuring that appropriate accounting procedures and controls are in place;

- liaising with paid staff and volunteers about financial matters;

- advising on the financial implications of the charity's strategic plans;

- ensuring that financial investments are consistent with the aims and objects of the charity;

- monitoring the charity's investment activity and ensuring its consistency with the charity's policies and legal responsibilities;

- ensuring that the accounts are prepared in the form required by law, included in the annual report and submitted to the relevant statutory bodies, e.g. the Charity Commission, the Registrar of Companies, Inland Revenue etc.;

- ensuring that the accounts are audited in the manner required by law and the charity's governing documents, and that any recommendations made by the auditors are implemented;

- keeping the board informed about its financial duties and responsibilities;

- contributing to the fund-raising strategy of the charity;

- making a formal presentation of the accounts at the annual general meeting and drawing attention to important points in a coherent and easy to understand manner; and

- sitting on appraisal, recruitment and disciplinary panels as required.

62.23   In addition to the qualities needed by all trustees, the treasurer should also possess the following:

- financial knowledge and experience;

- a willingness to be available to staff for advice and enquiries on an ad hoc basis;

- some experience of charity finance, fund-raising and pension schemes;

- the skills to analyse proposals and examine their financial consequences;

- a preparedness to make unpopular recommendations to the board.

63   Human Rights Act 1998

63.1   The *Human Rights Act 1998* came fully into force on 2 October 2000 and effectively incorporated most of the European Convention on Human Rights into UK law. The act allows people to claim their rights under the European Convention on Human Rights in UK courts and tribunals, instead of having to go to the European Court of Human Rights in Strasbourg. It affects all public authorities in the UK (including the Charity Commission) and all private and voluntary bodies carrying out public functions.

63.2   The *Human Rights Act 1998* gives every citizen statutory rights based on the European Convention on Human Rights that can be enforced against public authorities and private bodies carrying out public functions. The Act:

- obliges UK Courts and Tribunals to take into account (but not necessarily follow) the decisions and opinions of the European Court of Human Rights;

- requires that all legislation is interpreted in a way compatible with the Convention;

- makes it unlawful for a 'public authority' to act, or fail to act, in a way that is incompatible with the Convention. Where a public authority breaches this requirement the Act allows a person affected (a 'victim') to bring proceedings against that public authority;

- the Act permits a victim to rely on the Convention in any legal proceedings involving a public authority.

63.3   There are a number of rights and freedoms listed in the European Convention on Human Rights. They are:

- The right to life (Article 2)

- The right to freedom from inhuman or degrading treatment or punishment (Article 3) (this can be relevant to conditions in a residential care facility)

- The right to freedom from slavery and enforced or compulsory labour (Article 4)

- The right to liberty and security of person (subject to a derogation applicable to Northern Ireland) (Article 5)

- The right to a fair hearing within a reasonable time (Article 6) (this applies not only to criminal trials but also to things like planning enforcement procedures or housing benefit review boards)

- The right to freedom from retrospective criminal law (Article 7)

- The right to respect for private and family life, home and correspondence (Article 8) (this can be relevant to issues involving respect for someone's private information or privacy in a residential care facility)

- The right to freedom of thought, conscience and religion (Article 9) (this would apply, for example, to situations in which a person's religious beliefs require or prevent them from doing something, or wearing particular clothes, or working on a holy day)

- The right to freedom of expression (Article 10)
- The right to freedom of assembly and association (Article 11)
- The right to marry and found a family (Article 12)
- The right to prohibition of discrimination and the enjoyment of the Convention rights (Article 14)
- The right to peaceful enjoyment of possessions and protection of property (Article 1 of Protocol 1) (this could be relevant to decisions affecting someone's ability to carry out a trade)
- The right to education (subject to a UK reserve) (Article 2 of Protocol 1)
- The right to free elections (Article 3 of Protocol 1)
- The right not to be subject to use of the death penalty (Articles 1 and 2 of Protocol 6).

INTERFERENCE WITH A PERSON'S HUMAN RIGHTS

63.4   Some human rights are absolute (for example the prohibition on slavery), some are limited, i.e. the Convention provides explicit and finite circumstances in which the general right can be interfered with (for example the right to liberty) and some are qualified. If there is to be an interference with a qualified right, any interference:

- can only be 'prescribed by' or 'in accordance with' the law (in other words there must be clear legal rules which apply and which justify the interference);
- must have a legitimate aim;
- must be 'necessary in a democratic society' (this implies that any interference must be as small and as reasonable as possible).

WHAT IS MEANT BY 'PUBLIC AUTHORITY'?

63.5   The meaning of 'public authority' or 'public function' is deliberately not defined in the *Human Rights Act 1998*. The Houses of Parliament are specifically excluded from the definition, apart from the House of Lords when it is sitting as a Court. To date the Courts have been slow to identify charities to be public bodies. Poplar Housing Regeneration Community Association which had taken over a lot of the London Borough of Tower Hamlets housing stock was found to be a public body for the purposes of the *Human Rights Act* in *Donoghue v Poplar Housing Regeneration Community Association [2001] EWCA Civ 595, [2002] QB 48*, but in *R (on the application of Heather) v Leonard Cheshire Foundation [2002] EWCA Civ 366, [2002] 2 All ER 936* it was held that the Leonard Cheshire Foundation was not a public body.

63.6   Although the term 'public authority' is not defined, there are three broad categories of public authorities:

- Public authorities whose functions are all public, such as Government Departments, Non-Departmental Public Bodies (NDPBs) (including the Charity Commission), local authorities, health authorities and trusts, the armed forces, the police, prison and immigration authorities, public prosecutors, courts and tribunals.

- Persons or organisations that carry out a mixture of public and private functions, such as Railtrack, and the privatised utility companies.

- Private organisations, including charities, that carry out functions that central or local government would otherwise have to undertake.

63.7   Many charities believe they are unaffected by the Act as they do not regard themselves to be public authorities. However, many charities will be considered as public authorities for the purposes of the Act, particularly those that have been given a statutory authority to carry out work on behalf of a local authority.

63.8   Indeed, all charities should have procedures in place to alert them to breaches of the Act. Even if a charity does not fall under the definition of 'public authority', the Courts do. Therefore, any action before them has to be considered in light of the Act. Any charity facing Court action must ensure compliance, as any breach of the Convention will damage their public image.

PRIVATE BODIES WITH PUBLIC FUNCTIONS

63.9   Examples of private bodies with public functions are:
- privatised utilities that exercise public functions;
- regulatory bodies;
- professional bodies in their regulatory capacities;
- charities and voluntary organisations that carry out public functions for central or local authorities, such as running a residential home;
- private or independent schools;
- private companies managing contracted-out prisons;
- bodies that are legally public corporations.

KEY CHARACTERISTICS OF A PUBLIC AUTHORITY

63.10   In some cases it may be difficult to decide whether or not an organisation is a public authority. Organisations may need to take legal advice to clarify this, but the characteristics of a public authority would include:
- the body performs or operates in the public domain as an integral part of a statutory system that performs public law duties;
- the duty performed is of public significance;
- the rights or obligations of individuals may be affected in performance of the duty;
- an individual may be deprived of some legitimate expectation in performance of the duty;
- the body is non-statutory but is established under the authority of a national or local government body;
- the body's work is supported by statutory powers and penalties;

- the body's work involves regulating the activities of the public or section of the public;

- the body performs functions that national or local government bodies or a health authority would otherwise perform;

- the body is under a duty to act judicially in exercising what amounts to public powers.

63.11   Charities should carefully consider whether or not their functions, i.e. their legal powers and duties, render them likely to be considered as a public authority for the purposes of the *Human Rights Act 1998*. They should look carefully at each of the Convention rights and freedoms and consider whether what they do is likely to affect those rights. If so, they should ensure that their procedures and policies are compatible with the Convention.

CHARITIES WITH PUBLIC AND PRIVATE FUNCTIONS

63.12   Charities with both public and private functions are often referred to as 'hybrid' bodies. They will be carrying out a public function if they are doing work that would normally be the responsibility of central government or a local or health authority. Therefore charities contracting to do statutory work for local or health authorities will fall within the scope of the *Human Rights Act 1998* in relation to this work. In determining whether or not they are carrying out a public function charities should consider:

- Does the work depend on powers from an Act of Parliament or other legislation such as rules and regulations?

- Was the work, or part of it, once done by central or local government or a public utility?

- Is the work something that would be done by central or local government if the charity was not doing it?

- Does the work involve regulating the activities of the public or a section of the public?

If the answer to any of these questions is 'yes' advice about whether or not the charity is likely to be treated as a public authority should be sought from a suitably qualified lawyer.

63.13   Examples of charities with public functions might include:

- residential homes;

- hospices;

- healthcare and advice centres;

- child care agencies;

- housing associations;

- family planning and abortion advice centres.

However, when doing work that they fund themselves charities are acting privately and would not be directly liable under the Act as regards their private work.

63.14　While the finding that a charity is a public authority for the purposes of the *Human Rights Act 1998* will not mean that their every act is susceptible to challenge under the *Human Rights Act 1998*, it carries one crucial and far-reaching disadvantage: they will lose their status as a victim under the Act and therefore their ability to take action as victims under the Act.

TAKING ACTION UNDER THE ACT

63.15　The Act aims to prevent public authorities from acting in ways that are incompatible with a Convention right, but it is possible that parties in private law actions may be able to use the Act in their proceedings.

63.16　Only someone who is, or would be, a victim of an action by a public authority can take action under the Act. A victim can be an individual, a company or other organisation. An indirect victim, for example a spouse, can bring a human rights challenge if the victim is dead or unable to bring proceedings themselves. Interest groups will not be able to bring actions unless they meet the 'victim' test, but they will be able to assist individuals who bring actions. Professional bodies and trade unions will be able to claim on behalf of their members provided that they identify the individual victims.

63.17　Victims of an infringement of their rights or freedoms under the Convention can take the public authority concerned to Court for breaching their rights, or rely on Convention rights in the course of any other Court proceedings involving a public authority. Victims will still be free to take their case to the European Court of Human Rights but only after they have exhausted all domestic remedies.

63.18　Victims must bring proceedings under the Act within one year of the act complained of, although the Courts can extend this period under certain circumstances.

63.19　The Courts can grant a wide range of remedies including damages, declarations, quashing, mandatory and prohibitive orders and, in certain circumstances, injunctions.

IMPLICATIONS FOR CHARITIES THAT FALL WITHIN THE SCOPE OF THE HUMAN RIGHTS ACT 1998

63.20　The *Human Rights Act 1998* makes it unlawful for any organisation to carry out a public function in a way that is incompatible with the rights and freedoms guaranteed by the European Convention on Human Rights. The Act does not create any new offences. To act unlawfully under the *Human Rights Act 1998* does not mean that a charity (or its trustees) will have committed a criminal offence. Charities do not risk prosecution if they have acted unlawfully under the Act unless they have at the same time breached the existing criminal law.

63.21　However, if a charity does breach the *Human Rights Act 1998* it would be liable to the remedies available to the Courts. For example, if someone brings a case against a charity under the *Human Rights Act 1998* they could apply to the Courts for damages against it. There is also the possibility that a claim that a charity has acted unlawfully under the *Human Rights Act 1998* could arise during the course of other litigation against the charity. For example, if a charity were facing an action for negligence there is a likelihood that the prosecution could claim that the charity had also breached the *Human Rights Act 1998*.

63.22   Damages are restricted to civil proceedings as criminal courts do not have the power to award damages or compensation in respect of Convention violations. However there are other remedies open to criminal courts to grant, such as staying proceedings, quashing indictments and excluding evidence.

63.23   Before damages are awarded the court must be satisfied that the award is necessary to afford just satisfaction to the person in whose favour it is made (*s 8(3)(4)*). As often happens with decisions of the Court of Human Rights a simple finding that an unlawful act has occurred may be considered a sufficient remedy in all the circumstances. The level of damages awarded by UK courts must be commensurate with the level of damages awarded by the Court of Human Rights. Such awards usually range between £5,000–£15,000.

63.24   The *Human Rights Act 1998* would not apply if the charity could not have acted differently because of existing primary legislation.

CONVENTION RIGHTS MOST LIKELY TO AFFECT CHARITIES

63.25   Some Convention rights are likely to have more impact on charities and voluntary organisations than others do. Examples of those that are likely to affect such organisations are:

- Article 3 – Right not to be subjected to torture or inhuman treatment. This includes the right not to be subjected to degrading treatment and so could apply to organisations providing care, such as hospitals, residential homes etc.

- Article 6 – Right to a fair trial. This right might affect procedures for case reviews, complaints hearings, tribunals and appeals conducted by charities.

- Article 8 – Right to respect for private and family life. This has relevance for organisations providing care homes or domiciliary care and to any organisation with a public function that holds personal information.

- Article 9 – Freedom of thought, conscience and religion. This might affect, for example, a charity running a care home where one of the patients is Muslim and wishes to wear the chadoor. The home may find this inconvenient and contrary to its policies but it could not insist that the chadoor is not worn because under Article 9 the patient has a right to manifest her religion.

- Article 2 of the First Protocol – Right to education. This may be relevant for issues involving special educational needs provision, access to, or expulsion or exclusion of children from, schools, and (when taken together with Article 14: Prohibition of discrimination) the provision of education which is discriminatory between sexes, races or other categories (although this is only likely to be an issue where adequate educational provision is not available elsewhere locally for children excluded from schools that do discriminate, such as single sex schools).

63.26   Some rights are not absolute and they can come into conflict with other rights in the Act or be subject to limitations at law. In such cases it is for the Courts to decide how the competing rights were to be balanced.

63.27   If a charity's trustees think some of its procedures are in conflict with human rights they may wish to consider seeking legal advice.

BENEFITS FOR CHARITIES OF THE HUMAN RIGHTS ACT 1998

63.28   The implementation of the *Human Rights Act 1998* has brought new responsibilities for some charities, but it will bring opportunities. Charities are able to take advantage of the Act to challenge the activities of others where the rights of their organisation are being infringed. For example, charities are able to take action against public authorities, including the Charity Commission, where they believe that a public body has infringed their rights, for example under Article 9 (freedom of thought, conscience and religion), Article 10 (freedom of expression) or Article 1 of the First Protocol (protection of property).

63.29   Charities can also use the Act as an opportunity to build the principles of human rights into their policies and procedures to help develop and implement good practice and improve attitudes and behaviour towards people who they help and work with.

FURTHER INFORMATION

63.30   Responsibility for giving general advice on the *Human Rights Act 1998* moved to the Ministry of Justice in May 2007. Information about the *Human Rights Act 1998* is available from:

The Commission for Equality and Human Rights
www.cehr.org.uk

British Institute of Human Rights
www.bihr.org

The Council of Europe, Human Rights Directorate: *www.dhdirhr.coe.fr* (this site contains details of the Council's work in the human rights field)

The European Court of Human Rights: *www.dhcour.coe.fr* (this site contains details of the Strasbourg Court's judgments).

Your Rights: the Liberty Guide to Human Rights

64   Human Rights Charities

64.1   In 1983 the Charity Commission recognised racial harmony and good community relations as being a charitable purpose by analogy with other purposes recognised as charitable, such as the preservation of public order, mental and moral improvement and the promotion of equality between men and women. In 2002 the Commission recognised the promotion of human rights as charitable by analogy with mental and moral improvement. It also recognised the promotion of religious harmony as charitable using as analogies the promotion of gender equality, the promotion of racial harmony and mental and moral improvement. Finally it recognised the promotion of equality and diversity as charitable, using as analogies the promotion of gender equality, the promotion of religious harmony, the promotion of human rights and mental and moral improvement. In 2004 the Charity Commission recognised international conflict resolution and reconciliation as charitable by analogy with the relief of poverty, sickness and distress, the protection of human life and property, the preservation of public order and mental and moral improvement.

64.2   All these charitable purposes fell under the traditional fourth head, i.e. other purposes beneficial to the community. The *Charities Act 2006* now defines the advancement of human rights, conflict resolution or reconciliation or the promotion of religious or racial harmony or equality and diversity as a charitable purpose. Organisations wishing to register under this new head will have to state clearly the types of human rights, or conflict resolution, etc, that it will be addressing and its areas of operation.

64.3   The advancement of conflict resolution or reconciliation includes the resolution of international conflicts and relieving the suffering, poverty and distress arising through conflict on a national or international scale by identifying the causes of the conflict and seeking to resolve such conflict. It includes the promotion of restorative justice, where all the parties with a stake in a particular conflict or offence come together to resolve collectively how to deal with its aftermath and its implications for the future. It also includes purposes directed towards mediation, conciliation or reconciliation as between persons, organisations, authorities or groups involved or likely to become involved in dispute or inter-personal conflict.

64.4   Charities established for the advancement of human rights, conflict resolution or reconciliation or the promotion of religious or racial harmony or equality and diversity will have to demonstrate that they provide public benefit. They are likely to have to demonstrate that they are altruistic, not too political and not too propagandist. The Charity Commission's awaited revised guidance on political activities and campaigning will need to be considered.

64.5   Examples of the sorts of charities and charitable purpose that will fall under this head include:

•   Charities concerned with the promotion of human rights, at home or abroad, such as relieving victims of human rights abuse, raising awareness of human rights issues, securing the enforcement of human rights law;

•   Charities concerned with the promotion of restorative justice and other forms of conflict resolution or reconciliation;

64.6   Human Rights Charities

- Charities concerned with the resolution of national or international conflicts;
- Mediation charities;
- Charities promoting good relations between persons of different racial groups;
- Charities promoting equality and diversity by the elimination of discrimination on the grounds of age, sex or sexual orientation;
- Charities enabling people of one faith to understand the religious beliefs of others.

FURTHER INFORMATION

64.6   Charity Commission RR12 'The Promotion of Human Rights'.

65   Income Tax

TAX ON CHARITABLE INCOME

65.1   As most charities are corporate bodies or unincorporated associations they are liable to corporation tax on their income subject to specific exemptions. Charitable trusts, however, are subject to income tax on their income unless a tax exemption or extra-statutory concession applies and the income that would otherwise be taxable is used only for charitable purposes.

65.2   Charitable trusts enjoy the same exemptions from tax on their income as do charities subject to corporation tax and the same rules for non-qualifying payments apply for income tax purposes as they do for corporation tax (see 31.23ff). Charitable trusts must make a return of any taxable income and account for any tax payable under the procedures for self-assessment and must notify HMRC of liability to tax within six months of the end of the year of assessment (i.e. by 5 October) if no tax return has been received. In most instances a tax return will be unnecessary as no tax will be payable and HMRC will not normally issue a tax return.

RECLAIMING TAX PAID

65.3   Charities, whether trusts or companies, will receive income net of tax deducted at source from payments made under Gift Aid. Tax should not be deducted at source, however, from interest on bank or building society deposits or government securities (gilts). Assuming the charity qualifies for tax exemption on its income, any income tax suffered by deduction at source can then be reclaimed.

DEDUCTING INCOME TAX

65.4   A company which borrows money, other than from a UK bank, on a loan which lasts or is intended to last for not less than a year, is required to deduct tax at source from any interest paid to the lender. The tax so deducted must be accounted for to HMRC on a quarterly basis using form CT61. The form, together with the payment, should be sent to the Collector of Taxes within 14 days of the end of each calendar quarter and, if different, 14 days from the company's year-end. HMRC will charge interest on any tax not paid by the due date. The lender will be treated as having received income net of UK tax and the company should be able to obtain a deduction for the gross interest paid. These provisions can apply to the trading subsidiaries of charities which have had to borrow funds to finance their operations. The rules do not apply to overdrafts or loans that are to be repaid within a year.

65.5   Charities are also, of course, required to deduct income tax from payments to individuals in return for work under HMRC's Pay As You Earn (PAYE) scheme. Employers have a duty to register for PAYE, and operate it by sending tax and national insurance payments to the collector of taxes on a monthly basis. Charities are required by law to keep PAYE records. Failure to do so can result in the employer being held liable for all tax and national insurance payments that should have been deducted and paid to the collector of taxes, plus interest for late payment, plus penalties. (See CHAPTER 89 – PAYE Administration.)

66   Incorporation of Trustees

ADVANTAGES OF INCORPORATING THE TRUSTEE BODY

66.1   Trustees of unincorporated charitable trusts or associations usually have to enter into legal agreements in their individual names, or in the names of holding or custodian trustees, because the charity has no legal personality of its own. Trustee incorporation is a process by which the charity trustees of an unincorporated trust or association can incorporate themselves as a body. The charity can then vest its property in the name of the incorporated body. This avoids the need to execute deeds transferring land or investments every time new trustees are appointed to an unincorporated charity. Incorporation of the trustee body also allows trustees to enter into contracts and sue, or be sued, in the name of the incorporated body.

66.2   The *Charitable Trustees Incorporation Act 1872* enabled the trustees of charities established for religious, educational, literary, scientific or public charitable purposes to apply to the Charity Commission for a certificate of incorporation. The *1872 Act* was substantially amended by the *Charities Act 1992* and the provisions are now contained in *Part VII* of the *Charities Act 1993*.

66.3   *Section 50* of the *Charities Act 1993* gives the Charity Commission power to grant a certificate of incorporation provided that the Commission considers that incorporation of the trustees would be in the interests of the charity. It allows the Commission to include any conditions or directions it judges to be desirable in the certificate. The Commission cannot issue a certificate of incorporation to a charity that is required to be registered under *s 3* of the *Charities Act 1993* but is not so registered.

IMPACT ON TRUSTEE LIABILITY

66.4   Incorporation of the trustees gives the governing body, not the charity, legal personality, permanent succession, and the right to own property, enter into legal agreements and take legal action in the name of the governing body. However, it does not limit the liability of members and trustees in the way that the incorporation of the charity would, so they continue to remain liable to the same extent as if they had not incorporated.

66.5   If a charity's trustees do not consider that they need the additional protection that incorporating as a charitable company or industrial and provident society would bring, but do own property and/or investments or enter into leases and/or contracts, trustee incorporation could be an appropriate and cost-saving option.

PROCEDURE

66.6   Trustees of registered charities and charities that are exempt or excepted from registration with the Charity Commission can apply to the Commission for a certificate of incorporation. An application pack CHY–1093: 'How to Apply to the Charity Commission for a Certificate of Incorporation' is available from the charity support staff at any of the Commission's offices. They will need to send the following with their application:

- a copy of the governing document, if the Charity Commission does not already have a copy;

- a list of the charity's property or any property held in trust for the charity;

- the names of the current trustees, and evidence of their appointment in legal terms;

- the proposed name with which the trustees wish to be incorporated;

- a statement of why the trustees consider that incorporation of the trustees would be in the best interests of the charity.

NAMING THE INCORPORATED BODY

66.7   The Charity Commission advises that the name of the incorporated body should contain either the word 'trustees' or some similar word such as 'governors'. It should not contain the word 'registered', as this could lead the public to believe that the charity is registered under the *Companies Acts*. Suggested forms are 'The Trustees of the Charity of A N Other', or 'The Incorporated Trustees of the Charity of A N Other'.

TRANSFERRING PROPERTY TO THE INCORPORATED BODY

66.8   Once granted, the certificate of incorporation automatically vests all the property of the charity in the incorporated body, with the exception of any property vested in the Official Custodian. Land vested in the Official Custodian can remain so, but may be transferred by a Charity Commission Order to the incorporated body at the trustees' request. If individuals, such as holding trustees, hold equities, bonds, etc. in trust for the charity they must transfer them into the name of the incorporated body.

CONTINUING TRUSTEES

66.9   Incorporation of the trustee body does not affect the governing document of the charity. It therefore does not change the composition of the trustee body or the provisions in the governing document that relate to the appointment, retirement and removal of trustees. These provisions should be followed in detail as before.

REGISTER OF CHARITIES

66.10   In the case of a registered charity the certificate of incorporation will be placed on the charity's file, which is available for inspection by members of the public. A note that the trustee body has been incorporated will be made on the Register of Charities computer database and the Register of Charities on the Commission's website.

SEAL

66.11   Trustees incorporated under the *Charities Act 1993, s 50* are no longer required to have a common seal. If they choose to have a common seal, documents must be executed using the seal. The trustees must ensure that:

- the design of the common seal includes the name of the incorporated body;

- they have agreed proper measures for the seal's safe keeping; and

- they have agreed regulations for the use of the seal.

If an incorporated body of trustees does not choose to have a common seal, perhaps because of the associated costs, they can execute documents by either:

- having them signed by a majority of the trustees and thereby expressed as being executed by the incorporated body; or

- using an authority granted by the trustees, which should be in writing or by resolution of the trustees, that allows for documents to be executed by two or more trustees in the name of, and on behalf of, the incorporated body.

AMENDMENT

66.12   The trustees cannot amend the certificate of incorporation. However, the Charity Commission has powers, under *s 56* of the *Charities Act 1993* to amend a certificate of incorporation in response to a request from the incorporated body or, on rare occasions, because the Commission believes the conditions in the certificate need amendment. Amendments are made by making an Order or by issuing a new certificate of incorporation.

DISSOLUTION

66.13   Similarly under *s 61* of the *Charities Act 1993* the Commission has power to make an Order for dissolution of an incorporated body either at the trustees' request or because the Commission believes that the incorporated body has no assets and does not operate, or because the charity's objects have been achieved or are incapable of being achieved, or because the charity has either ceased to exist or was not a charity at the time of incorporation. If the trustees wish to dissolve the incorporated body they must demonstrate to the Charity Commission that this is in the best interests of the charity. Unless the trustees can do this the Commission cannot make an Order dissolving the incorporated body.

GIFTS

66.14   Gifts made around the time of incorporation of a trustee body are treated as if they had been given to the incorporated body, even if they were actually given to the charity or for the purposes of the charity. [*Charities Act 1993, s 59*].

67   Industrial and Provident Societies

67.1   Most industrial and provident societies are not charities. However, many registered social landlords (RSLs),of which many will be charities, and a small number of other charities use this legal structure. The registered social landlords may also be registered with the Housing Corporation, Scottish Homes or Tai Cymru under the *Housing Acts*. They are primarily affected by two pieces of legislation, the *Friendly and Industrial and Provident Societies Act 1968* and the *Industrial and Provident Societies Act 1965*. The *1968 Act* is mainly concerned with accounting and audit and the *Industrial and Provident Societies Act 2002* updated the *Industrial and Provident Societies Act 1965*, bringing it into conformity with certain aspects of the law relating to companies.

67.2   Under the *Financial Services and Markets Act 2000* the Mutual Societies Registration section of the Financial Services Authority took over the registration and regulation of industrial and provident societies in England, Wales and Scotland from the Registrar of Friendly Societies, a post which then ceased to exist. In Northern Ireland the Registry of Companies, Credit Unions and Industrial and Provident Societies regulates industrial and provident societies. Registration is considered only where there is a special reason for adopting this particular legal structure.

67.3   A society must therefore be able to demonstrate that it has special reasons for registering as an industrial and provident society, rather than as a company under the Companies Acts. The FSA state that there is no statutory definition of 'special reasons'. The reasons for registration as an industrial and provident society rather than as a company should be 'special' in that there is some concrete advantage or benefit to be gained which would be lost or unobtainable as a company. The fact that the society is to be run for the benefit of the community is not itself a special reason. Each application will be judged on its own merits.

67.4   Genuine and persuasive reasons might be for example:

●   a society might wish to operate on the basis of 'one member, one vote';

●   there might be practical business reasons;

●   a society might be part of a group structure of societies sharing common accounting or IT systems; or

●   a society, which is already registered, might find the costs involved in converting to a company prohibitive and likely to result in its own demise.

67.5   Industrial and provident societies adopt a set of model rules, which are then submitted to the Financial Services Authority for registration in return for a fee. These rules have to include 14 matters set out in *1 Sch* to the *1965 Act*, including matters such as name, objects, meetings, shareholdings, provision for audit and borrowing and investment powers. The rules also set out the powers of remuneration in respect of the committee and officers: this takes into account a clear authority for members of the committee to be paid expenses, without which such payments would be *ultra vires*.

67.6   Charitable industrial and provident societies are exempt charities under the *Charities Act 1993, s 46*. This means that they cannot be registered with the Charity Commission, or quote a charity number. If they need to obtain the tax benefits of being wholly charitable, then they apply direct to HMRC and will be given a Revenue Reference number which they can use on their stationery. Under the *Charities Act 2006* exempt charities which are not regulated by any other principal regulator (such as the Housing Corporation) will register with the Charity Commission.

67.7   *Section 13* of the *Charities Act 2006* gives the Minister for the Cabinet Office power to make regulations prescribing a body or a Minister of the Crown as the principal regulator of an exempt charity. Under a Memorandum of Understanding between the Charity Commission and the Housing Corporation, the Housing Corporation will become the principal regulator of the exempt registered social landlord sector, i.e. registered social landlords that are industrial and provident societies, when the relevant regulations have been made under the *Charities Act 2006*.

67.8   A society may be registered as an industrial and provident society if it is carrying on any industry, business or trade, and is either a co-operative society, or is conducting its business for the benefit of the community and there are special reasons why the society should be registered as an industrial and provident society rather than as a limited company. The term 'business' is not a strictly defined one in this context, and charities will often be able to fit within its scope.

67.9   Only industrial and provident societies established for the benefit of the community are eligible for charitable status. A society 'for the benefit of the community' must principally show that:

● the business must be run primarily for the benefit of people who are not members of the society and must be in the interests of the community at large;

● the rules of the society must not allow distribution of profits or assets to the members: any profits must be ploughed back into the business;

● the organisation has special reasons for registering under this part of the industrial and provident society legislation rather than as a company;

● on dissolution, the assets of the society must pass to some other body with similar objects, not to the members.

67.10   Once registered, an industrial and provident society has similarities to a company: it is a body corporate, with legal identity, perpetual succession and limited liability. Unlike a company the legislation governing an industrial and provident society is not as detailed, although the registration process can be cumbersome, and the structure of management may also be unfamiliar to those involved. It must be democratically controlled by its members.

67.11   Every society must:

● keep proper books of account and maintain satisfactory systems of control of those books, cash holdings and all receipts and payments;

● submit an accounting return every year, by the due date, accompanied by a set of accounts.

- give notice of any change of its registered office; and

- apply to the FSA to amend any of its rules or to change its name, as no amendment is valid until it has been registered.

STRUCTURE

67.12   Although an industrial and provident society is similar in its democratic structure to a charitable association, it differs in being a body corporate: it has a share capital, and all members have to hold at least one share, which must be recorded in the register of members. There is no equivalent to the authorised share capital of a Companies Act company and therefore no limit to the number of shares that may be issued. It is unusual for a benefit of the community society to issue more than nominal share capital (for example, one £1 share per member). Where it does issue more than nominal share capital or where members make loans to the society, or both, any interest paid must not be more than a reasonable rate necessary to obtain and retain enough capital to run the business.

67.13   An industrial and provident society must have a minimum of three members. Eligibility for membership is usually set out in the society's rules and is frequently related to criteria such as living or working in the area of benefit, or sharing a common ethnic origin, or supporting the society's objectives. Members must be aged 16 or over. Members may be individuals or corporate bodies, or a combination of the two. Admission to membership may be at the discretion of the directors or it may be open, for example anyone living on a particular estate may be eligible for membership.

67.14   An industrial and provident society is not a common form of structure for a charity to adopt, partly because the structure came into existence to serve a particular, not exclusively charitable, purpose, and partly because the company limited by guarantee structure can achieve the same ends and is more commonly understood. The *Industrial and Provident Societies Act 2002* included detailed provisions setting out how an industrial and provident society can be converted into a company. The *Charities Act 2006* contains provisions to enable charitable industrial and provident societies to convert to charitable incorporated organisations.

REGISTERS

67.15   Every registered society must keep at its registered office a register recording:

- the names and addresses of members;

- the number of shares per member;

- a statement of other property in the society held by each member;

- the date at which a person started or ceased to be a member;

- the names and addresses of the officers of the society, noting the office and the date of appointment.

ACCOUNTS

67.16   The *Charities Act 1993* requires exempt charities to prepare accounts at least every 15 months, unless other legislation includes another requirement. A trustees' or auditor's report is not required by the *Charities Act 1993*, but accounts must be made available to the public, for a reasonable fee if necessary, within two months of being requested.

67.17   Industrial and provident societies, as exempt charities, have their own legislation governing accounts and audit set out in the *Friendly and Industrial and Provident Societies Act 1968*. All industrial and provident societies have year-ends between 31 August and 31 January, unless otherwise agreed with the Regulator. Every society must keep proper books of account, and establish and maintain a satisfactory system of financial control. Annual accounts have to include revenue accounts dealing with one or more aspects of the society's business, and a balance sheet, duly audited (subject to exemptions) and signed by the secretary of the society and two members of the committee, acting on behalf of the committee. Because the specification of the accounts is so brief, charitable industrial and provident societies are able to comply with the charities SORP in full: the distinction between a revenue account and the SOFA is carried through into the SORP in the consideration of FRS 3 and the need for a summary income and expenditure account where appropriate.

67.18   Every registered society must keep a copy of the latest balance sheet, together with its audit report, hung in a conspicuous position at the registered office of the society at all times.

ANNUAL RETURN

67.19   All industrial and provident societies have to submit an annual return, including the accounts. These then go on public record and are open to inspection.

AUDIT

67.20   The audit regime for industrial and provident societies is set out by the FSA as follows:

> 'The accounts must be audited by a qualified auditor (that is someone who is eligible for appointment as a company auditor under s 25 of the Companies Act 1989), even if the lighter 'accountant's report' is used. In some circumstances your society may be able to substitute a full audit or accountant's report' with a lay audit, or submit unaudited accounts. The type of audit depends on a number of factors:

> i   Financial thresholds, namely:

> - the turnover of the society in the preceding year of account, and

> - the total assets in the preceding year of account;

> ii   Whether the society is required by law to have a full professional audit;

> iii   The current rules of the society;

> iv   Assent by the membership in general meeting.'

In all instances all published accounts, whether audited or not, must be signed by the secretary and two committee members of the society on behalf of the society's committee.

Societies which require a full professional audit by a qualified auditor

67.21   A full professional audit by a qualified auditor is always required by societies which in the preceding year of account had a turnover in excess of £5,600,000 (£250,000 if charitable) or total assets in excess of £2,800,000.

67.22   Any society, irrespective of its level of turnover or assets, which falls under any of the following categories must also undertake a full professional audit:

- Housing associations registered with the Housing Corporation, the National Assembly or Scottish Homes;

- A subsidiary of another society;

- A society with one or more subsidiaries (whether those subsidiaries are companies or societies);

- A society that must prepare accounts under the *Insurance Accounts Directive* (*Miscellaneous Insurance Undertakings*) *Regulations 1993*;

- A society which takes deposits or has taken in the past and continues to hold deposits, within the provisions of the *Financial Services and Markets Act 2000*, other than a deposit in the form of withdrawable share capital.

Societies eligible to substitute an accountant's report for a full professional audit

67.23   Societies are eligible to substitute an accountant's report for a full professional audit only if all of the following criteria are met:

- the society's rules allow it to disapply the requirement to undertake a full professional audit. If the rules only permit the society to conduct a full professional audit, then the appropriate rule amendments must first be registered with the FSA.

- the society's membership has passed at a general meeting a resolution allowing the society to disapply the requirement to undertake a full professional audit for the year of account in question.

- in the preceding year of account its turnover exceed £90,000, but did not exceed £5,600,000 (£250,000 if charitable) and its total assets were below £2,800,000.

- If is not a society falling under any of the five categories listed in **67.22** above, which are required by law to have a full professional audit.

67.24   The accountant's report must state whether, in the opinion of the qualified auditor making the report:

- The revenue account or accounts, the other accounts (if any) to which the report relates, and the balance sheet are in agreement with the books of account kept by the society;

- On the basis of the information contained in the books of account, the revenue account(s) comply with the requirements of the *Industrial and Provident Societies Act 1965* and the *Friendly and Industrial and Provident Societies Act 1968;*

- The financial criteria allowing the production of a report instead of a full audit have been met.

Societies eligible to forward unaudited accounts

67.25   A society may produce unaudited accounts only if all of the following criteria are met:

- The society's rules allow it to disapply the requirement to undertake a full professional audit. If the rules only permit the society to conduct a full professional audit, then the appropriate rule amendments must first be registered with the FSA;

- The society's membership has passed at a general meeting a resolution allowing the society to disapply the requirement to undertake a full professional audit for the year of account in question;

- In the preceding year of account its turnover did not exceed £90,000 and its total assets are below £2,800,000;

- It is not a society falling into any of the five categories listed in **67.22** above, which are required by law to have a full professional audit.

67.26   Where the relevant conditions are met, and the society produces unaudited accounts, the revenue account(s) and balance sheet must still be signed by the secretary and two committee members of the society acting on behalf of the society's committee.

Societies eligible to substitute a lay audit for a professional audit by a qualified auditor

67.27   A society may appoint two or more lay auditors in place of a qualified auditor only if **all of the following criteria are met:**

- The society's rules allow it to disapply the requirement to undertake a full professional audit. If the rules only permit the society to conduct a full professional audit, then the appropriate rule amendments must first be registered with the FSA.

- The society's membership has passed at a general meeting a resolution allowing the society to disapply the requirement to undertake a full professional audit for the year of account in question.

- The total of the society's receipts and payments (income and expenditure) in the preceding year of account was below £5,000 and the total number of members at that year end was below 500 and the total assets did not exceed £5,000. This is the total of the society's receipts added to the payments figure.

- It is not a society falling into any of the five categories listed in **67.22** above, which are required by law to have a full professional audit.

67.28   A lay audit is an audit by two or more lay auditors. A person may be a lay auditor if he/she is not an officer or servant of a society and is not a partner of or in the employment of, or does not employ, an officer or servant of the society. A society might use lay auditors if it wishes people other than its committee to check the accounts against its books.

DISSOLUTION

67.29   The society's rules must not allow its assets to be distributed to its members on dissolution. The rules should state that on dissolution the assets should be transferred to some other body with similar objects. If no such body exists, the rules should state that the assets must then be used for similar charitable or philanthropic purposes.

68   Inheritance Tax

68.1   Inheritance tax is chargeable on the value of a person's estate at the day of their death, plus the value of gifts made by them during the previous seven years. Legacies, bequests and lifetime gifts to charities are exempt from inheritance tax. [*Inheritance Tax Act 1984*].

QUALIFICATIONS OF EXEMPTION

68.2   To qualify for exemption from inheritance tax the gift must be irrevocable and used only for charitable purposes.

68.3   The charity exemption applies to transfers of value attributable to property which is given to a charity. It is essential that the gift becomes the property of a charity or is held on trust for charitable purposes only. No relief is available, however, if the property or any part of it may become applicable for non-charitable purposes, so that a gift to a temporary charity would not qualify. Relief is also not available if the property is not immediately vested in the charity. Therefore, a gift in a settlement where an individual has a life interest is not exempt from inheritance tax.

68.4   There is no general restriction on the charity exemption under the reservation of benefit rules where the donor retains some benefit. However, if the property given is land and the donor, their spouse or a person connected with the donor is entitled to possession or occupation of the land rent free, or at a rent below the full market rent, then the charity exemption will not apply.

DEED OF VARIATION

68.5   It is possible for the beneficiaries of a person's estate to enter into a Deed of Variation which claims that for inheritance tax purposes the variation shall have effect as if the provisions of the Deed were included in the will. The beneficiaries can also transfer part of the estate to a charity and qualify for the charity exemption, even though there is no such provision in the original will. As the variation applies only for inheritance tax and capital gains tax purposes, the gift is treated for all other purposes as if it had been made by the beneficiary.

68.6   There have been cases where the beneficiary has then applied the provisions of the Gift Aid scheme so that the charity receives a further repayment of income tax and the beneficiary receives relief from income tax at the higher rate on the gross amount. This arrangement was successfully challenged by the Inland Revenue in a case taken to the Special Commissioners who decided that the Gift Aid rules could not apply because the beneficiary had received a benefit. The benefit in question was the saving in inheritance tax, thus increasing the value of the estate (before the charitable donation) which passed to him (*St Dunstan's v Major [1997] STC (SCD) 212*).

68.7   As HMRC are challenging arrangements which seek to utilise both income tax and inheritance tax reliefs any person considering entering into such an arrangement may have to take the case to appeal before the courts and should therefore take professional advice.

69   Insolvency

INSOLVENCY

69.1   'Insolvent' is the technical term for what the layman may describe as bankrupt, bust or broke. It has a specific meaning in legislation, and it is important to identify when a charity has become insolvent. Failure to do so can lead to increased financial losses, a deterioration of the position of creditors and the exposure of trustees to personal liabilities and to possible criminal penalties. There are two main tests to assess solvency: the 'cash flow' test and the 'balance sheet' test. Depending on the outcome of these tests, and the nature of the charity's constitution, the trustees will need to act appropriately. These tests are enshrined in the principal legislation governing insolvent companies, the *Insolvency Act 1986*, which partly applies to unincorporated organisations. Because of the extremely complex situations that can arise during an insolvency, and the risks involved, trustees should take appropriate professional advice as soon as possible if they think that their organisation might be insolvent.

Cash flow test

69.2   An organisation is insolvent if it cannot pay its debts as they fall due. The *Insolvency Act 1986, s 123*, specifically in the context of companies and Industrial and Provident Societies, states that this situation arises where:

- a creditor to whom the organisation is indebted in a sum exceeding £750 has served a statutory demand on the organisation requesting payment of the amount due, and for a period of three weeks thereafter the organisation has neither paid nor made satisfactory arrangements to pay the debt, or

- the execution or other process issued on a judgment or order of any Court in favour of a creditor of the organisation is returned unsatisfied in whole or in part, or

- the Court is satisfied that the organisation is unable to pay its debts as they fall due.

69.3   Trustees and management should be alert to creditors pressing for the repayment of debts by presenting a winding-up petition on the basis that the company has failed to pay a debt within 21 days of a statutory demand being made. This may result in a winding-up Order under which the company is placed into compulsory liquidation. Although a winding-up Order will not be made on the basis of a debt which is genuinely disputed or where the company has a genuine counter-claim that would reduce the company's net indebtedness below the statutory minimum of £750, the Court must be satisfied that the dispute or counter-claim is well founded.

Balance sheet test

69.4   Where an organisation has passed the cash flow test, it may yet fail another test based on the organisation's current balance sheet. The *Insolvency Act 1986* states that an organisation is insolvent if its total assets are less than

350

its total liabilities, taking into account contingent liabilities and prospective liabilities. The inclusion of prospective and contingent liabilities make this a very wide definition of insolvency. A contingent liability is one which potentially exists now, but the circumstances which may trigger the payment have not yet occurred, for instance, a claim for unfair dismissal being heard by a tribunal, where the verdict is still uncertain. A prospective liability is one which the organisation knows it will have in the future. This category is so wide as to make many organisations potentially insolvent using this test. Many organisations may have some long-term financial commitments that are certain, whereas raising a matching amount of income is not certain. A good example of this is the requirement for organisations to recognise the full extent of liabilities pertaining to pension fund deficits. This is as true for organisations that trade, as it is for those which rely exclusively on voluntary income. Thus many organisations may find themselves in this position before it is clear that they are insolvent on a cash flow basis.

IMPLICATIONS OF INSOLVENCY

69.5   The implications of insolvency on an organisation that has no realistic chance of a recovery of its financial position can be dramatic. The organisation will be unable to continue to operate, and it must take all steps possible to preserve the position of creditors. The nature of the process of closing down and finalising the affairs of the insolvent organisation will depend on its legal structure.

Limited companies and industrial and provident societies

69.6   An insolvent charitable company may be placed into liquidation or into some other formal insolvency process. In the meantime, however, the key considerations in the minds of the trustees will be twofold: to reduce the risk of loss to the creditors, and to preserve the work of the charity.

69.7   A company or industrial and provident society is obliged, when insolvent, to act in the best interests of its creditors. Whilst this duty may sometimes seem to conflict with the charitable company's duty to its members and beneficiaries, it is of paramount importance and enshrined in the UK insolvency legislation. In practice, this means that from the moment that the trustees are aware of the insolvent position of the organisation, they must collect all possible sums owing from debtors, they should not incur any expenditure that does not preserve value and/or create an asset of at least an equivalent value, and they should not pay off any creditor in preference to another. This latter point means that money should not be paid into an overdrawn bank account: a credit-only account at a separate bank should be opened. The trustees should also carefully consider whether the charitable company should accept any further donations.

69.8   There are a number of insolvency processes available and it is essential that the company seek professional advice regarding the most appropriate process in the circumstances. A reputable insolvency practitioner will usually provide initial advice to the company without charge. The processes available are:

- **Creditors' voluntary liquidation.** This is commenced by a winding-up resolution passed by the members at an extraordinary general meeting. The creditors will then ratify the liquidator's appointment at a meeting of the company's creditors. The liquidator must be a licensed insolvency practitioner. This type of liquidation may result in a better outcome to creditors when compared with a compulsory liquidation, due to the statutory fees and charges that are applied in a compulsory liquidation.

- **Compulsory liquidation.** An Order for the compulsory winding-up of a company may be made by the Court following its consideration of a winding-up petition. Whilst the winding-up petition can be issued by the company, it is usual for a petition to be issued by a creditor with an unsatisfied debt exceeding £750. However, given the length of the Court process, directors of a charitable company facing an unavoidable insolvency procedure would generally be expected to have taken appropriate steps to place the company into a voluntary insolvency procedure to safeguard the position of creditors.

- **Administration Order.** This is a process that can be instigated by a company, its directors, or a creditor. Due to recent legislative changes, this is a relatively quick and simple process with no Court involvement, although in certain circumstances it will be necessary to petition the Court for an administration order. An administrator must be a licensed insolvency practitioner. The administration process is primarily applicable where all or part of the business of a company can be saved as a going concern, or where the administration process is likely to result in a more advantageous realisation of assets compared to liquidation.

- **Administrative receivership.** This occurs where a secured creditor with a floating charge registered before 15 September 2003, over the whole or substantially all of the assets of a company, can appoint an administrative receiver, who must be an insolvency practitioner. The administrative receiver's function is to sell sufficient of the company's assets to repay the debts of the secured and preferential creditors. Additionally, a creditor with a fixed charge over the assets of a company can appoint a fixed charge receiver, sometimes called an 'LPA Receiver', who will deal solely with the assets specified in the charge (most often land and property).

- **Company Voluntary Arrangement.** This is where a company enters into an arrangement with its creditors in order to compromise its debts, usually involving a reduced and/or delayed repayment of the debts. Such a process is carried out under the control of an insolvency practitioner, who acts as supervisor of the arrangement.

- **Informal arrangement/moratorium.** Such an arrangement is made informally between a company and its creditors and the process is not governed by the insolvency legislation. In practice the company would need expert professional advice in order to reach such an arrangement, as without the protection offered by a formal insolvency process any informal arrangement could be compromised by a single creditor taking action against the company.

69.9   A number of the processes outlined above can be used to facilitate the transfer, for value, of a charity's assets and/or charitable activities to a charity with similar objectives. This will ensure that the charitable activities and objectives of the charity are not destroyed by the insolvency of the charitable company.

69.10   It should be noted that of the processes outlined above, only the two types of liquidation and the informal arrangement process are generally available to industrial and provident societies, and some registered societies may not be able to enter into voluntary liquidation. Additionally, if the society has granted a fixed or floating charge to a creditor, it is possible that the creditor could place the society into receivership or administration.

69.11   Assuming that the directors/trustees of a company have not been guilty of trading whilst insolvent, breaching their fiduciary duties, preferring one creditor to another, or of entering into any other transaction contrary to the provisions of the *Insolvency Act 1986*, they should be able to rely on the protection afforded to them by the incorporation of the company. This means that any debts which remain unpaid when all the assets of the company have been exhausted simply remain unpaid, and the company is eventually struck off the Companies' Register and dissolved. This protection is important as the general position is that not all creditors will be paid in full. This is not only due to the fact that the value of claims by creditors may exceed the value of the company's assets, but because there are strict priorities to the order in which creditors may be paid, the value of assets realised during an insolvency process may be substantially less than would normally be obtained in a business trading as a going concern, and the costs of conducting the insolvency must be paid before any distributions are made to creditors. It should be noted that many charitable companies are limited by guarantee and, upon an insolvency process, the amount of such guarantee is likely to be called (i.e. required to be paid to the company).

69.12   It is essential to remember that assets held by a charitable company are not part of its corporate property if held within permanent endowment or restricted income funds. These assets cannot be pooled with unrestricted funds and distributed to the company's creditors. Failure to separate, or the distribution of, these funds could expose the directors to personal liability in respect of the value of the funds. In addition, when permanent endowment or restricted income funds are included on a charitable company's balance sheet, they may flatter the financial position of the company and hide the actual financial difficulties that may exist. It is therefore important that funds are correctly analysed and that 'free cash reserves' are identified when determining the actual financial position of the company.

Company Directors Disqualification Act 1986

69.13   The *Company Directors Disqualification Act 1986* applies to limited companies and partnerships. A person will be disqualified as a company director if that person was a director of an insolvent company, and their conduct as a director makes them unfit to be involved in managing a company. For every formal insolvency process, other than the company voluntary arrangement procedure or an informal arrangement (see **69.7**), a confidential report is made to the DTI by the office holder (or the Official Receiver in the case of a compulsory liquidation), who will then decide whether to take action against the director(s) concerned. Under the provisions of the legislation, an individual can be disqualified from acting as a director for a period of up to 15 years.

69.14 Insolvency

Unincorporated organisations

69.14 These organisations do not have limited liability, and therefore the trustees are personally liable for the outstanding debts of the charity. Whilst the constitution may govern what happens in an insolvency situation, it is again essential that professional advice is sought as early as possible, as no statutory insolvency processes exist for unincorporated charities. The order of priority for the payment of creditors is also not defined in the same way as for charitable companies and industrial and provident societies.

69.15 In this situation, because each of the trustees is personally liable for the debts of the charitable organisation, they should take professional advice on their own personal position. The trustees would normally fund this themselves, rather than look to the charity to pay for the advice, although the charity can pay for advice regarding the position of the charity and the body of trustees as a whole. In certain circumstances, it may be appropriate or necessary for a trustee to take action against a fellow trustee. By this stage, the charity is likely either to have had a receiver and manager appointed by the Charity Commission, or to have ceased operations.

INSOLVENCY INDICATORS

Going concern

69.16 The accounts of a charity will indicate an insolvent position where the balance sheet as a whole is negative, or where the balance sheet remains positive only by virtue of assets such as functional land or buildings, or intangible assets, that cannot readily be used to pay debts as and when they fall due. It may be possible to borrow against certain tangible assets, thus repaying short-term debts with longer-term borrowing. Whilst this will not alter the total balance sheet position, it will enable the organisation to meet its short-term cash requirement and help to reschedule the financial position of the charity.

Cash strains

69.17 The presence of high cash balances does not always indicate a solvent charity. Many organisations receive income in advance, especially subscription-based charities where members will pay a proportion of next year's dues before the current year-end. In this case the income is treated as deferred income, i.e. a liability. The difficulty with this sort of liability is that in day-to-day terms it never needs repayment and no apparent cost has to be incurred to meet any obligation against it. Trustees should be very aware that this is a perception and not reality: the receipt of deferred income, even subscriptions, involves some future cost against that same income.

69.18 Additionally, and as described at 69.9, high cash balances can also camouflage insolvency where the fund analysis is incomplete. It is possible for a restricted fund to be in deficit, if expenditure has been incurred in advance of anticipated funding. In general, though, restricted funds will be in credit, pending application of the balances. These positive fund balances can appear to offset negative balances on general funds. The charity may therefore have a positive balance sheet, but in reality be insolvent if the positive fund balances can only be spent on the purposes for which they were given.

69.19   In both of the above cases there may be no apparent cash strain in the organisation, and the accounts may only indicate insolvency on the harshest interpretation of the *Insolvency Act 1986*. However, the reality of the situation is that the charity is operating whilst insolvent, and by doing so the trustees are potentially exposing themselves to personal loss. They must therefore be aware of this and ensure that they are taking all possible steps to protect the position of creditors.

69.20   Often the reality of insolvency is only starkly apparent when the auditors report on the financial accounts. Whatever the state of a charity's management information, however, there are usually other signs of an insolvent position developing, and these should be regarded seriously. Typical indicators are an inability to operate within agreed borrowing facilities, pressure from creditors, failure to observe credit limits or terms, and having to reschedule or cancel payments. These pressures are not simply routine financial management, but may indicate either insolvency, poor cash management or a combination of both. A reduction in donation income or funding can also cause significant financial difficulties. In these situations, the trustees should immediately investigate whether any steps can be taken to improve the financial position of the charity, for example, if there are assets not being properly employed, debts or grants uncollected, or whether operating costs can be reduced.

Forecasts

69.21   As with any other commercial business, all charities should be operating to budgets. A forecast has a slightly different function in that it predicts the most likely outcome over a period of time, whereas the budget is usually the target result. At the start of a financial period the budget and the forecast for the period are likely to be very similar or the same, but as time progresses the forecast results will identify likely future variances from budget.

69.22   Where an organisation is potentially facing insolvency the need for sensible forecasts is enhanced, and these forecasts must take into consideration the effect of variations in income streams. Whilst voluntary income may be difficult to predict, on the basis that it is by definition not contractual and therefore must be classed as uncertain, generally the various strands of income will have established patterns. The degree of risk to the going concern of the organisation is therefore the sensitivity of the charity to a downturn in income and/or an increase in costs. Where a charity's financial position is very sensitive and small changes in income and cost streams could lead to a potential insolvency, the risks to the charity should be carefully evaluated.

STEPS TO BE TAKEN BY TRUSTEES

69.23   The following is a brief list of practical steps that trustees should consider taking where there is a risk of insolvency:

- Act early, on the first suspicions of potential insolvency issues – the longer the delay in dealing with issues, the harder they will be to resolve;

- Seek timely, specialist advice from insolvency practitioners, lawyers, auditors and other advisors;

- Ensure that the organisation has accurate and up-to-date financial information, on which the trustees and management can base their decisions, and that the information is regularly reviewed and any issues identified immediately acted upon;

- Ensure that Trustees meet regularly and that all their decisions are documented;

- Ensure that the trustees and management team has sufficient commercial and business skills to guide the organisation through its difficulties. Where the skill base is insufficient, consider formal training or the recruitment of staff with relevant skills;

- Maintain constant communication between the management, trustees, advisors and key creditors and stakeholders;

- Ensure that trustees and management understand the distinction between restricted, endowed and designated funds, and that the management information provides an accurate fund analysis;

- Consider obtaining trustees' indemnity insurance to mitigate the risk of personal liability;

- Consider using trading subsidiaries to reduce exposure to the charity itself.

AVOIDING INSOLVENCY

69.24   Insolvency is usually apparent when debts are unpaid due to a lack of cash, and so struggling organisations need to concentrate especially on their cash management. Sometimes this is beyond their power, and there is no easy answer for charities that are dependent on annual grant receivable at a certain point in the year, or where funding is delayed. However, charities should ensure that funding problems are not exacerbated by poor management. Options to improve the cash position include:

- renegotiation of timing of grant receipts;

- using, and trying to negotiate the best, supplier credit terms;

- making regular claims for income tax recoveries;

- attracting interest-free loans from supporters;

- obtaining security from third parties for financing the charity.

69.25   Insolvency may alternatively result from lack of income or over-expenditure. If possible, steps must be taken to resolve the situation, however, unpalatable they may appear to the trustees, as it must be remembered that by law the interests of creditors are of paramount importance. It may be wise to consult with the Charity Commission in advance, especially if these measures are likely to generate complaints or adverse publicity, such as the closing of an entire operation.

69.26   Finally, the lack of cash may represent a lack of support that cannot be managed because the charity simply no longer has an important function to fulfil, either because it has achieved its purpose, or because its objectives are out of date. When a fund-raising strategy cannot revitalise the organisation then insolvency may be unavoidable unless there is an opportunity to merge with, or be taken over by, another charity with similar charitable objectives.

69.27   The Charity Commission publishes a guidance booklet CC12 'Managing Financial Difficulties and Insolvency in Charities', that provides further information.

RECEIVERS

69.28   Confusion can exist because an insolvent charity may encounter this term in three differing contexts. For the sake of clarification, these are set out below.

Administrative receiver

69.29   An administrative receiver is an insolvency practitioner who may be appointed by a lender under the powers contained in a debenture securing the charity's assets by way of a floating charge. The lender will generally be a bank or other financial institution, but it can also be an individual. Charities should be aware of any such powers which exist in their finance arrangements. As described at **69.7**, a lender may also be able to appoint a fixed charge or LPA receiver over certain specified assets covered by a fixed charge.

Official Receiver

69.30   The Official Receiver is an officer of the Court working for the Insolvency Service (an agency of the Department for Business, Enterprise and Regulatory Reform), which deals with compulsory liquidations and personal bankruptcies. In certain situations, the Official Receiver may pass the conduct of the liquidation or bankruptcy to an insolvency practitioner. In Scotland, the Accountant in Bankruptcy carries out functions similar to the Official Receiver.

Receiver and manager

69.31   A receiver and manager is a person appointed by the Charity Commission under *s 18* of the *Charities Act 1993*, to take over some or all of the duties of the trustees of a charity. This will occur if the Commission is satisfied that there has been misconduct or mismanagement, or that the charity's assets are in need of protection, after a *s 8* inquiry has been instituted. The receiver and manager acts to protect the assets of the charity, and eventually either closes the charity down or stabilises the charity's financial affairs so that it can continue to operate. The Charity Commission has a panel of professional firms from which it will make receiver and manager appointments.

DISSOLUTION

69.32   When a registered charity ceases to operate, the Charity Commission will remove it from the register using its powers under *s 3(4)* of the *Charities Act 1993*. In addition to removal from the register, a charitable company would also be dissolved under the provisions of the *Companies Act*. (See CHAPTER 38.)

70   Insurance

70.1   Charity trustees have a duty to safeguard the assets of the charity, both tangible and intangible, and any trading companies it may own, from direct loss or damage and from third party liabilities which would otherwise have to be satisfied out of the property of the charity. They also have responsibilities towards any staff or volunteers who work for the charity. Cover may be required for a wide range of items, including the property of the charity (such as land, buildings, plant, furniture, vehicles, equipment and computers); its liabilities to employees, volunteers and the public; accidents, sickness and costs arising from staff taking maternity leave; cash on the premises or in transit; motor insurance; insurance for fund-raising or special events; and loss of key people. An up-to-date inventory of all property, furniture and equipment must be kept for insurance and other purposes.

70.2   Under statute it is compulsory for organisations to take out certain types of insurance, for example employers' liability insurance and motor insurance, but insuring other risks will be a matter for discretion, and in some instances the governing document may specify the types of insurance that should be taken out. In most cases the trustees will have to make a judgement, balancing risk against the cost of insurance. However, if they are found to have neglected their responsibility to safeguard the property of the charity, trustees may be personally liable to make good the charity's losses.

70.3   Under the *Trustee Act 2000* trustees of unincorporated charities have a clear power to:

●   insure any trust property against risks of loss or damage due to any event; and

●   pay the premiums out of the charity funds.

70.4   The power in the *Trustee Act 2000* does not apply to charitable companies (except where they are trustees) but the powers expressed in a charitable company's memorandum of association will normally be wide enough to authorise the purchase of this sort of insurance. *Section 39* of the *Charities Act 2006* gives trustees a clear power to purchase indemnity insurance against their personal liability, and to pay the premiums out of charity funds (see *Chapter 122*).

Risk management

70.5   Where a certain type of insurance cover is not compulsory, the trustees should conduct a risk analysis to determine whether insurance would be the best way of managing the risk. They will need to address the following questions:

●   Does the nature of the charity's business present risk of a particular form of loss or liability? This clearly will involve an analysis of the nature of the charity's business activity, and the practical risk of liability occurring. The risk of vicarious liability for the acts of the charity's employees or volunteers should not be overlooked when conducting this analysis, because in certain circumstances a charity or its trustees may be directly liable for the wrongful acts of its employees or volunteers. The larger the number of a charity's employees and volunteers the greater the risk.

- How much would it cost to pass the risk to an insurer?

- Can anything be done to reduce this cost? For example:

  - By taking steps to reduce the likelihood that a claim will need to be made against the insurer and/or to reduce the size of any claim. Examples include enhanced security measures and the display of disclaimer notices.

  - By instructing the charity's broker to seek competitive quotes, and not automatically accepting the first terms which are offered.

  - By using a broker who can and will engage positively with insurers about the assessment of risk. A well-informed broker may be in a position to 'educate' insurers, for example by drawing comparisons between claims experience in charities and claims experience of non-charitable bodies of a similar size, and so obtain a more realistic premium for his client.

  - By collaborating with other charities in the purchase of insurance.

- Can anything be done to increase the charity's funding to meet the cost of insurance? For example, can the cost of insurance be built into the fees for contracts?

- Is it reasonable for the charity to carry part or all of the risk of loss or liability itself? Trustees should take into account:

  - The size of the charity. A charity with a large-scale operation might think it appropriate to accept the consequences of its exposure to risk without taking out insurance. The need for insurance may be more obvious where the charity risks losing all or most of its assets as a result of a single claim.

  - The type of charity, specifically the risk to the charity trustees of personal liability. The use of a company structure usually protects the directors and members of the company from personal liability for its debts. Trustees of unincorporated charities need to consider the potential risks to themselves in relation to liabilities of the charity. If the charity's assets are insufficient to meet the liabilities, the trustees may possibly find themselves with a personal liability through no fault of their own. Incorporation would mitigate this risk.

  - The importance of the charity and the number of other charities working in the same field. How damaging would the social consequences be if the charity was put out of business by a claim or series of claims?

  - The possibility of reducing premiums by accepting a higher excess.

- Should the charity reduce, or abandon altogether, the activity which gives rise to the risk?

INSURING PROPERTY

70.6   If a charity owns the freehold of the premises it occupies it will be solely responsible for insuring them against the main material damage risks of fire, explosion, aircraft, lightning, storm and tempest, and subsidence. The Charity Commission recommends that trustees should insure buildings for their full reinstatement value, even if the governing document does not require reinstatement. They should take professional advice about this amount, which may need to include any necessary:

- demolition work;

- site clearance;

- architects, surveyors and other professional fees;

- costs associated with compliance with planning requirements and building regulations;

- rebuilding.

70.7   The buildings insurance should be regularly reviewed to check that cover is adequate and has kept apace with fluctuations in property prices and the cost of building materials. The amount of cover should take into account the fact that a building could be burnt down on the last day before renewal. Therefore, it needs to be sufficient to cover the cost of replacement at that time, if this is likely to be greater than the cost at the start of the insured period. If a claim is made and the charity is found to be under-insured, the trustees could be personally liable to make up the shortfall.

70.8   If a charity's premises are leased, then the lease should specify whether the landlord or the lessee, i.e. the charity, is responsible for insuring the property and/or the contents. If a charity is a landlord then the trustees should consider who will be responsible for insuring the building when they draw up a lease. It may well be in the charity's best interest to retain responsibility for insuring the building, but if this is the case then the costs should be reflected in the rents charged. If the charity passes responsibility to the lessee or lessees then it must ensure that the lessee has taken out adequate insurance cover.

CONTENTS

70.9   Insurance should be taken out against physical damage to the contents arising from fire, flood or explosion, theft, and 'all risks'. Some 'all risks' policies do not include cover for loss or damage caused by war, nuclear contamination, riot and civil commotion. Lessees are usually responsible for insuring the contents of the part of the building which they occupy. An 'all risks' policy will generally cover damage to contents from most events, but the trustees may need to consider whether the insurance should:

- be on a 'new for old' basis;

- be index linked;

- cover losses from theft;

- cover accidental damage;

- cover goods or cash in transit;

- cover specified high-value items such as computers.

70.10   In some instances charities will be unable to afford the cost of insurance. This could well be the case for a charitable art gallery or museum. Where this is so, trustees should seek advice from the Charity Commission. This could protect them from being found guilty of a breach of trust should under-insured items go missing. Computer insurance is an area where a charity can easily find itself over-insured, as costs are declining. The cost of replacing a two-year-old computer would be much less than the computer's cost at the time of purchase.

BUSINESS INTERRUPTION/ADDITIONAL COST OF WORKING

70.11   Cover for consequential loss that indemnifies an organisation against loss of income or profit will often be inappropriate for a charity. However, cover against the additional cost of working, such as the cost of renting alternative premises if the charity's premises are unusable as the result of any of the material damage risks listed at **70.3** and hiring equipment whilst awaiting repairs or replacements, is often more appropriate and may be advisable for some charities.

EMPLOYERS' LIABILITY INSURANCE

70.12   Charities employing staff are required under the *Employers' Liability (Compulsory Insurance) Act 1969*, as amended by the *Employers' Liability (Compulsory Insurance) Regulations 1998*, to have a minimum employers' liability insurance cover of £5 million for injury, illness or disease suffered or contracted by employees whilst carrying out their duties. Most insurance companies will offer cover of £10 million. All individuals who have a contract of employment with the charity must be covered. Some volunteers, for example, those in receipt of honoraria, may be regarded as employees for the purposes of this Act. A copy of the certificate of insurance must be displayed at all premises where employees are based. Failure to take out employers' liability insurance or to display the certificate showing that a valid policy is in force will be subject to a heavy fine.

EMPLOYERS' LEGAL EXPENSES

70.13   Employers' legal expenses insurance is not compulsory. It provides cover against losses related to employment matters, such as legal expenses and compensation arising from industrial tribunal awards. This is probably the most useful form of cover for potential legal liabilities that a charity needs.

PUBLIC LIABILITY INSURANCE/PRODUCT LIABILITY INSURANCE

70.14   There is no statutory requirement for charities to take out public liability insurance or product liability insurance. However, it is prudent for every charity that occupies premises, holds public events or sells or distributes products to have these types of insurance. If they do not, the trustees could be found to have breached their duty of trust.

70.15 Insurance

70.15 Public liability insurance protects charities from claims arising from members of the public for any death, injury, illness, and/or loss of, or damage to, property incurred as the result of negligence on the part of the charity or one of its employees or volunteers whilst on the charity's premises or as a result of the charity's activities. It is generally linked to premises or to fund-raising events. It does not cover liabilities arising from the charity's work, for example, liabilities arising as the result of being given incorrect information, or to products manufactured or supplied by the charity.

70.16 'Members of the public' normally includes the charity's volunteers (including the trustees), users and beneficiaries, but policies should be checked to make sure this is in fact the case. This is particularly important if volunteers, including trustees, are not explicitly included in the employers' liability insurance. Volunteers should be informed about the extent of cover provided for them by the charity and made aware of any exclusions, and of any alternative arrangements the charity has made to protect them. For example, some policies exclude cover for volunteers over the age of 70 working in charity shops.

70.17 *Section 2(2)* of the *Unfair Contract Terms Act 1977* means that positioning a disclaimer notice, such as those frequently seen in car parks and cloakrooms, may not be an effective way of restricting the charity's liability for loss or damage resulting from negligence except in so far as the notice satisfies the requirement of reasonableness, while *s 2(1)* of the Act states that disclaimer notices cannot exclude or restrict liability for death or personal injury resulting from negligence.

70.18 Product liability insurance will be needed by charities that sell products to the public to protect them from liabilities arising under the *Consumer Protection Act 1987*, the *Sale of Goods Act 1979* or under Common Rules of Negligence. For example, a consumer who sustains serious injuries from using an item purchased from a charity's trading company's mail order catalogue could sue the trading company. Without adequate product liability insurance such a claim could result in the trading company becoming insolvent, and the trustees having to write off the charity's investment in the trading company.

MOTOR INSURANCE

70.19 If a charity owns or operates vehicles it must comply with the *Road Traffic Act 1988* which stipulates third party insurance as a minimum requirement. If volunteers drive their own vehicles in the course of their volunteering work, the charity must ensure that the volunteers have suitable insurance. If a volunteer's insurance provider levies a higher premium as a result of the car being used for the charity's business, the volunteer can be reimbursed from charity funds for the additional premium.

FIDELITY GUARANTEE INSURANCE

70.20 If employees or volunteers handle large amounts of cash or other valuables, the charity should consider taking out fidelity insurance to protect against any possible fraud or dishonesty. The insurer will usually insist on background checks with the police. If this is the case the trustees will have to put their duty to protect the charity's property before any personal distaste at appearing not to trust staff and volunteers. Fidelity guarantee insurance, now commonly known as 'theft by employee insurance', also protects against theft of money by a forged signature on a cheque or the fraudulent use of computer equipment. Fidelity guarantee insurance is not a substitute for sound financial and personnel risk management and is usually provided only if the charity can demonstrate that its internal controls are both adequate and properly supervised.

PROFESSIONAL INDEMNITY INSURANCE/ERRORS AND OMISSIONS

70.21   Professional indemnity/errors and omissions insurance protects against claims arising from a charity's work. The use of 'Professional' in this instance can be misleading as this insurance applies not only to traditional professionals, e.g. lawyers, accountants, etc., but also to care workers, carpenters, gardeners, etc. This type of insurance would, for example, protect the charity against a claim for a loss, injury or damage suffered by an individual or an organisation as the result of following incorrect advice given by an employee or volunteer of the charity. This type of insurance is particularly useful for charities providing professional services or complex, and potentially contentious, advice.

TRUSTEE INDEMNITY INSURANCE/DIRECTORS' AND OFFICERS' INSURANCE

70.22   For details of this see CHAPTER 122.

OTHER TYPES OF INSURANCE

70.23   It is possible for a charity to insure against any risk providing that no illegality is involved, an insurer is willing to cover the risk and the charity can justify that the degree of risk or potential consequences for the charity are such as to warrant the expenditure on the premium. Risks that charities have insured against include:

● legal expenses;

● staff sickness, to cover the cost of paying sick pay;

● pregnancy, to cover the cost of maternity pay and temporary replacement staffing;

● rain/bad weather, to cover loss of income from a fund-raising event (pluvius insurance);

● personal accident or assault, to protect employees and volunteers from claims made against them by members of the public for personal injury or assault in the course of their duties;

● life of a key member of staff;

● loss of computer data;

● non-appearance, to protect against the withdrawal of a celebrity from a fund-raising event;

● loss of revenue, e.g. in a charity shop that has had to close because of damage to it;

- glass, e.g. to cover breakage of charity shop windows;

- goods in transit;

- travel insurance for personnel travelling abroad against medical expenses, repatriation costs and detention;

- defamation in a charity's publications;

- medical malpractice, to cover risks faced by those in the healthcare sector over and above those covered by professional indemnity insurance.

Charities operating internationally

70.24   Charities that operate internationally, and particularly those operating in war zones and areas of conflict, have to consider complex risks to personnel and property. Having adequate safety measures may help to reduce both the risk to personnel and the cost of insurance premiums. The charity People In Aid, an international network of development and humanitarian assistance agencies, provides information on personnel safety and the management of risk associated with overseas activities.

OBTAINING INSURANCE COVER

70.25   Insurance cover can be obtained directly from an insurance company or from an intermediary, such as a broker. If an intermediary is approached, care should be taken to ensure that they are offering independent advice and are not tied to a particular insurance company. It is good practice to obtain up to three comparable quotes from insurers or brokers.

70.26   When choosing a policy charities should look at their past claims record in order to decide the most appropriate excess, which is in effect a partial retention of risk. The trustees' duty to act prudently makes them risk averse and prone to choose low excess levels, with correspondingly high premiums. However, examining the history of losses may indicate that they are quite steady from year to year and it may be better for the charity to accept the cost of covering some losses themselves rather than insuring against them. By opting for a higher excess, the charity can reduce costs of its insurance premiums. The overall level of risk to the charity remains unchanged.

FULFILLING CONDITIONS

70.27   It is essential that the person responsible for the charity's insurance understands any conditions stipulated in the insurance policies and ensures that they are fulfilled. Failure to do so can be costly. Consequential loss insurance, for example, may be dependent on the charity taking proper precautions against loss. For example, the reimbursement for damage to information held on computer is often conditional on the maintenance of regular back-ups, which the fire insurance may in turn require to be stored at different premises. Some computer policies exclude damage to computers from water, so it will be important to ensure computers are not located under sprinklers installed to limit fire damage.

FURTHER INFORMATION

70.28   Charity Commission CC49 'Charities and Insurance' May 2007

Advice on reviewing and renewing insurance and on insuring volunteers is available from NCVO (*www.ncvo-vol.org.uk*)

People In Aid
Development House
56–64 Leonard Street
London
EC2A 4JX
Tel: 020 7065 0900
Fax: 020 7065 0901
Website: *www.peopleinaid.org*

British Insurance Brokers' Association
BIBA House
14 Bevis Marks
London
EC3A 7NT
Tel: 020 7623 9043
Fax: 020 7626 9676
Website: *www.biba.org.uk*

71   Internal Audit

71.1   As charities become increasingly complex and face an increasing number of changes each year in areas such as governance, controls assurance and fund-raising demands, this in turn focuses attention on risk and the need to ensure that the link between risk management and control is kept under review. As a result, charities have an increasing need to focus attention on their internal audit functions and, in particular, the quality of the resources available.

71.2   'Internal auditing' is defined as an independent, objective assurance and consulting activity designed to add value and improve an organisation's operations. It helps an organisation accomplish its objectives by bringing a systematic, disciplined approach to evaluate and improve the effectiveness of risk management, control and governance processes.

71.3   This definition recognises the significance of corporate governance and the need to manage risk with appropriate controls. The internal audit function becomes a process by which a charity can gain assurance that the risks it faces are understood and adequately managed in the context of dynamic change.

MONITORING CONTROL EFFECTIVENESS

71.4   An integrated risk management and internal audit process will ensure that the senior management team identify risks to charity objectives and assess the controls in place to manage them; however, this will not work without monitoring control effectiveness. Once risks and appropriate controls have been identified, an effective monitoring process will check to see that those controls actually work. Charities may rely entirely on site visits by the internal auditors to fulfil this role but this may provide little indication as to whether controls are working in the time between site visits, especially if only addressed say once in a three-year cycle.

71.5   The internal audit team appraises, monitors and reviews the accounting and internal control systems and reports directly to the trustees. Internal audit does not replace the function or need for external statutory audit, but may usefully supplement it.

71.6   Generally internal audit will undertake the following:

- reviews of accounting and internal control systems, often including a review of the design of systems, monitoring their operation and recommending improvements;

- examination of financial and operating information – this may include a review of the means used to identify, measure, classify and report such information, supported by detailed testing of transactions, balances and procedures;

- reviews of the economy, efficiency, and effectiveness of operations including non-financial controls of an organisation;

- reviews of compliance with laws, regulations and other external requirements, and with internal policies and procedures; and

- special investigations, such as a fraud enquiry.

WHY HAVE INTERNAL AUDIT?

External requirement

71.7   In some circumstances an organisation is automatically required by external factors to operate an internal audit function, either because of the type of organisation it is, or because of an external funder's specific requirement. Frequently, organisations set up internal audit functions voluntarily, before any of the external factors come into play. The following circumstances all have a bearing in deciding whether or not an internal audit function is either useful or necessary.

71.8   When a charity's affairs become of a scale or degree of complexity that the trustees or the finance department conclude that a failure to comply with laid down procedures would be difficult to identify in a timely manner through routine controls, then the need for an internal audit function is indicated. It will allow the charity to devote more attention to the effectiveness of the control procedures themselves, rather than rely on detection of errors or non-compliance well after the event.

71.9   Often a charity will be operating through locations remote from head office control. These local operations may be in the form of non-autonomous branches, shops, or projects, and may be in the UK or overseas. In these situations it may be difficult for the finance department to confirm that procedures which appear to be operating properly are in fact doing so: the additional resource of internal audit can help in these circumstances.

71.10   Some charities regularly find themselves in need of additional finance related services, such as creating new systems for new projects, updating procedures manuals, and carrying out routine procedures such as stock counts and ad hoc investigations, including fraud enquiries or efficiency reviews. There comes a point when the number of such occasional pieces of work becomes disruptive to the finance department's normal pattern of work, or the costs of outsourcing such work become prohibitive. At this point the formalisation of the role into some form of internal audit function becomes desirable.

71.11   As is the case in many situations, charities will often consider implementing an internal audit function before a comparably sized commercial operation would. The reasons for this are partly to do with the factors already listed: charities become more complex, specialist and diversified before most similarly sized commercial organisations. However, other factors may also encourage charities to consider internal audit sooner, rather than later. Internal audit can play a valuable role in providing support to staff and volunteers who are struggling with understanding financial matters, or with the internal procedures and reporting requirements of the charity as a whole. Not all local staff will have the degree of training necessary for them to be ideally qualified for their job and many charities will use volunteers in administrative capacities, typically in running charity shops, or acting as branch treasurers.

71.12   Internal audit staff can visit these staff and volunteers, and not only carry out the traditional functions of that department, but also provide guidance and on the spot training on relevant issues. In this way the overall operation of the charity is strengthened, and internal audit is not seen as merely a policing function, which in turn helps the internal auditor in his or her role. With each such visit the amount of knowledge within the internal audit department develops, allowing procedures to be modified and targeted more effectively in future.

CREATING AN INTERNAL AUDIT FUNCTION

71.13   As with any department or function, clear terms of reference and guidelines need to be established in advance. Normally an internal audit team should have direct access to the trustees or to the audit sub-committee and be able to report independently of the finance function if necessary. The definition of the internal auditor's role becomes even more important where it is envisaged that the support element will be an intrinsic part of the job: there is a real danger that the internal auditor may subconsciously 'change sides' unless the brief is very well defined. Internal audit can be carried out either in-house or using an external provider, i.e. 'outsourcing', although co-sourcing is becoming more popular where an employed Head of Internal Audit will draw on outsourced specialist internal audit expertise.

In-house internal audit

71.14   Charities operating full-time internal audit functions are unusual, simply because the costs of maintaining them often outweigh the benefits. However, for larger and more complex organisations this may be possible, with full-time qualified staff. More often it will be appropriate for costs to be contained either by using part-time staff, or by the use of volunteers.

71.15   Volunteer internal audit functions are rarely formally set up. It is not uncommon, however, for charities to ask a suitably qualified individual to carry out occasional pieces of review work and where this is the case, such individuals can be considered as acting as internal auditors.

71.16   All internal auditors should have job descriptions, suitable training, adequate direction, a reporting format and a programme of work designed to cover the essential areas normally over a three to five-year cycle. With volunteers even more care will be needed in ensuring that those involved are indeed adequately qualified and suitably motivated for the task.

Outsourced internal audit

71.17   Internal audit services can be purchased from accountancy practices or other firms offering these services. Usually a programme of work is agreed and a certain number of days work is purchased at an agreed fee. Internal audit differs markedly from external audit and it should not be assumed that all firms offering external audit services can automatically conduct efficient internal audits.

71.18   It is generally recommended that the same firm should not carry out both external and internal audit work.

71.19   Several consortia of charities operate systems where the costs of an internal audit team are shared between a number of participating organisations. This can provide the benefits of cost control, with the advantages of developing a stronger relationship more often associated with an in-house team.

INTERNAL AND EXTERNAL AUDITS

71.20   The two types of audit are fundamentally different. Internal audit is a continuous process to do with procedures, transactions, systems and effectiveness. External audit is a statutory requirement designed to express an extremely stylised opinion on the accuracy of the financial accounts once a year. The two types of audit may or may not be interested in the same areas.

71.21   Most external audits of charities will not concentrate on detailed assessments of internal control systems, but will rely on a blend of some such assessment, along with testing of closing figures and analytical review. In larger organisations, systems become more important to the external auditor and there may be greater overlap. As a result, internal audit should not be seen as a substitute for external audit. However, it will certainly complement it and the two sorts of auditor should work together. For instance, the external auditor should plan his work having regard to the internal auditor's work programme and work performed. The external auditor should review the internal audit papers where relevant, and be involved in the implementation of any recommendations which have a bearing on his/her function. Conversely, the internal auditor should be aware of the external auditor's programme, simply for administrative convenience, and may expect feedback out of the external audit on the efficacy of the internal audit function.

71.22   The external auditor may (in certain circumstances) rely on the work of the internal audit department and this may lead to some savings in professional fees. This should not, however, be seen as the prime reason for establishing an internal audit function.

71.23   The external auditors should obtain a sufficient understanding of internal audit activities to assist in planning the audit and developing an effective audit approach. Where much of internal audit is geared towards the support role, or concentrating on immaterial areas, then the external audit procedures may be unaffected. Nevertheless, the external auditor may find it helpful to be aware of any conclusions drawn by the internal audit team.

71.24   During the course of their planning the external auditors should assess the internal audit function to see if it is either possible or desirable to rely on it. Important criteria for the auditor are as follows:

- The internal audit department's organisational status. Can the department report direct to the trustees, or audit committee, and the external auditors? Does it have any other operating responsibility which might impair its independence?

- The nature and extent of the assignments carried out. The nature of the assignments carried out is self-explanatory, and the extent is usually a matter of ensuring not a broad coverage of issues, but proper coverage of a selected area. This can be particularly frustrating for the external auditor, where there may have been useful work done on, for instance, branch activities. However, the reliance on the work done is reduced simply by the number of branches visited or by the failure to address a key aspect relevant to the auditors.

- The technical competence of the personnel. This will depend on the nature of the work being performed. Certainly one would expect any internal auditor operating in a charity not only to have the necessary

369

71.25 Internal Audit

finance and audit skills, but also to have an understanding of charities' regulatory framework generally, and the specific framework, including the governing document, applicable to the charity in question.

- Whether the internal audit work is done properly: that is, the work is planned, supervised, reviewed and documented. Whether or not the work is done properly is often a matter of communication between the two sets of auditors, as this is often an issue of quality control rather than the quality of the work itself. The introduction of some simple procedures may enable the external auditor to place more reliance on the internal auditor's work.

71.25 Once the audit is past the planning stage, then the two sets of auditors should meet to co-ordinate their work and exchange information where appropriate. If the internal audit work is to be relied upon, then it should be treated in a very similar way to work carried out by the external auditor's own staff: for instance, it should be subject to proper supervision and review, be supported by sufficient appropriate evidence, with appropriate conclusions drawn. Sometimes the internal audit work itself will need testing to confirm its adequacy.

71.26 The external auditor should also seek to comment on the efficacy of the internal audit function to the charity, especially where they have sought to rely on it. In this way weaknesses in this aspect of the internal controls of the charity can be identified and improvements suggested.

FURTHER INFORMATION

71.27 CC9 'Internal Controls for Charities', Charity Commission

72   Internal Controls

72.1   A charity's internal control system has a key role in the management of risks that are significant to the fulfilment of its charitable objectives. Trustees should establish a system of internal control that helps to facilitate the effectiveness and efficiency of operations, helps ensure the reliability of internal and external reporting and assists compliance with laws and regulations. Such a system will protect the property of the charity and ensure that it is applied only towards its objects. The operation of the control system will often be a matter for the executive staff, but this does not absolve the trustees of their ultimate responsibility.

72.2   Effective financial controls, which are part of the overall internal control framework, are also important, including the maintenance of proper accounting records. They help the charity to ensure that it is not unnecessarily exposed to avoidable financial risks and that financial information used within the charity and for publication is reliable. They are as relevant to the smaller charity as they are to the larger one, but naturally their nature and sophistication will be different.

72.3   Many charities now maintain various registers which help to identify when internal controls fail and how the problem has been addressed. The information contained in these registers can also then inform the risk assessment process and internal audit. Many charities operating overseas will keep some sort of fraud register, and this is becoming more commonplace with UK based charities too. Following a Charity Commission report on complaints procedures, many charities also keep a register of complaints, although these are often not comprehensive. When things do go wrong, the charity should know how to respond. There should therefore also be procedures for dealing with crisis management by way of business continuity plans.

72.4   In smaller charities much of the day-to-day administration may be undertaken by the trustees themselves. In these instances trustees should divide responsibility for functions so that no one trustee has too much authority, or has the ability to conceal or misrepresent transactions.

72.5   An internal control system needs to be clearly documented, communicated and maintained. It should also be monitored for compliance. The external audit is not necessarily designed to ensure that all internal control procedures are adhered to and therefore trustees may wish to create their own procedures for ensuring compliance. In larger charities this may take the form of an internal audit function, but in smaller ones it may take the form of occasional reviews carried out by disinterested parties. Where a finance or audit committee exists, this can be a suitable forum for reviewing such matters.

72.6   All internal control systems should identify the charity's structure, show who is responsible for what and the reporting lines. Where authority is delegated within the structure, then all such delegation should be formally recorded by the trustees and regularly reviewed. Often the extent of such delegated authority will be included in a job description and can be updated at staff reviews. All delegated authority must always be within the scope of the governing document.

72.7   The system of internal control should be embedded in the operations of the charity and form part of its culture. Further guidance and best practice can be

72.8 Internal Controls

found in the publication 'Internal Control: Guidance for Directors on the Combined Code' (also known as the Turnbull Report).

SEGREGATION OF DUTIES

72.8 Wherever possible different people should be responsible for different aspects of an operation, so they can serve as a cross-check on each other. For instance, a trainer should not arrange a course, take bookings, dispatch invoices and bank payments for the event. The administration of the event may be carried out by the trainer, but the cash bankings should be controlled by the accounts staff. In this way, and subsequently, numbers attending and monies received can be separately compared and verified.

COMPETENCE

72.9 Staff and trustees should have the degree of competence necessary to undertake their respective roles. In growing charities the level of competence needed is likely to increase as activities become more complex. Staff will need training if they are to keep abreast of developments or new staff with appropriate qualifications and experience will have to be recruited. Frequently, charities outgrow their people as the complexities of the systems become too great for the original staff and trustees. Typical areas that can lead to breakdowns are the diversification of activities into potentially taxable areas and transactions involving other legislation, such as licences, property transactions and investments. Trustees and staff should be conscious of the dangers of getting out of their depth and take future developments into consideration when appointing new trustees, staff or advisers.

BUDGETS

72.10 Where realistic budgets are prepared before an accounting period they provide an easy means by which the charity can be managed and help the charity in planning to use its resources in fulfilment of its charitable objectives. Most budgets are based on a realistic estimate of what may be achieved in the coming period and will incorporate certain key targets. Commonly, the crucial target will be levels of voluntary income. Results should be reported to the trustees regularly, ideally monthly, but at least quarterly, and the reports should focus on the key areas of the operation drawing attention to the achievement or otherwise of the targets.

72.11 Budgets only operate effectively as a control tool where the trustees understand the numbers and the underlying assumptions, and can then challenge the variances between the actual results and the budgets.

SYSTEMS

72.12 The system of internal financial controls should accommodate the following key areas: income, expenditure and assets. The Charity Commission's leaflet CC8: 'Internal Financial Controls for Charities' sets out the basic requirements. It includes a self-checklist that a charity can use to assess its degree of compliance and identify areas where it should reassess its procedures.

INCOME

72.13   Trustees should consider the nature of the charity's income and ensure that controls are appropriate. Sources of income may include:

- grants;

- contract income;

- donations;

- legacies;

- trading income and fees;

- investment income.

72.14   Probably the most difficult area to control adequately is the complete record-ing of unsolicited donations received through the post. All incoming money and cheques should be recorded at the time of opening of the post with two responsible people present whenever possible. Where the size of the organisa-tion prevents this, the charity may consider publicising a policy of acknowl-edging donations as a further deterrent to misappropriation at this first stage of the cycle. In larger organisations closed circuit television cameras may be installed in a room specifically designated for cash and post handling. All of these procedures should also ensure the safe custody of the unopened post. All moneys received should be banked promptly, on the same day. Records of the postal receipts should be reviewed and the nature of the item also recorded and reviewed. In this way a pattern can be established and unexplained fluctuations identified. The initial recording of the cash receipts is designed to trap the information at the earliest opportunity, so that subsequent transac-tions or losses can be investigated. It follows that the record is only of any real value if it is used subsequently on either a regular or occasional basis to validate subsequent bankings.

72.15   Other types of income may be received which are not unsolicited. These may include fees, responses to grant applications and investment income. In all cases a register should be established against which any subsequent receipts can be checked. Amounts received can thereby be verified for accuracy and the supporting records can also be reviewed for omissions.

72.16   A register is particularly desirable for monitoring planned giving schemes. This is because a register not only helps income to be properly controlled, but it also enables the charity to submit accurate tax reclaims reducing the risk of an overclaim, which might only be detected after a visit from the Inland Revenue.

72.17   Income received electronically should be subject to the same controls as any other income, with logs kept of receipts which can be audited and checked later on.

Public collections

72.18   Similar controls to those recommended for unsolicited donations should be operated for the opening of collecting boxes, or envelopes. In addition, however, there should be controls over the number, location and opening of the boxes. For instance, each receptacle should have a unique number and its location recorded. Boxes should be emptied regularly and agents should report to the charity on their collecting cycle.

Trading and service income

72.19   Income is usually easier to record and control where a service or goods are being exchanged. This is for two reasons. Firstly, because it is possible to identify the costs of provision and look for a matching source of income (for instance, the revenue generated by the theatre seat) and secondly, the purchasers will often require proof of purchase for their own reasons. This means that it will be possible to use pre-numbering systems which can be reviewed subsequently for omissions.

72.20   Some trading income can also be effectively recorded as soon as it is received by the use of tills that can analyse sales by item and provide a ready source of information to compare with bankings.

RECORDING OF INCOME

72.21   It is important for charities to identify any terms of trust which may attach to income received. This is because the trustees may be in breach of trust if the money is misapplied, and because the final statutory accounts will have to disclose the various types of fund. Those receiving and recording income should therefore be alert to the nature of the income received and record it accordingly.

EXPENDITURE

72.22   Whether expenditure is to acquire an asset or to meet a revenue cost, the process should be subject to authorisation and control. The same principles of documentary evidence and custody apply as they do to income. Where supporting documentation is required, these should always be originals and not photocopies.

72.23   The Charity Commission guidelines are helpfully brief.

- All expenditure and investment should be authorised against supporting documentation.

- Cheque books should be kept in safe custody with limited access.

- The preparation of documentation for authorisation should be undertaken by someone other than the persons authorising the payment.

- There should be clear written procedures setting out who is authorised to incur expenditure.

72.24   In some smaller organisations having detailed written procedures and separation of duties may be impractical, if not impossible. In these instances alternative controls may be applied, such as lists of payments being authorised by the trustees as a body, or even by the charity obtaining all cheques back from the bank for subsequent review.

72.25   Expenditure from cash should be restricted as much as is practicable. Cash raised from events or donations should not be used to subsidise petty cash expenses. This is to ensure that expenditure authorisation procedures cannot be bypassed and because gross accounting gives a more accurate picture of the relevant items.

72.26   Controls over expenditure are only of any value if there are equivalent controls over the ability of the charity to incur liabilities. Authorisation levels for the placing of orders should be documented, and suppliers can be notified that invoices will only be paid if raised against purchase orders in an approved format.

72.27   In larger charities a high level of control needs to be delegated to the executive staff operating these expenditure procedures. Sometimes this may extend to the trustees not being represented on the bank mandate at all. This is an undesirable extreme, as it makes it even more important that no two individuals are capable, through collaboration, of misapplying funds. If trustees are not represented on the bank mandates, then details of larger transactions should be reported regularly to them, and the treasurer could augment this with a closer review of all transactions.

72.28   In no cases should blank cheques be used. However rarely or exceptionally this practice may occur, it offers an unparalleled opportunity for easy fraud, and it can become a habit in an organisation simply to avoid inconvenience, for example, when one cheque signatory has to travel some distance to sign cheques. In leaflet CC8, the Charity Commission has stated that 'the practice of signing blank cheques would be regarded as neglecting the duty of care owed by trustees'.

72.29   Payments to employees and volunteers should follow similar procedures, with adequate personnel records maintained for all staff. This should include records of rates of pay and expenses arrangements. Such records should also ensure that staff are properly identified as self-employed or employees.

72.30   Expenses should only be paid against supporting documents, in the same way as any other expense item. Wherever possible round sum allowances should be avoided since they are more likely to be regarded as taxable, and subject to deduction for national insurance. They are also less susceptible to monitoring and control.

72.31   Records of expenses need to be maintained as employees may require details in order to complete their own tax returns under the self-assessment regime. It is also a requirement of the SORP for the annual accounts to disclose the amounts of expenses paid to charity trustees, including a nil return.

72.32   Payments by other methods, e.g. BACS, direct debit, etc., should be authorised in the same way as other payments. Where regular payments are established, and the transaction is only authorised on inception, the signatory should take particular note of the termination date for the arrangement. Where a number of payments are authorised in a batch, as with BACS, each item should be within the relevant signatory's powers. The Charity Commission website provides additional guidance and best practice on electronic banking.

ASSETS

72.33   Certain assets require particular forms of control. Fixed assets (cars, equipment, buildings, etc.) should be listed, checked and adequately insured. To record these assets adequately it will often be necessary to assign a unique number to the item and record it in a fixed asset register. Often the fixed asset register is the supporting evidence to the cost figure in the annual accounts. Sometimes, however, an accounting policy may require certain items to be written off and never capitalised, although they still have a value to the charity and should therefore be subject to recording and control.

INVESTMENTS

72.34   Investments should be safeguarded by the charity and full records kept of any holdings. Where a substantial sum is held in investments an independent investment manager should be appointed provided that the trustees have the appropriate powers of delegation. If they do not, they should approach the Commission to ascertain whether or not their powers of delegation can be widened. The investment manager should be regulated under the *Financial Services Act 1986*.

72.35   Reporting on investments held and their performance should be an intrinsic part of the management reporting of the charity. Further consideration of the role of investments in a charity is set out separately in CHAPTER 75. However, the basic controls that should always operate include:

● taking professional advice before selecting or disposing of investments;

● ensuring that all dividends or interest payments are received; and

● portfolio diversification to prevent one major failure seriously impacting on the charity.

REPORTING

72.36   Internal financial controls require documenting, updating and monitoring. The management accounts will provide evidence of the effectiveness of the control system, as will an internal audit function. The external auditors should also submit a management letter addressed to the trustees that draws attention to any shortcomings in the system of internal controls. Whilst the auditor's comments will never be comprehensive, any matters arising should be brought to the attention of all the trustees as a body and the trustees should respond formally to them.

73   Internet

BACKGROUND

73.1   The Internet is a loose association of thousands of networks and millions of computers across the world that all work together to share information. The Internet 'information superhighway' is like a road system. There are a number of major routes that meet at particular points. Lots of smaller roads spread out across the countryside and feed the major routes. On the smaller roads, devices such as PCs and servers are connected and are provided with their own address, the Internet Protocol (IP) address. On the Internet, the main lines carry the bulk of the traffic and are collectively known as the 'Internet backbone'. The backbone is formed by the biggest networks in the system, owned by major Internet service providers (ISPs) such as XO Communications, Sprint, UUNet, and PSINet. The backbone has so many intersecting points that if one part fails or slows down, data can be quickly re-routed over another part. This is known as 'redundancy'. In some places (e.g. offshore islands), the network may have less redundancy and so be more vulnerable to slowdowns or breakdowns.

73.2   The Internet's ability to handle an enormous amount of data every day trades flexibility for speed. Everyone who uses the Internet shares 'bandwidth', the data-carrying capacity of a network. Every time you send an email or down-load a file, you contribute to the load. Web pages can take up a lot of bandwidth given the quantity of graphics and animations they may contain, as can such technologies as streaming media (like videos) and telephony. Although as technologies improve bandwidth 'contention' is becoming less of an issue.

E-COMMERCE

73.3   E-commerce is normally divided up as follows:

- business to consumer (b2c);

- business to business (b2b);

- consumer to consumer (c2c).

73.4   The b2c segment gets the most publicity but the fastest growing area is b2b. Business to business is all about electronic transactions between business, email, purchasing, invoicing and payments.

The Internet and not-for-profit organisations

73.5   The Internet can offer important opportunities to charities, but can also create a variety of problems for the unwary. As with the introduction of any other business tool, the business case for exploiting the potential of the Internet should be considered and endorsed at a senior level as part of the normal business planning process.

73.6   The implementation of an Internet strategy comprises two parts:

- eVision;

- delivery.

73.7 The first stage deals with the ebusiness concept; evaluating its potential and feasibility, how this fits in with and complements the 'business' plan, and assessing the real value of the opportunities. If this is acceptable, it will be necessary to refine the proposed strategy, identify the enabling technologies and solutions required, and ensure that approval for any necessary funding is put in place.

73.8 The delivery phase is concerned with ensuring that the vision is realised. This will involve:

- Scope and definition phase: defining in detail the scope and objectives of the ebusiness delivery stage(s), identifying the detailed requirements, costs and plans;

- Develop and implement phase: building and delivering each of the requirements set out in the delivery stages;

- Operate and enhance phase: managing the running of the business environment and planning for the next phase of enhancement or additional solution.

EMAIL

73.9 Email offers significant benefits:

- You can prepare and send emails for less money than either letters or faxes.

- Emails are faster than a letter and sometimes faster than fax.

- Provided precautions are taken, email can be a secure communications medium.

- It is unimportant where the recipient is physically located and, unlike a telephone call, does not need to be available to receive a message.

- Emails can be addressed to multiple recipients which provides mass mailing or collaboration possibilities.

- Email attachments ensure:

  — the recipient gets documents exactly as they were sent without any corruption or degradation;

  — one can work on documents with other people in ways that are simply not possible with other media.

73.10 Email is, however, different from other forms of communication and some of the issues it raises are not immediately apparent. Bad use of email can irritate colleagues, clients, customers and suppliers.

73.11 Another drawback of the widespread use of email systems is the increased volume of unsolicited electronic mail (Spam). Due to its low cost to produce, Spam is used to advertise services or products, commonly for non-reputable ones such as fraudulent claims for investment or pornography. However, one thing that Spam mails have in common is that they place an unnecessary load on email systems and organisations should ensure they have protective measures in place to stop users from receiving unnecessary, sometimes offensive, email.

73.12   Email alone should not be used for any document that has a contractual implication. Emails, in common with faxes, have dubious value in court because they are so easy to forge. Drafts and copies of contractual documents may be sent by email, but security is required to ensure that the integrity of the final version has been assured.

Internet Telephony

73.13   As the speed and reliability of the Internet increases, so has the growth of real time applications such as Voice over IP (VoIP). Providing companies and individuals witha a low-cost alternative to the public telephone exchanges, VoIP provides telephony via the Internet, typically across fast connections using PCs with special software and headsets or dedicated VoIP telephone handsets. Many organisations are employing internet telephony to connect multiple office telephone systems as internal calls are then born without cost as they occur across the Internet. This is also typical of individuals who can now make local or long distance telephone calls to other VoIP users without incurring any call charges. Developments in VoIP also include the ability to make calls via a VoIP system, but for the call to be transferred across onto a public telephone exchange providing full compatibility with existing telephony infrastructures.

Streaming media

73.14   Another technology that has benefited from speed enhancements across the Internet is that of streaming media. Streaming media provides users with the ability to watch and listen to feature rich content such as video, either live in real time or through pre-recorded content that is watched or listened to as it is downloaded – or streamed. This has provided an opportunity for amateur film makers to make their work accessible and could be useful for not-for-profit organisations to disseminate information. The danger for organisations is that streaming media can hog bandwidth, and can also put them at risk due to issues of copyright; access to streaming media therefore needs to be managed closely.

SECURITY AND THE INTERNET

73.15   There is much talk of the Internet's security problems. To a certain extent, the sheer volume of traffic travelling over the Internet reduces the risk that someone will pick on a specific message, intercept it and understand enough about its contents to use it maliciously. The risk, however, exists. For a high profile charity or not-for-profit organisation, the risk is increased where those with malevolent intent may be specifically targeting the organisation.

73.16   To secure documents, encryption is one of the most popular techniques used. This involves encoding the file using an algorithm that is agreed in advance between the sender and the recipient.

73.17   There are two simple ways to encrypt documents:

● many programs, such as Word and Excel, have options on their 'Save as …' panel to enter a password to save the document in encrypted form;

- the 'Zip' utility encrypts documents as they are being compressed.

73.18   Another area of concern is that of 'hacking', the practice of gaining unauthorised access to a company or individual's computer or network. Hacking has received a great deal of press in recent years with many highly publicised occurrences such as attacks against well-known organisations which resulted in customer credit card details being compromised. To protect against such attacks common practice is to install firewalls to protect the office systems. These come in a number of guises including individual PC based solutions and dedicated corporate hardware devices. Update and maintenance of these devices is essential.

Viruses

73.19   Some of the most infectious viruses are transmitted by email. They can be embedded in attachments so that just opening a Word document or an Excel spreadsheet, for example, infects a PC. Some viruses spread themselves by identifying people in address books and sending them emails containing the virus, others detect network drives and replicate themselves to file servers ready to infect other PCs attached to the network.

73.20   The only guaranteed way to completely protect against viruses is to remove network connectivity and use of external media altogether. Fortunately there are some less draconian measures that can provide reasonable protection:

- Install virus-checking software. Some products will check emails as they are received.

- Keep virus-checking software up to date. One should usually expect to have to load updates at least monthly, though with today's anti-virus products this is typically performed automatically on a daily basis.

- Be wary of unsolicited programs and documents. Even if the email comes from someone trustworthy, do not open any attached documents if the covering note appears strange or uncharacteristic (it might have been sent by a virus on that person's computer). Suspicious emails should be checked before use or deleted.

- Treat with caution any unfamiliar messages passing through outboxes or appearing as sent items that do not arise from known users.

'SIGNATURES' AND DISCLAIMERS

73.21   It is important to recognise that emails are considered to be 'published' company documents. Thus, when an email is sent, it is considered to be from the originating organisation. In these circumstances it is important that the email should carry a signature identifying the sender to comply with the *Company Names Act 1985* and *Business Names Act 1985*. The signature may simply be text added either to the top or bottom of a mail message, giving the company name, registered office and company number.

73.22   It is also regarded as good practice to include a disclaimer to remind the reader that the mail may be confidential and privileged (this is particularly important as emails can be easily forwarded) and can help reduce liability. It is very important to seek the appropriate legal advice to formulate a disclaimer to meet the needs of your particular organisation. However an indication of a typical disclaimer (for a company 'ABC Limited') follows:

> 'This email is confidential and may be privileged; it is for use of the named recipient(s) only. If you have received it in error, please notify us immediately; please do not copy or disclose its contents to any person or body, and delete it from your computer systems. ABC Limited does not guarantee the security of any information electronically transmitted. ABC Limited is not liable for the proper and complete transmission of the information contained in this communication, nor for any delay in its receipt. THE USE OF EMAIL FOR ANY ILLEGAL PURPOSE OR FOR ANY PURPOSE OTHER THAN AS PERMITTED BY ABC Limited IS STRICTLY PROHIBITED. ABC Limited Registered Office 123 Acacia Avenue. Registered Company Number: 123456'

73.23   In certain circumstances special signatures or disclaimers should be added for particular departments or people within the organisation. For example, the Human Resources department may wish to explain the data protection policy or a department that sells financial services may want to stipulate its accreditation with the relevant statutory bodies.

ACCEPTABLE USE POLICY

73.24   There may be occasions when it is necessary to monitor a colleague's use of the charity IT systems, for example if they are unavailable or if there is a suspicion of malpractice of some kind. In certain circumstances such as email abuse, it is not advisable to view the person's mailbox unless the employee has been told that this may be done and that the organisation reserves the right to inspect mailboxes at any time. Otherwise, opening someone's emails may constitute an infringement of their rights under the *Data Protection Act 1998*.

73.25   It is best practice to set up the correct framework at the outset, with a policy such as an Acceptable Use Policy (AUP). Such a policy stipulates the terms and conditions on which email and Internet use is granted to an employee, and is agreed by an employee before they are granted access. Typically, a policy covers at least three areas.

●   It should contain a core definition which scopes the systems covered and the basic policy tenets (e.g. protection from illegal and immoral use);

●   It should define the ownership of the IT systems, stating that use of the systems is a privilege and they are wholly owned by the organisation;

●   It should include specific details and prohibitions, for example stating that junk email should not be propagated, or that non-work related internet access should only be used outside working hours.

73.26   The construction of a policy requires expertise. It is important that if that expertise is not available in-house, external assistance should be sought.

THE INTERNET AND FUNDRAISING

73.27   The Internet offers a new opportunity when running fundraising campaigns. Charities can reach a much larger audience at relatively low cost. Targeted campaigns are also easier to run, focusing resource and effort where needed. Donors can access a greater amount of information and any additional detail can be added with ease to the site.

73.28   Online fundraising may also improve the charity's overall carbon footprint as the size and scale of mail-outs can be reduced. It may also assist with the amount of donations received if the donor knows that they are dealing directly with the charity.

73.29   For donors Internet fundraising is like buying items from an online retailer. Large charities may look after the processing of credit and debit card transactions on a secure site themselves. This will be dependent on whether or not they have the appropriate hardware and software, or the resources and funds to set this up. Smaller charities on the other hand may look to use an agency to collect funds on their behalf. Another alternative is for the charity to affiliate themselves with a company selling goods or services, and this company will collect the funds on their behalf. So for example, 'AAA Company' will donate 0.20p to 'B charity' for every £5 spent in their online store.

74 Investigations and Inquiries

CHARITY COMMISSION POWERS

74.1 The statutory power for the Charity Commission to investigate a charity is found in the *Charities Act 1993, s 8*: 'The Commissioners may from time to time institute inquiries with regard to charities or a particular charity or class of charities, either generally or for particular purposes, but no such power shall extend to any exempt charity' – unless under the *Charities Act 2006* the inquiry has been requested by another principal regulator. The power therefore extends to excepted charities and also to any Scottish charity which is largely controlled from within England and Wales.

74.2 The Commission's powers in relation to such an inquiry are not open ended but well defined. They may demand accounts and written explanations relating to the matter in question, if necessary by statutory declaration, and copies of any relevant documents held. They may also require people to attend at a stipulated place and give evidence, some of which may be required to be under oath. The power does not extend merely to trustees or employees of a charity. Any person with information relevant to the inquiry can be asked for information and copy documents, and following the *Charities Act 2006* this even applies if they relate solely to an exempt charity.

74.3 The Commission does not have the power to investigate criminal matters. If an inquiry uncovers a possible criminal offence, such as fraud or child abuse, the Commission will notify the police.

74.5 Anyone who, knowingly or recklessly, provides misleading information to the Commission in the context of these powers is guilty of an offence punishable by either a fine or up to two years' imprisonment, or both.

74.6 Having instituted an inquiry under *s 8*, the Commission has further powers under *s 18* to act for the protection of charities (other than exempt charities). It first has to satisfy itself that there has either been misconduct or mismanagement in the administration of the charity, or that it needs to act to safeguard the property and assets of the charity, or the proper application of existing or future property. Once this is established then the Commission can independently do one or more of the following by Order:

(*a*) suspend any trustee, officer, agent or employee of the charity, pending consideration of his removal, for up to 12 months. Any such suspension must be preceded by written notice;

(*b*) appoint new or additional trustees;

(*c*) transfer property to the Official Custodian;

(*d*) forbid the disposal of charity property without the Commission's consent;

(*e*) forbid debtors making payments to the charity without the Commission's consent;

(*f*) restrict the charity's transactions; and

(*g*) appoint a manager, referred to as an 'interim manager'.

74.7 Investigations and Inquiries

74.7   If an inquiry has been instituted and both conditions referred to above apply (misconduct or mismanagement, and the need to protect property) then the Commission may remove those individuals listed at (a) above, and may establish a Scheme for the better administration of the charity.

74.8   The exact nature of misconduct and mismanagement has been the subject of some attention over the years, as it covers the largest numbers of cases where the Charity Commission, having instituted an inquiry, has identified a cause for concern. Although there are many instances which could appear under this heading, the legislation specifically refers to only one situation: excessive payments for administrative purposes.

74.9   The Charity Commission has powers to replace a trustee, or to appoint additional trustees, if it considers this to be in the interests of the charity, irrespective of an inquiry being conducted. Trustees may be removed where a trustee has been bankrupt within the last five years or becomes incapable of acting due to mental disorder. If a corporate trustee goes into liquidation the Commission will remove it from trusteeship. All of these cases are rare, but two other instances are more probable: where a trustee has not acted and will not declare whether he is prepared to act or not, and where a trustee is absent, maybe outside England and Wales, and thus impeding the efficient functioning of the charity.

PROCESS: WHAT INITIATES AN INQUIRY?

74.10   An inquiry is usually initiated either as a result of the Charity Commission's internal monitoring procedure or as a result of external comment. Matters requiring investigation may emerge from internal monitoring of annual returns, reviews of annual reports and accounts, or from routine visits to charities. External comments come from a variety of sources but most frequently from press comment and from individuals, many of whom have mixed motives for referring the matter to the Commission. The advent of the wider whistle-blowing regime for auditors may also be expected to contribute to the initiation of inquiries. The Charity Commission publication 'The Charity Commission and Regulation' sets out, amongst other things, seven principles applied in regulating charities: accountability, independence, proportionality, fairness, consistency, equality and diversity, and transparency. Charities subject to an inquiry may therefore want to reflect on the degree to which these principles are applied during the process.

74.11   All complaints are first considered by an evaluation officer who takes a view on whether or not:

- the complaint is groundless;

- the problem is minor and can be put right by the Commission giving the charity some advice;

- the problem is more serious, but can best be dealt with by the Commission providing the charity with substantial help;

- from the evidence to date the matter is sufficiently serious to warrant the launch of a formal s 8 inquiry;

- Another regulator should be involved.

74.12   The Commission has repeatedly made it clear that it will not get involved in matters relating to the internal administration of a charity, where the matter is simply one of internal politics. The introduction to its leaflet CC47 'Investigating Charities' says, 'The Commission cannot act in the administration of a charity, nor can we interfere in its affairs, where the trustees have acted properly. We will not mount an investigation without establishing that there is good reason to do so'. The good reasons are set out most fully in a supplementary leaflet. They include:

- a lack of proper prudence, conduct or control in the administration of a charity's affairs such that funds or other assets of the charity are at risk;

- incompetent management;

- disclosure of activities which would be likely to damage the reputation of charities generally;

- misuse or misapplication of the assets or the funds of the charity;

- failure to operate within the charity's constitution or the law;

- provision of false information to the Commission, or misleading the public and others with an interest in the charity (e.g. beneficiaries or employees) in a material way;

- remuneration of the trustees where there is no power to pay them or receipt of benefits by trustees when this is not explicitly permitted by the governing document;

- significant non-compliance with the accounting requirements of the *Charities Act 1993* or with any other statutory responsibilities of charity trustees;

- actual or incipient insolvency;

- unnecessary accumulation of income or a large and increasing revenue deficit;

- any other matters arising from examination of a charity's accounts which give cause for concern;

- breach of obligations imposed on trustees by the general law, for example, trustees buying property from, or selling their own property to, their trust, or exploiting for their own benefit opportunities of which they have become aware in their capacity as trustees, or any dealing between a charity and one or more of its trustees which has not been conducted at arms' length, or without proper authority;

- unacceptably high administration or fund-raising costs;

- excessive payments to any trustee or employee, or for any services rendered to the charity; and

- improper political activities.

74.13   Charities report serious incidents to the Commission as part of their annual return process or beforehand, and these are likely to lead to evaluation or inquiry. Serious incidents include significant fraud, theft or loss of funds, significant sums of money or other property donated to the charity from an unknown or unverified source, a known link with terrorism, proscribed organisations or unlawful activities, a disqualified trustee, a lack of policy for protecting vulnerable beneficiaries, a lack of staff and trustee vetting procedures, or a criminal or other regulatory investigation.

74.14   If a charity is subject to an inquiry the trustees will be informed of its terms of reference and the name of the relevant case officer. Sometimes professionals external to the Charity Commission will also be employed. In all cases further guidance notes expanding on the Commission's leaflet CC47 'Investigating Charities' will be provided to the trustees.

74.15   The person conducting the inquiry will act impartially, in the best interests of the charity. As their inquiry progresses other matters may come to their attention which merit further investigation, and these too will be looked at.

74.16   The outcome of any inquiry may vary. The commission posit the following scenarios:

- The evidence does not indicate issues of relevant misconduct or mismanagement and so no remedial action is necessary. In this situation the charity may wish to wonder why an inquiry was opened in the first place, and be especially vigilant about any wording in a final report which might appear to justify the Commission's initial concerns and thereby stigmatise the charity or trustees;

- There is evidence of misconduct or mismanagement, but as a result of actions already taken in the course of the inquiry there is no longer any need to act to protect the property of the charity, or rectify other causes for concern;

- There is evidence of unintentional misconduct or mismanagement, but willingness and ability on the part of the trustee body to put matters right. The Commission will then want to monitor trustee action against a future action plan;

- Serious irregularities are identified that require use of formal remedial powers (such as appointing an interim manager), or which may be dealt with by the Statement of Results of Inquiry setting out those irregularities and close monitoring;

- The commission institutes legal proceedings under *s 32* of the *Charities Act 1993*. This may be necessary where the trustees are unable or unwilling to remedy such matters that require remedy (e.g. restitution claims for unauthorised remuneration) or to compromise claims with a view to avoiding or ending such proceedings.

74.17   At the end of the inquiry a report will be prepared and published on the Commission's website, usually within three months. Usually anybody likely to be strongly criticised will be given the opportunity to respond to those criticisms, although the Commission is not obliged to accept or note any of the comments made. Where action is to be taken then the charity will be informed in writing of the proposed action. Results may be used in court proceedings and those of particular public interest will be published.

74.18   Each year the Charity Commission report on their activities. During the year to 2006 they reported that the asset value directly protected by their investigations amounted to some £30m, and that 90% of their investigations involved substantiated concerns which were resolved.

74.19   It is apparent even from these summary figures that only a tiny minority of charities each year are subjected to the regulatory powers of the Charity Commission. The matters reported are instructive as to which matters have created the most concern. Four particular issues which are referred to in the context of recurring themes are as follows.

- The dominant founder/administrator: 'It is essential that each and every trustee is aware that they are individually and collectively responsible for the administration of their charity and must insist on full information and an equal say and involvement in the policy and activities of the charity';

- Lack of control by the trustee body: one report drew attention to the case of a trust, where 'the founder trustee effectively ran the affairs of the charity without reference to the other trustees, two of whom were resident in the USA';

- Rapid expansion: 'In many cases the internal controls and financial arrangements are not sufficient to cope with this change. Eventually the administration of the charity breaks down resulting in loss of funds or failure to achieve the purposes of the organisation';

- Disaster relief efforts: 'Where an organisation launches into a small relief programme without having prepared the ground, or without any practical experience of what is required, the result can be disastrous. It is not uncommon for the following problems to be encountered:

  — loss of funds or goods resulting from inadequate organisation or controls;

  — ineffective control over the activities of the volunteers while abroad;

  — unnecessary risk to the employees and volunteers abroad; and

  — loss of confidence by the local communities in aid organisations generally which can undermine the patient planning of the larger or more skilled charities'.

Interim manager appointments

74.20   A manager appointed under the *Charities Act 1993* has a different function to one appointed under the terms of a debenture in an insolvency case. An appointment is only usually made where there is evidence that the administration of a charity has completely broken down, or if assets or income are at risk. The role and function of the receiver is determined in part by the *Charities (Receiver and Manager) Regulations 1992* and partly by the Order appointing the receiver. He or she acts under the supervision of the Charity Commission.

74.21   The regulations authorise the Charity Commission to seek security from the receiver, and to determine fees. Within three months after appointment the receiver must report to the Charity Commission setting out the asset value of the charity on appointment, the strategy for discharging their duties as set out in the Order, and other relevant matters.

74.22 Investigations and Inquiries

74.22 In practice the receiver takes responsibility for running the charity with the usual powers in place of the trustees. This may involve putting it on to a sounder financial or administrative base, or it may be a matter of working alongside existing and new trustees and assisting them in the better performance of their duties.

74.23 The Charity Commission also have powers under the *Regulation of Investigatory Powers Act 2000* (RIPA). Specifically, the Commission is able to operate directed surveillance operations, use covert human intelligence sources (CHIS) and to obtain communications data, for the purpose of preventing and detecting crime. The use of these powers is strictly controlled both by internal procedures and by the framework imposed by RIPA to ensure that their use is proportionate and necessary in the circumstances.

OVERSEAS

Overseas activities

74.24 In November 2006 the commission clarified their position in relation to compliance issues arising overseas.

> 'The Commission's registration of charities and its powers of investigation and remedy extend only to charities established in England and Wales. Where compliance issues arise in relation to charities operating overseas, the Commission's powers of investigation into the administration of a charity and its powers to act to safeguard charities and their property are effective only within this jurisdiction. Consequently the Commission may formally exercise its powers only against charities, persons, and property within the jurisdiction and not outside of it.

> Where it is necessary for the Commission in the course of its compliance work to verify facts about the application of funds overseas, they may ask trustees to undertake an independent professional audit or ask another charity working in the region to verify the way funds have been applied. Alternatively, the Commission might seek the assistance of the overseas regulator in the relevant country or, subject to necessary diplomatic clearances and to security issues, send its own staff to carry out inquiries overseas. In this way it can safeguard the application of funds overseas and where appropriate, hold trustees to account.'

SCOTLAND

74.25 The statutory basis for the regulation of charities in Scotland is provided by the *Charities and Trustee Investment (Scotland) Act 2005* ('the Act') and supporting regulations. As in England and Wales inquiries may arise as a result of internal monitoring or an external complaint. OSCR can inquire into charities, or their subsidiairies or organisations representing themselves as charities while not on the Register. The power to make that inquiry is contained in *ss 28* and *29* of the Act. Every inquiry will be made in line with OSCR's published enquiry and intervention policy. Most inquiries will be conducted under *s 28* but sometimes OSCR will use the powers of compulsion in *s 29* if there is an offence of failure to comply with a requirement made by OSCR.

74.26   OSCR generally will seek to resolve matters without use of formal powers. However they state that in cases of more serious mismanagement or misconduct, the options open to OSCR after inquiry include the suspension of persons from management or control, directing a charity or other body not to take the action that is the cause of concern or in the most extreme cases to take formal action.

75 Investments

INVESTMENT POWERS

75.1   Charities, with the exception of charitable common investment or common deposit funds, are not established for investment purposes. Therefore most charities can only invest in funds if their investment activities are ancillary to achieving their charitable objects.

75.2   The investment powers of charity trustees are defined mainly by the *Trustee Act 2000* and by the charity's governing documents. Where the governing document narrows the investment powers available under statute with the deliberate intention of prohibiting the trustees from making investments that would be permitted by law, the powers in the governing document take precedence. However, where a governing document contains wording to the effect that the trustees' powers of investment are as described in the *Trustee Investments Act 1961*, the trustees now have the general power of investment set out in the *Trustee Act 2000*. Trustees are likely to be personally liable for losses that arise if they act outside their powers, therefore it is important that they and charity administrators know exactly what their investment powers are, and also ensure that their professional advisers are aware of them.

THE TRUSTEE ACT 2000

75.3   The *Trustee Act 2000* replaced the *Trustee Investment Act 1961* which had become out of date and was preventing many charities from achieving the maximum rate of return on their investments. It introduced:

- new, wider powers of investment;
- new powers for the appointment of nominees and custodians;
- new powers to acquire land and to insure property;
- appropriate safeguards, including a duty to take proper advice in relation to investments and a statutory duty of care.

75.4   *Section 3* of the *Trustee Act 2000* allows trustees to invest trust funds in any kind of investment, excluding land, in which they could invest if they were the absolute owner of those funds. Therefore, unless a charity's governing document includes an explicit provision that restricts or excludes the trustees from investing the charity's funds, trustees have a statutory power to invest funds held on trust. The *Trustee Act 2000* only applies to property (money) held on trust. It does not apply to the corporate property of charitable companies (though it does apply to assets they hold on trust, i.e. assets that cannot be freely used for any of a charitable company's purposes) or to the property of charities incorporated by or under legislation. Although the *Trustee Act 2000* does not apply to the corporate property of charitable companies, such charities usually have express powers of investment that are similar to those contained in the *Trustee Act 2000* in their Memorandum of Association.

75.5   Although investment in land (including buildings) is not included in *s 3* of the *Trustee Act 2000*, *s 8* gives trustees the power to acquire freehold or leasehold land in the United Kingdom as an investment or for any other purpose, subject to any restriction or exclusion in the charity's governing document. If trustees wanted to invest in land outside the UK they would need an explicit power to do so in their governing document.

DUTY TO REVIEW INVESTMENTS

75.6   These wider powers of investment allow trustees to consider investing in a wider range of investments than many were previously allowed to consider. *Section 4(2)* of the Act requires trustees of charities whose investment powers have been extended since the Act came into force in February 2001 to review their existing investment portfolios and consider if changes would be advantageous. The Charity Commission expects these reviews to have taken place by now.

STATUTORY DUTY OF CARE

75.7   The *Trustee Act 2000* states that when exercising any of the powers, or discharging any of the duties set out in *Schedule 1* to the Act, trustees must exercise such care and skill as is reasonable in the circumstances, having particular regard to:

- any special knowledge or experience that a trust holds themselves out as having;

- where a trustee acts as a trustee in the course of business or a profession, to any special knowledge or experience that it is reasonable to expect of a person acting in the course of that business or profession.

75.8   This duty of care applies to the way in which trustees exercise their new, wider powers of investment, their obligation to review the charity's investment portfolio, and the obligation to review arrangements with an agent, nominee or custodian. The duty can be excluded, modified or extended by provisions in the charity's governing document.

75.9   The new duty of care does not mean that all trustees must now be experts in investment. People without investment expertise can continue to act as trustees but the duty of care will require trustees who do have some expertise in this area to use it when considering issues relating to investment.

75.10   In deciding 'what is reasonable in the circumstances' account can be taken of the charity's size, nature and purposes. So, for example, the time taken to monitor the performance of an investment manager should be proportionate to the size of funds under management.

75.11   In addition to discharging their duty of care, all trustees (not just those to whom the *Trustee Act 2000* applies) are also required by *s 5* to take proper advice from a person or body reasonably believed by the trustees to be qualified to give investment advice, unless they reasonably conclude that this would be unnecessary or inappropriate, for example if the cost of obtaining advice would be disproportionate to the benefit to be gained from the investment. Trustees must also have regard to standard investment criteria.

STANDARD INVESTMENT CRITERIA

75.12   *Section 4* of the *Trustee Act 2000* lays down the following standard investment criteria. When investing, trustees must:

- diversify their investment portfolio to reduce the risk of loss should one investment fail;

- consider the suitability of all investments for the charity's needs (i.e. the balance of long-term capital growth or income generation required to meet the needs of present and future beneficiaries);

- consider the suitability of particular investments on ethical grounds (for example, they should consider whether investing in a tobacco company would be contrary to a charity's objectives).

POWERS TO EMPLOY AGENTS

75.13   The powers that trustees have to delegate certain investment functions to agents are set out in *section 11* of the *Trustee Act 2000*. These powers are subject to any restrictions or exclusions in the charity's governing document. They permit agents to:

- carry out decisions that trustees have taken;

- invest assets;

- raise funds from investments;

- carry out other functions prescribed by an order made by the Secretary of State.

75.14   Trustees may authorise one or more of their number to act as an agent or someone who is also appointed to act as their nominee or custodian. Where two or more people, including trustees, are appointed as agents for the same function they must exercise the function jointly. *Section 12* of the *Trustee Act 2000* prohibits the appointment of a 'beneficiary' to act as an agent, but in this context 'beneficiary' means someone with a legally enforceable proprietary interest in a trust. Beneficiaries of a charity are not 'beneficiaries' in this sense, so someone who is receiving help from the charity could be appointed to act as an agent.

75.15   Trustees can pay agents if they see fit, though they can only pay trustees to act as agents if the governing document contains an explicit power to pay trustees, or if they get permission from the Charity Commission, and if they regard paying the trustees to be in the best interest of the charity.

75.16   Trustees should not generally authorise a person to act as their agent on terms that allow the agent to appoint a substitute, or that restrict the liability of the agent, or permit the agent to act in circumstances that could give rise to a conflict of interest. The agent will not be bound by the statutory duty of care, but will owe a duty of care to the trustees under the contract that the agent has with the trustees.

POWERS TO APPOINT NOMINEES AND CUSTODIANS

75.17   In this context a nominee is a person appointed by the trustees to hold trust property in his or her own name. A custodian is a person who undertakes safe custody of some or all of the assets or of documents or records relating to the assets. Nominees and custodians are used to:

- eliminate the need to transfer the title of trust property when changes to the trustee body take place;

- facilitate the transfer of trust property, for example selling or buying shares;

- reduce the risk of important trust documents being lost.

75.18   The new powers in the *Trustee Act 2000* to appoint nominees and custodians apply in addition to any powers already in a charity's governing document. They do not apply to trusts which have a custodian trustee, or where the assets are vested in the Official Custodian for Charities, or where the governing document explicitly prohibits the appointment of nominees or custodians.

75.19   Trustees may remunerate nominees or custodians as they see fit, unless a nominee or custodian is also a trustee of the charity, in which case they can only be remunerated if the governing document contains provision for the payment of trustees or permission is obtained from the Charity Commission. As with agents, trustees may not authorise a person to act as their nominee or custodian on terms that allow the nominee or custodian to appoint a substitute, restrict the liability of the nominee or custodian, or permit the nominee or custodian to act in circumstances that could give rise to a conflict of interest.

75.20   A person can only be appointed as a nominee or custodian if they carry on a business that consists of or includes acting as a nominee or custodian, or are a body corporate that is controlled by the trustees as determined by *s 840* of the *Income and Corporation Taxes Act 1988*, or are a body corporate recognised under *s 9* of the *Administration of Justice Act 1985*. Trustees can appoint as a nominee or custodian one of their own number if that is a trust corporation, or two or more of the trustees if they are to act as joint nominees or custodians. Trustees can appoint as a nominee someone that they have appointed to act as their custodian or authorised as their agent. Similarly, trustees can authorise someone to act as a nominee who has been appointed to act as custodian.

75.21   Trustees should keep their agents, nominees and custodians under review to ensure they remain suitable, their performance is satisfactory and that their terms of appointment and remuneration are still appropriate.

SECURITY OF ASSETS

75.22   Charity Commission guidance reminds trustees:

- that it is important to ensure that the charity retains legally provable ownership of any trust assets held by a nominee or custodian;

- that there are particular risks associated with appointing as nominee or custodian people or companies whose main affairs or business has no connection with the UK;

- that they need to balance the advantages and disadvantages of appointing people as nominees or custodians who are independent of each other and of any investment manager used;

- that they should require nominees and custodians to report to them regularly on the controls in place to safeguard the charity's assets.

INSURANCE

75.23   The *Trustee Act 2000* confers a general power on trustees to insure any trust property up to its full value and to pay the premiums out of trust funds.

COMMON INVESTMENT FUNDS

75.24   Unless forbidden by their governing document, trustees in England and Wales also have power under the *Charities Act 1993, s 24(7)* to invest in a special range of investments which include common investment funds and common deposit funds. (See CHAPTER 25.)

WIDENING INVESTMENT POWERS

75.25   Trustees wishing to widen their powers of investment, for example because the governing document contains restrictions or exclusions on the trustees' powers of investment that no longer seem appropriate, may amend their governing document, providing it contains a power of amendment and they obtain written consent from the Charity Commission (HMRC Charities (Scotland) (formerly FICO) in Scotland). If the governing document does not contain a power of amendment the Court may grant or vary powers of investment. Normally, this will not be given for charities with investments of less than £750,000.

INVESTMENT DUTIES

75.26   Charity trustees have a duty of care to the charity's beneficiaries when investing the charity's funds. They must act with the same degree of care that a prudent business person would exercise when investing on behalf of someone for whom they had a moral obligation to provide.

75.27   Trustees also have a duty to invest the charity's funds in ways that are likely to produce the highest level of return consistent with minimising the charity's exposure to risk. This duty means that trustees who do not invest surplus income or, for example, merely put it in a bank account which earns a comparatively low rate of interest, have breached their duty and could be personally liable to compensate the charity for lost investment income.

ETHICAL INVESTMENT

75.28   When investing, trustees have a general duty to maximise financial return which must override the trustees' personal code of ethics, or their preferred types of investments, and has implications for the extent to which a charity can adopt an ethical investment policy. However, having an ethical investment policy may be entirely consistent with the principle of seeking maximum return as companies that behave in a socially responsible way are more likely to flourish in the longer term.

75.29   The circumstances in which a charity can adopt an ethical investment policy were defined in 1993 by the judge in a case brought against the Commissioners of the Church of England by the Bishop of Oxford, Richard Harries. The Bishop argued that the Church's policy of investing in arms companies and companies that perpetuated apartheid in South Africa was against the ethical principles of the church and was therefore in breach of trust and should cease.

Although the Bishop lost this particular case, the judgment clarified the circumstances in which trustees should take ethical considerations into account when defining their investment policy (*Harries (Bishop of Oxford) v Church Commissioners for England [1992] 1 WLR 1241*). The Charity Commission's leaflet, CC14 'Investment of Charitable Funds', takes account of the judgment in the *Harries* case. Where trustees are considering establishing an ethical investment policy they should bear in mind the following:

- Trustees should keep in mind the fundamental principle of maximising return. Where an ethical policy is adopted it should be set out in writing and be clear on the positive aims and any exclusions. If companies or sectors are excluded the reasons for exclusion should be clearly thought through. Trustees may need to take professional advice to evaluate what the effect of exclusions or inclusions would have on the likely investment return. (The Government's Strategy Unit report recommended that trustees of larger charities should be required by law to state their investment principles in their annual report.)

- Any ethical criteria adopted must reflect the needs of the beneficiaries of the charity, not the trustees' personal views.

- Trustees should avoid investments that directly impede the furtherance of the charity's objectives, e.g. a cancer charity should exclude investments in tobacco companies and a charity for the relief of alcoholics should exclude investments in breweries or pubs.

- Trustees should avoid investments that might be to the charity's financial detriment, e.g. investments that would result in a loss of financial support from donors or members.

- Trustees should avoid investing in companies that potential beneficiaries regard as acting against their interests, and which could deter potential beneficiaries from accepting help from the charity.

- While in most instances it should be possible to identify investments with at least a similar potential return to those excluded on ethical grounds, where this is not possible it may be necessary for the trustees to take a less principled approach. In order to avoid having a portfolio that is not sufficiently diverse to ensure good enough financial returns, the trustees may have to exclude investments in companies with more than a certain proportion of their turnover linked to the unacceptable product, rather than impose an absolute ban.

THE NEED FOR AN INVESTMENT STRATEGY/POLICY

75.30   If a charity has surplus assets that the trustees believe would be prudent to set aside, they will need to develop an investment strategy or policy. As the latest guidance from the Charity Commission on reserves makes clear, charities should set aside funds to protect the charity from fluctuations in income, to fund future commitments they have made to beneficiaries, or to fund repairs or a planned development (CC19 'Charities' Reserves'). However, the Commission warns that trustees should not allow excessive reserves to accumulate without good reason. If they do, HMRC could require tax to be paid on the investment income, as it would not be being spent on charitable purposes.

75.31 Investments

75.31 The investment strategy should facilitate the achievement of the charity's objectives by creating sufficient income to enable the charity to carry out its purposes consistently year by year, whilst maintaining, and if possible enhancing, the value of invested funds. The strategy should be set out in writing together with any policy constraints. These could include for example:

- liquidity – the need for a certain proportion of funds to be kept readily accessible;

- ethical constraints – no investments in companies that impede the achievement of the charity's objects or that deter supporters;

- diversification – no more than x% of funds to be invested in any single company;

- asset allocation – set parameters for the percentage to be held in equities, bonds, cash, hedge funds, property, commodities, private equity, etc;

- restrictions – limitations on the charity's powers of investment;

- risk – the acceptable level of risk;

- monitoring – trustees to receive written reports on investment at specified intervals.

PROFESSIONAL ADVICE

75.32 Investment advice should be written, impartial and given by someone with sufficient experience of charities and the types of investments they are permitted to use. This could be an accountant, bank manager, stockbroker, investment manager, a member of the charity's staff or one of the trustees. However, if trustees give investment advice they should consider the extent of any professional negligence liability which they may incur by so doing. If the trustees decide to disregard professional advice they have received, they should minute their reasons for taking an alternative course of action.

75.33 Once a charity's investments have reached a size where they could benefit from specialist attention, the trustees may wish to appoint investment managers and delegate day-to-day investment management to them, providing their governing document contains a power to do so, or consent is obtained from the Charity Commission.

75.34 *Section 11* of the *Trustee Act 2000* gives trustees powers to delegate certain investment functions, including the power to employ investment managers, that are in addition to any powers in the charity's governing document. However, when trustees delegate functions it does not mean that they can abdicate responsibility. For example, they must always retain control of investment policy, ensuring that there are adequate controls in place to check that the investment managers' powers are being exercised prudently, within the law and the powers in the charity's governing document, and that their performance is reviewed regularly. Any investment manager appointed must be authorised to conduct investment business by the *Financial Services and Markets Act 2000*.

75.35 Trustees have wide discretion under *s 14* of the *Trustee Act 2000* as to the terms on which investment managers are employed. However, trustees should provide investment managers with a written statement of their investment powers and their detailed investment policy. This should specify:

- the overall level of return expected and the minimum yield required;

- the income and/or capital requirements;

- the ability to use a total return approach;

- the nature and timing of any liabilities;

- the liquidity requirements including dates of planned expenditure;

- the marketability of the investments, in case capital needs to be raised quickly;

- the time horizon of the trust;

- the time horizon over which performance will be assessed and the benchmarks that will be used;

- any particular currency requirements;

- any tax or legal constraints;

- any cap on the percentage to be invested in particular asset classes.

75.36   The agreement with the investment manager and the terms of delegated authority should be clearly set out in writing or evidenced in writing and trustees should monitor that these are observed. Trustees should not enter into agreements that allow the investment manager to appoint a substitute, or reduces the manager's duty of care, or allows the investment manager to act in circumstances that could give rise to a conflict of interest. Further details on delegation to investment managers can be obtained from the Charity Commission, in their leaflet CC14 'Investment of Charitable Funds'.

LIABILITY FOR INVESTMENT LOSSES

75.37   Trustees are not personally liable for a charity's investment losses if they have acted within their powers and discharged their duties properly. However, they may be personally liable if they fail to do this. For example trustees may be liable if losses arise from unauthorised investments, or trustees may be liable if they have acted outside their powers, or if they have failed to take professional advice, or if they have failed to monitor their investment managers, or if they had an undeclared personal interest in a charity making or retaining an investment.

ENDOWED CHARITIES

75.38   The Charity Commission has authorised some endowed charities to adopt a 'total return' approach to investment. This allows the trustees to decide the amount of income that is retained for investment and the amount that is applied for charitable purposes, thus helping them balance the needs of present and future beneficiaries. A total return approach allows trustees to invest to achieve optimal performance in their overall return, rather than having to invest in a way that is likely to produce a certain amount of income and a certain amount of capital growth.

75.39 Investments

PROGRAMME-RELATED OR SOCIAL INVESTMENT

75.39   Programme-related' or 'social' investment is not 'investment' in the sense the word is used in this chapter. The terms are used to describe the ways in which charities pursue their objectives by providing loans or loan guarantees, or purchasing shares, or by letting land or buildings. Such investments may generate a financial return, but the charity's main objective in making them is to help its beneficiaries. Therefore legislation such as the *Trustee Act 2000* does not apply to programme-related or social investment.

REPORTING REQUIREMENTS

75.40   The policies that trustees have adopted (if any) for the selection of investments must be described in the charity's statutory annual report. Larger charities must include a statement in their annual report setting out the performance during the financial year of any investments belonging to the charity.

76   IT Planning

IT STRATEGY MUST SUPPORT THE BUSINESS PLAN

76.1   IT strategy should support an organisation's overall business strategy to facilitate its long-term goals and vision. As a charity evolves, so should the IT strategy to ensure that the supporting systems are extended or even replaced and remain appropriate. The strategy therefore needs to be continually reviewed and if necessary revised to take account of changing circumstances, both internal and external. Only in this way can an organisation expect its IT to continue to be effective and cost efficient. The alternative, 'reactive' approach to IT change inevitably leads to compromises, unanticipated shortcomings and, at worst, project failures and wasted resources.

76.2   For a number of reasons, an organisation's IT systems can become out of date or no longer fully support the charity's objectives, for example:

- organisational growth, both size and complexity may place strains upon the capacity of existing systems. For example, changes in methods of fund-raising activities, the introduction of new charitable activities or the establishment of a trading arm may mean that existing systems can no longer cope with current organisational needs;

- external factors can force the replacement of outdated systems, such as new accounting regulations, phasing out of supplier support for bespoke and obsolete systems or suppliers ceasing to trade;

- inefficiencies and shortcomings of systems will become increasingly apparent as the volume of work increases. Users can find it difficult and frustrating having to work around problems when operational activities are no longer served well by the systems that were designed to support them;

- advances in telecommunications and computing particularly through the global reach of the Internet mean that technology can be applied in ways that weren't possible only a few years ago.

76.3   Unlike the commercial sector where the cost of IT projects can often be written off over the life of a profitable venture, charities are often expected to stretch the life of a system, avoiding the cost of significant enhancement or replacement until it becomes unavoidable. This can lead to operational inefficiency and increased manual effort and work-arounds to cope with changing needs and obsolete, slow equipment. In terms of management and staff time, this can be expensive. These costs can be hidden as the resulting inefficiencies are spread across the organisation and not easily isolated.

76.4   Those charged with making investment decisions often feel vulnerable when presented with bids for IT funding. They do not always consider themselves to be computer literate and can be nervous of the jargon and the way in which computer systems are often described and presented. However, the decision to change or upgrade systems is, irrespective of the type of organisation, primarily a business decision. If the costs and benefits cannot be explained in a language understandable by those who will use new systems, or ultimately benefit from them, or who have responsibility for authorising the project, approval should not be given.

76.5   IT Planning

PRACTICAL STEPS

Justification – getting approval

76.5   In justifying the time and resources required to prepare an IT plan, the following should be borne in mind.

- Organisations that have no means of measuring the success of their fund-raising initiatives and performance indicators on financial performance, income and costs will fall behind those that are able to interpret results and make changes that result in improvements. By incorporating performance indicators within new systems, the organisation will be best placed to measure success and take appropriate timely action.

- Planning encourages creativity and fresh ideas that simply reacting to problems as they arise can never accomplish. Leaving IT decisions to the last minute leads to compromises that could have been avoided.

- Holding on to systems that are burdensome and no longer support the business objectives can result in greater staff and management time, opportunity costs and reduced efficiency and effectiveness. Anticipating future needs and planning ahead provides an opportunity to compare the costs and benefits of available courses of action whilst there remains time to select the best stratagem.

- Recent attention to matters of corporate governance and accountability coupled with public scepticism emphasises the importance of improved budgeting and transparency of reporting.

- It is essential to future-proof current and planned investment as far as practically possible, but equally important to recognise when it is time to move on. Trends and current supplier offerings should always be monitored to ensure that existing systems continue to provide good value for money against current products.

Preparing an IT plan

76.6   The IT plan should address three simple questions.

- Where are we now?

- Where do we want to be (in support of the "business")?

- How are we going to get there?

76.7   The starting point would be to summarise the current computer equipment and systems and propose changes in hardware, software and infrastructure supported by an argued business case as to the costs, benefits and risks associated with degrees of change and investment in support of the organisation's plans and objectives. In doing so it should be borne in mind that the real costs of supporting obsolete systems are often hidden or overlooked. For example, not only is it harder to find IT professionals familiar with obsolete systems, but when found they do not really want to spend time looking after them if they can be working on more up-to-date and more interesting systems.

76.8   Once the proposed new systems and equipment have been approved, their introduction can be planned. All projects should be properly managed, but it is often helpful to start by asking the question 'What has got to be done, by whom and by when?' It would be useful to show the answer to this diagrammatically, for example using Gantt charts showing time along the horizontal axis and the various tasks to be performed along the vertical axis. Each task can then be shown by a horizontal line between the start and end dates of each. In this way, a view of the project can be shown including those tasks that are dependent on the completion of earlier steps or tasks and the critical path through the project. The chart can then be regularly updated with actual progress.

Involving the people – needs analysis and resistance to change

76.9   Resistance to and fear of change are enemies of successful IT projects. A participative approach promotes ownership. Ideally, no one should be made to feel left out and it is important that those who will work most closely with the new system should feel committed to its success and comfortable when using it. Everyone should be regularly appraised of progress and expectations managed.

76.10   It is a good policy to welcome and listen to the views of staff in advance of the introduction of change. The extent to which staff and volunteers should become involved in selecting new systems will vary according to their duties, roles and responsibilities. They may not have a role in making the final investment decision but those who feel involved and share a sense of commitment and ownership of a plan are most likely to support it and make it work.

76.11   Therefore, it is always useful to seek staff input in identifying:

●   the strengths, shortcomings and inadequacies of present systems, as a basis for agreeing the essential needs of the new system;

●   areas where workloads and tasks can be tackled more efficiently and productively by better use of IT or by streamlining processes;

●   the strengths and weaknesses of candidate systems under consideration, for example in demonstrations, workshops or pilot studies as appropriate; and

●   alternative systems that may be suitable candidates to meet the needs of the organisation based on their experience.

76.12   Where small numbers of staff and volunteers are involved, an appraisal of system requirements can be obtained through focused meetings and workshops. In a larger organisation, detailed questionnaires may be prepared to obtain information according to particular areas of individual staff expertise. One to one interviews with individual staff members or workshop sessions for groups of users can be arranged to discuss views and needs. Whatever the approach, the deliverable should be a clearly articulated expression of what the new system should do together with a list of key areas of required functionality, especially those that are non-routine or unique to the organisation. It would be useful for subsequent tasks if those needs were prioritised between the essential and those considered nice-to-have. It is worth remembering that the definition of requirements that comes from this process should be concerned only with the business need and need not consider the technical solution to it, that is for the supplier to use his expertise to determine.

76.13   Finally, unless senior management take an active interest in the project and champion its success, staff may reflect the perceived view of management and assign the project a low priority. Experience suggests that successful IT projects are those where the senior management take a personal interest in its success and a 'champion' drives the process. It is for this reason that there should always be a board 'sponsor'. This will allow the board to make known its views to the team at project review meetings and also to receive feedback on project status and progress.

Research – information sources and issues

76.14   There is no shortage of information on all aspects of IT. The difficulties lie in distinguishing fact from fiction, optimism from reality and promises from working solutions. To help keep abreast of IT matters, it is wise to choose one or two regular information sources of which the independence can be assured, such as publications by the IT Faculty of the Institute of Chartered Accountants of England and Wales. For information on popular matters, the Internet is the best source of information (but it is sometimes hard to find what you want) and the weekly technology supplements of some newspapers can be more relevant than magazines aimed at home users or the technically minded. Charities and community organisations can get free advice and support from the ICT Hub website (*www.icthub.org.uk*), or by calling the Hub's helpdesk on 0800 652 4737.

76.15   The software market is constantly changing through consolidation, innovation and development. Up-to-date, comprehensive information on specific, specialist software products for charities can be difficult to obtain, and time can be wasted investigating unsuitable products. Magazine articles and reference publications may be helpful, but can be incomplete, quickly out of date, misleading or poorly researched. Charity sector exhibitions and conferences are often useful sources, both for the information they provide and as a means of linking up with other similarly interested parties keen to exchange experiences and ideas. However, system implementations are only as good as the planning, effort and project management that went into them. One person's unconfirmed adverse testimony may have nothing to do with the capability of the software but the way it was installed and used.

Economic use of external expertise

76.16   The decision whether to manage a specification, procurement and implementation project in-house or employ external consultants can be a difficult one. Many organisations, particularly charities, believe that they do not have sufficient in-house skill and resources for the staffing of IT projects. The most common argument is that other duties will inevitably result in an inability to devote sufficient time to the project resulting in loss of control, mistakes and time delays. Conversely, external consultants should have practical experience of systems implementation but any additional knowledge and experience they possess or gain will depart with them at the end of the project.

76.17   As a possible solution to this problem, and recognising the need to drive value from the process, it is possible to use focused external consultancy expertise whilst retaining overall control of the project. For example, it may be cost-effective to engage a consultant's services for some aspects of the selection process, to supplement a known shortfall in expertise and as a sounding board or as a mentor in making sure that all-important matters have been given adequate prominence. In this way, the external consultant may complement the skills of internal staff, provide guidance and confidence and fill specific gaps in knowledge and experience, on an as-needed rather than a full-time basis.

SOFTWARE AND HARDWARE

For not-for-profit organisations

76.18   It is important to bear in mind the diversity of the specialist software now available. It can range in price, from a few hundred to many thousands of pounds. In addition, after-sales support arrangements can range from virtually nothing, online support by modem to permanent on-site presence. The mainstream accounting software industry does not look upon the not-for-profit sector as a significant target and has traditionally made little effort to cater for its specialist needs, but there are a number of smaller suppliers offering specific solutions that do not always have the backup of resources or client base to guarantee continued support or investment in the product. There is, however, a variety of specialist software available to cater for the needs of the charity sector in the recording, analysis and administration of revenue. Requirements specific to the trading arms of charities are generally available within the commercial sector. Great care must be taken in assessing the viability of less well-known software products as their continued ability to meet needs unique to the not-for-profit sector, for example the SORP requirement for fund analysis, may be limited.

Accounting software

76.19   Given the shortcomings described above, organisations are often forced to compromise their particular requirements with the features and functionality present within mainstream accounting software applications designed for the commercial sector. As a general rule, if no charity-specific solution can be found, a market-leading accounting software product with backup of resources and a number of not-for-profit customers may be worth investigating.

76.20   The need to analyse transactions according to the fund to which they are to be applied is usually the primary consideration for charities choosing accounting software. The leading products differ significantly in their ability to meet this need. The number of levels or dimensions over which a package is capable of analysing transactions is often a key indicator of their ability to meet fund reporting requirements, both on the balance sheet and within the revenue and expenditure statement.

Fund-raising software

76.21   There is a variety of fund-raising software products available. The marketplace is constantly changing and consolidating, such that there are now only a

403

handful of major players at the top end of the market offering products essentially similar in functionality. The differentiating factors tend to be price, specialist add-on modules and the style and quality of implementation, training and support.

76.22   At the lower end of the market, there is a wider variety of products and much greater disparity in functionality, price, operating system and quality of support. Generally speaking, the level of functionality is directly reflected in the price of software. Great care should be taken in assessing the suitability of these products and whether they meet an organisation's particular needs.

76.23   Some or all of the following areas of activity are catered for in specialist charity systems:

- contacts, relationships and donor database;

- diary facilities;

- receipt administration;

- receipts analysis to nominal ledger interface;

- receipt analysis (by fund, project, appeal, etc.);

- covenant and gift aid tax claim management;

- grant-making and applications management;

- membership and subscription management;

- event management;

- volunteer management;

- office automation software.

76.24   Word processing, spreadsheet, database and presentation software applications can be most economically purchased in integrated suites. Practical advantages of integration include the ability to cut and paste between applications in the same suite incorporating, for example, a graph produced in a spreadsheet into a report in the word processing application. Ideally, the spreadsheet should integrate seamlessly with fund-raising and accounting systems to allow the transfer of information for further manipulation and analysis.

76.25   A variety of Human Resource systems specifically designed to assist in the administration and management of personnel is available. As a general guide, systems become cost-effective from about 50 employees upwards, although some are designed to cater for 500 employees or more. For further information contact the Institute of Personnel and Development or visit the exhibitions at which the market-leading suppliers exhibit.

Selecting software – general guidance

76.26   It is important to have a clear understanding of the organisation's needs, which of these are important, and thus, which are not. One way to express this is to list the organisation's functional requirements distinguishing between those needs that are essential and those that are desirable or of little interest. This document is often called a 'Statement of (Functional) Requirements'.

76.27   The level of detail provided in a Statement of Requirements will vary according to the type of application and the complexity of the function it will be required to support. It could act as a discussion document for use within the organisation, can be used as the basis of an invitation to tender, a checklist to ensure that the requirements have been met, form a schedule to the contract as to what is to be supplied and may later form the basis of an implementation plan. Provided it is unambiguous and concise, it can ensure that there is no misunderstanding between users and the supplier as to what is required. It can also be useful in ensuring that internally the need is agreed and understood by all. It is clearly an important document and it is essential to get it right.

76.28   The extent to which the essential needs can be met at a reasonable price and without major modifications to the packaged system will be a key factor in the selection process. It is not uncommon for users to declare initially that most of their needs are 'essential'. This means that the selection exercise could become bogged down in making sure these 'essential' requirements have been met when some of the work could have been avoided by being more rigorous with the prioritisation of needs. It is interesting to note that essential needs are often no longer considered quite so 'essential' when faced with a large bill for changing the system to meet them.

76.29   The question of whether software should be bespoke or off the shelf is one that sometimes arises. Usually in any normal business function, a packaged application is the right way forward. Some organisations regard themselves as unique in the way they operate and managers believe that only a bespoke solution will meet their particular needs. It is worth reflecting on whether this is indeed true or whether the organisation's processes have simply not kept pace. While bespoke applications have their place, they should only be considered if there is no packaged application that can deliver the majority of the requirements. In software, the pareto rule applies – you can usually get 80% of what you want for 20% of the price of the full solution. While bespoke (and heavily modified application) software should do everything the charity wants, it will be significantly more expensive to maintain and to change, the requirements will need to be specified very carefully, upgrades will not usually be provided free of charge, and it is inherently more risky.

Selecting hardware

76.30   The selection of hardware is often dependent upon the choice of software as sometimes there are restrictions as to the platforms upon which it can run. It is wise to seek advice from the software supplier on the minimum hardware and communications specification required to ensure that the performance of the software will not be inhibited, and to select hardware brands that will be reliable, enhanceable and maintainable.

76.31   Software resellers are usually happy to advise on hardware suitable for the software they distribute but increasingly do not wish to become involved in the supply and maintenance of hardware where the profit margin is comparatively low. It is now common for the purchaser to obtain IT equipment from other, less expensive sources.

76.32   However, whilst there is no obligation to buy hardware from the software supplier, it may be convenient to arrange a single-source agreement such that one party takes responsibility for the supply and maintenance of all facets of the system. This avoids the problem of disagreement between the various suppliers for each component of the system over responsibility for fixing a fault, especially where it cannot be determined initially where the problem has arisen. For example, faults could arise as a result of software, hardware, the communications system or operating system failure. The circumstances under which a single-source agreement is appropriate depends on a number of factors, not least of which is the size and sophistication of the system and the extent of in-house expertise to handle and manage the relationship with all the parties that may be involved.

Implementation guidelines

76.33   The most important element of implementation planning is to consider fully and agree what has to be done and by whom. In addition, any risks to the successful completion of the project also need to be identified and managed. An implementation plan is a collaborative effort involving all parties with the output of agreed tasks, resources and milestones together with a realistic timetable embracing installation, set up, testing and acceptance of the system. This will include the physical delivery, assembly and configuration of the system so that it can be seen to be functioning throughout. Where there is a network, cabling will have been laid, connected and tested to all workstations and equipment.

76.34   Pre-installed software is usually only tested in so far as its facilities or modules can be accessed and not that it has been set up to meet any predetermined requirements. Before a system can be used it needs to be configured and tested. Users should be satisfied that it can deliver the functionality set out in the Statement of Requirements. For example, the set-up of accounting systems requires user input. This includes defining the chart of accounts and report layouts. Someone will need to decide upon and set up all the reference information within the new system. Once everything is set up, it will need to be checked not only to ensure that it is correct and operates correctly within each area but that it also works correctly across the system as a whole. In all cases, someone will need to clean up data from the old system and determine the best way in which it can be transferred to the new one.

Project management

76.35   In any implementation there will be certain tasks which cannot be carried out unless other tasks have been completed. Success of the project will require people and resources to be available to carry out their tasks at the right time, as envisaged in the project plan. It is this vital stage of the planning process that requires someone to take overall responsibility for the implementation. Project management is required therefore from drafting and agreeing the implementation plan through to ensuring achievement of the agreed milestones and ensuring that all resources are made available at the right level of priority through all stages up to the system going live on a timely basis. This is the role of the Project Manager.

76.36   The software supplier will also normally provide a Project Manager. This person will often be very useful to the organisation and drive the project forward. However, the primary role of this person is to manage the project from the supplier's perspective. The supplier's project manager may not necessarily be focused on ensuring that all the customer's obligations and tasks have been satisfactorily completed or that they have used the system to best advantage, especially where they have no impact on what the supplier has to deliver. It is important, therefore, for the customer to appoint a Project Manager representing their own interests. This is normally an internal role reinforcing a sense of commitment and ownership although an external consultant may also have a role to play. This may include, for example, a mentoring role, attending project review meetings to ensure that progress is being made or independently confirming that the correct course of action is being taken.

77 Joint Ventures

77.1   Where several organisations work together in partnership it may be advisable to set up a formal joint venture. Charities typically enter into joint ventures to carry out joint trading enterprises, or to work together on a particular initiative to promote a mutual charitable interest, for example, relief of Third World debt. Although many joint working arrangements do not need a separate legal identity it is often advisable to set up a joint venture company, or at least a formal agreement, in order to minimise the risk of disputes should things go wrong, particularly if losses are incurred.

JOINT VENTURE AGREEMENT

77.2   All the parties to a joint venture should be clear about their rights and obligations. Therefore, a joint venture agreement is drawn up setting these out, including the purpose of the venture, who owns it, how profits are to be shared, how it is to be governed, restrictions on competitive behaviour and arrangements for terminating the agreement. Other provisions will cover problem areas such as dispute resolution, inquorate meetings and partners who want or need to withdraw.

77.3   The issues to be considered before entering into a joint venture are much the same whether the venture is charitable or commercial. The charity should consider its legal capacity to enter into such an arrangement, the financial commitment and risk involved and whether or not the joint venture is in line with the objects of the charity and its strategic plan. As with sponsorship and commercial participation, charities may need to consider the extent to which a relationship with the other venturers is compatible with the good name of the charity and the degree of control they will have over the future direction of the venture.

ACCOUNTS

77.4   The financial statements will need to take account of the joint venture, although the precise accounting will depend on the charity's stake in the joint venture company and whether that company is a subsidiary, associate or joint venture for accounting purposes. Associate and joint venture accounting is governed by FRS 9 and the accounts of subsidiary companies should be consolidated as required by the SORP. If a charity has a participating interest (within the meaning of *Companies Act 1985, s 260*) in an undertaking which is not a subsidiary and exercises significant influence over its operating and financial policy (usually presumed if one holds beneficially 20% or more of the voting rights), then it is probably an associated company.

77.5   The accounting treatment of an associate or joint venture will depend on the exact nature of the relationship:

- associates should be included in group accounts on the net equity method, i.e. just the net results and assets are included in the accounts;

- joint ventures should be included in the group accounts under the gross equity method, under which joint ventures receive the same treatment as associates, except that items relating to the joint venture must be expressed separately rather than as part of the group figure. Additionally, the investor's share of the gross assets and liabilities of the joint venture must be separately disclosed, rather than being expressed as a net figure. Also, the disclosure requirements of the SORP will need to be included in the notes to the financial statements. This presentation looks peculiar on the face of the Sofa, and so treasurers should be prepared to explain it!

77.6   Less formal joint arrangements (sometimes referred to as a 'JANE' or 'joint arrangement that is not an entity') should be treated like a branch, with the charity showing its share of income and expenditure as determined per the agreement governing the arrangement.

78   Land and Buildings

78.1   Dealings in property are frequently complex and often carry underlying risks which may not be immediately apparent. Although this chapter can indicate some general principles, in most instances it will be necessary to take special-ist legal advice. Reasons for this include the topic's history, reaching back to the Middle Ages, and the variety and breadth of issues to which this chapter can do no more than allude. The principles set out below are of general application to all charities, including charitable industrial and provident societies although most of the sections of the *Charities Act 1993* relating to land do not apply to industrial and provident societies.

78.2   For registered charities in England and Wales, the *Charities Act 1993* sets out the statutory regime for the disposals of charity land and relieves the Charity Commission of the need to give consent to most charity land transactions, placing increased responsibility on charity trustees.

GENERAL DUTIES OF TRUSTEES

78.3   The Charity Commission has set out trustees' duties regarding land in a number of leaflets, i.e. CC3 'The Essential Trustee – what you need to know', CC28 'Disposing of Charity Land', and CC33 'Acquiring Land'. In this context land is taken to mean land in England or Wales with or without buildings and includes any estate or interest in land, such as a lease or right of way. Trustees' duties apply whether the land is used by the charity for its own purposes, or if it is let to produce income for the charity, and are as follows:

- Trustees are individually and jointly responsible for the protection, management and supervision of the land.

- In managing the land trustees must act only in the interests of the charity and its beneficiaries, which means, for example, obtaining the best price on a disposal.

- Trustees must act honestly and must use the same degree of care as they would prudently exercise in dealing with their own business affairs, which means, for instance, that they must maintain overall control of the management of their land and ensure that the charity can afford a prospective purchase.

- Trustees must seek professional advice when purchasing or disposing of land.

- Any decision to dispose of, or mortgage, land must be taken by the trustees acting together.

- A disposal or mortgage of land is always a matter which should be undertaken and controlled by the trustees as a whole.

- Trustees must always have the necessary power or authority for the transaction.

REASONS FOR HOLDING LAND

78.4   The reasons that charities hold land will have bearing on some of the processes involved in relevant transactions.

Functional property

78.5 Functional property is property, such as an almshouse, which is held on trusts which stipulate that it is to be used for the purposes of the charity. This is not the same as the charity simply allowing the asset to be used for charitable purposes.

Permanent endowment

78.6 Land will form permanent endowment if the capital cannot be expended. The charity may or may not be allowed to dispose of the land, but in either case it will not be able to dispose of the proceeds, which may require reinvestment in line with the original terms of the trust.

Investment property

78.7 Under *s 8* of the *Trustee Act 2000* charities have a general power to acquire freehold or leasehold land, including buildings, in the UK for investment, subject to any restriction or exclusion in the charity's governing document. If trustees want to acquire land outside the UK for investment purposes the charity's governing document must contain a power that permits this.

WHO CAN HOLD LAND

78.8 Incorporated bodies, such as limited companies, industrial and provident societies and incorporated trustees can hold land in their own name since they are recognised legal persons. Unincorporated bodies such as associations and trusts cannot hold land or rent property in the same way; they must therefore vest title in the asset in a small group of holding trustees or a custodian trustee or the Official Custodian for Charities. Where a charity has several properties, it will often establish its own trust company for this purpose. The company never trades, it simply is a vehicle for holding title. In all these cases the person who holds the legal title is not the beneficial owner. They have no rights over the asset, but merely hold it on behalf of the charity. Vesting charity land in the Official Custodian does not change any of the powers the charity trustees have to dispose of it.

ACQUIRING AND DISPOSING OF LAND

78.9 Before acquiring or disposing of land the trustees must be certain that the proposed action is in the best interest of the charity and that an alternative course of action would not be more beneficial. For example, before disposing of investment land the trustees should take professional advice on the long-term potential of the land, to see if it is suitable for development or if a higher rate of return could be achieved if the land were enhanced in some way.

78.10 Apart from where a mortgage is required, or where the purchase is subject to an Order of the Charity Commission, the acquisition of land by a charity is essentially the same process as that undertaken by a commercial organisation or an individual. Where trustees are considering purchasing land for the charity's purposes or for investment they should remember that:

- Land can depreciate as well as appreciate in value;

411

78.11   Land and Buildings

- Land may require more active management than other forms of investment;

- Land cannot be quickly changed into cash;

- Purchase of a sufficiently diversified portfolio of investment land can be difficult, especially for a smaller charity. Investment in a land-based common investment fund may be more suitable;

- Ownership of investment land may impose financial obligations on the charity.

78.11   Before purchasing land trustees should obtain a report from a qualified surveyor acting solely for the trustees. The report should contain:

- a description of the land;

- details of any planning permission needed;

- a valuation of the land;

- advice on the price the trustees ought to offer, or on the maximum bid they should make at auction;

- a description of any repairs or alterations the trustees would need to make, together with the estimated costs;

- a positive recommendation that purchasing the land is in the best interests of the charity, and the reasons why this is the case;

- a description of any restrictive or other covenants to which the land is subject;

- any other information the surveyor thinks is relevant.

78.12   Before commencing a disposal of land charities must ensure that they have a legal power to dispose of the land. This will need reference not only to the governing document, but also to the terms relating to the original acquisition of the property and to *s 36* of the *Charities Act 1993* (this does not apply to exempt charities). Where the relevant power does not exist, or where it is unclear as to what the original terms were, then the Charity Commission should be consulted. CC28 'Disposing of Charity Land' sets out the Charity Commission's latest advice on this subject.

78.13   The statutory procedures on a disposal do not necessarily apply in relation to a disposal to another charity, if the trusts do not prohibit such a disposal and the disposal is a means of furthering the charity's purposes. Similar conditions apply on the granting of a lease to another charity. The landlord should not automatically charge less than the full market rent when selling or letting to another charity. This should be done only where it is clear that such a transaction furthers the landlord charity's objects in a way that is preferable to a transaction at market value. The exception does not extend to supporting all charities or to charities with which the trustees have an empathy. Decisions about selling or letting at below market value should be made by trustees.

Charity Commission consent

78.14   Since the introduction of procedures under *ss 36–40* of the *Charities Act 1993* it is not normally necessary for a charity to seek the Charity Commission's consent for the sale of property. The detailed procedures differ depending on the transaction.

Granting leases for seven years or less where no premium is paid to the charity

78.15   No consent is required to the granting of such a lease if:

- trustees obtain and consider the advice of a person they reasonably believe to have the ability and experience to advise them competently on the granting of the lease;

- trustees satisfy themselves, taking into account the views of their adviser, that the terms they are receiving for the lease are the best that can reasonably be obtained in the circumstances; and

- the land is to be leased to someone who is not a connected person (see **79.27**).

Other transactions

78.16   No consent is required for other transactions, including the granting of leases for more than seven years, leases for premiums, freehold sales, grants of easements, rights and options, exchanges of land if:

- trustees obtain and consider written advice on the proposed disposal from a qualified surveyor instructed by the trustees and acting exclusively for the charity;

- trustees advertise the property in accordance with the surveyor's advice, unless the trustees are advised not to advertise the property;

- based on the surveyor's report, the trustees are satisfied that the terms of the disposal are the best that they can reasonably achieve; and

- the disposal is not to a connected person.

78.17   The surveyor's report is governed by regulations issued under the *Charities Act 1993*. It should comment on the following:

- Whether or not the land or buildings are in good order and what work, if any, needs to be done before the sale;

- Whether or not the land or buildings are subject to any restrictions, easements, etc;

- The best approach to selling the land; and

- The value of the property.

78.18   In general trustees should be satisfied that they have secured the best terms reasonably available in the circumstances, though occasionally there may be situations in which it is in the best interests of the charity to accept a lower offer, for example if it allows them to include a covenant restricting the use of the land being sold. Trustees cannot sell at less than the highest offer simply to avoid selling to a purchaser they find objectionable. They may, however, reject an offer if they believe that the purchaser will use the land in a way which will affect other land they are retaining, or which will be contrary to the purposes of the charity. Where a lower price is accepted the trustees must be convinced that this is in the overall best interests of the charity.

78.19   The surveyor used to give advice must be a fellow or professional associate of the Royal Institution of Chartered Surveyors or the Incorporated Society of

Valuers and Auctioneers, and must have experience relevant to the type of property he is being asked to advise upon. The regulations themselves are available from HMSO, although trustees are encouraged by the Charity Commission not to rely upon the regulations alone, but to ensure that the report takes into account any other factors which may have specific bearing on this particular transaction.

Functional land

78.20   Trustees must advertise the fact that a disposal of functional land is intended, unless it is to be replaced on the same trusts, or the trustees are granting a lease for only two years or less, receiving only a rent and levying no premium, or the Charity Commission have issued a direction that these rules need not apply.

Mortgages

78.21   Special rules apply where a charity wishes to acquire property using mortgage finance, or indeed even if a mortgage is taken out on property already owned by a charity. A mortgage in this instance includes a charge over the property. These rules do not apply to exempt charities.

78.22   As with disposals, there is no need for a charity to obtain the consent of the Charity Commission to take out a mortgage as long as certain procedures are properly followed, although even the procedures set out below are unnecessary where a higher authority (e.g. a Scheme) already exists. Usually the trustees must obtain and consider the advice of someone who is reasonably believed to have sufficient ability in, and practical experience of, financial matters to give them sound advice. This person can be an officer or employee of the charity, but must have no financial interest in the loan. The adviser must provide the trustees with advice in writing about whether or not the loan is necessary in order for the trustees to be able to pursue the particular course of action in connection with which the loan is sought, whether or not the loan's terms are reasonable (in view of the charity's own credit status), and the charity's ability to repay the loan on the proposed terms.

78.23   These requirements are set out in s 38 of the Act, but occasionally prospective lenders require charities to obtain the advice set out above from an independent adviser, such as the auditor, as though confusing the requirements on disposal and mortgaging. Where a charity is asked to obtain such a report, it should ensure that the lender is fully aware of the exact requirements of s 38 before incurring what may be otherwise unnecessary professional costs.

78.24   The Charity Commission has also made it clear that if a charity takes out an unsecured loan, and its assets comprise mainly land, then they will not necessarily grant their consent to any subsequent sale of land to repay the loan unless the borrowing had originally been authorised by the Charity Commission.

Register of charges

78.25   Limited companies have to maintain a register of charges as part of their statutory books. As a mortgage is a charge it should be recorded in the register, setting out the date of the charge, the name of the lender, details of the property concerned, and the amount. Notice of the creation of a charge must be given to Companies House within 21 days. Similarly an industrial and provident society must notify the Financial Services Authority about the creation of charge or mortgage within the same period.

Additional statements

78.26   Whenever a registered charity makes a disposal of land, including taking a mortgage, the trustees are required under *s 37* of the *Charities Act 1993* to make certain statements and issue certain certificates, some of which have prescribed wording and some of which will be drafted by solicitors. These statements are designed to demonstrate that the charity is acting within its powers in the transaction, and has complied with relevant statutory requirements. If the statements are wrong, and the charity has not complied in the appropriate way, then the purchaser's title will still be good, but the trustees may be liable for any loss arising from their actions.

Connected persons

78.27   These are defined in *Sch 5* of the *Charities Act 1993* as follows:

(*a*)   a charity trustee, or trustee for the charity (e.g. a custodian trustee);

(*b*)   a person who is the donor of any land to the charity (whether the gift was made on or after the establishment of the charity);

(*c*)   a child, parent, grandchild, grandparent, brother or sister of any such trustee or donor;

(*d*)   an officer, agent or employee of the charity;

(*e*)   the spouse of any person falling within any of (*a*) to (*e*) above;

(*f*)   an institution which is controlled

(i)   by any person falling within (*a*) to (*d*) above, or

(ii)   by two or more such persons taken together; or

(*g*)   a body corporate in which

(i)   any connected persons falling within (*a*) to (*f*) above has a substantial interest (that is, more than 20% of either the share capital or the voting power in general meeting), or

(ii)   two or more such persons, taken together, have a substantial interest.

78.28   For the purposes of this definition, 'child' includes a stepchild and an illegitimate child, a 'spouse' includes someone living with another as that person's husband or wife or civil partner, and a person controls an institution if he is able to secure that the affairs of the institution are conducted in accordance with his wishes.

78.29   The definition of connected persons for Scottish charities is given in FRS 8, which applies to the whole of the UK.

SPECIAL CASES

78.30   There are a number of situations where a land transaction will be complicated by specific circumstances, some of which are unique to charities or certain types of charity. These cases will need expert legal advice, and may include the following.

Rentcharges

78.31   A rentcharge is a regular payment (usually very small) which the owner of a particular piece of land is obliged to make to another person, often a charity, other than under a lease or mortgage. Rentcharges are usually payable annually. Because the amount payable is fixed, its real value falls each year in line with inflation. Under the *Rentcharges Act 1977* nearly all rentcharges will be extinguished without compensation in the year 2037. The Charity Commission has advised trustees of charities that receive rentcharges to consider releasing any rentcharge to which they are entitled by voluntary agreement with the landowner in exchange for a lump sum payment, equivalent to the annual payments for a number of years. Most landowners will agree to this as it relieves them of the time and cost involved in making a small payment each year.

78.32   The *Charities Act 1993* treats rentcharges in a different way from other interests in land. The Charity Commission's consent will not be required if a charity releases the rentcharge for a sum of money not less than ten times the annual rentcharge payment (e.g. a rentcharge of £10 is released for more than £100). The Commission's consent will be required, and will rarely be given, if the release payment is less than ten times the annual payment. If the sum received by the charity for the release is less than £500 then any costs incurred by the charity in proving its legal title to the rentcharge must be paid by the landowner.

Auctions

78.33   Although a charity may sell property through auction, it cannot control who will purchase it. If it subsequently transpires that the purchaser is a connected person, then the consent of the Charity Commission will be required. This should be made clear in advance.

Reverter

78.34   Under legislation such as the *Literary and Scientific Institutions Act 1854*, individuals were encouraged to pass property to relevant charitable institutions on condition that the property would revert back to the donor, or his successors, if the property ceased to be used for the purpose for which it was given. Other types of property affected include libraries, schools, burial grounds, places of worship and clergy houses. Charities holding such properties might not benefit from any sale proceeds on disposal of such a property.

Church halls

78.35   The Charity Commission have issued specific guidance on the use of church halls for other charitable purposes, including as village halls. Broadly this follows guidance in other parts of this chapter concerning the need for the trustees to take due note of their own particular terms of trust. It also points out that if a church hall is no longer needed at all for church purposes, then the trusts of the charity can be said to have failed and the property should be sold. Other legislation will need consulting, such as the *Parochial Church Council (Powers) Measures*.

Churches

78.36   There are further specific provisions relating to churches, related properties and cathedrals. For instance the definition of charity in the context of the *Charities Act 1993* does not apply to some ecclesiastical corporations (that is, in the Church of England in respect of certain corporate property, nor to diocesan glebe land) nor to any trust of property for purposes for which the property has been consecrated. Cathedral land transactions are governed by other legislation, as are transactions relating to redundant churches (*s 96(2)*).

TAXATION

78.37   Property transactions, whether on disposal and acquisition, or as rental or lease payment may all be subject to tax. Income tax or corporation tax may be due on amounts received, VAT may be charged on rent, gains may be subject to capital gains tax (for instance on a reversion), and council tax and business rates may apply. These taxes are addressed in their relevant chapters. Charities are exempt from stamp duty on conveyances, transfers of securities, assignments of existing leases or grants of new leases to the charity. [*Finance Act 1982, s 129(1)*].

78.38   Stamp duty land tax, introduced in *Finance Act 2003*, is a charge on transactions and replaced stamp duty on land and buildings. It affects land transactions involving any estate, interest, right or power in or over land in the United Kingdom. Documents evidencing an acquisition of land or an interest in land not chargeable to stamp duty land tax remain chargeable to stamp duty.

78.39   Relief from stamp duty land tax, similar to the relief from stamp duty, is available where a charity, or a charitable trust, purchases an interest in land, subject to certain conditions.

78.40   Generally it would be accepted that the purchase of property by a charity

- registered with the Charity Commission in England and Wales; or

- recognised as a charity by OSCR in Scotland or HMRC Charities in Northern Ireland

which is not bought for resale, qualifies for relief.

78.41   Where a registered social landlord grants a lease with either an indefinite term, or terminable by notice of a month or less, to one or more individuals that transaction is exempt from stamp duty land tax. The exemption only applies to arrangements entered into between the registered social landlord and a housing authority whereby the landlord provides accommodation for individuals nominated by the authority.

ACCOUNTING FOR PROPERTY

78.42   Property owned by a charity will normally be classified as a fixed asset and shown on the face of the balance sheet. Property donated to a charity will appear as an incoming resource in the year when it is receivable in accruals accounts. Expenditure on the acquisition of a property is capital, and may include enhancement and installation costs. It is often a matter of fine judgement whether certain costs on a property constitute repairs and mainte-nance, or some sort of capital expenditure improving the property. FRS 15, which governs all fixed assets accounting and depreciation, draws a distinc-tion between expenditure which enhances performance and expenditure which maintains performance of a fixed asset. All fixed assets except land, but including buildings, should be subject to depreciation unless it is immaterial or unless the property is inalienable: both these exemptions are narrowly drawn and if a charity wishes not to depreciate buildings and associated works it should consult the SORP and FRS 15 for more detailed guidance.

78.43   The accounting value attributed to a property will depend on its purpose and nature of title:

- Freehold land and buildings held for charity's own use: at cost or valuation, less depreciation on the buildings.

- Leasehold property held for charity's own use: at cost or valuation, less amortisation, usually over the unexpired term of the lease.

- Investment property: at market value.

- Rented property: no value will appear in the accounts, as the charity has no legal interest in the land.

- Inalienable buildings: in principle such assets should be accounted for as any other asset, although sometimes the nature of the asset itself might preclude its inclusion on cost-benefit grounds.

- Heritage assets: at the time of writing a debate rages over the appropriate treatment for heritage assets, which includes certain property such as stately homes and special coastlines, for instance. Current proposals require inclusion of such assets at market value, unless it is impracticable to do so.

78.44   FRS 15 requires revalued assets, usually land and buildings, to be profession-ally revalued every five years. For charities (but not their subsidiary com-panies) this valuation may be based on any reasonable approach, thus avoiding the cost of professional fees, subject to gaining advice as to the possibility of material movements in value. Investment properties should be accounted for at market value each year, and property brought into the accounts as a result of a gift at market value will not be treated as having been revalued, so the five-year rule does not apply.

78.45   Property donated in the past can be a problem, but generally only where the SORP is being implemented for the first time or when there is a change in accounting policy. The value to the charity at the time of the donation (probably equivalent to cost at that time) is often neither known nor relevant. Revaluing may be an expensive option, but is often the only option. Once all property has been identified a register should be established to control future transactions. Anglican parishes are required to maintain this as a terrier (register of property), subject to inspection by the Archdeacon every three years.

78.46   Revaluation movements will be shown in the accounts within the statement of recognised gains and losses, except for depreciation and permanent diminutions in value which will form part of outgoing resources.

78.47   As with other fixed assets, trustees should be alert to property values being overstated in their accounts. Where this is the case the charity should conduct an impairment review under FRS 11 and amend the values accordingly. The application of impairment reviews to charities is usually straightforward, except for specialised properties such as hospices and historic assets such as monuments. In such cases the SORP asks charities to consider using alternatives to net realisable value, such as the intrinsic worth of the property, its service potential, or the depreciated replacement cost.

79 Legacies

79.1   Legacy income is worth an estimated £1.6bn a year to charities, representing around 12% of all voluntary income received by charities. Health related charities, animal welfare charities, disability organisations, and armed services charities are the main recipients, though the highest legacy growth rate is currently amongst charities operating in welfare and housing, conservation and environment, animal welfare, and international aid/human rights.

79.2   Legacy fundraising is the most cost-effective form of fundraising, though its future is uncertain. The percentage of people who remember a charity in their will is smaller than the percentage who regularly support charities but between 2000 and 2005 the percentage of will makers who included a charity in their will increased from 10 to 15%. This fact, combined with increasing house prices, has led some commentators to argue that there is significant potential for growth. Others argue that inadequate pensions, the high cost of long-term care, the increasing popularity of equity release schemes, and increasing levels of debt, will lead to a reduction in legacy income.

79.3   Legacies often give rise to complex legal and tax issues, especially when residuary legacies are shared by a number of charities and tax paying beneficiaries. Smaller charities are likely to need legal advice. Occasionally situations may arise in relation to wills where charities will have to seek consent from the Charity Commission to make an ex gratia payment, for example, where a codicil leaving a legacy to an individual is unexecuted and therefore invalid, but there is clear evidence that the testator wanted the individual to receive the legacy, the trustees may regard themselves as having a moral obligation to make a payment to the individual.

79.4   Most charities will benefit from producing a legacy pack to encourage legacy giving. Income from legacies is likely to decline over time unless proactive work is done to promote legacy giving. Providing clear guidance can also help to prevent the common problems that are likely to arise. For example, people may leave a legacy for 'research into heart disease' rather than to a particular charity that carries out or funds research into heart disease. Where charities have branches or a federated structure it is not always clear whether someone intended to leave a legacy to the national umbrella organisation or to a local branch.

TAXATION

79.5   The tax status of legacies is discussed elsewhere (see CHAPTER 68). To ensure that charitable bequests are not subject to inheritance tax the bequest should be clearly and exclusively charitable, and the charity recipient should ensure that any receipts have not been inadvertently subjected to tax either on the capital sum, or on any income arising in the period pending distribution. For instance, the sale by an executor of an asset forming part of an estate will be subject to capital gains tax unless the executor is acting as bare trustee for a charity.

79.6   Charities may also wish to confirm the basis of any allocation of inheritance tax. It is normal practice for charities to receive their share of any residuary legacy before any deduction of inheritance tax, with that burden falling on the non-exempt beneficiaries. This practice was reversed in *Re Benham's Will Trusts, Lockhart v Harker [1995] STC 210*, but the HMRC have subsequently confirmed that this was not a precedent to be applied generally in future, but was specific to the rather unusual wording used in the will concerned.

79.7   Not all apparently charitable bequests escape inheritance tax. In *Chichester Diocesan Fund and Board of Finance Inc v Simpson (Re Diplock) [1944] AC 341, [1944] 2 All ER 60* the wording of the will was judged to be too wide in its purposes, i.e. charitable or benevolent, to be a charitable bequest. Although many charities would like to become involved with the drafting of wills to prevent this sort of thing occurring, the Charity Commission has repeatedly warned charities not to get too involved in drafting legacies or codicils for individuals. If a charity is involved in drafting a will in which it is a beneficiary, the will may be subsequently challenged on the grounds that it was drafted under undue influence (see 79.18). Charities should follow the Institute of Fundraising's Code of Practice on Legacy Fundraising and the Charity Commission's guidance.

79.8   These factors suggest that charities must take care in advising potential donors, and should investigate legacy receipts to ensure that no unnecessary tax has been borne by the charity.

CONTROL

79.9   As with other sources of voluntary income, it is important to ensure that records of income are not only accurate, but also complete. Where it is unusual for a charity to receive legacies, then only normal controls are expected over non-contractual income: dual opening of post, cash receipt registers and maintenance of correspondence files all being important.

79.10   Where legacies are received fairly frequently, other controls can be implemented. A register of legacies should be maintained, which should record a legacy as soon as any notification of its existence is received. The income received can then be cross-referenced to this register, and the entry only closed when it is confirmed that all sums due have been received. Some organisations also keep records of legacies written in their favour, so that they can judge the effect of any legacy campaign, and ensure that legacies do not get diverted when due.

79.11   Specialist agencies exist which record details of charitable legacies left to specific charities or for specific or general charitable purposes. Charities may subscribe to these services in order to identify potential legacy income. Where a legacy has been left for a purpose that falls within a charity's objects, the charity can write to the executors asking for all or part of the legacy to be given to the charity.

79.12   It is possible to budget for legacy income. Legacy income is broadly predictable when measured as a four-year moving average, though it can fluctuate widely on an annual basis and just one legacy can have a substantial effect on the annual performance of a small charity. According to the Charity Finance 100 Index, legacy income has shown steady growth ever since 1992. Where a charity has an established pattern of legacy income, then external information, such as the index, can give useful guidance to the organisation in determining whether an unexpected change in the pattern can be explained satisfactorily, or whether a control breakdown has occurred.

ACCOUNTING

79.13   In the past charities operated legacy equalisation accounts, which released legacy income over a number of years. These had usually been initiated by prudent treasurers wishing to avoid wild fluctuations in legacy income. However, the SORP requires all legacy income to be recognised as income when receivable unless it is incapable of financial measurement. This means that it is incorrect to defer the recognition of income simply because it is a large and apparently distorting figure. This position was underlined in the case of an incorporated charity which was in insolvent liquidation when the testator died. The liquidator was able to enforce collection of the bequest and use it towards paying the creditors *(Re ARMS (Multiple Sclerosis Research) Ltd [1997] 2 All ER 679)*.

79.14   The SORP requirement means that charities should not only recognise legacies already received, but also those notified. In other words it would be correct to treat as income a pecuniary legacy to which a charity is entitled, where probate has been granted, and where there is no doubt about the amount or certainty of receipt. An example of this would be where the charity has received notification from the personal representatives of the estate that a payment will be made. Administrators may take the view that this situation can only truly occur where the bequeathed amount is actually received after the year-end but before the accounts are signed off. Residuary legacies are often difficult to value, but if they are likely to have a major impact on the charity's financial position it is good practice to refer to them in the notes to the accounts.

79.15   This accountancy requirement applies only to where the legacy is capable of financial measurement. Very often a residuary legacy will fall outside this definition. Where this happens, the notes to the accounts should give an indication of the estimated amount receivable (where material).

79.16   For charities that are still uneasy about incorporating too much income into their day-to-day operations, placing legacies over a certain size in a designated fund may be a sensible option. Sometimes legacies will be restricted funds in their own right, but otherwise there is nothing to stop trustees regarding legacies as being in some way special, and setting them on one side for particular purposes. As long as this does not represent an unauthorised accumulation of funds, then representing such funds as part of designated funds would seem reasonable.

PAYING FOR WILLS WITH CHARITY FUNDS

79.17   Charities pay for wills to be prepared either because it is a way of pursuing their charitable objects, for example if they are established to provide support for the terminally ill, or because they judge it to be a cost-effective way of generating income from legacies. The Charity Commission has no objection in principle to either of these activities, but recommends that charities should follow best practice if they are to avoid damage to their reputation.

79.18   The Commission strongly advises that a charity's employees should never become involved in drafting an individual's will, as this could lead to a legacy left to the charity in the will being challenged on the grounds of undue influence, or want of knowledge and approval. Where a charity offers to meet the cost of drafting a will the Commission recommends that the will is drafted by the individual's own solicitor, or where the individual does not have a solicitor the charity should recommend that a solicitor is used, but it should not recommend a particular individual or firm of solititors. The charity can provide a list of solicitors, provided the individual chooses from the list themselves.

79.19   Charities paying for wills should avoid inadvertently creating a contractual relationship between the charity and the solicitors who actually draft the wills, so that the charity will have no financial liability if a solicitor's conduct of business proved to be negligent, and to minimise the risk of any legacy to the charity in the will being invalid on the grounds of undue influence or want of knowledge and approval.

79.20   The Charity Commission advises charities to seek written confirmation from any solicitor who prepares a will for a client at the charity's expense that in any case where the testator after advice decides to leave a legacy to the charity, that they are fully satisfied that the testator:

- was **not** subject to any influence;

- **did** fully understand and intend what he or she was doing; and that

- the charges made (indirectly) to the charity will correspond to those normally charged for preparing a will.

79.21   The Law Society has stated that where clients are referred to a solicitor by a third party the solicitor can agreed to be paid by the third party provided the referral arrangement complies with The Solicitors' Introduction and Referral Code 1990. This code governs all arrangements between solicitors and third parties thatrefer clients to them. It requires the solicitor:

- to act exclusively in the interests of the testator;

- to retain the freedom to advise the testator impartially;

- to keep the testator's instructions confidential, unless the testator authorises these to be disclosed.

79.22   Where the third party is paying the solicitor's fees the code additionally specifies that:

- the terms of the referral agreement between the charity and the solicitor are set out in writing, with a copy available for inspection by the Law Society and the Office for the Supervision of Solicitors; and

- the terms of agreement between the charity and the testator, relating to the payment and the preparation of the will, includes specified information relating to the solicitor's independence and their duties to the testator.

LEGACIES AND MERGERS

79.23   The *Charities Act 2006* allows merged charities to continue to receive legacies even if the original charity named in a will has been removed from the register as a result of the merger. Some mergers can be registered with the Charity Commission voluntarily and some will have to be registered because a vesting declaration has been made.

79.24 Trustees of a merged charity need to tell the Commission:

- what has been transferred and the date(s) the transfer(s) took place;

- that appropriate arrangements have been made for meeting any liabilities of the charity that is transferring its assets; and

- if a vesting declaration has been made, and if it has, certain details about it.

79.25 A 'vesting declaration' essentially means that any charity transferring assets only has to use one deed to cover the transfer of all its assets to the new merged charity, rather than separate transfers to cover the transfer of the various assets included in the merger.

79.26 When a merger is registered with the Commission legacies left to the charity which 'disappears' as a result of the merger will automatically be transferred to the new merged charity.

SCOTLAND

79.27 Whilst the tax and accounting regimes for legacies are the same for the whole of the UK the law relating to wills is different in Scotland and professional advice should be sought. For example, residuary legacies are often promoted in Scotland where descendants and a spouse have an automatic right to claim part of the moveable estate, instead of accepting whatever provision the deceased has made for them in the will.

FURTHER INFORMATION

79.28 Institute of Fundraising *www.institute-of-fundraising.org.uk*

Remember a Charity *www.rememberacharity.org.uk*

Charities Aid Foundation *www.cafonline.org*

80   Light Touch Regime

80.1   The light touch regime applies to 75% of registered charities in England and Wales, i.e. those that are unincorporated, have no external scrutiny requirement in their constitution and that have neither income nor expenditure above £20,000 a year. It simplifies their accounting and reporting requirements and the way in which their accounts must be scrutinised, in order to balance the need for public accountability with the burden and cost of compliance on the trustees of small charities.

80.2   Unless their governing documents set out more stringent requirements light touch regime charities must:

- maintain proper accounting records showing and explaining all sums of money received and paid out, the date, and what it was received for or spent on, and a record of the charity's assets and liabilities, and keep them together with copies of the annual accounts, for at least six years;

- prepare annual accounts on either a receipts and payments basis or an accruals basis, together with a statement of assets and liabilities;

- prepare a simple annual report describing the main activities and achievements;

- make a simple annual return so the Charity Commission can keep its Register up to date; and

- make copies of the accounts available to the public on written request.

80.3   Unless specifically requested a light touch regime charity does not have to send its accounts or annual report to the Charity Commission each year.

80.4   Charities in the light touch regime do not have to have the accounts independently examined or audited unless their governing document requires this.

80.5   If trustees elect to prepare their accounts on an accruals basis they must be prepared in accordance with the Regulations, though they can take advantage of certain concessions permitted in the Regulations, of which the most useful is the exemption from presenting costs on an activity basis.

80.6   As with other variations in the accounting regime, no formal election is required for trustees to operate within the light touch regime.

81 Local Authorities

81.1 A local authority is defined as a county council, a district council, a London borough, a parish council, a community council (Wales), the Council of the Isles of Scilly, or the Common Council of the City of London. [*Local Government Act 1988 Sch 2*].

81.2 Charities and local authorities work together in a number of ways. Services that local authorities have a statutory duty to provide are often funded by local authorities but run by charities under contract agreements. Charities have to apply to local authorities for permits or licences to run certain fund-raising events and for exemption from business rates. Local authorities sometimes act as a charity trustee or as a custodian trustee and they sometimes have powers to appoint charity trustees.

LOCAL AUTHORITY AS TRUSTEE

81.3 Local authorities can hold or accept gifts of land or other property for the benefit of people living in the whole of, or part of, their area (*Local Government Act 1972, s 139*) although they cannot be the trustee of an ecclesiastical charity or a charity for the relief of poverty. Having the local authority as trustee has the advantage over a trustee body made up of a group of individuals in that, as a body corporate, it has perpetual succession so there is no need for legal expense vesting property each time there is a change of trustees. More importantly, it has the advantage that the local authority may be willing to subsidise the charitable work if it can see that it is of benefit to the local community. It may do this through grants, or by providing premises or professional services free of charge.

81.4 However, there are also disadvantages in having a local authority as trustee. For example, the local authority may not appreciate that it cannot deal with charitable property in the same way that it would its own corporate property, and, as a result, may breach the charitable trusts. Conflicts of interest can arise between a local authority's responsibilities to its council tax and business rate payers and its duty, as charity trustee, to act in the best interests of the charity's beneficiaries. The management of the charitable activities may not be given the same priority by the local authority that it would receive if managed by a group of trustees focused solely on the charity. Finally, if the local authority is restructured or reorganised a successor authority may not be aware that certain property is held on trust and is not part of the local authority's corporate property.

81.5 When the Charity Commission considers a proposal for a local authority to be appointed as trustee it will only consent if it is sure that the proposal is the best arrangement that could be made after taking into account the possibility of conflicts of interest and the need to safeguard both the charity's property and the beneficiaries' interests.

81.6 When dealing with a charity where the local authority is trustee the Commission will sometimes suggest that other arrangements might be more appropriate. For example, they might suggest that the local authority stands down as trustee and is replaced by a new, independent group of individuals. If the local authority wishes to retain some influence then they might retain the right to appoint some of the trustees. However, trustees appointed by local authorities must act in the best interests of the charity's beneficiaries even when this is in conflict with the interests of the local authority that appointed them.

81.7   In some instances a charity's governing document gives a local authority the power to appoint some or all of the trustees. Trustees appointed by a local authority have exactly the same responsibilities and duties as other trustees, i.e. they must act in the best interests of the charity, even if this conflicts with the best interests of the local authority that appointed them.

81.8   *Section 79* of the *Charities Act 1993* gives some local authorities the power to appoint trustees of parochial charities that are not ecclesiastical charities and that were founded more than 40 years ago. Where this is the case appointments are usually for a period of four years.

LOCAL AUTHORITY AS CUSTODIAN TRUSTEE

81.9   Under *s 139* of the *Local Government Act 1972* local authorities can act as custodian trustee for unincorporated charities that are for the benefit of people in the local authority's area, apart from ecclesiastical charities or a local charity for the relief of poverty. This saves the charity from the expense of transferring title to property every time there is a change of trustee. The scope for a conflict of interest between the charity and the local authority is less when the local authority acts as the custodian trustee, rather than as trustee, because custodian trustees take no part in the management of the charity.

PROPERTY

81.10   There is limited scope for some charities to transfer property to local authorities, with the consent of both the Charity Commission and the authority concerned. The property in question must not belong to an ecclesiastical charity, and must comprise either a public recreation ground or allotments, or be held for other charitable purposes connected with a parish or community council. A local authority also has powers to create enforceable bye-laws for recreation grounds of which it is a trustee or custodian trustee, or to which it has given money, or supplied goods or services such as grass cutting. This can be very helpful to a charity, since they can allow fines to be imposed on people who misuse the recreation ground, or allow officials of the local authority or the police to remove anyone disregarding the bye-laws.

RATES

81.11   Charities are entitled to rate relief of 80% on non-domestic rates charged on properties if:

- the property is occupied by a charity and used wholly or mainly for charitable purposes; or

- the property is used wholly or mainly for selling goods donated to the charity and the net proceeds are spent on charitable purposes.

81.12   Local authorities have power to extend rate relief further, even up to 100%. If the property is unoccupied and the next envisaged use will be for wholly or mainly charitable purposes, only 10% of the standard rate is charged. There is no relief for charities, however, from water and sewerage charges.

81.13   Non-domestic property exempt from local rating includes agricultural land and buildings, places of religious worship including church halls, and property used for people with disabilities.

FUND-RAISING

81.14   When *s 48* of the *Charities Act 2006* comes into force (this is likely to be in 2009) charities holding street collections and door-to-door collections will need a permit from the local authority in which the collection is to be held and will need to give the local authority a copy of its public collections certificate, which will be issued by the Charity Commission. In the meantime most house-to-house collections, street collections and some lotteries will need a permit or licence from the local authority. House-to-house collections include collections in offices, factories and pubs. Similarly, street collections include collections in any public place. A licence will be needed for a house-to-house collection and many local authorities have regulations covering street collections. For more detail see CHAPTER 82 and CHAPTER 95.

CONTRACTING

81.15   With the growth of the contract culture, charities increasingly find themselves entering into relationships with local authorities under a variety of documentation variously termed 'grants', 'service level agreements', 'contracts' and so on. Contracts and service agreements are described in CHAPTER 29.

81.16   Before seeking funding, whether by contract or by grant, from a local authority, a charity should establish how the authority in question approaches the matter. Local authorities have widely differing structures to deal with charities, and also will have widely varying priorities as to the services which they feel they should provide or purchase. Local authorities provide services which fall into defined categories, but they also have powers under the *Local Government Act 1972, s 137* to give limited grants to charities where that will be of benefit to the local population.

81.17   The variety of services that a local authority may provide is so extensive as to permit most charities to be able to find at least one category within which it can validly seek to obtain funds either under grant or contract. For instance, local authorities are variously required to provide accommodation for a wide range of people in need and to provide childcare services. They can enjoin charities in an even wider range of activities including historic building conservation, the provision of country parks, contributing towards the costs of maintaining recreational amenities such as swimming pools and playing fields, and the provision of premises for the arts. This great diversity of activity indicates that a charity ought at least to explore the potential for either obtaining assistance from the local authority, or for assessing its own plans in the light of the authority's own priorities. It may be that resources have already been committed to the same issue elsewhere, or that a changed approach by the charity to the same problem could better complement existing provision.

COMPACTS

81.18   Compacts are designed to help build the partnership between central and local government and the voluntary sector. They set out a code for the relations between central and local government and voluntary organisations and can help resolve potential conflicts between voluntary organisations and local councils or government departments and agencies.

81.19   The Compact with central government sets out undertakings by both government and the voluntary sector.

For the government, these undertakings cover four areas:

● Independence — recognising the independence of the voluntary sector.

● Funding — paying attention to the need for strategic funding and developing a code of good practice (now published) on government funding of the voluntary sector.

● Policy development and consultation — taking account of effects of new policies on the voluntary sector; consulting the sector on issues that are likely to affect it; taking account of those parts of the sector that represent women, minority groups and socially excluded people; and developing a code of good practice on consultation (now published).

● Better government — promoting effective working relationships between government and the sector; reviewing the operation of the Compact; and promoting the adoption of the Compact by other public bodies.

The voluntary sector undertakings cover three areas:

● Funding and accountability — maintaining high standards in funding and accountability, respecting and being accountable to the law, and developing quality standards.

● Policy development and consultation — ensuring that service users, volunteers, members and supporters are informed and consulted about activities and policy positions.

● Good practice — promoting effective working relationships with government; involving users in activities and services; promoting best practice and equality of opportunity.

Codes of practice

81.20   In addition to the basic principles of the Compact, the voluntary sector set up working parties with representation from Government Departments, and developed Codes of Good Practice on the following issues:

● Funding and procurement

● Consultation and policy appraisal

● Black and minority ethnic groups

● Volunteering

● Community groups.

81.21   Local Authorities

Local Compacts

81.21   Most voluntary sector organisations are based at a local level. Much of their funding comes from local authorities and the relationship can sometimes be problematic, drawing in local politicians and MPs. Almost all of England is now covered by local compacts designed to help partnership working between local government, local public bodies and local voluntary and community organisations. Local Compacts are living documents that inform the whole range of joint working at a local level, from police working with the community sector to tackle antisocial behaviour to social services improving their contracting with social care organisations. Local compacts mirror the national Compact and have been drawn up in consultation between the voluntary sector at a local level and local councils and other local public bodies. They do not set out a prescriptive course of action but are designed to help local communities in drawing up effective agreements based on local circumstances.

81.22   More information about the Compacts and the Codes of Good Practice is presented in Chapter 27 and is available from *www.thecompact.org.uk*.

BEST VALUE

81.23   From 1 April 2000 all local authorities were required under the *Local Government Act 1999* to seek continuous improvement to services and functions through regular reviews of their economy, efficiency and effectiveness. Services provided by charities under contracts or service level agreements are subject to review. The reviews use performance indicators and if charities considering entering into contracts with local authorities have not already developed indicators for their own internal use, they may find it advantageous to do so. Otherwise they may find that their services are assessed exclusively by indicators developed by the local authority. Further information about best value performance indicators is available from *www.communities.gov.uk*.

LOCAL AUTHORITY CONTROLLED OR INFLUENCED COMPANIES

81.24   A local authority may control a company in much the same way as any entity may do so, that is by shareholding or controlling the composition of board of directors. Local authority controlled (or influenced) companies have additional requirements relating to disclosure and financing arrangements. This situation may become relevant to a charity particularly where the local authority has the power to appoint, or control the appointment of, trustees.

LOCAL AUTHORITIES' POWERS IN RELATION TO LOCAL CHARITIES

81.25   *Section 76* of the *Charities Act 1993* permits local authorities to maintain an index of local charities, which is open to public inspection. *Section 77* empowers local authorities to review the working of any group of local charities with the same or similar purposes within its council's area and to make recommendations to the Charity Commission. This review must be with the individual charity trustees' approval, and cannot extend to ecclesiastical charities. Charity trustees are specifically permitted to co-operate in such procedures under *s 78*. One of the purposes of these sections is to aid the efficiency of the sector by facilitating the merger of similar organisations, or the closure of dormant ones.

FURTHER INFORMATION

81.26   CC29 'Charities and Local Authorities'. Charity Commission, 2001.

82 Lotteries

82.1 Charity lotteries can be a cost-effective way of fund raising for many charities. They also provide charities with a way to reach those who would not normally donate money to charities. There are 660 society lotteries registered with the Gambling Commission, the majority of which are run by charities or sports clubs. In 2005/06 the proceeds from society lotteries amounted to £138.7m according to statistics published by the Gambling Commission.

82.2 Charities running raffles, tombolas, lotteries, 100 clubs, etc often do not see themselves as part of the gambling industry and assume that gambling regulation does not apply to them. However, these activities are a form of gambling and those involved in running them cannot be exempt from the obligations of social responsibility applicable to all gambling operators. The *Lotteries and Amusements Act 1976*, as amended by the *National Lottery Etc Act 1993*, has been the main piece of legislation regulating lotteries conducted in Great Britain for the last thirty years. It was repealed by the *Gambling Act 2005* when it came into force on 1 September 2007.

82.3 The *Gambling Act 2005* introduces a new regulator, the Gambling Commission, for all gambling except the National Lottery and spread betting. It also introduces a new licensing regime for society lotteries and a registration system for small society lotteries. The *Gambling Act 2005* creates two broad classes of lottery:

- Large society lotteries which will be licensed by the Gambling Commission; and

- Exempt lotteries, including small society lotteries, which will be registered with licensing authorities (local authorities).

82.4 The *Gambling Act 2005* relaxes previous legislation regulating lotteries. In particular it:

- Relaxes the limits on the percentage of the proceeds that can be spent on prizes or expenses;

- Allows rollovers of the prize fund from one lottery to another;

- Removes the maximum price for a lottery ticket (£2 before 1 September 2007).

- Allows for the sale of tickets by an automated process.

WHAT CONSTITUTES A LOTTERY?

82.5 *Section 14* of the *Gambling Act 2005* introduced the first statutory definition of a lottery. An arrangement is defined as a simple lottery if:

- Persons are required to pay in order to participate in the arrangement;

- In the course of the arrangement one or more prizes are allocated to one or more members of a class; and

- The prizes are allocated by a process which relies wholly on chance.

82.6 An arrangement is defined as a complex lottery if:

- Persons are required to pay in order to participate in the arrangement;
- In the course of the arrangement one or more prizes are allocated to one or more members of a class;
- The prizes are allocated by a series of processes; and
- The first of those processes relies wholly on chance.

TYPES OF LOTTERY

82.7   There are several types of public lotteries in Great Britain:

- **Society lotteries** are promoted for the benefit of a non-commercial society. A society is non-commercial if it is established and conducted:

    (a)   for charitable purposes;

    (b)   for the purpose of enabling participation in, or support of, sport, athletics or a cultural activity;

    (c)   any other non-commercial purpose other than that of private gain.

- **Exempt lotteries,** which include:

    — Incidental, non-commercial lotteries, which are often held at charity fundraising events, such as fêtes, balls or jumble sales;

    — private society lotteries, in which only members of the society and those on its premises can participate;

    — work lotteries, in which only people who work together on the same premises can participate;

    — residents' lotteries, in which only those living at the same premises can participate;

    — customer lotteries, in which only customers at the business premises can participate.

- **Local authority lotteries**: these lotteries are run by and for local authorities and are regulated by the Gambling Commission.

- **The National Lottery,** which is regulated by the National Lottery Commission (see **Chapter 85**).

SOCIETY LOTTERIES

82.8   Society lotteries are potentially large income generators for charities. They are allowed to sell tickets up to the value of £2m for a single lottery or an aggregate value of £10m in a calendar year. The Charity Commission has no objection to charities running society lotteries provided that the trustees adopt a prudent approach and that the running of the lottery does not become an end in itself.

82.9   Society lotteries include prize draws run by large organisations such as the National Trust, and lotteries similar to the National Lottery, which many hospice charities run. If the total proceeds (ticket sales) exceed £20,000 or, if when added to the proceeds of tickets sold in the charity's lotteries that have already taken place in the same calendar year, they exceed £250,000 the lottery will be a 'large lottery' and it may only be run under an operating licence issued by the Gambling Commission. The licence will set out specific conditions and codes of practice that the licence holder must comply with.

82.10   If a society promotes a lottery which is a large lottery, then every subsequent lottery it holds in that year and in the following three years will be a large lottery and will require the society to hold a lottery operating licence issued by the Gambling Commission.

82.11   If a society promotes a lottery that allows players to participate by means of remote communication (internet, telephone, etc) it is required to hold a remote lottery operating licence, regardless of whether it is required to hold a non-remote lottery operating licence.

82.12   Small society lotteries are those in which the proceeds are less than £20,000, or where the total proceeds from all lotteries run by the society in the year are less than £250,000. Small society lotteries may operate without a Gambling Commission licence, provided that they register with their local authority. The promoting society must be registered for the whole of the period during which the lottery is promoted with a local authority in England and Wales, or licensing board in Scotland.

82.13   Societies running small lotteries under registration with a local authority and who sell tickets using remote means of communication are not required to hold a remote gambling licence issued by the Gambling Commission.

OPERATING LICENCES

82.14   Under the *Gambling Act 2005*, any operator promoting a lottery, or managing a society lottery on behalf of a charity, will be required to hold an operating licence unless they qualify under a general exemption such as that for small society lotteries. An operating licence must specify:

- The person to whom it is issued;
- The period during which it is to have effect;
- Any condition(s) attached by the Gambling Commission.

82.15   A lottery operating licence may only be issued to:

- A non-commercial society (such as a charity);
- A local authority; or
- A person proposing to act as an external lottery manager on behalf of a non-commercial society or a local authority.

82.16   A lottery operating licence may authorise:

- Promotion generally or only specified promoting activities;
- The promotion of lotteries generally or only the promotion of lotteries of a specified kind or in specified circumstances;
- Action as an external lottery manager (in which case it is known as a 'lottery manager's operating licence'.

82.17   A lottery operating licence allows charities to send lottery tickets by post.

PERSONAL MANAGEMENT LICENCES

82.18   The effect of *ss 80(1)* and *129(1)* of the *Gambling Act 2005* is that any operating licence holder, other than a small-scale operator, must have at least one personal management licence (PML) holder if they have more than three people in 'qualifying positions'. A qualifying position is one which is held by a person who, by the terms of his or her appointment, has primary responsibility for certain functions. In the context of a society licensed to run lotteries the relevant functions are:

● the management of the lottery;

● the management of the financial affairs of the society;

● ensuring that the society's lottery operations comply with the *Gambling Act 2005*, any relevant regulations and the relevant parts of the Commission's Licence Conditions and Codes of Practice;

● the marketing/promotion of the lottery;

● the management of the IT system used for the lottery. (Where a society uses an 'off the shelf' IT system (e.g. Combase or Starvale) which does not allow anyone in the society to gain access to alter its operation, then people in jobs such as managing data input do not count under this category).

82.19   The relevant licence condition provides that the PML holder must be the person who has overall management responsibility for running the lottery. If the society is a charitable company, the PML holder must be one of the company's directors (i.e. one of the directors registered as such at Companies House and not just a staff member who uses the title of director). If the society is an unincorporated charitable association, the PML holder must be an officer of the association such as a trustee, chairman, secretary, treasurer, or chief executive. If there is a change in the identity of the person who meets these criteria, the new person will need to apply for a PML as soon as is reasonably practicable.

82.20   The Commission has power to require licensees who are not small-scale operators to have more than one person holding a PML. In most sectors of the gambling industry the Commission will be doing this by way of licence condition. However, the licence condition on lottery operating licences issued to non-commercial societies, such as charities, only requires one PML holder.

82,21   A small-scale operator is not required to have a PML holder. A small-scale operator is defined in the *Gambling Act 2005 (Definition of Small-scale Operator) Regulations 2006*. In summary, a society will be a small-scale operator if:

● its organisation has no more than three 'qualifying positions'; and

● each qualifying position is occupied by a qualified person.

82.22   Once a society acquires a fourth person occupying a qualifying position it will cease to be a small-scale operator and the appropriate person within the society (as to which see above) will need to apply for a PML.

EXTERNAL LOTTERY MANAGERS

82.23   Society lotteries can be such large-scale operations that licensed or registered societies may employ an external lottery manager (ELM) to run all or part of its lottery. An ELM is defined in *s 257* of the *Gambling Act 2005* as someone who makes arrangements for a lottery on behalf of a society of which he is not a member, an officer, or an employee. All ELMs must hold a lottery managers' operating licence issued by the Gambling Commission before they can manage a licensed society lottery or a society lottery registered with a local authority. It is the responsibility of the society to check before employing an ELM that they hold a lottery managers' operating licence. A list of those holding a lottery managers' operating licence is available on the Gambling Commission's website.

82.24   Employing an ELM does not absolve a society from its responsibility for ensuring that its lotteries are carried out lawfully and in compliance with all licensing conditions and codes of practice.

82.25   ELMs are required to hold a PML for a range of directors and senior managers. ELMs are also required to hold a remote gambling licence if they intend to sell lottery tickets through remote communications.

82.26   External Lottery Managers holding the Gambling Commission's certificate are required to submit annual audited accounts to the Commission for inspection.

PROMOTING A LOTTERY

82.27   The trustees of a charity running a society lottery must nominate, in writing, one of their members (in charitable companies this means a member in terms of company law) to act as promoter. If a charity uses an ELM, both the charity and the ELM will be regarded as the promoters. *Section 252* of the *Gambling Act 2005* states that a person promotes a lottery if he makes or participates in making the arrangements for a lottery including:

- making arrangements for the printing of tickets;

- making arrangements for the printing of promotional material;

- making arrangements for the distribution or publication of promotional material;

- possessing promotional material with a view to its publication or distribution;

- making other arrangements to advertise a lottery;

- inviting a person to participate in a lottery;

- selling or suppling, or offers to sell or supply, a lottery ticket;

- possessing a lottery ticket with a view to its sale or supply;

- doing, or offer to do, anything by virtue of which a person becomes a member of a class among whom prizes in a lottery are to be allocated;

- using premises for the purpose of allocating prizes or for another purpose connected with the administration of a lottery.

82.28   A company that provides services such as printing or distributing lottery tickets is not considered to be a promoter.

RESTRICTIONS ON PROCEEDS, EXPENSES AND PRIZES

82.29   The following rules apply:

- The total of expenses and prizes must not exceed 80% of the proceeds, ensuring that at least 20% of the proceeds are available to the charity;

- The maximum value of tickets that can be sold in a single large lottery is £2m;

- The maximum aggregate value of lottery tickets that can be sold in a calendar year is £10m;

- The maximum prize in a single lottery is £25,000 in the case of a small lottery, and £25,000 or 10% of the total value of tickets sold, whichever is greater (i.e. a maximum of £200,000 if all tickets are sold) in the case of a large society lottery;

- Rollovers are permitted provided the maximum single prize limit is not breached;

- There is no maximum price that can be charged for a lottery ticket;

- The price of every ticket in the lottery must be the same, i.e. there can be no discounts for buying several tickets, and the cost of purchased tickets must be paid to the society before entry into the draw is allowed;

- No lottery may operate in such a way that a player can win a prize greater than the statutory prize limit of £200,000;

- No lottery may be linked to any other lottery in such a way that a person who wins a prize in one also wins a prize in another unless the aggregate of those prizes is less than or equal to the statutory prize limit of £200,000;

- Where separate lotteries have a feature that allows a player to win a larger prize than the statutory maximum of £200,000 by selecting the same numbers in different lotteries and these lotteries are decided by the same draw, no advertisement or other marketing of the lottery may refer to this.

TICKET INFORMATION

82.30   All tickets in a society lottery licensed by the Gambling Commission or registered with a local authority must state:

- the name of the society on whose behalf the lottery is being promoted;

- the name and address of the promoter(s);

- the price of the ticket;

- the date of the draw, or the means by which the date can be determined;

- the fact, where that is the case, that the society is registered with the Gambling Commission.

82.31 Lotteries

82.31   Tickets which are issued through a form of remote communication or any other electronic means must specify this information to the purchaser of the ticket and ensure that the message can be either retained or printed.

SALE OF TICKETS

82.32   Tickets in society lotteries promoted under licence from the Gambling Commission must not be sold to any person under the age of 16. Tickets must not be sold in any street, tickets may be sold by a person in a kiosk or from door-to-door, though regulations concerning door to door collections may apply (see Chapter 52).

82.33   Societies licensed by the Commission should consider adopting one or more of the following measures to limit the risk of fraud when sending unsolicited mailings of lottery tickets:

- Prohibit mailings to non-members of the promoting society;

- Limit the value of tickets sent to any one address that is not that of a member of the promoting society to £20;

- Maintain records of tickets distributed but not returned, including the serial numbers.

RECORDS

82.34   For society lotteries promoted under licence from the Gambling Commission accounting records must be retained for a minimum of three years from the date of the lottery to which they relate. The records must be available for inspection by the Commission on request. The accounts should show the results of the society's activities on an accruals basis. Records must contain, in respect of each lottery, details of:

- Total proceeds;

- Expenses;

- The number of sold and unsold tickets.

82.35   It is advisable for societies to keep records of:

- Details of tickets ordered and received from the printers;

- Details of all tickets issued to each point of sale, details of those sold, those returned unsold and those not returned;

- Details of all expenses with relevant invoices, including (*a*) those met directly from the proceeds; (*b*) those met by the charity; and (*c*) those met by donations from a third party;

- Details of all prizes together with relevant invoices;

- Details of winners (not including 'instant' winners) and winning tickets;

- Details of the distribution of proceeds and receipts from beneficiaries where relevant;

- Where agents are employed, details of their remuneration and the number of tickets sold and returned.

82.36   Where a society promotes a number of separate lotteries (e.g. one a week or one a month), periodic expenses, such as insurance, rent and rates, should be apportioned between the lotteries and depreciation on start-up and capital costs should be accounted for.

82.37   Unsold tickets may be destroyed after completion of the lottery and the submission of the necessary return to the Commission.

Lottery Returns

82.38   Every society licensed by the Gambling Commission must submit a Lottery Return (form GCL12) to the Commission within three months of the date of the draw showing, for each lottery, details of the total proceeds, any interest earned on the proceeds, the amount spent on expenses and prizes, and the amount applied directly to the society's purpose. The Return must be verified by a PML holder, or a qualified person in the case of a small-scale operator, or the person named on the lottery tickets as the promoter. This applies irrespective of whether the society employs the services of an ELM and whether or not the ELM prepares and/or submits the forms to the Commission.

82.39   Where Value Added Tax (VAT) is payable on an individual item of expenditure or on a prize, it should be included in the amount shown for that item on form GCL12, unless it is reclaimable. Where VAT is reclaimable it should be shown in brackets beside the item in question and not included in the total expenses or prizes.

82.40   If the duration of a lottery exceeds 15 months the Commission requires the society to complete an interim return on form GCL12A every 12 months after the first ticket is placed on sale.

82.41   Every society registered with the local authority to run small society lotteries must submit a statement certified by two other members of the society, appointed by the Board for that purpose, within three months of the date of the draw containing the following information:

- the date on which tickets were available for sale or supply;
- the total proceeds of the lottery;
- the amounts deducted by the promoters to provide prizes, including rollovers;
- the amounts deducted by the promoters in respect of the costs of organising the lottery;
- the amount applied directly to the society's purposes (this should be at least 20% of the gross proceeds);
- whether any expenses incurred in running the lottery were not paid for out of the proceeds, and, if so, the amount of these expenses and the sources from which they were paid.

EXEMPT LOTTERIES

Incidental non-commercial lotteries

82.42   An incidental non-commercial lottery is one that is incidental to a non-commercial event. Examples include raffles, tombolas, and 'guess the name of the teddy', lotteries held at bazaars, sales of work, fêtes, dinner dances, sporting or athletic events or other entertainment of a similar character, whether limited to one day or extending over two or more days. They do not have to be licensed by the Gambling Commission but should be registered with a local authority.

82.43   The *Gambling Act 2005* specifies that:

- The promoters may not deduct more than an amount prescribed by the Secretary of State (Scottish Minister) from the proceeds in respect of expenses, such as tickets, hiring equipment, etc. The amount prescribed is currently £250, though this is likely to increase to £500;

- No more than £250 of the proceeds can be spent on prizes, though this is likely to increase to £500. There are no restrictions on the value of donated prizes;

- The lottery cannot involve a rollover of prizes from one lottery to another;

- All tickets must be sold at the location during the event and the result must be declared during the event.

Private lotteries

82.44   There are three types of private lotteries that qualify as exempt lotteries: private lotteries, work lotteries and residential lotteries.

- Private lotteries are those where the sale of tickets is restricted to people who belong to the same membership organisation or club established for purposes not connected with gambling, betting or lotteries, such as a sports club or art appreciation society. They can only be promoted by members of the club or society and tickets can only be sold to other members or to people on premises used for the activities of the club. The proceeds must go to the club for the purpose for which it is established.

- Work lotteries must be promoted by a person who works on the premises and tickets can only be sold to other people who work at the same premises. They must be run on a not-for-profit basis. All the proceeds must be spent on prizes or any reasonable expenses incurred in running the lottery.

- Residential lotteries must be promoted by someone who lives on the premises and tickets can only be sold to other people living at the same premises, e.g. a nurses' home or care home. They must be run on a not-for-profit basis and all the proceeds must be spent on prizes or any reasonable expenses incurred in running the lottery.

82.45   '100 Clubs', where up to 100 people contribute usually £1 a week to a kitty in the hope that their name will be drawn out and they will win the kitty, will usually qualify as private lotteries, work lotteries or residential lotteries depending on the nature of the participating group.

82.46   Private lotteries must comply with the following:

- Private society, work or residents lotteries can be advertised only at the society's premises, or the work premises, or the relevant residence;

- Tickets in private lotteries may be sold or supplied only by, or on behalf of, the promoter;

- Tickets and the rights they represent are non-transferable;

- Each ticket must state the name and address of the promoter of the lottery, the persons to whom the promoter can sell or supply tickets, and the fact that they are non-transferable;

- Private lotteries cannot be held on vessels;

- The price paid for each tickets must be the same, i.e. 25p each or 5 for £1 type arrangements are not permitted;

- The price must be shown on each ticket and must be paid to the promoter of the lottery before any person is given a ticket.

Customer lotteries

82.47　A customer lottery is a lottery run by the occupiers of business premises who sell tickets only to customers present on their premises. The *Gambling Act 2005* requires customer lotteries to meet the following conditions:

- Customer lotteries must be run on a non-profit making basis;

- Tickets can only be sold or supplied by, or on behalf of, the promoter;

- The lottery must not be advertised except at the business premises;

- Another customer lottery cannot take place within seven days on the same premises;

- Tickets and the rights they represent are non-transferable;

- No ticket may result in the winner receiving a prize worth more than £50;

- No rollovers of prizes are permitted;

- Each ticket must state the name and address of the promoter of the lottery, the persons to whom the promoter can sell or supply tickets, and the fact that they are non-transferable.

RAPID DRAW/ONLINE LOTTERIES

82.48　Some charities are moving their raffles and lotteries online. The *Lotteries and Amusements Act 1976* prohibited the sale of lottery tickets solely by means of a machine. However, some society lotteries lawfully run online and mobile phone lotteries by introducing an element of human intervention at the point of sale. Under the *Gambling Act 2005* remote gambling, including online, mobile phone, and interactive TV gambling, will be lawful for the first time. Those wishing to operate remote gambling, including lotteries, will be required to hold a licence issued by the Gambling Commission.

PRIZES

82.49　Participators have to pay in order to have a chance of winning a lottery prize. The payment does not have to be specifically for the chance to enter the draw. It could be included in the price of an admission ticket for an event or the price of a programme.

82.50 Lotteries

82.50   Lottery prizes must be of some value. Many charities appeal for donated prizes such as holidays, flights, cars, restaurant meals, theatre tickets, electrical equipment, toys or bottles of alcoholic drink. Charities are permitted to offer liquor prizes in lotteries held at incidental non-commercial lotteries without the need to obtain a liquor licence. Donated prizes do not need specific accounting as they are treated as donated assets whose value is accounted for upon realisation, i.e. when they are sold or won. Any prize won in a society lottery and donated back to the society by the legal owner of the winning ticket ought to be shown in the accounts as a donation.

82.51   Prizes must be distributed solely according to chance. If any skill, however slight, is required the distribution will be a competition, not a lottery. However, where a promotion involves a skill, but there are likely to be a number of people giving the correct answers and the ultimate winner is selected by drawing one of the correct entries from a hat, this will be a lottery. A competition to guess the correct number of buttons in a jar was held to involve skill and was therefore a prize competition and not a lottery (*R v Jamieson* (*1884*) *7 OR 149*). However, competitions in which the correct answer is determined by the entrants themselves, such as placing different brands of dog food in order of merit, are lotteries (*Hobbs v Ward* (*1929*) *45 TLR 373*).

TRADING SUBSIDIARIES

82.52   Some charities prefer to operate large-scale lotteries through their trading subsidiaries to minimise risk to the charity and avoid tax. At first sight this would appear to be excluded by the *Gambling Act 2005* as the charity's trading company will be established for commercial purposes. However, the Gambling Commission permits a charity's trading company to register with the Gambling Commission, provided that the trading company covenants all its taxable profits to the charity.

82.53   Even if the lottery is run by the charity no tax is payable because an amendment to the *Finance Act 1995* resulted in *ICTA 1988, s 505(1)(f)* exempting charities from tax on society lotteries provided the income is applied solely for the charity's charitable purpose.

FURTHER INFORMATION

82.54   The Gambling Commission
Victoria Square House
Victoria Square
Birmingham B2 4BP
Tel: 0121 230 6666
Fax: 0121 233 1096
info@gamblingcommission.gov.uk
www.gamblingcommission.gov.uk

The Lotteries Council
www.lotteriescouncil.org.uk

The Hospice Lotteries Association
Tel: 01442 891459

www.hospicelotteries.org.uk

Charities that wish to sell tickets in Northern Ireland should contact:
Social Policy Unit
Department for Social Development
James House
2–4 Cromac Avenue
Gasworks Business Park
Belfast
BT7 2JA
Tel: 028 9081 9142

83 Memorandum and Articles of Association

83.1 The memorandum and articles of association (often referred to as the 'mem and arts') are the governing documents of a limited company, which need to be filed with the Registrar of Companies before any company can be issued with a certificate of incorporation. Currently the memorandum sets out the organisation's purpose and powers and the articles its internal rules and procedures. Sections of the memorandum are known as 'clauses', sections of the articles are known as 'articles'.

MEMORANDUM

83.2 The memorandum of association is the document that formally records that one or more legal persons (i.e. individuals or limited companies themselves) have formed the company. For a charitable company, the memorandum sets out:

- the charity's name;

- the address of its registered office;

- the charitable objects;

- the powers of the trustees to pursue the objects;

- the beneficiary group;

- the names of the members; and

- the size of their guarantee or share holding.

[*Companies Act 1985, s 35*].

83.3 The objects of a charitable company are usually stated in broad terms, i.e. 'to relieve poverty, distress and suffering amongst refugees', though they are often supplemented by a more detailed list of the types of activities or services the charity will provide to achieve its objects, e.g. 'by the provision of a helpline'. This gives a charity the flexibility to develop its work in the future without the need to get the Charity Commission's consent to broaden the objects, as would be the case if they were defined more precisely.

83.4 The objects of a charitable company must be charitable within the law. Powers will be restricted to prevent transfers of funds to members or to third parties except in the pursuit of the charity's objects or to organisations bound by similar restrictions.

83.5 A company is limited to carrying out those activities which fall within its objects, although transactions undertaken outside them cannot be declared void in order to avoid contractual liability. Although directors of commercial companies can subsequently ratify an *ultra vires* transaction, directors of charitable companies do not have the same power to ratify such transactions after the event. A commercial company's object can be all-embracing, e.g. 'to carry on business as a general commercial company'. Charitable companies cannot use such a phrase, however, as it would not be a charitable object.

83.6 The objects of a company can be changed by special resolution, though in the case of a charitable company registered in England and Wales, Charity

Commission consent will be required. Changing the objects will be necessary if they have become too restrictive or out of date.

ARTICLES

83.7   The articles of association give the rules and regulations that govern the internal proceedings of a company. They usually include:

- the membership of the company;

- details of directors/trustees including procedures for election, length of term that can be served, restrictions on eligibility, powers, expenses, etc.;

- procedures for calling and holding meetings, the annual general meeting and extraordinary general meetings;

- voting procedures;

- financial procedures;

- procedures for the appointment of auditors;

- use of the Seal;

- winding-up procedures.

83.8   Many charitable companies' articles contain potentially restrictive clauses that serve no useful purpose. For example, there may be an article requiring the annual accounts to be audited, even though the charity is small and an audit would not be mandatory if this article had not been included. Trustees should periodically review their memorandum and articles of association to identify any such clauses and seek to amend or delete them and to ensure that they are complying with their governing document.

83.9   In addition companies limited by share will include rules concerning the share capital and membership. In the case of a company limited guarantee this section will be much reduced and will cover the terms and rights of members.

83.10   In practice many companies do not create their own rules, but follow models published with the *Companies Act 1985* known as Tables A to F. Table A is the most commonly adopted format, being applicable to private companies limited by shares as many subsidiary trading companies are constituted. Table C relates to companies limited by guarantee. The Charity Commission and the Charity Law Association have published model memorandum and articles of association for charitable companies. There is less of a need for tailored models for subsidiary trading companies as they have even more standard formats. Companies can either be formed from scratch or bought 'off the shelf', already incorporated from incorporation agents. If this is the case the memorandum and articles of association will need to be reviewed and a number of changes will usually need to be made, not least the company name.

83.11   The memorandum and articles of association can be altered, but only by a formal process of a general meeting of the members and the passing of a special resolution. The meeting will usually require 21 days' notice, setting out the proposal. It is possible to waive this notice period if 90–95% of the membership so agree. The exact percentage will depend on whether the company has made the relevant elective resolution. It is also possible for a special resolution to be passed not by an actual meeting, but by the circulation of the resolution in writing, and its signature by or on behalf of all members. [*Companies Act 1985, s 381*]. As mentioned above, however, certain changes including alterations to the charity's objects or powers, or to any clause relating to how the charity's income or property is to be used, will need the consent of the Charity Commission.

COMPANIES ACT 2006

83.12 Some of the provisions of the *Companies Act 2006* came into force in January 2007, but many of the changes will not be implemented until 2008 or even 2009 because of the size and complexity of the new legislation. The Act should, however, simplify the administration of charitable companies limited by guarantee and reduce costs.

83.13 Under the *Companies Act 2006* the memorandum will serve a more limited purpose. It will evidence the intention of the subscribers to the memorandum to form a company and to become members of that company on formation. The objects will be included in the articles. The memorandum of a company formed under the *Companies Act 2006* will therefore look very different from that of a company registered under the 1985 Act. It will not be possible to amend or update the memorandum of a company formed under the *Companies Act 2006*, though it will be possible to amend the articles.

83.14 Under *s 28* of the *Companies Act 2006* provisions in the memoranda of existing companies will be treated as provisions in the articles if they are of a type that will not be in the memoranda of companies formed under the 2006 Act. Existing companies will therefore not need to amend their articles to reflect these changes, but may do so if they wish. They will, however, be able to alter or update provisions that are now set out in their memoranda by amending their articles.

83.15 Amending the memorandum and articles of association of an existing charitable company may become easier under the *Companies Act 2006*. The notice period for holding a general meeting reduces from 21 days to 14 days, though it is not yet certain whether or not provisions relating to notice periods contained within the existing articles will continue to apply. The consent of only 90% of members would be needed to hold a general meeting at short notice. Under the *Companies Act 2006* written ordinary resolutions will only require a simple majority of members to pass them (i.e. 50% +1) and written special resolutions will only require a 75% majority. Notice for general meetings can now be given in electronic form, as well as in hard copy, or by means of a website, although in this case members must be notified that the notice is on the website.

83.16 Trustees of charitable companies should consider amending their memorandum and articles of association if they contain restrictions that prevent them from taking advantage of the new provisions in the *Companies Act 2006*. In the majority of instances Charity Commission consent will not be required, though it will still be required for amendments to:

- the objects of the charity;

- provisions dealing with what happens to property on the dissolution of the company;

- provisions where the amendment would authorise any benefit to the directors or members, or to people connected to them.

84 Mergers

REASONS FOR MERGERS

84.1 Mergers used only to be associated with the commercial sector but the growing number of registered charities chasing reduced funding has meant that charities, both large and small, are now considering merger to increase their effectiveness or their chances of survival. Merging can do away with the duplication of effort that charities are sometimes criticised for, providing economies of scale and greater efficiency. *Sections 74* and *75* of the *Charities Act 1993* introduced powers for small charities that facilitate and encourage merger and *s 44* of the *Charities Act 2006* included further provisions to remove obstacles to mergers.

84.2 The trustees of charities considering merger must always be satisfied that merger is in the best interest of their charity and its present and future beneficiaries. Merger may not always be a viable solution. There are complex legal issues and some charities may not have powers in their governing document permitting a merger. Even if merger is legally possible, in some cases having more than one charity working in the same field is regarded as advantageous and there are emotive and cultural reasons why a merger may not always be successful.

REGISTER OF MERGERS

84.3 The *Charities Act 2006* requires the Charity Commission to keep a public Register of Mergers holding details of charity mergers. The Act sets out what types of mergers can be recorded on the Register. Usually these will be where:

- One or more charities dissolve and pass their assets to another existing charity (i.e. a consolidation);

- Two or more charities dissolve and pass their assets to a newly created charity with compatible objects (often known as a true merger or an 'amalgamation');

- A unincorporated charity winds up and transfers its assets to a newly created charitable company (usually known as incorporation).

84.4 Registering a merger with the Charity Commission is voluntary, but compulsory if a charity wishes to use a vesting declaration. A vesting declaration means that any charity transferring assets only has to use one deed to cover the transfer of all its assets to the new merged charity, rather than separate transfers to cover the transfer of the various assets included in the merger. Charities that wish to register their mergers will have to give the Commission the following information:

- What has been transferred and the date(s) the transfer took place;

- Confirmation that appropriate arrangements have been made for meeting any liabilities of the charity that transferred its assets;

- Whether or not a vesting declaration has been made and, if so, certain details about it.

84.5   When a merger is registered it does away with the need to keep a charity that is essentially dissolving as a shell or dormant organisation, in order to ensure that gifts and legacies received after the charity has 'dissolved' are not lost. Gifts and legacies left to charities that have merged, and disappeared in the process, will automatically be transferred to the new successor charity.

IS MERGER LEGALLY POSSIBLE?

84.6   Whether or not a merger is legally possible is determined by a charity's legal structure, the powers in its governing document and its charitable objects.

Trusts

84.7   Modern charitable trusts will usually have the power to dissolve or transfer property to other charities or amalgamate with other charities. Problems can arise with older trusts that may not have the power to spend capital. The *Charities Act 2006* extends the circumstances in which unincorporated charities can spend permanent endowment as if it were income. They will be able to do this without needing the Commission's consent if they have annual income of £1,000 or less, or where the market value of the endowment fund in question is £10,000 or less. Should the trust have no power to amalgamate or dissolve, a Charity Commission Scheme will usually be required.

Unincorporated associations

84.8   Most modern unincorporated associations will have powers in their constitutions to dissolve the charity and transfer remaining assets to another charity. Certainly the Charity Commission model constitution provides powers for dissolution if it is 'necessary or desirable' and powers for the transfer of assets. Again, it is with older associations that assistance from the Charity Commission may be required.

Charitable companies

84.9   It is usually relatively straightforward for charitable companies to merge, as most memoranda of association will contain powers to merge with other charities with similar purposes.

COMPATIBLE OBJECTS

84.10   Whatever the legal structure, and even if a charity's governing document holds powers that enable a merger, it will only be possible if the two charities involved have compatible objects. It will be usual for the acquiring charity to have broader objects. If the objects are not compatible then an approach will need to be made to the Charity Commission.

84.11   For an unincorporated charity, the approach will be a for a *cy-près* application under *s 13(1)(c)* of the *Charities Act 1993* on the basis that the property of the merging charity could be used more effectively in conjunction with the property of the acquiring charity with similar purposes. For a charitable company the Charity Commission will need to give written consent for a Special Resolution amending the objects under *s 64(2)* of the *Charities Act 1993*. Again the Commission will only give consent in line with *cy-près* principles.

COMMON TRUSTEESHIP AND JOINT VENTURE AGREEMENTS

84.12   If the possible options for full merger have been exhausted, the standard alternative is for a common trusteeship arrangement where one charity is appointed trustee of another. A corporate charity appointed as a trustee by the Charity Commission under s 35 of the *Charities Act 1993* will be a trust corporation and can thus act as sole trustee. Under a common trusteeship arrangement the two charities remain separate and must keep their own funds and accounting records. There can be practical difficulties in maintaining such an arrangement.

84.13   Another possibility to consider is setting up a joint venture agreement which enables two charities whose objects are not wholly compatible, but who have some overlap in their activities, to establish a separate charitable venture that can utilise the resources of both the charities in that area of work.

IMPLEMENTING THE MERGER

84.14   If the merger is an amalgamation (as described above) then the new charity is starting afresh and as such it is easy to establish suitable constitutional and operational arrangements. This is the more desirable form of merger if a change of legal structure is required. However, the more common form of merger is consolidation and the successor charity will need to ensure that its constitution is suitable to meet the requirements of the charity that is being absorbed and the demands of the combined organisations.

84.15   The most important considerations are:

- the name of the merged charity;

- whether the new constitution will need to include additional powers to allow the merged charity to meet its charitable purposes;

- what governance structure should be established, for example, what should be the representation of trustees from the original charities; and

- whether new membership provisions need to be put in place.

FUNDS HELD ON SPECIAL TRUSTS

84.16   A problem that can arise with merger is where a merging charity holds funds on special trusts. If the amount of the funds are small, it may be possible to use the small charities provisions in *ss 74* and *75* of the *Charities Acts 1993* (as amended by the *Charities Act 2006*), which will come into force in 2008, to wind up the trusts and transfer them to another charity or to spend the permanent endowment. The small charities provisions cover those with gross income in the last financial year not exceeding £10,000.

84.17   If the funds are too great for these provisions to be applied, or if the land is held on trust, then it may be necessary to amend the trust deed if there is an express power to do so, or to obtain a Scheme from the Charity Commission.

TRANSFER OF ASSETS OR UNDERTAKING

84.18   There are a number of other legal matters that need to be addressed aside from the constitutional issues raised by merger. There are two forms that the merger can take: either there is a simple transfer of assets or, as is more common, a transfer of the whole undertaking to the acquiring organisation. In this instance the acquiring organisation will need to investigate fully the assets, liabilities and risks being taken on including funding, contractual agreements, VAT and property. This process is often referred to as 'due diligence'. There will normally be a transfer agreement between the two charities covering the transfer of assets, liabilities and any indemnities.

84.19   A major consideration for service providing charities will be contractual relations and funding arrangements with third parties. The usual arrangement is for the existing contracts to be taken over by the successor charity. The consent of third parties will be needed for the transfer of contractual obligations and there may need to be a novation (substitution of new contract for former one) of existing contracts.

84.20   The merging organisation will need to protect its position, and that of its trustees' with regard to any future liability. There will be a potential personal liability for the charity trustees in an unincorporated charity. A charitable company will normally be wound up using the striking off procedure, which will then render the company directors (the trustees) personally liable for any debts arising after the company has been struck off. The transfer agreement will need to include indemnities to protect the trustees of the merging charity against this.

EMPLOYEES

84.21   Charities should be aware that the *Transfer of Undertakings (Protection of Employment) Regulations 2006* apply to mergers (for more information about *TUPE* see CHAPTER 42. This means that all the employees of the merged charity are taken on by the successor charity. Dismissal of an employee could be considered as unfair, and therefore lead to an unfair dismissal case being brought against the charity, unless evidence can be shown of an economic, technical or organisational motive for an employee's dismissal. A change in terms and conditions of employment is not recognised as an economic, technical or organisational motive.

WINDING UP OF MERGING CHARITY

84.22   Once the transfer of assets or undertakings has been completed, it is usual for the merging charity to be wound up. For an incorporated charity, the normal procedure is to make an application to be struck off the Register of Companies and to then send closing accounts to the Charity Commission so that the charity can be removed from the register. For an unincorporated charity, a copy of the Resolution winding up the charity and the closing accounts should be sent to the Commission.

FURTHER INFORMATION

84.23   Charity Commission CC34 'Collaborative Working and Mergers' 2006

Charity Commission RS4 'Collaborative Working and Mergers' 2003

85   National Lottery

85.1   The National Lottery was originally established by the *National Lottery Act 1993*. It has become an important, though sometimes controversial, source of funding for the voluntary sector. For every £1 spent on a National Lottery ticket, 50p goes towards prizes, 28p goes to 'good causes', (mainly, but not exclusively, charities). 12p goes to the Treasury in duty, 5p goes to Lottery retailers, and 5p to the game operator (0.5p of this is profit, the remainder covers operating costs). Since its launch, ticket sales have totalled over £70 billion and £20 billion has been distributed to 250,000 good causes.

85.2   National Lottery distribution was reformed in 2006 by the *National Lottery Act 2006*. Key changes introduced by the Act were:

- The establishment of the Big Lottery Fund as a single body replacing the Community Fund, the New Opportunities Fund and the Millennium Commission;

- Increased public involvement in the Lottery with distributors able to consult and take account of public views in making distribution decisions;

- Measures to ensure that the licensing and regulation of the Lottery continues to maximise the returns to good causes.

85.3   In 2006 the distribution between the good causes was as follows:

- Health, education, and the environment – 33.33%

- Sports – 16.67%

- Arts – 16.67%

- Heritage – 16.67%

- Charities – 16.67%.

85.4   There are currently 14 distributing bodies responsible for awarding Lottery grants. Each is independent of Government and the Department for Culture, Media and Sport (DCMS), but each has to follow guidelines set by DCMS when deciding who should receive National Lottery funding. The 14 distributing bodies are:

- The Big Lottery Fund

- Arts Council England

- Arts Council of Northern Ireland

- Arts Council of Wales

- Scottish Arts Council

- Scottish Screen

- UK Film Council

- Sport England

- Sportscotland

- Sports Council for Wales

- Sports Council for Northern Ireland
- UK Sport
- Heritage Lottery Fund
- The Olympic Lottery Distributor.

85.5   Information about applying for funding and the different funding streams is available from the National Lottery Funding Helpline on 0845 275 0000, or from a joint website run by all Lottery funders in the UK. (*www.lotteryfunding.org.uk*). Details of all Lottery grants that have been made are available on the National Lottery section of the DCMS website at *www.culture.gov.uk*. Although the Big Lottery Fund is seen as the main source of lottery funding for charities, a proportion of the funds dispersed by the other distributing bodies is given to charities and non-charitable voluntary organisations.

THE BIG LOTTERY FUND

85.6   The Big Lottery fund was formed in 2004 from the merger of New Opportunities Fund and Community Fund. It currently distributes around £600 million each year to projects in the UK and overseas that improve health, education and the environment and it supports voluntary groups helping those most in need. It seeks to regenerate and revitalise communities, with a particular emphasis on tackling disadvantage. Contact details are as follows:

Big Lottery Fund
1 Plough Place
London
EC4A 1DE
Tel: 020 7211 1800
Advice line: 0845 4 10 20 30
www.biglotteryfund.org.uk
Email: general.enquiries@biglotteryfund.org.uk

ARTS

85.7   The Arts Councils in the UK aim to promote access, education and excellence in the arts through partnership by bringing the arts to a wider audience, encouraging individuality and experimentation, nurturing creativity across the generations, embracing the diversity of our culture and exploring new forms of expression. Grants are available for individuals, arts organisations, national touring companies and others who use the arts in their work, and support activities that benefit the public or that help artists and arts organisations to carry out their work.

85.8   The UK Film Council uses National Lottery money to develop new filmmakers, fund exciting British films such as 'Touching the Void' and 'Vera Drake' and give audiences the opportunity to see the best of world cinema. Scottish Screen development funding helps Scottish production companies with the development of feature film, live action drama, theatrical documentary and animation projects and its production funding supports the production of feature films and documentaries, short dramas, documentaries and animations, and also supports organisations that want to run independent short film schemes.

85.9   Contact details for the four national Arts Councils and two film councils are as follows:

Arts Council of England
14 Great Peter Street
London SW1P 3NQ
Tel: 0845 300 6200
Fax: 020 7973 6590
Textphone: 020 7973 6564
www.artscouncil.org.uk

Arts Council of Northern Ireland
77 Malone Road
Belfast, BT9 6AQ
Tel: 028 90385200
Fax: 028 90661715
Email: info@artscouncil-ni.org

Arts Council of Wales
South Wales Office
9 Museum Place
Cardiff
CF10 3NX
Tel: 029 2037 6525
Fax: 029 2022 1447
Text phone: 029 2039 0027
Email: south@artswales.org.uk

Arts Council of Wales
Mid and West Wales Office
6 Gardd Llydaw
Jackson's Lane
Carmarthen SA31 1QD
Tel: 01267 234 248
Fax: 01267 233 084
Textphone: 01267 223 496
Email: midandwest@artswales.org.uk

Arts Council of Wales
North Wales Office
36 Prince's Drive
Colwyn Bay
LL29 8LA
Tel: 01492 533 440
Fax: 01492 533 677
Textphone: 01492 532 288
Email: north@artswales.org.uk

Scottish Arts Council
12 Manor Place
Edinburgh
EH3 7DD
Tel: 0131 226 6051

Help Desk 0845 603 6000 (local rate)
Fax: 0131 225 9833
Typetalk: prefix number with 18001
E-mail: help.desk@scottisharts.org.uk

The UK Film Council
10 Little Portland Street
London
W1W 7JG
Tel: 020 7861 7861
Fax: 020 7861 7862
Email: info@ukfilmcouncil.org.uk
www.ukfilmcouncil.org.uk

Scottish Screen
249 West George Street
Glasgow
G2 4QE
Tel: 0845 300 7300
Email: lottery@scottishscreen.com
www.scottishscreen.org

HERITAGE

85.10   The Heritage Lottery Fund allocates money to safeguard and enhance the heritage of buildings, objects, collections and the environment, to assist people to appreciate and enjoy their heritage and to allow them to hand it on to future generations. Funding is given for projects related to natural habitats and countryside, urban green spaces including parks, historic buildings and sites, historic library collections and archives, museum collections, archaeological projects and industrial, transport and maritime heritage that are of outstanding interest and importance at a local, regional or national level. By 2007 the Heritage Lottery Fund had awarded over £3.6 billion to projects that open up our nation's heritage for everyone to enjoy.

85.11   The Heritage Lottery Fund is currently helping groups and organisations of all sizes with projects that aim to:

● conserve and enhance the UK's diverse heritage;

● encourage more people to be involved in, and make decisions about, their heritage;

● make sure that everyone can learn about, have access to and enjoy their heritage.

The Heritage Lottery Fund also aims to achieve a more equitable distribution of grants across the UK.

85.12   Contact details for the Heritage Lottery Fund are as follows:

Heritage Lottery Fund
7 Holbein Place
London
SW1W 8NR

85.13 National Lottery

Tel: 020 7591 6042.
Fax: 020 7591 6271
E-mail: enquire@hlf.org.uk
www.hlf.org.uk

SPORTS

85.13 The four national Sports Councils operate lottery programmes that provide funding for both capital projects and revenue schemes to increase active participation in sport and recreation. Applicants can apply under the capital programme for building and construction, the purchase of land and/or the purchase of capital equipment. Projects must meet defined standards of good design, quality and technical requirements for the relevant sport or sports. Buildings must provide access for people with disabilities. Projects will only be considered for funding from the Lottery Sports Fund if they involve a sport or sports recognised by the Sports Councils.

85.14 Capital projects must be of demonstrable benefit to the local community and command a good level of support from the public. Applicants must have attracted significant partnership funding to ensure that the project can be completed and sustained.

85.15 Revenue programmes run by the Sports Councils can fund individual athletes and their governing body's performance plans. Revenue funding is also used to support major sporting events.

85.16 UK Sport is the Government agency responsible for maximising British success in the Olympic and Paralympic Games through investing in the most talented British athletes. Lottery funding is targeted at athletes capable of delivering medal-winning performances, and at sports national governing bodies. UK Sport also distributes funds to sporting and other organisations to bid for and stage world class events in the UK.

85.17 The Olympic Lottery Distributor is an independent, UK-wide, Non-Departmental Public Body which distributes Lottery funds from the Olympic Lottery Distribution Fund to support the provision of facilities, services and functions necessary for the hosting of the 2012 Olympic Games. When making grants it will ensure that the principles of a lasting legacy, environmental and social sustainability, that were set out in the bid which won the Games for London, are put into practice. It is expected that the Olympic Lottery Distributor will be responsible for disbursing £1,835m of Lottery funds. Sport England will also be providing £50.5m to support elements of the facilities necessary to host the London 2012 Games, bringing total Lottery investment to £1,885.5m.

85.18 Contact details for the four national Sports Councils, UK Sport and the Olympic Lottery Distributor are as follows:

Sport England
3rd Floor Victoria House
Bloomsbury Square
London
WC1B 4SE
Tel: 020 7273 1551
Fax: 020 7383 5740

Email: info@sportengland.org
www.sportengland.org

Sports Council for Northern Ireland
House of Sport
Upper Malone Road
Belfast BT9 5LA
Tel: 028 90 382222
Fax: 028 90 383822
E-mail: info@sportni.net
www.sportni.net

Sports Council for Wales
Sophia Gardens
Cardiff,
CF11 9SW
Tel: 029 2030 0500
Fax: 029 2030 0600
Email: scw@scw.co.uk
www.sports-council-wales.co.uk

Sport scotland
Caledonia House
South Gyle
EDINBURGH
EH12 9DQ
Tel: 0131 317 7200
Fax: 0131 317 7202
Email: library@sportscotland.org.uk
www.sportscotland.org.uk

UK Sport
40 Bernard Street
London
WC1N 1ST
Tel: 020 7211 5100
Email: info@uksport.gov.uk
www.uksport.gov.uk

Olympic Lottery Distributor,
1 Plough Place
London
EC4A 1DE
Tel: 020 7880 2012
Fax: 020 7880 2000
Email: info@olympiclotterydistributor.org.uk
www.olympiclotterydistributor.org.uk

86 Non-departmental Public Bodies

86.1 A non-departmental public body (NDPB) is: 'an entity which has a role in the process of national government but is not a government department nor forms part of a department. It is established at arms' length from departments recognising that a degree of independence from Ministers in carrying out its functions is appropriate.' There are three broad types of NDPB:

- Executive — these are generally bodies which carry out prescribed functions within government guidelines. Typically, they have a separate legal identity under specific statute and employ their own staff. Some may exercise administrative or regulatory functions, supported by staff from the sponsor department.

- Advisory — these are mainly bodies set up by Ministers to advise them on matters pertinent to their department's functions. They are normally serviced by staff of the sponsor department.

- Tribunals — these are bodies whose functions are essentially judicial. They are again normally serviced by staff of the sponsor department

Executive NDPBs can incur expenditure on their own account and are usually financed at least in part from public funds. The use to which a body puts these funds is governed by a financial memorandum issued by the sponsoring department'. (APB Practice Note: Audit of Central Government Financial Statements in the United Kingdom).

86.3 Executive NDPBs are similar to quangos, but often exist to deliver a charitable service, and may be registered charities in their own right. A number of museums for instance fall into this category.

86.4 Of the registered charities with annual income in excess of £10m, a small proportion are NDPBs or quangos. In Scotland NDPBs include the regional health boards, local enterprise companies as well as organisations such as Scottish Homes and UVAF (Unemployed Voluntary Action Fund).

STRUCTURE

86.5 Charities that are NDPBs are often established as limited companies. They may use terminology and systems that would be more at home in the public sector and often have to operate under an even wider range of regulation than other similar charities.

86.6 The funding of a typical NDPB is provided, at least in part, by parliament via a sponsoring department. The terms of the funding will be governed by a financial memorandum, and the financial reporting requirements will be set out in an accounts direction, both issued by the sponsoring department. Funding may be by grants, or by grant in aid. The treasury provide the following example to distinguish the two:

1The distinction between grants and grant in aid

86.7 If a department decides to fund the purchase of works of art by the British Museum (an NDPB) under a grant system, it would issue the grant as the museum acquired each item. Evidence of the purchase price would be required before individual payments were made. The museum would not have uncommitted funds in hand, nor would it be allowed to carry over grant money at the end of the year. Under a system of grants in aid, the department would issue the grant in aid in full or by instalments during the financial year, the timing and amounts of which would reflect the need for funding. The museum would have discretion over the spending of that money within the general framework of controls agreed amongst it, the relevant government department and the NDPB itself, and set out in a financial memorandum.

86.8   Annual accounts for all NDPBs are prepared on an accruals basis, and charitable NDPBs should adopt the Charities SORP, although sometimes in a slightly modified format depending on the nature of their activities.

86.9   An NDPB has an accounting officer, who is formally responsible for the performance and stewardship of the charity, for ensuring that the body has in place sound systems for financial management and for accounting to parliament each year. Normally the Chief Executive is the accounting officer, assisted by the Finance Director. The accounting officer is responsible for the propriety and regularity of the financial activity, keeping proper accounts, prudent and economical administration, the avoidance of waste and extravagance and the efficient and effective use of resources. The finance director (sometimes referred to as the principal finance officer) is responsible for ensuring the charity's effective financial management and for the production of the annual accounts. The duties of the accounting officer, and the accounting requirements generally of NDPBs are set out in 'Government Accounting' (the manual setting out the accounting rules and requirements in the central government sector — available on line at www.government-accounting.gov.uk). More specific guidance on annual accounts is set out in 'Executive NDPB Annual Report and Accounts Guidance' which is available on the Treasury website (*www.hm-treasury.gov.uk*). This guidance is updated annually with amendments agreed by the Financial Reporting Advisory Board (an independent body which advises the Treasury on its financial reporting standards and principles) to reflect new Financial Reporting Standards and developments in UK GAAP, adapted, where appropriate, to take account of the public sector context.

86.10   Where a charity receives any form of government funding, it should clarify whether the terms of the funding are such as to impose these additional requirements. For instance the trustees may be required to take account of compliance with relevant authority, known as regularity. Regularity is defined as the requirement that a financial transaction should be in accordance with the legislation authorising it, regulations issued by a body with the power to do so under the governing legislation, parliamentary authority, and treasury authority. The financial memorandum may require the auditors to report not only on the accounts as prepared under the accounts direction, but also to report on non-financial measurements of performance which may or may not be specified.

MANAGEMENT

86.11   The Cabinet Office issued Guidance on *Codes of Practice for Board Members of Public Bodies* in February 2000. All executive NDPBs are required to adopt codes taking account of the guidance. It covers, among other things, public service values; the role of the chairman; the corporate and individual respon-

sibilities of board members; the handling of conflicts of interest; and accountability for public funds. The guidance recommends that all public bodies
should establish an audit committee as a committee of the board and envisages
that the Accounting Officer will normally attend its meetings.

86.12   The management of an NDPB is also expected to meet a requirement of
propriety, which is the behavioural aspect of regularity. It is concerned with
standards of behaviour and corporate governance. Matters that would fall
under this definition include open and fair competition in letting contracts,
the avoidance of unnecessary extravagance, avoiding conflicts of interest or
making a personal profit from public money. Propriety is not subject to any
formal report, but auditors are expected to have regard to matters of propriety and to report any shortcomings to the relevant body.

86.13   In dealing with charitable NDPBs, or organisations which are required to
account in similar terms, charities may therefore find themselves dealing with
unfamiliar terms and procedures. Apart from these areas though, the ability
of such an organisation to operate generally, or to enter into contracts, is
governed by general applicable legislation, such as tax law and the *Companies
Acts* and should not cause difficulties in a normal business relationship.

87   Northern Ireland

87.1   The regime governing charities in Northern Ireland is currently subject to sweeping changes. Whilst Company and tax legislation has applied to charities consistently across the UK, charity law itself has differed. Scotland has developed its own legislation since 1992, but Northern Ireland is currently introducing the *Charities (Northern Ireland) Order 2007*. This order is the equivalent of the charity legislation in England, Wales and Scotland, and is to be considered by the Northern Ireland Assembly. This means that a Northern Ireland Charity Commission may be established in 2008.

THE NEW REGIME

87.2   The order comprises 183 sections, nine schedules and covers 176 pages. In summary it:

• Provides a definition of charity and charitable purpose;

• Establishes the Charity Commission for Northern Ireland (CCNI), an Official Custodian, and the Charity Tribunal for Northern Ireland;

• Creates a register of charities;

• Provides for CIOs (charitable incorporated organsiations);

• Deals with the regulation of charities, public charitable collections and fundraising for charitable institutions.

87.3   The proposed order closely follows the Charities Acts for England and Wales with two differences:

• The public benefit test is more rigorous: the order requires public benefit to be considered in the context of benefit gained by non-beneficiaries, and disbenefit incurred by the public.

• All charities are required to register, with no exempt charitable status.

87.4   The CCNI has wide powers. It can institute inquiries, make schemes for the protection of charities, make common investment and common deposit schemes, can incorporate trustees, and establish a register of mergers.

87.5   Under the Order charities have a duty to keep accounting records, issue statements of accounts and arrange for external audit. The Department for Social Development can prescribe the form and content of such accounts for charities with income over £100,000. These charities will in practice use the Charities SORP 2005.

87.6   The Order permits smaller unincorporated charities to transfer their property to other charities or modify their objects.

87.7   In respect of fundraising, the Order defines 'charitable institutions' and 'collector', and regulates street collections and door to door collections, as well as other fundraising activity. Promoters are required to obtain a public collections certificate from the CCNI.

87.8   Northern Ireland

THE OLD REGIME

87.8   The Department for Social Development is the charity authority for Northern Ireland, and matters are handled by its Charities Branch. The relevant main legislation, before the commencement of the 2007 order, comprises the *House to House Collections Act (NI) 1952*, *Charities Act (NI) 1964*, and *Charities (NI) Order 1987*.

87.9   Until the Order is in place as legislation, it is inappropriate for Northern Ireland charities to refer to themselves as 'registered'. Charities should instead use phrases like 'recognised as a charity by HMRC' and may quote their HMRC reference number.

88   Overseas Activities

88.1   Charities may be involved in overseas activities in a variety of ways. In some cases they may simply send money or goods overseas, in others they may have overseas branches or projects and finally some may be part of an international organisation overseas grouping, with funds and facilities being shared around the international organisation. There are a number of issues common to all these scenarios, and some specific to individual cases.

88.2   Just as the Charity Commission has no power to prevent a charity from setting up in England and Wales because there are already others addressing the same purpose, there is no international regulatory body that can regulate the number of agencies responding to overseas needs. Sudden emergencies can lead to a spate of new relief organisations seeking to help in an overseas area, often where other UK charities, or local or international agencies from other countries, are already established. Where a charity wishes to act in such circumstances it should first make enquiries through the overseas country's embassy, and through other organisations, in order to co-ordinate activities and maximise effectiveness.

CONSTITUTION

88.3   A charity may be registered to carry out charitable purposes abroad. In their first published 'Decisions of the Charity Commissioners', the Commission set out its position, i.e. that the first (old) three heads of charity are charitable wherever the purpose is fulfilled. International charities set up for the relief of poverty, and the advancement of education or religion, were assumed to be for public benefit. Old fourth head charities, 'purposes beneficial to the community', have a wide range of activities within them, from preserving old buildings to preventing cruelty to animals. A charity working overseas qualified under this head if the Commission considered that its activities overseas would so qualify if undertaken in the UK, and as long as its activity is not contrary to public policy. A charity cannot be registered with objects that are unlawful in the country or countries in which it intends to carry out its charitable activities. Once the public benefit requirements of the *Charities Act 2006* comes into force in 2008 all overseas charities will have to demonstrate that they provide a public benefit.

REGULATION

88.4   Regulating a charity's overseas activities is more difficult than regulating its affairs in this country. In its annual report for 1996, the Charity Commission, in relation to its investigation of the Palestinians Relief and Development Fund (Interpal), commented that, 'Where a charity's beneficiaries are overseas our powers of investigation in the locations where funds are distributed are often limited'. Interpal was registered in 1994 with the principal aim of providing aid to the poor and needy, including sick children and widows suffering as a result of civil or military action or national disasters. The charity confines its activities to Palestine and Palestinian refugees. Articles had appeared in the press alleging that there was a connection between Interpal and the alleged terrorist wing of Hamas and that Interpal part-funded Hamas. The Commission reported that it had carried out a detailed scrutiny of the charity's controls and records. It found them to be well-organised and there was no evidence of any donations being made for political purposes or that could not be accounted for. Scrutiny of the charity's publicity and documentation provided no evidence of pro-terrorist propaganda and interviews with staff and trustees showed they were 'motivated by faith and altruism rather than fanaticism'. The Commission recognised that Hamas would have supporters in the areas where Interpal was distributing aid but agreed that aid could not be denied to such people because of that support. On the basis of its work, the Commission was able to conclude that there was no evidence linking Interpal with support for terrorism and that funds were not being given solely because of an individual's support for Hamas but on the basis of their poverty and need. The trustees had taken all reasonable steps to ensure that the funds were being used within the objects of the charity and within the law. Interpal is one of a number of similar cases, and has contributed to the current proposals promulgated in the Government "Review of safeguards to protect the charitable sector from terrorist abuse". At the time of writing this consultation is incomplete, but it seems likely to lead to a greater emphasis on 'know your beneficiary'.

88.5   The law permits trustees of UK based charities to be based overseas, although the Charity Commission has expressed unwillingness to permit this where it applies to a majority of the trustees, arguing that in order to discharge their responsibilities effectively trustees need to be able to meet on a regular basis. Some charities use telephone or video conferencing facilities to conduct some of their meetings, or use them to allow overseas based trustees to participate in meetings held in the UK. The Charity Commission has permitted some international organisations whose funding and support is international to have the majority of their trustees based overseas.

TRUST OBLIGATIONS

88.6   The fact that money or other resources of a charity are to be applied abroad in no way diminishes the trustees' duty of good stewardship, or their responsibility to ensure that funds are applied only in furtherance of the objects of the charity. It is still surprisingly common to find organisations that treat any activity overseas as automatically not under the control of the trustees, as though once the funds or goods have left the UK, there the responsibility ends. This is not true – the trustees are responsible for ensuring that the resources are applied for the relevant charitable objects, wherever that application may be carried out.

TAX

88.7   Charities working overseas have to be registered in the UK to qualify for UK tax reliefs (*Camille and Henry Dreyfus Foundation Inc v Inland Revenue Commissioners [1954] 2 All ER 466*). They need to take particular care that expenditure incurred is actually charitable expenditure for tax purposes. Where this is not the case, then an element of tax relief available under *ICTA 1988, s 505* may be withdrawn. In short, for every pound spend on non charitable activity the charity can be taxed on the income that has been subject to tax relief. See 31.23ff.

Grants to overseas organisations

88.8   A payment made, or accrued, to a body situated outside the United Kingdom is not necessarily charitable expenditure unless the charity has taken reasonable steps to ensure that the payment will be applied for charitable purposes. HMRC have published guidance on this matter which reads as follows:

> 'When a payment is made or is to be made to a body outside the UK, this will only be considered charitable expenditure if the charity takes reasonable steps to ensure the payment is applied for charitable purposes. 'Applied for charitable purposes' means applied for purposes, which are regarded as charitable under UK law. It is not sufficient for the charity to establish that the overseas entity is a charity under the domestic law of the host country'.

88.9   The charity trustees must be able to describe the steps they took, demonstrate that those steps were reasonable and produce evidence that the steps were, in fact, taken.

88.10   When considering whether the steps taken by the charity were 'reasonable in the circumstances', HMRC will have regard to:

- the charity's knowledge of the overseas body;

- previous relations with and past history of that body.

88.11   Trustees are expected to make adequate enquiries to find out such information as is reasonably available about the overseas body, and establish what evidence will be provided by that body to show that the payment(s) will or have been applied for charitable purposes. The nature of the steps will depend upon the scale of operations and size of the sums involved.

88.12   In the case of small one-off payments, an exchange of correspondence between the charity and the overseas body will normally be sufficient. Where possible, the correspondence should be on headed paper and:

- give details of the payment and the purpose for which it was given; and

- provide confirmation that the sum has or will be applied for the purpose given.

88.13   More thorough work by the trustees will be required where the sums involved are large or where a transfer forms part of an ongoing commitment. This might include independent verification of the overseas body's status and activities, and reporting and verification of the manner of application of resources provided. The steps required can be reviewed in the light of evidence of proper use of funds and resources from earlier involvement with a particular project.

88.14   The steps taken are to 'ensure' that the payment will be applied for charitable purposes. If the recipient overseas body is not bound by its own domestic law to apply all of its income for charitable purposes, then the UK charity should consider seeking a legally binding agreement to ensure that their payment will be applied charitably. If the overseas body declines to enter into such an agreement, the trustees may have difficulty ensuring that the payment is applied for charitable purposes. If an agreement is entered into, the UK charity will need to have a means of establishing whether the agreement has been complied with.

88.15   Where a charity makes a series of payments to the same overseas body for the same charitable purpose, it is not necessary for fresh enquiries to be made in respect of each new payment. If the trustees have just reviewed the bona fides of the overseas body and are satisfied that they are bound to apply payments from the charity for charitable purposes, then it is not unreasonable for them to rely on the results of this review for a payment shortly thereafter.

88.16   From the above it is clear that the UK charity needs to be quite clear that the payment is within its own charitable objects, and also that the application of the funds in the foreign country will meet the criteria set out above, i.e. would the activity be charitable if it was carried out within the UK?

88.17   Within the UK charities can ensure that their expenditure is 'charitable expenditure' by operating within the terms of their trust and rigorously checking the use to which funds will be put if they are donated to another organisation or charity. Equal rigour should be applied when making donations to overseas organisations. An English charity, for instance, will often be regulated by the Charity Commission and its trustees' behaviour is governed by various legislation. In an overseas context the relevant legislation may be much less developed, there may be no regulatory body, and so the chances of error or corruption may also be greater. These factors should be considered, and, if necessary, appropriate controls and accountability introduced to ensure that payments are properly applied.

88.18   Note that *s 506* of *ICTA 1988* refers to accrued payments. Under the SORP they would only be accrued in the accounts if there existed a claim against the charity which arose from a duty or responsibility which obligates the entity either legally, or practically, because it would be financially or otherwise operationally damaging to the entity not to discharge the duty or responsibility. A moral obligation – such as results from the making of a non-contractual promise – does not create a liability unless it meets the definition of a liability (SORP Appendix I, para 19). Where trustees enter into long-term commitments, then they should be clear about how the funding sent overseas will continue to meet the charitable expenditure criteria and not just concentrate on the application of funds despatched during the accounting period.

Overseas expenditure incurred by the charity

88.19   When an organisation is operating overseas it is sometimes true that the level of accountability to the head office in the UK is less stringent than applies in the UK itself. There are a number of reasons for this, and it will often depend on whether the structure of the charity is project or branch based and whether it is run by local staff and volunteers, or by employees recruited in the UK. Whatever the situation, it is equally important that expenditure incurred overseas is properly accounted for and controlled to ensure that no breach of trust occurs and no tax liability is generated.

Overseas income

88.20   Income paid to UK charities from abroad, such as rents and bank interest, is generally exempt from tax. A UK charity that receives income from which foreign taxes have been deducted may be able to recover the tax from the relevant tax authorities.

VAT

88.21   VAT is an indirect tax which operates, under different names, throughout Europe. Charities may incur similar indirect taxes in other countries. These taxes are not recoverable in the UK.

88.22   Charities often give goods and equipment away to organisations in countries outside the European Community. HMRC accepts that the goods and equipment can be treated as exports by the charities. As exports these can be treated as a zero-rated business activity, allowing the charity to register and reclaim the VAT on the purchase. HMRC strongly advises charities to retain documentary evidence that the relevant items have indeed been exported. A donation of goods to a charity for export can be zero-rated by the person making the gift.

88.23   Where goods are bought in a different EU Member State by a charity which is not VAT registered, then VAT will be charged in the Member State of supply and this tax will not be recoverable. Where goods are brought in from another Member State by a VAT registered charity the supplier can usually zero-rate his supply if he is provided with the charity's VAT registration number and evidence of the removal of goods to the UK. The charity will then be liable to account for UK VAT on the purchase – declaring this as 'acquisition' VAT in box 2 of its next VAT return. The extent to which the charity can make a deduction of this VAT will be determined by the usage of the goods, e.g. if the goods will be used for non-business purposes or to make only exempt sales no recovery is allowed.

88.24   A VAT registered charity may be able to zero-rate certain eligible goods when supplied to charities in other Member States, that are not registered for VAT in their own state, provided that evidence is retained to show that all the conditions of the appropriate relief are met.

88.25   Wherever overseas activities are involved, and especially where supplies involve different Member States, then a charity may need to take specialist advice. A number of special schemes exist to reduce diversity in the tax treatment, covering a wide variety of topics, including the Tour Operators Margin Scheme, triangulation and place of supply.

ACCOUNTING

88.26   The accounting requirements for overseas activities are the same as for activities carried out within the UK. There are, however, real practical difficulties in attempting to account centrally for overseas work as though it were a project based at headquarters. Therefore before embarking on these activities, the trustees should consider and establish an appropriate level of accountability which recognises certain factors. Issues to consider may include the extent to which it is necessary or practicable for financial reports to be regularly conveyed to headquarters. For established projects, or branches, with their own bank accounts this is certainly feasible, but it is impracticable where projects are carried out in remote locations or where much of the financial activity is based on barter. In these cases the trustees may have to accept that project accounts cannot always be submitted on a regular basis. Also, exchange risks will affect the amount of funding to be placed in the relevant country. The risk may not only be adverse fluctuations in the exchange rate, but also restrictions on the accessibility of funds for withdrawal. Where the risk is material, these sorts of problems can sometimes be addressed by hedging, or by partnerships with other charities operating in the same country.

88.27   Assuming that overseas activities are to be brought into the annual accounts, then more planning will be needed in the accounts production process. An extended timetable is needed for the consolidation of branch activities within the UK, and so even more time may be required to consolidate overseas activities, especially if they are sufficiently material to merit the attention of the auditors. In some cases it will be necessary for auditors to visit the overseas operation. Usually it will be more efficient and cost effective for the charity to retain a firm of auditors with international representation in the relevant countries.

88.28   Financial information submitted by local branches will need conversion to sterling. This can be done either by the main charity informing the local operation of a standard conversion rate to apply, or by the headquarters converting all the returns on receipt. Exchange gains and losses would normally be regarded simply as part of the cost of the project, although not all funders will pay for exchange losses. Good treasury management should reduce exchange risk. Although the position will vary from country to country, it is sensible to minimise holdings in unstable currencies, or use a locally acceptable stable equivalent such as US dollars.

88.29   If the UK charity is buying or supplying equipment, goods or services overseas, then exchange differences are likely to arise on transactions. These are treated as part of the relevant income or expenditure. Where assets held overseas are converted to sterling they may also give rise to an exchange gain or loss, which should be recognised through the SOFA in the statement of recognised gains and losses.

OVERSEAS CHARITIES OPERATING IN THE UK

88.30   Charities based overseas that operate or fund-raise in the UK may suffer the following tax disadvantages:

- tax on UK income such as interest will be deducted at source and will be irrecoverable;

- tax-efficient giving incentives such as Gift Aid or payroll deduction schemes cannot be used to recover income tax paid by donors;

- they will not be able to take advantage of tax exemptions available only to charities registered in the UK.

88.31   The exact impact of tax legislation on an overseas charity operating within the UK will also depend on the tax regime of the country in which the charity is based and the status of the UK tax treaties. International tax advice may be necessary.

88.32   An overseas charity can overcome these tax disadvantages by registering its UK activities as a UK registered charity with the Charity Commission (England and Wales) or with OSCR (Scotland). The Charity Commission is likely to insist that a majority of the trustees are UK citizens or at least UK based.

UK CHARITIES FUND-RAISING OVERSEAS

88.33   A UK charity that raises funds overseas may have to register in the countries in which it is fund-raising in order to qualify for any tax exemptions or tax-effective giving concessions operated by those countries.

ADMINISTRATIVE MATTERS

88.34   Apart from the financial aspects covered above the charity working overseas will also have to address wider and more complex issues in terms of volunteer management, employment law and ethics. Many of these are discussed in the Charity Commission's 'Useful Guidelines — Charities Working Internationally'. This especially draws attention to the need to understand local culture and regulation, and the effects of the *Anti-terrorism, Crime and Security Act 2001*.

88.35   Charities will draw up appropriate policies governing the areas that affect them in the light of this guidance. Apart from the normal administrative matters, these policies are also likely to cover local and overseas employment policies, including per diems, loans and ex pat arrangements, security procedures, bribery and corruption policies.

89 PAYE Administration

89.1 Every employer has a duty to operate PAYE in respect of payments made to employees. It is the employer's responsibility to ensure that all persons who are employees are treated as such for tax purposes and that the PAYE regulations are then operated properly. Failure to operate PAYE results in the employer being responsible for any tax which should have been deducted from an employee's pay. Penalties are levied for failing to deduct tax as well as for failing to complete and submit the necessary forms correctly or on time.

PAYE AUDITS

89.2 HMRC send their officers to check that employers are operating PAYE correctly. These inspections check that proper procedures are being followed, that calculations are carried out in accordance with the regulations, that PAYE is applied to all persons who should be treated as employees and that, where benefits are provided to employees, they are correctly recorded on the appropriate end of year returns. These inspections will typically cover a period of up to three years but may extend to six years or even longer if the employer is seriously in default. HMRC will seek to collect tax for any errors discovered in the period under review.

OPERATING PAYE

89.3 PAYE operates by recording the weekly or monthly pay of each employee and calculating the tax thereon. This is done using PAYE code numbers, which are provided by HMRC for each employee and which represent the allowances or tax-free pay to which an employee is entitled. In some cases where taxable benefits or other income exceed allowances the employee is given a negative PAYE code. The PAYE code by the employer used will depend upon the employee's circumstances when he joins the employer. Every employee who doesn't provide a valid form P45 should be asked to complete form P46 on which the employee certifies whether or not it is his main employment. These forms should normally be retained by the employer as long as the person remains an employee, as evidence of their status, unless the employer is instructed to send them to HMRC. Pay is calculated using working sheets and tax tables, supplied by HMRC, or a computerised payroll system, of which a number are commercially available. National insurance contributions, statutory sick pay and statutory maternity pay are calculated in a similar fashion. The amount due to HMRC for each month must be paid over by the 19th of the following month, covering both tax and national insurance contributions.

END OF YEAR PROCEDURES

89.4 At the end of the year, an employer is required to complete a form P35 showing each employee's yearly tax and national insurance and reconciling this with payments made. The form also contains a declaration to be signed by the employer certifying that all employees are included and that PAYE has been properly operated. At the same time, individual certificates of pay and tax deducted are provided to each employee (P60) and copies sent to HMRC.

These forms must be submitted to HMRC by 19 May following the end of the tax year and forms P60 must be given to employees by 31 May.

EMPLOYEES LEAVING

89.5   When an employee leaves during a tax year, he should be given a form P45, which certifies his pay and tax deducted for the year to date. This is then given to his new employer who operates PAYE based on the figures shown.

TAXABLE PAY

89.6   The amount of tax and national insurance to be deducted is calculated by reference to an employee's pay. The definition of pay is not always the same for both tax and national insurance purposes. Pay includes all salaries, wages, overtime, bonuses, pensions, commissions, etc. and includes holiday pay, Christmas boxes and any other cash payments. It also includes any liabilities of the employee that have been met directly by the employer unless these are genuine business expenses. The cost of meals and travel from home to normal place of work are not business expenses.

Termination payments

89.7   There are some payments on termination of an employment which are not taxable. Where an employee is entitled to a period of notice, which is not given but the employment contract does not provide for an alternative payment, the employee is nevertheless entitled to compensation in lieu of his notice period. This is not pay under the terms of the contract but compensation for breach of the contract and is not taxable up to a maximum of £30,000. Similarly, a compensation payment for a material alteration to a person's contract may also be non-taxable. Employers should, however, beware of making payments to persons who have reached or are near to retirement age as there are circumstances when HMRC can treat these as retirement benefits, in which case they are taxable. Sometimes, the position regarding such payments is not clear and it is as well for employers to seek professional advice rather than leave themselves open to a liability for failure to deduct PAYE.

Pension contributions

89.8   There are certain deductions which an employer may make from a person's pay before it is subject to tax. These are pension contributions to an approved occupational pension scheme and payments to charity under the payroll deduction scheme. Such deductions are, however, only allowable for tax purposes and not for national insurance. National insurance contributions are therefore calculated on the person's salary before such deductions.

STUDENTS

89.9   There are special rules and procedures for students working during their vacations, who will not earn sufficient to be liable to tax. The PAYE system assumes that a person will be paid at regular intervals throughout the year so that the allowances and rates of tax are apportioned on a monthly basis according to a person's earnings in the tax year to date of payment. This method of calculation can mean that persons who only work during part of a tax year may have too much tax deducted, which they can reclaim at a later date. This problem can be avoided for students by completing form P38(S) as soon as they start working and, if already employed, at the beginning of each tax year.

BENEFITS

89.10   Many employers provide staff with benefits as well as salary. While benefits cannot be subject to PAYE they must be declared to HMRC at the end of each tax year so that any tax liability can be assessed. For employees who are not directors and who earn less than £8,500 a form P9D is used. For directors and employees earning more than £8,500 per annum the rules on taxable benefits are more complex and a form P11D must be completed. There is a special exemption for directors of charities or non-profit making concerns who earn less than £8,500 per annum but directors of trading subsidiaries of a charity would not qualify for this exemption unless they are also a full-time working director of that company earning less than £8,500 per annum.

89.11   The form P11D should show all benefits, whether taxable or not, including all reimbursed expenses. This includes reimbursed travel and entertaining expenses even if incurred entirely on the business of the employer. It is then up to each individual to make a separate claim for these items not to be taxed. In completing the form, the employer is required to calculate the cash equivalent of the benefit. In the case of a company car, this will be the scale charge and in the case of a beneficial loan the amount based on the reduced interest rates applicable. HMRC publish a detailed guide to expenses and benefits (Booklet 480, 'Expenses and Benefits – A Tax Guide') and how they are calculated for tax purposes. Once completed, the forms P9D and P11D should be sent to the Revenue and a copy given to the employee by 6 July following the end of the tax year. The forms are designed to enable the employees to enter the necessary figures on their self-assessment tax returns, without themselves having to make complex calculations. The employer can, of course, be liable for penalties if a form P11D is incorrectly completed although in the case of a minor innocent error it is unlikely that HMRC would take any action.

Dispensations

89.12   Where an employer pays any expenses or provides any benefits which will not result in tax payable by the employee, the employer can apply to HMRC for a dispensation. If granted, those items need not be included on form P11D. This avoids the submission of details of routine expenses, such as travelling and subsistence expenses which are properly controlled and are genuine business expenses.

P11D errors

89.13   When carrying out inspections, HMRC often discover that employers have omitted certain benefits from the forms P11D, often because they were not aware that they should be included. This typically happens with such expenses as staff Christmas parties or similar functions which exceed the limit of £150 per head and other social events paid for by the employer. In such cases, the employer will often not wish the employee to incur a further tax charge, particularly where the mistake may have happened for a number of years. In these circumstances, HMRC will treat the value of the employee's benefit as being the benefit received by the employee after tax has been deducted and will collect the tax from the employer.

Employers paying tax

89.14   If an employer wishes to provide such benefits and does not wish the employee to be taxed on them, arrangements have been introduced known as PAYE Settlement Agreements. These are formal arrangements whereby the employer agrees to settle tax on certain classes of benefit on a global basis. This does not give rise to any tax liability for the employees. These arrangements can be made in respect of minor expenses such as taxi fares, small gifts etc., items paid on an irregular basis such as a holiday under an incentive award scheme or where it is impracticable to operate PAYE or to identify the precise benefit for each employee such as staff entertainment or the provision of company transport. Regular incentives should be dealt with under an HMRC approved Taxed Award Scheme (TAS). The employer must apply to HMRC for such an arrangement by 6 July following the end of the tax year and any tax payable becomes due on the following 19 October.

INLAND REVENUE GUIDES

89.15   When starting a PAYE scheme each employer is provided with detailed guides explaining how the scheme should be operated. These are updated by HMRC each year and a new supply of forms is distributed. Employers should be familiar with these guides because not knowing what is in them is not considered an acceptable excuse by HMRC for failing to operate PAYE properly.

90   Pensions

STATE PENSION SCHEMES

90.1   The legislation covering State, occupational, personal and stakeholder pensions for employees in a voluntary sector organisation is exactly the same as for any organisation. People of State pension age, which is currently 65 for men and 60 for women (changing to 65 progressively between 2010–2020), are entitled to a basic State pension if they (or their husband for married women) have paid National Insurance Contributions for the required amount of years. The amount of this pension is fixed and bears no relation to the amount earned.

90.2   In addition to this, a State Earnings Related Pension Scheme (SERPS) is available for employees who paid full rate National Insurance Contributions for some or all of the period between April 1978 and April 2002. The amount received depends on the earnings on which National Insurance Contributions were paid. From April 2002 SERPS has been abolished and State benefits are now accrued under the State Second Pension (S2P). Ultimately, this will be a flat rate pension not linked to earnings but currently a very complex interim calculation applies based on relevant percentages of three bands of earnings. It is more generous to low earners.

90.3   At retirement, people who have accrued benefits under SERPS and S2P will receive a pension derived from a mixture of both benefits. Anyone who would like a forecast of their State benefits at retirement should obtain, complete and send a form BR19 to The Pension Service, who can be contacted on www.thepensionservice.gov.uk/pdf/br19.

90.4   Since 6 April 2006, the concept of full 'concurrency' has been introduced. This allows an employee to concurrently be a member of as many pension arrangements as he/she wishes. For example, an employee can be a member of his/her employer's occupational pension scheme, and, at the same time, be contributing, to a personal pension scheme.

OCCUPATIONAL PENSION SCHEMES

90.5   Although there is no legal requirement for employers to provide pensions for their employees, some charities choose to set up occupational pension schemes. Occupational pension schemes are regulated by the Pensions Regulator (formerly known as the Occupational Pensions Regulatory Authority). There are two types of occupational pension scheme: final salary or defined benefit schemes and money purchase schemes. A 'final salary' or 'defined benefit' scheme has a formal benefit structure that is set out in the scheme's Trust Deed and Rules. The benefit is salary related, with the a pension based on the employee's salary at retirement, the prescribed accrual rate, and length of service. The other type, 'money purchase' schemes, provide a pension which is bought by the accumulated value, at the time the pension becomes payable, of the contributions made to the scheme have been invested. Both types can also provide a tax-free lump sum in lieu of part of the pension. Money purchase schemes, which will have the advantage for the employer of a fixed contribution. However, the employer's pension will be dependent on how well the scheme's investments have performed. For salary related schemes, however, the commitment for the employer is open ended as they guarantee the benefit levels, irrespective of what it costs them. As different retirement ages for men and women contravenes *Article 141* of the *Treaty of Rome*, both sexes must be allowed to take their pension at the same age.

90.6 Whether or not an employee remains part of the S2P whilst also a member of an occupational scheme depends on whether the scheme itself is contracted out or not. If contracted out, an employee is excluded from S2P and broadly gains an equivalent pension from their occupational scheme. Both the employee and the employer pay a reduced rate of National Insurance Contributions. The rebate for those in final salary related schemes in tax year 2006/2007 is 5.1% (5.3% for tax years 2007/2008 to 2011/2012) of earnings between the lower and upper earnings limits. The rebate for an occupational money purchase in tax year 2007/2007 arrangement is 2.6% (3.0% for tax years 2007/2008 to 2011/2012) plus an age related rebate. The total amount of rebate for money purchase schemes must be paid into the occupational scheme. Part of the rebate is deducted by the employer and the remainder is paid by the Inland Revenue National Insurance Contributions Office at the end of the tax year.

90.7 The level of contribution made by the employee to an occupational scheme is set by the employer. In non-contributory schemes, employees make no contribution. The Pensions Regulator's new scheme funding requirements for defined benefit schemes came into force on 30 December 2005. The new rules require scheme trustees to deliver a statement of funding principles; obtain regular actuarial valuations and reports; prepare a recovery plan for any funding deficit; and ensure that members are kept informed about the scheme's funding position by releasing regular summary funding statements. The new rules supplement the Pensions Act 2004 and apply to valuations completed on or after 30 December 2005, which are based on a date on or after 22 September 2005.

90.8 Additional voluntary contributions (AVCs) offer members of an occupational pension scheme a cost effective way to increase their pension fund. However, since April 2006, there are more ways for employees to boost their pensions. Apart from AVCs and free-standing AVCs (FSAVCs), employees who are members of an occupational pension scheme can now save in any number of pension plans including personal pension and stakeholder plans.

90.9 Since April 2006, tax relief has been available on employee contributions up to the higher of £3,600 per annum and 100 per cent of earnings, subject to an overall maximum of the Annual Allowance. The Annual Allowance limits are as follows:

Tax Year	Annual Allowance
2006/07	£215,000
2007/08	£225,000
2008/09	£235,000
2009/10	£245,000
2010/11	£255,000

90.10 Pensions

90.10 An employer should seek independent advice before setting up an occupational scheme. They can be expensive to run and typically will suit larger employers, although there are a number of issues which should be considered. For smaller employers, an organisation such as the Pensions Trust, which runs multi-employer occupational pension schemes for the charitable, social, educational, voluntary and not-for-profit sectors, may be more appropriate. Personal Pensions or Stakeholder Pensions should also be considered (see below). Certain insurance companies may also offer suitable schemes.

90.11 Employees in occupational pension schemes who change job can leave their contributions in their old employer's scheme or take a transfer value to another occupational scheme or personal pension plan. If the employee has been in the scheme for less than three months it is possible to get a refund of their own contributions less tax and administrative costs and possibly with interest. If the employee has been in the scheme for more than three months, he/she may be entitled to a 'preserved benefit' within the scheme. This is a complex matter and individual independent advice should be sought on the best option.

PART-TIME EMPLOYEES

90.12 One area of particular concern to voluntary sector organisations is that in the past part-time workers were often excluded from occupational pension schemes. With effect from 1 July 2000 UK regulations came into force implementing an EU directive which directly prohibits treating part-time workers less favourably than comparable full-time workers.

90.13 For employment prior to that date exclusion of part-time workers may have been unlawful dating back to 8 April 1976 when European law required equal treatment for men and women. A claim may be brought by part-time workers that exclusion from pension scheme membership from this date amounted to indirect sex discrimination. Claims must be made through an Industrial Tribunal within strict time limits. The equal treatment requirement was strengthened by the *Pensions Act 1995* which explicitly required pension schemes to provide men and women with equal access and benefits from 15 May 1990.

90.14 If a part-time worker can satisfy an industrial tribunal that the equal treatment rule has been breached, he/she may be granted backdated admission to the scheme or otherwise compensated. The primary defence to such a claim is if the trustees or managers of the pension scheme (the defendant) can show that the exclusion is not related to gender but to some objective factor. The employer will be treated as a party to the proceedings and will be entitled to appear and be heard at the tribunal.

PERSONAL PENSION PLANS

90.15 Personal pension plans can be taken out by any employee regardless of whether or not he/she is also a member of an occupational pension scheme. A recent rule change also offers employees earning less than £30,000 per annum the opportunity to be a member of both the occupational scheme and a stakeholder pension scheme. Personal pensions are all of the money purchase variety (see 90.5). Some employers that do not operate their own pension occupational scheme are willing to contribute a fixed percentage of an employee's salary to the employee's own personal pension plan. However, some employers with occupational schemes may not be willing to offer that option, although this could change in the future.

90.16   The tax treatment of employer' pension contributions is identical for the employee and employer regardless of the type of pension scheme. Employers may seek relief as a normal trading expense. Employees are not taxed on employer contributions that are within the Annual Allowance amounts described above. Personal contributions to personal pension plans, are paid net of basic rate tax, which is reclaimed on the member's behalf by the personal pension plan provider. Higher rate tax, if paid, can be recovered through self-assessment. Pension schemes which are eligible for the above tax concessions, whether occupational or personal, are collectively known and recorded as "Registered Pension Schemes".

90.17   Personal pension plans approved by the Inland Revenue can be used by the individual to contract out of S2P, but, unlike occupational schemes, employees continue to pay full National Insurance Contributions. The difference between the full and contracted out rate is refunded by the Inland Revenue National Insurance Contributions Office to the employee's pension plan at the end of the tax year. The element within the employee's pension plan that is secured by the National Insurance refunds is known as 'Protected Rights'.

90.18   An employer may arrange a series of personal pension plans for a group of employees. This is known as a group personal pension plan. The advantage of a number of staff joining the same scheme is that administration costs are minimised, and the employer does not incur the costs of running an occupational scheme. In addition, virtually all new personal pension plans are 'single charged' plans, usually termed as an Annual Management Charge (AMC), and pension providers often charge a lower AMC for a group arrangement. Pension providers offer a wide range of investment funds to choose from and any lower AMC might not apply to all the available funds.

STAKEHOLDER PENSIONS

90.19   The *Welfare Reform and Pensions Act 1999* sets out the general principles for stakeholder pension schemes, so that all employees can have access to a simple, flexible and cost-effective method of pension provision.

90.20   Since October 2001 all employers with five or more staff have had to offer stakeholder pension schemes to 'relevant employees'. Although there are some specific exceptions, 'relevant employees' are all permanent employees. Where the employer has an occupational scheme or offers a group personal pension plan which meets certain criteria, the employer can be exempted from this requirement.

90.21   The stakeholder access requirement means that unless exempted, an employer must make a stakeholder scheme available to employees. Charities are obliged to provide employees with information about a chosen scheme and provide information for the employee to get in touch with the scheme administrator. The employer is not required to contribute to the scheme but can do so if they wish. The employer must facilitate the deduction of contributions from an employee's salary and onward transmission to the pension provider, if required by the employee. Charity trustees/employers are not liable for the performance of the scheme they offer to employees. The employee is able to select his/her own investment strategy from the investment funds available.

90.22   Individuals, even those without earnings, are able to contribute up to £3,600 per year into a stakeholder pension scheme. Contributions are paid net of basic rate tax, regardless of earnings level, as with personal pension plans, and higher rate taxpayers are able to claim extra tax relief. If an individual's earnings exceed £3,600 per year, it is possible to pay more than £3,600 a year into the scheme – see 90.9 above. The same contribution rules now apply to all types of pension arrangements.

ACCOUNTING FOR PENSION CONTRIBUTIONS

90.23   Contributions to money purchase pension schemes and stakeholder pensions are recognised as expenditure as the contributions become payable.

90.24   Assets in a defined benefit scheme should be measured at their fair value at the balance sheet date. This will require the scheme liabilities to be measured on an actuarial basis.

90.25   Any surplus or deficit in the defined benefit scheme normally gives rise to an asset or liability within unrestricted funds. Any movement in the surplus or deficit year on year should be allocated to the statement of financial activities as either expenditure, income or actuarial gains/losses in accordance with FRS17.

90.26   A charity participating in a multi-employer defined benefit scheme may not be able to identify its share of the underlying assets and liabilities on a consistent or reasonable basis. In this situation, the charity should account for its contributions to the scheme as if it were a money purchase scheme.

90.27   Further information on accounting for pension schemes can be obtained from both FRS17 and the Charities SORP.

91   Personal Liability

91.1   Questions of liability tend to arise when something goes wrong, such as the organisation running into financial difficulties, being taken to court for breach of contract, being fined, e.g. for failing to file accounts, or when it faces a loss that is not insured. Most people are unclear about who is liable in these situations and can become extremely worried in case they are personally liable.

FACTORS GIVING RISE TO A LIABILITY

91.2   Liabilities most commonly arise from organisations or people acting on their behalf committing:

- breaches of criminal law, e.g. corporate manslaughter;

- breaches of statutory duty, e.g. failing to put the charity's registered status on certain documents;

- breaches of covenants or other property rights or duties, e.g. selling alcohol on premises despite the existence of a covenant forbidding this;

- breaches of trust, e.g. spending money on activities outside the charity's objects;

- breaches of contract, e.g. failing to meet specified standards of service delivery;

- breaches of duty when facing insolvency, e.g. continuing to trade when there is no realistic hope of financial survival; or

- tort (a civil wrong), e.g. libel.

WHERE DOES LIABILITY REST?

91.3   Who is liable in any particular instance depends on:

- whether the organisation is incorporated or unincorporated;

- who authorised the action, and whether or not they were authorised to do so;

- who carried out the action and whether or not they were authorised to do so; or

- who omitted to do something which they had a duty to do.

91.4   If a member of the charity's governing body or someone else associated with the charity is held personally liable for an action, or for omitting to carry out some action, they may have to use their own money to:

- meet the organisation's obligations;

- make good losses suffered by the organisation as a result of their actions;

- repay to the organisation any personal profit they have made as a result of their action; and

- pay fines or penalties arising as a result of their action.

91.5   Personal Liability

91.5   In some instances someone held personally liable may be entitled to be reimbursed by the organisation, or their fellow members of the governing body or by the charity's members. The court has power to relieve directors of charitable companies, company secretaries or senior employees from personal liability arising from negligence, default or breach of duty (*Companies Act 2006, s 1157*) and any charity trustee from personal liability arising from a breach of trust if the person concerned was judged to have acted honestly and reasonably and ought fairly to be excused. [*Trustee Act 1925, s 61*].

91.6   Where the members of a charity's governing body are held liable, the liability is joint and several. That means that each member could be held liable for all or any part of the obligation. If only some members of a governing body are sued for tort or breach of contract they are entitled to recover a contribution from the other members. The court decides what each person's contribution will be depending on their degree of culpability for the loss or damage. [*Civil Liability (Contribution) Act 1978, ss 1 and 2*].

91.7   The liability of charity trustees does not cease on their retirement. They remain responsible for acts taken during their term as a trustee. New trustees are not generally liable for actions taken before they became a trustee. However, if on taking office they become aware of irregularities they must take action to put matters right, or else they too could become liable.

91.8   The *Charities Act 2006* introduced a new power, now in *s 730 Charities Act 1993* (as amended) of the for the Charity Commission to relieve trustees, auditors and examiners from liability for breach of trust or duty. Previously there was limited scope for the Commission to grant what was known as equitable relief for trustees in certain circumstances, but in fact this never actually relieved trustees of liability. The new power allows the Commission to make an Order relieving liability if the individual concerned has acted honestly, reasonably and ought fairly to be excused. This section cannot apply to any personal contractual liabilities.

VICARIOUS LIABILITY

91.9   The general rule of liability is that people are liable for their own acts. However there are many circumstances in which others may be held liable as well as, or instead of, the person who committed the act. In general charity trustees are liable for:

- their own acts or omissions;

- the wrongful actions or omissions of employees or volunteers that they have authorised or sanctioned;

- the actions or omissions of employees or volunteers that they have not expressly sanctioned or authorised, that take place in the course of a business which they conduct and where there is a close connection between the conduct and what the wrongdoer was employed to do (vicarious liability). For example, employers can be liable for unlawful race, sex or disability discrimination carried out by their employees, even if it was carried out without their knowledge, unless the employer can show they took all reasonable steps to prevent such discrimination from occurring.

91.10   Trustees can be liable for the acts or omissions of employees and volunteers but will not normally be liable for the acts or omissions of independent contractors, such as cleaners or consultants.

91.11   The trustee board, as employers, can be liable not only for employee acts that they have authorised but also for acts that they have not authorised or for conduct that has been specifically forbidden. Employers have vicarious liability for breaches of duty by employees and in certain circumstances could have vicarious liability for criminal offences committed by employees in the course of their employment. For example, following a disaster in which four teenagers were drowned during an activity holiday, the company operating the holiday was found to have vicarious liability and fined £60,000 and the managing director imprisoned. In other cases trustees have been found to have various liability when teachers and school caretakers have been found guilty of commiting acts of child abuse.

91.12   Vicarious liability does not depend upon the employer being at fault in any way. All that must be proved for an employer to be found vicariously liable is that the person who committed the act is an employee of the employer, that the act occurred during the course of the employee's employment and the act committed is one which entitles the person who has been injured to bring court proceedings. Vicarious liability normally extends only to employees but in some instances courts have found employers vicariously liable for the acts of volunteers, either because they judge that the 'volunteer' is in law an employee or because in their view the relationship between the employer and the volunteer was such that it justified a liability being imposed. Volunteers working regularly in charity shops could come into this category. Even if the employer was not found vicariously liable the charity might still face a claim for its own liability in not properly training and supervising the volunteers.

91.13   If charity trustees find themselves held liable for the default of an employee they will have to meet whatever sum the court awards in compensation. If the charity is incorporated the trustees will be able to recover the amount from the charity, unless the trustees themselves have been at fault or have breached some duty that they owe. If the charity is unincorporated the trustees will be sued as individuals but will have the right to be indemnified out of the assets of the charity in respect of their liabilities, costs and expenses if it can be shown that they have been properly incurred in connection with the due performance of their duties. So where an employee or volunteer has been properly selected and reasonably supervised in carrying out their work, the trustees will have no difficulty in establishing their right to indemnity. The trustees of an unincorporated charity will, however, be personally liable to pay any compensation awarded and their costs if the charity has insufficient assets to cover them.

91.14   Charities working with children or vulnerable adults in schools, residential care, prisons, etc., will be particularly at risk of vicarious liability. Trustees will need to ensure that:

● there is an effective vulnerable persons policy in place which is observed and enforced;

● there is imaginative and efficient administration and supervision designed to minimise any risk to the community from accidents or intentional harm;

481

91.15 Personal Liability

- they have suitable insurance.

91.15   Where trustees set charges for services the fees should include an element to cover any possible payment of compensation to victims of employees' wrongs.

92   Political and Campaigning Activities

92.1   A commonly held misconception is that charities are forbidden from engaging in any form of political activity. This is not the case, though there are some restrictions. Charities have a long history of legitimately using the political process to further their aims. From the campaign of the Anti-Slavery Society in the nineteenth century to more recent work on community care and environmental legislation charities have played an important role in shaping social policy.

92.2   In the forward to the April 2007 version of the Charity Commission guidance *Campaigning and political activities by charities – some questions and answers* Dame Suzi Leather states that 'Campaigning, advocacy and political activities are all legitimate and valuable activities for charities to undertake. In fact the strong links charities have into their local communities, the high levels of public trust and confidence they command, and the diversity of causes they represent, mean that charities are often uniquely placed to campaign and advocate on behalf of their beneficiaries. Charities are free to carry out campaigns in furtherance of their charitable purposes. Only where these are directed at changing the law or government policy do special rules apply.'

CHARITY COMMISSION GUIDELINES

92.3   The law makes a distinction between political purposes and political activities. Charities are not permitted to have directly political objects, so an organisation set up to achieve a political purpose, e.g. to further the interests of a political party or to change the law, policy or decisions of central or local government in this country or abroad, cannot be registered as a charity. This is because the question of whether the organisation is established for the benefit of the public, an essential feature of all charities could not be assessed by the Charity Commission, as it would involve looking at questions of political priority, resources, and possibly human rights implications and questions of compensation. These are political questions which neither the Commission nor the courts are in a position to answer. However, an organisation set up to achieve a charitable purpose may engage in campaigning and political activities, including lobbying for changes in the law, provided that the activities pursed are a legitimate means of furthering their charitable objects. Thus, an organisation established to promote people's health by encouraging them to give up smoking can be registered as a charity, and can campaign for changes in the laws on smoking, but an organisation set up merely to change the laws on smoking cannot be registered as a charity.

92.4   The law on campaigning and political activities is based on case law, rather than statute, and as relatively few cases have come before the Courts it is not always easy to determine whether or not a particular action would be regarded as coming within the law. The Charity Commission's inquiry into Oxfam's campaigning activities in 1991 highlighted just how difficult it can be to draw the line between acceptable campaigning activity and unacceptable political action. Largely as a result of this inquiry the Commission issued clearer, revised draft guidelines on political activities and campaigning in April 1994. These guidelines were revised in 2004 following the recommendations contained in the Government's Strategy Unit report *Private Action, Public*

92.5 Political and Campaigning Activities

Benefit and they are likely to be revised again in 2008, following the recommendations made by the Advisory Group on Campaigning and the Voluntary Sector, Chaired by Baroness Helena Kennedy QC.

92.5   When considering whether to engage in campaigning or political activities the Charity Commission states that trustees must be reasonably satisfied that:

- the activities will be an effective means of furthering the purposes of the charity;

- the activities will further the purposes of the charity to an extent justified by the resources applied;

- the activities are permitted by the governing document;

- any political or campaigning activities they are considering comply with the general law and any other regulatory requirements;

- the possible benefits for the charity and their beneficiaries outweigh any reputational or other risks.

DUTY TO TAKE POLITICAL ACTION

92.6   Despite the Charity Commission's guidance, some charities continue to come under criticism, even from their own supporters, when they take political action. As Brazilian Archbishop Dom Helder Camara so aptly put it: 'When I give food to the poor, they call me a saint. When I ask why the poor have no food, they call me a communist'. Sometimes this criticism of charities is regrettable, particularly given that the law not only permits charities to take action directed at securing, or opposing, changes in the law or in government policy in some circumstances, but also the law could find trustees guilty of acting in breach of their duties if they failed to take political action when this would be both within the law and the most effective way of meeting the needs of their beneficiaries.

CAMPAIGNING v POLITICAL CAMPAIGNING

92.7   Campaigning is a broad term that includes raising public awareness of an issue, public education, or seeking to influence and change public attitudes. Campaigning and political campaigning are distinct activities. Political campaigning is confined to campaigns and activities that advocate or oppose changes in the law or public policy. All campaigning activities conducted by a charity must be directly related to its work and designed to further its aims or charitable objects. A charity may choose to devote all of its resources to non–political campaigning if that is what the trustees decide is the most effective way of pursuing its objects.

92.8   Trustees can only use political campaigning and activities as a way of furthering a charity's purpose. They must not become the reason for the charity's existence. In its guidance the Charity Commission states that political activities cannot be the dominant means by which a charity carries out its charitable purpose. What is dominant is a question of scope and degree upon which trustees must make a judgement, taking into account factors such as the amount of resources applied and the period involved, the charity's objects, and the nature of the political activities. If a charity does engage solely or predominantly in political activities that may indicate that the organisation

484

has ceased to be a charity and has become a political organisation. On the other hand it may mean that the trustees have exercised their discretion properly and have decided that for the time being the charity objects are best pursued through political activities.

92.9   The Commission has clarified that in stating that political activities must be ancillary and incidental it did not mean that political activities could only amount to a small part of the charity's work, rather that they should be a means of pursuing the charity's objects and not an end in themselves. Political activities would not be incidental or ancillary if the political aim had become the charity's reason for existing.

92.10   Campaigning to change the law or public policy is political campaigning, as is campaigning targeted at public bodies such as the NHS, the UN and the World Bank. Campaigning targeted at a private company, such as a drugs company or a clothing manufacturer, is not political campaigning.

Other legislation and regulations affecting campaigning

92.11   Charities conducting campaigning activities have to abide by a number of legal and regulatory requirements including:

- The *Communications Act 2003*, which bans advertising by political bodies and adverts directed towards political ends on TV and radio. The *Serious Organised Crime and Police Act 2005* and the *Terrorism Act 2000* which have restricted protests and demonstrations, particularly those in the vicinity of Parliament.

- The *Protection from Harassment Act 1997*, which prevents campaigners from, for example, sending emails to the board of directors of a company and its employees claiming that the company's actions are damaging the environment.

- The British Code of Advertising, Sales Promotion and Direct Marketing Code, which ensure that all advertisements are legal, decent, honest and truthful (see CHAPTER 4).

PUBLIC MUST BE GIVEN INFORMATION

92.12   Charities can put their views to the government, and publish the advice or views they express to ministers. They can seek to inform and educate the general public, and advocate solutions to the problems they are trying to tackle, providing this campaigning and education work is based on a well-founded, reasoned argument based on research or direct experience. Charities must present their case in a way that enables people to make up their own mind, avoiding the use of data which the charity knows, or ought to know, is inaccurate or distorted by selection to illustrate a preconceived position.

92.13   Charities should provide the public with sufficient, accurate information to support the case they are promoting. Where the medium used makes this impractical (e.g. billboard advertising or a brief TV advertisement) the charity should be able to set out its full position if requested to do so.

92.14   Campaigning material may have an emotional content, but charities should not seek to persuade the public or the government on the basis of material that is merely emotive.

VOTING RECORDS

92.15 Charities are permitted to publish individual MP's or political parties' voting records on relevant issues provided that they do so in a way that is designed to enable their supporters or the public to encourage those MPs or parties to alter their position as a result of reasoned argument, rather than merely in response to public pressure.

RESEARCH

92.16 Charities can conduct and publish properly constituted research studies or surveys that use a methodology appropriate to the subject. If research is undertaken to test a hypothesis, it must be designed to test that hypothesis objectively and not merely to look for evidence to support that hypothesis. The aim of publishing research must be to inform and educate the public. Charities must not publish research which they know, or ought to know, is flawed and must not undertake research for another organisation in the knowledge that the other organisation intends to use the results for party political or propagandist purposes.

PRESENTING VIEWS TO GOVERNMENT

92.17 The Commission's guidelines allow charities to provide their supporters, or members of the public, with material to send to MPs or the government, provided that the material is sufficient to enable supporters to put forward a well-founded, reasoned argument. They are also allowed to provide and publish comments on proposed changes in the law or government policy contained in Green or White Papers, or other documents, to respond to invitations to comment on proposed legislation, to supply Members of either House with material for use in debate which would further the charity's purpose, and to advocate a change in the law or public policy by presenting the government with a reasoned memorandum setting out the charity's case.

PETITIONS

92.18 Charities are permitted to organise petitions to be presented to either House of Parliament or to national or local government. It is good practice to state the purpose of the petition on each page the public is asked to sign.

WHAT THE GUIDELINES PROHIBIT

92.19 Charities must avoid all party political activities and must not take part in party political demonstrations. They must not seek to persuade members of the public to vote for or against a candidate or a political party which advocates or opposes a particular policy supported or opposed by the charity. When a charity advocates a particular solution to a problem, and that solution is also advocated by a political party, the charity must make it clear that its views are independent of those of the political party.

92.20 Charities must not attempt to influence public opinion or put pressure on government using data they know, or ought to know, is inaccurate or misleadingly selective.

92.21   Charities must not claim public support for their position on a political issue unless they can substantiate their claim.

92.22   Charities whose objects include the advancement of education must not overstep the boundary between education and propaganda. Material supplied should be sufficient to enable a person to form their own judgement about an issue and not merely restricted to presenting one set of arguments designed to promote a particular point of view.

ACTING WITH OTHER BODIES

92.23   Charities are often invited to take part in joint action on political issues by other organisations working in the same field, such as the Make Poverty History campaign. Charities are not prohibited from joining alliances which contain non-charitable organisations provided that certain conditions are met. They may join only if:

●   The alliance can be reasonably expected to further the charity's own charitable objects;

●   Any expenditure can be justified;

●   The risks of participating are outweighed by the benefits;

●   The alliance activities would be permissible for a charity to engage in;

●   They dissociate themselves from any activities of the alliance that are not charitable and do not allow their name to be associated with such activities or their funds to contribute towards them.

ELECTIONS

92.24   Charities may comment on proposals put forward at local, national or European elections provided they relate to the charity's work and any comments are consistent with the Charity Commission's guidelines on campaigning and political activities and the requirements of electoral law. Charities may bring issues relating to their work to the attention of prospective candidates and raise public awareness about them provided that they do so in a way which is reasoned, well-founded, educational and informative.

92.25   The *Political Parties Elections and Referendums Act 2000* amended the *Representation of the People Act 1983* and brought in new rules on election expenses in relation to elections to the Westminster Parliament, European Parliament, Scottish Parliament, National Assembly for Wales, Northern Ireland Assembly and local councils. *Section 94(6)* of the Act provides that where controlled expenditure is incurred by or on behalf of a third party and that it is done 'in pursuance of plan or other arrangement' with other people in connection with the production or publication of election material 'which can reasonably be regarded as intended to achieve a common purpose' then that expenditure shall be treated as also having been incurred by the other third party or parties. Consequently if people act together to promote the success of a party or group of candidates, the aggregate amount of expenditure they incur will be treated as if it had been incurred by each of them. This means that if the joint expenditure goes above the £10,000 mark, they will both (or all) have to register with the Electoral Commission as recognised third parties. Failure to register may result in a fine of £5,000 for incurring controlled expenditure without authority.

92.26   Therefore charities incurring controlled expenditure in connection with the production or publication of election material should consider carefully whether they may be acting in concert for these purposes with like-minded charities. Charities working jointly with branches that are not legally part of the same organisation will be acting in concert with third parties.

92.27   Under the Charity Commission's guidelines charities should not support a political party or seek to persuade members of the public to vote for or against a particular candidate or party. Therefore the rules on election expenses may not at first appear to be of relevance to charities. However, they are relevant to those charities that, in the interests of their beneficiaries, analyse and comment on the proposals of political parties, or advocate changes in the law, or support or oppose proposed legislation or advocate particular solutions, even though also advocated by a political party. If a charity's views coincide with those of a candidate or political party, the charity's material may be deemed election material. The problem can also occur after a charity has published its materials if an election candidate or party adopts the views of the charity. If the charity then republishes the materials it could be caught by the controls.

DEMONSTRATIONS

92.28   Care must be taken if charities are considering taking part in some form of demonstration or direct action that goes beyond handing out informative leaflets in a public place. Such events can involve significant risk and may alienate supporters of the charity, or damage public support for it, or even for the charitable sector generally. Public rallies and demonstrations can easily get out of control and the charity, or its officers, or those taking part may find themselves charged with committing an offence and face potential civil or criminal liability. If a demonstration is likely to interfere with the rights of others it becomes increasingly unlikely that the trustees could justify exposing the charity's assets to risk. Should the trustees decide to proceed with a demonstration that in the event gets out of hand because they have failed to exercise sufficient prudence in its organisation and control, the trustees could face a claim for want of prudence in their administration of the charity. In these circumstances the trustees could find themselves having personally to make good any financial loss the charity suffers as a result of the demonstration.

92.29   Charities should also exercise caution before requiring their staff to take part in a demonstration, as employers must not require employees to do any unlawful act. Where staff or trustees of charities take part in demonstrations in a private capacity they should take care to ensure that they are not perceived as being official representatives of the charity, for example by carrying placards or wearing badges carrying the charity's name.

PENALTIES

92.30   In addition to the risk of damaging a charity's good name and losing public support, tax relief can be lost on funds applied for non-charitable purposes.

Trustees may be required to repay to the charity money judged to have been mis-spent on improper campaigning or political activities plus any additional tax liability incurred as a result.

CONTROLS AND ADVICE

92.31   Any charity engaged in campaigning or political activities must have in place adequate arrangements for the commissioning, control and evaluation of such activities by its trustees.

92.32   Charities that are uncertain about the legality of any proposed campaigning or political activities should seek advice from their legal advisers, or from NCVO, or the Charity Commission or in Scotland from SCVO or OSCR.

POSSIBLE DEVELOPMENTS

92.33   The Advisory Group on Campaigning and the Voluntary Sector, Chaired by Baroness Helena Kennedy QC, published a report in April 2007. The report found that 'Campaigning in the 21st century takes place in a minefield of confusion, obstruction and outdated interpretations of the law'. The report recommended that:

- Charities should be able to engage in political campaigning in further-ance of their charitable purposes as long as they do not support political parties. In particular:

    - Charity trustees should be free to decide to engage exclusively in political campaigning in furtherance of their charitable purposes.

    - A charity should not have limits placed on the resources that can be committed to political campaigning activities.

- A change in the interpretation of the law to remove the 'dominant and ancillary' rule would be of public benefit, where the purposes are otherwise charitable.

- The Charity Commission continue the more flexible approach that they have shown recently in interpreting court judgements on political activi-ties by charities.

- Parliamentarians should support the new *Public Demonstrations (Repeals) Bill* which calls for the repeal of those parts of the *Serious Organised Crime and Police Act 2005* that impose disproportionate restrictions on protests and demonstrations, in particular the provisions prohibiting unauthorised demonstrations in the vicinity of Parliament.

- Whilst recognising the effectiveness of the *Human Rights Act 1998* to restrict arbitrary interferences with the right to protest, the Commission for Equality and Human Rights should take up the active promotion of peaceful protest.

- *Section 44* of the *Terrorism Act 2000*, which allows for individuals to be stopped and search by a police officer without reasonable suspicion, should be re-drafted. In particular the time and geographical locale of any designated area should be restricted. Further guidance should be issued on the use of the powers to ensure its use is aimed at preventing terrorism, rather than restricting peaceful protest.

- Policing procedures and codes of practice should be amended to ensure that, in the discharge of their powers, police officers positively respect freedom of expression and assembly, and accord due weight to the legitimate rights of individuals to protest peacefully in public.

- Ofcom and the BACC should immediately recognise that registered charities are not permitted to have a political purpose and should apply a rebuttable presumption that charities are not political bodies, thus lifting the unreasonable prohibitions that the *Communications Act 2003* currently imposes on advertising by charities and NGOs.

- The ban in the *Communications Act 2003* on all advertising by 'political' organisations should be repealed.

- A new legislative framework should permit in principle non-political advertising by NGOs and charities.

- The definition of political in *s 321(3)* of the *Communications Act 2003* should be amended so as to permit the broadcast of social advocacy advertisements on radio and television but restrict the broadcast of advertising for political parties.

- A new regulatory framework for broadcast media advertising should be imposed in which any 'political' (excluding party political) advertising by NGOs should state that it contains political content and represents the opinion of the advertiser and should state the source of funding for the advertisement. Consideration should be given to a moratorium on all political and social advocacy advertising in the broadcast media during local and national election periods.

92.34   In his *Governance of Britain* green paper, the Prime Minister, Gordon Brown, stated that he would consider the report's recommendations.

FURTHER INFORMATION

92.35   Charity Commission CC9 *'Campaigning and Political Activities by Charities'* – *Some Questions and Answers*, April 2004

The Report of the Advisory Group on Campaigning and the Voluntary Sector Chaired by Baroness Helena Kennedy QC

93   Poverty Charities

93.1   Many older charities for the relief of financial hardship, particularly those
        which were originally set up before the advent of the State welfare system,
        have objects which refer directly to 'the poor' or to 'poverty'. The meaning of
        'poverty' can be interpreted in a broad sense, as poverty is a relative term. To
        qualify as 'poor' a person does not have to be destitute. People regarded as
        poor in the UK today have possessions, such as televisions and refrigerators,
        that were regarded as luxuries only 50 years ago. In comparison with many
        people living in the Third World, poor people in the UK are relatively rich.
        Charities for the relief of poverty often define their beneficiary group as
        'people who cannot afford the normal things in life that most people take for
        granted'.

93.2   The relief of poverty or financial hardship also includes giving help to people
        in financial need who are suffering from the effects of old age, sickness or a
        disability. To qualify for help a person's hardship does not have to be
        long-term. As well as helping those living below the poverty line, charities
        established for the prevention and relief of poverty can assist those who have
        fallen on hard times relative to their usual standard of living, because their
        circumstances have changed suddenly, perhaps due to job loss, bereavement
        or sickness.

93.3   People may qualify for help from a charity regardless of whether or not they
        are entitled to State benefits. Some people in receipt of a number of State
        benefits may need additional help and people who do not qualify for State
        benefits may need help in particular circumstances.

93.4   Depending on the wording of a charity's governing document there may be a
        number of ways in which charities can relieve poverty at home and abroad:

        • Gifts of money. These could be in the form of a one-off grant, for
          example to purchase furniture or clothing, pay utility bills or towards
          funeral expenses; a regular weekly allowance to supplement a person's
          income or a regular payment to purchase a particular item or service
          such as a television licence or telephone line rental; payments to cover
          travelling expenses to hospitals, children's homes or prisons where more
          frequent visits than public funds provide for are desirable.

        • Provision of goods, such as radio and television sets, washing machines,
          furniture, bedding, clothing, food, fuel, heating appliances, prams, used
          cars, etc.

        • Payment for services such as laundry, home insulation, decorating and
          repairs, meals on wheels, child-minding, respite care, and holidays.

        • Provision of items such as essential tools or books, lessons or equipment
          for children with particular talent in music, sport, ballet, art, etc; travel-
          ling expenses to enable someone to earn their living, training to enable
          someone to gain employment or to enhance the quality of their life.

        • Grants to organisations in less developed countries working to relieve
          poverty and encouraging the sale of fairly traded goods.

93.5   Charities for the relief of poverty often give extra help to those who are both
        poor and sick. They can provide grants towards the cost of special diets,

adapting a home to meet the needs of someone with a physical disability, or convalescent care. They can provide medical equipment such as a wheelchair, either outright or on loan. They can provide services such as personal or nursing care, physiotherapy or chiropody in the home, respite care, shopping, gardening, exchange of library books, counselling, befriending, etc.

STATE BENEFITS

93.6   Charities must take care that the assistance they provide is not replacing any State benefit that the recipient is entitled to, as the recipient would be no better off and the charity's funds would be merely relieving the State. Charities can, however, make grants or loans to relieve immediate need when there is a delay in the receipt of State benefits. Charities should encourage their beneficiaries to claim any State benefits to which they are entitled. When assessing a person's need for assistance the trustees should take into account all the State benefits a person should be claiming, even if they are unwilling to claim them.

SOCIAL FUND

93.7   People who cannot meet exceptional expenses from their regular income can apply to the Social Fund for a grant or a loan. However, people do not have a statutory right to assistance from the Social Fund and many applicants are turned away either because the grants budget has been exhausted or because the applicant has no means of repaying a loan. Social Fund officials are in some circumstances obliged by law to consider if an applicant could get help from another source such as a charity. Therefore trustees of charities that give help to needy people should establish good contacts with their local Jobcentre Plus office, so that the agency has a good understanding of the circumstances in which the charity can offer assistance. If trustees believe that the agency is using the charity in order to avoid Social Fund expenditure they should take the matter up with the Department for Work & Pensions.

93.8   A charity can assist a person who has been promised a Social Fund loan if:

- they are in urgent need and there is a delay in the receipt of the money;

- the person would clearly not be able to repay the loan in the time specified (this is an exception to the general principle that charitable funds should not be used to replace State funding);

- the Social Fund loan promised is insufficient to meet the person's need.

Organisations relieving hardship that are not for the public benefit

93.9   Organisations established to assist a particular named person or a specific, small group of individuals cannot usually be granted charitable status as they do not exist for the public benefit.

Prevention of Poverty

93.10   As well as dealing with the effects of poverty, organisations can tackle the root causes of poverty, and campaign for government action to tackle poverty, providing they do not overstep the Charity Commission's guidance on political activities, if they are registered in England or Wales. The Office of the Scottish Charity Regulator, which recognises charities in Scotland, could refuse recognition on similar grounds. Charities can also aim to prevent poor people from becoming poorer, or people who are not poor from becoming poor, for example by providing advice about finance, tax and debt management.

FURTHER INFORMATION

93.11   CC4 'Charities for the relief of financial hardship'. Charity Commission, August 2003.

94   Public Benefit

94.1   The *Charities Act 2006* introduced a statutory requirement for all charities to provide evidence that they operate for the benefit of the public. *Section 4* requires the Charity Commission to issue guidance in relation to public benefit, and the charity trustees must have regard to any such guidance when exercising their powers or duties.

94.2   The *Charities Act 2006* in some ways changed nothing, as it has always been a legal requirement that charities must provide benefit to the public in order to qualify for charitable status. However, in the case of the first three traditional heads of charity, i.e. the relief of poverty, the advancement of education and the advancement of religion, there was a presumption of public benefit. The *Charities Act 2006* changes this by abolishing the presumption, so all charities now have to provide evidence that they are operating for the benefit of the public.

94.3   There is no statutory definition of public benefit in the 2006 Act, although *s 8* of the Charities and Trustee Investment (Scotland) Act 2005 goes closer to a definition:

> 'In determining whether a body provides or intends to provide public benefit, regard must be had to:
>
> (a)   how any:
>
> > (i)   benefit gained or likely to be gained by members of the body or any other persons (other than as members of the public); and
> >
> > (ii)   disbenefit incurred or likely to be incurred by the public, in consequence of the body exercising its functions compares with the benefit gained or likely to be gained by the public in that consequence; and
>
> (b)   where benefit is, or is likely to be, provided to a section of the public only, whether any condition on obtaining that benefit (including any charge or fee) is unduly restrictive.'

94.4   Although the principles underlying this section are similar to those applied in England and Wales, there is no concept of 'disbenefit' there. The discussion that follows therefore does not strictly apply to Scottish charities, although the principles are very similar.

What is "public benefit"?

94.5   The Charity Commission has issued some draft guidance on this topic, which recapitulates existing law. It states that there are five main principles which show whether an organisation provides benefit to the public. These are:

The Benefit:	i	There must be an identifiable benefit, but this can take many different forms.
	ii	Benefit is assessed in the light of modern conditions.

The Public:	iii	The benefit must be to the public at large, or to a sufficient section of the public.
	iv	Any private benefit must be incidental.
	v	Those who are less well off must not be entirely excluded from benefit

94.6   When assessing benefit, trustees should consider whether there is any harm caused which outweighs the benefit. This is the closest the Charity Commission get to discussing dis-benefit.

94.7   The identifiable benefit might be tangible or intangible, direct or indirect. Clearly it is most straightforward if the benefit is both direct and tangible. Society's view on benefits can change over time and so for instance environmental benefits would now be considered much more positively than they would have been one hundred years ago!

94.8   Benefiting the public does not mean everyone benefits, but it does broadly mean that anyone could benefit without any undue restriction on their eligibility. This has nothing to do with numbers, but instead is to do with ensuring that the benefit is not unduly restrictive. So a charity for the education of family members would not represent public benefit, whereas a charity for the benefit of a small hamlet might.

94.9   In general, a private benefit is legitimately incidental if:

- it arises as a necessary, but secondary, consequence of a decision by the trustees; and

- that decision is directed only at furthering the organisation's charitable purposes; and

- the amount of benefit is reasonable in the circumstances.

How do charities ensure they meet the public benefit test?

94.10   Ensuring that they meet the public benefit test will be straightforward for many charities. However, a number of charities are having to think through the implications of this new emphasis. For instance, fee paying charities need to consider whether their fee structure effectively precludes sections of the public from receiving benefit, membership organisations need to ensure that there is no significant private benefit, and religious and cultural bodies need to consider to what extent they can demonstrate they provide public benefit.

94.11   The Charity Commission's consultation document provide four key principles that charities need to consider:

1   There must be an identifiable benefit;

2   Benefit must be to the public, or a section of the public;

3   People on low incomes must be able to benefit;

4   Any private benefit must be incidental.

94.12   These principles have already been discussed above, although the Commission expanded on what they meant by 'people on low incomes', stating *inter alia* that: 'in England and Wales for example, it would typically cover

94.14 Public Benefit

households living on less than 60% of the average income (both before or after housing costs are taken into account) and people living on or below the level of income support' and 'Charities can charge for their services but where the charges are so high that they effectively exclude people'.

94.14   Finally, the Commission provided a suggested list of questions for charities to consider in assessing whether or not a charity meets the public benefit test:

1   What benefit(s) does your organisation provide?

2   How do those benefits help fulfil your organisation's purpose(s)?

3   Who is your organisation primarily set up to benefit?

4   Does your organisation provide wider benefits to the community or society generally? If so, how?

5   What criteria does your organisation use to select beneficiaries? Is anyone excluded from being a beneficiary? If so, who is excluded and why?

6   Does your organisation have a membership where someone must be a member to benefit? If so, is it open to anyone to join? If not, who can join and why?

7   Does your organisation provide facilities for, or services to, the public? If so, what, if any, restrictions are there on what people can have access to or who can have access?

8   Does your organisation charge for its services? If so, how are charges set? Is everyone charged the full rate?

9   How are people on low incomes able to benefit from your organisation?

10   Does anyone receive private benefits from your organisation? If so, what benefits do they receive? How do those benefits contribute towards achieving your organisation's purposes and/or to what extent are they incidental?

94.14   What is clear from this list, from the legislation and from the various comments from the Commission, is that public benefit must be central to the charity's raison d'etre. It is not sufficent, for instance, to work out a few addons which benefit the local community, and point to it as 'doing your bit for public benefit'. The charity must exist for public benefit, and trustees need to ensure that the activites are delivering this.

94.15   At the time of writing it is proposed that all charities confirm within their annual reports that trustees have considered the public benefit test, and that trustees of larger charities should make it clear how they have done so. In lieu of further guidance from the Commission, the above list of questions is a useful starting point.

What happens if a charity fails the test?

94.16   There has been some concern that this test could be used to mask a political drive to secularise society by deregistering religious charities, or to attack fee charging schools. The Commission has denied this, and it is of course, independent from government – any such policy statements would instead be more likely to emanate from the Office of the Third Sector. Charities may be comforted by early work in Scotland, where OSCR carried out some initial 'rolling review pilot visits' looking at public benefit in a sample of charities. OSCR reported in the summer of 2007 on the following:

1   The High School of Dundee;

2   The University of Dundee;

3   Voluntary Action Fund, Dunfermline;

4   Eastriggs and Dornock Childrens' Gala Fund, Eastriggs;

5   Coalburn Miners Welfare Charitable Trust, Coalburn, South Lanark-shire;

6   Arniston Miners Welfare and Social Club, Arniston, Midlothian;

7   John Wheatley College, Glasgow;

8   Pollokshaws Methodist Church, Glasgow.

94.17   OSCR reported that some key lessons learned at this stage included:

● The annual report will be central to the assessment of how charities are addressing the public benefit requirement;

● That the most difficult area relates to fees and unduly restrictive conditions.

94.18   On fees, OSCR considered not only the fee level itself, but how it related to the cost of what was provided, the availaibility and extent of free and facilitated education, the provision of other facilities, the selction of beneficiaries and indirect benefits.

94.19   Where a charity fails to meet the public benefit test the regulator will seek to help the charity in doing so. In the Scottish pilot, for instance, a number of constitutional changes arose as a result of the study. The charity may then need to consider the range of activites it undertakes and alter them. This may be a matter of changing some fundamental policy, such as dealing with restrictive access, or re-routing some activity through a separate entity. If the matter is still not resolved the Commission, or OSCR, could direct the charity to change its behaviour, either by direction or by appointing an interim manager or new trustees. Finally a charity may cease to be a registered charity. In some cases this may happen sooner, where there has been a mistake in the original registration.

94.20   Where a charity ceases to be a registered charity, there will of course be serious tax implications affecting VAT, direct tax, capital gains tax and business rates relief. The exact tax implications will depend on how long the organisation has been a charity, where its wealth has been generated, and whether the organisation has ever been a charity at all in law.

95   Public Charitable Collections

95.1   The state of the law covering public collections, such as street collections, and door-to-door collections is highly unsatisfactory as the regulations accompanying *Part III* of the *Charities Act 1992* have never been brought into force. The *Charities Act 2006* addresses this by giving power to the Secretary of State to control charity fundraising by issuing regulations if he deems it necessary or desirable. In response to this the Institute of Fundraising has established a UK wide, self-regulatory scheme for fundraisers that could avoid or minimise the need for statutory controls.

95.2   A new self-regulatory body, the Fundraising Standards Board, is implementing the Institute's scheme. The Fundraising Standards Board is encouraging all charities that raise funds from the general public to join the scheme. Businesses and consultancies that raise funds from the general public on behalf of charities are also being encouraged to join the scheme.

95.3   Members of the scheme are required to:

- Adhere to the Institute of Fundraising's Codes of Fundraising Practice;

- Adhere to and promote the Fundraising Standards Board's Fundraising Standards Promise, whereby members of the scheme commit to adhere to the highest standards of best practice when fundraising;

- Use the Fundraising Standards Board's logo on all their fundraising communications and corporate literature wherever practical;

- Ensure that they have a robust complaints procedure in place for dealing with complaints from the public about fundraising;

- Nominate a complaints co-ordinator who will act as the primary point of contact with the Fundraising Standards Board.

95.4   There will, however, be statutory control of public charitable collections, though it is unlikely to be introduced before 2009. When enforced, *s 48* of the *Charities Act 2006* will require charities holding public appeals to have a public collections certificate (to be issued by the Charity Commission) and a permit issued by the local authority and *s 49* will require those conducting door-to-door collections to have a public collections certificate and to have notified the local authority and provided it with a copy of its public collections certificate. There will be exemptions for local, short-term collections (a collection is a local, short-term collection if the appeal is local in character and does not exceed a prescribed period) and for door-to-door collections of goods, providing prior notice is given to the relevant local authority. A charitable appeal is not a public appeal if the appeal is made:

- during a public meeting; or

- at a place of worship; or

- on land to which the public has unrestricted access, either because of the express or implied permission of the occupier of the land or where the public has a statutory right of access, for example under the *Countryside and Rights of Way Act 2000*, and where the occupier is the promoter of the collection. (This provision is intended to exclude collections undertaken by organisations such as the National Trust on their own land from the scope of the scheme.); or

- where the public are invited to place money or goods in an unattended receptacle.

95.5   Public charitable collections in the street are currently regulated under the *Police, Factories etc (Miscellaneous Provisions) Act 1916,* and the *Charitable Collections (Transitional Provisions) Order 1974,* contains a model licence that can be used by a local licensing authority that chooses to license street collections, but its use is not obligatory.

95.6   Public charitable collections conducted door-to-door are currently regulated by the *House to House Collections Act 1939* and the *House to House Collections Regulations 1947* which established a central licensing regime for such collections.

95.7   The *Local Government Act 1972* transferred responsibility for both forms of licensing to local authorities from the police, except in London where responsibility remains with the Metropolitan Police and the Common Council of the City of London.

95.8   The Cabinet Office is responsible for administering the national exemption order scheme for door-to-door collections under the current law. National exemption orders are generally available to organisations that have obtained house-to-house collection licences in at least 70 – 100 local authority licensing areas for the two preceding years.

STREET COLLECTIONS

95.9   The relevant local authority should be contacted before a charity attempts to hold a street collection, as street collections are usually required to have a permit or a licence. There is no obligation, however, for local authorities to license street collections and there are no national regulations controlling the collection on the streets of money, or the sale of articles, for the benefit of charities.

DOOR-TO-DOOR COLLECTIONS

95.10   Door-to-door, or as they are sometimes known, house to house, collections must be licensed or have an exemption. An application must be made at least a month in advance of the month in which the collection is due to start. The application must specify the purpose of the collection and the area in which the collection will be made.

95.11   Large charities planning to hold a nationwide collection, or a collection over a substantial part of England and Wales, can apply to the Cabinet Office for exemption from having to apply to each local authority. Local police can give exemption from the need to obtain a licence for a local collection to be completed within a short time period.

95.12   A 'house' in terms of the *House to House Collections Act 1939* includes certain business premises including public houses and places of business, so fund-raising pub crawls come within this legislation. The Act also covers the

95.13   Public Charitable Collections

collection of goods and the house to house sale of goods or services where at least part of the proceeds will be used for charitable purposes.

95.13   The licence is granted to the 'promoter' who is responsible for ensuring that the collection is carried out in accordance with the law. The promoter must keep a record of the name and address of each collector along with the numbers of the collecting tins or receipt book given to them. Collectors must be aged over 16 and they must carry a certificate of authority and wear an official badge, both of which they must sign. The certificate and badge must be returned to the promoter after the event and the promoter must then destroy them.

95.14   Money may only be collected in:

- a sealed tin or box which can only be opened by breaking the seal, and which shows the purpose of the collection and a distinguishing number;

- envelopes sealed by the donor, if authorisation has been obtained from the Secretary of State;

- any other way if the donor is given a receipt from a duplicate or counterfoil receipt book.

[*House to House Collections Regulations 1947, Reg 6(1)(13)*].

95.15   Money must be counted in the presence of the promoter and another responsible person unless the sealed tins are delivered unopened to a bank. The person counting the money must note the amount of money collected in each tin. A return must be made to the licensing authority listing all donations and expenses incurred in connection with the collection within one month of the expiry of the licence.

95.16   When *ss 45* to *66* of the *Charities Act 2006* are implemented the existing legislation covering public collections for charities will be repealed.

FURTHER INFORMATION

95.17   Institute of Fundraising
Park Place
12 Lawn Lane
London
SW8 1UD
Tel: 020 7840 1000
Fax: 020 7840 1001

Fundraising Standards Board
Hampton House
20 Albert Embankment
London
SE1 7TJ
Tel: 0845 402 5442
Fax: 0845 402 5443
Email: info@frsb.org.uk
www.frsboard.org uk/England

500

Fundraising Standards Board
22A/1 Calton Road
Edinburgh
EH8 8DP
Tel: 0845 688 9894
Fax: 0845 688 9895
www.frsb.org.uk/scotlandnorthernireland

Public Fundraising Regulatory Association
Unit 11, Europoint
5–11 Lavington Street
London
SE1 0NZ
Tel: 020 7401 8452
Fax: 020 7928 2925
Email:info@pfra.org.uk

96   Quality Initiatives

INTRODUCTION

96.1   Many voluntary sector organisations are introducing quality systems as a way to maximise their effectiveness. Four of the most common models and systems used in the voluntary sector are described here together with a brief commentary about their use and value. The four quality initiatives are:

- BS EN ISO 9000;

- Investors in People (IIP);

- EFQM Excellence Model;

- PQASSO.

Each of these quality initiatives has a distinctive contribution to make. They are complementary and can be used alongside each other. The 'best' quality models to use are the ones that best meet an organisation's particular needs.

BS EN ISO 9000

96.2   BS EN ISO 9000 is an international standard for quality management systems, developed from the British Standard BS 5750. Known as ISO 9000 for short, its full title reflects the fact that it is a British, European and International Standard. It is therefore well regarded as a 'badge of quality' worldwide and has been adopted by over 50,000 companies in the UK and over 127,000 worldwide.

96.3   The standard is written in a generic form that fits any type of organisation, for example, manufacturing, service industries, voluntary organisations and further education. ISO 9000 is based on the premise that in order to do things consistently well, everyone needs to know what to do and how to do it. The best way to do this is to have documented procedures, as knowledge can more easily be shared in this way and there is less chance of misunderstandings, especially over time.

96.4   Defining and documenting your procedures and practices can provide a powerful starting point for quality improvement. Besides encouraging consistent practice across the organisation and subsequent customer satisfaction, the actual process of documenting procedures encourages organisations to review current practice and to question whether things can be done any better. Gaps in people's knowledge of how things should be carried out can be identified and rectified and staff understand what is expected of them.

96.5   However, one of the many criticisms levelled at ISO 9000 is that too much of the focus is on documenting all procedures, and not enough on how effective they actually are. This is not quite fair for two reasons. First, the standard provides fairly prescriptive guidelines on how to manage quality throughout the lifecycle of a product or service and documented procedures must be in accordance with the requirements of the standard. Second, another fundamental principle of ISO 9000 is the notion of continual improvement, through both internal review and external assessment. In other words, as well as undergoing an external assessment, organisations are obliged to internally review procedures and systems for both compliance and effectiveness.

96.6   This notion of continual improvement is reinforced within the latest revision of the standard (ISO 9001:2000) which requires organisations to have specific measures of improvement. The new standard will also introduce increasing emphasis on relationships with, and understanding of, the customer, his/her needs and satisfaction as well as staff training. In this way, the revisions will move the standard nearer to Investors in People and the EFQM Model.

96.7   Once the quality system is in place and established, an independent assessment by a certified body is carried out to check conformity with the requirements of the standard and to ensure that declared procedures are working in practice. If certification is awarded, the organisation must continue to be regularly audited by an independent certification body.

96.8   There have been many debates about whether self-assessment or validation by a certification body is best for voluntary organisations. Improved public perception of the organisation's image may well result from external validation, but the downfall is that there is a temptation to view obtaining ISO 9000 certification as an end in itself. If this is the approach, then organisations will try to get there as quickly and as cheaply as possible and quality will suffer because important corners are cut. ISO 9000 is a good quality badge to have, but it is much more powerful as a tool to help set up and run a quality management system. Even if a charity does not choose to seek certification, the principles are sound and worth checking out.

INVESTORS IN PEOPLE

96.9   Investors in People (IIP) is a national standard for effective investment in the training and development of people in order to achieve organisational goals. It is a UK government business initiative, developed by the National Training Task Force and endorsed by the CBI and TUC. IIP is open to any organisation of any size from any sector and is now being introduced in a number of countries outside the UK.

96.10   IIP offers an invaluable alternative focus that other quality models (which tend to be more process driven) often gloss over, in other words, that effective quality management requires emphasis on the training and development of employees. While being about people, it is clearly directed at improving performance by linking training and development to the needs of the business.

96.11   The standard provides a set of criteria by which organisations can be assessed in terms of their effectiveness in using training and development to meet organisational targets and improve performance. These criteria are based on four key principles:

●   a commitment, from the top, to develop all employees;

●   a regular review of the training and development needs of employees and a plan to meet those needs;

●   action to train and develop individuals throughout their employment;

●   the measurement of the organisation's success in using its investment in training and development effectively.

96.12   The benefits of IIP can be seen both for the organisation and the individuals within it. The organisation benefits from a more systematic approach to training, improved employee communications and a more skilled and motivated workforce. Individuals often benefit from greater recognition, structured development and increased job satisfaction.

96.13   Learning & Skills Councils, Business Links, Education and Learning in Wales, Local Enterprise Company in Scotland and the Department for Employment and Learning in Northern Ireland can provide help and support to organisations implementing IIP. However, should a charity wish to pursue the IIP award, it only needs to involve other people when ready for an assessment, which is carried out by an independent assessor.

96.14   Following the assessment visit, if the charity meets the standard it will be formally recognised as an 'Investor in People' organisation and can publicise this through use of the IIP logo. Further reassessments will either take place after three years or every 12–15 months in order to ensure that continuous improvement becomes an integral part of organisational management.

EFQM EXCELLENCE MODEL

96.15   The EFQM Excellence Model was first introduced in 1991 and was developed by the European Foundation for Quality Management (EFQM), a body of 14 'leading' European companies. The EFQM was formed in order to promote business improvement through the use of Total Quality Management (TQM), and the group developed the model using considerable expertise developed from the Malcolm Baldrige (USA) and Deming (Japan) Award Models.

96.16   The EFQM Excellence Model was designed as a generic framework for assessing and then continuously improving the performance of an organisation across all its activities. The Model is applicable as much to 'non-business' orientated organisations, such as non-profit organisations, as to private sector organisations. However, a public and voluntary sector version has been published that recognises the richness of differences that exist between these different types of organisations and draws out some small differences. It is this Model that is keenly promoted to the voluntary sector by the National Council for Voluntary Organisations (NCVO).

96.17   The EFQM Excellence Model is not a standard (such as ISO 9000 and IIP). The Model is a non-prescriptive framework that recognises that there are many approaches to achieving sustainable organisational excellence. The Excellence Model is a self-assessment tool, although it can also be used to obtain external validation through participation in the European Quality Award (or a national equivalent) which uses the model as the assessment criteria.

96.18   The Excellence Model's key distinction, when compared with the other 'quality' models, is that it attempts to link organisational processes with actual results. Unlike ISO 9000, for example, this Model places as much emphasis on the necessity to measure outputs, outcomes and impacts as it does on the processes available to enable these.

96.19   The model has nine elements, which have been identified as the key components of business excellence. There are five 'enabler' and four 'result' criteria. The 'enabler' criteria are concerned with what is done to run the organisation and how it is operated, how it manages its staff and resources, how it plans its strategy and how it reviews and monitors key processes.

96.20   The 'result' criteria are concerned with what the organisation has achieved and is achieving as seen by those who have an interest in the organisation, for example, its customers, employees, the community and funders. These cover the level of satisfaction among the organisation's employees and customers, and its impact on the wider community. The framework places percentage weightings on each of the nine criteria, representing a consensus view of their relative importance, but these are only of direct relevance to applicants for quality awards.

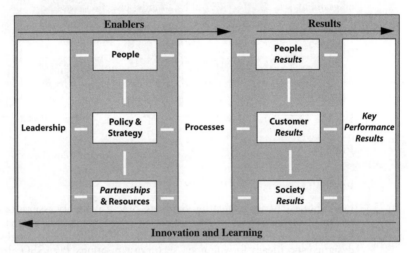

Fig 4: The EFQM Excellence Model

96.21   The starting point for most organisations is to conduct a self-assessment against the Model, which can range from a quick assessment to a fully evidenced and externally validated report. A key part of the detailed 'health check' is that it highlights those areas where an organisation is performing well, as well as those where it is performing poorly. The typical outputs are a score profile against the Model, and much more importantly a prioritised improvement action plan that can provide a valuable input to the annual organisational planning process.

96.22   The EFQM Excellence Model is a non-prescriptive framework that recognises there are many approaches to achieving sustainable excellence in organisations. This lack of prescription for specific controls and procedures allows organisations to build their own underlying tools and procedures. However, the Model's flexibility and non-prescriptive style may frustrate organisations if their priority is to determine clear standards and measure achievement against them.

96.23   It is for this reason that many organisations may find value in referring to more prescriptive standards, such as IIP and ISO 9000, as complements to the Excellence Model. There is no duplication or complication and each of them can contribute to improving the performance of an organisation within one or more of the nine boxes of the Excellence Model.

96.24　Quality Initiatives

96.24　The relationship between the Excellence Model and IIP/ISO 9000 is diagrammatically expressed below.

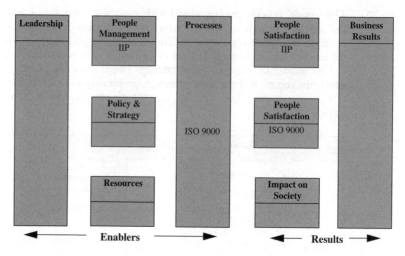

Fig 5

PQASSO

96.25　PQASSO is Charity Evaluation Services' practical quality assurance system for small organisations, or for projects within larger organisations. It is a low-cost, straightforward quality system, written in plain English and designed specifically for voluntary sector organisations. PQASSO provides a flexible, step-by-step approach to working out what an organisation is doing well and what could be improved.

96.26　PQASSO is designed as a self-assessment work pack, which helps a charity administrator to:

- focus on what the organisation is doing;
- bring people together to identify areas for improvement;
- facilitate discussion to ensure all stakeholders are aware of policies, procedures and plans;
- motivate people to make visible progress;
- use a clear language for negotiating with funders.

96.27　The twelve PQASSO quality standards are:

1.　planning for quality
2.　governance
3.　management
4.　user-centred service
5.　staff and volunteers
6.　training and development

7.   managing money

8.   managing resources

9.   managing activities

10.   networking and partnership

11.   monitoring and evaluation

12.   results.

96.28   Each area has three levels of achievement, with details of what the organisation should be doing to achieve each of these levels. Very small or newly
formed charities may decide to choose level 1 as their entry point, with the
option of progressing to levels 2 and 3 as they develop and grow. More
established or complex organisations may decide to begin at level 2 or level 3.

96.29   Each area has 'suggested evidence' to help identify how to demonstrate a
charity's achievements. This leads on to a 'self-assessment' page, which helps
the organisation to decide what action needs to be taken, by specific people
and within specific timeframes to meet the 'levels of achievement. Users are
encouraged to set a review date to evaluate progress.

CONCLUSION

96.30   All four quality initiatives described above have their own specific characteristics. The quality path chosen for a particular organisation will depend on its
particular circumstances. The Business Excellence Model and PQASSO
provide an overall look at performance, Investors in People looks at developing staff, and ISO 9000 helps improve the way processes are managed.
Collectively they can help improve all aspects of organisational performance,
encouraging the constant review and improvement of performance.

FURTHER INFORMATION

EFQM

The British Quality Foundation
32–34 Great Peter St
London SW1P 2QX
Tel: 020 7654 5000
Fax: 020 7654 5001
E-mail: mail@quality-foundation.co.uk
www.quality-foundation.co.uk

Investors in People

Investors in People UK
7–10 Chandos Street
London W1G 9DQ
Tel: 020 7467 1900
Fax: 020 7636 2386
E-mail: information@iipuk.co.uk
www.investorsinpeople.co.uk

96.30 Quality Initiatives

BS EN ISO 9000
BSI British Standards
389 Chiswick High Road
London W4 4AL
Tel: 020 8996 9001
Fax: 020 8996 7001
E-mail: cservices@bsi-global.com
www.bsi-global.com

PQASSO

Charities Evaluation Services
4 Coldbath Square
London
EC1R 5HL
Tel: 020 7713 5772
Fax: 020 7713 5692
E-mail: enquiries@ces-vol.org.uk
www.ces-vol.org.uk

For details of accredited certification bodies:

United Kingdom Accreditation Service
21–47 High Street
Feltham
Middlesex TW13 4UN
Tel: 020 8917 8400
Fax: 020 8917 8500
E-mail: info@ukas.com
www.ukas.com

97   Rates and Council Tax

BUSINESS RATES

97.1   A local authority calculates the rates bill by multiplying the rateable value by a factor set by central government each year called the multiplier, or Uniform Business Rate (UBR). The local authority then applies any applicable reliefs. Rates bills are received sometime between February and April each year. Business rates apply to non-domestic property. Other property used solely for residential purposes is subject to council tax. Rates are due from the owner as long as the property is occupied. No rates are payable in respect of voids of between six weeks and three months, and most empty premises attract half rates thereafter. Properties used for a mixture of purposes are assessed on a case by case basis.

Exemptions

97.2   Certain churches enjoy full relief from rates. These are the Church of England, the Church in Wales, and those certified under the *Places of Worship Registration Act 1855*. The relief extends to their administrative buildings, church halls and similar buildings used in connection with a place of worship. This phrase encompasses a range of other buildings operated in connection with the church. Where property is used for the day-care of those who are ill or disabled, or the provision of welfare or workshops for people with disabilities, then full rate relief is available under the *Rating (Disabled Persons) Act 1978*.

97.3   Apart from these specific exemptions, all charities are entitled to 80% rate relief under the *Local Government Finance Act 1988, ss 43* and *45*, as long as the property is used wholly or mainly for charitable purposes and the charity is the ratepayer. Under *Local Government Finance Act 1988, ss 47* and *48* further discretionary relief is also available up to another 20%, thus allowing local authorities to grant charities complete exemption from rates. Full relief, though on a discretionary basis, is also available to not-for-profit organisations which use the property for educational, social welfare, philanthropic, religious, literary, artistic or scientific purposes, and not-for-profit clubs using the property for recreational purposes. This discretionary relief is less likely to be granted if the organisation does not make its facilities widely available. Under separate regulations the relevant authority has to give one year's notice of a reduction in these reliefs, and the change must take effect at the end of a financial year.

Mixed use

97.4   The reliefs almost exclusively operate where the property is 'wholly or mainly used' for the charitable or similar purposes referred to. 'Mainly used' is defined as more than half (*Fawcett Properties Ltd v Buckingham County Council [1960] 3 All ER 503*). Charitable purposes normally exclude fundraising but include the sale of donated goods. Premises used partly by a charity for its purposes and partly by a non-charitable subsidiary trading company will qualify for relief only in respect of the part actually occupied by the charity.

509

Charity shops

97.5   Charity shops selling donated goods are often operated as trading subsidiaries, in which case they are not automatically entitled to 80% relief, though some local authorities are prepared to grant it. Even where shops are operated by the charity itself, relief could still be restricted if all the proceeds, minus expenses, are not paid to the charity.

97.6   In some instances where donated goods are sold alongside ordinary trading goods the trading activity may be carried out by the charity acting as an agent for the trading company. The charity may claim that it is occupying the whole premises, for the sale of both donated and bought-in goods. The charity would therefore be occupying the shop partly for charitable purposes and partly for another purpose. However, the charity will not necessarily lose its rates relief because it may still be able to satisfy the local authority that the shop is occupied mainly for charitable purposes. Where a charity shop is selling a mixture of new and donated goods then the rating authority can use different bases to assess whether or not the proportion of activity comprises charitable use. Whatever system is used, be it the proportion of floor space, volume, or sales etc, it should be applied consistently and not mean that the shop moves in and out of charitable relief as a result of minor fluctuations.

COUNCIL TAX

97.7   Council tax relates to domestic property, defined as that used wholly for residential accommodation, and is payable by the occupier. Charities do not get any general relief from council tax. Therefore council tax has to be paid on some charitable property which, if it were not residential, would qualify for relief from uniform business rates, for instance hostels, nursing homes and almshouses.

97.8   Although the tax is usually payable by the occupier, there are specific cases relevant to charities where the owner, rather than the occupier, is liable. These are:

- nursing homes, residential care homes, student halls of residence, dwellings occupied solely by students, hostels, dwellings in multiple occupation;

- dwellings occupied by religious communities whose main activities are prayer, education, the relief of suffering, or contemplation;

- dwellings occupied by a minister of religion in connection with the performance of his or her duties; and

- dwellings occupied by staff who live there in order to carry out work for their employer.

97.9   Charities that are liable for council tax will need a clear policy on whether or not they wish to recover it, or part of it, from the occupiers, particularly where there is a chance that by not trying to recover it they could be argued to be replacing statutory provision.

97.10   Because council tax is assessed partly on the value of the property, and partly on the basis of occupancy, some charities will be able to obtain reliefs because of exemptions granted to classes of people with whom they work. These may include:

- full-time students;
- those in hospital or in care, or severely mentally impaired;
- those in hostels or night shelters;
- careworkers;
- members of religious communities;
- certain international visitors (soldiers); and
- prisoners.

97.11   Unoccupied property owned by a registered charity is also exempt from council tax. The property must be unoccupied, but need not be unfurnished and must be owned or leased by a registered charity. It must also have been last occupied by the charity for the purpose of the charity's objectives. The exemption will apply for a maximum of six months from the date last occupied. After this 90% of the charge is payable if the property remains unoccupied and furnished or the full charge is payable if the property is unfurnished.

Scotland

97.12   A similar regime operates for rates and reliefs in Scotland. Where an organisation is registered with the Office of the Scottish Charity Register (OSCR), and the property is used 'wholly or mainly for charitable purposes', charities may be entitled to 80% mandatory rates relief, again with a further 20% discretionary relief.

97.13   Other types of non-profit-making organisation are not automatically entitled to relief, but councils have discretionary powers to grant up to 100% rate relief. To qualify, the organisation must be charitable, religious, or concerned with education, social welfare, science, literature or the fine arts, or the property must be used by a non-profit-making organisation and used wholly or mainly for the purpose of recreation.

97.14   Community amateur sports clubs registered with HMRC may be entitled to 80% mandatory rates relief, with discretionary 100% relief available. Sports clubs that do not meet the requirements for mandatory rates relief may be eligible for up to 100% discretionary rate relief from their local authority.

98   Receipts and Payments Accounting

INTRODUCTION

98.1   Accounts prepared on a receipts and payments basis summarise all the cash transactions that actually took place during the year and show the remaining cash and non-cash assets and liabilities. They do not purport to show a true and fair view of a charity's financial position. Unlike accruals accounts, receipts and payments accounting makes no adjustments to allow for expenditure made in one accounting period that relates to costs incurred in another.

98.2   Unincorporated charities with annual income of £100,000 or less are permitted to prepare receipts and payments accounts and a statement of assets and liabilities if they wish rather than accruals accounts, provided that they do not have another statutory obligation, or are required to do so by their governing document, to produce accruals accounts. Larger unincorporated charities, charitable companies and industrial and provident societies do not have an option to produce accounts prepared on a receipts and payments basis. They must produce accruals accounts.

PRINCIPLES

98.3   Although accounting on a receipts and payments basis is simpler than on an accruals basis it in no way lessens the trustees' responsibility for maintaining the accounting records and ensuring accountability. Consequently many of the fundamental principles set out in detail in the main SORP for Charities follow through into receipts and payments accounting. For instance, the year-end accounts should still distinguish between restricted, unrestricted and designated funds and indicate the existence of liabilities and certain assets that may be recoverable. To an extent these accounts are not pure receipts and payments, they are a hybrid format. The main differences between these and accruals accounts are that:

● accruals, prepayments, depreciation of fixed assets and valuation movements can be ignored; and

● there is no need to present a traditional balance sheet — a statement of assets and liabilities is required instead (or in Scotland a statement of balances).

Income and expenditure

98.4   Many donations to charities are not in cash form and therefore will not feature in receipts and payments accounts. Therefore in some cases the choice of accounting presentation will determine the accounting presentation that must be adopted. For instance, accruals accounting requires donated assets for functional use and receivable items, such as pecuniary legacies, to be treated as income, whereas they are excluded from income in accounts prepared on a receipts and payments basis. Preparing a charity's accounts on an accruals basis could show the charity's income as being more than the £100,000 threshold, so the charity will have to produce accruals accounts, whereas preparing the accounts on a receipts and payments basis might record the income as being less than £100,000, giving the charity the option of preparing accounts on either a receipts and payments or on an accruals basis.

98.5   No formal guidance exists for organisations that find themselves in this position but there are some commonsense guidelines. First, it is important that the accounts are at least internally consistent. Second, the accounts must be comparable from one year to another so that if a charity's income or expenditure is fluctuating around the £100,000 threshold, it would be advisable for it to adopt the higher requirement, i.e. accruals accounts, in order to avoid the expense of having to restate a previous year's figures. Where timing determines on which side of the threshold a charity falls, such as deferred legacy income recognition, then it will be particularly important to consider the impact of the transaction in the foreseeable future.

98.6   Charity accounts must include all the charity's activities including those carried out by, or otherwise relating to, branches. Receipts and payments accounts may only be prepared if the charity's gross income, including that of branches, is under the relevant threshold. Care must be taken to assess the effect of this amalgamation process in advance. If the combined results of the headquarters and branches exceed the threshold, then the accounts will need revision to an accruals basis and the information already obtained from the branches may need to be revised and supplemented.

Assets and liabilities

98.7   The statement of assets and liabilities is not a balance sheet. It is simply a list setting out the charity's assets and liabilities. Appropriate values may be added if available. The assets and liabilities will mainly comprise monetary items such as cash and bank deposits, debtors, loans and tax recovery claims. Other assets such as investments and stock can be included at cost. It is recommended, however, that their estimated value should be set out in a note to the accounts, but this is not a compulsory requirement. In some instances the insured value will be adequate.

98.8   Fixed assets should be included in the statement of assets and liabilities, whether owned or financed through lease or hire purchase, and even when the charity's governing document prohibits their resale. Where future lease payments (e.g. to finance an asset) do not constitute a liability, then the future commitment should be disclosed as related to the relevant asset. Other liabilities should be disclosed with any other commitments disclosed separately.

98.9   If possible, conditional liabilities (e.g. where a charity has agreed to make a grant of £2,000 to an organisation on condition that the organisation itself raises £1,000 from other sources) should be listed separately and guarantees and contingent liabilities should also be listed together with their estimated value wherever possible.

98.10   The Charity Commission has issued standard forms which can be used to submit receipts and payments accounts. They are not statutory filing documents. There is no obligation to use them; they are merely produced to assist smaller charities. To underline this point, the Commission's guidance leaflet (CC16 'Receipts and Payments Accounts Pack') includes a specimen form of accounts prepared without using the standard forms. In practice the standard forms will be of most use to small charities with simple financial affairs, and where there is only limited demand from the public for information about their affairs.

99   Reclaiming Tax

99.1   Charities have a wide range of tax exemptions and generally have no liability to corporation tax or income tax as a result. Nevertheless, charities will have received income from which income tax will have been deducted at source. Where the charity has no liability or the liability is less than the income tax suffered, the charity can obtain a repayment of all or part of this tax.

99.2   In order to obtain a tax repayment, the charity must submit a claim to HMRC. Such claims must be sent to HMRC Charities (Repayments) at their office in Bootle. Before any such claim can be considered by HMRC, they will need the appropriate forms and supporting documents. A charity can submit a repayment claim as often as it wishes but most charities find it convenient to make an annual claim at the end of each tax year. Larger charities, however, often make claims quarterly or monthly.

FORM FOR CLAIM

99.3   To reclaim tax a charity must complete an R68 claim form, and an R68 Gift Aid schedule if it is reclaiming income tax paid by donors who have completed a Gift Aid declaration, or an R68 other income schedule if it is claiming a repayment of tax withheld on certain income taxed at source, for example, bank or building society interest, royalties, legacy income, etc. Proof of tax deducted at source in the form of a tax voucher from the payer should be submitted with the form. These forms can be obtained from HMRC or can be downloaded from HMRC's website. New forms are usually issued each time a repayment claim is made. The R68 claim form requires details of the amount of tax being reclaimed, the period the claim relates to, whether the claimant is a charity or a community amateur sports club, and details of where the repayment should be sent.

INCORRECT FORMS

99.4   HMRC will not accept the form unless the declaration has been completed and signed by an appropriate official of the charity, who will normally be the company secretary, treasurer or a trustee. In that declaration the person signing it claims exemption from tax on the basis of the claimant being a charity or a community amateur sports club and states that to the best of their knowledge and belief the information given on the form is correct and complete. The form makes it clear that false statements can lead to prosecution and this could happen where there was a deliberate attempt to defraud or cheat HMRC. Prosecutions are, however, relatively rare. What is perhaps more common is that insufficient checks are carried out by the charity to ensure that the form is properly completed and that the charity is entitled to a full exemption from tax. If HMRC discover this situation after the repayment has been made they can, of course, assess the charity for the amount of tax overpaid. If they then consider that this resulted from negligent conduct on the part of the charity, interest and penalties can also be charged. HMRC provide a good deal of help and guidance to charities to ensure that their tax affairs are dealt with properly. They are not always sympathetic, therefore, when charities have not been following the correct procedures or have been careless in dealing with their tax affairs.

99.5   Reclaiming Tax

REPAYMENT PERIOD

99.5   A charity has six years in which to make a repayment claim and HMRC normally has six years in which to make any assessment to collect tax. If, however, the Inspector discovers at a later date that a repayment claim is incorrect due to the fraudulent or negligent conduct of the charity, then HMRC have 20 years to make an assessment for the tax due. Full disclosure of all relevant facts is, therefore, extremely important if the charity is to avoid the risk of any later discovery by HMRC.

99.6   HMRC have stated that they no longer want charities to send their accounts with their repayment claims and even if they do HMRC will not look at them. Instead HMRC issue a self-assessment tax return and then open an enquiry if they require further information to see whether any tax is payable or if excessive repayments have been claimed. A charitable trust may be asked to submit its accounts. A company is required to submit its accounts with its tax return. If HMRC find something wrong they may well start an investigation into earlier years.

HMRC PROCEDURES

99.7   HMRC have a statutory power to require a charity to produce its books and records for inspection by an Inland Revenue officer of HMRC. This power extends to all books, documents and other records in the possession of, or under the control of, the charity, that contain information relating to the claim. Where a charity fails to produce the necessary documents, it can be liable to a penalty of £300 with an additional penalty of £60 per day until the documents are produced. HMRC now have a continuous programme of on-site visits to charities to examine their books and records.

99.7   If the repayment claim appears to be in order and is supported by the necessary tax certificates and vouchers, HMRC will normally make the repayment without delay. It is in the interest of the charity to ensure that all such documents are properly completed, if only to avoid unnecessary enquiries from HMRC, which can be time consuming and administratively expensive.

100   Registered Social Landlords

CONSTITUTION

100.1   Registered Social Landlords (RSLs) are independent, not-for-profit organisations providing homes for people in housing need. In addition to permanent general needs housing, this provision extends to supported housing for residents with special needs, shared ownership properties for sale, temporary accommodation, leasehold schemes for the elderly, sheltered housing, student accommodation and key worker accommodation. The *Housing Act 1996* established the term 'Registered Social Landlord' to supersede that of 'Registered Housing Association'. To be 'registered' means inclusion on the Housing Corporation's register of social landlords.

100.2   The Housing Corporation (*www.housingcorp.gov.uk*) is a Non Departmental Public Body sponsored by the Department of Communities and Local Government (CLG) (*www.communities.gov.uk*). Its role is to fund and regulate RSLs in England. Communities Scotland (Scottish Homes transferred most of its functions to Communities Scotland on 1 November 2001 although it still exists as a residuary body), The National Assembly for Wales and the Northern Ireland Housing Executive perform the equivalent role in other parts of the UK.

100.3   The Board or Management Committee of a registered social landlord comprises members without executive director responsibilities. They have legal responsibility for the policies and running of the organisation and usually delegate the day-to-day management to a senior management team comprising executive officers. Board members of registered social landlords are now entitled to receive remuneration in their capacity as Board members although many have not yet introduced this in their organisations.

100.4   There are three types of body eligible for registration:

- a registered charity that is a housing association;

- an industrial and provident society (provided it fulfils certain conditions);

- a company (also subject to conditions).

100.5   The principal condition referred to above is that the body is non-profit making. This is defined as not trading for profit or having a constitution that prohibits the issuing of capital with interest or dividend exceeding a rate determined by the Treasury.

CHARITABLE STATUS

100.6   A registered social landlord can be charitable or non-charitable depending upon its objects. An RSL may have charitable status if its objects are restricted to measures for the relief of poverty, for example the objects of many RSLs refer to housing being provided for persons in 'necessitous circumstances'. However, there is no statutory definition of 'necessitous circumstances' and in practice this is usually taken to mean those on less than average incomes or those in receipt of benefit.

100.7 Charitable industrial and provident societies which are registered social landlords do not register with the Charity Commission as they are independently regulated by the Housing Corporation. Other charitable social landlords must be registered with the Charity Commission.

100.8 Specific tax exemptions are available to charitable RSLs but charitable status does not give a blanket exemption from tax. Confirmation of exemption should be sought from the Inland Revenue.

REGISTRATION

100.9 The Charity Commission and the Housing Corporation have streamlined the process for the registration of RSLs which are also seeking charitable status. The Housing Corporation, as the principal regulator of RSLs, will now carry out the bulk of pre-registration scrutiny and then confirm to the Commission that the body meets certain criteria. The Commission and the Corporation will be concerned to ensure that a prospective RSL:

- has an effective governing document;

- is independent of other bodies (particularly of a local authority which is transferring its housing stock to the RSL);

- is fully able to take decisions in its own interests and those of its beneficiaries.

100.10 Particular areas of interest and concern will be:

- nomination agreements with local authorities. A charitable RSL must be able to consider applicants who are not on the local authority's waiting list and must have the final choice over all tenants;

- group structures. Charitable RSLs may be part of a group structure. The Charity Commission will be concerned to establish that the trustees are able to take decisions that are demonstrably in the best interests of the RSL and independent of the group parent;

- governing body membership. Neither the Commission nor the Corporation will want local authority nominees to make up more than a third of the governing body. Procedures for dealing with conflicts of interest will need to be in place.

RESIDENTS ON THE BOARD

100.11 A charitable RSL can have tenants on the governing body providing that this is permitted by the governing document. There is no legal bar on the number of tenants who can be trustees, so an RSL with a resident majority on its board can be a charity. However, all trustees must act, and be seen to act, in the best interests of the RSL and not for their own private interest or gain. Many RSLs follow the stock transfer governance model of one-third independent board members, one-third resident-elected board members and one-third local authority nominated board members.

FUNDING

100.12 The *Housing Act 1996* replaced Housing Association Grant with Social Housing Grant which may be paid by the Housing Corporation to RSLs to assist with their expenditure on housing activities. The Corporation lays down certain principles about how social housing grant can be applied for, the types of housing activities it will cover, how it will be calculated, and how it will be paid. It will also attach conditions to the receipt of grant and these apply to the RSL to which it is paid and to any other RSL that subsequently comes into possession of the property funded by grant.

ACCOUNTING REQUIREMENTS

100.13   The *Housing Act 1996* gives the Housing Corporation the power to lay down accounting requirements for RSLs. The current accounting requirements are set out in the Accounting Requirements for Registered Social Landlords General Determination 2006. This Determination draws on many features of the *Companies Act 1985* with alternative disclosures to reflect the activities of a housing association. In particular, an analysis of social housing activities and non-social housing activities is required. In some cases an RSL may have to supply further additional information to satisfy the requirements of another body with which it is registered.

100.14   The Statement of Recommended Practice (SORP): 'Accounting by Registered Social Landlords' (RSL SORP) was first published jointly in March 1999 by the National Housing Federation, the Welsh Federation of Housing Associations and the Scottish Federation of Housing Associations and was then updated in 2002 and again in 2005. The SORP outlines the requirements for the primary financial statements and other disclosures to be given in the notes to the accounts. It explains how RSLs should interpret and apply the requirements of applicable Financial Reporting Standards, especially in contentious areas such as major repairs expenditure on housing properties and housing property depreciation. This SORP requires housing properties to be shown either at historical cost net of social housing grant or at valuation. If properties are shown at cost, only costs that are directly attributable to bringing the properties into working condition for their intended use should be included. Any property valuation should use the existing use value for social housing (EUV-SH) as defined in the SORP.

100.15   With continual changes in financial reporting standards and other accounting practice, combined with changes in the social housing sector, a SORP Working Party continues to work on updates to the RSL SORP. The Update to the 2005 SORP is expected to be published before the end of 2007 and will be referred to as SORP 2008. The main changes affect accounting for shared ownership properties and mixed tenure developments. The effective date will be for accounting periods beginning on or after 1 April 2008, but earlier adoption will be encouraged. The majority of RSLs will therefore need to implement the changes in their 31 March 2009 financial statements but some are likely to adopt the changes for 31 March 2008.

100.16   Another update to the SORP is then expected in 2009 which will take into consideration the ASB's revised approach to conversion in respect of International Financial Reporting Standards.

AUDIT

100.17   Every registered social landlord is required, under legislation, to have an annual independent audit, although the specific auditing requirements vary depending on the legal status of the RSL. For example, some registered social landlords may be eligible to apply exemptions applicable to small companies, charities and industrial and provident societies. The thresholds have been amended by Statutory Instrument 2006/265 The *Friendly and Industrial and Provident Societies Act 1968 (Audit Exemption) (Amendment) Order 2006* and the *Charities Act 2006*. Advantage of these exemptions is only possible if permitted under the rules of the registered social landlord.

100.18   Auditors of RSLs must be registered auditors, i.e. eligible under the *Companies Act 1989* and registered with a supervisory body recognised under that Act.

ACQUIRING TENANTED HOUSING STOCK

100.19   A charitable RSL may only acquire tenanted housing stock, including local authority housing stock, when it is satisfied that the acquisition:

- will enable it to further its charitable objects; and

- is capable of being regarded objectively in that way.

100.20   The two main reasons for charitable RSLs considering the acquisition of tenanted stock are:

- that they can provide a better service for the tenants than that provided by the current landlord; or

- in the longer term it will increase the RSL's ability to provide for people qualified to be its beneficiaries, as it can offer them housing as vacancies arise.

100.21   Trustees considering acquiring tenanted stock will need to consider the following factors and take advice from their lawyers, the Housing Corporation and the Charity Commission:

- how the intended acquisition fits in with the RSL's policy for fulfilling its charitable objects;

- what would be the ratio of non-beneficiaries in the properties to existing tenants;

- the expected rate of turnover of non-beneficiary tenants;

- statutory rights to buy;

- the opportunity to buy on advantageous terms.

LETTINGS POLICY/HOUSING OF NON-BENEFICIARIES

100.22   Charitable RSLs should have a lettings policy that seeks to ensure that each housing unit is let in accordance with the charity's objects, or alternatively that it is let at market rates as an investment. This can be complex in practice, as on the one hand it is not appropriate to means-test beneficiaries and terminate their tenancies if the economic circumstances improve, but on the other hand the RSL's charitable support can only be offered to those whose circumstances as such that the need the help the charity offers. One way of dealing with this is for the RSL to offer an incentive scheme leading to full or shared ownership of the dwelling.

NATIONAL HOUSING FEDERATION (NHF)

100.23   The National Housing Federation (*www.housing.org.uk*) is the body that represents the independent social housing sector. It has approximately 1,300 non-profit housing organisations in its membership. The NHF represents and negotiates in the interest of its members to help them in providing affordable homes to meet housing needs. It also provides information and support for its members and helps to shape policy in the social housing sector.

101 Registration with the Charity Commission

THE REGISTER

101.1 *Section 3(1)* of the *Charities Act 1993* as amended by the *Charities Act 2006* requires the Charity Commission to keep a register of those charities in England and Wales that are required to register with the Charity Commission. Scottish charities do not register with the Commission and are considered in CHAPTER 108. The Commission has a computerised register that can be consulted by the public via the Internet or at the Charity Commission's offices.

WHICH CHARITIES HAVE TO REGISTER?

101.2 Section 3A of the *Charities Act 1993* states that all charities must be registered except for:

- those with a gross annual income of £5,000 or less (effective from April 2007);

- excepted charities with a gross annual income of £100,000 or less (likely to be effective from 2008);

- exempt charities supervised by a principal regulator, such as the Housing Corporation or the Financial Services Authority (likely to be effective from 2008);

- other exempt charities with a gross annual income of £100,000 or less (likely to be effective from 2008).

101.3 All charities that opt for the new status of Charitable Incorporated Organisation must when it is introduced in 2008 register with the Commission regardless of their income.

101.4 If a charity is not registered, but should be registered, it is the duty of the trustees to apply for registration. Similarly if a charity has ceased to exist, or if there are changes to the particulars entered on the Charity Commission's register, it is the duty of the trustees to inform the Commission.

CHARGES

101.5 At present there is no charge for registration. However, charges may be introduced in the future to cover the cost of the service under *s 85(1)* of the *Charities Act 1993*.

THE PROCESS

101.6 Those thinking about setting up a charity should start by getting a copy of the Charity Commission's booklet CC21 'Registering as a Charity' available at *www.charity-commission.gov.uk/publications*. This explains the types of organisations that can be registered as charities, the advantages and limitations of being a charity and the registration process. If having read this booklet it looks as if the organisation is likely to be charitable, and would be required to register with the Commission, the next step is to legally constitute the organisation (for example as a trust or a company) if this has not already been done, and apply to the Commission for a Registration Application Pack (call 0845 300 0218 or download one from *www. Charity-commission.gov.uk*). This includes an application form (APP1) and a declaration form (DEC1) that must be completed by all trustees. Apart from providing the Charity Commission with routine administrative information, the application form is intended to confirm that the activities of the proposed charity are indeed going to be in line with its declared objects. The questionnaire asks for information about the intended activities of the charity, about the proposed trustees and other relevant information including details of how the charity will meet the public benefit test.

101.7   The next step is to send the Commission:

- the completed application form (APP1);

- two copies of the organisation's governing document;

- copies of the financial accounts for the last three years where these are available;

- the declaration form (DEC1);

- supporting information, such as a business plan, independent expert assessment, publicity literature, newspaper cuttings, written pledges of funding, etc.

101.8   The governing document should have been incorporated, executed or adopted as appropriate, and evidence provided that this has happened. This evidence will differ for each type of constitution. A limited company should provide a certified copy of the Certificate of Incorporation, the pages of the memorandum and articles listing the subscribers, and copies of any special resolutions. A trust should provide a certified copy of the executed trust deed after it has been signed, witnessed, dated and sent to the HMRC Office of the Controller of Stamps in case it attracts stamp duty. The Commission recommends that the promoters of a trust should always refer to the nearest Stamp Office to check on the necessary procedure. An unincorporated association should provide a certified copy of the minutes of the general meeting at which the constitution was adopted and copies of the minutes of any subsequent meetings reflecting changes to the constitution. The Commission emphasises that the constitution, and any changes to it, must be approved by the members, not by the trustees alone.

101.9   Once the documentation is received by the Commission it will be checked to see if the objects are charitable in law, the proposed activities are capable of furthering the stated purpose and the public benefit test is satisfied. Other checks may also be necessary. For example, if the beneficiaries are vulnerable children or adults the Commission may carry out checks with other government departments and statutory bodies, such as the Criminal Records Bureau. HMRC may also be consulted.

101.10   The Charity Commission aims to reply to applications within 15 working days, either approving the application, requesting further information, or rejecting the application and setting out the reasons for this. The letter will name the officer dealing with the application and give a contact number and a reference number to be used in any further correspondence.

101.11　Registration with the Charity Commission

101.11　The process can be as quick as a few days, as in the case of the Diana, Princess of Wales Memorial Trust, but in 2006 the average time for processing an application was 87 working days. Applications are dealt with more speedily when the Charity Commission's or the Charity Law Association's model governing documents are used or where a standard governing document is used without amendment and with the agreement of the issuing body (see CHAPTER 55). In cases of dispute, for instance where an organisation is seeking charitable status in an area hitherto not considered as charitable, the process of arguing the point with the Charity Commission may take several months or even years before it is resolved. An initial rejection can be reviewed and an appeal can be brought in the High Court. An appeal in the High Court can be brought not only by the promoters, but by any person, apart from the Attorney-General, who is, or may be, affected by the registration. If a charity's registration has gone to appeal in the High Court, then it will be suspended from the register pending the outcome of that appeal and will not be conclusively presumed to be a charity during this period. [*Charities Act 1993, s 4*]. Most appeals against registration are made by HMRC, as it stands to lose money if an organisation is granted charitable status.

101.12　Once the Charity Tribunal provided for in the *Charities Act 2006* is established, appeals against the Charity Commission's legal decisions can be taken to the Tribunal. This process will be cheaper, more convenient and less formal than appealing to the High Court. Access to the High Court will still be possible on appeal against a decision of the Charity Tribunal.

101.13　Once registration is approved the charity will be entered on the register and the promoter will be sent the registration number and a certificate (form RE5) setting out the details of its entry on the register. Inclusion on the register is, for legal purposes, proof that the organisation is a charity. The registration may not be backdated, although HMRC may backdate tax exemption if the organisation can demonstrate that from an earlier point in time exclusively charitable activities were undertaken.

REMOVAL FROM THE REGISTER

101.14　Existing registered charities with an annual income below the £5,000 threshold for registration can ask to be removed from the register. They will, however, continue to be charities and will have to continue to abide by charity law.

101.15　If the trustees wish to wind up a registered charity they must send the Charity Commission evidence that the procedures for dissolving the charity have been properly completed. These procedures are usually set out in the charity's governing document. They must also send the Commission a copy of the charity's final accounts and of the minutes of the meeting where the resolution to terminate the charity was passed.

101.16　If a charity no longer appears to the Charity Commission to be meeting the criteria for being a charity, *s 3(4)* of the *Charities Act 1993* requires the Commission to remove it from the register. This sub-section also gives the Commission power to remove from the register any charity that has ceased to exist or is not operating.

DECLARATION OF REGISTERED CHARITABLE STATUS

101.17　Registered charities with a gross income of over £10,000 in the previous financial year must state that they are registered charities on certain specified documents such as fund-raising literature, bills of exchange, cheques, receipts and invoices. [*Charities Act 1993, s 5*]. The Charity Commission has indicated that the following statements would satisfy the requirement.

- 'A Registered Charity'
- 'Registered Charity No' (followed by the charity's registration number)
- 'Registered as a Charity'
- 'Registered with the Charity Commission'

PENALTIES FOR NON-COMPLIANCE

101.18 Many organisations are required by the *Charities Act 1993* to register with the Charity Commission have not registered. Although trustees have a duty to register it is not actually an offence not to register. However, an organisation that does not register is unlikely to get the tax benefits to which it is entitled. If the Charity Commission becomes aware of the organisation's existence and orders it to register, the trustees could be found in contempt of court if they continue to fail to register the organisation.

101.19 Failing to comply with the provisions of *s 5* of the *Charities Act 1993*, which requires the organisation's charitable status to be declared on certain documents, is a serious matter as it is a criminal offence punishable by a fine. Liability rests with the individual who issues, authorises or signs the document, regardless of whether they are a trustee or a member of staff.

102   Religious Charities

102.1   The advancement of religion is a charitable purpose. The *Charities Act 2006* states that 'religion' includes a religion which involves belief in more than one god (e.g. Hinduism), and a religion which does not involve belief in a god (e.g. some forms of Buddhism). The criteria used by the Charity Commission since 1999 to decide if an organisation is advancing religion are:

- Do adherents have a belief in a Supreme Being?
- Do adherents worship the Supreme being?
- Does the organisation advance the religion?
- Is the organisation established for the benefit of the public?

102.2   The criteria refer to a 'Supreme Being', rather than a god, because belief in a Supreme Being is a necessary characteristic of religion in charity law. The law allows theistic, non-theistic and polytheistic faiths to be regarded as religions. A Supreme Being does not have to be in the form of a personal creator god. It may be in the form of one god or many gods, or of no god at all in the accepted understanding of the word. This allows Jainism, for example, to be regarded as a religion because although it does not involve a belief in god, it does involve a belief in a Supreme Being.

102.3   The Charity Commission have indicated that the definition of religion contained in the *Charities Act 2006* may need further clarification. When the Commission carry out public consultations on the public benefit of religious charities they will consider what further guidance on the definition of a religious charity may be required.

102.4   There are over 22,000 faith based charities on the Charity Commission's register, including those whose sole aim is to advance a particular faith (e.g. Christianity, Islam or Sikhism) and those where a particular faith is the driving force behind the charitable activity (e.g. to advance education or relieve poverty). The Charity Commission is actively seeking to engage with faith based groups, and in 2006 conducted a programme of visits to mosques, churches and temples all over the country to listen to the experiences of faith communities and understand better their activities in order to improve the services the Commission provides to such groups.

102.5   Examples of religious charities include:

- those advancing particular religions, for example Christianity, Judaism, Islam, Hinduism and Buddism, in the UK and overseas;
- those conducting religious services and promoting public worship;
- those distributing religious literature;
- those providing and maintaining places of worship, churchyards and other religious burial grounds;
- those providing spiritual guidance and spiritual retreats;
- those supporting ministers of religion, including those housing ministers and others employed by religious charities orders and those caring for ministers and former ministers and their families;

- those set up in general terms for religious purposes and to support religious institutions and communities.

102.6   Under the *Charities Act 2006* religious charities must be able to demonstrate that they are of public benefit. The public benefit test means that religious cults can be registered if the public benefit is proved, whereas an enclosed order of nuns who spend their time in contemplation and prayer cannot be registered. This interpretation is not intended to cast doubt on the intercessory value of prayer, it simply means that charitable status requires the advancement and promotion of religion, not merely the practice of that religion. Similarly the Courts have held exorcism to be charitable, whilst freemasonry was not.

102.7   The Charity Commission recognises the promotion of religious harmony between religions and between believers and non-believers as charitable. It is judged to be for public benefit as promoting harmony and tolerance could lead to reductions in crime and conflict, though to be recognised as charitable the organisation will need to demonstrate that disharmony between people from particular groups is apparent, or has the potential to arise, or is already causing conflict. Having an understanding of others' beliefs can also be an important factor in determining the quality of care provided by some charities, for example those providing health care or care of the elderly.

PLACES OF WORSHIP

102.8   Individual local places of worship may be:

- excepted from registration with the Charity Commission, for example if they are registered under the *Places of Worship Registration Act 1855* (once the provisions in the *Charities Act 2006* relating to excepted charities come into force excepted charities will have to register if their annual income is above £100,000);

- designated religious bodies (Scotland);

- too small to be required to register with the Charity Commission, i.e. their gross annual income does not exceed £5,000; or

- registered charities.

102.9   There is often a misconception amongst religious groups, especially those that are not aligned to any particular denomination, that they do not have to register as charities. This is not so. If their activities are charitable and they provide public benefit, then most are required to be registered under the *Charities Act 2006*. Exception under the *Places of Worship Registration Act 1855* only applies to charities established for the provision and maintenance of places of worship, and not to those, for example, conducting religious services and promoting public worship The specific church organisations that are excepted from registration are set out in *Charities (Exception from Registration) Regulations (SI 1996/180)*. (See CHAPTER 48.)

CHURCH OF ENGLAND

102.10   The Church of England has an extremely formalised structure with many of its powers and duties deriving from legislation. Its parish structure covers the whole of England, and many of its office bearers have powers which extend beyond the confines of the church context. At the top of the structure are the provinces of Canterbury and York, together comprising 43 dioceses, each of which is overseen by a bishop, some of whom sit in the House of Lords. Anglican Dioceses are divided into archdeaconries, which are subdivided into rural deaneries. These are augmented by diocesan courts, provincial courts, and the court of ecclesiastical causes reserved. Between them these courts will deal with matters such as faculties and proceedings against priests including matters concerning doctrine, ritual or ceremony. A faculty is the legal granting of permission for altering a consecrated building or its contents, or other areas which may be determined by the bishop.

102.11   Synods, comprising elected lay and clerical members exist at different levels: deanery, diocesan and General. The General Synod has legislative powers.

102.12   The parish is led by the incumbent, who is priest in charge, vicar or rector. The terms 'vicar' and 'rector' are now almost synonymous, the original distinction dating back to the dissolution of the monasteries. Once instituted only the incumbent (apart from the bishop) has the duty and right to minister within the parish, and to receive a stipend. Since 1993 women may be ordained to the priesthood, although individual parishes still have the right to pass a resolution to the effect that they will not accept a female incumbent.

102.13   Churchwardens are responsible for the fabric of the church and have powers, along with the incumbent, which include the right to prevent people from entering the church. They may also remove people who cause a disturbance. The incumbent and wardens may be assisted by other lay officers, such as the verger (responsible for the internal fabric), readers (who assist with pastoral work), a sexton (usually responsible for the churchyard, grave digging and bell ringing) and side-persons.

102.14   The Parochial Church Council (PCC) (not the same as a parish council) is elected from the electoral roll of the parish at the annual general meeting, and functions like a board of trustees administering the church's affairs in, and sometimes beyond, the parish. Its chairman is the incumbent, but the treasurer will normally be a member, or co-opted member, of the PCC, which is a body corporate with perpetual succession. Its powers are derived from various pieces of legislation, principally the *Parochial Church Councils (Powers) Measure 1956* and the *Church Representation Rules* although much of its work is delegated to the standing committee, comprising the incumbent and wardens.

102.15   The annual general meeting of the church must be held each year by 30 April. Amongst its business will be the receiving of the accounts and annual report, prepared and audited or examined under the *Charities Act 1993* and the *Church of England Accounting Regulations* requirements. Although these accounts and report do not need to be filed with the Charity Commission as long as the PCC continues to be excepted. They must be sent to the local Diocesan Board of Finance within 28 days of the AGM. Other business will include reports from various committees responsible for fabric and the electoral roll, and from the deanery synod. The Central Board of Finance of the Church of England publishes its own guidance on PCC accounting.

CHARITIES ACT 1993 AND ECCLESIASTICAL PROPERTY

102.16   *Section 96(2)* of the *Charities Act 1993* states that the expression 'charity' is not applicable, in the Act, 'to any ecclesiastical corporation (that is to say, any

528

corporation in the Church of England, whether sole or aggregate, which is established for spiritual purposes) in respect of the corporate property of the corporation, except to a corporation aggregate having some purposes which are not ecclesiastical in respect of its corporate property held for those purposes; or to any Diocesan Board of Finance within the meaning of the *Endowments and Glebe Measure 1976* for any diocese in respect of the diocesan glebe land of that diocese within the meaning of that Measure; or to any trust of property for purposes for which the property has been consecrated'.

ROMAN CATHOLIC CHURCH

102.17   In the UK the Roman Catholic Church has a similar structure to the Anglican Church but there are several important differences. Both Anglican and Roman Catholic dioceses are registered charities, but Catholic parishes (unlike Anglican parishes) are not autonomous – their accounts are consolidated into the diocesan accounts. Canon law determines much of the Roman Catholic Church's activity but within the UK this does not have the same force of law as the Church of England's legal framework.

CHURCHES IN SCOTLAND

102.18   Certain religious charities in Scotland are treated similarly to excepted charities in England and Wales. The Office of the Scottish Charity Regulator included a religious organisation in its 2007 pilot review of Scottish charities and how they meet the public benefit test. The paragraph reproduced below is instructive, although it should be remembered that this report is an extract from a pilot, and specifically applies the Scottish law.

> 'The primary activity of Pollokshaws Methodist Church is the provision of public worship. OSCR is satisfied that the provision of worship provides benefit to those attending by enhancing their spiritual wellbeing and sense of spiritual and moral fellowship, and providing spiritual, moral and social instruction. The other activities provide benefit to those attending in terms of social and moral instruction and pastoral care and to the wider community through enhanced social solidarity. There was no evidence of private benefit or disbenefit resulting from the activities of the Church'.

103   Research

RESEARCH IS NOT CHARITABLE PER SE

103.1   Carrying out research is not, of itself, a charitable objective. However, charities are permitted to carry out research, or to commission others to carry out research on their behalf, provided that research is included in the charity's objects, falls within its powers, and is for the public benefit. The research must be balanced and objective and the results must be made publicly available. Charities are under no obligation to publish their research, they are merely required to make the public broadly aware of the results and the conclusions that can be drawn from the results and make the results available to any interested party who wishes to scrutinise the results. Charities can charge a reasonable fee for access to the results of their research. Such trading would be regarded as primary purpose.

INTELLECTUAL PROPERTY

103.2   In general charities should make the results of their research available reasonably promptly. However, the Charity Commission will sanction a delay if the results could be exploited commercially. Charities should protect the valuable intellectual property arising from research under patent, or in other ways. They should use intellectual property for the purposes of the charity or exploit it commercially to raise funds for the charity.

103.3   In some instances it will be necessary for a charity's trading subsidiary rather than the charity to conduct research, for example if a third party sponsoring the research wishes to delay or restrict making the results publicly available for commercial reasons, or if a public body wishes to keep secret the results of research it wishes to commission a charity to conduct on its behalf. If this is the case the charity must not pass any intellectual property rights to its trading company free of charge. It must charge a fee or arrange for an annual royalty payment to be made. And, as with any other such arrangement, the trading company must pay the charity a fee which covers the cost to the charity of the use of any of the charity's assets.

COMMISSIONING RESEARCH

103.4   Charities commissioning others to undertake research on their behalf must either directly supervise and monitor the research themselves, or arrange for this to be done on their behalf, in order to ensure that the charity's funds are being properly applied. They should have a written contract that includes details of:

- how the research will be supervised;

- who will evaluate the results;

- who will own the results, and what share of the proceeds the charity will get if they are exploited commercially; and

- how the results will be published.

103.5   The trustees must be satisfied that the public benefit of the research will outweigh any potential private benefit to the researchers.

VAT

103.6   Research that consists of original investigation is exempt from VAT if it is conducted by an eligible body (usually an educational charity) and supplied to another eligible body. Research that is routine analysis rather than original investigation is not VAT exempt and will normally be standard rated.

CHARITY COMMISSION GUIDANCE

103.7   In October 2000 the Charity Commission published guidance on charities and research. The guidance explains that trustees have a duty to ensure that any research carried out, or commissioned or funded by a charity remains within the charity's purposes and powers, is well managed and cost effective, is of good quality, and has a public benefit.

104   Reserves

104.1   When individuals give money to charities they want it to be spent on charitable activities, not hoarded in a bank. Charity law requires that a charity's income is applied within a reasonable time of being received, unless the charity has specific, express powers in its governing document allowing it to hold income in reserve rather than spending it promptly. Failure to consider the matter and allow income to accumulate without good reason amounts to a breach of trust.

104.2   Charities, just like other businesses, need to hold reserves in order to protect their cash flow position, meet their liabilities and honour their commitments to users and beneficiaries. At times Trustees will face a conflict between their duty to act prudently, safeguarding the welfare of future beneficiaries, and their duty to apply income quickly. Some charities have been the subject of media criticism because of their high reserves, particularly those with reserves equivalent to between five, ten or even 20 years of their current annual expenditure. This type of publicity can bring a charity, or even charities in general, into disrepute, particularly if the charity is continuing to fund-raise.

104.3   Having too much or too little in reserve can deter funders. Grant-making trusts and other funders scrutinise the amount a charity is holding in reserve and will be unwilling to fund projects if the charity clearly has sufficient reserves to fund the project itself, or where the charity has too little in reserve to ensure its medium to long-term survival. Holding too little in reserve can be costly, particularly when a blip in fund-raising means having to cut back on staff, with the associated redundancy costs, only to have the expense of recruiting new staff a few months later when funding has picked up.

104.4   At the time of writing a new version of the Charity Commission's publication CC19 'Charities' Reserves' is in preparation. However, RS13 'Tell it like it is. The extent of charity reserves and reserves policies' can be downloaded from the Commission's website (*www.charitycommission.gov.uk/publications*). The Commission's last guidance was not prescriptive. Recognising the lack of homogeneity in the sector, it did not attempt to define what level of reserves a charity should have. Rather, it stated that a charity should have a reserves policy and must be able to justify why it is holding a particular amount in reserve at a particular point in time. The level of reserves should be justified with reference to the charity's current position and future prospects. Where a charity holds income in reserve, the Commission, in its role as regulator, seeks evidence that the trustees have given proper consideration to the level of reserve, can justify the position, and have included an explanation of their reserves policy in their annual report.

GUIDANCE COMPLEMENTS SORP

104.5   Paragraph 55 of the Statement of Recommended Practice: Accounting by Charities (SORP) requires charities to include in their annual report a statement of the charity's policy on reserves, stating 'the level of reserves held and why they are held. Where material funds have been designated, the reserves policy statement should quantify and explain the purpose of the designations and, where set aside for future expenditure, the likely timing of that expenditure'. The Charity Commission's last guidance supplemented this by requiring trustees to explain clearly in their annual reports:

- whether or not they hold reserves;

- the reasons why they do, or do not, hold reserves;

- if they hold reserves, the future needs, opportunities, contingencies and risks the reserves are intended to provide for or be a buffer against;

- the level of reserves at the end of the financial year to which the report relates.

104.6   The definitions of terms used in the Commission's guidance were the same as those used in the SORP. 'Free reserves' were defined as 'the resources the charity has or can make available to spend, for any or all of the charity's purposes, once it has met its commitments and covered its other planned expenditure'. The definition of reserves therefore excluded:

- permanent endowment – capital, such as a building or sum of money that has been given to the charity on condition that it must be retained by the charity to be used or invested indefinitely and the income used to further the charity's objects;

- expendable endowment – capital that has been given to the charity on terms that allow the trustees to convert part, or all of it, to income to be spent on charitable purposes if they wish;

- restricted funds – capital or income funds given to be used only for a specified charitable purpose;

- designated funds – unrestricted funds earmarked by the trustees for a particular purpose, such as future requirements of beneficiaries, or to fund repairs, but which the trustees are under no legal obligation to apply in the way they have designated, and which the trustees remain free to change the designation of should they so wish; and

- certain income funds – funds which could only be realised by disposing of fixed assets held for charity use.

104.7   Although designated funds are excluded from its definition of reserves, the guidance made it clear that the Commission would frown upon trustees who set up designated funds principally in order to show a reduced level of free reserves. Therefore designated funds should be incorporated into any reserves policy, both practically and in disclosures.

RESERVES POLICY

104.8   There is no legal rule about the proportion of its income that a charity may hold as a reserve. The Commission's last guidance merely stated that the level must be the result of a well-considered reserves policy, based upon the charity's current position and its future commitments and prospects.

104.9   Trustees holding income in reserve must have power to invest. Some will have an express power in their governing document allowing them to hold income in reserve, but others will have to rely on an implied power by which they can hold income in reserve if it is their considered view that this is necessary in the best interests of the charity. Trustees holding reserves without justification could be acting in breach of trust.

104.10   Reserves

104.10   A reserves policy should include:

- the reasons for holding reserves;

- the level, or range, of reserves that the trustees aim to hold, based on an assessment of their reserve needs;

- the trustees' strategy for maintaining, achieving or reducing reserves to that level or range; and

- details of how and when the reserves policy will be monitored and reviewed.

104.11   To determine the level of reserves needed trustees should take account of:

- forecasts of future income, including the risks to each income stream and possible new sources of income;

- forecasts of expenditure on planned activities;

- an analysis of future needs, possible opportunities and contingencies or risks where the cost could not be met out of income; and

- an assessment of the risk of not being able to fund future needs and the consequences of this for the charity.

104.12   Trustees also need to ensure that they fully understand the activities undertaken in other funds. For instance a restricted fund in deficit may need to be financed from unrestricted funds, or future overheads may need to be paid out of unrestricted funds which are currently absorbed by restricted grant funding.

104.13   In its guidance on reserves the Commission stresses that the amount of time spent preparing the reserves policy, and the detail in which it is set out, should be in proportion to the scale and complexity of the charity's affairs. However, there is no absolute guidance on the right level of reserves; each charity will be different.

REINVESTED INCOME

104.14   Some charities have not been spending income earned from their expendable or permanent endowment, but have been adding it to the principal. Reinvesting income generated from capital does not convert the income to capital. The Commission expects trustees to give, or at least estimate, the proportions of any retained funds that represent income and capital respectively.

TAX

104.15   If income from investments is reinvested it could be liable for tax. The exemptions from tax on a charity's income contained in *s 505* of the *Income and Corporation Taxes Act 1988* relate only to income spent on charitable purposes. Investment does not qualify as a charitable purpose. However, in practice, the Inland Revenue normally exempts from tax investment income which is accumulated provided that the charity can show that the income is being accumulated for some specific future purpose, rather than merely to avoid tax.

MISREPRESENTATION

104.16   The Commission's guidance reminds charities that when appealing for money they should not give the wrong impression about the extent or urgency of their need for funds.

104.17   The Commission also say that trustees should not:

- use restricted funds to provide reserves for general funds;

- attempt to hide or reduce the appearance of reserves in their accounts; or

- retain resources received to be spent as income in, for example, a designated fund or in reserves, for the sole purpose of generating future income.

FUTURE ACTION

104.18   Charities finding that their reserves are too high have to reduce them gradually, either by expanding their existing work programme or by introducing new types of work. If necessary, they will have to apply to the Commission for permission to broaden their charitable objects.

104.19   If the Charity Commission comes across a charity that does not appear to have applied the principles set out above it will explore the reasons with the trustees and encourage compliance. As a last resort the Commission will use its statutory powers in cases where mismanagement or misconduct persist, where charity resources are at risk, or where the law continues to be breached.

105   Resolving Charity Disputes

BACKGROUND

105.1   Disputes within a charity, or between charities, or between a charity and a third party such as a supplier, can be costly and damaging. Charity disputes come in all shapes and sizes, ranging from disagreements about policy, via employment disputes, to disagreements with funders or suppliers. Dealing with a serious dispute can divert a considerable amount of the trustees' time, or the time of senior staff, from advancing the charity's mission. In addition, bad publicity can damage a charity's ability to raise funds. Disputes can also seriously damage staff morale and cause stress to trustees and staff. Charities should therefore consider mediation as a speedy and less costly way of resolving disputes than litigation.

105.2   Traditionally, if disputes could not be settled by negotiation, they were dealt with through the litigation process. Litigation is time consuming, distracting and can be extremely costly. Moves towards the adoption of less adversarial and simpler means of resolving disputes were made in the early 1990s firstly by the Commercial Court and later by the Queen's Bench and Family Divisions. In the mid 1990s the Court of Appeal started to encourage what has become known as Alternative Dispute Resolution (ADR).

105.3   The Woolf Report into the Civil Justice System which was published in 1996 sought not only to simplify court procedures but also to encourage the settlement of disputes outside the Courts. The Civil Procedure Rules which followed came into force on 26 April 1999. They introduced active case management, limitations on the requirement for disclosure of evidence and measures to support the efficient management of proceedings where litigation cannot be avoided. However, at the same time, it was made clear that the Courts would encourage parties to avoid litigation altogether by means of ADR.

105.4   ADR encompasses arbitration, expert determination, adjudication and mediation. There is also a process termed Early Neutral Valuation where, with the consent of the parties, a judge will assist in the resolution of the matters in dispute by providing a non-binding assessment of the strengths of the litigation. The most widely used procedures are Arbitration and Mediation.

ARBITRATION

105.5   It has long been the practice to incorporate arbitration clauses into legal contracts and these were in existence long before the wider development of ADR. Contracts will generally specify that, in case of dispute, the matter should be referred to a professional body who will nominate an arbitrator. Arbitration is governed by the *Arbitration Act 1996*.

105.6   The parties will make their cases to the arbitrator in a similar manner to a court hearing. On the basis of the evidence, the arbitrator will make an award which is binding on the parties. There is a process of appeal to the Courts but only in the case of 'serious irregularity'. Whilst a settlement under arbitration may be achieved more quickly, it can nevertheless be time consuming and costly where complex claims and counterclaims need to be argued in front of the arbitrator. Charities are unlikely to favour arbitration as an alternative method of resolving disputes due to its cost.

MEDIATION

105.7   Mediation has been practised in the United Kingdom since the early 1990s, but its use has received a significant boost from the new *Civil Procedure Rules*. At case management conferences and pre-trial reviews the parties are required to state (*a*) whether they have discussed the question of ADR, (*b*) if not, why not and (*c*) if so, the result.

105.8   If ADR has not been discussed, the judge is likely to suggest that the parties should consider it.

105.9   An essential element of the process is its voluntary nature. Thus, disputes will only proceed to mediation where all the parties agree and, as a result, there will generally be a strong motivation to achieve a settlement. By contrast, Courts in the USA can mandate the parties to use mediation.

105.10   A mediator is an independent person whose function is to facilitate an agreement between the parties. The mediator does not pass judgement on the merits of the respective cases and, except on the rare occasions when he or she is asked to do so, will not give advice to the parties or suggest solutions.

105.11   There are a number of organisations which both train and accredit mediators and also provide mediation services. The parties, having agreed to mediate, will typically ask one of those organisations to put forward a name or names from those who are on their panel so that the parties can agree between them who the mediator should be. In larger cases there are sometimes two experienced mediators acting jointly as co-mediators and, in most cases, the mediator will have the assistance of a pupil who is training or gaining experience.

105.12   If two or more parties agree to use a mediator, they will start by each sharing information with the appointed mediator. The parties will meet in confidential discussions with the mediator and face to face with each other as appropriate. The parties may be accompanied by legal or other experts or representatives agreed between the parties at the outset. Most mediations are settled in one day. Where agreement is reached, it is drawn up immediately in writing and its implementation is planned. While the mediator facilitates the process, it is the parties themselves that are responsible for the outcome.

105.13   Mediation is becoming widely used for commercial disputes, negligence and liability matters, matrimonial settlements, social and community disputes, employment problems and many other situations of conflict both national and international. Mediations are also used effectively to deal with internal disputes.

105.14   The London County Court is referring matters to mediation and the Independent Housing Ombudsman is also using mediation services. The National Council for Voluntary Organisations offers mediation services for charities through a joint venture with the Centre for Dispute Resolution (CEDR). Costs are on a sliding scale depending on the charity's financial resources. The cost of a one-day mediation can be as little as £250 for a small charity. Experience shows that there is a high success rate from mediation proceedings.

105.15 Resolving Charity Disputes

105.15   If mediation is used to settle litigation the proceedings will be stayed while the mediation takes place. The timing of the mediation can affect the likelihood of success and not all cases will be suitable for mediation. Successful mediation will require all parties to want a settlement and all parties will need to have enough information to assess the strengths and weaknesses of their own and the other parties' cases. It is common, therefore, for mediation to take place when the litigation is at an advanced stage. There is, however, a trend towards earlier mediation to further minimise costs and the technique of 'preventative mediation' has been developed to guard against conflict in highly complex contract arrangements. In this case, a mediator may be briefed at the implementation of the contract in order to deal with problems before they escalate.

105.16   The format for a mediation is necessarily flexible and the mediator will tailor it depending upon the circumstances. The mediation will normally involve a series of joint meetings between the parties under the mediator's chairmanship and also separate private meetings with the parties individually. The process is designed to generate a better mutual understanding of the position of each of the parties and also to test the reality of their positions. The private sessions enable the parties to reveal matters to the mediator without the mediator necessarily passing that information on to the other party. Private sessions are confidential.

105.17   The mediator, or the organisation which has provided the mediator, will arrange a convenient venue, date and time ensuring that rooms are available for each of the parties and for the mediator. Each party will be asked to submit a case summary to brief the mediator on the issues. These case summaries will normally be provided also to the other parties.

105.18   Through the series of meetings, the mediator will attempt to bring each of the parties to the point where they gain a realistic appreciation of a basis for agreement. They may reveal to the mediator what their 'bottom line' would be in any settlement. In this way a mediator can assist the process of settlement by being an instrument of negotiation between the parties to the point where they can discuss together the basis of settlement.

105.19   Once agreement is reached the settlement will be committed to writing and considered binding upon the parties. The settlement is confidential unless the parties agree otherwise. Should they fail to reach agreement, then litigation may proceed. In these circumstances, nothing which has been revealed in mediation may be used in evidence, neither may the mediator be called as a witness.

105.20   Where settlement is not achieved at the time of the mediation, there can still be significant benefits. The issues in dispute may have been narrowed which may result in simplified litigation. Alternatively, the parties may decide to reinstate negotiations. In any event, the mediator will normally keep in touch with the parties and continue encouraging them to settle or reactivate the mediation.

105.21   A successful mediation will have facilitated communication between parties who are often estranged and enabled the resumption of negotiations in a calm atmosphere. (It is often important to the parties that they should have a continuing relationship.) It will often also have focused on the causes of the conflict in a way which was not possible at arm's length or in court. As the process is non-binding until an agreement is reached and without prejudice, the parties are able to explore any possible avenue for compromise which would not be the case in court.

105.22   Mediations may be limited in smaller cases to a few hours but even large cases would not be expected to take more than a few days. The costs are therefore considerably less than those of a court hearing which additionally involves preparation time, an uncertain outcome and the risk of an adverse costs award.

105.23   As it is particularly important to charitable organisations that their funds should be maximised and their costs minimised, should they be involved in a dispute, mediation can be an effective and certainly less costly means of settlement than litigation. Above all, mediation offers a certainty of outcome should it be successful. Its confidential nature means that conflicts, particularly internal ones, can be resolved without funders and beneficiaries necessarily being aware of them and the loss of confidence that might ensue.

CHARITY COMMISSION'S POWERS TO RESOLVE DISPUTES

105.24   The Charity Commission expects those involved in charity disputes to do all they can to settle them responsibly and with goodwill. Where necessary, the Commission will advise on the financial, accounting and governance matters at issue. Where the effects of a dispute threaten a charity with harm, the Commission may decide to intervene but it will always be concerned primarily with putting the charity on a sound and effective footing. This is more important from the point of view of the charity's beneficiaries than saying who is in the wrong in a dispute, especially where matters of judgement are concerned, or than punishing members of a party to a dispute who may have erred in good faith. The only 'side' that the Commission will seek to take will be that of the charity and its beneficiaries.

105.25   The Commission will consider cases where:

- the way in which the charity is being run is putting significant assets or funds at risk;

- the charity's income is not being used for its charitable purposes;

- the trustees are not acting in accordance with the charity's governing document, or charity law or trust law;

- there is a real danger of the charity's name being brought into disrepute;

- the administration of the charity has broken down.

105.26   The Charity Commission will not become involved where the dispute is about how the trustees are managing the charity on a day-to-day basis as the trustees have broad discretion to manage the charity as they see fit. Therefore it will not become involved in cases where the dispute is:

- about a matter of policy or administration and the trustees are acting correctly;

- between trustees themselves, or between trustees and members;

- a contractual dispute or other dispute about property rights between the charity and a third party;

- about criminal matters unconnected with the running of the charity or furtherance of its objects;

- between charities or people or organisations that have entered into contracts with the charity;

- about matters that the Charity Commission has already considered or investigated unless circumstances have materially changed or significant new evidence has come to light.

105.27   The Charity Commission will ask the complainant to supply details of the dispute and details of efforts the complainant has already taken to resolve the dispute. If the Commission then decides the matter is something that they can deal with and their intervention would be in the public interest they will notify the complainant and invite the trustees and anyone else involved in the dispute to respond to the allegations.

105.28   Once the Commission has all the necessary information and is satisfied that the allegation is well-founded it will consider how to act. In less serious instances it will deal with it by providing information and advice to the trustees. If the issue is more serious the Commission will use its powers to intervene and put things right or prevent a reoccurrence. If necessary, it will use its powers to suspend or remove trustees or employees, appoint new trustees, freeze bank accounts, or, if the matters are criminal refer them to the police or other appropriate authorities.

EMPLOYMENT ACT 2002

105.29   The *Employment Act 2002* and the detailed regulations made to implement the provisions of that Act, namely the *Employment Act 2002 (Dispute Resolution) Regulations 2004 (SI 2004/752)* introduced statutory minimum internal disciplinary and grievance procedures for all organisations that employ staff and encourages employers and employees to use them. The employee must set out their grievance in writing and send a copy to their employer. The employer must have a meeting with the employee to discuss the grievance and the employee has a right to be accompanied by a work colleague or trade union representative. The employer must then inform the employee of the decision and give them details of their right of appeal. If the employee wishes to appeal they must inform their employer in writing. The employer must then invite the employee to attend a further meeting and the employee must attend that meeting. Following that meeting the employer must inform the employee of their final decision. An employee cannot go to an employment tribunal unless they have already been through this statutory process.

105.30   The *Employment Act 2002 (Dispute Resolution) Regulations 2004* have been widely criticised because they have created complex legal issues and have failed to achieve their key objectives such as reducing the number of tribunal claims. In March 2007 the Department of Trade and Industry published an independent review of the dispute resolution procedures which recommended the repeal of the procedures in their entirety. The Department are currently consulting on these proposals and for the time being, employers should continue to follow the current statutory procedures. But whatever the outcome, behaving reasonably in handling disputes remains crucial and disciplinary, grievance and dismissal procedures will still be essential to ensure that such behaviour is adopted.

105.31   ACAS (Advisory, Conciliation and Arbitration Service) can help resolve disputes or disagreements at work, whether they involve individuals, groups of people, or the whole workforce ACAS aims to help organisations reach an acceptable solution without having to go through any kind of court hearing, such as an employment tribunal. ACAS can advise on ways of managing conflict and dealing with disputes or act as a neutral third party or 'honest broker'. Their services are confidential and voluntary. The ACAS Code of Practice *Disciplinary and Grievance Procedures* provides detailed guidance for employers and will continue to be crucial both before and after the proposed reforms.

FURTHER INFORMATION

105.32   Centre for Effective Dispute Resolution (CEDR)
International Dispute Resolution Centre
70 Fleet Street
London EC4Y 1EU
Tel: 020 7536 6000
Fax: 020 7536 6001
Email: info@cedr.co.uk
www.cedr-solve.com

ACAS
Brandon House
180 Borough High St
London
SE1 1LW
www.acas.org.uk

106   Risk Management

106.1   The increasing importance of corporate governance, both in the commercial sector and for charities, has led to it becoming a key driver for implementing sound risk management strategies. Many will have heard of the Combined Code which provides guidance for listed companies on internal control and risk management. For registered charities, the Charities SORP sets out additional reporting requirements for trustees on the identification of major risks, their review and the systems or procedures established to manage those risks.

106.2   'Risk' is an event or action that may adversely affect an organisation's ability to survive and compete in its chosen market as well as to maintain its financial strength, positive public image and the overall quality of its people and services. Risk can arise from failure to exploit opportunities as well as from threats materialising.

106.3   The Charity Commission defines risk as 'The uncertainty surrounding events and their outcomes that may have a significant effect, either enhancing or inhibiting operational performance, achievement of aims and objectives, or meeting expectations of stakeholders'.

106.4   Controlling risk depends on understanding it, measuring it and determining its consequences. Charity staff and external stakeholders will interact and will make choices. They will respond to those choices in unpredictable ways and that will ultimately be the source of uncertainty – this is where risk management comes in.

106.5   Risk management should be:

- Comprehensive – covering all parts of the organisation

- Continual – not just a one-off exercise, but something that is maintained and kept up to date

- Integrated – not just an add-on, but part of all operations and systems

- Suitable – no 'one size fits all' but instead principles, policies and practices that can be adapted to any activity

- Proportional – maintain a sense of perspective and proportion between benefits and risks.

106.6   Successful risk management can add value to business performance by improving an organisation's focus on the achievement of strategic aims and objectives. Set out below is a simple six-point plan that should help with the successful implementation of a risk management strategy. Stages 1 to 3 cover the identification of risk. Stages 4 to 6 are about managing risk.

IDENTIFYING RISKS

Step 1

106.7   The key element here is to make the identification of risk integral to the strategic business planning and budget setting process. The questions to ask are 'What external and operational risks might prevent our organisation from achieving its strategic objectives?', 'What might happen and what would be the consequences for the charity if it happened?' and 'Are there any steps that might be taken to mitigate the risks?'

106.8   External risks tend to fall into one of six categories: political, economic, social, environment, technology, legal and environmental (or PESTLE for short). External risks tend to be beyond an organisation's control and the related risks should be identified where they may affect the ability to meet strategic objectives. For example, government policy, external competition, and increasingly in today's labour market the demand for high calibre staff all present charities with risks. A good place to start is with a market analysis and how performance may be affected by risks inherent in that market. Organisations need to consider the market's changing dynamic, their ability to adapt to market changes and the effect on performance of entering new markets or withdrawing from an existing market.

106.9   Operational risks derive from the day-to-day running of the business. Operational risk arises from doing the right thing strategically but doing it the wrong way. Again, operational risk identification should be linked to the possible non-achievement of strategic aims and objectives.

Step 2

106.10   Having identified the risks, they need to be prioritised. This takes the form of an impact analysis where the significance of a risk is measured against the certainty or likelihood of that risk actually arising. Significance should be considered in both financial terms and the possible damage to reputation. Likelihood is usually measured by reference to a three-year period. A high rating is given if there is a strong possibility that the risk will arise within that period and low if it is thought unlikely to happen in that same period. Once significance and likelihood are measured against each other, this enables the risks to be prioritised. High significance and high likelihood result in primary risks. If both categories are low, then the risk is minimal. High significance and low likelihood give rise to contingency risk, for example risks which require business continuity plans. Low significance and high likelihood result in housekeeping risks, for example the incidence of petty cash fraud.

106.11   Determining what is a high or low category for the purpose of the above analysis will depend on how much risk an organisation is willing to take, i.e. its 'risk threshold'. This may be influenced by the level of reserves, projected surpluses and risks already faced by the organisation. Commercial companies are likely to have a greater 'risk appetite' than charities.

Step 3

106.12   Recording the work carried out in Steps 1 and 2 above is important. The most practical form of documentation is a risk map or risk register which records the risk identification process, the risk impact analysis and the way that each risk is to be managed. Risk maps should be kept simple and ideally should not run to more than ten pages. There are many formats to choose from including software that electronically calculates the risk prioritisation for you based on the impact analysis set out in Step 2 above.

106.13   Risk Management

MANAGING RISKS

Step 4

106.13   Having identified and prioritised the risks, the next step is to decide whether to accept, limit or reject certain activities giving rise to the risks and whether to insure them or pass them on to third parties. Where risks can be managed by introducing internal controls or through insurance, the related cost should be compared to the possible cost that would arise if the risks were to materialise. It is also a worthwhile exercise to grade the effectiveness of risk management strategies and to then determine the residual risk.

106.14   Business plan objectives should be reviewed to ensure that the levels of risk are acceptable. For example, if the business plan includes diversification objectives but the identified risks and their impact are considered unacceptable, then the organisation may wish to withdraw from that plan or consider alternative strategies. This will include setting activity limits that will act as a control over an organisation's exposure to individual activities and the external environment. It is worth referring back to the definition of risk at the beginning of this chapter and to remember that risk management is as much about the realisation of opportunities as well as dealing with adverse events.

Step 5

106.15   Risk management is a continual process. Day-to-day activities will result in new risks. Also, risks will continue to materialise from external sources. Circumstances requiring a further risk assessment review could include:

- new projects or markets not foreseen when first setting strategic objectives;

- appraisal of new projects in the furtherance of existing business plan objectives;

- routine reporting and monitoring, for example in committee papers that alert the organisation to potential new risks.

Step 6

106.16   This final step is concerned with the corporate governance arrangement with regard to risk management and in particular, the role of the Board or the Trustees. They will have ultimate responsibility for ensuring that the risk management process is effective and for establishing the risk management framework. Terms of reference and delegated authorities should clearly set out responsibilities for business planning and the risk review process. Subcommittee performance should be regularly reviewed to ensure that the appropriate skills exist for the activities under their control and for managing the related risks.

106.17   The executive management team will be tasked with running the business effectively. The executive management structure and their responsibilities will also be key to ensure that risks arising from strategic objectives are identified and managed effectively.

544

FURTHER INFORMATION

106.18   *Charities and Risk Management* (available at *www.charitycommission.gov.uk*)

Good Governance – A Code for the Voluntary and Community Sector (available at *www.governancehub.org.uk*)

The Institute of Risk Management (*www.theirm.org*)

107 Schemes and Orders

107.1 A charity's governing document sets out its purposes and how it is to be run. However, after a number of years the governing document can become outdated and may need to be changed. Depending on the circumstances, trustees should start by considering if they can amend their governing document by using:

- a power of amendment in the existing governing document;

- the power in *s 74* of the *Charities Act 1993* that allows small, unincorporated charities to modify their trusts;

- the statutory power in *s 74D* of the *Charities Act 1993*, as amended by the *Charities Act 2006*, that enables the trustees of all unincorporated charities to modify their powers and procedures;

- the statutory power in the *Companies Act 1985* that enables the members of a charitable company to alter the memorandum and articles of association, subject to the prior written consent of the Charity Commission if the changes affect the objects clause or relate to the application of the charity's property;

- an Order under *s 26* of the *Charities Act 1993* which can confer discretionary authorities on the trustees.

A Scheme will be required if none of these options can be used to make the necessary changes.

ORDERS

107.2 A *s 26* Order is a legal document drawn up by the Charity Commission that gives new powers to the trustees. The authority the Order provides is discretionary. Trustees can choose whether or not to exercise the authority granted by the order. Orders will normally be sufficient to make the following sort of changes:

- Provide additional powers not included in the current governing document, e.g. a power to adopt a total return policy;

- Give the trustees power to add or amend specific administrative provisions in the governing document;

- Confer on the trustees a power of amendment, subject to certain limitations;

- Authorise a payment as being expedient in the interests of the charity, e.g. a severance payment to an employee made redundant that is above the legal requirement;

- Authorise the trustees of a charity to transfer its undertaking to another charity, providing this does not involve any alteration to the purposes of the transferor charity;

- Provide a power to spend capital on terms of replacement.

107.3 When the Charity Commission makes Orders which confer general powers, including powers of amendment, they include a duty of care that will require trustees, when exercising the powers, to discharge the statutory duty of care in *s 1* of the *Trustee Act 2000*. This means that when a trustee exercises the power they must exercise such care and skill as is reasonable in the circumstances and the skill and care must be commensurate with any special knowledge or experience that the trustee has.

107.4   Orders are less elaborate than Schemes and can be made without the need for a formal application. Where changes are sensitive or controversial the trustees will not be granted an Order and will have to apply for a Scheme. The request for an Order should come from a suitably authorised person, such as the registered correspondent of the charity, an officer of the charity, such as the chair, secretary or treasurer, or solicitors acting on behalf of the trustees. Orders can usually be made quickly and the Charity Commission normally attempts to agree the wording of the text at the time they offer to make the Order. Once the wording is agreed the Charity Commission seals the Order and it becomes effective. There is no need to publicise an Order before it is sealed, though the Charity Commission have powers to ask trustees to give publicity to a proposal to make an Order, or to publicise an Order that has been made.

SCHEMES

107.5   A Scheme is a legal document, usually made by the Charity Commission under *s 16* of the *Charities Act 1993*, that amends, replaces or extends a charity's governing document when a charity can no longer run effectively under the existing governing document and the trustees cannot make the necessary changes themselves. A Scheme may set out new objects and purposes, or changes to the existing objects and purposes, or new constitutional arrangements, or new powers for the trustees. Some of the provisions of a Scheme will require the trustees to carry out certain actions, whilst others will be discretionary: they enable the trustees to take certain actions if it is in the interests of the charity to do so. It is the Charity Commission's policy to use a Scheme only where there is no other way of changing the charity's trusts.

107.6   Schemes can be used for a wide variety of purposes including the following:

- To replace a governing document that needs changing completely;

- To clarify the objects if they are imprecise or ambiguous, e.g. if it is unclear whether the main purpose of a charity is to help children with a particular condition, or to support the parents of children with that condition, or to carry out research into the cause and treatment of the condition;

- To modernise or widen the objects. A charity may have been established to provide a service which is no longer regarded as the most effective way of meeting the needs of the beneficiaries, such as the provision of orphanages, or for a class of people that no longer exists, such as slaves;

- To amend the objects if the cause or need for which the charity was established is now met in some other way or by some other body. Charities frequently pioneer new services or approaches to dealing with social problems that are then adopted by statutory providers;

- To amend the objects if the service provided is no longer effective, for example if the grants made are too small to be of any significance;

- To amend the objects if the geographical limits specified in the charity's governing document need expanding, for example if a successful local service could be expanded into a national operation;

- To allow something that the constitutional arrangements or an Act of Parliament expressly prohibit;

- To permit trustees to spend permanent endowment or capitalise income of the charity (the rules about spending permanent endowment will change when *s 43* of the *Charities Act 2006* comes into force in early 2008);

- To confer a benefit on any or all of the trustees;

- To restrict the existing right of a person other than the trustees to appoint or remove a charity trustee;

- To allow the Charity Commission to administer a charity where, having opened a *s 8* inquiry, misconduct or mismanagement has been found and it is necessary that the Commission acts to protect or secure the charity's property.

CHANGES TO THE OBJECTS CLAUSE

107.7   If the trustees wish to change the charity's charitable purposes they can apply to the Charity Commission for a Scheme, under *s 16* of the *Charities Act 1993*, subject to *s 13* of the Act which states that charities can only amend their purposes where:

- the original purpose has been fulfilled or can no longer be carried out;

- the original purpose can only use part of the funds available;

- the funds could be used more effectively within the spirit of the gift;

- the charity was established for a purpose that has become outdated or harmful;

- the original purpose referred to a class of person (e.g. child chimney sweeps), or an area that no longer exists;

- the need is now provided for in some other way, e.g. out of public funds;

- the original purpose has ceased to be charitable in law.

107.8   The 1993 Act requires changes to a charity's objects clause to define a new purpose that is *cy-près*, i.e. as close as practicable to the original purpose, hence Schemes amending a charity's objects have become known as *cy-près* Schemes. However, *s 18* of the *Charities Act 2006* amends *s 13* of the 1993 Act, so that when applying charity property *cy-près* the court or the Charity Commission now have greater flexibility and can take the following three matters into consideration, giving them equal weight:

- the spirit of the original gift;

- the desirability of securing that the property is applied for charitable purposes which are close to the original purpose; and

- the need for the relevant charity to have purposes which are suitable and effective in the light of current social and economic circumstances.

107.9   When considering an application for a *cy-près* Scheme for a charity originally formed by a single donor, the court or the Charity Commission can take into account:

- the donor's religious beliefs;

- the donor's particular interests;

- what the donor believed to be worthy causes;

- the donor's interests in a particular locality; and

- any wishes the donor expressed outside their attested will.

107.10   Although charities that are companies limited by guarantee or industrial and provident societies have powers to amend their governing document under the *Companies Act 1989* or the *Industrial and Provident Societies Act 1965, s 64* of the *Charities Act 1993* requires any alterations to the objects clause of a charity to have the prior written consent of the Charity Commission in order to become effective.

107.11   A Scheme is not needed if the trustees merely want to update the wording used to define the objects and purposes of the charity, rather than to change the substance of the objects and purposes. In these circumstances a charity can use its power of amendment (where it has one) to make the changes, even if the power of amendment does not explicitly permit changes to the objects and purposes. However, if the power of amendment prohibits changes to the objects clause, as opposed to the objects, a Scheme will still be needed. Where a charity does not have a power of amendment the Charity Commission will make a *s 26* Order to change the objects and purposes.

POWER TO MAKE SCHEMES

107.12   The *Charities Act 1993 s 16* gives the Charity Commission concurrent jurisdiction with that of the High Court to make Schemes. In practice most Schemes are made by the Charity Commission. However, *s 16(3)* excludes the Charity Commission from making Schemes that determine questions of title to property or the existence of a trust and *s 16(10)* forbids the Commission to act in circumstances where the matters would be better left to the court to decide, such as complex questions of law.

APPLYING FOR A SCHEME

107.13   In most circumstances Schemes and Orders are made on the initiative of the charity's trustees, but the Charity Commission can instigate the making of a Scheme or Order if there are reasons to believe that the charity trustees should have applied for one, but have failed to do so, either through neglect or because they cannot agree among themselves. Applications can also be made by the court, the Attorney General or, in the case of a charity with income of less than £500 a year, by one or more of the trustees, or by a person interested in the charity, or by two or more inhabitants of the local area in which the charity operates.

107.14   The Charity Commission provides application forms for a Scheme though trustees are not obliged to use them. They can make their own application in writing. In most instances the application will arise from a resolution passed by the trustees. The resolution must have been taken strictly in accordance with the normal rules for the conduct of meetings of the trustees. Where the rules require a meeting it must be properly convened. The resolution may authorise a named individual or individuals to sign the application on behalf of the charity. The authorised individuals do not need to be trustees; they could be officers of the charity or professional advisers. Even if the charity cannot achieve a quorum, the Charity Commission may be willing to accept an application if they consider it to be appropriate. However, if a charity has an income of less than £500 a year, a Scheme can be applied for by one or more of the trustees, or by any person with an interest in the charity, such as a potential beneficiary, or, if the charity serves a local area, by two or more people resident in that area. If there are no trustees to apply for a Scheme the Charity Commission will appoint trustees who can then apply for a Scheme.

107.15   When the Charity Commission receives an application it will usually discuss the broad outlines with the trustees. Once agreement has been achieved on these, the Commission will invite the trustees to submit a formal application. The Commission will then send a detailed draft Scheme to the trustees for their comments and final agreement.

PUBLICITY

107.16   The *Charities Act 2006* amends *s 20* of the 1993 Act, speeding up the formal procedure for making Schemes and Orders and reducing the costs. The need to advertise a draft Scheme and publish the final Scheme after sealing is now a matter of Charity Commission discretion. The Commission will not require public notice to be given where it believes the Scheme is likely to be non-controversial. Where the Commission decides publicity is required the period for which the notice is displayed will usually be no more than one month.

SEALING

107.17   If the Charity Commission has decided that a draft Scheme should be given publicity it is obliged by law to consider and deal with all representations and objections received during the stated notice period. If representations appear to be based on a misunderstanding of what is being proposed, the Commission will write to the objector explaining the true position. If the objections appear to have some validity the Commission will ask the trustees for their views. If necessary, the draft Scheme will be amended. Once all the representations and objections have been dealt with satisfactorily the Commission will prepare the Scheme for sealing. After a Scheme is made it must be displayed publicly for at least a month in the Commission's office. If the charity in question is a local charity, the Commission also has discretion to decide to display the scheme publicly at a convenient place in the charity's area.

107.18   A Scheme comes into force on the date it is sealed. In many cases the sealed Scheme will be sent first to HMRC for confirmation that no stamp duty is payable, and then to the trustees. A sealed Scheme is a legal document and should be kept securely, preferably in a fireproof safe. Copies should be given to all current trustees and in the future to any new trustee together with a copy of the governing document.

APPEALS

107.19 The Scheme can be appealed against and although trustees can rely on the Scheme immediately, they should bear in mind the possibility of an appeal. If an appeal is made then it will be for the courts to rule on its long-term effectiveness.

FEES

107.20 At present the Charity Commission makes no charge for providing Orders or Schemes.

EXCEPTIONS

107.21 Unincorporated charities with a gross income of less than £10,000 in the last financial year, and that do not hold any land, do not require a Scheme, but can use the procedures set out in s 74 of the *Charities Act 1993* as amended by the *Charities Act 2006* if they want to transfer their assets to another charity or charities, change the charity's objects or modify the trustees' powers or procedures.

107.22 If a charity has permanent endowment that does not comprise any land, and a gross income of less than £1,000 in the last financial year, and is not a charitable company, then it does not require a Scheme if it wishes to spend the permanent endowment as income, but can use the procedures set out in s 75 of the *Charities Act 1993*, as amended by the *Charities Act 2006*. When all the endowment is spent the charity will cease to exist.

107.23 The Secretary of State for Children, Schools and Families has statutory powers to implement Schemes for educational charities without reference to the Charity Commission. However, neither the Charity Commission nor the Secretary of State for Children, Schools and Families have power to amend the objects clause of an educational charity within the first 40 years of its existence.

107.24 If a charitable school is unused or about to close the Secretary of State for Children, Schools and Families has the power to make a Scheme in the form of a statutory instrument to allow any endowment to be used for a different purpose. The Charity Commission also has powers to make Schemes for ecclesiastical charities or ecclesiastical property held under trusts which do not qualify as charities according to the definitions used in the *Charities Act 1960*.

108   Scotland

THE REGULATORY FRAMEWORK

Charities and Trustee Investment (Scotland) Act 2005

108.1   The 2005 Act repeals the *Law Reform (Miscellaneous Provisions) (Scotland) Act 1990* and the *Charities Accounts (Scotland) Regulations 1992.*

108.2   The Act gives full powers to the Office of the Scottish Charity Regulator (known as OSCR). The OSCR website can be accessed as *www.oscr.org.uk.*

108.3   OSCR's general functions are:

- to determine whether bodies are charities;

- to keep a public register of charities;

- to encourage, facilitate and monitor compliance by all charities with the provisions of the Act;

- to identify and investigate apparent misconduct in the administration of charities and to take remedial or protective action in relation to any misconduct to give information or advice, or to make proposals, to the Scottish Ministers on matters relating to OSCR's functions.

108.4   The register of Scottish charities was previously maintained by HMRC. That list will form the basis of the new list to be maintained by OSCR. Any new applications for charitable status must now be made to OSCR.

The Charity Test

108.5   One of the most important areas of the new Act is what is known as the charity test. Charities applying for registration now must prove that their purposes consist, only of one or more of the charitable purposes listed in the Act and that they provide, or intend to provide, public benefit.

108.6   Charities which were on the HMRC list will be assumed initially to be performing a charitable purpose and also to be providing public benefit. However, a rolling review is in place by OSCR who will be selecting certain existing charities to investigate whether they satisfy these conditions and in particular meet the public benefit test.

108.7   The listed charitable purposes within the Act are as follows:

(1)   the prevention or relief of poverty

(2)   the advancement of education

(3)   the advancement of religion

(4)   the advancement of health

(5)   the saving of lives

(6)   the advancement of citizenship or community development

(7)   the advancement of the arts, heritage, culture or science

(8)   the advancement of public participation in sport

(9)   the provision of recreational facilities, or organisation of recreational activities, with the object of improving the conditions of life for the persons for whom they are primarily intended

(10)   the advancement of human rights, conflict resolution or reconciliation

(11)   the promotion of religious or racial harmony

(12)   the promotion of equality and diversity

(13)   the advancement of environmental protection or improvement

(14)   the relief of those in need by reason of age, ill health, disability, financial hardship or other disadvantage

(15)   the advancement of animal welfare

(16)   Any other purpose that may reasonably be regarded as analogous to any of the purposes listed in 1–15 above.

108.8   The public benefit can be provided in Scotland or elsewhere. Benefit can be to the public as a whole or to part of it. However, there must not be undue restriction on any access to benefit by the imposition of any conditions, including charges or fees which restrict access too much.

108.9   In assessing whether any body provides public benefit, the Act requires the following to be considered:

●   benefit which will or is likely to be gained by persons not simply as members of the public (i.e. any potential private benefit); and

●   any disbenefit incurred or likely to be incurred by the public.

108.10   OSCR must, after consulting representatives of the charitable sector and such other persons as it thinks fit, issue guidance on how it determines whether a body meets the charity test.

108.11   While OSCR has no discretion in the application of the charity test, it will exercise discretion in not taking immediate action against a body, which is not entered in the Scottish Charity Register, calling itself a 'charity' after 22 February 2007, providing that it has an existing right to call itself a charity; that it has made an application to be entered in the Scottish Charity Register; and that it has confirmed to OSCR's satisfaction that it intends to take the appropriate action to allow it to meet the charity test within a reasonable timescale.

OTHER AREAS COVERED BY THE ACT

Charity Names

108.12   OSCR has the power to direct a charity to change an objectional name. It will also have the power to review a charity's name if another charity claims the name is too like its own name. If OSCR agrees that this is so, OSCR will then be obliged to direct one or both of the charities to change its or their names. A charity will have to obtain OSCR's advance consent to any proposed change of name.

108.13   Scotland

Changes

108.13   Charities must be aware that if they make any changes to the charity that this must be reported to OSCR within three months i.e. change of principal contact, any change to the details in the Scottish Charity Register, change to the constitution etc.

108.14   Certain other changes must be notified to OSCR within one month. These are appointment of a receiver in respect of any of the charity's property and any administration order or any other order for winding up made by the court in respect of the charity.

108.15   If the charity wishes to change its legal name then at least 42 days' notice must be given prior to the date of change, together with a copy of the founding deed/constitution.

108.16   If the charity wishes to change the constitution then at least 42 days' notice must be given to OSCR and a copy of the current constitution and a copy of the proposed new version, and new purposes must be clearly identifiable with the charitable purpose in the 2005 Act.

108.17   If the charity is amalgamating with another charity then 42 days' notice must be given to OSCR together with a copy of the constitution and a statement of assets and liabilities.

Enquiries

108.18   OSCR may at any time make enquiries either generally or for particular purposes into any charity. OSCR also has the powers to obtain any information or documents which it considers necessary for the purposes of its enquiries.

Charity annual returns

108.19   The full charity annual return regime was implemented by OSCR in 2006. All charities are required to prepare a basic annual return with the larger charities required to complete a monitoring return. The annual returns and monitoring returns will be issued to charities two months after their financial year end and will require to be submitted to OSCR together with a copy of the annual accounts no later than nine months after the charity's year end.

Duty of auditors

108.20   Any person who is appointed to carry out an independent examination or audit of the charity's statement of account and who becomes aware of any activity which they believe is likely to be of material significance for the purposes of the exercise by OSCR of its functions must immediately report the matter to OSCR.

Dormant accounts

108.21   OSCR has the power to transfer any dormant funds to any such charity as OSCR may determine, having regard to the purposes of the relevant body and the purposes of the charity.

108.22   Funds are classed as dormant where there have been no transactions over the previous five years and OSCR is unable to locate any person concerned in the management or control of the charity.

Scottish charitable incorporated organisation (SCIO)

108.23   This is a new type of proposed organisation which allows an organisation to have limited liability without being set up as a limited company. This will take away the need for the organisation to comply with the filing requirements of the Companies Act.

108.24   If a charity is set up as an SCIO this must be clearly stated on all documents issued by or on behalf of the SCIO.

108.25   Any two or more individuals may apply to OSCR for an SCIO to be constituted and for its entry in the register. The application must state the name of the SCIO, the proposed principal office and be accompanied by a copy of the SCIO's proposed constitution. OSCR will only grant the application if the SCIO meets the charity test.

108.26   A charity which is currently a company or a registered friendly society can apply to have its status transferred to that of an SCIO. Such an application cannot be made if the company has unpaid share capital or if the company only has a single member.

108.27   Any two or more SCIOs can apply to OSCR to be amalgamated and for a new SCIO to be constituted and entered into the register as their successor.

Religious charities

108.28   OSCR may designate a charity as a religious charity if it satisfies the following conditions:

- The advancement of religion as its principal purpose;

- The regular holding of public worship as its principal activity;

- Has been established in Scotland for at least ten years;

- A membership of at least 3,000 who are resident in Scotland and are at least 16 years of age; and

- Has an internal organisation such that one or more authorities in Scotland exercise supervisory and disciplinary functions in respect of the component elements of the charity, and those elements are subject to requirements as to keeping accounting records and audit of accounts which appear to OSCR to correspond to those required by *s 44*.

108.29   Charities which are classified as designated religious charities do not need to apply certain provisions within the *Charities and Trustee Investment (Scotland) Act 2005*. The relevant sections are; *ss 28(3), 31(4), (6), 34(5)(c)-(e)* and *69*.

Investment powers of trustees

108.30   The new Act has extended the powers of trustees so that they can now make any kind of investment of the trust estate and to acquire heritable property for any other reason. The new regulations override the *Trustee Investments*

Act 1961. The new regulations are aimed at simplifying investment administration and also assist to reduce transaction costs.

108.31 Before exercising their powers of investment the trustee must have regard to the suitability of the proposed investment and the need for diversification of the investments of the trust (subject to the charity's constitution). They must also obtain and consider proper advice about the way in which the power should be exercised. They also have the option to appoint a nominee or a discretionary manager.

Cross border issues

108.32 A cross-border charity is one which is regulated in England and Wales but has significant 'activities' in Scotland.

108.33 An 'activity' is classed as being any of the following;

- Owns/rents property, pays rates, claims rates relief;

- Holds open meetings; or

- Charges for events.

108.34 The following are **not** classed as 'activities';

- Advertising in Scotland;

- Awarding grants in Scotland; or

- Conducting street collections, occasional members' conferences and the administration of volunteers based in Scotland.

108.35 These charities will have a dual filing requirement and will be required to submit an annual return/monitoring return to OSCR as well as the Charity Commission in England and Wales.

108.36 OSCR will also look for these charities to refer to their Scottish activities within their annual report.

108.37 OSCR has identified a technical difficulty facing many bodies that are charities registered in England and Wales and that are applying for charitable status in Scotland. The wording of some of their constitution permits the disposal and use of assets for purposes that are not charitable in Scottish law. As a result these bodies do not meet the charity test in the *Charities and Trustee Investment (Scotland) Act 2005* and OSCR cannot grant them charitable status. This means that such bodies may not refer to themselves as 'charities'. OSCR and the Charity Commission have worked together to agree model clauses that may be adopted by these organisations to amend their constitutions so that they can meet the requirements of both regulators. OSCR has contacted those bodies affected to explain the situation and suggest how this may be resolved. This is likely to require only a minor amendment to the affected constitutions, for example, inserting a clause stating that 'charitable' is as defined in Scots, as well as English, law. However, it will be for the bodies concerned to consult their legal advisers on the most appropriate course of action to meet individual needs.

THE CHARITIES ACCOUNTS (SCOTLAND) REGULATIONS 2006

108.38 These regulations now apply to all charities with a financial year which begins on or after 1 April 2006.

108.39 The new regulations repeal the present legislative requirements in these areas which are the *Law Reform (Miscellaneous Provisions) (Scotland) Act 1990* and the *Charities Accounts (Scotland) Regulations 1992.*

Accounting records

108.40 The charity trustees must ensure that accounting records are kept which are sufficient to show at any time the financial position of the charity.

108.41 All charities must submit a statement of accounts to OSCR within nine months of its financial year end together with the annual return and monitoring return as required.

108.42 A charitable company must also send a copy of its statement of account to Companies House within a period of not more than ten months from the end of its financial year. Following amendments to the Companies Act this period will be reduced to not more than nine months.

108.43 Charitable companies entitled to prepare abbreviated accounts for filing with Companies House should file their full accounts with OSCR. There is no accounts exemption in relation to abbreviated accounts within Scots' charity law.

Consolidated accounts

108.44 Where a charity with one or more subsidiary undertakings has a combined gross income in excess of £500,000 after the removal of consolidated adjustments it must prepare consolidated accounts in accordance with the SORP.

Connected charities

108.45 Connected charities may prepare accounts collated into a single document to send to OSCR. Where connected charities choose to submit such accounts they must be audited or independently examined depending on which regulation the charity with the highest gross income is required to follow.

Statement of account

108.46 A charity with a gross income of less than £100,000 in a financial year is permitted to prepare receipts and payments accounts consisting of;

- A receipts and payments account
- A statement of balances
- Notes to the accounts
- An annual report.

108.47 The statement of balances and the annual report shall be signed by one of the trustees on behalf of all of the charity trustees.

108.48   Scotland

108.48   The required contents of the receipts and payments accounts can be found within *reg 9 – Schs 2* and *3* of the *Charities Accounts (Scotland) Regulations 2006.*

108.49   All other charities are required to prepare fully accrued accounts which must also comply with the current SORP requirements. Charities with gross income of less than £100,000 must also prepare fully accrued accounts if so required by the constitution of the charity, any other enactment or the charity trustees.

108.50   The required contents and principles of fully accrued accounts can be found within *reg 8 – Sch 1* of the *Charities Accounts (Scotland) Regulations 2006.*

Annual audit

108.51   A charity's statement of accounts must be audited if any of the following conditions are met:

- Gross income for the financial year is greater than £500,000;

- Aggregate value of its assets (before deduction of liabilities) in a financial year exceed £2.8 million;

- The charity has gross income less than £500,000 and has prepared fully accrued accounts and the charities constitution requires an audit;

- The charity has gross income less than £100,000 and has prepared receipts and payments accounts and the charities constitution requires an audit.

108.52   The statement of account must be audited by an auditor who is eligible to act as an auditor in terms of *s 25* of the *Companies Act 1989* or by the Auditor General for Scotland.

Independent examination

108.53   A charity with a gross income of less than £500,000 which is either required to prepare fully accrued accounts or receipts and payments accounts and which is not required to be audited must have its statement of account for that year independently examined by an independent examiner.

108.54   An independent examiner must be:

- A member of:

    — the Institute of Chartered Accountants in England and Wales;

    — the Institute of Chartered Accountants of Scotland;

    — the Institute of Chartered Accountants in Ireland;

    — the Association of Chartered Certified Accountants;

    — the Association of Authorised Public Accountants;

    — the Association of Accounting Technicians;

    — the Association of International Accountants;

    — the Chartered Institute of Management Accountants;

—   the Institute of Chartered Secretaries and Administrators;

—   the Chartered Institute of Public Finance or Accountancy;

• A full member of the Association of Charity Independent Examiners; or

• The Auditor General for Scotland.

109   Secondment

109.1   One way in which charities can contain their costs is to persuade another organisation to lend it an employee for a period. This arrangement is commonly called 'seconding'. The first employer continues to pay the secondees' salary while the secondee is working for the charity. Most secondments are of staff working in the private sector. Until recently, the typical secondee was a manager approaching retirement age employed by a large company. For the company the cost was not significantly greater than giving the employee early retirement and was easily outweighed by the public relations benefits. Now companies are increasingly willing to second younger staff, seeing charities as a suitable training ground for up and coming young managers. After all, marketing a charity, developing its internal communications strategy, or upgrading its computer system are not fundamentally different from carrying out the same tasks for a commercial organisation.

109.2   Many companies will have a well thought out business case underpinning their corporate community involvement strategy, knowing that in order to thrive, business needs communities with income to spend and people who are not deterred from leaving their homes by the fear of crime. In almost every case a company willing to second an employee will be looking to gain something from the relationship. Charity trustees should take care to ensure that the arrangement is not weighted too heavily in favour of the company. There are tax and other legal considerations that companies and charities entering into secondment arrangements must take into account. Any company, sole trader or partnership seconding a member of their staff to a charity can deduct the relevant costs from their taxable profits. If the employer agrees to pay the secondee's expenses as well as their salary these are also deductible to the extent that they would have been allowed had the employee's services continued to be available to the employer. [*Income and Corporation Taxes Act 1988, s 86*].

109.3   Secondees, unlike volunteers, are employees. It is good practice for all parties to a seconding arrangement to have a written agreement clarifying which party is responsible for matters such as insurance, discipline, management control and legal liability. In some cases where disputes have arisen the courts have ruled that the secondee is employed by the original employer but in others, particularly those over where vicarious liability rests if a secondee has caused loss or injury, they have held the recipient organisation to be the employer, as they are generally the one with control over the actions of the secondee.

109.4   Business in the Community is an organisation that has done much to further partnerships between business and the voluntary sector including promoting the benefits of staff secondments.

CHARITY TO CHARITY

109.5   Charities will sometimes second a member of their staff to another charity, usually to enable the staff member to gain wider experience. This is permissible provided that the secondee is working on a project that is within the charitable objects of the first charity. When considering such an arrangement the trustees should be satisfied that seconding a member of their staff to another organisation is the most effective way of deploying their resources to meet their goals.

109.6   In some circumstances the supply or loan of staff from one charity or voluntary organisation to another can be treated as non-business and outside the scope of VAT. There are conditions that need to be met, so further professional advice should always be taken.

110 Self-assessment

110.1   Self-assessment of income tax for individuals and trusts was introduced in respect of the tax year 1996/97 and self-assessment of corporation tax was introduced for accounting periods ending after 30 June 1999. The previous rules for the assessment and collection of tax required taxpayers to supply information to HMRC so that it could issue an assessment, which was the legal charge to tax. The responsibility for arriving at the correct tax liability was split between the taxpayer and HMRC.

110.2   Under self-assessment individuals, trusts, unincorporated entities and companies have a requirement to file tax returns by a fixed date and to pay all income tax, corporation tax and capital gains tax (as applicable) according to a fixed set of dates. There are penalties for late filing and late payment of tax, in addition to interest charges. While the self-assessment regime takes away the administrative burden of assessments from HMRC, it means that taxpayers are responsible for calculating the correct amount of tax due. Even where HMRC agree to carry out the necessary calculations for individuals and trusts if the return is submitted by a certain date, this is little more than a numerical process. HMRC then carry out sample checks on tax returns, either where something appears to be incorrect or by random sample.

110.3   Most charities have no taxable income and therefore will not need to complete a self-assessment tax return. However, HMRC send many charities tax returns to complete once every three to five years. If a charity receives a tax return then it is obliged to complete and submit it to HMRC by the due date (even if there is no taxable income to report). There are supplementary pages annexed to standard tax returns specifically designed for completion by charities. The self-assessment rules do not affect the tax repayment claims procedure.

110.4   Self-assessment for companies also has an impact on the trading subsidiaries of charities, as they are liable to pay corporation tax on their profits unless they donate them to the charity under Gift Aid.

110.5   The introduction of self-assessment has had an impact on charities as employers, as the PAYE administration rules have been changed to ensure that employees are given sufficient information to complete their own self-assessment tax returns. Employers are now required to supply all their employees with a P60 by 31 May and a copy of their P11D by 6 July.

111   Setting up a Charity

IS A NEW CHARITY NECESSARY?

111.1   The Charity Commission is currently registering about 5,000 new charities each year. However, before deciding to start up a new charity there are a number of issues to be considered. Firstly, is there a need for a new charity? Is there already a charity in the area doing similar work? If there is, it may well be more cost effective and efficient to work with an existing charity rather than set up another organisation. If the purpose of setting up the charity is to commemorate someone, it may be better to do this by setting up a named, restricted fund within an existing charity. If the purpose is to respond to a national or international disaster, it may be better to offer money, goods or services to the Disasters Emergency Committee. If the purpose is to help a specific individual, for example by raising funds to pay for their medical treatment overseas, an organisation helping one individual cannot be registered as a charity, as it will not be providing public benefit. The alternatives would be to set up a non-charitable trust to benefit the individual or raise funds for an existing charity established to help people facing similar difficulties. Secondly, what are the prospects of raising funds? Charity fund-raising is a highly competitive marketplace and people may prefer to give to organisations with a proven track record. Thirdly, is it advantageous to have charitable status? Charitable status brings with it the opportunity to raise funds from certain sources, certain tax advantages, relief from business rates, access to advice from the Charity Commission and it gives reassurance to donors. On the other hand charitable status limits the objects of the organisation to being wholly and exclusively charitable, places limits on political and trading activities, and it usually prevents trustees from receiving benefits.

PURPOSES

111.2   If a decision is made to go ahead the next steps are to consider:

- What will the purposes of the organisation be, both in the short term and in the longer term? Who will be the beneficiaries? What will be the geographical area of benefit? What type of methods or activities will be used to achieve the purposes?

- Who will be the charity trustees, responsible for controlling the organisation? Will there be members, and if so will the members be beneficiaries, or will they be supporters?

- Will there be a significant number of employees and will there be volunteers?

- How will the organisation be financed at the start and in the longer term? Is there an endowment and if so what restrictions are there on how it can be used? How will funds be raised? Will the organisation be entering into contracts? Will land or buildings be acquired?

LEGAL STRUCTURE

111.3   Once these issues have been decided it will probably have become apparent what would be the most suitable legal structure (i.e. trust, association,

563

company, charitable incorporated organisation, industrial and provident society, etc.) to use, bearing in mind how the charity is likely to develop over the next few years. However, before the governing document can be drawn up a number of other issues will need to be decided.

111.4   If the charity is to have a national remit and will have local groups or branches some thought must be given at the outset about whether to structure it as a single organisation or whether to adopt a federal structure with autonomous local branches.

NAME

111.5   At this point there will still be a number of important issues to decide, including the charity's name. This must not be misleading, must not cause offence and must not be the same as an existing charity's name or so similar that it could give rise to confusion. The names of existing charities can be checked by viewing the Register on the Charity Commission's website or telephoning Charity Commission Direct on 0845 3000 218. If a company wants to use the words 'charity', 'charitable', 'charities', 'charity's' or 'charities' in its name it requires approval from the Secretary of State for Business, Enterprise & Regulatory Reform before a Certificate of Incorporation can be issued.

TRUSTEES

111.6   The trustees must be over the age of 18 if the proposed charity is to be unincorporated (people under 18 can be trustees of incorporated charities) and not disqualified by law from acting as charity trustees (see CHAPTER 121). They must be willing and able to give the necessary time to take an active part in directing the charity. They should be selected for their relevant experience and skills, rather than their status or position in the community alone.

111.7   Decisions will need to be taken about how trustees will be appointed or elected. Will they be:

- appointed by the founder?

- appointed by the trustees?

- appointed by an outside body such as a local authority?

- elected by the membership?

- appointed by virtue of an office holder, such as the local vicar or mayor?

- appointed through trusteeship of another charity?

111.8   Will terms of office be fixed, and if so will there be a limit on the number of terms an individual can serve, so the board will get a regular infusion of new blood? How often will the trustees meet and will the trustee board have sub-committees? What will be delegated to sub-committees and staff? What powers will trustees need, for example will they need wide powers of investment or a power to accumulate?

REGISTRATION

111.9   Once a decision has been taken to establish a new charity and the issues described above have been decided the next step will be to draw up a governing document, either with the help of a lawyer or by using one of the model governing documents available from the Charity Commission or the Charity Law Association (see CHAPTER 55). Once this has been done an application can be made to the Charity Commission for registration as a charity (see CHAPTER 101).

112   Shops

112.1   In the 19th century the Salvation Army ran second-hand clothing shops to
provide the urban poor with cheap clothing. However, the first charity shop
set up primarily to raise money for charity was opened by Oxfam in 1947.
Oxfam had been swamped by donations from the public (mostly blankets and
clothing) following its appeal for aid to alleviate the post-war situation in
Greece. The success of this appeal yielded so many donations that it was
decided to set up a shop in Oxford to sell a proportion of these and to use the
profits to further fund aid in Greece.

112.2   There are now almost 6,000 Charity shops in the UK and they have become a
familiar sight on almost every high street, generating profits of over £101
million on a turnover of over £511 million. At first, most charity shops
opened for short periods taking vacant premises rent free. Now the trend is
for charities to take premises on a more permanent basis and budget for
takings to cover the rent and other expenses. Costs are kept down by using
volunteers to sort, price and sell donated goods, though many charity shop
chains find it cost-effective to have at least one paid member of staff.

FUND-RAISING OR TRADING?

112.3   Converting donated goods into cash is not regarded as trading, but merely as
realising the value of the gift. Charity shops selling mainly donated goods can
therefore be operated by charities and do not have to be run by trading
subsidiaries. The gross proceeds can be accounted for as voluntary income
and are exempt from corporation tax.

112.4   Charity shops that sell only bought-in goods are trading and therefore have to
be operated through a subsidiary trading company.

112.5   The sale of new goods that are made by a charity's beneficiaries, such as
handicrafts made in a workshop for people with visual impairment, is
regarded as primary purpose trading and therefore can be carried out by the
charity.

112.6   Charity shops selling wholly or mainly donated goods, or goods produced by
the beneficiaries, and operated by the charity also have the additional financial
benefits of 80% mandatory relief on business rates (this can be extended to
100% at the discretion of the local authority). Charity shops run by the
charity can sell some bought-in goods but must take care that these do not
constitute the majority of their sales. Bought-in goods should normally be
accounted for through the trading subsidiary. Direct costs of new goods are
charged to the trading company and the charity must charge its trading
subsidiary an amount to cover a proportion of the shop overheads, e.g. rent,
electricity, staff. Many charities use a method based on turnover, e.g. if 30% of
sales are of bought-in goods and 70% donated, then costs that cannot be
directly attributed are split on a 30:70 ratio.

112.7   For VAT purposes, donated goods are zero-rated, while new goods such as
Christmas cards, candles and stationery will be standard-rated. Usually, input
VAT relating to the shop should be recoverable since the shop will be selling
zero-rated and mainly standard-rated goods via the trading company.

REGULATIONS AND CONTROLS

112.8 Charity shops have to abide by a wide range of consumer protection legis-lation including the *Sale of Goods Act 1979*, the *Supply of Goods and Services Act 1982*, the *Sale and Supply of Goods Act 1994* and the *Sale and Supply of Goods to Consumers Regulations 2002*. All goods sold should be of merchant-able quality. The buyer of second-hand goods has exactly the same rights as the buyer of new goods. Customers may be entitled to a refund where the goods sold are faulty, not as described, not fit for their purpose or where the seller had no legal right to sell them. However, with older goods it is increasingly difficult for the buyer to prove that a fault was inherent at the time of sale.

112.9 The consumer's right to a refund cannot be taken away and any attempt by a charity shop to limit its liability under the Act by reference to an exclusion clause or similar notice will be void and therefore unenforceable. Under the *Consumer Transactions (Restrictions on Statements) Order 1976* it is also a criminal offence to display a notice saying:

- 'No Refunds Given'
- 'Goods can only be Exchanged'
- 'Only credit notes will be given against faulty goods'.

112.10 Charity shops may not sell electrical equipment unless it has been tested by a qualified electrician and carries a label to that effect. Other items they should not sell include:

- anoraks with drawstring hoods
- safety equipment, such as children's car seats, cycle helmets, motorcycle helmets
- upholstered baby items
- firearms (unless pre-1850)
- certain knives
- spectacles
- alcohol, unless the shop has a licence
- tobacco products
- videos that have not been classified by the British Board of Film Classifi-cation or that are not labelled according to the regulations.

112.11 Some items can only be sold if they conform to certain safety standards. These include:

- toys;
- prams, pushchairs and cots;
- nightwear;
- upholstered furniture;
- oil heaters;
- gas appliances.

567

112.12   Shops

112.12   Many charities will have a policy of not selling certain items even though there is no legal reason to prohibit their sale. This is usually for reasons of hygiene or public health. Examples of items not sold by many charity shops include second-hand children's shoes, underwear, and earrings for pierced ears.

112.13   Care needs to be taken whenever plastic bags are used for display and particularly when distributing unsolicited plastic sacks to homes in order to encourage people to donate goods, because of the potential suffocation hazard posed to young children. Sacks should be perforated or sealed in an outer envelope and labelled as to the dangers of suffocation.

112.14   The *Sunday Trading Act 1994* applies only to large shops, i.e. those with over 280 square metres of floorspace, so most charity shops are not restricted in the hours they can trade on Sundays. Large shops can only trade for six hours between 10am and 6pm.

HEALTH AND SAFETY

112.15   Charity shops must abide by the *Health and Safety at Work Act 1974* which sets out the duties of employers to employees and to others who may be affected by their work activities. It also sets out the duties of people who are in control of premises as well as employees' duties. The Act implied the need for employers to manage health and safety in a structured way. The *Management of Health and Safety at Work Regulations 1999* were subsequently introduced to make this requirement explicit.

112.16   Other relevant health and safety legislation includes:

- The *Workplace (Health, Safety and Welfare) Regulations 1992,* which cover a wide range of health and safety matters including ventilation, heating, lighting, seating and welfare facilities. If no employees work at the premises not all of the regulations apply, however it is good practice to follow them to ensure the safety of volunteers;

- The *Regulatory Reform (Fire Safety) Order* which replaced all previous fire safety legislation in England and Wales from October 2006. (Similar legislation took effect in Scotland and Northern Ireland on the same date.) The Order covers general fire precautions and other fire safety duties needed to protect people in case of fire in and around premises;

- The *Manual Handling Operations Regulations 1992;*

- The *Control of Substances Hazardous to Health Regulations 1999;*

- The *Health and Safety (First Aid) Regulations 1981.*

112.17   Equipment such as irons, steamers and kettles should be maintained in effective working order and volunteers and staff should be trained how to operate them safely. Floors should be kept clear of clutter and materials stored in such a way that they are unlikely to fall on anyone and cause injury. Fire exits must never be blocked. The use of step ladders should be avoided as much as possible and any step ladders provided should be suitable for use by elderly volunteers.

112.18   Staff and volunteers should be trained in the correct procedures for lifting goods in order to minimise the risk of back injury. They should also be trained in sorting techniques to minimise the risk of injury from broken glass, crockery or hypodermic syringes. Many charities provide their volunteers with protective overalls and disposable gloves to wear when sorting.

112.19   Staff and volunteers should be trained to deal with incidents, that could give rise to threats to their personal safety, such as threats, abuse and assaults by customers. Staff should be told to always put their safety and that of their fellow shop helpers first. If someone demands money from the till all staff, voluntary or paid, should hand it over rather than risk their safety. Where shop takings are high, money should be removed from the till several times a day and stored in a safe until it can be banked. Staff and volunteers should also be given training in how to deter shoplifting and what to do if they see or suspect someone of shoplifting.

112.20   Banking should be done frequently. The route to the bank, the times at which money is banked and the container in which money is taken to the bank should all be varied to minimise the risk of robbery.

112.21   Shops should have good internal control procedures including making sure that two people are present whenever takings are counted, a reconciliation is made between the takings and the till roll, till 'z' readings (summaries of daily takings) are sequentially numbered, and there is a secure place for cash or valuables stored overnight on the premises.

112.22   Charity shop till receipts must state that the shop is a registered charity in order to comply with s 5 of the *Charities Act 1993*. Failure to do this is a criminal offence punishable by a fine of up to £1,000.

PERFORMANCE

112.23   The performance of charity shops is regularly monitored in an annual survey carried out by *Charity Finance* magazine. The 2007 survey showed that profits had increased by 3.5% compared with a 3.2% fall in the previous year. Oxfam remains the market leader with 746 shops generating an annual profit of £20.1m, followed by Cancer Research UK with 582 shops generating a profit of £15.9m and the British Heart Foundation with 546 shops generating profits of £12.7m. Overall profit per shop per week was £349 and while the three market leaders all exceeded this, some very small chains of shops run by hospices achieved even higher levels of profit per shop per week. St Rocco's Hospice's eight shops were the market leaders with profits per shop per week averaging £1,202.

ASSOCIATION OF CHARITY SHOPS

112.24   The Association of Charity shops is a membership organisation formed in 1999 to support registered charities that run shops, or are interested in running shops, as part of their fundraising activities. Members range from the largest national charities running hundreds of shops to locally based charities running just one shop. The Association:

● Develops good practice in charity shops;

● Publishes a useful range of guidance;

● Commissions research on relevant issues;

112.25   Shops

- Lobbies local and national government and the European Union on key policy issues;
- Provides training and support;
- Promotes charity shops to the general public;
- Facilitates networking between members;
- Provides legal advice;
- Provides resources and marketing materials.

112.25   In 2005 the Association launched the Code of Charity Retailing, in response to the Government's encouragement of increased self-regulation in charity fundraising. The Code promotes best practice, high standards and increased public support for charity retailing and has received high levels of support from existing members – 98% of the shops run by members in 2006 are signed up to the Code. Currently voluntary, the Code becomes a mandatory part of membership of the Association in 2008.

112.26   The aims of the Code are:

- To promote good practice and high standards in charity retailing;
- To promote public confidence in and support for charity shops;
- To increase donations to charity shops, both straight into the shops and through house-to-house collections and textile and book banks;
- To get positive publicity for charity shops;
- To promote awareness of legitimate charity shops and to help stamp out dishonest and bogus house-to-house activities.

112.27   Those charities signed up to the Code can display the Code's logo in their shops, on their textile and book recycling banks, on house-to-house collection sacks and on their vans. The logo should reassure the public that the charity will sell all saleable donated goods and the rest will be sold for further reuse and recycling, maximising the amount of money that can be raised for the charity.

FURTHER INFORMATION

112.28   Association of Charity Shops
Central House
14 Upper Woburn Place
London WC1H 0AE
Tel: 020 7255 4470
Fax: 020 7255 4475
Email – mail@charityshops.org.uk
www.charityshops.org.uk

Setting Up and Running Charity Shops – An Essential Guide, John Tough, Association of Charity Shops, June 2006, ISBN 0-9553376-0-7

Charity Shops Survey 2007 Plaza Publishing Limited

113   SOFA — Statement of Financial Activities

113.1   The Statement of Financial Activities (SOFA) was first introduced in the Statement of Recommended Practice on Accounting by Charities (SORP) issued in October 1995 and applies to all charities preparing accruals accounts under the SORP. In the majority of cases this statement replaces the traditional income and expenditure account in a set of annual accounts, although in certain cases, as discussed below, it will also be necessary to present a separate income and expenditure account. The traditional income and expenditure account was not thought to be the most suitable way of explaining a charity's activities, as the charity's primary purpose concerned the provision of benefits to its beneficiaries, rather than gain for shareholders. Also, as many charities receive significant amounts of restricted income, their accounts must show this if the reader is to have a clear understanding of a charity's financial position.

113.2   The SOFA is a primary statement in a set of annual charity accounts. It analyses all amounts coming into the charity, the resources expended and contains a reconciliation of all movements of the charity's funds. It should be given equal prominence with other primary statements such as the balance sheet.

113.3   The SOFA comprises three broad elements: income and expenditure, investment gains and losses, and the reconciliation of opening funds to closing funds. All these figures are analysed over the three main types of fund: capital, restricted income, and unrestricted funds. A possible presentation of the SOFA is shown in Table 10.

INCOME

113.4   The following principles should be applied in the preparation of a SOFA, except in the case of immaterial items.

- All figures should be shown gross, not net. For instance, if a professional fund-raiser has been paid £90,000 to raise £100,000, then both of these figures should be shown, not just £10,000 as net income.

- Incoming resources should be recognised as soon as it is prudent and practicable to do so based on an assessment of entitlement, certainty, and measurement. In particular grants receivable should be accounted for when due, not on receipt. Similarly, legacies notified but not yet received should be brought into account when receipt is reasonably certain and they can be measured with some certainty.

- Incoming resources should all be accounted for irrespective of the source and analysed by source and nature into the following categories:

  - Incoming resources from generated funds:
    - Voluntary income;
    - Activities for generating funds;
    - Investment income;
  - Incoming resources from charitable activities;
  - Other incoming resources.

571

113.4 SOFA — Statement of Financial Activities

Table 10   Possible layout of a SOFA

Description	Unrestricted funds	Restricted (income) funds	Endowment funds	Total funds in current year	Total funds in previous year
Incoming resources (analysed)	–	–	–	–	–
Total incoming resources	A	A	A	A	A
Resources expended (analysed)	–	–	–	–	–
Total resources expended	B	B	B	B	B
Net incoming resources = (A–B)	C	C	C	C	C
Gross transfers between funds	D	D	D	Total = Nil	Total = Nil
Net incoming resources after transfers	E	E	E	E	E
Gains and losses on revaluations of fixed assets for charity's own use	F	F	F	F	F
Gains and losses on revaluation and on investment asset disposals	G	G	G	G	G
Actuarial gains and losses on defined benefit pension schemes	H	H	H	H	H
Net movement in funds = (E+F+G+H)	I	I	I	I	I
Total funds brought forward	J	J	J	J	J
Total funds carried forward = (I+J)	K	K	K	K	K

Note: Where necessary the detailed headings may be expanded or amended. The columnar analysis shown above is the minimum requirement where the relevant types of fund exist. Further analysis may be presented. In particular, some charities may wish to insert rows showing the cost of generating funds and a sub-total showing total charitable expenditure.

113.5   This means that any incoming resources, regardless of whether they are subject to specific terms of trust or form the capital of the charity, should be included as income on the face of the SOFA. This method of accounting for capital movements is contrary to normal, commercial accounting principles, and means that company accounts with a SOFA including such items cannot present a true and fair view of the charity's financial transactions and position unless a separate, summary income and expenditure account is also presented.

113.6   The SOFA should reflect resource movements, not just inflows and outflows represented by cash. This may require the recognition of income not captured in traditional accounting systems, such as donated items, facilities and services.

EXPENDITURE

113.7   Expenditure should be analysed as follows:

- Costs of generating funds:

  — Costs of generating voluntary income

  — Trading (non-primary purpose): cost of goods sold and other costs

  — Investment management costs

- Charitable activities

- Governance costs

- Other resources expended.

Supporting notes should show the main components of each category.

113.8   Costs of generating funds may relate to more than just fund-raising expenditure. This category may also include some publicity expenditure, but only if that relates to fund-raising rather than promoting the mission of the charity.

113.9   Grants payable will form one of the elements of charitable activities. Grants payable should include both legal and constructive obligations, and further analysis of institutional grants should be made in the notes. Although the precise amount of disclosure is a matter of judgement, the SORP requires disclosure of a sufficient number of grants to provide a reasonable understanding of the range of institutions it has supported.

113.10   Costs of charitable activities will comprise direct and allocated costs and may be expanded on the face of the SOFA or in a note. The headings should reflect income headings wherever possible. For instance, if one of the income headings is 'care services', then the related expenditure should be similarly labelled. The headings should also correlate to the review of activities in the trustees' report.

113.11   Governance costs are the costs associated with the governance arrangements of the charity which relate to the general running of the charity as opposed to those costs associated with fundraising or charitable activity. The specific examples quoted in the SORP include such items as the costs of compliance with constitutional and statutory requirements, internal audit, legal advice for trustees and costs associated with the strategic as opposed to day-to-day management of the charity's activities. However, these costs will include a proportion of management time and overheads.

113.12 Support costs are those costs that, whilst necessary to deliver an activity, do not themselves produce or constitute the output of the charitable activity. Similarly, costs will be incurred in supporting income generation activities such as fundraising, and in supporting the governance of the charity. Support costs include the central or regional office functions such as general management, payroll administration, budgeting and accounting, information technology, human resources, and financing.

113.13 Support costs should be allocated across the expenditure headings which are shown on the face of the SOFA. The basis of this allocation and the impact on the reported results should be shown in the notes to the accounts.

113.14 It can often be difficult to establish where some types of expenditure should be allocated on the face of the SOFA. Any changes made in the underlying principles adopted year on year need to be carefully thought through and documented to ensure comparability from year to year.

113.15 Costs disclosed on the SOFA will often be an amalgam of nominal ledger cost items, allocated to the appropriate heading. For consistency and accuracy therefore, costs should always be allocated on a basis that is both consistent and reasonable. For instance, a childcare charity may spread the costs of its facilities between running playgroups and counselling, two functional cost categories, which it may choose to disclose on the face of the SOFA or in a note.

TRANSFERS

113.16 Transfers between funds will be comparatively rare as, generally, Charity Commission consent will be needed for the release of restricted funds and similarly for the formation of restricted funds by internal transfer. All transfers between different funds should be shown gross and not netted off. It is possible for the depreciation of restricted assets to be reflected through unrestricted funds and then a transfer made from the restricted fund balance to meet this cost.

RECOGNISED GAINS AND LOSSES

113.17 This part of the SOFA should show:

- realised and unrealised gains and losses on investments
- revaluation gains and losses on other fixed assets unless they represent impairment losses
- actuarial gains and losses on defined benefit pension schemes.

LIMITED COMPANIES

113.18 Limited companies are required to comply with the accounts formats under the Schedules to the *Companies Act 1985*. However, there is no fundamental conflict between the *Companies Act 1985* and the SORP although the SOFA may appear to alter the formats of the profit and loss account. As both accounts formats in the Act may be amended to use headings marked by Arabic numbers, the profit and loss account should be presented as a SOFA, subject to the clear identification of income and expenditure.

113.19 Where the income and expenditure account cannot be separately identified from within the SOFA, or there are such items as movements on the endowment fund or unrealised gains arising during the year, then a separate income and expenditure account is needed.

INDUSTRIAL AND PROVIDENT SOCIETIES

113.20 The layout of the SOFA does not conflict with the requirement for Industrial and Provident Societies to present a revenue account.

SMALL CHARITIES

113.21 Where full SORP accounts are prepared by charities that are not subject to a statutory audit (currently those with income below £250,000 but this will increase to £500,000 as a result of the *Charities Act 2006*), certain minor disclosure exemptions are available. The most significant is probably in respect of the SOFA, where small charities can choose expenditure categories to suit their needs.

NOTES

113.22 In all cases the SOFA requires a number of notes supporting the figures and providing more analysis. The more significant of these are notes explaining any trading subsidiary's performance, supporting analysis of costs, and specific disclosures in relation to such items as audit fees, trustees' expenses and employees' remuneration.

114   SORP — Statement of Recommended Practice

114.1   The Statement of Recommended Practice on Accounting by Charities – the Charities SORP – applies to all charities in the United Kingdom and the Republic of Ireland regardless of their size, constitution or complexity. This includes charities financed from permanent endowments, public appeals, regular subscriptions or Gift Aid, as well as from the proceeds of trading profits or from any other sources. However, where a Statement of Recommended Practice exists for a particular class of charities, such as housing associations or higher education institutes, charities in that class should adhere to that more specialised SORP. Like other accounting guidance, the SORP only applies to material items in the accounts. An item is material if its inclusion or exclusion makes a significant impact, either on the overall accounts or in the section of which the item forms a part. When in doubt, trustees should assume that an item is material. This materiality rule does not apply in respect of all disclosure requirements, for example the amount of trustees' benefits and the size of audit fees must be disclosed even if the amounts are not material.

GENERAL PRINCIPLES

114.2   The Charities SORP sets out the requirements in respect of the trustees' annual report (described in CHAPTER 123), the annual accounts, and summarised accounts (described in CHAPTER 3). It stresses that it is essential for a charity's accounts to be accompanied by an explanation of the basis on which they have been prepared. The accounting policies adopted for accrual accounts must be relevant, reliable, comparable, and understandable and be consistent with two fundamental accounting concepts:

- The 'going concern' concept, i.e. the charity will continue in operational existence for the foreseeable future.

- The 'accruals' concept, i.e. income is recognised when earned or receivable and expenditure when incurred, and not just when paid in or out.

114.3   In considering which accounting policies to apply trustees of charities are expected to apply the principles of the SORP.

114.4   Recognising the skill required to produce accruals accounts and the small size of the majority of charities, the *Charities Act 2006* provides for the alternative 'receipts and payments' basis of accounting for charities with gross income below the applicable level, currently £100,000 in England and Wales (£25,000 in Scotland), in the relevant year.

114.5   Income is all resources which become available to the charity and which the trustees are legally required to apply in furtherance of its charitable purposes within a reasonable time of receipt. Income includes all trading and investment income, legacies (unless they are incapable of financial measurement) and all donations, fund-raising proceeds, grants, gifts in kind, gains from disposals of fixed assets and investments, and asset revaluation gains. All incoming resources should be reported gross as far as practicable.

114.6   Expenditure should include all outgoing payments, all losses on the disposal of fixed assets, provisions for depreciation and all claims against the charity when recognised as liabilities by the trustees.

114.7   The underlying objectives of the SORP are to improve the quality of charities' financial reporting and to enable charities to account in a more consistent
manner making comparisons across the sector more meaningful. The
accounts presentation has therefore moved away from the traditional income
and expenditure format and adopted a different primary statement, the
Statement of Financial Activities (SOFA) that shows the sources and application of all incoming and outgoing resources, analysed by fund. The detailed
breakdown of the charity's activities by type of fund, and even by individual
fund, is followed through in the balance sheet and in the notes to the accounts.

114.8   The SORP is a recommendation, not an accounting standard, although FRS
18 effectively requires an industry SORP to be the basis of an entity's
accounting policies. The principles of the SORP are specifically referred to in
the *Charities (Accounts and Reports) Regulations 2005*. For instance, *reg 5* states
that the accounts shall be prepared in accordance with the methods and
principles set out in the SORP. Within the overall framework of the SORP
there is still considerable flexibility over how figures are presented and what
additional information should be provided. This is because the aim of the
SORP was to introduce greater consistency and comparability in charity
accounting, rather than to set up a straightjacket.

114.9   The SORP specifies that where a charity is preparing accounts on an accruals
basis, and not on a receipts and payments basis, then the charity's accounts
should always comprise a SOFA (see CHAPTER 113), a balance sheet, and
supporting notes. In certain cases two other statements will also be required, a
cash flow statement and a separate summary income and expenditure
account.

BALANCE SHEET

114.10   The balance sheet shows the assets, liabilities and funds of the charity. Assets
should be analysed between fixed assets and current assets. The balance sheet
should show, or indicate in notes, how the funds may be utilised, or must be
utilised because of restrictions imposed by donors. The format adopted in the
SORP is essentially the same as that in the *Companies Act 1985 Sch 4 Part 1*.
Investments held for long-term gain, which are therefore classified as fixed
assets, should be carried at market value. Other fixed assets may be shown at
either cost or valuation, less a provision for depreciation. However, at the time
of writing there are discussions taking place which propose that heritage
assets should be recorded at market value.

114.11   The balance sheet may be presented in one continuous vertical format or
analysed by columns into various types of fund.

114.12   Some fixed assets can be excluded from the balance sheet. These are certain
assets which are inalienable, historic or not susceptible to valuation. If they
are excluded, then a note should indicate the extent to which such assets exist.
However, as mentioned above, accounting for heritage assets is currently
under review. FRED40 is likely to require that all such assets are capitalised at
valuation, unless it is unpredictable to do so. Because much of the wealth of
many charities, especially older ones, is represented by their fixed assets, it
may be appropriate to create a fund which equates to the value of functional
fixed assets, to make clear to the reader that much of the charity's apparent
wealth is not readily available for immediate application.

114.13   Current assets and liabilities should be included in the accounts at their conventional valuations: cost, or net realisable value if lower, of current assets and the settlement value of liabilities. Liabilities should be analysed between current and long-term liabilities. Liabilities should only include genuine liabilities existing at the balance sheet date. Moral obligations and informal commitments are not liabilities. Where a charity has an enforceable commitment to funding, for instance a grant given for research over a period of several years, then this should be included as a liability, split between short term and long term. In exceptional circumstances it may be appropriate to exclude such liabilities on the basis that the charity is anticipating matching income to meet this cost. However, this cannot be done simply on the expectation that general fund income will be sufficient to meet the future liabilities. The anticipated income should relate specifically to the future expenditure, such as is the case when a child sponsorship programme is undertaken on the basis of continuing support pledges: the SORP equates this to reimbursement.

114.14   Liabilities will only include deferred income if the income is due to the charity in a future period or receivable when certain conditions are met. Current income relating to a specific purpose or geographical area should be treated as current year's income, within restricted funds if necessary. Income will only be deferred if the trustees are not entitled to draw upon it until the relevant period is reached (effectively it is not theirs until that date) or where conditions attached to performance related grants have not been met.

114.15   The other side of the balance sheet is analysed by type of fund, distinguishing between unrestricted funds, designated, restricted and endowment funds. Where consolidated accounts are prepared the balance sheet also shows funds retained in subsidiaries.

114.16   Apart from other specific designated funds, the unrestricted funds may be split into separate reserves as necessary, including the following referred to in the SORP or accounting standards:

- Free reserves – effectively the charity's working capital;
- Functional fixed assets – funds held in fixed assets;
- Intentions – funds for commitments which are not liabilities;
- Pensions reserve – required for deferred benefit schemes under FRS 17;
- Contingent liabilities – setting aside funds for contingencies;
- Revaluation reserve – for limited companies' revalued assets.

NOTES TO THE ACCOUNTS

114.17   The supporting notes should explain the accounting policies, expand upon the information in the financial statements, and provide other useful information. The SORP sets out the following items for disclosure and expansion.

- Accounting policies: these should explain the policies applying to material items in the accounts, and may cover income streams, recognition of expenditure, asset valuations and recognition of gains, netting off, and the use of designated funds.

- An analysis of material funds by types of fund, showing the movement in the year and how the fund is represented: this analysis will show the opening balance, incoming resources, other movements and the closing balance. Where there are immaterial funds they can usefully be grouped together to save cluttering the notes with unnecessary detail. The only exception to this is any fund which is in deficit. This should always be disclosed separately and explained. If designated funds are shown on the face of the SOFA, then the note showing movements on these funds will usually show transfers only, not incoming and outgoing resources separately.

- A breakdown of fixed assets by cost and depreciation, the purposes for holding the relevant assets, and details of any revaluations: the basis of valuing assets and the depreciation policy will usually be set out in the accounting policies.

- An analysis of investments and investment income: both should be analysed out into their distinct types, such as properties, listed investments, investments in subsidiaries and connected persons, unlisted securities, and cash. All of these should be split between UK and overseas holdings. Further details of how the portfolio is structured should be set out as appropriate, showing for instance where any one investment represents more than 5% of the portfolio, or where there are significant restrictions on the realisation of any asset.

- An analysis of debtors and both short-term and long-term liabilities: where the charity's assets have been offered as security, details should be provided.

- Details of any loan made to a subsidiary.

- Transactions with trustees and connected persons: these should include expenses (a nil return must be made if there are no transactions).

- Allocation of support costs: the methodology of allocating support costs to expenditure categories and the actual amount allocated in the year to each expenditure heading.

- Staff costs: the total emoluments (i.e. remuneration and benefits-in-kind, as defined for taxation purposes) paid to the charity's employees should be shown and the average number of employees (full-time equivalents) employed during the year. The note should also show the number of employees whose emoluments (including taxable benefits but not pension contributions made by the employer) for the year were £60,000 or more in bands of £10,000. Bands in which no employees' emoluments fell should not be listed.

- The total amount payable to the charity's auditor or independent examiner: this should distinguish between fees paid for the audit/examination itself, and fees paid for other services, such as tax advice.

- *Ex gratia* payments: these include any payments, non-monetary benefits, other expenditure or the waiver of rights to property to which the charity is entitled made not as an application of funds or property for charitable purposes, but in fulfilment of a compelling moral obligation. Where the charity has obtained the consent of the court, the Attorney-

General or the Charity Commission, then the nature and date of the authority should be disclosed. Payments that the trustees reasonably consider to be in the interests of the charity, for example a gratuity to a long-serving employee on his retirement, or an additional severance payment to an employee made redundant, which confirm the charity as being a good employer should not be treated as *ex gratia*.

- Details of indemnity insurance: the cost and the nature of any insurance purchased with the charity's funds to protect the charity from losses arising from the neglects of defaults of trustees, employees or agents, or to indemnify the trustees should be disclosed.

- Other commitments, guarantees and contingent liabilities: commitments which are legally binding should have been accounted for as liabilities, but charitable commitments payable by instalments to be funded out of future income should be described in the notes to the accounts. Other commitments may not be charitable, for instance operating leases. Particulars of all such material binding commitments should also be disclosed. Material guarantees, and the conditions under which they might result in liabilities, need setting out, along with details of contingent liabilities. Where a contingent loss is material and probable it should be accrued in the accounts. Where loss is less certain, but not remote, then disclosure should be by way of note. This should set out the nature of each contingency, the uncertainties that are expected to affect the outcome, and a prudent estimate of the financial effect where an amount has not been accrued. If such an estimate cannot be made a note in the accounts should show why it is not practicable to make such an estimate.

OTHER STATEMENTS

Cash flow statement

114.18   The cash flow statement is a separate statement required only for larger charities, i.e. those which exceed two of the following three thresholds:

- gross income in the year in excess of £5.8 million;

- balance sheet total in excess of £2.8 million; or

- more than 50 employees.

114.19   Where an accounting period is not 12 months long, the figures should be pro-rated as appropriate. 'Balance sheet total' refers to the total balance sheet values of assets. 'Employee numbers' means the average monthly number of full-time equivalent persons employed. [*Companies Act 1985, s 247*]. The thresholds are applied to the current and two previous years and a cash flow statement must be produced if they were breached in any two of those years. The content of the cash flow statement is set out in Financial Reporting Statement No 1 (revised).

Summary income and expenditure account

114.20   An income and expenditure account is required for limited companies if the SOFA includes movements on endowment funds that are regarded as capital, not revenue, transactions. This will be a summary income and expenditure account, derived from and cross-referenced to the corresponding figures in the SOFA. The summary need not distinguish between restricted and unrestricted funds, but should show income, expenditure and transfers separately in respect of continuing operations, acquisitions and discontinued operations.

115 Sponsorship

115.1   The term 'sponsorship' is used to describe many different types of funding arrangement. Charities can only engage directly in certain types of sponsorship and the tax treatment will depend upon the precise nature of each arrangement.

115.2   At one extreme some sponsorships are simply donations. For example, a runner in the London Marathon may ask for 'sponsorship', a swimmer taking part in a 'sponsored' charity swimming gala asks for 'sponsorship', or a company 'sponsors' a charity event or service in return for a simple acknowledgement of the company's support. What is being sought in all these examples is a donation to a charity, the amount of which may vary according to criteria such as the distance completed or time taken. Where this is the case, the sponsorship money can be accepted by a charity as a donation and will be free of both corporation tax and VAT. Because these types of sponsorship payments are genuine donations, companies and individuals can make them tax effectively by using Gift Aid. However, the gift aid always relates to the original donor, rather than the individual handing the money over: sponsorship forms should therefore be prepared in such a way that allows each sponsor to make a gift aid declaration.

115.3   At the other extreme, some types of 'sponsorship' are essentially business transactions in which the sponsor offers the charity money, or goods or services, but in return expects the charity to provide a significant benefit such as valuable advertising, publicity or entertainment for the sponsor. This type of sponsorship is essentially trading, as the charity is providing advertising, publicity or other services for the sponsor in return for the sponsorship payment. Such sponsorship arrangements will usually have to be structured through a charity's trading subsidiary, as the provision of advertising or publicity for commercial companies is not a charitable purpose and therefore cannot be carried out by a charity. When a sponsoring company receives a benefit in return for their sponsorship the payments will not normally be eligible for Gift Aid, but it can be deducted from the company's total income when calculating its taxable profits.

TAX IMPLICATIONS

115.4   Sponsorship can have VAT and tax implications. If the sponsorship is correctly a payment for services supplied, then the organisation supplying those services has to account for VAT on everything received under the sponsorship agreement. Where the amount of sponsorship is agreed without reference to VAT, it must be treated as VAT inclusive. Where a charity makes supplies to sponsors as part of a fund-raising event, such as sponsorship of the event or the sale of advertising space in a brochure, the supplies may be exempt. (*VATA 1994, Sch 9, Group 12*)

115.5   If the sponsorship represents a trade, then the profits earned will be subject to corporation tax, subject to one of the trading exemptions or concessions applying. [*ICTA 1988, s 18*]. Any tax liability can be avoided if trading type sponsorship is handled by a subsidiary company that donates its profits to its parent charity under a profit-shedding deed of covenant or by Gift Aid. [*ICTA 1988, s 339*].

115.6   Sponsors will wish to be associated with the name of a charity, rather than its trading subsidiary. Therefore if a sponsorship agreement is made between the sponsor and a charity's wholly owned trading subsidiary, either because the legal restrictions on trading by charities prevents the charity from entering into a proposed sponsorship agreement, or because the charity needs to structure the agreement with its trading subsidiary in order to avoid paying corporation tax on profits arising from the sponsorship, then the charity should set up a licence agreement allowing the trading subsidiary to use its name.

115.7   Many sponsorship agreements fall between the two extremes, i.e. a pure donation or a purely commercial business transaction. Often the value received by the sponsor is worth significantly less than the amount of sponsorship they give or the services they supply. If this is the case, it is possible to split the sponsorship payment into two parts, though this must be done at the commencement of the agreement. The first part is regarded as the 'business' payment for the expected value of the anticipated benefits, attracting VAT and possibly some corporation tax, and the second is regarded as a voluntary donation which could be paid using Gift Aid tax to avoid any tax liability.

115.8   Where it is intended to apportion income for VAT purposes and the arrangement does not fall within clearly published guidelines (such as that given in VAT leaflet 701/1/95 in relation to affinity cards) it is sensible to obtain HMRC's written agreement in advance.

POINTS TO CONSIDER

115.9   Charity staff and trustees should remember that a charity's name is one of its most valuable assets, as it is the means by which the charity is known and by which its reputation will be judged. So before launching a sponsored event, or entering into a sponsorship agreement with a commercial company, there should be a minuted discussion showing that the relevant points on the following checklist have been taken into consideration.

- Could the sponsored event/association with the sponsoring company damage the charity's relationships with its beneficiaries, donors, funders, supporters or the general public?

- Is the type of activity to be sponsored in keeping with the charity's values?

- Does the charity's insurance cover give adequate protection against claims that might arise from the event/sponsorship?

- What risks does the charity face from this event/sponsorship?

- Is the sponsorship agreement generally to the benefit of the charity?

- Could the charity use its resources more effectively to raise money?

- Could the sponsorship agreement lead to the charity's name being exploited for non-charitable purposes?

- Does the agreement give the charity the right to terminate it if the commercial sponsor misuses or improperly exploits the charity's name?

115.10   Sponsorship

115.10   If charities enter into sponsorship agreements with retailers, including banks, the sponsors are likely to come within the *Charities Act 1992, s 58(1)* definition of a commercial participator. This means that there will need to be a written agreement between the charity and the sponsoring company

116   Staff Recruitment and Development

116.1   One of the most important parts of any organisation is the people who work for and with it to achieve its aims and objectives. Attracting the right people and enabling them to work effectively and efficiently are key management tasks. A sure foundation is good and fair policies and working practices. Much of the work in charities is carried out by volunteers so it is necessary to decide how staff and volunteers are to be integrated into personnel policies. Key elements in the good management of staff and volunteers are:

- good practice in setting staff conditions, policies and procedures within the legal framework;

- effective recruitment; and

- appraisal, development and training.

Together they all help to attract, motivate and retain good staff and volunteers.

STATUTORY OBLIGATIONS AND THE LEGAL FRAMEWORK

116.2   Staff who are paid are in a contractual relationship with their employer, governed by employment law. Staff undertake to perform an agreed range of tasks and the organisation rewards them for doing so. These tasks must be legal and the person carrying them out must be controlled by the organisation. This element of control differentiates the employed from the self-employed and has implications for how income tax is deducted from payments made by the organisation.

116.3   Both sides in this relationship owe a duty of care to the other. The employer must ensure that the place of work meets health and safety regulations and the needs enshrined in common law, i.e. to pay what has been agreed and not to make unreasonable demands; the employee must work safely and be loyal and conscientious in carrying out their side of the contract.

116.4   The trustees of a charity are obliged to use the charity's funds in the most effective way to achieve its aims and objectives. There are sometimes hard decisions to be made about the level of salaries and rewards that need to be paid to attract people of sufficient calibre to be effective and those that could lay the organisation open to charges about the misuse of funds.

116.5   A contract of employment exists as soon as an employee agrees to start work for an employer, and by doing so shows that they accept the terms and conditions offered by the employer. Both employer and employees are bound by the terms offered and accepted. All employees taken on for one month or more are entitled by law to be given a written statement of employment particulars within two months of the date the employment starts. The written statement sets out the main particulars of the terms and conditions of employment. Usually it will have already been discussed with prospective employees at interview. The written statement must cover:

- the names of the employer and the employee;

- the date when the employment (and the period of continuous employment) began;

585

- remuneration and the intervals at which it is to be paid;

- hours of work;

- holiday entitlement;

- entitlement to sick leave, including any entitlement to sick pay;

- pensions and pension schemes;

- the entitlement of employer and employee to notice of termination;

- job title or a brief job description;

- where it is not permanent, the period for which the employment is expected to continue or, if it is for a fixed term, the date when it is to end;

- either the place of work or, if the employee is required or allowed to work in more than one location, an indication of this and of the employer's address; and

- details of the existence of any relevant collective agreements which directly affect the terms and conditions of the employee's employment – including, where the employer is not a party, the persons by whom they were made.

116.6   If an employee is normally employed in the UK but will be required to work abroad for the same employer for a period of more than one month, the statement must also cover:

- the period for which the employment abroad is to last;

- the currency in which the employee is to be paid;

- any additional pay or benefits; and

- terms relating to the employee's return to the UK.

116.7   The statement must also include a note giving certain details of the employer's disciplinary and grievance procedures and must state whether or not a pensions contracting-out certificate is in force for the employment in question.

116.8   The requirement to issue the written statement prompts the need for policies on remuneration and all the items that follow it in this list. However, these are only the bare bones and the policies need to reflect the type of organisation (membership, philanthropic etc.) its culture, the staff's expectations, custom and practice to date, what can be afforded and what accords with the nature of the organisation's aims and objectives.

116.9   Many charities have found it convenient to tie their salaries to a relevant, nationally set scale, e.g. universities, local government etc. However, this is not suitable for all organisations and many of the scales that were nationally agreed are breaking down, so more organisations are having to devise their own scales. Whichever approach is taken, it is still worth defining a pay policy for the organisation and this will include a system to reward extra individual effort or contribution to organisational success.

116.10   Salaries are not the only 'compensation' to be considered: holidays, hours of work, how sickness is dealt with, training, the amount of maternity and paternity pay, pensions and retirement all need to be taken into account, as well as other benefits that might be considered such as season ticket loans, cars, and even private health insurance.

116.11   The statutes that make up employment law are complicated. The essentials are: the *Equal Pay Act 1970* which enshrines the concept that people should be paid the same for doing the same job. This principle has been extended by EC directive to say that work of equal value must be paid at the same rate. The same principles of equality also apply to conditions such as hours of work and how pay is determined. The *Employment Protection Act 1975* introduced basic principles and established an employee's right to go to an industrial tribunal if they believed they had been dismissed unfairly or that 'constructive dismissal' had taken place. The way that the dismissal is handled is also important. The Act has subsequently been amended and a huge body of practice and case law has been amassed.

Discrimination

116.12   Unfair discrimination in employment is wrong. Sex discrimination is prohibited by the *Sex Discrimination Act 1975* (as amended), discrimination on the grounds of racial or ethnic origin by the *Race Relations Act 1976* (updated by the Race Directive), discrimination on the grounds of disability by the *Disability Discrimination Act 1995*, discrimination on the grounds of religion or belief by the *Employment Equality (Religion or Belief) Regulations*, discrimination on the grounds of sexual orientation by the *Employment Equality (Sexual Orientation) Regulations*, and discrimination on the grounds of age by the *Employment Equality (Age) Regulations*. There are exceptions, particularly in cases where a person's sex or religion is a genuine occupational qualification for the job, e.g. workers at a womens' refuge, or head teachers of religious schools.

116.13   As well as direct discrimination indirect discrimination is also banned. Indirect discrimination involves applying a requirement or condition, even if it applies to everyone equally, if the condition is not justifiable and has a detrimental effect on people with disabilities, or of a particular racial group, or sex, or age group, because they disproportionately cannot comply with the requirement or condition. For example, requiring a certain number of years of continuous experience may indirectly discriminate against women who have taken time off to raise a family.

DATA PROTECTION

116.14   Recruitment processes involve the collection of personal data so have to comply with the *Data Protection Act 1998* (see CHAPTER 32). The Employment Practices Data Protection Code, published by the Information Commissioner, is a useful tool in helping develop good data protection practice. The code is available at *www.dataprotection.gov.uk/dpr/dpdoc.nsf*.

116.15   Taking notes at an interview will constitute the processing of personal data, so job applicants have normal subject rights of access to them. Therefore care should be taken in writing notes during an interview. A discriminatory statement recorded as the reason for non-appointment could have legal repercussions for the employer.

116.16   Examples of benchmarks for the collection and handling of data in the recruitment and selection process are:

- When responding to job advertisements, applicants should be aware of the employer's name to which their information will be provided.

- The application form should deal with how the information will be used. The information requested should be relevant to the recruitment decision. If further checks are going to be made this should be made clear at the outset.

- Following the interview, personal data should be recorded and retained. The employer must ensure that interview notes can be justified as relevant to, and necessary for, the recruitment process itself or for defending the process if challenged.

- It should be made clear to the applicant at the outset if the employer intends to undertake pre-employment vetting and, if so, how this vetting will be conducted. Comprehensive vetting should only be conducted on successful applicants. Where information is collected about a third party, e.g. the applicant's partner, employers must ensure the third party is made aware of this so far as practicable.

116.17   Organisations are required by the Code to set up their own policy for the retention of recruitment records, based on fair business need. Information obtained following a vetting exercise should be destroyed as soon as possible, or in any event within six months. The applicant should be made aware if it is the employer's practice to keep an unsuccessful applicant's details on file for future vacancies and the applicant should be given the opportunity to have his/her details removed from the file. Personal data obtained during the recruitment process must be securely stored or destroyed by the employer.

EMPLOYMENT CONDITIONS

116.18   The *Employment Relations Act 2004* updates collective labour law and trade union rights. It established a statutory procedure for the recognition of trade unions by employers for collective bargaining purposes.

116.19   The *Transfer of Undertakings (Protection of Employment) Regulations 2006 (TUPE)* protect conditions such as pay and other benefits when staff are transferred from one employer to another. This is a complicated area and expert guidance is advised.

HEALTH AND SAFETY AT WORK

116.20   Health and safety legislation imposes the same standard of care on all organisations regardless of their size and whether they are run by staff and/or volunteers. The *Management of Health and Safety at Work Regulations 1999* require employers to assess risks to employees, other workers, clients, members of the public and anyone who comes onto the organisation's premises or uses its services. Employers must draw up a health and safety scheme setting out a programme to reduce risks or minimise the negative impact of risks that cannot be avoided. Employers with more than four employees must put the risk assessment and health and safety scheme in writing.

116.21   Where employees are aged under 18 the Regulations require the employer to carry out a specific assessment taking into account the fact that young people may be inexperienced, immature and/or less aware of risks than adults.

116.22   The Health and Safety Executive has produced guidelines and a training video specially tailored for use by charities called 'Charities and Voluntary Workers: A Guide to Health and Safety at Work'.

FINDING THE RIGHT PEOPLE

116.23   Recruiting new staff is often difficult. The whole future of the organisation hangs on finding and keeping the right people for the tasks to be undertaken and on those people working well together. The costs of changing staff are high, not only in terms of the funds actually spent on the recruitment process, but also the time that must be invested by colleagues while the new person grows to performing at the required level. Throughout, the process should be conducted in a fair and open manner and fit within the organisation's equal opportunities policy. Thinking in advance will reduce the likelihood of mistakes, though some things are very difficult to detect, no matter how good your process. Success depends upon being clear about several factors.

The job

116.24   The job description and person specification define the job to be done and the key skills, competencies, qualities and experience needed to do it.

Finding the right candidate

116.25   There are a number of options available. An organisation can:

- promote a member of staff;

- appoint someone from outside and exclude applications from members of staff; or

- consider internal and external candidates.

116.26   Unless a staff member is to be promoted, the position should be made known to the widest possible range of potential candidates in the most cost-effective way, and applications encouraged from appropriately qualified and experienced candidates. Places to look for candidates other than amongst the existing staff might well include:

- the organisation's own networks;

- advertising in national and/or local newspapers;

- using confidential registers maintained by recruitment consultancies or agencies; and

- search, sometimes known as headhunting. This usually means finding and approaching candidates who are not actively looking for another post and persuading them to apply. It is generally best left to professional consultants as potential candidates often feel more comfortable if approached by a third party.

116.27   Though many organisations in the sector would prefer not to use a proactive search agency to find candidates as doing so appears to conflict with their equal opportunities policy, it is becoming increasingly used to recruit chief executives and specialists in short supply.

Attracting the right applications

116.28   Attracting the right applicants will depend on how well the job description, person specification and the advertisement are written. They should give an idea of the scope of the job and the ethos of the organisation, and state clearly any skills, competencies or experience that are *essential* for the post so that time is not wasted processing applications from unsuitable candidates. In drawing up the advertisement charities should consider the benefits the job will offer to candidates in terms of career development, interest, public profile, etc. It may be necessary to 'sell' the job to candidates if the post is hard to fill, the conditions are particularly onerous or the salary rather low.

The form of interview and other selection methods

116.29   Interviews always form part of the process, but are not the only way to select people. Increasingly, charities are using psychometric tests to assess critical numerical and verbal reasoning skills. Personality questionnaires and tests of management style, where appropriate, can provide useful information about how the applicant would fit into the organisation. The results can indicate areas to probe more deeply during the interview. Such tests should always be carried out by properly qualified people.

116.30   Interviews should be planned carefully so that by the end all the information needed has been gained. It is important to give candidates the opportunity to ask questions about the post and the organisation. Candidates should be put at ease so that they are able to think clearly and develop their replies to questions. Interviewers should not make assumptions – if something is important they should ask the candidates. As well as their skills, interviewers should look for the special contribution a candidate could make to the organisation, which may come from their social networks rather than their professional or work experience.

WOULD AN OUTSIDE RECRUITMENT ADVISER HELP?

116.31   Outside help might come from an individual personnel consultant, from a recruitment consultancy or from an agency. Each makes a different contribution.

The individual consultant

116.32   A personnel consultant or an occupational psychologist brings an outside perspective to the process. This is particularly useful when making senior appointments and when a change of direction in management is required.

Recruitment consultancies

116.33   Sometimes called Search and Selection, recruitment consultants bring the same skills and expertise as an individual consultant and add expertise in finding and attracting the best candidates. They may have a confidential register of potential candidates and they will provide the administrative services involved in recruitment.

116.34   The consultant will expect to carry out preliminary interviews with perhaps two or three times the number of candidates that the organisation wishes to interview and will assist with producing the shortlist. They should also be able to help with planning the interview.

Agencies

116.35   An agency is primarily a source of candidates through a register. They do not offer search, though the agency staff will have experience in advertising. They will be able to undertake the administrative tasks involved in recruitment.

116.36   The services offered by consultancies and agencies often overlap and so it is advisable to contact several to find out exactly what they offer and for what fee.

TRAINING AND DEVELOPMENT

116.37   For any organisation to achieve its aims and objectives effectively and efficiently, its people need to be knowledgeable and skilful. This applies to all workers, whether paid staff or volunteers, including the trustees.

116.38   However well staff with the requisite skills are recruited, they still need training to keep up to date and develop so that they can move up the organisation. Changes in legislation, such as employment and data protection legislation, produce a need for staff training as do developments in technology, particularly database management systems.

116.39   Training in skills for a particular job is not enough. Staff need the opportunity to develop generic skills such as budgeting, report writing, presentation and evaluation. They also need opportunities to practise their newly developed abilities so that they and the organisation get the best value from the training. Encouraging staff and volunteers to gain and practise new skills can be a powerful way to build loyalty to the organisation.

116.40   As well as developing individuals' skills, it is worth developing their ability to work as team members. Few jobs require people to work in isolation. Team working is the norm and often people need to learn how best to work as a member of a team – and as a member of a particular team. This does not apply only to staff. Many volunteers, including trustees, work in teams and would gain from training in team development.

116.41   Charities must reconcile meeting the individual's needs with spending the charity's funds wisely, so any training and development provided should contribute actively to the betterment of the organisation in fulfilling its aims and objectives.

GOOD MANAGEMENT

116.42   Perhaps the most important factor in recruiting and retaining staff is good management, providing adequate resources to do the job, recognising an individual's contribution, keeping everyone informed and not allowing staff to burn themselves out. Management as a skill is frequently undervalued in charities and many make false economies by not providing adequate training to staff being promoted to managerial positions. Management training is an ongoing process and identifying training needs should be an integral part of any appraisal system. Training should be viewed as an investment, with an expected return for the charity that can be monitored. There is now a wide

116.42   Staff Recruitment and Development

range of training tailored to the needs of the voluntary sector, including some excellent and highly cost-effective distance learning provided by the Open University Business School.

117   Tax Effective Giving

GIFT AID

117.1   The Treasury launched a consultation on Gift Aid in June 2007 with the aim of examining and identifying measures to drive up charitable giving through Gift Aid.

117.2   At the time of writing, December 2007, the consultation period has closed and the Treasury are in the process of assimilating the responses received from various interested organisations including charities, professional advisors and fundraising organisations. The Treasury envisage a further short period of consultation with selected respondents to the original consultation and hope to announce any changes to the Gift Aid scheme in the spring 2008 budget.

117.3   The present Gift Aid scheme for tax effective charitable giving was substantially changed in the *Finance Act 2000* and applies to all donations large or small, regular or one-off, except payroll donations. Prior to April 2000 the scheme only applied to donations of £250 or more (£100 in the case of Millennium Gift Aid).

117.4   The new legislation replaced that relating to Deeds of Covenant. Payments made under Deeds of Covenant in existence on 5 April 2000 now qualify for relief for tax purposes under the Gift Aid scheme. Two quite separate pieces of legislation were amended by the *Finance Act 2000* (*Finance Act 1990, s 25* and *Income and Corporation Taxes Act 1988, s 339*) relating to gifts by individuals and gifts by companies. Some factors are common to both, but there are also notable differences. The rules concerning Gift Aid in relation to individuals have now been rewritten in the *Income Tax Act 2007* (*ss 412 to 429*), which broadly applies from 2007/08. The legislation does not refer to the term Gift Aid, but to 'qualifying donations'. Nevertheless, Gift Aid is a term which has been adopted by HMRC.

117.5   There is no limit to the number of Gift Aid donations an individual or company can make to a single charity, or to a number of charities, in the same tax year.

117.6   A qualifying donation must be a gift which satisfies the following conditions:

- It must be a payment of a sum of money. A promise to make a payment at some later date is not sufficient and any form of gift in kind or a gift of an asset will not qualify.

- It must not be subject to a condition that any part of it can be repaid.

- It must not be a payment from an individual under the payroll deduction scheme, since these payments qualify for tax relief in their own right.

- Neither the donor nor any connected person may receive a benefit above a certain limit in consequence of the gift.

- The payment must not be conditional on, or associated with, the acquisition of any form of property by the charity from the donor or a connected person. Therefore, a donor cannot make a qualifying donation to the charity, which then uses the money to purchase something from the donor. The fact that this extends to persons connected with the donor makes this restriction difficult to circumvent.

117.7   Tax Effective Giving

Gift Aid by companies

117.7   From 1 April 2000, companies (including companies owned by a charity) and unincorporated associations, such as clubs and societies, must make Gift Aid donations gross, rather than deducting tax from them. They also do not have to complete any forms or give the charity a Gift Aid declaration. The charity does not therefore have any tax to reclaim or have any administrative procedures to follow, other than entering the amount in its accounting records. These rules also apply to payments due under a Deed of Covenant which was executed prior to 1 April 2000. Therefore tax should not be reclaimed on donations received from companies after 1 April 2000. These rules apply to all companies whether or not they are resident in the UK.

Gift Aid by individuals

117.8   Individuals still have to deduct tax from their Gift Aid donations and make a Gift Aid declaration. Therefore the amount paid by an individual is treated as a sum net of basic rate tax. The tax withheld can be reclaimed by the recipient charity. Fluctuations in the basic rate of tax will impact on the amount of tax recoverable by charities. The basic rate of tax reduces from 22% to 20% in April 2008 and this will result in a reduction in the amount of tax recoverable by charities from 28 pence to 25 pence for every pound donated under Gift Aid.

117.9   An individual who is a higher rate taxpayer can obtain tax relief at the higher rate on the gross amount of the gift. The donor claims tax relief by giving details on their tax return or by writing to their tax office asking for an adjustment to be made to their PAYE code number or self-assessment tax calculation. The donor must have paid an amount of income tax or capital gains tax, at either the basic rate or some other rate, that is equal to or more than the tax deducted from their donation. This includes any tax suffered by deduction at source and tax credits on dividends.

117.10   Individuals who make Gift Aid donations after 5 April 2003 may elect to carry back the donation and be treated as if the qualifying donation was made in the previous year of assessment (*Income Tax Act 2007, s 426*).

117.11   In addition to individuals who are resident in the UK, Gift Aid donations can be made by:

- Crown servants and members of the UK armed forces serving overseas;

- non-resident individuals, provided they have income or capital gains charged to UK tax that are at least equal to the gross amount of the donation.

117.12   Gift Aid certificates have been replaced by simpler and more flexible Gift Aid declarations. There is no specified format for Gift Aid declarations, provided that all the required information is shown (see below). HMRC has issued a model Gift Aid declaration form for guidance but charities are free to design their own if they prefer to do so. There is no requirement to ask HMRC to approve a self-designed declaration form, but HMRC Charities are happy to advise or approve forms if requested.

117.13   Charities should ensure that their declaration forms comply with any other relevant legislation. If the charity intends to use the data provided by the donor for any purpose other than reclaiming tax, for example to build a mailing list, the form must comply with the *Data Protection Act 1998*. The *Charities Act 1993* requires registered charities to include a statement that they are a registered charity in fund-raising literature.

117.14   A charity must have received a Gift Aid declaration from the donor containing certain information and confirming that the donation is to be treated as a Gift Aid donation before it can be treated as a qualifying donation, i.e. before the charity can reclaim tax. The details required on a Gift Aid declaration are:

- the donor's name and home address;

- the charity's name;

- a description of the donations to which the declaration relates, e.g. 'the enclosed donation' or 'all donations I make on or after the date of this declaration' or 'all donations I make under the direct debit mandate below';

- a declaration that the donation is to be treated as a Gift Aid donations;

- except where given orally, a note explaining the requirement that the donor must pay an amount of income tax or capital gains tax at least equal to the tax deducted from the donation;

- the date of the declaration.

117.15   The declaration can be written or oral, so donations can now be made tax effectively by telephone or over the Internet. However, if a charity receives an oral declaration, it will not be effective unless the charity sends the donor a written record showing:

- all the details provided by the donor in their oral declaration;

- a note explaining the donor's entitlement to cancel the declaration retrospectively;

- a note explaining the requirement that the donor must pay an amount of income tax or capital gains tax at least equal to the tax deducted from the donation;

- the date on which the donor gave the charity the declaration;

- the date on which the charity sent the written record to the donor.

Signature

117.16   There is no need for a Gift Aid declaration to be signed.

Declarations for gifts made by partnerships

117.17   A partnership is not a legal entity in England, Wales and Northern Ireland, so a donation by a partnership is treated as being made by the individual partners. However, one partner may make a Gift Aid declaration on behalf of all the other partners, provided that partner has the authority to do so. The declaration need only show the name and address of the partnership. Otherwise it will be necessary for each partner to make their own Gift Aid declaration. The partners can do this on a single declaration form provided it shows all their names and addresses. In Scotland, a partnership has a legal identity, so one of the partners can make a Gift Aid declaration on behalf of the partnership, and give just the name and address of the partnership.

117.18   The donation will normally be apportioned between the partners in accordance with the way they share profits. Each partner can claim higher rate tax relief by entering their share of the donation on their own self-assessment tax returns.

Declarations on collection envelopes

117.19   A Gift Aid declaration can be included on envelopes used for collecting cash, such as those used for house to house collections or those used by many churches for regular giving, provided there is a means of identifying the donor. This could be done by asking donors to write their name and address on the envelope or to give a reference number that can be checked against a donor register. Gift Aid declarations can also be included on forms for sponsored events. However, it is the sponsor who is making the donation that must make the Gift Aid declaration, not the person participating in the event.

Cancellation

117.20   Gift Aid declarations can be cancelled at any time. Donors can do so by notifying the charity in any communications medium. Charities should keep records of cancelled declarations, including the date on which the charity received notification of cancellation. The cancellation takes effect either on the date the charity is notified or on a later date specified by the donor.

117.21   If a donor cancels an oral declaration within 30 days of the charity sending a written record, the cancellation has a retrospective effect so it will be as if the declaration had never been made.

DONOR BENEFITS

117.22   Charities may only provide a limited amount by way of thanks or benefit to its donors if their donations are to qualify as Gift Aid donations. A benefit is any item or service given to the donor, or to a person connected with him or her, in consequence of the donation and includes benefits provided under a membership scheme. However, a mere acknowledgement of the donation in the charity's literature will not amount to a benefit provided that it does not take the form of an advertisement. Newsletters and publications produced for the purpose of describing the work of the charity, are considered to have no value even if the literature has a cover price and is also on sale to members of the public.

117.23   The donor benefit rules contain two limits on the value that a donor, or someone connected with them, may receive as a consequence of making a donation. First, the maximum value of the total benefits that a donor may receive from the same charity in the same tax year is £500 after 6 April 2007 or £250 prior to this date (the aggregate value test). Second, the value of benefits received must not exceed the limits set out in Table 11 below (the relevant value test).

Table 11   Benefit limits

Amount of Donation £	Maximum Value of Benefits that can be received
£0–100 £101–1,000 >£1,000	25% of donation £25 5% of donation (2.5% of donation pre 6 April 2007)

117.24   The limits in Table 11 apply separately to each donation. However, special rules are used to 'annualise' the amount of certain donations and the value of certain benefits for the purposes of applying the limits. In order to assess whether the benefit exceeds the relevant limits, the total value of the benefits due over a 12–month period must be taken. This must then be compared with the total value of donations made in connection with those benefits over a 12-month period. The limits are then applied according to the 'annual value' of the benefits and the 'annualised' donations. These will usually apply where a donor makes a single donation but receives free of charge a monthly periodical, which has a face value. Alternatively, a charity may make a single gift to a donor who has agreed to make regular monthly donations.

Gift Aid on donations that attract a right of free admission to charity property

117.25   Prior to April 2006, where a charity's main purpose was the preservation of property or conservation of wildlife for the public benefit and it charged for admission to view property or observe wildlife, the value of free admission was excluded from the calculation of the benefit in consequence of making a Gift Aid donation. Such charities could therefore allow free admission on payment of a Gift Aid donation equivalent to the admission price, and claim basic rate income tax from the Exchequer in respect of the amounts donated under Gift Aid.

117.26   From 6 April 2006, changes introduced in the *Finance Act 2005* (now rewritten to *s 420* of the *Income Tax Act 2007*) extended the application of these rules, subject to certain conditions outlined below, to any rights of admission granted by a charity for the purpose of viewing property preserved, maintained, kept or created by a charity for its charitable purposes.

117.27   Property is not restricted to land and/or buildings. It also includes:

- artefacts

- works of art (but not performances)

- plants

- animals

- property of a scientific nature.

This list is not exhaustive, however, it clearly expands upon property of heritage and wildlife charities which enjoyed the earlier relaxation of the benefits rules.

117.28   If the benefit of any right of admission received in consequence of making a donation is to be disregarded the opportunity to make a donation and receive free admission must be available to the general public and one of the following conditions must also be satisfied:

- either a donation is made of at least 10% more than the cost of admission to the general public and in return the charity grants an equivalent right of admission to the donor, or the donor and his family; or

- the donation secures admission to the property for a 12-month period for the donor or the donor and his family, for example through a season ticket or a membership scheme. Access should in general be unlimited whenever the property is open to the public during that 12-month period but charities may exclude from the right of admission up to five days in each 12-month period when the property is otherwise open to the public and still qualify.

The 'admission charge plus 10%' option

117.29   Where a visitor chooses to make an additional donation that it as least 10% more than the cost of admission the whole amount paid is treated as a donation for Gift Aid purposes, not just the additional amount.

117.30   Many charities use this option for daily admissions, but in fact any period of admission less than 12 months can be included within this option as long as members of the public could purchase an equivalent right of admission.

117.31   Each visitor must be made aware at the time he is asked for payment that he can choose to pay the admission charge or make a voluntary donation of 10% more than the admission charge and receive the same right of admission. HMRC have made it clear that blanket requests for the additional 10% without clearly advertising normal admission charges or denial of entry if a visitor chooses not to pay the additional 10% will mean the amount paid will not qualify as a Gift Aid donation and the charity will not be able to reclaim any income tax (nor will the visitor be able to claim tax relief on the amount paid).

The annual right of admission option

117.32   Charities are free to decide what minimum level of donation they will accept before granting a right of admission for a year or more (so for example can choose to allow annual admission for a donation equal to the daily admission charge), but must always give an equivalent right of admission to all donors including those who do not make a Gift Aid declaration.

117.33   Charities do not have to be open all year or every day to grant a right of admission for a period of a year or more. Gift Aid can apply as long as the right of admission is available to donors at all times when the property is open for viewing by members of the public.

Provision of other benefits

117.34   A charity may decide to provide visitors with additional benefits, for example a guide to the property being visited, as a thank you or an incentive for making an optional 10% donation or buying an annual pass; this is acceptable providing the benefits do not exceed the normal benefit rules described above.

Joint admission arrangements

117.35   Gift Aid can apply to donations which give the donor a right of admission to the property of more than one charity. The visitor who chooses to make a donation must, however, know which charity or charities are sharing his donation, and in what proportions.

Mixed Sites

117.36   Charities must also be very careful when they consider offering multiple admissions to a mixture of charity and non-charity properties. The right of entry to a non-charity property may have to be considered as a benefit received in consequence of the donation (unless it is clearly priced and paid for separately).

117.37   Charities in this position should contact HMRC Charities for guidance about specific scenarios or proposals.

Reciprocal arrangements with other charities

117.38   Gift Aid can apply to qualifying donations which grant a right of admission to the property of more than one charity as long as there is an equivalent right of admission granted to donors who opt not to make a Gift Aid declaration. For example, two museums in different parts of the country may have a reciprocal arrangement to allow donors annual admission to each other's property.

Performances

117.39   Performances are specifically excluded from the category 'works of art' but Gift Aid may still be available on donations made for admission to view property where performances also take place as long as the performances are merely incidental to the viewing of a charity's property. For example, historic re-enactments illustrative of the property's former use.

Charity auctions

117.40   If a person buys an item at a charity auction and intentionally pays more than the market value of that item in order to support the charity, the amount paid over and above the market value can be treated as a Gift Aid donation, provided any necessary declaration is made and the limits on donor benefits (see **117.22** above) are not exceeded. For example if someone pays £10,000 at a charity auction for two tickets to a gala concert performance that sell at the box office for £150 then as the market value of the tickets does not exceed the limits of the relevant value test (i.e. £150 is less than 5% of £10,000) and the total benefit received by the donor in that year does not exceed the aggregate benefits test (i.e. the benefit of £150 is less than the permitted limit of £500) the payment of £10,000 can qualify as a Gift Aid donation.

117.41   Other payments for goods and services can also be split between the amount required to purchase the item and the amount that is really a donation. This treatment, however, is only permissible if the item is commercially available (so its value can be ascertained) and the donor is aware, at the time he makes a successful bid, that the item could be purchased separately and for what price. Where the item being auctioned is not commercially available valuation of the benefit will be extremely difficult and a charity should seek professional advice in such a situation.

KEEPING RECORDS

117.42   A charity has to keep records to show that its tax reclaims are accurate. As far as Gift Aid from individuals is concerned, these records must show an audit trail linking each donation to an identifiable donor who has provided a valid Gift Aid declaration. In addition to accounting records, therefore, the charity will need to keep copies of all Gift Aid declarations. Where declarations cover donations the donor intends to make in the future it is important to keep those declarations for as long as they are needed to support tax reclaims.

117.43   If a charity fails to keep adequate records it may be required to repay to HMRC the tax it has reclaimed, plus interest and may also be liable to a penalty.

117.44   Records need not be kept on paper. They can be held on the hard drive of a computer, floppy disk, microfiche or CD ROM. Digital records of oral declarations given during a telephone call are also accepted by HMRC on condition that individual oral declarations can easily be identified and accessed.

117.45   Charitable companies should keep records for a minimum of six years after the end of the accounting period to which a tax claim relates. There is, however, a shorter period for charitable trusts, which is the normal time limit for keeping records in respect of an income tax return. If, however, a tax reclaim is made late, the records need to be kept until the end of the quarter following the first anniversary of making the reclaim. The normal date for income tax returns is the first anniversary of the 31 January filing date following the end of the tax year. Clearly, if an audit is in progress then the records must be retained until it is completed.

DONATIONS FROM JOINT ACCOUNTS, ETC.

117.46   Charities often receive donations drawn on joint bank accounts and need to decide if the donation has been given by someone who has already given the charity a Gift Aid declaration. It is reasonable to assume that the donation is from the person who has signed the cheque, debit card slip, standing order mandate, or direct debit mandate. Credit card donations can similarly be made from accounts that have more than one authorised signatory and it is reasonable to assume that the person signing the slip or authorising a telephone donation is the donor. Where donations are made by telephone or through the Internet it is reasonable to assume that the donation is from the person who authorises the transaction. Where there is doubt the charity should ask the person who signed the documentation or authorised the transaction to confirm that the donation is from them.

DEEDS OF COVENANT

117.47   From April 2000 there is no longer separate tax relief for payments made under Deed of Covenant as all future tax relief for such payments will be under the Gift Aid arrangements. As a transitional measure a Gift Aid declaration is not needed for payments already in existence under Deed of Covenant before 6 April 2000. However, any donations made outside the terms for the Deed or after it expires must be covered by a Gift Aid declaration as should payments under a Deed of Covenant executed on or after 6 April 2000. Although there is no longer any tax advantage to setting up payments under a Deed of Covenant, it may be a way for a charity to ensure committed giving from a donor.

GIFTS OF SHARES AND SECURITIES

117.48   From April 2000, individuals and companies, whether resident or non-resident in the UK, are able to get tax relief for gifts of certain shares and securities to charity when calculating their income or profits for tax purposes. This tax relief will be in addition to the existing relief for gifts of shares, securities and other assets to charity when calculating capital gains.

117.49   The tax relief will apply where an individual or a company disposes of the whole of the beneficial interest in any qualifying shares or securities to a charity either by way of gift or by way of a sale at undervalue.

117.50   Donors will be able to claim a deduction in calculating in the case of an individual, his or her income for the tax year in which the disposal takes place, and in the case of a company, its profits for the accounting period in which the disposal takes place.

117.51   The amount that donors can deduct will be the market value of the shares or securities at the date of disposal plus any incidental costs of disposing of the shares (brokers fees, etc.) less any consideration given in return for disposing of the shares, and the value of any other benefits received by the donor, or a person connected with the donor, in consequence of disposing of the shares.

117.52   Donors will claim the tax relief, at their top rate of tax, on their self-assessment or corporation tax return. Charities should not reclaim tax on gifts of shares and securities.

Qualifying shares and securities

117.53   The following categories of shares and securities can be donated:

- shares and securities listed or dealt in on a recognised stock exchange, whether in the UK or elsewhere;

- units in an authorised unit trust;

- shares in a UK open-ended investment company;

- holdings in certain foreign collective investment schemes.

117.54   Shares and securities listed or dealt in on a recognised stock exchange include shares traded on the Alternative Investment Market.

Qualifying interest in land

117.55   From April 2002, individuals and companies, whether resident or non resident in the UK, are able to get tax relief, for gifts of a qualifying interest in land to a charity when calculating their income or profits for tax purposes.

The relief is in addition to the existing relief for disposal of assets to charity when calculating capital gains. A qualifying interest in land includes buildings sited on the land in question and is either:

- a freehold interest in land, or

- a leasehold interest in land, where the land in question is in the United Kingdom.

117.56 The tax relief will apply when an individual or company disposes of the beneficial interest in a qualifying investment in land. In order to make a claim the individual or company must have a certificate issued by or on behalf of the charity which:

- specifies the description of the qualifying interest in land which is the subject of the disposal;

- specifies the date of the disposal, and

- contains a statement that the charity has acquired the qualifying interest in land.

117.57 The amount that donors can deduct will be the market value of the qualifying land at the date of disposal, plus any incidental costs of disposal, less any consideration given in return for the disposal of the land and the value of any other benefits received by the donor, or a person connected with the donor, in consequence of disposing of the land.

117.58 Where two or more persons have a beneficial interest in the land the relief is only available where each of them disposes of the whole of his beneficial interest in the land to the charity. The relief available will be such share of the amount above as agreed between the parties.

117.59 Where, within the relevant period, a person, or any one of the persons, who made the disposal, or any person connected with him, or any one of them:

- becomes entitled to an interest or right in relation to the land to which the disposal relates, or

- becomes party to an arrangement under which he enjoys some right in relation to all or part of the land,

he shall be treated as never having been entitled to tax relief in the first place.

117.60 The relevant period for the purpose of **117.59** above is a period commencing with the date of disposal and ending with:

- in the case of an individual, the fifth anniversary of the 31 January next following the end of the year of assessment in which the disposal was made, and

- in the case of a company, the sixth anniversary of the end of the accounting period in which the disposal was made.

PAYROLL DEDUCTION SCHEME

117.61 The payroll deduction scheme came into effect in April 1987 as a method of encouraging charitable giving. Employees can make donations from their own gross pay, before tax has been deducted thus effectively increasing the value of their donation. Employees automatically get tax relief at their highest rate of tax. Such schemes can therefore only be used by those in employment or those receiving a company pension from which tax is deducted under PAYE. The total payment an employee may make under this scheme has been increased from time to time since it was introduced but from 6 April 2000 the limit was abolished. The rules are governed by both statute and regulations.

117.62   If an employer operates a payroll deduction scheme it must be approved by HMRC. It is up to the employees to decide whether or not they wish to join the scheme (which cannot be compulsory), the amount they wish to donate and the charity or charities that will benefit.

117.63   The employer deducts the amount authorised by each employee from their salary and this is paid monthly to a charity who has agreed to act as agent and been approved by HMRC. The best known agency is Give as You Earn (GAYE) operated by the Charities Aid Foundation. The agency distributes the payments to the charities nominated by the employees. The regulations lay down conditions with which the agency must comply, which include having a contract with each employer, providing receipts to the employer and certificates to the employees if requested, maintaining records for three years, which must be available to HMRC for inspection, and the agency must neither retain money nor repay it to the employer or employees. The agency is, however, allowed to deduct charges from amounts paid to the nominated charities. Any charges made to the employer, or administrative expenses incurred by the employer, are deductible in arriving at the taxable profits of the employer's business.

117.64   Employees do not pay tax on the payments they make by deduction from their salaries, however, national insurance remains payable on their full salary. [*Income and Corporation Taxes Act 1988, s 202*].

117.65   The Government provided various incentives in the early years of the scheme to encourage employers to set up payroll giving schemes and employees to donate to charity through payroll giving schemes as follows:

- A 10% supplement was paid on donations under payroll giving schemes in the four years from 6 April 2000 to 5 April 2004.

- A grant was paid to employers setting up schemes between 6 April 2004 and December 2006 which was dependant upon the number of employees, as follows:

1–99 employees	300
200–249 employees	400
250–499 employees	500

In addition the Government matched the monthly donation of an employee up to a maximum of £10 per month for the first six months.

117.66   Payroll deduction schemes are administratively simpler than Gift Aid for both charities and HMRC, as the charity does not have to reclaim tax paid. However, they do place an administrative burden on employers and for this reason some employers are reluctant to take part in the scheme.

117.67   An individual can elect to have the gift treated as if it were made in the previous year of assessment. The election must be in writing before the self-assessment tax return for the previous year has been submitted and in any case not later than 31 January next following that year. The effect of the

117.68 Tax Effective Giving

election is that the gift will be treated as a qualifying donation for the previous year by the donor but will not affect the position of the recipient.

117.68 From April 2004 individuals who are due to a tax refund when submitting their self-assessment tax return will be able to nominate a charity to receive the refund and HMRC will pay this directly to the charity.

118   Taxation

118.1   It is a common misconception that charities do not pay tax. In fact charities are liable to pay most taxes unless they take care about the activities they undertake and the structures they use. This chapter provides a brief overview of the main taxes and their bearing on charities, while specific taxes are dealt with in more detail in other chapters.

INCOME AND CORPORATION TAX

118.2   Tax matters relating to charities and their subsidiary companies are all dealt with by HMRC: the HMRC Charities office based in Bootle.

118.3   Where charities receive voluntary income or operate only within the terms of the basic tax exemptions then they should not be subject to tax on their income. The Charity Commission has made it clear that they expect charities to adopt appropriate strategies to mitigate tax liabilities where it is appropriate and cost effective to do so, but that in some cases it may be appropriate for the charity to accept a small tax charge rather than set up expensive and cumbersome structures to avoid a liability.

CAPITAL GAINS TAX

118.4   *Section 256* of *Taxation of Chargeable Gains Act 1992* exempts charities from capital gains tax, as long as the gain in question is applied for charitable purposes. Normally, an individual who disposes of a chargeable asset at less than its value (i.e. gives it away) would be charged tax as though the disposal was at full value. Because there is an annual exemption (£9,200 in 2007/2008) this could otherwise be used as a way of arranging a sale through someone to whom the asset was gifted just prior to sale, and who had not already used their exemption. These rules do not apply to a gift to a charity and so chargeable assets may be transferred tax free. Where an asset is likely to create a gain of an amount within the donor's exemptions, it may be worthwhile to ask the donor to sell the asset personally, and for the proceeds then to be donated (net) by Gift Aid to the charity. Assuming that the donor has enough relevant taxable income, this not only avoids any charge to capital gains tax, but also increases the value of the gift as the charity can reclaim the basic rate tax paid on the donation.

INHERITANCE TAX

118.5   No inheritance tax is payable on transfers to charities, whether made as lifetime gifts or on death. A gift which is conditional, and where the condition is not met within 12 months, will then cease to be exempt. Similarly, a gift which can be retracted, or which is dependent on a period of time elapsing, will also not be exempt.

NATIONAL INSURANCE

118.6   As an employer no special rules operate for charities in respect of National Insurance.

STAMP DUTY AND STAMP DUTY LAND TAX

118.7   Stamp duty is payable by the purchaser on a range of transactions, but since December 2003 has been largely restricted to transfers of shares and securities. Stamp Duty Land Tax ('SDLT') was introduced from 1 December 2003 to tax the transfer of land.

118.8   A series of *Finance Acts* has ensured that charities are exempt from stamp duty on stock and share transfers, provided that the share transfer is adjudicated as not liable to tax.

118.9   A land transaction is exempt from SDLT provided that the subject matter of the transaction is to be used in furtherance of charitable purposes or the profits there from are so applied. The SDLT exemption is withdrawn if, within three years, the charity ceases to hold the land for charitable purposes.

118.10   Transactions by non-charitable subsidiary companies are subject to stamp duty and SDLT in the normal way.

VAT

118.11   VAT is a European wide indirect tax which is administered by HMRC in the UK. There is no blanket VAT relief for charities and any charity which undertakes taxable business activities (i.e. standard and/or zero-rated) must register for VAT if these exceed the registration limit, (£64,000 per annum in 2007/8). Most charitable activities are either "non-business" activities or VAT exempt and therefore no right to recover VAT arises on related costs. However, certain goods and services can be supplied VAT free to charities which helps them to mitigate their irrecoverable VAT. These reliefs are very specific and should be considered on a case by case basis. Charities will therefore often have a very complex VAT position. The reliefs are discussed in more detail in CHAPTERS 50 and 130.

118.12   There are a number of special schemes that operate for certain types of business, e.g. the Tour Operator's Margin Scheme. Where a charity's activities come within one of these areas the charity will need to comply not only with the general VAT rules, but also with the specific rules for charities and those for the special scheme.

118.13   Charities that have business activities with turnover in excess of £600,000 may also be required to disclose the use of specific schemes under anti-avoidance legislation. Of particular relevance to charities are the schemes listed pertaining to property transactions and those relating to the provision of education. Furthermore, businesses with turnover in excess of £10 million are required to notify HMRC of schemes bearing the 'hallmarks' of VAT avoidance, such as certain property transactions between related parties.

OTHER TAXES

118.14   Charities have no general exemption from other forms of taxation, such as insurance premium tax, air passenger duty, council tax and excise duties. Mandatory relief of 80% exists for business rates and a further 20% relief is at the discretion of the levying council. The non-charitable subsidiary trading company of a charity is not entitled to business rate relief.

119   Terrorism

119.1   The incidence of charity involvement with terrorist organisations is very rare, however the possibility of involvement exists. Methods of using charities by terrorist organisations may include:

- using money raised by charities to fund terrorist organisations;

- using charities to smuggle people into countries illegally;

- using residential schools as military recruitment and training centres;

- using charities set up for providing facilities for young people for organisation and recruitment;

- using charities as a base to spread propaganda; or

- using charities for money laundering purposes.

119.2   Trustees need to take great care to ensure that their charity is not inadvertently assisting a terrorist organisation by allowing the charity to be used for money laundering purposes. Although the following offers of donations may well be legitimate, trustees are right to be suspicious if:

- offered large donations from persons unknown to the trustees or senior staff;

- donations are offered conditional upon particular individuals or organisations being used to do work for the charity;

- offers are made of donations in cash, for a certain period of time, the charity to receive the interest, but the principal to be returned to the donor at the end of the specified period.

Trustees should report any suspicions they may have to the Charity Commission and/or the police.

119.3   The Charity Commission has been alert to potential links between charities and terrorism for a number of years and has worked to three basic assumptions:

- The Commission would not register an organisation that had support of terrorism explicitly or implicitly as an object.

- That use of an existing charity's assets for support of terrorist activity is not a proper use of those assets.

- That links – or alleged links – between a charity and terrorism corrode public confidence in the integrity of charity.

119.4   The Commission's principles when looking at charities with potential links to terrorism are:

- Any links between charities and terrorist activity are totally unacceptable. 'Links' in this case might include fund-raising or provision of facilities, but also include formal or informal links to organisations 'proscribed' under the *Terrorism Act 2000* and any subsequent legislation.

- The Charity Commission will deal with any allegation of links between a charity and terrorist activity as an immediate priority.

- Where such allegations are made the Charity Commission will liaise closely with relevant intelligence, security and law enforcement agencies to facilitate a thorough investigation.

- Active collaboration between charities and terrorist organisations is a police matter that may lead to serious criminal charges. Where allegations are made to the Commission or suspicions arise as a result of the Commission's work (e.g. monitoring or casework), the Commission will inform the relevant law enforcement agencies immediately and co-operate fully with the criminal investigation.

- Where a charity's activities may give, or appear to give, support or succour to any terrorist activity, the Commission expects the charity's trustees to take immediate steps to disassociate the charity from the activity.

- The Commission expects trustees to be vigilant to ensure that a charity's premises, assets, volunteers or other goods cannot be used for activities that may, or appear to, support or condone terrorist activities. Examples include the use of a charity's premises for fund-raising or meetings.

- Charities should take all necessary steps to ensure their activities could not be misinterpreted. The Commission expects trustees or charities to ensure their activities are open and transparent, for example, when transferring assets abroad. It holds trustees accountable for ensuring that procedures are put in place to ensure that terrorist organisations cannot take advantage of a charity's status, reputation, facilities or assets.

- The Charity Commission expects any person connected with a charity, whether a trustee, employee, volunteer, adviser or beneficiary to bring evidence of a charity's possible links with terrorism to its attention immediately.

119.5   There is debate about the scale of the problem. The Charity Commission disclosed the following when responding to the Home Office review of the matter in 2007:

> 'The Commission's current experience in operational compliance work is that:
>
> - dealing with allegations of and concerns about charity links with terrorism is an increasing area of work. This is likely to continue to be the case in the future;
>
> - our compliance function currently has 121 open cases dealing with all types of serious problems in charities. 40 of these are formal statutory inquiries, with seven of these inquiries involving allegations of charity links with terrorism; and
>
> - we are also assessing and actively monitoring an increasing number of allegations of links between charities and terrorism.'

LEGISLATION

119.6   The main legislation relating to terrorism is the *Terrorism Act 2000* and the *Anti-terrorism, Crime and Security Act 2001*. The *Terrorism Act 2000* came into force in February 2001. It gave the Secretary of State power to proscribe any organisation that is believed to be concerned with terrorism, either by committing or participating in acts of terrorism, preparing for terrorism, or promoting or encouraging terrorism in the UK or abroad. It is against the law to be a member of a proscribed organisation and it is illegal to assist, raise money for, or send money to a proscribed organisation or to anyone who is a member of one.

119.7 A list of proscribed organisations is published on the Charity Commission's website as part of its operational guidance on terrorism, and the Bank of England website (*www.bankofengland.co.uk/sanctions/main.htm*) contains a list of people and organisations that have been named by the UN, the EU, and by UK orders and statutory instruments as having possible links to terrorist organisations or to be involved in terrorist activities.

119.8 The *Anti-terrorism, Crime and Security Act 2001* augmented the *Terrorism Act 2000*. This Act contains provisions relating to the seizure and forfeiture of terrorist cash found at any place in the UK.

TRUSTEES' DUTIES

119.9 Trustees should be aware that *s 19* of the *Terrorism Act 2000* provides that a person who receives information in the course of a trade, profession, business or employment that leads him/her to believe or suspect that another person has committed an offence under *ss 15–18* (which relate to money or other property being used for the purposes of terrorism) is guilty of an offence if s/he does not disclose this to a constable as soon as is reasonably practicable.

119.10 Likewise, *s 39* of the Act provides that where a person, who knows, or has reasonable cause to suspect, that a constable is conducting, or proposes to conduct a terrorist investigation, the person commits an offence if s/he discloses to another anything which is likely to prejudice the investigation or interferes with material which is likely to be relevant to the investigation.

119.11 Both the Home Office and the Charity Commission recognise that certain charities are more at risk than others. Their approach to regulation is therefore risk based. Trustees should adopt the same approach and recognise that certain activities and affiliations create a greater exposure to terrorist abuse. A principal of 'know your beneficiary' is proposed and supported in principle, although at the time of writing the exact mechanics of this have yet to be worked out. OSCR has yet to make a pronouncement on charities in Scotland and links to terrorism.

CHARITIES WORKING OVERSEAS

119.12 Charities that operate overseas should ensure that all overseas money transfers and transfers of goods are fully documented and that there is a clear audit trail to satisfy the public that the charity's funds are being used appropriately. The documentation should be retained in the UK as part of the accounting records. Such documentation should include the names of the intermediary(ies), the beneficiary, the commission paid, the gross and net value of the transactions and the countries of transaction. The Charity Commission does not advocate using the hawala or other informal money transfer systems to send money abroad. However, the Commission will accept this if assured by the charity trustees that this is the best way to transport cash in the circumstances prevailing at the time.

120 Trading Subsidiaries

120.1 Many charities wish to undertake regular trading activity as a means of raising income. Where this extends much beyond a primary purpose of the charity, however, the exemption the charity has from paying corporation tax (or if the charity is a trust, income tax) will be lost. The charity is also at risk of committing a breach of trust if it carries on such a trade, as it does not constitute a charitable activity. A charity should therefore consider setting up a separate non-charitable trading company that donates its profits to the charity. The trading company can be either a wholly owned subsidiary of the charity or can be jointly owned by a number of charities. A wholly owned subsidiary company is generally preferable in that it does not cause problems in dividing up and distributing the profits as would be the case when a number of charities are shareholders.

120.2 For the profits of certain small trading and other fund-raising activities carried on by a charity, the Charity Commission has confirmed that if the charity is governed by one of its model governing documents, which contain prohibitions on 'any substantial trading activity', the charity may lawfully carry on activities falling within the tax exemption, without having to set up a trading company.

120.3 The exemption applies to the profits of all trading and most other incidental fund-raising activities, provided that the total turnover from all of the activities does not exceed the annual turnover limit or, if it does, there was a reasonable expectation at the beginning of the period that it would not. The profits must also be used solely for the purposes of the charity. The annual turnover limit is £5,000 or, if greater, 25% of the charity's total income from all sources, subject to an overall turnover limit of £50,000.

INVESTING IN A TRADING COMPANY

120.4 Forming a trading company must be considered by a charity as the making of an investment and must therefore be within the charity's investment powers and policy. Any funding from the charity which the subsidiary may require must also be similarly viewed. The Charity Commission will not normally object to a nominal subscription of share capital but prefers to see the initial funding coming from commercial sources, to minimise the risk to charitable assets. However, the trading company will find it difficult to raise a loan without a guarantee from the parent charity, so the charity's funds would still be at risk. A loan from a charity to its trading subsidiary may well be considered non-charitable expenditure by HMRC, which could result in the charity losing tax exemptions.

TRANSFERRING PROFITS

Profit-shedding covenant or Gift Aid payment

120.5 The most tax efficient method of donating the profits of a subsidiary trading company to the parent charity is through Gift Aid. Until April 2000, a company could obtain tax relief for a payment under a deed of covenant but this relief was replaced by Gift Aid. Companies that are wholly owned by one or more charities have nine months from the end of the company's accounting period to make the Gift Aid payment. This means that companies have time to calculate their taxable profits and complete their accounts and corporation tax computations before the payment has to be made.

120.6   Some companies still have deeds of covenant in place. Where this is so, then any payment made in respect of a financial year should be reflected in the accounts for that period. Where a payment is simply made under Gift Aid, and there is no legal or constructive obligation to make such a payment, then this may be reflected in the following year's accounts.

Dividends

120.7   A trading subsidiary can also pass its profits to its parent charity using a dividend. The payment of a dividend is not generally a tax efficient method because it still leaves the company with a corporation tax liability and the tax credit on dividends that charities used to be able to reclaim has been withdrawn.

FINANCING THE TRADING COMPANY

120.8   A trading subsidiary should be financed on a commercial basis. Any loan should bear interest at a reasonable rate and there should be a repayment schedule. Any payments of capital or interest should actually be made, rather than just recorded in the accounts. Because companies have working capital commitments, they often do not generate enough cash to repay loans without incurring tax liabilities. This problem is exacerbated by the interaction of the calculation of profit on an accounts and tax basis.

120.9   The taxable profits of a company often exceed the profits shown by the company's accounts, for example because the company has incurred expenses which are not allowable for tax purposes, such as entertaining its customers, or because the tax relief for capital expenditure is less than the depreciation charged in the accounts, which is not itself allowable. If a Gift Aid payment equals the whole of the company's taxable profits, the company will be unable to build up reserves and can actually become insolvent if it has insufficient capital to cover this deficit. The parent charity may well be unable to provide additional funding in these circumstances because to do so would breach its investment powers. The charity may lose some of its tax exemption if it makes a further non charitable payment to the company to help refinance it. An investment is only a qualifying payment for tax purposes if it is made for charitable purposes, i.e. for the benefit of the charity and not for the avoidance of tax. Unless it were in itself a commercially sound investment, ignoring the fact that the profits of the company were to be donated for charity, a loan or subscription for further shares by a charity would not fulfil those criteria. To resolve these problems, the charity should plan the setting up of a trading subsidiary carefully and prepare proper business plans, cash flow forecasts and profit projections.

120.10 To deal with such situations some charities decide that it is better to allow their trading companies to retain some of their profits each year so that the trading company has sufficient funds for working capital. This leaves part of the company's profits subject to corporation tax but may be preferable to the charity losing its tax exemptions or the trading company becoming insolvent.

120.11 Trading Subsidiaries

120.11   The subsidiary company can, of course, seek external finance. Anyone considering making an external loan will, however, look at the trading company's ability to make the necessary interest and loan repayments and would be unwilling to lend money to a company which cannot build up any reserves because it donates all of its taxable profits to its parent charity. The trustees of the charity should regularly review its subsidiary company's performance and the viability of the charity's investment in the subsidiary. Once a trading company is established the Charity Commission expects funds to flow only in one direction, namely from the trading company to the charity. Trustees who continue to fund loss making trading companies could be judged to be acting in breach of trust or breach of their fiduciary duty.

MANAGING A TRADING COMPANY

The Directors

120.12   Trustees and staff of the charity are permitted to be directors of the trading company and staff, but not trustees, can be paid for their service as directors. However, in order to avoid conflicts of interest it is advisable to ensure that some trustees are not directors of the trading company and that some directors of the trading company are neither trustees nor staff of the charity. The Charity Commission suggests that there should be at least one truly independent director: this director would be neither an employee nor a trustee of the holding charity.

Staffing

120.13   The trading company is legally a separate organisation from the charity, so care must be taken that the correct contracts of employment are in place. In some instances it may be appropriate to have joint contracts of employment.

Accounting and administration

120.14   Bank accounts and financial records must be kept separate and any paperwork and records should clearly indicate whether they relate to the charity or to its subsidiary trading company. The charity can make a management charge to cover the management of its trading company in addition to charging for providing premises or shared resources, but this in itself may lead to a tax liability if it represents a trade in its own right. Similarly, failing to maintain a separate bank account can generate a tax liability since a Gift Aid payment cannot be made without the separate account. Note that rate relief may not be available for the portion of a building used by a trading company. The loss of relief should be borne by the trading company. Charities should also beware of falling foul of the transfer pricing rules, which affect larger entities: those with more than 250 employees and either a turnover of assets of more than about £35 million or assets of less than about £30 million. Above this level all transactions should be costed on an arm's length basis, including loan interest. Where entities are established in countries where there is no provision for double taxation relief, then all sizes of entity are caught within the transfer pricing mechanism. Tax computations submitted under self assessment should reflect the arm's-length value.

Insurance

120.15   A charity's insurances will not cover its trading company unless the policies specifically state that they do.

VAT

120.16   The relationship between a charity and its trading subsidiary gives rise to a number of complex VAT issues. CHAPTER 125 touches on these but professional advice is usually called for.

Rates relief

120.17   Trading subsidiaries do not qualify for rates relief.

121   Trustee Duties and Responsibilities

121.1   In its leaflet CC3 'The Essential Trustee: what you need to know', the Charity Commission defines charity trustees as 'the people who serve on the governing body of a charity. Many charities do not use the term 'trustee' but refer to the members of their governing body by some other term, for example 'the council', 'the management committee, 'the board', 'the directors', 'the executive committee', or 'the governors'. However, no matter what they are called, those defined in the governing document as the charity's governing body are the charity's trustees. It is increasingly regarded as good practice for charities to include the word 'trustee' in the name of the body of people who bear the legal responsibilities of trusteeship. For example, many charities now refer to their governing body as 'The Trustees', 'The Board of Trustees' or 'The Council of Trustees'.

121.2   Charity trustees have legal, financial and managerial duties, i.e. legal obligations, and responsibilities. Although many of these are set out in guidance issued by the Charity Commission, the principles apply equally to trustees of Scottish charities.

LEGAL DUTIES AND RESPONSIBILITIES

121.3   Trustees are responsible for the proper administration of the charity in accordance with the law and its trusts, as set out in its governing document. As the governing body of a charity, the trustees have both ultimate power and ultimate responsibility for everything the charity does and how it does it. Their overriding duty is to pursue the objects of the charity as set out in its governing document. They must ensure that the charity is solvent, well-run and its activities are having the desired impact on the lives of its beneficiaries. The trustees must apply the income and property of the charity exclusively for the charity's objects, applying it fairly between those qualified to benefit from it now and in the future.

121.4   Charity trustees must not use the charity's resources to provide or subsidise statutory services (unless their governing document explicitly permits this). They can run services which central or local government have a statutory duty to provide, as long as the services are fully funded by the relevant statutory body. Charity resources can be used, however, to complement or supplement statutory services by providing additional benefits or higher standards of service.

121.5   Trustees have a fiduciary duty to the charity as a whole. 'Fiduciary' means 'in good faith', so trustees must always act in good faith (i.e. in the belief that what they are doing is correct), and in the interests of the beneficiaries, setting aside their own interests, preferences and prejudices.

121.6   Trustees also have a duty of care. Therefore they must act reasonably and prudently, with the same degree of care that a prudent business person would exercise in managing their own affairs. Note that this is a higher duty of care than that required of company directors who merely have to act honestly and in good faith with a degree of skill commensurate with their knowledge and experience. When dealing with investments the standard of care which trustees must exercise is higher still. They must act with the degree of care that a prudent business person would exercise in managing the affairs of someone for whom they were responsible. In practice this means that trustees need to know about the legal, financial and managerial issues affecting the charity, though they are not expected to have expert knowledge. If they hold themselves out as having expertise in a given area, however, they will be expected to act with a higher duty of care, and this will be taken into account should any issue come to the attention of the courts or the Charity Commission.

121.7   The *Trustee Act 2000* (which applies to the trustees of unincorporated charities and not to the trustees of incorporated charities) introduced a new 'duty of care' for the trustees of both charitable and non-charitable trusts to minimise the risk of loss or injury to the trust. It states that in exercising any of their powers trustees 'must exercise such care and skill as is reasonable in the circumstances, having regard in particular to any special knowledge or experience he has, or holds himself out as having'. In addition, if someone acts as trustee in the course of a business or profession, they must exercise such care and skill as is reasonable in the circumstances, having regard to any special knowledge or experience that it is reasonable to expect of a person acting in the course of that kind of business or profession. The duty of care applies to a trustee when they are:

- dealing with the trust's investments;

- acquiring land;

- entering into arrangements for others to act as agents, nominees or custodians;

- insuring the trust's property;

- dealing with reversionary interests, valuations and audit.

The duty of care does not apply if, or in so far as, it appears from the trust deed that the duty is not meant to apply.

121.8   If trustees do not seek advice on matters on which they are not experts, be they legal, financial or managerial, they could be judged as having acted imprudently and could be personally liable for the consequences. The *Charities Act 1993* requires trustees to seek professional advice in some instances, for example, in relation to certain land transactions.

121.9   Trustees have a duty to avoid conflict of interest and should not take part in any discussion or decision where they have a conflict of interest. If ever a trustee's personal, business or professional interests are likely to conflict with those of the charity, the trustee should disclose that interest to their fellow trustees. As a matter of good practice many charities now keep a public register of their trustees' interests. In some instances trustees may face not a conflict, but a duality of interest. For example, they may be a trustee or staff member of another charity working in a similar field and owe a loyalty to both organisations. Where this is the case the trustee must act in the best interest of the charity whose affairs they are then considering.

121.10   Trustees also have a duty not to profit from their position as trustees, unless the charity's governing document explicitly specifies otherwise or the court or Charity Commission authorises a payment. Therefore the majority of trustees must carry out their duties without payment, either in the form of money or preferential access to services. The *Charities Act 2006* contains provisions, likely to come into force in 2008, which will allow the payment of trustees, in certain circumstances, for the provision of goods or services to the charity over and above their normal trustee duties.

121.11 Trustees cannot usually be employed by the charity, as they must not benefit from their position. The rule still applies even where the trustee has resigned as a trustee before or after taking up employment. In exceptional cases the governing document may permit a trustee to be employed by the charity, or the Charity Commission may give permission.

121.12 Trustees of unincorporated charities have a statutory right to be reimbursed for any out of pocket expenses incurred in connection with their service as trustees. Trustees of charitable companies can have their expenses reimbursed if the governing document permits this.

121.13 Trustees must take their responsibilities seriously. Trusteeship is not a position of honour without responsibility: it requires time, understanding and effort. Trustees are required to act personally (i.e. to play an active role), meeting as often as is necessary for the proper administration of the charity, giving the time necessary to study board papers before the meetings, and keeping themselves informed about the charity's activities. They must also avoid conflicts of interest and must not profit from their position as trustees.

121.14 The time trustees need to devote to their trusteeship will vary considerably from one charity to another depending on a number of factors including:

- the size and complexity of the charity;

- whether or not the charity has volunteers and/or employs paid staff;

- the nature of the charity's work and how it is carried out, i.e. if the charity makes grants to others to carry out activities or if it carries out activities itself;

- whether or not the governing body has to represent the views of its members; and

- the stage of its organisational development.

In some organisations the trustees will have both a governing and a 'hands on' operational role, whilst in others their role will be restricted almost entirely to the charity's governance.

121.15 In their governing role, the trustees must ensure that the charity's mission is still relevant and that the charity has clear direction and purpose and a sense of urgency to get on with the work it is established to do. They should develop and agree the charity's strategic objectives and major policies and guard the charity's ethos and values. The board of trustees must set clear objectives, establish the charity's priorities, safeguard its assets (money, property, equipment, human resources), by ensuring that there are adequate financial controls (see CHAPTER 72) and that any land or buildings the charity owns are well maintained and insured, identify risks and take steps to mitigate those risks, and use the assets efficiently, effectively and exclusively to benefit those the organisation exists to help. Where day-to-day management and operations are delegated to staff, the board of trustees still remains ultimately responsible for all the charity's activities, so a key responsibility is to appoint the right chief executive, give that person clear direction regarding the charity's objectives, policies, values and ethos, clear guidance about the degree of authority the board of trustees is delegating to them, monitor their performance, offer support and assistance as required and take appropriate action if their performance falls below that expected.

Delegation

121.16   Trustees are required to act in person and any decisions affecting the charity must be made by the trustees acting together. However, the duty to act personally does not mean that the trustees have to do everything themselves. They can delegate a wide range of tasks to committees, staff or others but must give them clear instructions that define:

- the functions or tasks that are being delegated, and the results that the trustees expect;

- the limits of the authority that the body or person may exercise on the trustees' behalf;

- the types of decisions that can be made by delegates in the course of their work and the types that must be referred back to the trustees;

- how and at what intervals those to whom work has been delegated are to report progress to the trustees.

121.17   If the charity's governing document gives the trustees the power to delegate authority for a particular aspect of the charity's work to a subcommittee of the trustee board, or to delegate authority to a task group or committee whose members need not necessarily all be trustees, or to staff, they may do so. However, any decisions made by such groups or staff remain the responsibility of the full board of trustees. The terms of reference and reporting-back procedures of any committees, subcommittees, task groups or staff should be laid down in writing and agreed by the board of trustees. Decisions about important matters must be reported to the board of trustees as quickly as possible.

121.18   Trustees of charitable companies must also comply with the legal requirements placed on company directors since that is part of their dual role. They must ensure that the charity keeps up to date with its company returns and record-keeping and must not continue trading as a company if they know, or should have known, that the company is insolvent. They must also avoid conflicts of financial interest between the charity and themselves or any person connected with them such as a partner, spouse, child or stepchild, or business partner of themselves, their partner, spouse or child.

121.19   The following matters should not be delegated and should be handled by the whole board:

- Approval of the long-term objectives and strategy;

- Approval of annual plans and budgets;

- Approval of board appointments;

- Approval of terms of reference and membership of board committees;

- Approval of membership of the boards of subsidiary companies;

- Approval of the terms of reference for honorary officers and the chief executive;
- Setting the reward package for the chief executive;
- Approval of major capital projects;
- Approval of major contracts;
- Approval of the investment strategy;
- Approval of major investments or disinvestments;
- Approval of the risk management strategy;
- Approval of the statutory annual report and annual accounts;
- Approval of any significant changes to the accounting policies;
- Appointment or removal of the company secretary;
- Setting the remuneration of the auditors;
- Approval of press releases on Board decisions;
- Reviewing the Board's structure and performance;
- Approval of major changes to the staff pension scheme;
- Approval of the internal control procedures;
- Approval of major strategic policies.

Joint responsibility

121.20   Trustees are jointly responsible for the activities of the charity and must act together. No trustee acting alone can bind his or her fellow trustees, unless specifically authorised to do so. However, the board's decisions do not have to be unanimous, so the majority bind the minority. Trustees are bound by the decisions of their fellow trustees even if they were not present at a meeting where the decision was taken. Trustees may protect themselves to some extent by having their dissenting vote recorded in the minutes, but if the matter is serious, particularly if a decision constitutes a breach of trust, they should consider resigning.

Joint and several liability

121.21   A board of trustees has joint and several liability. This means that if the board of trustees agrees to do something under a contract then the multiple parties that make up the board make one promise which binds all of them, and, in addition, each party also makes a separate promise binding him or herself to honour the contract. This does not entitle the person or corporate body to whom the board of trustees has made that promise to receive more in total than they were promised, but it does entitle them to obtain what they were promised either from the board of trustees or from any one or more members of the board.

FINANCIAL DUTIES AND RESPONSIBILITIES

121.22   The financial responsibilities of charity trustees are wide ranging and should not be left to the treasurer or finance committee alone. All the trustees have a duty to be aware of the charity's financial position and they can be personally liable for the misuse of charity funds. They must protect the charity's assets and make sure that the charity complies with the accounting and audit regulations contained in the *Charities Act 1993*, as amended by the *Charities Act 2006* and any relevant Statements of Recommended Practice (SORP) such as the SORP for charities or for housing associations, or the *Companies Acts* if the charity is a company.

121.23   Trustees are responsible for:

- approving and monitoring budgets;

- ensuring that the charity has adequate resources to meet its commitments;

- ensuring that proper control is exercised over both income and expenditure;

- approving fund–raising policy and activities;

- overseeing any trading activities;

- ensuring the tax affairs of the charity are managed effectively;

- establishing policies for reserves and investments;

- ensuring that any investments earn the best possible return without putting the capital at risk and are in accordance with both the charity's investment policy and its powers of investment;

- making sure that the assets and income are used exclusively to pursue the charity's objects, adequately protected and managed efficiently and effectively.

121.24   In addition, trustees are responsible for ensuring that reasonable steps are taken to prevent and detect fraud and other irregularities. Trustees should make sure that the charity has adequate controls for operating the charity's bank account which cannot be abused by unscrupulous people. Cheques over a certain amount should normally be signed by at least two people, including one trustee, unless there are other controls which give a similar or greater degree of protection. If the charity is large enough to warrant having internal audit staff, these staff should report directly to the trustees.

121.25   Any money that a charity has should be placed on deposit if it is needed in the near future, or, if it is not needed in the immediate future, it should be invested in accordance with the *Trustee Act 2000*, subject to any restrictions in the charity's governing document. However, money must not be allowed to accumulate unless the trustees have decided to set it aside in a designated fund for a specific charitable purpose, or unless the governing document contains a power to accumulate.

121.26   Any funds, land, buildings or other assets which form part of the charity's permanent endowment (that is, assets which have been given to the charity to keep in perpetuity but with the charity benefiting from the income that can be earned from the asset) should be preserved and invested to produce a good income while protecting the real value of the capital.

MANAGERIAL DUTIES AND RESPONSIBILITIES

121.27   Trustees have a number of important managerial responsibilities, which may include responsibilities in relation to:

- setting strategic objectives;

- strategic planning;

- policy making;

- employing, managing, appraising and rewarding staff;

- managing volunteers;

- giving account to statutory and regulatory bodies as required by law, to funders and to other stakeholders (beneficiaries, volunteers, staff, the general public etc.);

- monitoring the work of the charity;

- evaluating the impact and effectiveness of the charity's work;

- managing the charity's property and land;

- managing the charity's public relations; and

- representing the views of the charity.

121.28   In addition, depending on the work of the charity and whether or not it employs staff, the charity may have to comply with the legislation covering such matters as employment, health and safety, environmental matters, data protection, child protection and trading standards.

121.29   The board of trustees, or a sub-committee of it, may also have to act as the final internal group to which senior staff can appeal against decisions made in relation to disciplinary or grievance matters.

121.30   In seeking to carry out their responsibility to manage the charity's affairs effectively the trustees should periodically review their own performance and take any steps needed to improve it. If necessary trustees should review their governing structure, the size and composition of the board, its method of recruitment and ways of working, and its need for training or other support.

ELIGIBILITY

121.31   Most people are eligible to become charity trustees. People under the age of 18 can be trustees of an incorporated charity, but not of an unincorporated charity. The governing documents of some charities may include eligibility criteria, such as requiring trustees to practise a particular faith or to reside in a particular area, and some may exclude people over a certain age. People who are beneficiaries of a charity may not serve as trustees unless the governing document specifically provides for this.

121.32   *Section 72* of the *Charities Act 1993* disqualifies people from becoming trustees of a charity if they:

- have unspent convictions for offences involving deception or dishonesty;

- are undischarged bankrupts;

- have been at any time removed from trusteeship of a charity by the Charity Commission or the Court in England, Wales or Scotland, because of misconduct;

- are disqualified from being company directors under the *Company Directors Disqualification Act 1986*;

- have failed to make payments under county court administration orders; or

- have made compositions (i.e. come to an arrangement) with their creditors and have not been discharged.

121.33 When appointing new trustees it is important to check that they are not legally barred from trusteeship of a charity.

COMPANIES ACT 2006

121.34 The *Companies Act 2006* lists a number of directors' duties that will apply to the trustees of charitable companies and charitable incorporated organisations, as well as to the directors of non-charitable trading subsidiaries:

- Duty to act within powers;

- Duty to promote the success of the company;

- Duty to exercise independent judgement;

- Duty to exercise reasonable care, skill and diligence;

- Duty to avoid conflicts of interest;

- Duty not to accept benefits from third parties;

- Duty to declare interest in proposed transaction or arrangement.

121.35 Many of these duties already apply to charity trustees, e.g. the duty to act in accordance with the company's constitution and to only exercise powers for the purposes for which they are conferred. However, trustees who are company directors should be aware of the duty to promote the success of the company for the benefit of its members. This is modified for charitable companies that are established for purposes other than the benefit of their members. When these provisions are implemented trustees of companies will have a duty to act in a way which is most likely to promote the success of the company to achieve its objects and purposes.

121.36 Trustees who are directors of both a charitable company and an associated trading company should be aware of the two versions of this duty and take care that they apply the correct criteria in the relevant circumstances.

122   Trustee Indemnity Insurance

122.1   If trustees act prudently, lawfully, and in accordance with the charity's governing document, then any liabilities (i.e. debts or financial obligations) that they incur as trustees can normally be met out of the charity's resources. However, if trustees incur liabilities or debts that amount in total to more than the total value of the charity's assets they may face a personal loss if the charity is not incorporated (i.e. if it is a trust or an unincorporated association), even if the liabilities have been properly incurred.

122.2   If the trustees act recklessly or imprudently, or are otherwise in breach of the law or the charity's governing document, then the position is different. Trustees may be personally responsible for liabilities incurred by the charity, or for making good any loss to the charity. Since trustees act collectively in running a charity, their liabilities are 'joint and several' which means that each trustee could be held liable for all or any part of the loss..

122.3   The main types of situations in which trustees may face a liability, depending on the circumstances, are where there are:

- Breaches of trust or fiduciary duty: for example, doing something which is outside the charity's charitable objects, failing to show a proper duty of care, failing to implement Health and Safety legislation, borrowing money if this is not permitted by the governing document, or failing to take professional advice about investment decisions;

- Breaches of statutory duties: for example, failing to submit accounts on time, to deduct PAYE, to declare the organisation's charitable status on all its financial documents, discriminating on the base of race, gender or disability, unfairly dismissing staff, or failing to provide employees with a written contract of employment;

- Breaches of contract: for example, failing to pay utility bills, builders, or suppliers, or to repay debts, or entering into contracts on onerous terms;

- Tort or breaches of common law duty: for example, acting negligently, causing nuisance, or libel.

122.4   All charity trustees could face personal liability for the first two types of wrongful actions listed above. Incorporation will protect some trustees from liabilities for breach of contract and tort. However, the trustees of charitable companies will have additional responsibilities as company directors. For example, they will have to comply with regulations regarding the proper recording of minutes of meetings, filing of returns etc. and these can be protected by taking out directors' and officers' liability insurance.

122.5   Trustees cannot be held responsible for the wrongful actions of staff or agents provided that they exercise proper care in their appointment and supervision.

122.6   The Charity Commission has powers to take proceedings in court to recover from trustees personally any funds lost to the charity as a result of a breach of trust or breach of duty. However, *s 38* of the *Charities Act 2006* gives the Charity Commission the power to relieve trustees from liability for breach of trust or breach of duty if it considers that they have acted honestly and reasonably and ought fairly to be excused for the breach of trust or duty.

122.7   Trustees cannot be indemnified against fines or penalties, such as fines for failing to submit accounts on time or breaching health and safety regulations, as this would be contrary to the public interest.

122.8   The main difference between trustee indemnity insurance, or trustee liability insurance as it is sometimes known, and other types of insurance taken out for the benefit of a charity is that trustee indemnity insurance directly protects an individual trustee rather than the charity itself. In practice trustee indemnity insurance is often provided under a single policy in combination with other types of cover. These could include:

- Professional liability insurance: covering errors or omissions resulting in a civil liability for the charity, where the charity provides counselling, advice, or an information service;

- Fidelity or 'theft by employee' insurance: covering fraud or loss through criminal acts by officers or employees;

- Trustee reimbursement insurance: covering residual liability for a claim which ought to have been met out of the charity's assets, but for which trustees may be held liable because those assets are insufficient to meet the claim.

122.9   Trustee indemnity insurance offers trustees some protection against their personal liability as trustees. It covers trustees against having to personally pay legal claims made against them (by their charity or by a third party) for a breach of trust, or a breach of duty or negligence, committed by them in their capacity as trustees. Provided that trustees have authority, they are entitled to be insured against claims that may arise from their legitimate actions as trustees, and will be covered against liability as long as they have acted honestly and reasonably. In most cases, this authority will be provided by the statutory power to purchase trustee liability insurance brought in by the *Charities Act 2006*.

122.10 Provided the cost is reasonable, *s 39* of the *Charities Act 2006* permits charity trustees to use the charity's funds to purchase trustee indemnity insurance designed to indemnify the charity trustees, and any holding or custodian trustees, against personal liability for:

- Any breach of trust or breach of duty committed by them in their capacity as charity trustees or holding trustees;

- Any negligence, default, breach of duty or breach of trust committed by them in their capacity as directors or officers of a charitable company or of any company carrying out activities on behalf of the charity.

122.11 The Act requires that the terms of any trustee indemnity insurance must exclude indemnity for any person in respect of:

- Any liability incurred by him to pay a fine imposed in criminal proceedings or a sum payable to a regulatory authority for non-compliance with regulations, such as a fine for late filing of accounts at Companies House;

- Any liability incurred by him in defending any criminal proceedings in which he is convicted of an offence involving fraud or dishonesty, or his wilful or reckless misconduct;

122.12   Trustee Indemnity Insurance

- Any liability incurred by him to the charity that arises out of any conduct that he knew, or reasonably should have known, was not in the interests of the charity, or in the case of which he did nor care whether or not it was in the best interests of the charity.

122.12   Under the duty of care provisions in the *Trustee Act 2000* (*s 1(1)*) charity trustees may not use the statutory power to purchase trustee liability insurance contained in the *Charities Act 2006* unless they are satisfied that it is in the charity's best interests for them to use the charity's money to purchase trustee liability insurance.

122.13   The *Charities Act 2006* does not authorise the purchase of trustee liability insurance where this is expressly prohibited by the charity's governing document but it does allow trustees to purchase trustee liability insurance where the governing document contains a general prohibition on trustees receiving a personal benefit from the charity. It is rare for a governing document to include an express prohibition on trustees taking out trustee liability insurance, but where this is the case trustees will need to apply to the Charity Commission for a Scheme to overturn the provision if they wish to take out trustee liability insurance. The Commission will make a Scheme providing they agree that this would be in the interests of the charity. It will look in particular at whether or not the charity is having difficulty in recruiting trustees because it does not have trustee liability insurance.

122.14   Where the governing document contains an express power to purchase trustee liability insurance, if the power is narrower than the statutory power, the trustees can rely on the statutory power. If it is *wider* than the statutory power, the trustees can rely on the power in the governing document. They should, however, be able to demonstrate why they consider it is in the best interests of the charity to provide this wider insurance for their benefit.

WHAT RISKS ARE COVERED?

122.15   Most trustee indemnity policies cover:

- poor investment decisions resulting in a loss to the charity;
- claims for wrongful advice or negligence in service delivery;
- industrial tribunal awards; and
- maladministration resulting in a loss to the charity.

Some policies will also cover:

- fraud or dishonesty by trustees, staff and/or agents;
- libel;
- negligence;
- legal costs;
- inadvertant breach of confidentiality or copyright/intellectual property rights; and
- contractual liabilities.

Risks not covered:

- fines or penalties; and

- claims arising out of death or injury on charity property.

122.16   Trustees could be held vicariously liable for acts committed by employees in the course of their work and may be held liable for acts by other members of the board of trustees if it can be shown that they authorised the action and/or that they were negligent in allowing it to take place. For example, in 1994 a company was convicted of corporate manslaughter after four teenagers were drowned while on a canoeing trip organised by the company's activity centre. The company was fined and the managing director imprisoned for three years.

122.17   Charity trustees who seek and act upon advice from the Charity Commission under *s 29* of the *Charities Act 1993* are protected from liability if they are later judged to have committed a breach of trust.

DISCLOSURE

122.18   Details of trustee indemnity insurance paid for by an unincorporated charity must be disclosed in the charity's annual report in compliance with the *Charities Act 1993*. For limited companies the same disclosure will be made in the notes to the accounts in accordance with the SORP.

ASSESSING RISK

122.19   Where a charity simply distributes income periodically the risks (to the trustees) are likely to be negligible or non-existent. On the other hand, for the trustees of a charity that is a major provider of services, such as a school or hospital, the potential risks may be considerable. When trustees are considering taking out trustee indemnity insurance they should take into account:

- the degree of risk to which they are exposed;

- the value of the indemnity required;

- the cost of the premiums; and

- whether or not the insurance is likely to be in the interests of the charity.

122.20   Trustees who are considering using charity funds to purchase trustee indemnity insurance should consider whether other steps should be taken to reduce the risk of personal liability, such as:

- recruiting trustees with business and professional acumen;

- providing trustee induction and other training;

- having clear internal procedures;

- having clear management structures and controls; and

- having clear internal financial controls.

122.21   Most professional advisers see limited benefit in a well-run, professionally staffed charity taking out trustee indemnity insurance as protection for their trustees because:

122.22   Trustee Indemnity Insurance

- the risks faced by trustees can be minimised by good management and clear controls and procedures;

- the Charity Commission restricts the risks that may be covered by trustee indemnity insurance purchased with a charity's assets to those where trustees are at very low risk, either because they would be indemnified by the charity or because the Charity Commission would be most unlikely to require the trustees to make a payment to the charity; and

- trustees are more likely to become the subject of claims if it is known that they have insurance.

However, this type of insurance may still be well worth considering if it protects the charity from the wrongful actions of its trustees.

122.22   A decision about whether or not to take out trustee indemnity insurance should be made by the whole body of trustees. The case for taking out such insurance must depend upon what is in the best, overall interests of the charity. Trustee liability insurance is no panacea. It should be viewed as catastrophe insurance – most unlikely ever to be needed, but invaluable if it is. Trustees should be reminded that even if they have trustee indemnity insurance there remain some situations in which they could be personally liable.

Scotland

122.23   Scottish charity law currently contains no general statutory power allowing trustees to use the charity's funds to purchase trustee liability insurance, which the Office of the Scottish Charity Regulator regards as a form of trustee remuneration.

FURTHER INFORMATION

122.24   Charity Commission CC49 'Charities and Insurance'

Charity Commission Operational Guidance 100 A1 'Trustee Indemnity Insurance'

123   Trustees' Annual Report

123.1 The requirement for registered charities to prepare an annual report for each financial year springs from the *Charities Act 1993, s 45*, although for many charities the production of a narrative document which describes the work of the organisation during the year has been a long-standing practice. Scottish charities are also required to produce an annual report . The detailed contents of the annual report are, to some extent, up to the trustees, as long as they meet the minimum requirements stipulated in the *Charities (Accounts and Reports) Regulations* (for registered charities) and comply with the Charities SORP. There are special rules for smaller charities, limited companies and Industrial and Provident Societies, which are described later in this chapter.

123.2 The purpose of the annual report is to discharge the trustees' duty of accountability and demonstrate their good stewardship by describing what the charity has achieved during the financial year. Charities in England and Wales with a gross income of more than £10,000 are required by *s 45* of the Act to send an annual report to the Charity Commission within ten months of the end of the financial year, together with their accounts and the report of the auditor or independent examiner.

123.3 The annual report is a statutory document and should not be confused with other documents which a charity may produce, such as progress reports or an annual review published for publicity and marketing purposes. It should be signed and dated by at least one of the trustees who has been authorised to do so. Any annual report sent to the Charity Commission must be open to public inspection at all reasonable times. [*Charities Act 1993, s 47(1)*].

123.4 The detailed requirements for the annual report are set out most fully in the SORP, which introduce the annual report as follows:

'The Trustees' Annual Report should be a coherent document that meets the requirements of law and regulation and provides a fair review of the charity's structure, aims, objectives, activities and performance. Good reporting will explain what the charity is trying to do and how it is going about it. It will assist the user of accounts in addressing the progress made by the charity against its objectives for the year and in understanding its plans for the future. Good reporting will also explain the charity's governance and management structure and enable the reader to understand how the numerical part of the accounts relates to the organisational structure and activities of the charity.'

123.5 In all the sections described below, the information can be restricted to some extent for smaller charities – that is, those below the audit threshold.

CONTENTS OF THE ANNUAL REPORT

123.6 The SORP requires the annual report to cover the following:

- Reference and administrative details of the charity, its trustees and advisors;
- Structure, governance and management;
- Objectives and activities;

123.7 Trustees' Annual Report

- Achievements and performance;

- Financial Review;

- Plans for future periods;

- Funds held as custodian trustee on behalf of others.

123.7   Charities are not required to use these headings but the report must contain the information described under these headings. In additionto the above requirements it has been proposed that trustees should also be required to confirm that they have considered or meet the public benefit test.

Reference and administrative details

123.8   This is usually the driest part of the report, and it is often relegated to the back of the document or appended to it. Details to be included here are:

- the name of the charity as it appears in the Charity Commission register and any other name by which it is known;

- the charity registration number (in Scotland the Scottish Charity Number) and, if applicable, the registered company number;

- the names of all trustees who have acted at any time throughout the financial year in question or who were trustees on the date the report was approved. Where there are more than 50 trustees, the names of at least 50 of those trustees should be provided. Where there is a corporate trustee the names of the directors or other persons managing the corporate trustee should be disclosed;

- the principal address of the charity and the address of the registered office if the charity is a company;

- the name of any Chief Executive Officer or other senior staff members to whom trustees delegate the day to day management of the charity;

- the names and addresses of any other relevant organisations or persons including those acting as auditor (or independent examiner or reporting accountant), bankers, solicitors, investment managers, or other principal advisers.

123.9   In exceptional circumstances where the disclosure of the names of trustees, or staff, or persons with the power of appointment, or the charity's principal address, could lead to that person being placed in personal danger (e.g. trustees of medical research charities that conduct experiments on animals) trustees may dispense with the disclosure provided that the Charity Commission has given its consent. In this instance it is recommended that a note giving the reasons for the non-disclosure should be included in the report. In the case of a charitable company, if the trustees' annual report is also to serve as the statutory directors' report, the trustees do not have the option of withholding their names, though under *s 163* of the *Companies Act 2006* directors can register a service address, which can be the company's registered office, rather than their home address.

Structure, governance and management

123.10   This section covers how the charity is constituted, its organisational structure
and how trustees are appointed and trained. The level of detail provided will
depend on the size and complexity of the charity. The report should explain:

- the type of governing document;

- the methods used to recruit and appoint new trustees;

- the policies and procedures for inducting and training trustees;

- the organisational structure and how decisions are made;

- where the charity is part of a wider network, e.g. if the charity is
affiliated to an umbrella body, the relationship should be explained if it
impacts on the operating policies adopted by the charity;

- the relationships between the charity and related parties, including
subsidiaries and other charities with whom the charity co-operates to
pursue its objects;

- the risk management statement. Trustees of larger charities are
required to confirm that the major risks to which the charity is exposed,
as identified by the trustees, have been reviewed and that systems or
procedures have been established to manage those risks (see
CHAPTER 106).

Objectives and activities

123.11   The SORP sets out a hierarchy, requiring charities to describe:

(a)   a summary of the objects of the charity as set out in its governing
document.

(b)   An explanation of the charity's aims including the changes or differences it seeks to make through its activities.

(c)   An explanation of the charity's main objectives for the year.

(d)   An explanation of the charity's strategies for achieving its stated objectives.

(e)   Details of significant activities (including its main programmes,
projects, or services provided) that contribute to the achievement of the
stated objectives.

123.12   This list effectively takes the reader from the mission and objects of the
charity, through the high level aims and strategy, to the activities actually
undertaken, as reflected in the accounts. This hierarchy has lead to some
confusion. By charities focusing on activities, many annual reports and
accounts read as though they are still focused on some sort of functional cost
allocation derived from the old SORP. It is difficult to relate this to achieving
strategic objectives and reporting on impact. Other charities have tended to
focus at the strategic level.

123.13   This section should also include details of the charity's grant making policies,
where these are relevant, and policies relating to the use of social or programme related investment. Where a charity makes significant use of volunteers this should be mentioned. The SORP prevents the use of an estimate of

the economic value of the contribution made by volunteers, the report should include sufficient information to enable the reader to understand in the accounts, but the contribution that volunteers make to the charity. Some charities disclose an analysis of what volunteers do, the amount of hours they contribute, and an indicative value of this contribution.

Achievements and performance

123.14   In this section, smaller charities can present a summary, but larger charities should try to set out what has been achieved by the charity and its subsidiaries in the financial year. Charities should provide a review of their performance against the objectives they set. The report should contain both quantitative and qualitative information that helps to explain achievement and performance. The report should contain:

- a review of charitable activities;

- details of fundraising, showing performance against objectives and the expected future return on current investments in fundraising;

- where the charity has material investments, details of the performance of those investments against the objectives set;

- other factors both within and outside the charity's control which are relevant to the achievements of its objectives, such as relationships with employees, or beneficiaries, or funders, or the wider community.

123.15   Companies reporting under the enhanced business review will also include financial and non-financial key performance indicators in this section. Where key performance indicators are used, they should be thought through carefully, so that they can be used consistently over a number of years.

Financial Review

123.16   This section should contain a review of the financial position of the charity and its subsidiaries and a statement of the principal financial management policies adopted in the year. Companies should also report on any use of financial instruments. This section of the report should also include the reserves policy, stating the level of reserves held and why they are held. Care should be taken to make sure that the figures disclosed in the policy can be readily identified within the body of the accounts. If the charity holds designated funds, the reserves policy should quantify and explain the purpose of the designations and the likely timing of future expenditure from these funds. Where any fund is materially in deficit the circumstances giving rise to the deficit should be explained, together with details of the steps being taken to eliminate the deficit.

123.17   This section should also give details of:

- the charity's principal funding sources and how expenditure during the year under review has supported the key objectives of the charity;

- where material investments are held, the investment policy and objectives, including the extent to which social, environmental or ethical considerations are taken into account.

123.18   It is common for a financial review to be illustrated by graphics. Many charities use imaginative ways of presenting some financial analysis to support the narrative: pie charts and bar charts are common, and histograms are also used. Whatever method is used, graphs should not simply be a way of saving words or breaking up the text: they should be considered as a means of effectively communicating complex ideas. Simply showing an analysis of expenditure in a pie chart may communicate little more than is obvious from the SOFA, whereas a graph depicting longer term trends and demonstrating good stewardship or greater financial needs may be more informative.

Plans for future periods

123.19   This section should explain the charity's plans for the future, including the aims and key objectives it has set for future periods, together with details of any activities planned to achieve them. In practice, many charities only comment on the forthcoming financial year, which is usually half over by the time the report is published. Quoted companies are encouraged to report along appropriate timescales for their organisation, and this is a good practice for charities too. That means that a charity seeking to deliver emergency aid might have specific aims relating to immediate needs, whereas a charity working towards the eradication of a disease might put its aims in the context of a long-term programme covering many years.

Funds held as custodian trustee on behalf of others

123.20   If the charity acts as a custodian trustee, then the report should disclose details of the assets it holds in this capacity, the name and objects of the charity or charities on whose behalf the assets are held and how this activity falls within their own objects, and details of the arrangementsfor safe custody and segregation of such assets from the charity's own assets.

LIMITED COMPANIES

123.21   Although smaller limited companies are entitled to prepare brief directors' reports, in practice this is overridden by the requirements of the SORP, so charities which are limited companies should ensure that they follow the SORP.

123.22   Companies should set out what they have done under the Information and Consultation of Employees Regulations to provide employees with information about the company's economic situation, employment prospects and about decisions which may lead to substantial changes in work organisation or contractual relations, including redundancies and transfers. When the regulations were first introduced they were restricted to organisations with 150 or more employees but by 2008 these regulations will apply to organisations with 50 or more employees. In addition, companies must also include a statement of policy concerning employment and career development of disabled persons. This disclosure requirement only applies if the organisation employs over 250 people in the UK.

123.23   Public companies are required to set out creditor payment policies. Some larger charities choose to follow this as a matter of good practice.

123.24   Charitable companies have to prepare both a directors' report and a trustees' annual report. These can be produced as two separate documents or they can be combined into one provided that it contains the information required by both company and charity law. Where the reports are combined the title page should clearly indicate this.

INDUSTRIAL AND PROVIDENT SOCIETIES

123.25   *Section 45* of the *Charities Act 1993* does not apply to exempt charities, so there is no mandatory requirement for Industrial and Provident Societies to produce an annual report unless they are required to do so by other legislation or their own rules, or unless they are specifically requested to do so by the Charity Commission under *s 46(5)*.

PUBLIC ACCOUNTABILITY

123.26   The trustees' annual report is a public document, in the same way that the accounts are. For registered charities outside the light touch regime this means that the annual report must be filed with the Charity Commission, along with the accounts, within ten months of the year-end. Where the Charity Commission request an annual report from a charity which falls within the light touch regime, then if the request is made within seven months after the year-end the ten-month filing rule applies, otherwise the charity has three further months in which to produce the report from the date of the request.

123.27   *Section 47* of the *Charities Act* requires the trustees to provide a copy of the charity's most recent accounts to any member of the public who requests a copy in writing, within two months. (In Scotland accounts must be provided within one month.) The charity can charge a reasonable fee for a copy. This *section* does not specifically refer to annual reports as well, but the purpose of the annual report is to put the accounts in context, and therefore most charities would automatically provide the two together.

THE AUDIT OF THE TRUSTEES' ANNUAL REPORT

123.28   The auditor of an unincorporated charity has a duty to review the trustees' annual report. When the annual report is being planned, if it is to be anything more than a routine statement attached to the main accounts, then the finance staff and auditor need to liaise carefully in advance of production.

123.29   Audits under the *Charities Act 1993* provisions for accounts prepared on an accruals basis require the auditor to consider whether any information contained in the accounts is inconsistent in any material respect with the information presented in the trustees' annual report. Similarly an independent examiner has the same duty, again only in respect of accruals accounts. No such requirement exists under receipts and payments accounting. However, auditors have a further duty, under the Auditors' Code, to prevent their reports from being included with other information which they may consider misleading. Therefore auditors will usually want to check such information to ensure that there are no inconsistencies which could confuse readers of the accounts, or cast doubt on the reliability of the audited information.

123.30   The *Companies Act 2006, s 496* explicitly requires auditors of limited companies to state in their report whether the information given in the directors' report is consistent with the accounts.

124   Trusts

124.1   A trust is the traditional legal structure used by charities in England and Wales. The concept of trusts dates back at least as far as the Middle Ages. Three parties are involved in the setting up of a trust. The first is the donor or settlor who gives the second, the trustee, money or other assets to be used to benefit the third, the beneficiary, sometimes in a particular area, known as the area of benefit. The trustees become the nominal owners of the trust property but they may not benefit personally from it. They hold it in trust on behalf of the beneficiaries and have a duty to ensure that it is used exclusively for the purposes set out in the trust deed. The beneficiaries have a beneficial interest in the trust property.

TERM 'TRUST' CAN BE MISLEADING

124.2   The term 'trust' is widely used with a number of different meanings. Most trusts are private trusts, set up to benefit an individual or a specific group of people, such as family members. Private trusts are not charitable as they do not benefit the public. Public trusts are established to benefit the public, or a relatively large section of the public, rather than identifiable individuals. Most public trusts are charitable. Charitable trusts are different in that they are established for the benefit of the public, or a substantial section of the public, and for purposes, or objects, that are recognised as being wholly and exclusively charitable (see CHAPTER 18). The governing document of a trust is usually a trust deed, or a declaration of trust, but charitable trusts can also be created under the terms of a will.

124.3   All charities are subject to trust law and all hold their assets on trust. However, not all are legally structured as trusts and even having the word 'Trust' in the name of an organisation does not necessarily imply that the organisation is legally structured as a trust. For example, the National Meningitis Trust is a company limited by guarantee.

ADVANTAGES

124.4   Trusts are relatively cheap and simple to set up. There are few statutory requirements specifically governing trusts, so the formalities and expense of administering one are minimised. The number of trustees can be as small as two, though the Charity Commission usually insists on a minimum of three. Trustees are generally appointed by the existing trustees so it is easier to create a board with a balance of skills and experience than it is for organisations with democratically elected boards. Unless the governing document specifies otherwise, the *Trustee Act 1925* gives trustees the power to replace trustees when they retire or when:

- they are out of the UK for a continuous period of more than 12 months;

- they refuse to act as a trustee; or

- they are unfit or incapable of acting as a trustee.

124.5   Most trust deeds contain a power to amend the powers and administrative procedures so changes can be made quickly, easily and relatively cheaply by each trustee executing a supplemental deed. The Charity Commission has to be informed of any amendments.

124.6 Trusts

DISADVANTAGES

124.6 Trusts are unincorporated organisations so the trustees are personally liable for the trust's debts if the trust cannot meet them.

124.7 Charitable trusts may not amend their objects clauses without first obtaining the consent of the courts or the Charity Commission.

124.8 Trustees are usually appointed rather than elected and this lack of democracy may be regarded as a disadvantage. It certainly makes the trust structure unsuitable for many membership organisations.

124.9 A trust's assets are held by the trustees, rather than the trust, so if a trustee changes the new trustee must be appointed to hold the land or investments. However, this disadvantage can be overcome by incorporating the trustee body (see CHAPTER 66), or by appointing holding trustee (see CHAPTER 32).

USING THE TRUST STRUCTURE

124.10 A trust is a suitable legal structure for an organisation such as a grant-making foundation that has substantial assets but does not deliver services or employ a large number of staff. It may also be suitable for organisations that have very secure funding, or that do not have long-term financial commitments and so are extremely unlikely ever to be in a position where they cannot meet their financial obligations. Trusts are not suitable structures for organisations with an active membership because the governing body is not democratically elected.

'PRIVATE' CHARITIES

124.11 When individuals use their own money to set up charitable trusts to support causes they believe in, they sometimes make the mistake of thinking that these trusts are private and that their affairs should not be open to public scrutiny.

124.12 No such category is recognised either at law or indeed in the Charity Commission's administration of charities, which classifies charities into those established for local, national or overseas benefit, charities connected with the Armed Forces and charities administered by the National Health Service. A so-called private charity should therefore be registered with the Charity Commission unless its income from all sources does not exceed £5,000 per annum, or unless it is an excepted charity with an annual income of less than £100,000.

124.13 All registered charities are required to make their accounts available to the public both through the general filing requirement and the requirements of the *Charities Act 1993, s 47*. The *Charities Accounts (Scotland) Regulations 2006* similarly require accounts to be made available to any member of the public, and also for the accounting reference date to be provided on request.

125   VAT

VAT GENERAL ADMINISTRATION

Introduction

125.1   VAT legislation contains no general relief for charities, and this aspect is often widely misunderstood. There are some specific reliefs contained within the *VAT Act 1994*, which are explored in greater detail at CHAPTER 130. As far as charities are concerned, their VAT accounting requirements and rules are probably more complicated than those imposed on any commercial business, despite their need to constrain administration costs. The nature of activities carried on by charities can cause problems, especially in the area of recovery of VAT on costs. Great care, therefore, needs to be taken to avoid pitfalls and to maximise VAT opportunities.

125.2   On a general basis, most charitable activities are either non-business activities from a VAT point of view or they are VAT exempt. In either case, this means that input tax on related costs is not recoverable and, indeed, many charities are unable to register for VAT as they do not have any taxable income. As a consequence, many charities have extremely significant irrecoverable VAT costs. The zero and reduced rates provide a measure of relief, but a 17.5% standard rate and the block of recovering VAT on the costs of making exempt supplies and on the costs of non-business activities account for the unfair VAT burden placed on charities.

VAT registration

125.3   Charities are required to register for VAT if their taxable turnover exceeds the registration threshold: at the time of writing, this is £64,000. In considering its taxable turnover, a charity must include branch taxable turnover unless the branches are autonomous. A liability to register arises if taxable turnover (the combined value of positive and zero-rated supplies made by the charity) in the last 12 months exceeds the threshold or if it is expected to be exceeded within the next 30 days.

125.4   Voluntary registration will normally be allowed if taxable turnover does not exceed the registration threshold. Such registration would allow the recovery of VAT incurred on goods or services used in making taxable supplies and a proportion of general overhead VAT. It would be worth considering where the recipients of the charity's positive rated supplies can recover the VAT charged, for example supplies made to local authority or public sector bodies, or where most of the taxable supplies made by the charity are zero-rated.

Business and non-business activities

125.5   As already mentioned, charities that only have non-business activities may not register for VAT. The dividing line between business and non-business activities can often be a very fine one.

125.6   There is no comprehensive definition of 'business' in *VATA 1994*. Nonetheless, it is much wider in scope than the definition associated with direct taxes, and a profit motive is not necessarily decisive. Therefore, although a charity may not be deemed to be in business for direct tax purposes, many activities in the course or furtherance of the charity's objectives are deemed to be business for VAT, even though they may be performed for the benefit of the community. It is therefore crucial for charities to recognise that, for VAT purposes, they are likely to engage in business activities. They therefore need to identify those activities to avoid the risk of exposure to assessments to tax, and possible penalties and interest. It is also important to recognise that VAT incurred on costs in connection with non-business activities (as well as VAT on costs used in making exempt supplies) is not recoverable. In determining whether a charity's activities are business or non-business, HMRC set out a number of tests by way of guidance, some of which include:

- whether the activity is concerned with the making of supplies for a consideration;
- whether the activity has a degree of frequency or scale; and
- whether the activity is continued over a reasonable period of time.

However, HMRC's policy is to determine a charity's business or non-business status on a case by case basis.

125.7 It may not matter whether the amount charged for the supply equals or is greater than the cost to the charity of making that supply, nor indeed whether the charge is below cost, although special rules do apply for non-business supplies of welfare as dealt with in CHAPTER 50.

125.8 The following activities by a charity are generally considered as being non-business:

- the receipt of donations, bequests, grants etc. (Care needs to be taken in the area of grants, because they can sometimes be consideration for services rendered, making them business income. A donation must not generally give rights or benefits to the donor beyond a simple acknowledgement and mention in programmes, etc.);
- voluntary services performed free of charge;
- sale of shares and other investment activities.

125.9 The following activities are generally regarded as being business activities:

- the sale of donated goods;
- sales of Christmas cards and other trading items;
- grants of sponsorship rights;
- grant of rights to use the charity's name or logo, for instance, under affinity credit card scheme arrangements;
- admissions to premises for a charge (e.g. to concerts etc.);
- the provision of membership benefits by clubs, associations and similar bodies in return for a subscription or consideration.

BUSINESS ACTIVITIES

125.10 Supplies made by a charity in the course of a business can be taxable at a positive rate or zero-rated, or can be exempt from VAT. Many charities will become involved with making exempt supplies, for instance in connection with welfare, education or the provision of healthcare. Further details on the making of exempt supplies are contained in CHAPTER 50.

Recovery of VAT on costs

125.11 This is a very complex issue for most charities. It is complicated by their mixture of non-business, exempt and taxable income. VAT is only recoverable to the extent that it relates to the making of taxable supplies or supplies made outside the UK which would be taxable if made in the UK. The following steps usually have to be taken by a VAT registered charity to calculate deductible VAT.

- Step 1: classify all the activities of the charity into:

  — non-business activities;

  — taxable supplies made by the charity (i.e. positive rated and zero-rated supplies);

  — 'out of country' supplies made by the charity (i.e. supplies treated as made outside the UK but which would be taxable if made in the UK, e.g. consultancy services supplied to a foreign NGO);

  — 'specified supplies' which are made to a person who belongs outside the EU, that are directly linked to the export of goods to a place outside the EU (including the making of arrangements for such supplies), or where supplies would have been exempt insurance or financial supplies if they have been made in the UK;

  — exempt supplies made by the charity.

- Step 2: Attribute VAT on costs (to the greatest extent possible) to each of the above activities. VAT incurred on goods/services used exclusively in making taxable or 'out of country' supplies is fully recoverable. The VAT on goods/services used exclusively for non-business activities, or in making exempt supplies, is generally not recoverable. VAT not exclusively used for any of the above activities, e.g. general overheads, is 'residual' and must be apportioned.

- Step 3: Residual VAT has to be apportioned in a way that HMRC accept is fair and reasonable. First of all it has normally to be apportioned between business and non-business activities (but see exceptionally 125.13 below re the 'Lennartz' option where capital costs are involved). There is no statutory method for doing this. The ratio of business to non-business income is the norm. In many cases an apportionment based on directly attributed input VAT will produce a result acceptable to the charity and to HMRC. Although there is no formal requirement to clear the business/non-business apportionment formula with HMRC it is highly advisable to do so. The proportion of residual VAT attributed in Step 3 to business activities is carried forward to Step 4. The residual VAT attributed to non-business activities is not deductible.

- Step 4: If the charity makes 'out of country' or 'specified' supplies it must determine how much of the remaining residual VAT is used to make these supplies. There is no set method, but the charity cannot use a formula based on income. Apportionment must be based on 'use' and generally this means either using a ratio based on input VAT or expenditure or staff numbers. The proportion attributed to out of country supplies is deductible. The remaining residual VAT is carried forward to Step 5.

- Step 5: This is the 'partial exemption' apportionment, i.e. the apportionment of remaining residual VAT between taxable and exempt supplies. The 'standard' method does not need permission from HMRC and apportions remaining residual VAT in the ratio that taxable turnover (positive and zero-rated turnover) bears to taxable and exempt turnover. The result is rounded up to the nearest whole percentage point. The proportion attributed to taxable supplies is deductible. The proportion attributed to exempt supplies cannot be deducted unless the VAT on costs directly and indirectly attributed to exempt supplies is *de minimis* (see below). If the 'standard' method does not produce a fair and reasonable result the charity can propose a 'special' method that does so. This might involve an apportionment based on input tax or expenditure or staff numbers, and in some cases, different departments or cost centres within the charity may have their own apportionment formula. All 'special' methods have to have approval from HMRC and since 1 April 2007 such approval will not be given unless the charity has made a written declaration to the effect that to the best of its knowledge and belief the method fairly and reasonably represents the extent to which goods or services will be used by it in making taxable supplies. The declaration must also include a statement that the person signing has taken reasonable steps to ensure that he/she is in possession of all relevant information. HMRC can direct a charity to use a special method in some cases. For example, some educational establishments provide exempt education or training, which is subsidised from public funds. HMRC do not accept that the 'standard' method will produce a fair and reasonable result in such cases because the grant income would be excluded from the calculation.

125.12   VAT attributed to exempt supplies can be recovered if it is *de minimis*, i.e. is not more than £625 per month on average (£7,500 in the VAT year) and also not more than 50% of total input tax, i.e. the VAT on costs attributed to business activities. Applying this test to each period means that in some periods a full recovery of VAT may arise but when applying the test to a full year, by means of an annual adjustment, a VAT restitution will arise. Where this occurs VAT previously claimed by applying the *de minimis* limit will be repayable to HMRC. Conversely, where the *de minimis* limit has been exceeded in one or more periods such that no VAT recovery was achieved, the annual adjustment may allow recovery if the figures for the full year are *de minimis*. An annual adjustment must be carried out each year and, in the case of a charity using the 'standard method', this may, in certain circumstances, be subject to an override calculation which takes account of the use to which goods and services have been or are intended to be put. This will usually arise only where the standard method gives an unreaonably high or low level of VAT recovery.

125.13   The 'Lennartz' option discussed below is disliked by HMRC, but requires to be available in respect of capital expenditure. At the time of writing a new European Council Directive has been proposed which would remove the use of the option in respect of land and buildings. Paragraphs 125.13 and 125.14 are therefore subject to change.

125.14   'Lennartz' is the name of a VAT judgment of the European Court of Justice which is of particular use to charities. Those which use goods and services for taxable and non-business purposes must normally apportion the VAT on such costs so that only the VAT element attributable to taxable supplies is recoverable. With VAT on capital costs, charities are entitled to recover all of the VAT in respect of non-business use upfront provided that the goods and services involved are being used to some extent (even if only minor) for taxable purposes. The charity is then required to account for VAT over the prescribed economic life of the asset (from 1 November 2007 ten years for buildings and land – otherwise five years) effectively repaying the VAT initially recovered on non-business use over that period via each VAT return. The input VAT attributable to the charity's exempt activities must continue to be treated as initially irrecoverable to the extent of that required by the charity's partial exemption method and is subject to adjustments over a similar ten- or five-year period in accordance with the Capital Goods Scheme (see HMRC Notice 706/2 'Capital goods scheme').

125.15   HMRC's Information Sheet 14/07 explains HMRC's interpretation of what goods and services are covered by Lennartz and how the calculations should be applied. For example, HMRC does not believe that refurbishment costs qualify for the Lennartz option. However, this is a complex area and all charities would be wise to seek professional advice particularly where large amounts of VAT are involved. In broad terms, Lennartz usually offers only a cash flow advantage with non-business VAT recovery having to be repaid over the life of the asset. Nevertheless the opportunity to be able to recover up front can be a significant one for a charity.

125.16   The same rules apply to trading subsidiaries as apply to charities. However, trading subsidiaries are unlikely to have non-business activities, but may well be partially exempt. One easily overlooked area that needs to be watched is the aspect of supplies between charities and their trading subsidiaries. These may arise in particular on recharges for staff and overheads. Where the charity and the trading subsidiary are separately registered, these supplies will be subject to VAT at the standard rate, subject to the normal rules for turnover etc. It may be possible to include a charity and its trading subsidiary in a VAT group to avoid this problem but the charity must be a corporate body for this to be the case. A special concession applies where staff seconded by the trading subsidiary to a charity work purely on the charity's non-business activities. However, this is often not the case in the area of shared staff. It may be possible to put into place joint employment arrangements which avoid a VAT charge needing to be levied. However, this area is complicated and both tax and legal advice will need to be sought.

CHARITY TAX REVIEW

125.17   The outcome of an earlier review of Charity Taxation was disappointing for those concerned about the impact of VAT on charities. The regime is still complicated and there has been no lessening of the irrecoverable VAT burden that charities suffer. Changes to the rules for advertising and fund-raising events were welcomed and are described in CHAPTER 4 and CHAPTER 40. In addition, the threshold below which charities and other businesses do not have to account for VAT when they deregister was raised from £250 to £1,000.

126   Volunteers

126.1   About 80% of charities are run entirely by volunteers and many of the largest professionally staffed charities such as Oxfam and Cancer Research UK also rely heavily on volunteers, particularly for fund-raising. Without volunteers much charitable work could not be done and much social need would go unmet. Volunteers are not just a source of unpaid labour. They often bring particular commitment and dedication to their work and can lend legitimacy and credibility to an organisation. Potential major donors are more likely to listen to an appeal from people they regard as their peers, who are themselves giving willingly of their time or money, than to an appeal from one of the charity's paid fund-raisers.

126.2   The use of volunteers may give rise to a number of legal issues. These should be given serious consideration to protect both charities and volunteers. Charities have legal responsibilities for the health and safety of their volunteers and must ensure that these are discharged. They also need to be clear about whether or not their volunteer management practices could be interpreted as establishing a contractual relationship between the volunteers and the organisation or its trustees, which could lead to the volunteers having rights in employment law. Volunteers should not find themselves with unexpected tax or national insurance liabilities or find that their volunteering has an unwelcome impact on any state benefits they may be receiving.

EXPENSES

126.3   The reimbursement of expenses is an equal opportunities issue. The cost of travelling and a meal eaten out is significant to someone on benefits or a low income. Any organisation serious about involving a diverse range of volunteers should reimburse expenses. Volunteer expenses should be built into any funding application. It is also worth remembering that volunteers are making a gift of their time – one that has substantial monetary value. They should not be expected to give up money as well. If volunteers say that they do not wish to receive expenses the charity can suggest that they claim their expenses and then donate them back to the charity under Gift Aid if they are taxpayers. This will be financially advantageous for both the charity and the volunteer if they pay income tax at the 40% higher rate.

126.4   In general any reasonable expense incurred as part of the voluntary work should be reimbursed. This can include:

- travel to and from the place of volunteering;

- travel while volunteering;

- meals taken while volunteering;

- care of dependants, including children, during volunteering;

- postage, phone calls, stationery etc;

- cost of protective clothing/special equipment etc.

126.5   Volunteers should be encouraged to use public transport wherever possible. Where they have to use their own transport it is good practice to reimburse them at the HMRC's approved mileage rates which for the period 1 January 2008 to 30 June 2008 are:

- Cars and vans – 40p per mile for the first 10,000 miles, 25p per mile over 10,000;

- Motorcycles – 24p per mile;

- Bicycles – 20p per mile.

126.6   Reimbursed expenses are not subject to tax or national insurance and do not affect a person's entitlement to benefits. In order to make it clear that any payment is a reimbursement and not a wage, volunteers should be given expense claim forms and asked to produce receipts. Reimbursement of genuine expenses does not turn a volunteer into an employee.

126.7   If volunteers are using friends or relatives rather than registered carers to care for their dependants while they are volunteering it is a good idea to produce a form for the carer to fill out as a receipt. As long as the charity reimburses expenses and does not pay the carer directly the legal relationship is between the volunteer and the carer. If something goes wrong and the carer is at fault the charity has no duty of care and cannot be sued. Equally the charity has no responsibility to ensure that the carer is declaring their earnings and paying tax and national insurance.

126.8   Some charities ask their volunteers to submit an expense claim at the end of each month. However, it may be difficult for some volunteers to fund their expenses for this length of time. It is generally much better for volunteers to receive their expenses in cash on a frequent basis rather than wait for a monthly cheque. Some people do not have bank accounts, and in any case cheques take time to clear.

Remuneration

126.9   Some volunteers also receive remuneration, often in the form of an honorarium or benefit in kind. Unless the person is on an official employment training or return to work scheme which specifically allows payment tax free, any remuneration will be taken into account when assessing an individual's liability for tax and national insurance and may affect their entitlement to benefits or the amount of benefit they receive. Payment of an honorarium, other than one which is totally unexpected and there is no precedent surrounding it, gives a volunteer employee status. Therefore payment of honoraria is best avoided.

126.10 A benefit such as free or subsidised accommodation is also generally regarded as remuneration, but perks such as discounts on the price of the charity's publications or events are generally not classed as remuneration for tax purposes.

126.11 Payment of remuneration does not of itself turn a volunteer into an employee for the purposes of employment law. It is legally possible to be a 'paid volunteer', i.e. an employee for the purposes of tax and national insurance but with no rights under employment law. It is the existence of a legally binding contractual relationship between the 'volunteer' and the organisation that gives the 'volunteer' rights under employment law. If there is a contractual relationship, and this does not need to be in the form of a written contract, then the 'volunteer' will no longer legally be a volunteer, but an employee or self-employed. For there to be a contractual relationship, there must be an agreement between the parties to the contract that some form of payment, or something else of material value, will be given in return for work, goods or services and the parties to the contract must intend there to be a legally binding relationship.

EMPLOYMENT LAW

126.12   Employment law was framed to protect employees and employers and does not always meet the needs of charities, particularly those charities that want to remunerate their volunteers but do not want to give them employment rights. Charities may wish to consider making it clear in all relevant discussions and documentation that their relationship with their volunteers is a voluntary one and is not intended to be legally binding. However, this may not be sufficient to protect the charity, as industrial tribunals generally assume that if one party agrees to pay another for work, the parties intend the relationship to be legally binding. In some circumstances, for example if payments are more than a token amount, it may not be advisable to state that the relationship is not intended to be legally binding, because such a statement could be interpreted as depriving an employee of their statutory employment rights. This would be an illegal act if done by an employer.

126.13   Applying employment law to volunteers is bound to give rise to decisions that appear contrary to common sense or to lack consistency. For example, in one instance a tribunal ruled that volunteers who were paid for their work were not held to have a contract of employment (*Milton v Department of Transport [1944] COIT 5086/44*) because they were carrying out a voluntary public service and in another a volunteer was held to have a contract of employment, although she did not receive payment, because she had received training and was under an obligation to repay the charity if she ceased to be a volunteer without good reason before working for the charity for a specified number of hours. Also there was an expectation that, after working for a certain number of hours without payment, at some time in the future the volunteer might be paid for further work (*Maria De Lourdes Armitage v Relate [1994] COIT 43538/94*).

126.14   Many charities regard having some sort of written agreement or contract with their volunteers as good practice. However, since some aggrieved volunteers have successfully obtained damages from charities as a result of tribunal hearings, much greater care has to be taken with the wording of such agreements. If a charity wants to ensure that its unpaid volunteers are engaged in voluntary work rather than employment, any volunteer agreement should make it clear that the relationship is binding in honour only and is not intended to be legally binding. It should refer to 'intentions', 'expectations' and 'privileges' rather than 'rights' and 'obligations'. Employment terms such as 'contract', 'leave', 'disciplinary and grievance procedures', 'promotion' and 'dismissal' should be avoided. For example, the volunteer agreement should include phrases such as 'Charity X expects its volunteers to turn up on the day they have agreed to work unless they are sick or have notified the charity in advance that they will be away on holiday' rather than phrases like

'Volunteer X's hours of work will be from 9.30am to 12.30 every Monday. Volunteer X will be entitled to take four weeks' annual leave'. Sample volunteer agreements are available on Volunteering England's website (*www.volunteering.co.uk*).

BENEFITS

126.15   The rules concerning the receipt of benefits by volunteers are complex and change frequently. It is good practice to check the position regularly with Volunteering England (or in Scotland the Volunteer Development Scotland, in Wales the Wales Council for Voluntary Action, or in Northern Ireland the Volunteer Development Agency) or the relevant benefits agencies. However, many benefits advisers are poorly informed about volunteering and often give incorrect advice.

126.16   At the time of writing people on Job Seekers Allowance can do as much voluntary work as they like as long as they remain available for and are actively seeking work. This will mean that they will have to show that they are looking for work and applying for jobs where appropriate. Charities will have to give their volunteers some flexibility, as they will need to visit the Job Centre for meetings and to sign on, and will need to attend interviews when they come up. If an individual is volunteering, then they are entitled to 48 hours' notice if they are asked to attend an interview, and a week's notice before starting work. These are concessions to the 24 hour's notice normally allowed.

126.17   Volunteering should not affect a volunteer's Income Support as long as they are not receiving any money other than reimbursement of expenses.

126.18   There is a lot of confusion over Incapacity Benefit because there used to be a rule that individuals in receipt of the benefit could only volunteer for 16 hours a week. This rule no longer applies, although many people are still being told that it does. Volunteers in receipt of Incapacity Benefit can volunteer to work for as long as they want. People often worry that starting to volunteer will automatically trigger an investigation into their need to claim Incapacity Benefit, but in fact this very rarely happens. Occasionally there is also some confusion about volunteering and 'permitted work' (similar to the old 'thera-peutic earnings'). The permitted work rule applies only to paid work and should not affect volunteers. Claimants should be entitled to volunteer without it being recognised as permitted work.

126.19   Disability Living Allowance is an allowance paid in acknowledgement of the fact that life for someone with a disability may be more expensive, for example, someone with mobility problems may be reliant on taxis. Volunteer-ing will not affect whether or not an individual receives this benefit.

126.20   It is good practice for charities to remind volunteers that it is compulsory for them to notify benefits advisers if they take up voluntary work. It is not the charity's responsibility to inform the benefits agency, it is entirely up to the volunteer whether they tell their adviser or not. Because of negative attitudes and lack of information on the part of advisers, many people feel more comfortable keeping their volunteering secret. Charities should bear in mind that if someone has not informed the benefits office that they are volunteer-ing, they may be wary of their name or photograph appearing in any publicity. Managers should always ask volunteers if they are willing to appear in any form of publicity.

126.21 Volunteers

126.21 State retirement pension, war disablement pension, war widow's pension and widow's benefits are not affected by paid or unpaid voluntary work. Housing benefit, council tax benefit and family credit are not affected by unpaid voluntary work but may be affected by paid voluntary work. Statutory maternity pay is not affected by volunteering, paid or unpaid. Maternity allowance is not affected by unpaid voluntary work but is not paid for any day on which paid voluntary work is done. Invalid care allowance is not affected by unpaid voluntary work unless it prevents the volunteer from caring for the invalid for at least 35 hours a week.

HEALTH AND SAFETY

126.22 All charities have a common law duty of care to protect the health and safety of their volunteers and if they are employers they have a statutory duty to protect the health and safety of the public which includes their volunteers. It is good practice to treat volunteers in exactly the same way as employees regarding matters of health and safety, even though health and safety legislation may not apply to volunteers in exactly the same way as it does to employees. Volunteers should be trained to carry out their work safely, in ways that do not put them or the public at risk.

INSURANCE

Employer's liability insurance

126.23 Employer's liability insurance protects paid employees in the event of accident, disease or injury caused or made worse as a result of work or the employer's negligence. There is no statutory duty for charities to extend their employer's liability insurance to cover volunteers, but it is good practice for them to do so. The policy must explicitly mention volunteers if they are to be covered by it.

Public liability insurance

126.24 Public liability insurance covers the organisation for claims from members of the public for death, illness, loss, injury or accident caused by the negligence of the organisation. This type of insurance should always explicitly mention volunteers. If a charity's public liability insurance covers volunteers it is not necessary to extend employer's liability insurance to cover volunteers. Public liability insurance also protects for loss or damage to property caused through the negligence of someone acting with the authority of the organisation which will include the actions of volunteers. Public liability cover should also cover loss or injury caused by a volunteer. If a volunteer is sued by a third party the organisation's public liability insurance should indemnify them against the claim.

Personal accident insurance

126.25 As employer's liability insurance and public liability insurance only cover claims arising from negligence many charities also take out personal accident insurance to cover accidents or death that happen in the course of volunteering but which do not result from the charity's negligence.

Professional indemnity insurance

126.26   Professional liability, professional indemnity errors and omissions or mal-practice insurance covers the organisation for claims arising from loss or injury caused by services provided negligently or without reasonable care. Such losses might arise, for example, from incorrect care or inaccurate advice. An organisation can be sued for claims arising from incorrect advice or information even if it is given free or via a telephone helpline. Professional liability insurance should also cover defamation, inadvertent breach of copyright, confidentiality and loss of documents. Depending on the type of work they do, volunteers may also need to be covered by the charity's professional indemnity insurance. This would provide protection against claims for loss or injury caused by services provided negligently or without reasonable care, such as inaccurate information provided on a telephone Helpline or a breach of confidentiality.

126.27   Insurance policies should specifically mention volunteers, as cover may not automatically include volunteers. Where possible cover should be extended so that it includes all volunteers, including those under the age of 16 years or over the age of 80. If this is not possible volunteers should be warned that they are not insured and the charity should carry out a risk assessment to determine the risks associated with using uninsured volunteers.

126.28   Charities have vicarious liability for the acts of their employees but not for the acts of their volunteers. Therefore a member of the public could bring a claim against a volunteer, for example for damages resulting from being given incorrect advice by the volunteer. Charities should protect their volunteers by making sure that either their public liability insurance, or their professional indemnity insurance, or their product liability insurance indemnifies volunteers if any claim is brought against them.

DRIVING

126.29   If a charity provides a volunteer with a vehicle then it is the charity's responsibility to ensure that there is proper insurance cover. If volunteers use their own vehicle only between their home and their usual place of volunteering they do not need to notify their insurer. However, if they use it during the course of their volunteering activity they must notify their insurer in writing. Otherwise the policy can be invalidated, which could result in the driver being personally liable for any damage or injuries sustained in an accident. Many charities have a standard form that volunteers can use to inform their insurers that they are using their car for voluntary work, otherwise there is a form that volunteers can use to inform their insurers that can be downloaded from Volunteering England's website. A volunteer's insurance premium should not be increased because the vehicle is used for voluntary work, but if it is they are entitled to be reimbursed by the charity for the additional premium.

126.30   Charities should check that volunteers using their own cars have informed their insurance companies and that their cover is up to date. Legally, only third party insurance is required, but it is good practice for the driver to have comprehensive insurance. Charities may want to take out contingent motor liability insurance to protect the organisation against any legal liability that may arise as a result of a volunteer being involved in an accident in the course of their volunteering and failing to inform their insurance company.

126.31   Volunteers

126.31   Charities should also check that volunteers have full, not provisional, licences, preferably without endorsements. Driving licences should be inspected when the volunteer is taken on, and then at regular intervals, to check that the volunteer does not have any recent or serious driving convictions.

126.32   If a volunteer driver is driving a vehicle that is over three years old the charity should check that the vehicle has an MOT certificate. The charity needs to be reasonably confident that the vehicle is safe. It can do this by looking to see if the vehicle has any obvious defects and asking the volunteer what maintenance is carried out. The charity should also check that cars have front and rear seatbelts and remind volunteers of their duty to wear them. In rear seats the passenger is legally responsible for wearing a seatbelt. Passengers who are not prepared to wear seatbelts should not be carried unless there are medical or disability grounds. Even in the later stages of pregnancy, women should wear a seatbelt, with the lap strap fitted under the abdomen.

126.33   Volunteer drivers should be trained if they are carrying elderly or disabled people or children. Particular training should be given in picking up and setting down passengers, disability awareness and customer care.

126.34   Volunteer drivers should not receive any payment other than for expenses actually incurred. A driver's insurance policy can be invalidated if the driver appears to be making a 'profit' and the driver could be prosecuted for running an unlicensed taxi service.

Discrimination

126.35   Although some anti-discrimination legislation does not apply to volunteers, as a matter of good practice charities should recruit and treat their volunteers in the same way that they would recruit and treat employees, i.e. they should not discriminate against volunteers on the grounds of race, colour, ethnic origin, religion or belief, gender, sexuality, marital status, age or disability, unless such action can be justified. For example, a women's refuge could refuse to take on male volunteers.

AGE RESTRICTIONS

126.36   There is no statutory minimum or maximum age for volunteering, but some local authorities have by-laws restricting the number of hours children can work and some organisations follow the *Children and Young Persons Act* which limits children aged 14 years and over to a maximum of two hours paid work on Sundays or school days. These hours must be between 7am and 7pm and must not be in school hours. Some insurance policies will also include restrictions. Where this is the case volunteers should be informed. The common law duty of care a charity has to protect the health and safety of their volunteers will be higher where the volunteers are children or young people. If volunteers are under the age of 16 years a risk assessment needs to be carried out so a judgement can be made about whether placing the young person in a voluntary role would place them, or the people they work with, at risk.

126.37   Most charities with young volunteers will operate a policy that:

   •   young people should not be left alone;

- young people should be supervised by two or more adults;

- any potentially dangerous activity should have constant adult supervision;

- a parental/guardian consent form should be obtained for volunteers aged under 16. If the volunteer is to work away from the premises where they normally volunteer additional consent should be obtained.

126.38   The *House to House Collections Act 1939* requires children under the age of 16 to be accompanied by an adult if they take part in house to house fund-raising.

Screening and police checking

126.39   Staff and volunteers, including trustees working with, or applying to work with, children or vulnerable adults, must be checked with the Criminal Records Bureau (CRB) prior to their employment (see CHAPTER 23). Under the *Criminal Justice and Courts Services Act 2000* it is an offence to knowingly employ anyone with a conviction for offences against children namely; murder, manslaughter, rape, GBH and a number of sexual offences, to work with children and young people under the age of 18. The *Care Standards Act 2000* requires a list to be maintained of people who are considered unsuitable to work with vulnerable adults because they have previously either harmed, or placed at risk of harm, vulnerable adults in the course of their work.

126.40   Other charities could be regarded as failing in their duty of care towards the people they work with if they did not screen their volunteers. Such charities should carry out a risk assessment to decide whether clients could be at risk if volunteers are not screened.

126.41   The Criminal Records Bureau will provide details of a person's records held by the police, the Department of Health and the Department for Children, Schools and Families. However, just because these organisations have no records of an individual, there is no guarantee that the individual has not committed an offence that would make them unsuitable as a volunteer or might commit such an offence in the future. Vigilance will always be necessary.

126.42   Charities should not, however, refuse to take on all volunteers with a criminal record. If they did so they would be in breach of their equal opportunities policies and would be cutting themselves off from a large number of potential volunteers. According to the Chartered Institute of Personnel and Development,

- More than five million people in the UK have convictions for crimes that could have involved imprisonment;

- One in three men under 30 years of age have criminal records;

- It is estimated that at least 20% of the working population has a criminal record.

126.43   When considering volunteers with criminal records each case should be judged on its own merits. For example, a ten-year-old conviction for shoplifting should not prevent someone from volunteering on a gardening project, whereas they might be judged unsuitable for a post involving handling large amounts of cash. The considerations that should be taken into account include:

- whether the conviction is relevant to the position;

- the seriousness of the offence;

- the length of time since the offence occurred;

- whether the applicant has a pattern of offending behaviour;

- whether the applicant's circumstances have changed;

- the circumstances surrounding the offence and the explanation offered by the applicant.

VULNERABLE VOLUNTEERS

126.44   Some excellent volunteers will themselves fall within the definition of a vulnerable person (see CHAPTER 23). Care should be taken that these volunteers are not put at risk and are given adequate support to carry out their role.

VOLUNTEERS FROM OVERSEAS

EU nationals

126.45   There are no restrictions on volunteering by people from Austria, Belgium, Bulgaria, Cyprus, Czech Republic, Denmark, Estonia, France, Finland, Germany, Greece, Hungary, Ireland, Italy, Latvia, Lithuania, Luxembourg, Malta, Netherlands, Poland, Portugal, Romania, Slovakia, Slovenia, Spain and Sweden (i.e. Member States of the European Union). The same freedom is extended to nationals of Iceland, Norway, Liechtenstein and Switzerland (i.e. members of the European Economic Area).

Non-EU nationals

126.46   People from outside the European Economic Area are not allowed to take up work, paid or unpaid (which includes volunteering) without a work permit. Given that work permits are only issued where a genuine vacancy exists and where particular qualifications or skills are required that are in short supply in the British and EEA labour force, there is little chance of obtaining a work permit solely to volunteer. However, the Home Office has allowed a concession to permit people from outside the EEA to volunteer if the work meets the following criteria:

- the activity is purely voluntary and does not involve taking up a salaried post or permanent position of any kind within the charitable organisation or entering into any arrangement that is likely to constitute a contract of employment;

- the activity is either for a charitable organisation listed in Home Office guidance or a registered charity whose work meets the criteria set out in the Home Office instruction;

- the activity is unpaid, or is not likely to be subject to payment of the National Minimum Wage, and directed towards a worthy cause;

- it is closely related to the aims of the organisation;

- the voluntary work should involve direct assistance to those the charitable organisation has been established to help (i.e. not clerical, administrative or maintenance work);

- the passenger (volunteer) intends to leave the United Kingdom at the end of their stay.

126.47   Different regulations apply to people coming into the UK to volunteer according to whether the person is from a country for which a visa is required to enter the UK (visa nationals) or not (non-visa nationals). The UK Visas website lists which countries fall into which category. People from countries for which a visa is needed to travel to the UK must obtain one before travelling. People who have arranged their voluntary work before travelling to the UK and who do not need a visa can seek entry clearance before travelling. This takes the form of a certificate placed in their passport. This is not a requirement and does not guarantee entry into the UK, but it may make passage through immigration control easier. Application for entry clearance is made to the British Embassy or High Commission in the volunteer's country. A fee is charged for entry clearance.

126.48   If someone wants to apply for permission to volunteer once they are in the UK, again different regulations apply according to whether the person is a visa national or a non-visa national. Visa nationals must have the appropriate visa, e.g. a volunteer visa, or one that allows them to work, such as a working holiday visa. If they wish to switch to a different visa they have to return to their home country and apply from there. Visitor visas prohibit volunteering. Non-visa nationals can apply while in the UK to change their immigration status to allow them to volunteer. Applications are considered under the Home Office concession described above.

Overseas students

126.49   Students from outside the European Economic Area no longer need permission to take part-time or holiday work, including volunteering. Some restrictions remain in place, including a limit of 20 hours per week during term time, unless the college agrees otherwise.

Refugees

126.50   People who have refugee status, or who have exceptional leave to remain in the UK, and their families are allowed to do any type of work including volunteering.

Asylum seekers

126.51   Asylum seekers and family members are allowed to do voluntary work, including during an appeal against a decision to refuse them asylum, provided that they receive no payment, other than genuine reimbursement of expenses, and do not receive any benefits apart from the training necessary for them to do their volunteer assignment. Home Office guidance states that care should be taken to ensure that any activity undertaken by an asylum seeker is genuinely voluntary and does not amount to either employment or job substitution.

126.52 Volunteers

The Asylum and Immigration Act 1996

126.52 *Section 8* of the *Asylum and Immigration Act 1996* makes it a criminal offence to employ a person who does not have the right to work in the UK. It does not apply to volunteers.

Police-checking volunteers from outside the EU

126.53 In order to secure a visa to enter the UK all applicants are police-checked in their country of origin. Applicants are not usually let into the UK if they have been convicted of an offence which if committed in the UK would be punishable with a term of imprisonment of at least 12 months. Therefore individuals entering the UK on a visa are not likely to have been convicted of a serious offence. Police checks can be carried out in the normal way to check if they have a police record for the period they have been resident in the UK.

Organisations supporting volunteering

Do-it

126.54 Do-it's website provides details of volunteering opportunities throughout the UK and is powered by an on line database of current vacancies. Do-It allows users to search by postcode, type of organisation and type of work: *www.do-it.org.uk*

Time Bank

126.55 The Time Bank is a BBC supported campaign that gives people the opportunity to share their time and skills with their community. The website allows people to register their details in order to receive a list of organisations in their area that need help, and which match their interests: *www.timebank.org.uk*

Youth Action Network

126.56 Youth Action Network supports and develops a range of youth volunteering projects across England: *www.youthactionnetwork.org.uk*

Volunteering Wales

126.57 Volunteering Wales provides a website for people who want to find out about specific volunteering opportunities in Wales: *www.volunteering-wales.net*

CSV (Community Service Volunteers)

126.58 CSV is a large-scale provider of volunteering opportunities in the UK. CSV also supports training and education initiatives: *www.csv.org.uk*

Retired and Senior Volunteer Programme (RSVP)

126.59 A free-standing programme within CSV, RSVP promotes volunteering by people aged 50+ and matches individuals with local voluntary opportunities: *www.csv-rsvp.org.uk*

Reach

126.60 Reach recruits volunteers of all ages and backgrounds throughout the UK with specific business, professional, managerial or technical career experience: *www.volwork.org.uk*

V

126.61 V aims to inspire young people (16–25) into volunteering: *www.wearev.com*

FURTHER INFORMATION

126.62 Volunteering England
Regent's Wharf
8 All Saints Street
London
N1 9RL
Freephone/textphone: 0800 028 3304 (M–F, 9.30 – 5.30)
Email: Information@volunteeringengland.org
www.volunteering.org.uk

Volunteer Development Scotland
www.vds.org.uk

Wales Council for Voluntary Action
www.wcva.org.uk

Volunteer Development Agency, Northern Ireland
www.volunteering-ni.org

National Association of Voluntary Service Managers
www.navsm.volunteering.org.uk

Association of Volunteer Managers
www.volunteermanagers.org.uk

Refugee Council
Bondway House
3–9 Bondway
London
SW8 1SJ
Information line: 020 7820 3085
Email: info@refugeecouncil.org.uk
www.refugeecouncil.org.uk

127   Wales

REGULATION

127.1   There are approximately 11,000 registered charities in Wales. Welsh charities are regulated by the Charity Commission for England and Wales and are subject to the same charity legislation as English charities, apart from minor differences relating principally to the use of the Welsh language. Similarly, UK-wide legislation, such as company law, employment law, tax law and the law on human rights, also applies to Welsh charities.

127.2   The Commission has a permanent office in Newport and staff there handle the majority of casework for Welsh charities. The Newport office acts for Welsh charities, and undertakes the Commission's advice and guidance work, registration of new charities, maintenance of the Register of Charities, Scheme and Order making, and some Review visit work, as well as maintaining the Welsh language elements of the Commission's website.

WELSH ASSEMBLY

127.3   *Clause 114* of the *Government of Wales Act 1998* required the Welsh Assembly 'to make a scheme setting out how it proposes, in the exercise of its functions, to promote the interests of relevant voluntary organisations'. Under the *Government of Wales Act 2006* the statutory duty to promote the interests of the Voluntary Sector (i.e. the Voluntary Sector Scheme) is transferred to the Assembly Government.

LANGUAGE

127.4   Special provisions exist recognising the right of Welsh organisations to use the Welsh language in their official documents. These apply separately to limited companies and registered charities.

Limited companies

127.5   Documents delivered to the Registrar of Companies under either the *Companies Act 1985* or the *Insolvency Act 1986*, which relate to a company whose registered office is in Wales, may be in Welsh as long as they are accompanied by a certified translation into English. This requirement is amplified in the legislation specifically to cover areas such as group accounting and filing, but also the annual accounts, directors' report and audit report filed with the Registrar, as well as subsidiary accounts which are not included in a group consolidation.

127.6   Under the *Companies Act 1985* Welsh companies are required to state that they are limited companies, even if they are incorporated under the Welsh equivalent 'cyfngedig' (shortened to 'cyf').

Registered charities

127.7   Registered charities with income of over £10,000 are required to disclose their charitable status on their official documents. The Charity Commission has clarified in their guide to the legislation that where a document is produced entirely in Welsh, then the equivalent 'Elusen cofrestredig' is permissible.

127.8   A limited company whose name does not include the words 'charity' or 'charitable' must disclose its charitable status on all correspondence and similar material. This does not apply if the Welsh equivalents ('elusen' or 'elusennol') are used and the related documents are entirely in Welsh.

FURTHER INFORMATION

127.9   Further information can be obtained from the Wales Council for Voluntary Action at help@wcva.org.uk, tel 0870 6071666.

128   Welfare to Work

128.1   People living on benefits are amongst the poorest in society. The government believes that the most effective way to tackle poverty, while at the same time keeping public spending down, is to help people off welfare dependency into employment. 'Welfare to Work' is the generic term for a series of Government initiatives to help specific groups of people into work by giving them advice, work experience and the chance to obtain qualifications and includes the New Deal programmes and the Pathways to Work programme which aims to help people on incapacity benefit return to employment. Welfare to Work impacts on the voluntary sector in three ways. Firstly, it reduces the number of people needing to seek help from welfare charities. Secondly, the initiatives allow some voluntary organisations to help their beneficiaries in a totally different way. Instead of 'giving them a fish to feed them for a day', employment training will be equivalent to 'teaching them to fish so they can feed themselves for life'. Thirdly, the funding provided for the Voluntary Sector Option provides a source of subsidised labour that should enable charities to expand their work. However, the costs of training and managing those taking part in the scheme have to be offset against the reduced labour costs. The main New Deal initiatives are described below.

NEW DEAL FOR YOUNG UNEMPLOYED PEOPLE

128.2   Young people aged 18 to 24 who have had a continuous claim to Jobseeker's Allowance for six months or more qualify to take part in this initiative. It provides each young person with a personal adviser and offers short basic skills courses, opportunities for work in a subsidised job with an employer, work in the voluntary sector, or with the Environmental Task Force, help with setting up and running a business, or full-time training and education to build on basic skills and obtain a recognised qualification.

NEW DEAL FOR PEOPLE AGED 25 OR OVER

128.3   This initiative is for people aged 25 or over who have had either a continuous claim to Jobseeker's Allowance for 18 months or who have been claiming Jobseeker's Allowance for 18 out of the last 21 months. It provides each person with a personal adviser and offers help in finding a job or training or work experience to improve skills.

NEW DEAL FOR LONE PARENTS

128.4   The government has recognised that one of the main barriers preventing lone parents from seeking employment is the lack of low-cost childcare provision. Therefore, this initiative, which focuses on helping people who are bringing up children as a lone parent who want to work but who are unemployed or working for less than 16 hours a week, and whose youngest child is under 16 years old to find work. Again participants are provided with a personal adviser who offers help with personalised job search. The adviser will also offer practical advice and help about finding childcare and training, much of which may be provided by voluntary organisations. The adviser will also be able to explain how benefits will be affected when the person starts work and help with applications for any in work benefits or tax credits.

NEW DEAL FOR DISABLED PEOPLE

128.5   The New Deal for Disabled People aims to help people with disabilities and those who have experienced long-term illness to reduce their dependency on benefits. It is entirely voluntary and open to people who are claiming disability or health related benefits that do not require them to be available for work or to seek work, namely:

- Incapacity Benefit;

- Severe Disablement Allowance;

- Income Support including a Disability Premium;

- Housing Benefit or Council Tax Benefit including a Disability Premium providing that the disabled person is not in paid work of 16 hours a week or more, or getting Jobseeker's Allowance;

- Disability Living Allowance;

- War Pension with an Unemployability Supplement;

- Industrial Injuries Disablement Benefit (IIDB) with an Unemployability Supplement;

- National Insurance credits because of sickness or disability;

- Equivalent benefits to Incapacity Benefit being imported into Great Britain under European Community Regulations on the co-ordination of social security and the terms of the European Economic Area Agreement.

128.6   The New Deal for Disabled People provides job brokers who help and support people by matching their skills and capabilities to what employers need, by identifying training needs and identifying suitable local trainers.

NEW DEAL FOR THE OVER 50S

128.7   New Deal 50 Plus is for people aged 50 or over who are in receipt of and have been receiving one or more of the following benefits for at least six months:

- Jobseeker's Allowance;

- Income Support;

- Incapacity Benefit;

- Severe Disablement Allowance;

- Pension credit.

128.8   New Deal 50 Plus is also available for people whose husband/wife or partner has been receiving benefits for them for at least six months, or for people who have been receiving National Insurance Credits, or Carer's Allowance, or Bereavement Allowance.

128.9   The scheme offers:

- Work advice and job search support from a Personal Adviser, including help with interviews.

- Access to in-work financial support, paid as part of the Working Tax Credit. This is a payment to top up the earnings of working people. The basic Working Tax Credit is paid for as long as the person stays in work, and the extra '50 Plus' element is paid for the first 52 weeks in work. The amount paid depends on the household's income.

- A Training Grant of up to £1,500 when starting work. £1,200 can be used to improve existing skills and up to £300 can be used to learn new skills.

- Advice on starting up a business if the person wants to move into self-employment, including access to business start-up courses and help with developing a business plan.

NEW DEAL FOR PARTNERS

128.10   This initiative is targeted at the partners of people claiming one or more of the following benefits:

- Jobseeker's Allowance;

- Income Support;

- Incapacity Benefit);

- Carer's Allowance (ICA); and

- Severe Disablement Benefit;

- Pension Credit.

People can also join New Deal for Partners if they are working for less than 24 hours a week and their partner gets Pension Credit, or if they are working for less than 16 hours a week and their partner gets Working Tax Credit.

128.11   A person is a partner if they are:

- married to,

- living with, or

- being supported by someone who is claiming one of the benefits listed above.

128.12   People joining the New Deal for Partners who want to find a job will get:

- help with looking for a job or practising interview skills if they are ready to start work straightaway;

- a chance to train for something new;

- a short course to refresh or boost existing skills before starting a job; or

- help and support with setting up a new business.

128.13   A New Deal personal adviser will support the partner during their time on the programme. They will also work out with the partner how much better off the partner and their family could be if the partner was in work rather than on benefits.

NEW DEAL FOR MUSICIANS

128.14 New Deal for Musicians (NDfM) is intended to help aspiring unemployed musicians into a sustainable career in the music industry, either as artists under contract or self-employed artists within the music industry. All genres of music are catered for on NDfM – rock/ pop, dance, jazz, blues, country and western folk, classical and even DJs. It does not directly provide musical tuition, which is provided by other formal training routes, rather it provides advice and guidance on the business aspects of work in the music industry.

128.15 NDfM offers specialist help to those who wish to, and are able to, pursue a career in the music industry, through:

- a range of specialist music industry related open learning materials;
- access to advisory support from specialists Music Industry Providers (MIP);
- self-employment flexibilities.

128.16 A set of specialist open learning materials can be accessed by anyone via the following website: *www.ndfmlearning.com* They cover the following subjects:

- Music Industry and You
- Work and Jobs
- Creating
- Performing
- Recording and Production
- Marketing, Distribution, Promotion and Retails
- Copyright, Legal and Management
- Business and Money
- Teaching Music

128.17 New Deal for Musicians is also part of New Deal for Young People and New Deal 25 plus. Those who qualify for the New Deals can get further support at the Option/IAP stage through Music Industry Providers, who provide one-to-one support through industry experts. Those wishing to try self-employment can also access specialist support. Whilst on the programme, participants will also receive the continuing help and support from a New Deal Personal Adviser whose main aim is to meet their needs of finding and keeping a job.

NEW DEAL FOR COMMUNITIES

128.18 New Deal for Communities (NDC) is a key programme in the Government's strategy to tackle multiple deprivation in the most deprived neighbourhoods in the country, giving some of our poorest communities the resources to tackle their problems in an intensive and co-ordinated way. The aim is to bridge the gap between these neighbourhoods and the rest of England.

128.19 The problems of each NDC neighbourhood are unique, but all the NDC partnerships are tackling five key themes of: poor job prospects; high levels of crime; educational under-achievement; poor health; and problems with housing and the physical environment.

128.20   Welfare to Work

EMPLOYMENT ZONES

128.20   Employment Zones complement the New Deal for Communities, tackling problems faced by areas where unemployment is particularly high and persistent and where a core of benefit claimants have been out of work for a considerable length of time. Many have multiple problems, others have simply found themselves with the wrong skills in the wrong place at the wrong time.

128.21   Personal job accounts combine monies previously available for benefits, Jobcentre Plus support and training to provide individually tailored packages designed to help people aged 25 and over to find and keep work.

128.22   Areas selected as employment zones were amongst the worst 150 unitary authorities/local authority districts in Great Britain when ranked by the share of unemployed claimants, aged 25 and over, who were long-term unemployed. Employment Zones are therefore located in the most disadvantaged labour market areas.

Pathways to Work

128.23   Between 80–90 per cent of people living on incapacity say that they want to get back into work. The Pathways to Work process aims to help them become independent and earn a living by targeting some of their health-related barriers and by providing financial support. Since December 2006, Pathways support has been delivered across 18 districts to 40 per cent of all new and repeat incapacity benefits customers. From 3 December 2007, Pathways provision was available in a further 15 Jobcentre Plus Districts, delivered by contracted providers. The final phase of Pathways to Work aims to deliver the programme in the remaining 16 Jobcentre Plus districts from April 2008, completing the national rollout across Great Britain.

TAXATION OF NEW DEAL PAYMENTS

128.24   The full wages of New Deal participants in the Employment Option or who are in waged placements under the Voluntary Sector or Environmental Task Force Options are taxable in the same way as the wages of any other employee. The weekly subsidies paid to employers do not affect the amount of tax that is due on the wages.

PARTICIPATING IN THE VOLUNTARY SECTOR OPTION

128.25   Jobseekers who don't find work during the Gateway period will be able to move on to a New Deal option, either the Voluntary Sector Option or the Environmental Task Force Option. The Voluntary Sector Option provides at least 30 hours work a week over five full days for up to six months with a voluntary organisation. Jobseekers with a disability that prevents them from working full time can still take part in the option. At the start of the option, the New Deal Personal Adviser will set up a proper induction session setting out the aims of the option and an outline of what young people can expect to get out of their work within the voluntary sector. The adviser will also draw up a personal development plan, tailored to each individual's needs, to use as a guide and provide structure. There is support available all the way through the option, with help and advice in finding work and regular progress checks.

128.26   While they are on the option, young people may be offered a wage. Otherwise, they will receive an allowance equivalent to their Job Seeker's Allowance entitlement plus a payment of £400 divided into weekly or fortnightly instalments. Providers get a payment for delivering the option and, if they choose to offer a wage, New Deal will make a contribution equivalent to the average Job Seeker's Allowance rate for 18 to 24-year-olds. There is financial help on offer for jobseekers, too: if they are getting an allowance, New Deal will also reimburse travel costs above £4.

PARTICIPATING IN THE ENVIRONMENT TASK FORCE OPTION

128.27   The Environment Task Force provides at least 30 hours work a week over five full days for up to six months plus the chance to study for an approved qualification. Jobseekers with a disability which prevents them from working full time can still take part in the option. The Environment Task Force gives young people a chance to get involved in a wide range of environmental projects at the same time as acquiring skills and gaining experience they can use in the future. The aim is to benefit the environment on a local, regional or even global level.

128.28   Work with the Environment Task Force can mean dealing with housing, managing parks or forests or reclaiming derelict or waste land. For example, in Cumbria, New Deal participants have been working with the Salterbeck Project, an initiative concerned with urban regeneration. The government is especially keen to encourage projects which will conserve energy and water or protect the environment, and projects which give young people a chance to get involved in their local community. Over time, this should lead to the regeneration of local communities and the 'greening' of urban areas.

128.29   At the start of the option, the New Deal Personal Adviser will set up a full induction session setting out the aims of the option plus an outline of what the young person can expect to gain from working with the Environment Task Force. The adviser will also draw up a personal development plan, tailored to each individual's needs, to use as a guide and provide structure. There will be support available all the way through the option, with help and advice in finding work and regular progress checks.

128.30   While they are on the option, young people may be offered a wage. Otherwise, they will receive an allowance equivalent to their Job Seeker's Allowance entitlement plus a payment of £400 divided into weekly or fortnightly instalments. Providers get a payment for delivering the option and, if they choose to offer a wage, New Deal will make a contribution equivalent to the average Job Seeker's Allowance rate for 18 to 24-year-olds. There is financial help on offer for young people too. New Deal will also reimburse travel costs above £4 for participants receiving an allowance.

FURTHER INFORMATION

128.31   Further information is available at *www.newdeal.gov.uk*.

129   Youth, Age, Ill-health, Disability, Financial Hardship or Other Disadvantage Charities

129.1   While charities for the relief of those in need by reason of youth, age, ill-health, disability, financial hardship or other disadvantage are defined as a charitable purpose in the *Charities Act 2006*, this head does not create any new charitable purposes as such. The head draws extensively on existing charity law and much of it dates back to the *Preamble* to the *Charitable Uses Act 1601*, known as the *Statute of Elizabeth 1*. The *Preamble* referred to 'the education and preferment of orphans', the 'supportation, aid and help of young trades- men, handicraftsmen and persons decayed (fallen into misfortune', and ' the relief of aged, impotent and poor people'.

129.2   *Section 2(3)(e)* of the *Charities Act 2006* states that the relief of those in need by reason of youth, age, ill-health, disability, financial hardship or other disadvantage includes 'relief given by the provision of accommodation or care'.

129.3   The Charity Commission gives the following as examples of the sorts of charities and charitable purposes that will fall under this head:

• Charities concerned with the care, upbringing or establishment in life of children or young people, e.g. children's care homes; apprenticing; etc;

• Charities concerned with the relief of the effects of old age, such as those providing specialist advice, equipment or accommodation, drop-in cen- tres, etc;

• Charities concerned with the relief of disability, such as those providing specialist advice, equipment or accommodation or providing access for disabled people; etc;

• Charities concerned with the provision of housing, such as almshouses, housing associations and Registered Social Landlords.

129.4   At first sight there would appear to be some overlap between the types of charities that fall under this head and those that fall under other heads. The relief of ill-health and disability is not concerned directly with healing or health care, that would fall under the head of the advancement of health, but with the particular needs that ill-health or disability can generate and the relief of those needs. Charities providing specialist equipment, assistance with hospital visiting, counselling for the terminally ill or home helps would fall under this head. Similarly the relief of need by reason of financial hardship is not the same as the relief of poverty. Relieving financial hardship is not designed to relieve a person's poverty, but the social and economic conditions that are engendered by poverty, such as the inability to have a holiday or engage in recreational pursuits.

129.5   The provision of accommodation and care, such as almshouses, cheap hostel accommodation, homes for the impoverished, elderly actors, and soup kitch- ens, comes within this head.

129.6   'Other disadvantage' is a sufficiently broad term to encompass many activities recognised as charitable under the traditional fourth head, such as the relief of suffering caused by drug or alcohol abuse, or the victims of crime or disasters.

129.7   Many charities falling under this new head will have already been required to demonstrate that they provide public benefit, as they previously came within the fourth head. Charities coming under this new head that were previously regarded as coming under one of the first three heads, i.e. the relief of poverty, advancement of education or the advancement of religion, will now have to meet the public benefit test.

129.8   This head is likely to be very susceptible to changes in society, focussing as it does on the relief of need as a consequence of social, economic and medical conditions or other disadvantage. In the future it may be used to relieve need caused by discrimination on the grounds of age, race, religion, or gender, or other needs that arise from changes in society.

130   Zero and Reduced Rates

130.1   Certain supplies of goods and services made to and by charities are zero-rated under UK law to assist them in their work. This relief is estimated to save charities about one-third of their potential VAT costs. The zero-rating provisions are found in the *Value Added Tax Act 1994 Sch 8* and those that particularly assist charities are as follows.

- *Group 3* — books, etc;
- *Group 4* — talking books for the blind and handicapped and wireless sets for the blind;
- *Group 5* — construction of buildings, etc;
- *Group 6* — protected buildings;
- *Group 8* — transport;
- *Group 12* — drugs, medicines, aids for the handicapped, etc;
- *Group 15* — charities, etc.

130.2   A zero-rated supply is the most favourable for VAT purposes. This is because the supplier can reclaim the VAT incurred on the costs of making the supply but does not have to charge VAT to the customer.

130.3   If a charity makes only zero-rated supplies it may ask to be exempted from VAT registration. Exemption saves the charity the trouble and expense of having to keep proper records and accounts for VAT purposes and to render returns, but it will bear the cost of the total VAT incurred on its purchases of goods and services..

130.4   A charity should take professional advice as to whether it is required to register for VAT and, if not, whether it would be beneficial to register voluntarily.

130.5   HMRC Notices mentioned in this chapter are available from the National Advice Service and at *www.hmrc.gov.uk*. The information contained in these Notices and in this section is for general guidance only, and can never be a substitute for detailed professional advice which will take into account a charity's precise circumstances. The zero-rated supplies made by and to charities are considered in greater detail below.

ZERO-RATED SUPPLIES MADE TO OR BY CHARITIES UNDER GROUP 15

Sales and hires of donated goods

130.6   The sale or hire of donated goods by a charity, or a trading subsidiary of a charity that arranges to give all the profits of the sale to the charity, is zero-rated under the provisions of *VATA 1994, Sch 8, Group 15, item 1* provided:

- the goods have been donated to the charity or its trading subsidiary with the intention that they will be sold or hired;

- the sale or hire takes place as a result of the goods having been made available for purchase or hire (whether in a shop, at a charity auction or elsewhere) to the general public, to two or more disabled people or people receiving means tested benefits. (Donated goods that are of too poor a quality to be sold to the public, e.g. unsaleable clothing that is sold to rag merchants or items for scrap, still qualify);

- the charity has not used the goods for any other purpose apart from being available for sale or hire by the charity; and

- the sale does not take place as a result of any arrangements relating to the goods entered into by the parties to the sale before the goods were made available to the general public.

A trading subsidiary of a charity may zero rate sales or hires of goods if the entity is registered for VAT and states in writing that the profits will be transferred to a charity, or the profits are otherwise payable to a charity. An entity under these arrangements is a 'profits–to–charity person'.

130.7   These provisions assist charity shops in particular as they do not have to add VAT to their sales. However, these shops often sell trade goods that they buy in, as well as donated goods, and the zero rate does not extend to the resale of purchased goods, e.g. new T-shirts, gift items or confectionery.

130.8   HMRC takes the view that the sale of bequeathed land or buildings by a charity does not qualify for zero-rating under this provision where the charity has not taken legal title. Their argument here is that, in most cases where dwellings or land are bequeathed to a charity, the property would not have been a business asset of the deceased person or the charity. Any supply of the property is thus normally outside the scope of VAT and the charity is thus not able to recover VAT on expenses connected with the sale. Any subsequent land or property sales will follow the specific rules for land and property (see 130.41 below, and CHAPTER 50).

130.9   *Item 2* of *Group 15* zero-rates goods donated by businesses to charities for sale, hire or export. Ordinarily, a business donor would have to account for VAT on such goods. Also, goods donated for the charity's own use do not qualify.

Export of goods

130.10   *Item 3* zero-rates the export of any goods by a charity to a place outside the EU whether or not in return for consideration. This provision enables a charity to recover VAT on goods which have been donated or purchased by the charity for export. As such activities are zero–rated, charities are entitled to reclaim VAT incurred on the goods themselves and any handling, transport, storage or associated overheads, subject to the normal rules.

130.11   Charities must be able to satisfy HMRC that the goods have been exported. They are required to keep records of exports and should be able to provide a clear and ready link between these records and the proof of export required. For example, the normal evidence of sea freight exports is a copy of the bill of lading or sea waybill or equivalent.

Medical and scientific equipment, etc.

130.12   Zero-rating applies under *item 4* of *Group 15* to the supply of 'relevant goods' (see 130.19 below) for donation to a nominated 'eligible body' where the funds for the purchase or hire are provided by a charity or from voluntary contributions. The goods must be supplied for onward donation to a nominated 'eligible body'. Where the donee of the goods is not a charity it must not have contributed wholly or in part to the purchase or hire of the goods.

130.13   The supply (including hire) of 'relevant goods' to an 'eligible body' may be zero-rated under *item 5* if that body pays for them with funds provided by a charity or from voluntary contributions.

130.14   Zero-rating also applies under *item 5* to the supply (including hire) of 'relevant goods' to an 'eligible body' which is itself a charitable institution providing care or medical or surgical treatment for 'handicapped' persons. 'Handicapped' means chronically sick or disabled. Where the 'eligible body' is a charitable institution, it is not regarded as providing care or medical or surgical treatment for handicapped persons unless the supply is made in a 'relevant establishment' and the majority of the recipients are 'handicapped' persons. A 'relevant establishment' is:

- a day centre other than a day centre which exists primarily as a place for activities that are social or recreational or both; or

- an institution which is approved, licensed or registered under the relevant social legislation or which is exempt from those obligations by that legislation.

130.15   Notwithstanding the above, a supply will qualify for zero-rating where an 'eligible body' provides medical care to handicapped persons in their own homes, and the 'relevant goods' are used in or in connection with the provision of that care.

130.16   By concession, where 'relevant goods' are supplied (including hired) to a charity:

- whose sole purpose and function is to provide a range of care services to meet the needs of handicapped people (of which transport might form a part); or

- which provides transport services predominantly to handicapped people;

the supply of those goods will be zero-rated, as will the repair and maintenance of those goods and the supply of any further goods in connection with that repair or maintenance. In order to be eligible for this concession, a charity must be able to demonstrate that it meets either of the principal conditions through its charitable aims and objectives, its publicity and advertising material, its day-to-day operations, any documents which it has issued for the purpose of obtaining funding from a third party such as a local authority and any other evidence that may be relevant.

130.17   The repair and maintenance of 'relevant goods' is zero-rated under *item 6* provided they are owned by an 'eligible body' and the services are paid for by a charity or from voluntary contributions. It does not matter how the goods themselves were bought in the first place. Spare parts etc. supplied in connection with the repairs and maintenance are also relieved under *item 7*. If the owner or hirer of the goods repaired or maintained is not a charity, it must not have contributed, wholly or in part, to the cost of the repairs or spares.

130.18   The goods and services can only be zero-rated if the supplier is registered for VAT and he is given a declaration in a prescribed form that the goods are either being purchased by an 'eligible body' or are to be donated to an 'eligible body'.

130.19   'Relevant goods' cover the following areas:

- medical equipment;
- scientific equipment;
- computer equipment;
- video equipment;
- sterilising equipment;
- laboratory or refrigeration equipment for use in medical or veterinary research, training, diagnosis or treatment;
- ambulances;
- parts or accessories for use in connection with the above;
- rescue equipment solely for the purpose of rescue or first aid services undertaken by a charity providing such services;
- vehicles designed or adapted for transporting the sick or handicapped, including minibuses adapted for the carriage of handicapped persons in wheelchairs. There are minimum statutory limits to the number of wheelchair spaces required in such a vehicle based on its seating capacity – for example a 27 seat vehicle requires a minimum of three spaces to attract the zero rating. In addition, the vehicle must be fitted with a lift or an access ramp if the vehicle has fewer than 17 seats,
- unadapted motor vehicles that have between 7 and 50 seats, and are purchased or hired for use by an eligible body mainly for the transportation of blind, deaf, mentally handicapped or terminally ill people.

130.20   'Eligible body' covers all health authorities and NHS trusts in England and Wales and their equivalents in Scotland and Northern Ireland. It also covers hospitals and research institutions whose activities are not carried on for a profit; and charitable institutions providing care, medical or surgical treatment for handicapped persons, rescue or first-aid services.

Advertising

130.21   With effect from 1 April 2000 the range of charity advertising qualifying for zero-rating was extended. It includes certain fund-raising products such as collection boxes, envelopes and label stickers. More details are given in CHAPTER 4.

Medicinal products

130.22   *Item 9* zero-rates the supply to a charity, providing care or medical or surgical treatment for human beings or any animals, or engaging in medical or veterinary research, of a medicinal product where the supply is solely for use by the charity in such care, treatment or research. This relief is restricted to charities that will be using the products or substances themselves; a charity which donates these items to another charity cannot obtain relief.

130.23   HMRC are wary of attempts to obtain relief under *item 9* for 'equipment' which does not qualify under *items 4* and *5* above, on the grounds that it is a medicinal product. Such attempts will generally fail on the basis that an explanatory note to this item explicitly excludes from relief 'an instrument, apparatus or appliance'. Medicinal products which qualify for relief are those capable of being consumed or otherwise absorbed into the body. For example, a pill to be taken orally would fall within this description, whereas a syringe would fall outside it. HMRC have provided the following guidance on *item 9* in their internal guidance to officers. Medical and veterinary research should be given its technical meaning, i.e. it is restricted to activities which are directed towards opening up new areas of knowledge or understanding, or initial development of new techniques, rather than towards mere quantitative additions to human knowledge. Medical or veterinary treatment includes the administration of medicines, physiotherapy and surgery.

130.24   Imports by charities of medicinal products can be zero-rated provided the charity gives the supplier a certified declaration that the goods are to be used for the specified purpose. The appropriate declaration must be presented with the HMRC entry form. This relief also applies to imports of talking books for the blind and handicapped and wireless sets for the blind (see 130.65 below) subject to the same condition.

130.25   *Item 10* zero-rates the supply to a charity of a substance directly used for synthesis or testing in the course of medical or veterinary research.

130.26   Further helpful guidance on this complex area of VAT reliefs is given in HMRC Notice 701/6, available from the National Advice Service or at *www.hmrc.gov.uk*

CONSTRUCTION OF BUILDINGS, ETC.: GROUP 5

130.27   It is important that planning advice is taken at an early stage in relation to any construction or property development to be carried out by a charity. This is an area where costs are high, but equally an area where high savings are potentially available. *VATA 1994, Sch 8, Group 5* provides a number of reliefs for buildings (or parts of buildings) intended for use solely for a relevant residential or charitable purpose (referred to as 'qualifying buildings').

Construction services

130.28   The supply of services and related supplies of goods in the course of construction of the following attract zero-rating:

- a building intended for use solely for a 'relevant residential purpose';
- a building intended for use solely for a 'relevant charitable purpose'; and
- the conversion by a housing association of a non-residential building (or part of) into a building designed as a dwelling(s) or a building (or part of) intended for use solely for a relevant residential purpose.

130.29   Use for a relevant residential purpose is defined as use as:

    (i) a home or other institution providing residential accommodation for children;

    (ii) a home or other institution providing residential accommodation with personal care for persons in need of personal care by reason of old age, disablement, past or present dependence on alcohol or drugs, or past or present mental disorder;

    (iii) a hospice;

    (iv) residential accommodation for students or school pupils;

    (v) residential accommodation for members of any of the armed forces;

    (vi) a monastery, nunnery or similar establishment; or

    (vii) an institution which is the sole or main residence of at least 90% of its residents.

130.30   Note that the above do not include use as a hospital, prison or similar institution or a hotel, inn or similar establishment. However, where, for instance, relief is available under (ii), the fact that the building is licensed as a hospital may not preclude zero-rating.

130.31   Use for a relevant charitable purpose means use by a charity in either or both of the following ways, namely:

    (*a*)   otherwise than in the course or furtherance of a business;

    (*b*)   as a village hall or similarly in providing social or recreational facilities for a local community.

130.32   Examples of buildings falling within 130.31(a) are places of worship and offices used by charities solely for administering a non-business activity or activities. Examples of non-qualifying buildings include youth group huts where the organisation charges a membership fee, some child nurseries where a fee is charged, school buildings in a fee-paying school, sports pavilions where membership is restricted to a particular section of a community, and offices used solely or partly for administering the business activities of a charity.

130.33   A building qualifies for zero-rating under 130.31(b) when:

- it is owned, organised and administered by the community for the benefit of the community at large;

- the facilities on offer are multi-purpose;

- it is situated in a location which is easily accessible to the community;

- the facilities are available for use by a local community at large rather than just particular sections of it;

- the facilities are available for use for a variety of public and private purposes.

Examples of non-qualifying buildings include those dedicated for use as a sports centre or swimming pool, a theatre, a membership club or a child nursery.

130.34   The zero-rating provisions only relate to that part of the building intended solely for a qualifying purpose, i.e. for a relevant residential or charitable purpose. Thus, if a builder constructs a shop with a flat above it, the construction work on the flat will be zero-rated, whilst that relating to the shop will be standard-rated.

130.35   The existence of an office is ignored in relation to a building intended to be used for a relevant residential purpose. Similarly, where a building is to be used for a charitable purpose, HMRC operates a concession (see paragraph 3.29 of Notice 48, 'Extra-Statutory Concessions') whereby business use will be ignored provided that this is likely to constitute less than 10% of the total usage. However, there is no provision for apportionment if the qualifying use falls below 90%.

130.36   For the purposes of the above concession, the non-business/business use of a building can be measured by reference to:

- time (entire building);

- time (parts of a building only);

- floor space (entire building); or

- head count (entire building).

However, if a method other than a time-based method applied to the entire building is used, prior written approval from HMRC must be obtained.

130.37   The zero-rating relief is conditional on the charity providing the contractor carrying out the construction work with a certificate specifying that the building is intended to be used for a qualifying purpose before the supply is made. Zero-rating by certificate is only available to contractors or others making supplies direct to the charity. Certificates must not be given to subcontractors.

130.38   The construction of a building does not include the conversion, reconstruction or alteration of an existing building. However, the construction of an annexe to an existing building is eligible for zero-rating if it is intended for use solely for a relevant charitable purpose and is capable of functioning independently of the existing building. Additionally, the main access to the annexe must not be via the existing building and the supply must be covered by a qualifying use certificate.

130.39   The contractor can also zero-rate the supplies of building materials used in the course of construction, with broad exceptions including carpets, built-in furniture (other than kitchen units and some basic bedroom wardrobes), and appliances such as cookers, fridges etc.

Design and build contracts

130.40   The services of an architect, surveyor or any person acting as a consultant or in a supervisory capacity are standard-rated regardless of whether zero-rating is available for the works. However, a charity may obtain relief from VAT on those services if they are subsumed in a design and build contract. Therefore, if under the terms of the contract between a charity and a contractor, the design, construction works and materials are supplied without any separate identification of the design element, the VAT liability of the design element follows that of the building. For example, it will be zero-rated if the supply by the contractor is zero-rated. HMRC will need to be satisfied the supply is a composite one of zero-rated construction services.

Disposal of interests in qualifying buildings

130.41   Zero-rating relief is available where the developer of a building is either selling for the first time the freehold interest, or is granting, assigning or surrendering a lease of over 21 years (or at least of 20 years in Scotland) in a building intended solely for a qualifying residential or charitable purpose.

130.42   Where only part of the building qualifies for zero-rating under these provisions, the consideration for the supply must be apportioned. Further, the supplier must obtain a certificate with regard to the intended use of the property before the supply takes place in order for the zero-rating provisions to apply. These conditions are consistent with the provisions relating to the construction of such buildings explained above.

130.43   In relation to a lease or tenancy zero-rating is restricted to the premium, if any, or if not to the first payment of rent due. This limits the recovery of VAT incurred to the construction of the building and not to the ongoing upkeep and maintenance of the building which is in principle irrecoverable. A zero-rating relief also applies to the first grant of a major interest of a 'converted' building, part thereof or its site. This applies where the developer has converted a building or part that was previously non-residential into a residential building. The relief might arise, for instance, in the case of the conversion of an office block into a student hall of residence. Unfortunately, it does not assist in the conversion into an otherwise charitable building that is not residential.

130.44   Buildings which were originally constructed as dwellings which have not been used as such or for a relevant residential purpose for a period of ten years since they were built are deemed to be 'non-residential' for the purposes of the reliefs on conversions. Thereby, the first grant of a major interest of such a building which has been converted will also qualify for the zero rating relief.

130.45   In the above cases, the zero-rating does not extend to carpeting materials, soft furnishings, built-in electrical appliances such as cookers, etc, when the developer must disallow the VAT incurred on purchase.

Change of use

130.46   The zero-rating relief for the first grant or construction of qualifying use buildings will be withdrawn if the building is used for non-qualifying purposes. [*VATA 1994, Sch 10, para 1*]. A charge to VAT is triggered where, within a ten- year period, the person to whom the relevant zero-rated supply was made:

● grants an interest in, right over or licence to occupy all or any part of the building, after which the building (or part of it) is not intended to be used for a relevant residential or charitable purpose; or

● uses the building for a non-qualifying purpose.

Where there is a grant of an interest in land within ten years VAT must be charged at the standard rate.

130.47   From 21 March 2007, HMRC no longer requires charities that obtain zero-rating on relevant charitable purpose buildings or their construction under Extra Statutory Concession, para 3.29 to suffer a VAT charge when they change the use of the building. This is on the condition that the change of use was not anticipated at the time that the zero-rating was obtained under the Concession.

130.48   As a consequence, charities that have suffered such a 'change of use' or self-supply charge in the preceding three years may now be entitled to a refund, whether they continue to be VAT registered or not.

130.49   The value of any self-supply is equal to the VAT that would have been chargeable had the original supply not qualified for zero-rating, subject to a favourable adjustment of 10% for each complete year since the day the building was completed.

130.50   For example, if a charity paid £1m for a new zero-rated building for its non-business use and at the time of purchase the standard rate of VAT was 17.5%, then after two and a half years the building was used for business purposes, the amount due to HMRC would be £1m × 17.5% × 80% = £140k.

130.51   Under the new rules, if there is an intention to use the building for non-qualifying use which would exceed that allowed by the concession (i.e. in excess of 10% in the ten-year adjustment period), HMRC will deem the original supply never to have been zero-rated in the first place.

130.52   It is thus imperative to document the intended use of a building prior to the supply being made, in order to protect the zero-rating status of the construction services should the non-qualifying use subsequently exceed 10%.

Conversions of non-residential buildings – concessions for charities

130.53   Some charitable organisations are prevented by legal constraints from selling a converted property, even to an associated organisation. They are, therefore, unable to sell the freehold or grant a lease of over 21 years (at least 20 years in Scotland) in order to qualify for zero-rate relief and recovery of their conversion costs. Nor do they qualify for a refund under the do-it-yourself scheme (see 130.61 below) if the conversion is carried out in the course or furtherance of business. However, HMRC will consider refunds of VAT on an extra-statutory basis. A charitable organisation that considers it may qualify is advised to write to HMRC about the matter.

PROTECTED BUILDINGS: GROUP 6

Approved alterations

130.54   Zero-rated supplies of alterations to buildings are restricted to supplies in the course of an 'approved alteration' to a 'protected building'. Generally speaking, an approved alteration means a major alteration which affects the character of a 'protected building' for which listed building consent has been obtained. In the case of a church which is a 'protected building', any alterations rank as 'approved' for this purpose. However, alterations to premises used as a minister's residence fall outside the relief.

130.55 Approved alterations do not include any works of repair or maintenance or any incidental alteration to the fabric of a building which results from the carrying out of repairs or maintenance work. A building separate from, but in the curtilage of, a protected building would not also be afforded protected building with approved alteration status unless on the facts there were other grounds for doing so, e.g. it qualified as a dwelling in its own right.

130.56 The supply of building materials in connection with the construction services are also zero-rated. The services of an architect, surveyor or any person acting as consultant or in a supervisory capacity are standard-rated. However, if a charity negotiates a design and build contract (see 130.40), the VAT liability of the design element of the project follows that of the building and may be zero-rated. A 'protected building' is strictly defined as a building which is:

● a listed building or scheduled monument within the meaning of the relevant statutes; and

● designed to remain as or become a dwelling or number of dwellings after the reconstruction or alteration; or which is

● intended for use for a 'relevant residential or charitable purpose' after the reconstruction or alteration.

130.57 Broadly speaking, a listed building is one which is included in a statutory list of buildings of special architectural or historic interest compiled by the Secretary of State for National Heritage in England and by the Secretaries of State for Scotland, Wales and Northern Ireland. A scheduled monument must be one that is included in a statutory schedule of monuments of national importance.

130.58 Where all or part of a 'protected building' is intended solely for use for a relevant residential or relevant charitable purpose, a supply of approved alterations to the building (or part of it) cannot be treated as such unless it is made to the person who intends to use the building for such a purpose and, before the supply is made, that person has given the supplier an appropriate certificate to that effect.

Substantial reconstructions

130.59 The grant of a major interest (the fee simple or a lease in excess of 21 years or at least of 20 years in Scotland) by a person 'substantially reconstructing' a 'protected building' is also zero-rated. The definition of 'protected building' covered in 130.56 above also applies for the purposes of this relief. A protected building is not regarded as 'substantially reconstructed' unless at least one of the following conditions is satisfied when the reconstruction is completed:

● at least 60% of the cost of the works carried out to effect the purported substantial reconstruction would, if carried out by a taxable person, be zero-rated as attributable to approved alterations;

● the reconstructed building incorporates no more of the original building than the external walls together with other external features of architectural or historic interest.

130.60 It should be appreciated that these reliefs are narrowly drawn and professional advice must be taken by a charity wishing to come within these provisions. Further details on these provisions are contained in HMRC's Notice 708 'Buildings and Construction'. The relevant certificates are also reproduced in this Notice.

DO-IT-YOURSELF CONSTRUCTION – VATA 1994 s 35

130.61   A person (including a charity) carrying out certain works which are lawful and otherwise than in the course or furtherance of any business may claim a refund of VAT charged to him on the supply of any goods (and not services) used by him for the purposes of the works. The works covered by *s 35* are:

- the construction of a building designed as a dwelling or number of dwellings;

- the construction of a building for use solely for a relevant residential purpose or relevant charitable purpose (referred to as 'qualifying buildings' — see 130.27 above);

- a residential conversion, i.e. the conversion of a 'non-residential' building or the non-residential part of a building into either a building designed as a dwelling or number of dwellings or a building intended for use solely for a relevant residential purpose.

130.62   Projects must involve the construction of a new self-contained building which is to be used for specified activities. The construction of a building by a charity intended for use as a communal residential building, benefiting either the aged, sick, disabled, needy or young people, or for the social, cultural or artistic benefit of the community in general would qualify. There must be a self-help element in the total project but what constitutes a self-help element often requires careful discussion with HMRC.

130.63   A building intended for use by a charity for non-business purposes or constructed by a charity and intended for use as a village, community, church or similar hall providing social or recreational facilities for the good of the local community would also qualify.

130.64   Relief is available for materials, builders' hardware, sanitary wear and other articles ordinarily installed by builders as fixtures. Refunds can be claimed on the building materials which would be zero or reduced-rated when supplied with zero or reduced-rated work but not on those which would be standard-rated. Thus carpets and built in appliances such as cookers etc. are not eligible for refund. The intention of *s 35* is that a refund is available if the supply of the relevant materials would have been zero or reduced-rated had the project been constructed by a contract builder. In relation to qualifying buildings, goods relating to other works on the site such as paths, patios, drives, car parks, boundary walls and fences will also qualify provided that they are built at the same time.

130.65   Charities cannot claim for refunds on conversions unless the conversion creates non-business residential accommodation. Where it does, then VAT recovery can be obtained on both the goods and services associated with the conversion, other than services of professionals such as architects. A charity carrying out a conversion in the course or furtherance of a business will not qualify for a refund under the DIY scheme (see 130.56 above).

130.66   Housing associations are regarded as being in business and cannot use the scheme.

130.67   Further details of the scheme may be found in HMRC's Notice 719 'VAT refunds for do-it-yourself builders and converters.'

DRUGS, MEDICINES, AIDS FOR THE HANDICAPPED: GROUP 12

Reliefs for charities looking after the handicapped

130.68   Various items in this group enable zero-rating to the supply to a charity making available to handicapped persons by sale or otherwise, for domestic or their personal use, of the following supplies:

- Medical or surgical appliances designed solely for the relief of a severe abnormality or severe injury. Also, certain other goods designed for invalids and handicapped persons including motor vehicles and boats designed or adapted for the disabled, lifts, hoists, special beds, sanitary appliances, etc;

- Services of adapting goods to suit a handicapped person's condition and subsequent repair and maintenance of the goods;

- Services of constructing ramps and widening doorways to facilitate access by a handicapped person;

- The provision, extension or adaptation of a washroom or lavatory for use by handicapped persons;

- Services necessarily performed in the installation of a lift for use by handicapped persons in a residential or day care centre;

- The supply to a charity for making available to a handicapped person, of an alarm system which will enable a handicapped person to alert directly a specified person or control centre;

- The supply of services by a control centre in responding to calls from an alarm as specified above.

130.69   HMRC recommend that the charity gives the supplier a certified declaration which the supplier can keep for production to HMRC if requested. Without such a declaration, HMRC may assess the supplier for the VAT on the supply.

130.70   Further description and explanation of these various statutory reliefs are included in HMRC's Notice 701/7 'VAT reliefs for disabled people'.

TALKING BOOKS FOR THE BLIND AND HANDICAPPED AND WIRELESS SETS FOR THE BLIND: GROUP 4

130.71   'Talking books' for the blind and severely handicapped when supplied to the Royal National Institute for the Blind, the National Listening Library and other similar charities are zero-rated. Included are certain apparatus and tapes designed or specifically adapted for such use and non-specialist sound recording equipment. Also zero-rated are wireless receiving sets and non-specialist sound recording equipment supplied to a charity for free loan to the blind. Further details of the relief are contained in HMRC's Notice 701/1 'Charities'.

BOOKS, ETC.: GROUP 3

130.72   This zero-rating group allows any business to buy publications, books, leaflets etc. on a zero-rated basis. It also enables aspects of a charity's supplies to be zero-rated, e.g. the quarterly magazine supplied as part of a membership package. It is thus a very useful relief, particularly when used in conjunction with the zero-rating for advertisements.

TRANSPORT: GROUP 8

130.73   This is a broad general zero-rating provision for the commercial transportation of passengers. It also affords some specific reliefs from VAT for the supply to a charity providing rescue and assistance at sea of lifeboats and associated equipment, together with their repair, maintenance and fuel. It also allows zero-rating for slipways for handling of lifeboats.

GOODS USED IN CONNECTION WITH THE COLLECTION OF MONETARY DONATIONS

130.74   Extra Statutory Concession 3.3 zero-rates the supply to charities of goods used in collecting donations. These include the following:

- Lapel stickers which may be given to donors as a token acknowledgement their donation, of at a low cost to the charity;

- Receptacles which have been manufactured solely for the purpose of collecting donations (and are subsequently solely used for this purpose).

- Pre-printed letters and pre-printed envelopes to be used to appeal for donations. It is not necessary to include the addressee's particulars on the pre-printed letters.

REDUCED RATES

130.75   Certain supplies of goods and services are taxable at a reduced 5% rate. *Schedule 7A* of the *VAT Act 1994* provides for the following reduced rate categories which normally assist or may be of interest to charities:

- *Group 1* — Supplies of domestic fuel and power

- *Group 2* — Installation of energy-saving materials

- *Group 3* — Grant-funded installation of heating equipment or security goods or connection of gas supply

- *Group 4* — Women's sanitary products

- *Group 5* — Childrens' car seats

- *Group 6* — Residential conversions

- *Group 7* — Residential renovations and alterations

- *Group 8* — Contraceptive products

- *Group 9* — Welfare advice or information by a charity

- *Group 10* — Installation of mobility aids for the elderly

- *Group 11* — Smoking cessation products.

Group 1 – Domestic Fuel and Power

130.76   Most charities will qualify for reduced rate (5%) gas and electricity supplies because 'qualifying use' means 'domestic use or use by a charity otherwise than in the course or furtherance of a business'. If at least 60% of the supply is used for a qualifying purpose the whole supply can be zero-rated. 'Domestic use' includes use by communal residential establishments, but excluding hotels, prisons, hospitals and similar establishments.

Group 2 – Installation of energy-saving materials

130.77   Supplies of energy-saving materials by the person installing them, and the installation services, are chargeable at the reduced 5% rate when installed in residential accommodation or in a building intended for use solely for a relevant charitable purpose. The materials are insulation for the structure or plumbing fittings, draught stripping for windows and doors, central heating and hot water system controls, solar panels, wind and water turbines, ground and air source heat pumps, micro combined heat and power units and boilers designed to be fuelled solely by wood, straw or similar vegetal matter. Consistent with the above paragraphs, 'residential accommodation' means dwellings, communal residential establishments (excluding hotels, hospitals, prisons and similar establishments), caravans and houseboats. 'Relevant charitable purpose' means use by a charity otherwise than in the course or furtherance of a business or as a village hall or similarly in providing social or recreational facilities for a local community.

Group 3 – Grant-funded installation of heating equipment or security goods or connection of gas supply

130.78   *Group 3* allows contractors to charge VAT at the 5% rate on grant-funded supplies of heating or security equipment to individuals aged 60 or over or individuals receiving certain public benefits such as a disablement pension.

Group 6 – Residential Conversions

130.79   A reduced 5% rate applies to the following building works:

- converting two or more dwellings into a different number of dwellings, or into bedsits, or into a residential home;

- converting bedsits into a dwelling or dwellings, or into a residential home;

- converting a residential home into a dwelling or dwellings, or into bedsits;

- converting a non-residential building into a dwelling or dwellings, or into bedsits, or into a residential home.

The position is complex and charities would be wise to look carefully at HMRC Notice 708 'Buildings and construction'.

130.80   The 5% rate does not apply to the services of architects or other members of the professional team. For conversions to residential homes the building does not have to be non-residential to start with. It can be any building that when last used was not used to any extent for a 'relevant residential' purpose. Note that the reduced rate will not apply to a building being converted into a residential home unless the conversion forms the entirety of the institution. For example, the conversion of stables into a residential annexe (with sleeping accommodation) at a home for the elderly will not qualify because the annexe will not form the entirety of the home. Note that the construction or conversion of a non–residential building (or part) into a garage qualifies for the 5% rate provided the work is carried out at the same time as a qualifying conversion and the garage is intended for use with the dwelling or the premises intended for use for a relevant residential purpose.

Group 7 – Residential renovations and alterations

130.81   The reduced 5% rate originally applied to the renovation or alteration (including extensions) of a dwelling or bedsits or a residential home provided that the property has been empty for at least three years. From 1 January 2008 this was reduced to two years.

Group 9 – Welfare advice or information

130.82   From 1 July 2006 charities and state-regulated private welfare institutions and agencies can reduce-rate advice or information which directly relates to the physical or mental welfare of elderly, sick, distressed or disabled persons or to the care and protection of children and young persons. The relief does not, however, extend to situations where the advice or information provided solely for the benefit of a particular individual or according to their personal circumstances. Nor does it include educational advice which would otherwise be exempt or to supplies of goods unless they are supplied wholly or almost wholly for the purpose of conveying the advice or information.

Group 10 – Installation of mobility aids for the elderly

130.83   From 1 July 2007 installation services, and the goods supplied in connection with these services, qualify for reduced rating when supplied to persons aged 60 and over for use in domestic accommodation. The goods comprise grab rails, ramps, stair and bath lifts, built-in shower seats or showers containing built-in shower seats and walk-in baths with sealable doors.

Index

Index

Index

Index

Index

Index

Index

Index

Index

Index

Index

Index

Index

Index

Index

Index

Index

Index

Index

Index